CW00734712

A CRITICAL INTRODUCTION TO INTI CRIMINAL LAW

International criminal law has witnessed a rapid rise since the end of the Cold War. The United Nations refers to the birth of a new 'age of accountability', but certain historical objections, such as selectivity or victor's justice, have never fully gone away, and many of the justice dimensions of international criminal law remain unexplored. Various critiques have emerged in sociolegal scholarship or globalization discourse, revealing that there is a stark discrepancy between reality and expectation.

Linking discussion of legal theories, case law and practice to scholarship and opinion, *A Critical Introduction to International Criminal Law* explores these critiques through five main themes at the heart of contemporary dilemmas:

- The shifting contours of criminality and international crimes
- The tension between individual and collective responsibility
- The challenges of domestic, international, hybrid and regional justice institutions
- The foundations of justice procedures
- Approaches towards punishment and reparation.

The book is suitable for students, academics and professionals from multiple fields wishing to understand contemporary theories, practices and critiques of international criminal law.

CARSTEN STAHN is a professor of international criminal law and global justice at the Leiden Law School, and is a former legal officer at the International Criminal Court. He is the project leader of Netherlands Organization for Scientific Research (NWO)-funded grants on *jus post bellum* and post-conflict justice and the winner of the Ciardi Prize of the International Society for Military Law and the Law of War for his work on international territorial administration. Professor Stahn is editor of the *Leiden Journal of International Law* and the *Criminal Law Forum* and correspondent of the *Netherlands International Law Review*. He has taught international criminal law in Geneva and Galway, and has published eleven books and more than seventy articles/essays in different fields of international law and international justice.

This title is also available as Open Access on Cambridge Core at https://doi.org/9781108399906

A CRITICAL INTRODUCTION TO INTERNATIONAL CRIMINAL LAW

CARSTEN STAHN
Leiden University

CAMBRIDGE
UNIVERSITY PRESS

CAMBRIDGE
UNIVERSITY PRESS

University Printing House, Cambridge CB2 8BS, United Kingdom

One Liberty Plaza, 20th Floor, New York, NY 10006, USA

477 Williamstown Road, Port Melbourne, VIC 3207, Australia

314–321, 3rd Floor, Plot 3, Splendor Forum, Jasola District Centre, New Delhi – 110025, India

79 Anson Road, #06–04/06, Singapore 079906

Cambridge University Press is part of the University of Cambridge.

It furthers the University's mission by disseminating knowledge in the pursuit of
education, learning, and research at the highest international levels of excellence.

www.cambridge.org
Information on this title: www.cambridge.org/9781108423205
DOI: 10.1017/9781108399906

First published 2019
Reprinted 2019

Printed in the United Kingdom by TJ International Ltd. Padstow Cornwall

A catalogue record for this publication is available from the British Library.

Library of Congress Cataloging-in-Publication Data
Names: Stahn, Carsten, 1971– author.
Title: A critical introduction to international criminal law / Carsten Stahn, Universiteit Leiden.
Description: Cambridge, United Kingdom ; New York, NY, USA : Cambridge University Press, 2019.
Identifiers: LCCN 2018027120 | ISBN 9781108423205 (hardback) | ISBN 9781108436397 (pbk.)
Subjects: LCSH: International criminal law. | LCGFT: Textbooks.
Classification: LCC KZ7000 .S73 2019 | DDC 345–dc23
LC record available at https://lccn.loc.gov/2018027120

ISBN 978-1-108-42320-5 Hardback
ISBN 978-1-108-43639-7 Paperback

Contents

Preface

International criminal law has been said to be overstudied and over-researched. There is no shortage of textbooks. Some may say there are already too many. There are books related to undergraduate and graduate students, critical accounts of jurisprudence, scholarly textbooks and several doctrinal treatises. Some works are geared towards public international law audiences, others address criminal law students or scholars and again others are directed at practitioners. Is it really necessary to publish one more? What can a new book add to the many foundational existing works, the growing list of commentaries and the ever-expanding world of commentary that dissects any new development with the precision that a surgeon applies to a patient?

I feel there is something more to say – something about the readings that underpin our current understandings of the law, the way the field constructs itself, and some of its inherent paradoxes and contradictions.

Many of the most relevant debates about international criminal law do not arise from conversations among lawyers, or endless doctrinal disputes over legal concepts, but rather from engagement with other disciplinary standpoints or critiques. This angle is often absent or sidelined in contemporary legal treatments. Classical positivist works tend to blend out political or other critiques that exceed legal argument. There is a risk that critical works or inputs from different fields do not reach legal audiences, since they are not directly related to positive law or practice, approach problems from distinct angles or use language and concepts that are not easily accessible. Something important gets lost in this. Getting a broader perspective that extends beyond law, in a form that lawyers can engage with, is not only important for those who are interested in theory but also (and perhaps precisely) for those who seek to apply the law or practice in the field.

Over the past decade, there has been a turn towards more reflexive scholarship, which has called into question certain foundations and methods of the field, i.e. its dominant narratives, its underlying concepts, its exclusions and effects. This is only gradually being reflected in existing textbooks. Members of different professional or scholarly communities easily remain entrenched in their own normative silos, or talk at each other rather than with each other. This causes disconnects, misunderstandings or at times superficial controversies. This work tries to relate international criminal law more closely to critiques from within and outside the field. It seeks to present critique alongside mainstream content. It might indirectly help to relate these critiques more directly to law.

This book has emerged as a result of teaching international criminal law at different places (e.g. The Hague, Geneva, Galway), discussions with students and scholars, talks with friends and colleagues, and comments on blogs and Twitter. It is thus the result of many people who have contributed to it – directly or indirectly, intentionally or unintendedly. The manuscript is like a book with many individual short stories. It started as a spin-off of a Massive Open Online Course (MOOC) on Investigating and Prosecuting International Crimes.[1] It complements this digital learning environment. It reflects in essence what I mean when I talk about international criminal law. The content reflects an attempt to cover main themes that have become part of the traditional curriculum, as well as some that are less frequently taught. Obviously, there is something inherently subjective to it: in the choice of themes, the type of judgments, decisions and policies discussed, the critiques formulated (and left out) and, most of all, the wealth of information that is excluded.

It is difficult to define what it is: a 'second generation' textbook, which builds to a greater extent on the rich discourse on international criminal law as a field? A scholarly account of contemporary concepts and problems? It is perhaps easier to say what it is not.

It is not a solution to the problems of international criminal law, or an exhaustive engagement with critique. There is a risk that 'mainstream' readers might find it not doctrinal enough, while sociolegal or 'critical' scholars might find it too conventional. The main purpose is to present key concepts and dilemmas and to set them into context from different perspectives: legal doctrine, jurisprudence and critique. While failing to provide full tribute to doctrinal or critical scholarship, it may nevertheless open certain new spaces by presenting divergent accounts in one and the same book.

The work is an introduction centred on five themes: evolving concepts of crimes, the tension between individual and collective responsibility, the international institutional architecture, foundations and dilemmas of procedures, and repairing harm (punishment, reparation). It focuses on macro-debates, rather than drowning the reader in technicalities. It is more a book about arguing about international criminal law than a conclusive account. It seeks to encourage readers to ask further questions.

The book draws on insights from different disciplines and invites reflection beyond the law. It seeks to critically portray international criminal law through some of its practices. But it remains grounded in law. It establishes links to scholarship and opinion in different fields (political science, criminology, anthropology, history) through a problem-oriented treatment and references.

---

[1] International Law In Action: Investigating and Prosecuting International Crimes, at www.coursera.org/learn/international-law-in-action-2.

It is in many ways imperfect – like international criminal law itself. It is meant to be timeless, but it is at the same time an expression of its time.

One of the dilemmas of international criminal law is unequal access to knowledge and information. International criminal law is taught in a broad range of contexts and places. But information is often a scarce resource in places where it is most needed. The book is thus made available open access, with the kind support of the Leiden University's Centre for Innovation which produced the MOOC.

I wish to thank a few persons: Professor Christian Tomuschat, who has been an academic mentor over the years and has provided invaluable guidance and insights; my colleagues at the Grotius Centre for International Legal Studies at Leiden, who have served as an important sounding board for discussions and ideas; Ciara Laverty and Carlos Fonseca Sánchez, who have provided helpful input to different parts of the book; the members of Leiden University's Digital Learning Lab team, as well as Lieneke Louman, Ioana Moraru and Martine Wierenga, who have supported the project and pushed it to successful completion; Ana Cristina Rodriguez Pineda, who has served as inspiration throughout the writing process; and the students of the Advanced LLM programme in Public International Law at Leiden, with whom I have had the privilege to discuss international criminal law over the past decade. Special gratitude is also owed to my friend Alexis Portilla, an abstract fine artist based in New York, who kindly allowed me to use his artwork 'Okinawa' as cover for the book. His work is often compared to aerial landscapes. This work reminds me of the flight of Icarus over urban and maritime landscapes, and the need to keep an equilibrium between proximity to sun and sea – a central theme discussed in the final section of the book. Finally, warm thanks to Marta Walkowiak, Caitlin Lisle and Marianne Nield at Cambridge University Press for their help and guidance in turning this book into a reality. It is dedicated to my father.

Abbreviations

AFRC	Armed Forces Revolutionary Council
AJIL	American Journal of International Law
AU	African Union
AZAPO	Azanian People's Organisation
CAR	Central African Republic
CDF	Civil Defence Forces
CEDAW	Convention on the Elimination of All Forms of Discrimination Against Women
CIA	Central Intelligence Agency
CIJA	Commission for International Justice and Accountability
CISA	Convention Implementing the Schengen Agreement
COPLA	Corte Penal Latinoamericana y del Caribe contra el Crimen Transnacional Organizado (Draft Statute of the Criminal Court for Latin America and the Caribbean Against Transnational Organized Crime)
DRC	Democratic Republic of the Congo
EAC	Extraordinary African Chambers
ECCC	Extraordinary Chambers in the Courts of Cambodia
ECOWAS	Economic Community of West African States
ECtHR	European Court of Human Rights
EJIL	European Journal of International Law
EU	European Union
EULEX	European Union Rule of Law Mission in Kosovo
GAOR	General Assembly Official Records
IAC	International Armed Conflict
IACtHR	Inter-American Court of Human Rights
ICC	International Criminal Court
ICCBA	International Criminal Court Bar Association
ICJ	International Court of Justice
ICRC	International Committee of the Red Cross
ICTR	International Criminal Tribunal for Rwanda

ICTY	International Criminal Tribunal for the Former Yugoslavia
IHL	International Humanitarian Law
IIIM	International, Impartial and Independent Mechanism to Assist in the Investigation and Prosecution of Crimes in Syria
ILC	International Law Commission
IMT	International Military Tribunal
IMTFE	International Military Tribunal for the Far East
ISIS	Islamic State in Iraq and Syria
JCE	Joint Criminal Enterprise
JICJ	*Journal of International Criminal Justice*
KLA	Kosovo Liberation Army
LGBT	Lesbian, Gay, Bisexual and Transgender
LJIL	*Leiden Journal of International Law*
LRA	Lord's Resistance Army
MICT	Mechanism for International Criminal Tribunals
MINUSCA	United Nations Multidimensional Integrated Stabilization Mission in the Central African Republic
NGO	Non-Governmental Organization
NIAC	Non-International Armed Conflict
OAS	Organization of American States
OECD	Organisation for Economic Co-Operation and Development
OTP	Office of the Prosecutor
PCIJ	Permanent Court of International Justice
R2P	Responsibility to Protect
RPF	Rwandan Patriotic Front
RTLM	Radio Télévision Libre des Milles Collines
RUF	Revolutionary United Front
SADC	Southern African Development Community
SC	Security Council
SCSL	Special Court for Sierra Leone
SD	Sicherheitsdienst
SFOR	Stabilisation Force in Bosnia and Herzegovina
SITF	Special Investigative Task Force
SS	Schutzstaffen
STL	Special Tribunal for Lebanon
TWAIL	Third World Approaches to International Law
UK	United Kingdom
UNCLOS	UN Convention on the Law of the Sea
UNIIIC	United Nations International Independent Investigation Commission
UNMIK	United Nations Mission in Kosovo
UNODC	United Nations Office on Drugs and Crime

UNTAES	United Nations Transitional Administration for Eastern Slavonia, Baranja and Western Sirmium
UNTOC	UN Convention against Transnational Organized Crime
UNTS	United Nations Treaty Series
UNWCC	United Nations War Crimes Commission
UPC	Union des patriotes congolais
US	United States

Introduction

In 1950, four years after the Nuremberg judgment, Georg Schwarzenberger wrote his famous essay on 'The Problem of an International Criminal Law'.[1] Schwarzenberger asked whether a global criminal law exists. He wrote:

When ... there is a new dernier cri, such as suggestions for the development of an international criminal law, it is advisable not to follow uncritically in the train of the enthusiastic protagonists of such an idea, but to pause and reflect on the meaning and value of it all.[2]

He came to the conclusion that '[i]n the present state of world society, international criminal law in any true sense does not exist'.[3] His main objection was that international criminal law cannot be applied universally due to the lack of central institutions. Today, this picture has changed fundamentally. International criminal cannot be criticized for underreach. On the contrary, it may suffer from overreach. There is a turn towards criminalization and accountability in many areas of international law. This is again a reason to 'pause and reflect'.

Few of the effects that international criminal law produces have been imagined in past decades. The International Criminal Court (ICC) is invoked in many situations of conflict. International criminal justice moves at such a rapid pace that it is difficult to follow its developments. Some speak of a 'new age of accountability'.[4] The UN Secretary-General Ban-Ki Moon used this term in 2010 at the Kampala Review Conference. He expressed an old cosmopolitan vision: '[t]hose who commit the worst of human crimes will be held responsible. Whether they are rank-and-file foot soldiers or military commanders ... whether they are lowly civil servants following orders, or top political leaders ... they will be held accountable'.[5] This vision deserves careful scrutiny. The idea of a modern age of accountability is grounded in the human rights movement. Accountability is related to certain key concepts: justice, truth and

---

[1] G. Schwarzenberger, 'The Problem of an International Criminal Law', (1950) 3 *Current Legal Problems* 263.
[2] Ibid., 263.
[3] Ibid., 295.
[4] See M. de Serpa Soares, 'An Age of Accountability' (2013) 15 *JICJ* 669.
[5] Secretary-General's 'Age of Accountability' address to the Review Conference on the International Criminal Court, Kampala, 31 May 2010, SG/SM/12930L/3158.

effective remedies. It has been promoted in the work of various UN agents and NGOs. It is frequently associated with the label of the 'fight against impunity'. The famous Joinet and Orentlicher principles relate the idea of accountability to four fundamental rights: The right to know the truth about gross human rights violations; the right to justice, which entails an obligation to investigate violations, and a right to fair and effective remedy; the right to reparation; and guarantees of non-repetition.[6]

International criminal courts and tribunals[7] play a key role in this process. They have to some extent reshaped contemporary understandings of justice.[8] In a traditional setting, criminal justice is primarily associated with ideas of fairness, retribution and justice for victims. The state is viewed as the guardian of legality. In the international arena, state agents often turn into criminals. In this context, justice is connected to a broader agenda, namely the 'fight against impunity'.[9] This determination features prominently in the preamble of the ICC Statute.[10] It implies that inaction, namely the failure to investigate and prosecute, may constitute a form of injustice.[11]

Repression of crime is only one element. International justice has been associated with a variety of goals, such as prevention and deterrence, the condemnation of specific patterns of atrocity violence, a catalytic effect on international on domestic society or a stabilizing effect on peace.

There are some reasons for optimism. In certain cases, international criminal justice may serve as a broader form of 'social deterrent'.[12] It creates greater awareness of atrocities, restricts the leverage and reach of political elites involved in crime, or may empower domestic constituencies (e.g. courts) and victim groups. Kathrin Sikkink went so far as to speak of a new 'justice cascade', arguing that prosecutions have a positive effect on human rights protection.[13]

In UN practice, international criminal justice has become part and parcel of the promotion of the rule of law. The turn towards accountability is reflected in a strengthening of the mandate of peace operations,[14] and a growing number of

---

[6] Commission on Human Rights, 'Updated Set of Principles for the Protection and Promotion of Human Rights through Action to Combat Impunity', UN Doc E/CN.4/2005/102/Add.1, 8 February 2005.

[7] The term is used in the abstract here. It includes the ICC, the International Criminal Tribunal for Rwanda (ICTR), the International Criminal Tribunal for the Former Yugoslavia (ICTY), the Extraordinary Chambers in the Courts of Cambodia (ECCC), the Special Court for Sierra Leone (SCSL) and the Special Tribunal for Lebanon (STL).

[8] See M. A. Drumbl, 'Policy Through Complementarity: The Atrocity Trial as Justice', in C. Stahn and M. El Zeidy (eds.), *The International Criminal Court and Complementarity. From Theory To Practice* (Cambridge: Cambridge University Press, 2011) 197, 212.

[9] See K. Engle, 'Anti Impunity and the Turn to Criminal Law in Human Rights' (2015) 100 *Cornell Law Review* 1070.

[10] Preamble, Rome Statute of the International Criminal Court (ICC Statute), opened for signature 17 July 1998, 2187 UNTS 3 (entered into force 1 July 2002).

[11] See L. Douglas, 'Truth and Justice in Atrocity Trials', in W. A. Schabas (ed.), *The Cambridge Companion to International Criminal Law* (Cambridge: Cambridge University Press, 2015) 34, 44.

[12] For an account, see B. Simmons, 'Can the International Criminal Court Deter Atrocity?' (2016) 70 *International Organization* 443, 449.

[13] K. Sikkink, *The Justice Cascade: How Human Rights Prosecutions Are Changing World Politics* (New York: W. W. Norton, 2011). For a critique, see P. McAuliffe, 'The Roots of Transitional Accountability: Interrogating the "Justice Cascade"' (2013) 9 *International Journal of Law in Context* 106.

[14] See e.g. para. 9 (d) of Resolution 2211 on the Intervention Brigade, UN Doc. S/Res/2211 (2015), 26 March 2015.

references in thematic and country specific resolutions.[15] There has been an unprecedented move to address accountability and international crimes in international fact-finding.[16] Hardly any situation of armed conflict or atrocity violence can be settled without engagement with the question of accountability. Violations are increasingly documented by eyesight witnesses or bystanders. The point when people start to ask questions about accountability moves ever closer to the actual events.

At the same time, international criminal justice continues to face criticism and rejection.[17] Several African states have threatened to withdraw from the ICC[18] or even advocated for a collective withdrawal from the ICC Statute.[19] In 2017, Burundi became the first state to withdraw from the ICC.[20] Enforcement of international criminal justice remains selective. It remains a challenge to bring hard cases that threaten powerful states.[21] From the perspective of the Global South, the 'fight against impunity' is sometimes perceived as a movement with certain disempowering features. It may dominate the discourse on peace, re-entrench inequalities or prioritize specific Western-liberal approaches to accountability and hide who benefits from such policies.[22] Where justice intervention occurs in ongoing conflict, or is carried out in conjunction with military action, such as in the Libyan context,[23] it may have certain destabilizing effects. The nexus between peace and justice remains a bone of contention. Although there is broad agreement that the two prerogatives are interconnected, timing, sequencing and the precise modalities of justice remain open to discussion. The slogan 'no peace without justice' is too general. Sometimes, there might be no justice without peace.

Experiences over past decades leave some doubts whether international trials can be expected to create security or an accurate account of the past.[24] There is typically a focus on spectacular trials. There are numerous historical examples: the Nuremberg and Tokyo trials which tried German and Japanese leaders after World War II,[25] the

---

[15] Findings include characterizations of certain acts as crimes under the Rome Statute, references to ongoing investigations, prosecutions or warrants of arrest, or recognition of the importance of cooperation with the Court. For a survey, see D. Ruiz Verduzco, 'The Relationship between the ICC and the United Nations Security Council', in C. Stahn (ed.), *The Law and Practice of the International Criminal Court* (Oxford: Oxford University Press, 2015), 30.

[16] Since the mid-1990s, more than twenty missions have been vested with an accountability mandate. See L. van den Herik, 'An Inquiry into the Role of Commissions of Inquiry in International Law: Navigating the Tensions between Fact-Finding and Application of International Law' (2014) 13 *Chinese Journal of International Law* 507.

[17] On the appeal of international tribunals to less powerful states, see A. A. Jacovides, 'International Tribunals: Do They Really Work for Small States?' (2001–2002) 34 *New York University Journal of International Law and Politics* 253.

[18] In 2017, Burundi became the first state to withdraw from the Rome Statute.

[19] P. Labuda, 'The African Union's Collective Withdrawal from the ICC: Does Bad Law Make for Good Politics?', EJIL Talk, 15 February 2017, at www.ejiltalk.org/the-african-unions-collective-withdrawal-from-the-icc-does-bad-law-make-for-good-politics/.

[20] The Philippines notified their withdrawal in 2018.

[21] See e.g. W. Schabas, 'The Banality of International Justice' (2013) 11 *JICJ* 545.

[22] See V. Nesiah, 'Doing History with Impunity', in K. Engle, Z. Miller and D. M. Davis (eds.), *Anti-Impunity and the Human Rights Agenda* (Cambridge: Cambridge University Press, 2016), 95, 111–112.

[23] See SC Resolution 1970 (2011), UN Doc. S/Res/1970 (2011). 26 February 2011. For an analysis, see L. Vinjamuri, 'The ICC and the Politics of Peace and Justice', in Stahn, *Law and Practice*, 13.

[24] See C. Stahn, 'Between Faith and Facts: By What Standards Should We Assess International Criminal Justice' (2012) 25 *LJIL* 251.

[25] On Nuremberg, see G. Mettraux (ed.), *Perspectives on the Nuremberg Trial* (Oxford: Oxford University Press, 2008). On Tokyo, see N. Boister and R. Cryer, *The Tokyo International Military Tribunal: A Reappraisal* (Oxford: Oxford University Press, 2008).

trial of Nazi leader Adolf Eichmann in Jerusalem,[26] the trial of Saddam Hussein after
the fall of the Iraqi regime,[27] the trials against Slobodan Milošević, Radovan Karadžić or Ratko Mladić before the International Criminal Tribunal for the former
Yugoslavia in The Hague,[28] or the trial of Charles Taylor which completed the work
of the Special Court for Sierra Leone.[29]

Such criminal trials are in many ways imperfect.[30] International criminal justice is
based on a rupture between past and present. It analyses historical events mainly
through the lens of crimes. As Hannah Arendt put it in her observations on the
Eichmann trial (*Eichmann in Jerusalem*): 'No punishment has ever possessed enough
power of deterrence to prevent the commission of crimes'.[31] Trials are highly selective.
They reflect only a fraction of incidents and charges. This compromises their ability to
contribute to prevention and justice. In proceedings, facts and events are filtered
through the rationality of the law. The legal process seeks to bring order into chaos.
It is geared at clarifying and simplifying social reality. It relates facts, conduct and
events to legal concepts and tangible normative constructs. It analyses human conduct
through certain ordering structures, hierarchies and chains of causation, and it uses
constructed knowledge and fictions to fill gaps. As a result, the judgment often reflects
at best one among multiple truths. Drawing on the experiences of post-authoritarian
transitions, scholars have made the argument that certain crimes are so outrageous
and complex that no punishment can suffice to render adequate justice.[32]

Proceedings are frequently criticized for being too long and too costly.[33] Some trials
are perceived as 'show trials',[34] or might even heighten tensions in local communities,
as shown by evidence in the Balkans.[35] Sometimes, a judgment produces injustice. For
instance, in the *Šešelj* case Judge Lattanzi argued that Šešelj's acquittal at trial by the
majority 'showed total disregard, if not contempt, for many aspects of the application
and the interpretation of that law as set forth in the case-law of the ICTY and the

[26] See W. Schabas, 'The Contribution of the Eichmann Trial to International Law' (2013) 26 *LJIL* 667.
[27] M. Newton and M. Scharf, *Enemy of the State: The Trial and Execution of Saddam Hussein* (New York: St. Martin's Press, 2008); J. E. Alvarez, 'Trying Hussein: Between Hubris and Hegemony' (2004) 2 *JICJ* 319.
[28] See generally T. Waters (ed.), *The Milošević Trial: An Autopsy* (Oxford: Oxford University Press, 2014); G. Boas, *The Milošević Trial* (Cambridge: Cambridge University Press, 2007).
[29] See C. Jalloh, 'Charles Taylor', in W. Schabas (ed.), *Cambridge Companion to International Criminal Law* (Cambridge: Cambridge University Press, 2016), 313–332.
[30] See G. Nice, 'Trials of Imperfection' (2001) 14 *LJIL* 383.
[31] H. Arendt, *Eichmann in Jerusalem: A Report on the Banality of Evil* (New York: Penguin, 2006), 273.
[32] C. Santiago Nino, *Radical Evil on Trial* (New Haven: Yale University Press, 1996).
[33] R. Zacklin, 'The Failings of the Ad Hoc International Tribunals' (2004) 2 *JICJ* 541, 543, 545.
[34] On the fine line between show trials and political trials, see J. N. Shklar, *Legalism: Law, Morals, and Political Trials* (Cambridge, MA: Harvard University Press, 1986); M. S. Ball, 'The Play's the Thing: An Unscientific Reflection on Courts under the Rubric of Theater' (1975) 28 *Stanford Law Review* 81; M. Koskenniemi, 'Between Impunity and Show Trials' (2002) 6 *Max Planck Yearbook of United Nations Law* 1.
[35] M. Milanović, 'The Impact of the ICTY on the Former Yugoslavia: An Anticipatory Post-Mortem' (2016) 110 *AJIL* 233; K. L. King and J. D. Meernik, 'Assessing the Impact of the International Criminal Tribunal for the Former Yugoslavia: Balancing International and Local Interests while Doing Justice', in B. Swart, A. Zahar, and G. Sluiter (eds.), *The Legacy of the International Criminal Tribunal for the Former Yugoslavia* (Oxford: Oxford University Press, 2010), 7.

ICTR', and reduced law to Cicero's old maxim 'In times of war, the law falls silent' (*Silent enim leges inter arma*).[36]

The turn to accountability and sanctions for violations has transformed human rights discourse and approaches towards human rights investigation and prosecution. It offers new prospects for enforcement. But it might easily take on certain missionary features. It is too simple to assume that international law can deal with evil by investigating and prosecuting 'bad actors'.[37] The concept of 'fight against impunity' can be used as a pretext by a government to silence political opposition. It induces pressures of compliance and emergence of justice mechanisms that are oriented towards global priorities. Coupled with socio-economic incentives, this approach may create strong discrepancies between 'ordinary' justice and elitist international justice regimes – which ultimately run counter to the objective of effective and long-term justice enforcement. As cautioned by scholars, there is a risk that the expansion of global accountability may effectively narrow or reduce, rather than broaden, the options of justice.[38] In certain contexts, international criminal law may impede peace efforts or humanitarian relief action. For instance, in Sudan the government expelled humanitarian NGOs following the issuance of ICC arrest warrants.[39]

I.1   Content

This book examines these dilemmas. It seeks to set the foundations and law and practice of international criminal law into context. It explores how international criminal law defines and legitimizes itself as a juridical field, how it works, what outcomes it produces and how it can be improved.[40]

International criminal law draws on a number of justifications: consent-based arguments, based on delegation of authority or social contract theory, process-based justifications (e.g. fairness and impartiality of proceedings), consequentialist arguments based on projected outcomes (e.g. deterrence, justice for victims) and expressivist claims, related to the affirmation of laws and social values. Many of these justifications are under challenge.

This work starts from the premise that justifications and critiques can be understood best through study of international practices and relations between agents and constituencies. It seeks to unpack some of the existing tensions in global discourse, such as the

---

[36] *Prosecutor v. Šešelj*, IT-03–67-T, Judgment, 31 March 2016 (*Šešelj* Trial Judgment), Partially Dissenting Opinion of Judge Flavia Lattanzi, paras. 143 and 150.

[37] M. J. Aukerman, 'Extraordinary Evil, Ordinary Crime: A Framework for Understanding Transitional Justice' (2002) 15 *Harvard Human Rights Journal* 39.

[38] See e.g. S. M. H. Nouwen and W. G. Werner, 'Monopolizing Global Justice: International Criminal Law as Challenge to Human Diversity' (2015) 13 *JICJ* 157.

[39] 'Sudan Expels 10 Aid NGOs and Dissolves 2 Local Groups', *Sudan Tribune*, 4 March 2009.

[40] On international criminal law as an object of study, see E. van Sliedregt, 'International Criminal Law: Over-studied and Underachieving?' (2016) 29 *LJIL* 1; M. Burgis-Kasthala, 'Introduction: How Should We Study International Criminal Law? Some Reflections on the Potentialities and Pitfalls of Interdisciplinary Scholarship' (2017) 17 *International Criminal Law Review* 227.

shifting contours of criminality and international crime, the relationship between 'the collective' and 'the individual', frictions between 'global' and 'local' visions of justice, foundations of the legal process, and divides between perpetrators and victims.[41]

The content is organized along five main themes that go to the heart of contemporary dilemmas of international criminal justice: the search for a definition of international crimes, the tension between individual and collective responsibility, the role and challenges of justice institutions, the organization of justice procedures, and approaches towards punishment and the repair of harm.

The first chapter introduces key concepts and foundations of international criminal law, including the evolving nature of the notion of international crimes. It shows that international criminal law struggles to identify a normative theory of international crimes. It illustrates how the fluid nature of international crime facilitated the framing of new labels of criminality. It revisits not only core crimes, but also contemporary understandings of historical crimes, as well as certain neglected crimes. It demonstrates how international crimes have been developed beyond their original context and practice. It argues that the distinction between international and transnational crimes is less fluid than traditionally assumed.

The second chapter examines the tension between individual and collective responsibility. It argues that international criminal law has developed a rigid distinction between individual criminal guilt and collective responsibility in order to counter critiques of victor's justice. According to this vision, individual guilt is expressed predominantly through criminal prosecution while collective responsibility is addressed through reparations. The book illustrates how existing concepts and theories struggle to translate the collective nature of criminality into an individualized framework of responsibility. It examines some of the contextual factors underlying international crimes, including typologies of group action. It then explores theories used to connect offenders to collective atrocities and grounds for excluding criminal responsibility.

The third chapter analyses some of the key challenges related to global justice institutions. It starts with an examination of the turn to institutions, and some of their justifications and critiques. It shows that international criminal courts and tribunals are not simply legal agents, but social actors whose actions are marked by investment by various agents and continuing strategies of goal adjustment. It analyses strengths and weaknesses of different justice models (domestic, international, hybrid and regional justice),[42] their links to politics, and approaches that institutions have developed to counter challenges to the enforcement of their mandates. It illustrates that there is a certain paradigm shift. Throughout much of the nineteenth and twentieth centuries, international criminal law has been driven by the ideal of international criminal jurisdiction. In contemporary practice, many limitations and

---

[41] On child soldiers, see M. Drumbl, *Reimagining Child Soldiers in International Law and Policy* (Oxford: Oxford University Press, 2012).
[42] See generally F. Mégret, 'What Sort of Global Justice is "International Criminal Justice"' (2015) 13 *JICJ* 77.

critiques of this universal model have become apparent. The accountability architecture is becoming more diverse and pluralist. Domestic jurisdiction, quasi-judicial or alternative forums are gaining broader importance. One of the key challenges is to develop a broader accountability texture that draws on the individual strengths of these diverse forums, and allows greater dialogue between their constituencies.

The fourth chapter examines justice procedures. It illustrates how international proceedings have been adjusted to capture the exceptional nature of international crimes. It analyses the different stages of the justice process, including the question of to what extent criminal processes and procedures promote justice and truth. It covers the role of different actors in the process, including prosecutorial strategies and dilemmas, Defence perspectives, the role of judges and the space of victims in international criminal proceedings. It shows that international justice cannot be measured simply in terms of 'bad guys' being convicted and innocent victims receiving reparation. Justice is largely about the justice process. Many important choices are made before the actual trial. The significance of proceedings extends far beyond the judgment, defendant or the Courtroom.

The final chapter addresses how harm is repaired. Traditionally, punishment is seen as the main instrument to remedy wrong. The book explains the complex functions of punishment and its different justifications. It traces the role and paradoxes of sentencing, including the difficulty of applying 'ordinary sentences' to extraordinary crimes.[43] It pleads for greater imagination in relation to punishment. It analyses contemporary trends to provide reparation through criminal proceedings, including differences between human rights-based and criminal justice approaches. It claims that reparative practices have an important symbolic space in international criminal proceedings, but should not be confused with national reparation programmes or other forms of humanitarian assistance.

The book concludes with some reflections on how to rethink the status quo of international criminal law. It argues that international criminal law as a field is likely to remain fundamental, despite the flaws and setbacks of specific global justice institutions. It pleads for greater modesty, and a fresh look on some fundamental conceptions, narratives and ambitions.

I.2   Foundations

The idea of justice can be traced back to ancient civilizations,[44] and is reflected in domestic criminal justice systems. However, as a field of international law,

---

[43] See M. Drumbl, *Atrocity, Punishment, and International Law* (Cambridge: Cambridge University Press, 2007), 1–22; M. B. Harmon and F. Gaynor, 'Ordinary Sentences for Extraordinary Crimes' (2005) 7 *JICJ* 683.

[44] On justice in pre-modern societies, see S. M. Shahidullah, *Comparative Criminal Justice Systems* (Burlington: Jones and Barlett, 2014), 130. On international criminal law specifically, see C. M. Bassiouni, *Introduction to International Criminal Law: Second Revised Edition* (Leiden, Boston: Martinus Nijhoff, 2013), 1047–1087.

international criminal justice is relatively young. It is in many ways a body of law in the making. It has a complex identity. Logically speaking, it has never been fully international, or purely criminal.[45] The connection between law and politics is porous.

Formally, international criminal law emerged at the boundaries of public international law and domestic law. Early works associated the idea of international criminal law with the exercise of jurisdiction by states over foreign crimes or domestic crimes committed by foreigners.[46] Throughout the twentieth century, it gained a special place in public international law. Public international law is traditionally focused on interstate relations and subjects of international law, such as international organizations. International criminal law deals with the rights and responsibility of individuals, and the mechanisms designed to promote individual criminal responsibility for violations of international law. Its sources are international, but the sanction is penal.

International criminal law is essentially a 'criminal law without a state'.[47] Unlike domestic criminal law, it is not grounded in the powers of a central sovereign institution. On the contrary, its essence and normative order transcends the authority of individual states.[48] Modern theorizations of international law have accepted the idea that international criminal law can exist as a body of law, despite the absence of one central sovereign institution at the international level that enforces it.[49] Cherif Bassiouni refers to the foundations of international criminal law as 'the convergence of two different legal disciplines', the 'international aspects of national criminal law' and the 'criminal aspects of international law'.[50] However, the ambiguous nature of international criminal law continues to pose tensions.[51] There is a conflict between realist and cosmopolitan visions of international criminal law.[52]

Realists argue that international criminal law is grounded in a state-centred international order. According to this view, international criminal law is essentially derived from state consent. Cosmopolitan approaches claim that international criminal justice derives from a human-centred order that places groups or individuals at the core of international society. A popular theory is that the commission of international crimes triggers a *jus puniendi*, i.e. a right to punish that is grounded in a responsibility of individuals towards the society of world citizens (*ubi societas ibi ius puniendi*).[53]

---

[45] C. Stephen, 'International Criminal Law: Wielding the Sword of International Criminal Justice' (2012) 61 *International and Comparative Law Quarterly* 55.

[46] E. Wise, 'Prolegomenon to the Principles of International Criminal Law' (1970) 16 *New York Law Forum* 562.

[47] K. Ambos, 'Punishment without a Sovereign? The Ius Puniendi Issue of International Criminal Law: A First Contribution towards a Consistent Theory of International Criminal Law' (2013) 33 *Oxford Journal of Legal Studies* 293.

[48] On the normative problems, see Schwarzenberger, 'Problem of an International Criminal Law', 263.

[49] See Q. Wright, 'The Scope of International Criminal Law: A Conceptual Framework' (1975) 15 *Virginia Journal of International Law* 561.

[50] C. M. Bassiouni, 'The Penal Characteristics of Conventional International Criminal Law' (1983) 15 *Case Western Reserve Journal of International Law* 27.

[51] E. van Sliedregt, *The Criminal Responsibility of Individuals for Violations of International Humanitarian Law* (The Hague: TMC Asser Press, 2003), 4.

[52] S. C. Roach (ed.), *Governance, Order, and the International Criminal Court: Between Realpolitik and a Cosmopolitan Court* (Oxford: Oxford University Press, 2009).

[53] See Ambos, 'Punishment without a Sovereign', 313.

According to cosmopolitan approaches, humanity is the sovereign and the *urbi* and *orbis* of international criminal law. Critical approaches, including Third World Approaches to International Law (TWAIL),[54] question some of the articulations of humanity represented by cosmopolitan approaches[55] and certain liberal premises of international criminal law, such as the virtues of juridification, criminalization and individualization.[56] They draw attention to limitations and tensions, such as the unequal effects of international criminal justice in international relations,[57] the narrow historical trajectory of atrocity trials, their selectivity, their limited attention to everyday forms of violence, or the gendered nature of doctrines and discourse.[58]

International criminal law seeks to protect different interests. As Herbert Packer has argued, the essence of criminal justice may be explained by two models: the 'crime control' model and the due process model.[59] The crime control model is grounded in the idea that the 'criminal process is a positive guarantor of social freedom'.[60] It stresses the value of criminal law enforcement to prevent the breakdown of public order. The due process model emphasizes the protection of the liberty of persons.[61] It introduces controls and safeguards against the abuse of power. International criminal justice encompasses both dimensions. However, it places special emphasis on the defence of international public order and peace and security. History has shown that these two conceptions may clash with each other.[62]

International criminal law is shaped by pragmatism. Initially, perpetrators were presented as outlaws of the international community, e.g. in the context of piracy. The international criminal law movement turned 'enemies' into criminals. It reduced at the same time the need for a turn to natural law. Early crimes, such as slavery or terrorism, were guided by the idea of sanctioning certain acts or practices that affected the common interest of states. In the course of the twentieth century, however, the

---

[54] According to Makau Mutua, TWAIL is driven by 'three basic, interrelated and purposeful objectives. The first is to understand, deconstruct, and unpack the uses of international law as a medium for the creation and perpetuation of a racialized hierarchy of international norms and institutions that subordinate non-Europeans to Europeans. Second, it seeks to construct and present an alternative normative legal edifice for international governance. Finally, TWAIL seeks through scholarship, policy, and politics to eradicate the conditions of underdevelopment in the Third World'. See M. Mutua, 'What is TWAIL?' (2000) 94 *American Society of International Law Proceedings* 31.

[55] For a critique of a 'monolithic' vision of international community' see I. Tallgren, 'The Voice of the International: Who is Speaking?' (2015) 13 *JICJ* 135.

[56] On the idea of 'TWAILing' international criminal law, see M. Burgis-Kasthala, 'Scholarship as Dialogue? TWAIL and the Politics of Methodology' (2016) 14 *JICJ* 921. See also A. Anghie and B. S. Chimni, 'Third World Approaches to International Law and Individual Responsibility in Internal Conflicts' (2003) 2 *Chinese Journal of International Law* 77; J. Reynolds and S. Xavier, '"The Dark Corners of the World": TWAIL and International Criminal Justice' (2016) 14 *JICJ* 959; A. Kiyani, 'Group-Based Differentiation and Local Repression: The Custom and Curse of Selectivity' (2016) 14 *JICJ* 939.

[57] On alleged 'inherent imperialism', see F. Cowell, 'Inherent Imperialism' (2017) 15 *JICJ* 667.

[58] K. Engle, 'Feminism and its (Dis)contents: Criminalizing Wartime Rape' (2005) 99 *AJIL* 778; F. N. Aolain, 'Gendered Harms and their Interface with International Criminal Law' (2014) 16 *International Feminist Journal of Politics* 622; D. Buss, 'Performing Legal Order: Some Feminist Thoughts on International Criminal Law' (2011) 11 *International Criminal Law Review* 409.

[59] H. L. Packer, 'Two Models of the Criminal Process' (1964) 113 *University of Pennsylvania Law Review* 1.

[60] Ibid.

[61] See D. Robinson, 'A Cosmopolitan Liberal Account of International Criminal Law' (2013) 26 *LJIL* 127. On fairness, see M. Damaška, 'Reflections on Fairness in International Criminal Justice' (2010) 8 *JICJ* 611–620; Y. McDermott, *Fairness in International Criminal Trials* (Oxford: Oxford University Press, 2016).

[62] D. Robinson, 'The Identity Crisis of International Criminal Law' (2008) 21 *LJIL* 925.

focus shifted. International criminal law developed mainly as a response to mass violations of human rights by states against citizens and persons within their territory.[63] It stresses the obligation-related side of sovereignty. It makes state action answerable, not only internally, in the domestic realm, but also externally, on the international plane. It has a dual function: it serves as a shield against violations, and as a sword to hold perpetrators accountable.[64]

International criminal law encompasses at least three types of offences: trans-national offences that affect certain global interests, offences relating to interstate relations (e.g. aggression) and offences protecting human beings.

The idea of protecting individuals has close synergies with two other bodies of law: international human rights law, which is designed to protect the basic rights and freedoms of all persons, and international humanitarian law, which protects citizens during armed conflict.[65] International criminal law seeks to reconcile three dimensions: the 'universalist' aspirations of public international law,[66] the 'humanist' dimensions of human rights law and the legality and fairness-oriented foundations of criminal law.[67]

International criminal law differs from human rights law and humanitarian law through its specific focus on individual criminal responsibility for violations. Unlike classical human rights law, it is not predominantly centred on obligations of states. The addressee of international criminal law is primarily the individual, as opposed to the state.

International criminal law at the same time overlaps with domestic criminal law. It includes offences, defences, modes of liability, as well as principles and procedures relating to evidence, sentencing, victim participation, witness protection or mutual legal assistance and cooperation.

A core foundation of international criminal law is the principle of legality, also called *nullum crime sine lege* ('no crime without law').[68] A person cannot or should not face criminal punishment except for an act that was criminalized by law before they performed the act. The principle was established as a reaction to the broad discretion of judges in the era of Enlightenment.[69] As the Permanent Court of International Justice held in 1935 in relation to changes of the German Penal Code

---

[63] For a critique, see S. Starr, 'Extraordinary Crimes at Ordinary Times: International Justice Beyond Crisis Situations' (2007) 101 *Northwestern University Law Review* 1257.

[64] See F. Tulkens, 'The Paradoxical Relationship between Criminal Law and Human Rights' (2011) 9 *JICJ* 577, with reference to the imagery used by Christine Van den Wyngaert.

[65] See R. Kolb, *Advanced Introduction to International Humanitarian Law* (Cheltenham: Edward Elgar, 2014).

[66] On 'universality', see B. Simma, 'Universality of International Law from the Perspective of a Practitioner' (2009) 20 *EJIL* 265.

[67] See also K. Ambos, *Treatise on International Criminal Law: Vol. I Foundations and General Part* (Oxford: Oxford University Press, 2013), 55, making reference to the principles of 'legality, culpability and fairness'. For an analysis of the tensions between these aspirations, see A. Clapham, 'Three Tribes Engage on the Future of International Criminal Law' (2011) 9 *JICJ* 689.

[68] C. Kreβ, 'Nulla Poena, Nullum Crimen Sine Lege', in R. Wolfrum (ed.), VII *Max Planck Encyclopedia of Public International Law* (Oxford: Oxford University Press, 2012), 889.

[69] R. Bellamy (ed.), *Beccaria, On Crimes and Punishments' and Other Writings* (New York: Cambridge University Press, 1995).

under the Nazi regime, it reconciles competing standpoints, namely 'that of the individual and that of the community':

From the former standpoint, the object is to protect the individual against the State: this object finds its expression in the maxim nulla poena sine lege. From the second standpoint, the object is to protect the community against the criminal, the basic principle being the notion nullum crimen sine poena.[70]

In a domestic context, the principle of legality imposes an obligation on the legislator to define offences and penalties with prospective force and precision. It protects the separation of powers. The understanding of the required degree regulation differs across traditions. Common law jurisdictions tend to have a wider understanding of 'lex' than Romano-Germanic traditions. In the international context, the principle is defined in more flexible terms since there is no general legislator. The basic test is whether the conduct is 'criminal according to the general principles of law recognized by the community of nations'.[71]

International criminal law has faced challenges in relation to the legality principle since its inception. In the aftermath of World War I, the US objected to the idea of holding German leaders accountable for breaches of 'the laws and principles of humanity', since it considered this notion too subjective and imprecise.[72] The standard under international law has developed over time. The Nuremberg judgment argued in a controversial fashion in 1946 that the legality principle is not binding per se. It held that the '[t]he maxim "nullum crimen sine lege" is not a limitation of sovereignty but is in general a principle of justice'.[73] Today, it is no longer only a doctrine of substantive justice, but a hallmark of the fairness and due process guarantees underlying international criminal justice.[74] As Geoffrey Robertson has noted, *nullum crimen sine lege* is more than only a protection against arbitrary governance. It 'provides the rationale for legislation and for treaties and Conventions, i.e., for a system of justice rather than administrative elimination of wrongdoers by command of those in power. It is the reason why we are ruled by law and not by police'.[75] The principle requires that the law be 'clear, accessible and predictable'.[76] It protects several interests: fair notice, the need to minimize arbitrariness and maximize certainty, respect for legislative

---

[70] PCIJ, *Advisory Opinion on the Consistency of Certain Danzig Legislative Decrees with the Constitution of the Free City*, 1935 PCIJ (Ser. A/B) No. 65, 41, 57.

[71] International Covenant on Civil and Political Rights (ICCPR), Art. 15.

[72] R. Lansing and J. Scott, 'Memorandum of Reservations' (1920) 14 *AJIL* 127, 134, 144.

[73] Trial of the Major War Criminals before the International Military Tribunal, Nuremberg 14 November 1945–1 October 1946, Vol. I (1947), 219. On Nuremberg, see R. K. Woetzel, *The Nuremberg Trials in International Law* (London: Stevens & Sons Limited, 1962), 111–112; G. Schwarzenberger, 'The Judgement of Nuremberg' (1947) 21 *Tulane Law Review* 329.

[74] A. Cassese, 'Nullum Crimen Sine Lege', in A Cassese (ed.), *The Oxford Companion to International Criminal Justice* (Oxford: Oxford University Press, 2009), 438–439.

[75] See SCSL, *Prosecutor v. Norman*, Decision on Preliminary Motion Based on Lack of Jurisdiction (Child Recruitment), Case No. SCSL-2004–14-AR72(E), 31 May 2004, Dissenting Opinion of Judge Robertson, para. 14.

[76] See H. Friman, 'Trying Cases at the International Criminal Tribunals in the Absence of the Accused?', in S. Darcy and J. Powderly (eds.), *Judicial Creativity at the International Criminal Tribunals* (Oxford: Oxford University Press, 2010), 332, 333.

action (e.g. drafter's intent) and prior law as the basis of punishment.[77] It is expressly codified in the ICC Statute, partly in reaction to the far-reaching interpretation of crimes by the ad hoc tribunals. It contains (i) the principle of strict construction of crimes, (ii) the prohibition of analogy and (iii) the mandate to interpret the definition of a crime in favour of the suspect or accused in case of ambiguity.[78] It is reinforced by prohibitions concerning retroactive application of the Statute and its applicable law,[79] and the corresponding mandate of ICC organs (e.g. principle of objectivity).[80]

The scope of application of international criminal law is in flux. It can be defined in three ways: (i) crime-based, that is by reference to crimes that involve direct individual criminal responsibility or a duty of states to investigate and punish; (ii) jurisdiction-based, that is by reference to the way in which it is enforced, internationally (through international actors) or transnationally (by states); and (iii) value-based, that is by reference to the interests and values that is seeks to protect, such as 'concerns' affecting 'the international community as a whole'.

The multi-layered accountability architecture of global criminal justice encompasses at least four layers: international justice, i.e. courts and tribunals deriving their powers and authority from universal legal instruments, such as international treaties (ICC) or Security Council resolutions; regional mechanisms, i.e. bodies created by international legal instruments whose membership is limited to a specific region; hybrid mechanisms, i.e. bodies that combine elements of domestic and international jurisdiction; and classical domestic courts and tribunals.

Conceptually, international criminal law is more than a set of norms and institutions. It is a juridical field[81] that defines itself through specific codes, rituals, representational features and processes. It can be understood as a normative project that establishes a special type of authority (*ordre public*) in relation to macro-criminality, a community of professionals, a 'special type of legal humanitarianism'[82] or a space of relations that inform and shape the content of international criminal justice. This perspective helps us understand international criminal law as a social reality, including clashes between different legal traditions, protagonists or approaches, and broader critiques about its construction as a field.[83]

---

[77] See L. Grover, *Interpreting Crimes in the Rome Statute of the International Criminal Court* (Cambridge: Cambridge University Press, 2014) 134–151.

[78] See Art. 22 (2) of the ICC Statute.

[79] See Arts. 11 (2), 22 (1), 24 (1) and 24 (2).

[80] See Art. 54 (1).

[81] P. Dixon and C. Tenove, 'International Criminal Justice as a Transnational Field: Rules, Authority and Victims' (2013) 7 *International Journal of Transitional Justice* 393, 395.

[82] See S. Kendall, 'Beyond the Restorative Turn: The Limits of Legal Humanitarianism', in C. De Vos, S. Kendall and C. Stahn (eds.), *Contested Justice* (Cambridge: Cambridge University Press, 2015), 352.

[83] Mégret lists no less than seven dichotomies: '(i) criminal lawyers who pride themselves in their focus on the rights of the accused vs "international human rights lawyers" who are suspected of privileging the injunction to repress grave crimes or to excessively side with victims ... (ii) "liberals" who argue that international criminal justice is no different from any form of domestic criminal justice and should above all concentrate on the fairness of the proceedings in any given case vs "show-trialists" who emphasize the expressive role of international criminal law, the implications of international criminal trials for transitional justice, and the need to appropriately politicize trials ... (iii) "supranationalists" for whom international criminal justice is above all about the "core" crimes and a vertical concept of repression vs "transnationalists" for whom the discipline is much broader and includes all variants of transnational crimes with

International criminal law operates at the intersection of peace and justice. Historically, it has been as much a peace project as a justice project.[84] One of the contemporary critiques is that 'the theory of international criminal justice is often understood as the theory of its institutions (primarily the tribunals) and its legal practices, rather than ... in terms of justice'.[85] The conceptions of justice that international criminal law pursues vary partly across institutions, and their underlying mandates and goals.[86]

The term 'justice' is broad and carries a number of different meanings.[87] International criminal law has been pragmatist and non-committal in relation to justice theories. It may be associated with at least four different 'ideal types' of justice: retributive justice, which is focused on the punishment of the perpetrator and the reaffirmation of norms through the legal process;[88] restorative justice, which is geared at repairing the damage caused rather than on penalizing the offender;[89] distributive justice, which is concerned with the just allocation of benefits and burdens, including resource allocation and distribution of blame;[90] and expressivist justice, which focuses on the communicative dimensions of the legal process, such as its ability to 'send messages', shape debates and discourse, and influence the generation and perception of norms.[91] The four dimensions of justice are interconnected.

Key elements ('international', 'criminal', 'justice') are disputed or evolving. Many normative assumptions require deeper theoretical analysis. Multiple institutions apply

global implications ... (iv) statists, who argue that international criminal justice is and should be primarily about punishing crimes of states vs non-statists who argue that violence should be prosecuted whatever its origin and extend to, for example, corporations ... (v) centralizers who consider that international criminal law should be marked by its universalism and impose a high degree of homogeneity vs pluralists for whom the idea of global common offences is compatible with a large "margin of appreciation" ... (vi) accused focused defense attorneys who consider that the defendant should have a particular pride of place in the criminal trial vs defenders of victims' rights who insist that the fate of victims should increasingly be borne in mind by the international trial ...(vii) common lawyers vs civil lawyers'. F. Mégret, 'International Criminal Justice as a Juridical Field' (2016) 13 *Penal Field* 34.

[84] Much of the focus of post-World War I and World War II responses was related to 'crimes against peace'. Efforts to institutionalize international criminal justice have been related to the goal of a thicker vision of peace which goes beyond the mere absence of violence. The preamble of the ICC Statute states expressly that 'grave crimes threaten the peace, security and well-being of the world'.

[85] Mégret, 'What Sort of Global Justice', 78.

[86] For a discussion of justice in international law, see S. Ratner, *The Thin Justice of International Law* (Oxford: Oxford University Press, 2015).

[87] On justice and fairness, see J. Rawls, *A Theory of Justice*, rev. ed. (Cambridge, MA: The Belknap Press of Harvard University Press, 1999).

[88] On retribution, see A. K. A. Greenawalt, 'International Criminal Law for Retributivists' (2014) 35 *University of Pennsylvania Journal of International Law* 969;A. Ahmad Haque, 'Group Violence and Group Vengeance: Toward a Retributivist Theory of International Criminal Law' (2005) 9 *Buffalo Criminal Law Review* 272.

[89] M. Findlay and R. Henham, *Transforming International Criminal Justice: Retributive and Restorative Justice in the Trial Process* (Devon and Portland: Willan Publishing, 2005).

[90] See Mégret, 'What Sort of Global Justice', 83 ('a comprehensive theory of the justice of international criminal justice must perforce be a theory of global distributive justice').

[91] See generally R. D. Sloane, 'The Expressive Capacity of International Punishment: The Limits of the National Law Analogy and the Potential of International Criminal Law' (2007) 43 *Stanford Journal of International Law* 39; M. deGuzman, 'Choosing to Prosecute: Expressive Selection at the International Criminal Court' (2012) 33 *Michigan Journal of International Law* 265; E. S. Anderson and R. H. Pildes, 'Expressive Theories of Law: A General Restatement' (2000) 148 *University of Pennsylvania Law Review* 1503; M. Drumbl, 'The Expressive Value of Prosecuting and Punishing Terrorists: Hamdan, the Geneva Conventions, and International Criminal Law' (2007) 75 *George Washington Law Review* 1165; M. Drumbl, *Atrocity, Punishment and International Law* 17 (Cambridge: Cambridge University Press, 2007), 175–176.

international criminal law. In some contexts, they create new realities and forms of power. The functioning and diverse effects of international criminal law are only gradually understood through insights from international relations, behavioural sciences, such as anthropology, criminology, social psychology and organizational theories.[92] There is an emerging new strand of reflective and critical research on international criminal law that sets existing approaches into a broader context, challenges existing assumptions or reveals tensions that are masked by legal accounts.[93] These lines of inquiry are often blended out. This work applies a broader analytical lens. It draws partly on these insights, in order to introduce readers to the foundations of international criminal law, as well as its tensions and critiques. It does not position itself within a particular tradition of critique or school of international criminal justice.[94] It rather engages with tensions and dilemmas in relation to five major challenges: the definition of global crime, approaches towards criminal responsibility, global institutional frameworks, criminal procedures and repair of harm. In this way, this book seeks to relate contemporary critique to the study of international criminal law as a field and to highlight its potential implications for theory and practice.

---

[92] See e.g. P. Roberts and N. McMillan, 'For Criminology in International Criminal Justice' (2003) 1 *JICJ* 315; D. L. Rothe and C. W. Mullins, 'Toward a Criminology of International Criminal Law: An Integrated Theory of International Criminal Violations' (2009) 33 *International Journal of Comparative and Applied Criminal Justice* 97; I. Bantekas and E. Mylonaki (eds.), *Criminological Approaches to International Criminal Law* (Cambridge: Cambridge University Press, 2014);K. M. Clarke, *Fictions of Justice: The International Criminal Court and the Challenge of Legal Pluralism in Sub-Saharan Africa* (New York: Cambridge University Press, 2009); J. Rowen and J. Hagan, 'Using Social Science to Frame International Crimes' (2014) 10 *Journal of International Law and International Relations* 92; R. Byrne, 'Drawing the Missing Map: What Socio-legal Research Can Offer to International Criminal Trial Practice' (2013) 26 *LJIL* 991.

[93] See e.g. I. Tallgren, 'The Sensibility and Sense of International Criminal Law' (2002) 13 *EJIL* 561; S. Kendall, 'Donors' Justice: Recasting International Criminal Accountability' (2011) 24 *LJIL* 585; Nouwen and Werner, 'Monopolizing Global Justice', 157–176; C. Schwöbel (ed.), *Critical Approaches to International Criminal Law: An Introduction* (London: Routledge, 2014); T. Krever, 'International Criminal Law. An Ideology Critique' (2013) 26 *LJIL* 701; G. Simpson, 'Linear Law: The History of International Criminal Law', in Schwöbel, *Critical Approaches*, 159–179; S. M. H. Nouwen, '"As You Set Out for Ithaka", Practical, Epistemological, Ethical, and Existential Questions about Socio-Legal Emperical Research in Conflict' (2014) 27 *LJIL* 227; J. Reynolds and S. Xavier, 'The Dark Corners of the World': TWAIL and International Criminal Justice' (2016) 14 *JICJ* 959; A. Bringedal Houge and K. Lohne, 'End Impunity! Reducing Conflict-Related Sexual Violence to a Problem of Law' (2017) 51 *Law & Society Review* 755.

[94] On the problem of situating critique, see D. Jacobs, 'Sitting on the Wall, Looking in: Some Reflections on the Critique of International Criminal Law' (2015) 28 *LJIL* 1.

1

International Crimes

According to contemporary understandings, the foundations of international criminal law are based on three fundamental precepts, namely 'that international law recognizes individuals, not merely as objects, but as subjects with rights and duties which it defines; that it defines certain crimes for which individuals are liable; and that it distinguishes this criminal liability from the civil responsibility of states under international law'.[1] These prerequisites have become hallmarks of the emancipation of international criminal law as a legal field.

The foundations of international criminal law are less developed than domestic criminal systems. This is a weakness from a due process perspective. One common critique is that it lacks coherence and common dogmatic foundations. However, the pragmatist approach towards the development of international criminal law is to some extent an asset for crime control. It has facilitated a dynamic understanding of the nature of international crimes and a certain degree of normative pluralism. The fluid nature of international crimes has allowed international criminal law to reinvent itself as a field. In many instances, crimes have been developed beyond their historical context through jurisprudence or institutional practices. This process of gradual adaption and normative expansion remains a source of friction from different angles: the *nullum crimen* principle, the role of judicial bodies and non-state actors in the process of lawmaking, and the interaction between international criminal law and other bodies of law (e.g. international humanitarian law, human rights law, the law on the use of force, or domestic law).

In current discourse and practice, most emphasis is placed on conflict- and atrocity-related crime. International criminal law as a field has a longer past, however, and a potentially more pluralist future. Some historic categories of crimes witness a postmodern revival (e.g. piracy, slavery and slavery-like practices, terrorism). Other crimes remain in legal grey zones, but deserve broader attention.

---

[1] See Wright, 'The Scope of International Criminal Law', 565.

1.1   Background

Criminologists have developed rich theories to explain why crime occurs. They have argued that certain social, historical or economic conditions can create 'cultures of criminality'.[2] Criminological research has defined different meanings of criminality, theories to explain deviant behaviour and critiques of formal legal labels. In international criminal law, the essential question of what an international crime is has received little structural attention.[3]

International criminal law deals with different types of violations, such as political violence, forced displacement and transfer of persons or protection of goods (e.g. cultural property). One approach is to define international criminal law based on the protection of certain public goods or interests. International criminal law protects individual and collective interests, such as peace and security, individual and group rights or human dignity. Unlike human rights law, it does not primarily seek to frame these interests as rights. It rather sets obligations. Individual or collective rights (e.g. civil and political rights, minority rights and certain socio-economic or cultural rights) are protected because of their relevance to broader community interests, or their context (i.e. the organized or systematic nature of violations, their relevance in situations of armed conflict or their transboundary nature). There is no unified theory on what ought to be protected by international criminal law, and what constitutes an 'international crime'. Rather, what international criminal law is has developed incrementally.

A second approach is to define an international crime by virtue of the nature of criminality. Criminologists have used different notions to describe the foundations of international crimes.

Some view international crimes essentially as 'state criminality', i.e. crimes undertaken in pursuit of state goals and interests, or resistance thereto.[4] Others link international crimes more broadly to a phenomenon of macro-criminality, i.e. crimes conditioned by macro-level events that affect not only individuals but also societies.[5] Yet others view international crimes as situational crimes that are driven by specific ideologies, such as nationalist ideas, patterns of victimization, dehumanization, scapegoating, absolutist worldviews or utopian ideologies,[6] or structures of obedience.[7] In legal circles, there has been a strong trend to define international criminal law as mass

---

[2] Roberts and McMillan, 'For Criminology in International Criminal Justice', 324.

[3] R. Haveman and A. Smeulers, 'Criminology in a State of Denial: Towards a Criminology of Crimes: Supranational Criminology', in A. Smeulers and R. Haveman (eds.), *Supranational Criminology: Towards a Criminology of International Crimes* (Antwerp: Intersentia, 2008), 3–26.

[4] See K. Lasslett, 'Understanding and Responding to State Crime: A Criminological Perspective', in Bantekas and Mylonaki, *Criminological Approaches to International Criminal Law*, 68–92, 68.

[5] See H. Jäger, *Verbrechen unter totalitärer Herrschaft: Studien zur nationalsozialistischen Gewaltkriminalität* (Freiburg-Olten: Walter, 1967).

[6] A. Alvarez, 'Destructive Beliefs: Genocide and the Role of Ideology', in Smeulers and Haveman, *Supranational Criminology*, 213–231, 216.

[7] See generally H. C. Kelman and V. L. Hamilton, *Crimes of Obedience: Toward a Social Psychology of Authority and Responsibility* (New Haven: Yale University Press, 1989), at 16–20. For a critique, see F. Neubacher, *Kriminologische Grundlagen einer internationalen Strafgerichtsbarkeit* (Tübingen: J. C. B. Mohr, 2005), 222–234.

atrocity crimes.[8] The term has been coined by former US Ambassador for War Crimes, David Scheffer.[9] It reflects the insight that modern conflict zones are social environments which produce cycles of criminality. The notion takes into account that the mandate of international criminal courts and tribunals is mostly tied to conflict-related crime.[10] It is, however, criticized for being overly narrow in scope and failing to include non-violent crime. The existing scope of criminalization appears to be richer. For instance, certain crimes with a transnational dimension may be better explained through economic opportunities, such as the exploitation of illegal markets (e.g. piracy, trafficking, slave labour, pillaging of natural resources), rather than a purely conflict-oriented lens.

A third approach defines international crimes by reference to the community whose interests are violated. This approach relies on the assumption that a crime is an attack on a society's normative order and collective conscience. It may be traced back to French sociologist Emile Durkheim, who sees the virtue of criminal law in the reaffirmation of a symbolic penal community.[11] For instance, large-scale atrocities, such as genocide, crimes against humanity or war crimes, might be broken down into many individual acts, such as murder, manslaughter, assault or torture. Many of the individual acts may be punished as 'ordinary crimes' under domestic law by states directly affected, such as the state of the nationality of the offender, the state where the crimes occur or the state of the nationality of the victim.[12] But 'the whole' is bigger than its individual parts. This vision is reflected in Telford Taylor's notorious claim at Nuremberg: An international crime 'is not committed only against the victim, but primarily against the community whose law is violated'.[13] According to modern constructivist understandings, international criminal law is not only a reaffirmation of a broader normative order, but a constant attempt by justice agents to create such a normative community or to reinstate beliefs in its existence.[14]

Qualifying conduct as an 'international crime', as opposed to an 'ordinary crime', may entail certain specific legal consequences. This explains why humanitarian and human rights agents have been eager to defend a pragmatic and dynamic conception of international crimes. It enlarges the scope of accountability for perpetrators. The most immediate consequence is that qualification of a crime under international law

---

[8] S. Karstedt, 'Contextualizing Mass Atrocity Crimes: The Dynamics of "Extremely Violent Societies"' (2012) 9 *European Journal of Criminology* 499–513.

[9] D. Scheffer, 'Genocide and Atrocity Crimes' (2006) 1 *Genocide Studies and Prevention: An International Journal* 229. See also W. A. Schabas, 'Atrocity Crimes' in W. A. Schabas (ed.), *The Cambridge Companion to International Criminal Law* (Cambridge: Cambridge University Press, 2016), 197.

[10] Bassiouni, *Introduction to International Criminal Law*, 142; G. Werle and F. Jessberger, *Principles of International Criminal Law* (Oxford: Oxford University Press, 2014), para. 90; K. J. Heller, 'What Is an International Crime? (A Revisionist History)', 58 *Harvard International Law Journal* 353–420.

[11] E. Durkheim, *The Division of Labor in Society* [1893] (New York: The Free Press, 1997), 60. For a discussion, see I. Tallgren, 'The Durkheimian Spell of International Criminal Law? (2013) 71 *Revue interdisciplinaire d'études juridiques* 137.

[12] G. Werle and F. Jessberger, *Principles of International Criminal Law* (Oxford: Oxford University Press 2014), para. 91.

[13] T. Taylor, 'Large Questions in Eichmann Case' New York Times (1961) 6, at 22, cited in Arendt, *Eichmann in Jerusalem*, 260.

[14] See Mégret, 'International Criminal Justice as a Juridical Field', 49.

allows investigation and prosecution, irrespective of whether the conduct is criminalized domestically.[15] A classic example is the prosecution of Nazi discrimination under the Holocaust, which was authorized under the legal order of the Third Reich.

The qualification has other important consequences. First, the nature of the offence may enable states to try perpetrators in the absence of any link between the accused and the state exercising jurisdiction, under the doctrine of universal jurisdiction.[16]

Second, the label as an international crime may bar the invocation of immunities in certain circumstances. A famous example is the *Pinochet* case, in which the House of Lords held that Chilean dictator Augusto Pinochet could not invoke immunity before British courts because torture does not form part of official functions.[17] The International Court of Justice specified that immunity does not bar investigation or prosecution before an international criminal court and tribunal.[18] These cases marked the beginning of a doctrine of exceptionality regarding the invocation of immunity before international criminal jurisdictions.

Third, the international character of the crime may further render statutes of limitations inapplicable.[19] This enables broader prosecution of crimes committed in the past.

1.1.1   Theories of International Crimes

One of the striking features of international criminal justice is that it does not contain a fully developed theory of international crimes.[20] A common perception is that international crimes are crimes so serious that they affect the international community as a whole. Or in other words: they injure something fundamental to being human in a way that domestic legal systems fail to address. Yet this conception is slightly misleading. Certain international offences, like rape, murder or torture, correspond largely to domestic offences. Some domestic crimes may be just as heinous or grave as

---

[15] G. Werle and F. Jessberger, *Principles of International Criminal Law* (Oxford: Oxford University Press 2014), paras. 91–93.

[16] On universal jurisdiction, see R. O'Keefe, 'Universal Jurisdiction. Clarifying the Basic Concept' (2004) 2 *JICJ* 735. There is a trend to limit universal jurisdiction to cases where the perpetrator is in the custody of the host state, or where the territorial state or the state of the nationality of the offender is either unwilling or unable to act (horizontal complementarity). See C. Ryngaert, 'Applying the Rome Statute's Complementarity Principle: Drawing Lessons from the Prosecution of Core Crimes by States Acting under the Universality Principle' (2008) 19 *Criminal Law Forum* 153.

[17] House of Lords, *R* v. *Bow Street Magistrates' Court ex parte Pinochet* (No. 3), 24 March 1999 ILM 38 (1999) 581; J. C. Barker, 'The Future of Former Head of State Immunity after ex parte Pinochet' (1999) 48 *International and Comparative Law Quarterly* 937; A. Bianchi, 'Immunity versus Human Rights: The Pinochet Case' (1999) 10 *EJIL* 237.

[18] ICJ, *Arrest Warrant of 11 April 2000* (*Democratic Republic of Congo* v. *Belgium*), 14 February 2002, para. 61 (*Arrest Warrant* Case).

[19] Both the UN and the Council of Europe have adopted conventions which render statutory limitations inapplicable to genocide, crimes against humanity and war crimes. See R. Kok, *Statutory Limitations in International Criminal Law* (The Hague: TMC Asser, 2007).

[20] A. Chehtman, 'A Theory of International Crimes: Conceptual and Normative Issues', in K. J. Heller et al. (eds.), *The Oxford Handbook of International Criminal Law* (Oxford: Oxford University Press), forthcoming.

international crimes.[21] Typically two theories are used to explain what an international crime is.

1.1.1.1 Evil Nature of the Offence (Malum in se)

According to one theory, the definition as an 'international crime' is tied to the nature of the offence. This theory draws on the Latin concept of *malum in se* (wrong or evil in itself). A crime is considered inherently wrong, independent of regulations governing the conduct, because of its evil nature. Factors that are taken into account are: its evil intent, such as an attack on humankind or fundamental human values, e.g. human dignity and humaneness; its gravity and scale ('grave matter of international concern'); its international or cross-jurisdictional dimension, including the need for international enforcement; and/or its perception, for instance as 'shock[ing] the conscience of humanity'.

This definition captures a wide range of crimes. A classic example is piracy – the first international crime.[22] Pirates on the high seas were called enemies of humankind (*hostes humanis generis*). Any state could prosecute them, regardless of nationality or place of commission of the crime. Later, new forms of international crimes developed. In the eighteenth century, origins of war crimes emerged. In 1915, what is today called 'the Armenian genocide' was qualified as a 'crime against civilization'.[23] After World War II, aggressive war was prosecuted under the notion of crimes against peace. It was seen as an attack on the 'society of states'. The notion of crimes against humanity emerged. It embraced the idea that violations by a state against its own population constitute an attack on humanity and humanness. It is grounded in a modern conception of international society as a 'society of peoples'.[24]

These notions were clarified and developed in post-war codification. In 1996, the International Law Commission of the United Nations provided a modern list of 'crimes against the peace and security of mankind', based on international practice since Nuremberg and Tokyo. It included the following categories of crimes: (i) aggression, (ii) genocide, (iii) crimes against humanity, (iv) crimes against United Nations and associated personnel and (v) war crimes.[25]

The main idea is that these crimes can be investigated and prosecuted internationally even though they are not enshrined in a universally applicable treaty. States which have custody over perpetrators have the obligation to take the necessary and reasonable steps to apprehend the offender and ensure the prosecution and trial by a competent jurisdiction.

---

[21] W. A. Schabas, *Unimaginable Atrocities: Justice, Politics and Rights at the War Crimes Tribunals* (Oxford: Oxford University Press 2012), 34–35.

[22] On piracy, see Section 1.2.1.

[23] See E. Schwelb, 'Crimes Against Humanity' (1946) 23 *British Yearbook of International Law* 178, 181.

[24] J. Rawls, 'The Law of Peoples' (1993) 20 *Critical Inquiry* 36–68.

[25] See ILC, Draft Code of Crimes against the Peace and Security of Mankind (1996), Arts. 17–20, in ILC, *Report of the International Law Commission on the Work of its Forty-Eighth Session*, UN GAOR, 51st Sess., Supp. No. 10, at 93, UN Doc. A/51/10 (1996).

A modern example that is increasingly invoked in doctrine is crimes against the environment.[26] They may be said to mark an attack against humankind since all human beings are seen to share an interest in suppressing grave acts of environmental destruction.

The *malum in se* theory has gained ground in the philosophy of international criminal law. For instance, Cécile Fabre has taken the view that from a *de lege ferenda* perspective all crimes that are dehumanizing and violate basic human rights should be regarded as international crimes.[27] The problem with this argument is that the concept of *malum* is inherently subjective and subject to abuse. It tends to downplay the power structures that underlie branding of crimes. What is wrong or evil depends on the speaker or agent. The theory suffers from an arbiter problem. It fails to determine who has the final say over what constitutes an international crime. It also lacks clear demarcation lines. For instance, even isolated attacks may 'shock the conscience', and yet they may not be recognized as international crimes.

1.1.1.2   *Prohibited Evil (*Malum Prohibitum*)*

A second theory relies more directly on regulation, in particular the level of prohibition. According to this view, an international crime is an act that is directly criminalized by international law.[28] A typical example is the violation of a criminal norm that is contained in an international treaty or international customary law.

Classic early examples are the United Nations Convention on the Prevention and Punishment of the Crime of Genocide[29] or the so-called grave breaches of the Four Geneva Conventions.[30] In line with this theory, it is increasingly accepted that crimes included in the jurisdiction of the ICC are international crimes.

Many international conventions contain an express obligation for states to investigate and prosecute the offence in question, or to extradite persons to another state that is willing to do so: the so-called to extradite or prosecute principle (*aut dedere aut judicare*).[31] This principle is included, for instance, in the Geneva Conventions, the

---

[26] See generally F. Mégret, 'The Problem of an International Criminal Law of the Environment' (2011) *Columbia Journal of Environmental Law* 195; T. Weinstein, 'Prosecuting Attacks That Destroy the Environment: Environmental Crimes or Humanitarian Atrocities?' (2004–2005) 17 *Georgetown International Environmental Law Review* 697–722. On ecocide, see L. Berat, 'Defending the Right to a Healthy Environment: Toward a Crime of Geocide in International Law' (1993) 11 *Boston University International Law Journal* 327.

[27] C. Fabre, *Cosmopolitan Peace* (Oxford: Oxford University Press, 2016), 181.

[28] See e.g. G. Werle, *Principles of International Criminal Law* (The Hague: T. M. C. Asser Press, 2005) ('[c]rimes under international law are all crimes that involve direct individual criminal responsibility under international law').

[29] See Convention on the Prevention and Punishment of the Crime of Genocide, 9 December 1948, 78 UNTS 277. The UN General Assembly recognized in GA Res. 180 (II) of 21 December 1947 that 'genocide is an international crime, which entails the national and international responsibility of individual persons and states'.

[30] Geneva Convention for the Amelioration of the Condition of the Wounded and Sick in Armed Forces in the Field, 12 August 1949, Arts. 49 and 50; Geneva Convention for the Amelioration of the Condition of Wounded, Sick and Shipwrecked Members of Armed Forces at Sea, 12 August 1949, Arts. 50 and 51; Geneva Convention relative to the Treatment of Prisoners of War, 12 August 1949, Arts. 129 and 130; Geneva Convention relative to the Protection of Civilian Persons in Time of War, 12 August 1949, Arts. 146 and 147. See Art. 85 Protocol Additional to the Geneva Conventions of 12 August 1949, and relating to the Protection of Victims of International Armed Conflicts, 8 June 1977. See generally W. Ferdinandusse, 'The Prosecution of Grave Breaches in National Courts' (2009) 7 *JICJ* 723.

[31] On *aut dedere aut judicare*, see M. C. Bassiouni and E. Wise, *Au Dedere Aut Judicare: The Duty to Extradite or Prosecute in International Law* (Leiden: Martinus Nijhoff, 1995).

1984 UN Convention against Torture,[32] the Convention against Enforced Disappearances[33] and many terrorism-related treaties.[34]

There are different conceptions of what constitutes an international crime. Under a narrow view, a crime is an international crime if it gives rise to individual criminal responsibility under international law, rather than under domestic law. Kevin Heller has called this the 'direct criminalization thesis'.[35] A more inclusive view includes norms that allow or require investigation or prosecution at the domestic level.[36] Typical examples are piracy or torture, as defined in the Convention against Torture. This approach covers in particular certain treaty crimes that are primarily subject to international cooperation and national prosecution (transnational crimes),[37] such as drug trafficking or trafficking in persons.

The distinction between these two categories is often difficult to draw.[38] Crimes in one category may become part of the other. There is thus fluidity between the narrow and the inclusive view. As Ethan Nadelmann has argued: 'just as few people during the eighteenth century could have imagined the emergence of a global antislavery regime ... few in this century can imagine that activities which are entirely legitimate today may evolve into targets of global prohibition regimes'.[39] The most convincing approach is to regard an international crime as a crime defined by international law.[40] The types of crimes covered depend on the factors and specificity of criminalization. For instance, Bassiouni has developed a typology of ten characteristics that define international criminalization, including recognition of the criminal nature of the act, the right or duty to prosecute, the establishment of a jurisdictional basis or reference to international jurisdiction.[41]

From a normative point of view, both the *malum in se* and the *malum prohibitum* theses are needed to understand the contemporary content of international criminal law. Some crimes are international crimes without being enshrined in an international treaty. For instance, aggression or crimes against humanity were initially dealt with in Nuremberg and Tokyo without a specific treaty base or prohibition. At the same time, the 'evil nature' of the act is not always the decisive criterion for international

---

[32] Convention Against Torture and Other Cruel, Inhuman or Degrading Treatment or Punishment, 10 December 1984, 1465 UNTS 85, Art. 7.

[33] International Convention for the Protection of All Persons from Enforced Disappearance, 20 December 2006, Art. 11.

[34] International human rights instruments, such as the International Covenant on Civil and Political Rights (ICCPR), the Optional Protocol to the International Covenant on Economic, Social and Cultural Rights (ICESCR), or the American Convention on Human Rights, accord to victims of gross human rights violations the right to an effective remedy for the breaches they have suffered.

[35] For a critique of the 'direct criminalization thesis', see Heller, 'What Is an International Crime?', 362–391.

[36] For a defence of a 'national criminalization thesis', see ibid., 391–407.

[37] N. Boister, *An Introduction to Transnational Criminal Law* (Oxford: Oxford University Press, 2012).

[38] A paradigm example is terrorism. Terrorism was traditionally a transnational crime. It was governed by specific counterterrorism convention that mandate states to criminalize specific acts of terrorism. Yet in 2011 the Special Tribunal for Lebanon found that terrorism qualifies as a crime entailing direct individual responsibility under customary law. See Section 1.2.3.

[39] See E. Nadelmann, 'Global Prohibition Regimes: The Evolution of Norms in International Society' (1990) 44 *International Organization* 479, 523.

[40] See R. O'Keefe, *International Criminal Law* (Oxford: Oxford University Press, 2015), 56.

[41] Bassiouni, *Introduction to International Criminal Law*, 143.

investigation or prosecution. In certain cases, the prosecution as international crime is driven by pragmatic considerations, such as the lack of capacity or failure of states to act, rather than the nature of the crime.

1.1.2 Structure of an International Crime

International crimes share structural resemblances with domestic offences. They typically encompass two classical elements known from domestic criminal law, namely an objective and a subjective element.

The material element (*actus reus*)[42] encompasses objective elements relating to the crime, such as the illegal conduct of the perpetrator (act or omission), its consequences, causation between act and consequence and, in some cases, specific circumstances related to the subject or object of the crime (such as the minimum age of victims) or its modalities.

The mental element (*mens rea*)[43] describes the culpable frame of mind of the perpetrator. The individual requirements depend on the crime and degree of responsibility. They encompass cognitive elements (knowledge), volitional elements (intent), as well as certain forms of awareness of risk or negligence.[44]

In many cases, international crimes share communalities with domestic categories of crime. For instance, offences such as rape, murder or torture can be found in domestic criminal codes. What makes international crimes distinct from 'ordinary' domestic crimes is the context in which they occur. It is factors such as the existence of an armed conflict or the systematic nature or scale of violations (i.e. the 'contextual elements') that mark the difference to ordinary offences.

International criminal law has been reluctant to admit exclusions from liability for crimes such as genocide, crimes against humanity or war crimes in light of their global prohibition and their nature. But in certain cases perpetrators may invoke grounds excluding criminal responsibility. They typically relate to individual circumstances, such as the situation or condition of the defendant.[45] These grounds have been limited over time.[46] They differ across institutions and jurisdictions.[47] The ICC Statute is more permissive than other international instruments. It includes several grounds

---

[42] See Ambos, *Treatise, Vol. I*, 100.

[43] See Art. 30 ICC Statute.

[44] On the complex ICC elements, see G. Werle and F. Jessberger, '"Unless Otherwise Provided": Article 30 of the ICC Statute and the Mental Elements of Crimes Under International Criminal Law' (2005) 3 *JICJ* 35. On *dolus eventualis*, see M. Badar, 'Dolus Eventualis and the Rome Statute Without It?' (2009) 12 *New Criminal Law Review* 433.

[45] The ICTY has made it clear that considerations relating to the state do not necessarily exclude individual criminal responsibility. It argued that the involvement of a person in a 'defensive operation' does not 'in itself' constitute a ground for excluding criminal responsibility. See ICTY, *Prosecutor* v. *Kordić and Čerkez*, IT-95-14/2, Judgment, 26 February 2001, para. 452.

[46] See K. Ambos, 'Defences in International Criminal Law', in B. Brown (ed.), *Research Handbook on International Criminal Law* (Cheltenham: Elgar, 2011), 299.

[47] Many of the grounds for excluding criminal responsibility under the ICC Statute are recognized in domestic jurisdiction. See Chapter 2.

excluding responsibility, such as intoxication, self-defence or duress,[48] and the principle of superior order.[49] They must be distinguished from procedural bars to investigation and prosecution, such as *ne bis in idem*[50] or immunities.

1.2 First Generation Crimes

The history of international crimes is marked by paradoxes. Today there is a strong focus on three categories of crime, namely genocide, crimes against humanity and war crimes, and, in some cases, the crime of aggression. These crimes are often referred to as 'core crimes', although that term is ambiguous.[51] These categories of crime are typically directly prohibited under international law and associated with individual criminal responsibility, rather than mere suppression duties of states. They are characterized by their systematic nature, i.e. their commission by entities, such as state agents, statelike entities or organized networks of criminality, or their harm relating to a large group of victims.[52] They are deemed to be marked by exceptional gravity, rather than cross-border harm that affects common interests of all or a number of states (transnational element).

However, there is a whole set of other crimes that enjoyed a high degree of recognition even before the emergence of these crimes. They are sometimes referred to as 'first generation crimes'.[53] They include certain 'private' forms of violence, i.e. crimes by non-state actors. Initially they were considered as international offences, because they target the common interests of states. In recent years, some of them have gained fresh attention in modified form.

1.2.1 Piracy

Piracy is usually considered to be the first universal jurisdiction crime. Pirates have been treated as outlaws for centuries since they targeted vessels at all times, without regard to the nationality.[54] Their activities have affected the security of navigation and commerce among nations, particularly on the high seas, a zone that falls outside the territorial jurisdiction of any state. The criminalization of piracy is closely related to the space of commission of the crime. It was declared a universal crime for pragmatic reasons, namely to facilitate the extraterritorial exercise of jurisdiction.[55]

---

[48] See Art. 31 ICC Statute.
[49] See Art. 33 ICC Statute.
[50] Art. 20 ICC Statute. See also Section 3.6.1.
[51] On the ambiguous nature of the term, see O'Keefe, *International Criminal Law*, 62–64.
[52] L. May, *Crimes Against Humanity: A Normative Account* (Cambridge: Cambridge University Press, 2005).
[53] Schabas, *Unimaginable Atrocities*, 29–32.
[54] M. Wachspress, 'Pirates, Highwaymen, and the Origins of the Criminal in Seventeenth-Century English Thought' (2015) 26 *Yale Journal of Law & the Humanities* 301.
[55] E. Kontorovich, 'The Piracy Analogy: Modern Universal Jurisdiction's Hollow Foundation' (2004) 45 *Harvard International Law Journal* 183.

In the sixteenth century, the nature of the crime was heavily debated.[56] Alberico Gentili argued that pirates were enemies of all. He claimed that pirates did not deserve the protection of the law of nations, since they violated obligations and placed themselves outside the community of humanity and the international order.[57] Hugo Grotius advocated that pirates should be extradited or punished.[58] Universal jurisdiction was justified on the ground that pirates challenged not only individual nations, but communication and trade within the community of nations and rules governing sea travel. The punishment of piracy rested on the individual nations which enacted piracy laws. Definitions of piracy varied across jurisdictions. They encompassed elements of treason, robbery and violence on the high seas by private vessels, without lawful authority. Pirates were distinguished from 'privateers', i.e. state-licensed sea-robbers.[59] Universal jurisdiction was an option, not a duty. Throughout the eighteenth century execution was deemed to be an appropriate punishment.

Under contemporary law, pirates are no longer subjects outside the law (i.e. 'enemies'), but criminals. Piracy is essentially a crime committed by non-state actors for personal gain. The modern law on piracy is enshrined in several UN conventions, such as the Convention for the Suppression of Unlawful Acts Against the Safety of Maritime Navigation[60] and the UN Convention on the Law of the Sea (UNCLOS).[61] UNCLOS, which is largely recognized as reflecting customary law, defines piracy as an illegal act of violence or detention committed by a private actor against another ship or aircraft on the high seas for private ends. It thereby differentiates piracy from naval warfare and acts of piracy committed in the territorial waters of states.

The UNCLOS definition poses difficulties for investigation and prosecution, due to the fact that it excludes acts on territorial seas or land, or crimes of financing and organizing acts of piracy and armed robbery at sea.[62] One key distinction from existing core crimes is that UNCLOS and UN resolutions only provide a framework for the repression of piracy under international law. They set obligations for states to criminalize piracy domestically and to enhance international cooperation for their

---

[56] For a survey, see M. Kelly, 'The Pre-History of Piracy as a Crime & Its Definitional Odyssey' (2015) 46 *Case Western Reserve Journal of International Law* 25.

[57] A. Gentili, *De Iure belli Libri Tres* (1612) (John C. Rolfe trans., Oxford: The Clarendon Press, 1933), 423 ('For pirates are common enemies, and they are attacked with impunity by all, because they are without the pale of the law. They are scorners of the law of nations; hence they can find no protection in that law. They ought to be crushed by us ... and by you in common, and by all men. This is a warfare shared by all nations').

[58] H. Grotius, *The Free Sea* (Indianapolis: Liberty Fund, 2004), 128 and, *De Iure Belli ac Pacis*, Book II, chap. XXI, paras. III and IV; English translation, *The Law of War and Peace*, Classics of International Law (F. W. Kelsey trans., 1925), 526–529.

[59] See Kontorovich, 'The Piracy Analogy', 210.

[60] UN Convention for the Suppression of Unlawful Acts Against the Safety of Maritime Navigation, 1678 UNTS 221, 27 ILM 668 (entered into force 1 March 1992). The focus lies on damage or destruction of a ship or its cargo and endangerment of safe navigation.

[61] UN Convention on the Law of the Sea, 10 December 1982, 1833 UNTS 3, 21 ILM 1261 (entered into force 16 November 1994)

[62] M. Scharf, M. Newton and M. Sterio (eds.), *Prosecuting Maritime Piracy* (Cambridge: Cambridge University Press, 2015).

prosecution. But they do not provide for individual criminal responsibility.[63] At present, piracy thus remains largely a transnational crime.[64]

There is no principal reason why certain forms of modern piracy could not develop into an international crime, especially if they affect more than one state.[65] Piracy may be more than simple 'robbery at sea'.[66] Acts of piracy off the coast of Somalia have shown that maritime piracy may reach beyond personal gain and involve organized criminal enterprise that is a threat to international peace and security. The Security Council requested the UN Secretary-General to report on accountability mechanisms, including an international tribunal for piracy offences.[67] The Secretary-General suggested several options: a hybrid court, a treaty-based regional court or an ad hoc tribunal under chapter VII for piracy. The idea of a special piracy court[68] was ultimately rejected for pragmatic reasons, such as set-up time, high costs, a large caseload and ongoing criminality. Instead special assistance was given to domestic jurisdictions.[69] The Protocol of Amendments to the Protocol on the Statute of the African Court of Justice and Human Rights (Malabo Protocol)[70] marks a step beyond the classical formulation as universal jurisdiction crime. It foresees the exercise of regional jurisdiction over piracy as a crime, modelled after the UNCLOS definition.[71]

1.2.2 Slavery and Slavery-Like Practices

Slavery is a second crime that has a long historical tradition. Its origins lie in the anti-slavery movement. Slave-trading counts among the first international crimes. It has a forgotten history that continues to be relevant, for instance in relation to 'combating illegal action by non-state, transnational actors'.[72] Bilateral anti-slavery courts count among some of the first experiments to combat transnational crime. The

[63] D. Guilfoyle, 'Piracy off Somalia: UN Security Council Resolution 1816 and IMO Regional Counter-Piracy Efforts' (2008) 57 *ICLQ* 690, 693.

[64] See M. Bo, 'Piracy at the Intersection between International and National: Regional Enforcement of a Transnational Crime', in H. van der Wilt and C. Paulussen (eds.), *Legal Responses to Transnational and International Crimes* (Cheltenham: Elgar, 2017), 71, 74.

[65] On the ICC and piracy, see Y. M. Dutton, 'Bringing Pirates to Justice: A Case for Including Piracy within the Jurisdiction of the International Criminal Court' (2010) 11 *Chicago Journal of International Law* 197; M. O'Brien, 'Where Security Meets Justice: Prosecuting Maritime Piracy in the International Criminal Court' (2014) 4 *Asian Journal of International Law* 81.

[66] Contra Bo, 'Piracy at the Intersection', 73.

[67] SC Res 1918, S/RES/1918 (2010), 27 April 2010.

[68] C. Thedwall, 'Choosing the Right Yardarm: Establishing an International Court of Piracy' (2010) 41 *Georgia Journal of International Law* 501.

[69] Report of the Secretary-General on possible options to further the aim of prosecuting and imprisoning persons responsible for acts of piracy and armed robbery at sea off the coast of Somalia, S/2010/394, 26 July 2010, paras. 97–102, arguing that '[t]he crime of piracy is well established under the United Nations Convention on the Law of the Sea and customary international law and should not present a difficulty of definition'.

[70] Protocol on Amendments to the Protocol on the Statute of the African Court of Justice and Human Rights, AU Doc. No. STC/Legal/Min. 7(1) Rev. 1, 14 May 2014, adopted by the AU Assembly on 30 June 2014.

[71] See Art. 28 F of the Malabo Protocol. In favour of regional jurisdiction, see Bo, 'Piracy at the Intersection', 90–91. For caution, see F. Jessberger, 'Piracy (Article 28F), Terrorism (Article 28G) and Mercenarism (Article 28H)', in G. Werle and M. Vormbaum (eds.), *The African Criminal Court* (The Hague: TMC Asser, 2017), 71.

[72] J. S. Martinez, 'Anti-Slavery Courts and the Dawn of the International Human Rights Law' (2008) 117 *Yale Law Journal* 550, 633.

1926 Convention to Suppress the Slave Trade and Slavery (1926 Slavery Convention)[73] required states to criminalize slavery, i.e. the exercise of the right of ownership
over persons (their treatment as property),[74] and the slave trade. It contained a
relatively far-reaching definition of slavery. It defined slavery as 'the status or condition of a person over whom any or all of the powers attaching to the right of
ownership are exercised'. The term 'status' bans *de jure* slavery, i.e. the recognition
of slavery in law. The second term ('conditions') captures factual relationships, i.e.
slavery in fact.

In 1956, the 1926 Slavery Convention was complemented by the Supplementary
Convention on the Abolition of Slavery, the Slave Trade, and Institutions and
Practices Similar to Slavery.[75] It extended the relationship between 'owner and
owned' to certain similar practices, such as debt bondage or serfdom. It stated that
'the act of mutilating, branding or otherwise marking a slave or a person of servile
status in order to indicate his status, or as a punishment, or for any other reason, or of
being accessory thereto, shall be a criminal offence'.[76]

The types of human exploitation have diversified throughout the twentieth century.
Ownership of another human is not legally recognized. Trafficking of humans for
purposes of forced labour, servitude, child begging or organ removal has become one
of the most profitable illegal businesses with a global reach.[77] The first conventions at
the beginning of the twentieth century were focused specifically on suppressing the
trafficking of women and girls for prostitution.[78] Modern types of slavery and slave-
like practices are characterized by economic exploitation, the lack of a human rights
framework and control over other persons through the prospect or reality of violence.[79] These wider forms of exploitation have been largely captured by the modern
law on human trafficking, most notably the Protocol to Prevent, Suppress and Punish
Trafficking in Persons, especially Women and Children (Palermo Protocol),[80] which
supplements the UN Convention against Transnational Organized Crime.

---

[73] Slavery Convention, 26 September 1926, 60 LNTS. 253.
[74] See Art. 6 of the 1926 Slavery Convention. Art. 1 defines a slave. Slave trade 'includes all acts involved in the capture,
   acquisition or disposal of a person with intent to reduce him to slavery; all acts involved in the acquisition of a slave with
   a view to selling or exchanging him; all acts of disposal by sale or exchange of a slave acquired with a view to being sold
   or exchanged, and, in general, every act of trade or transport in slaves'.
[75] Supplementary Convention on the Abolition of Slavery, the Slave Trade, and Institutions and Practices Similar to
   Slavery, 7 September 1956, 266 UNTS 3.
[76] Art. 5.
[77] From a phenomenological perspective, the majority of trafficked (exploited) persons are subjected to forced labour and
   sexual exploitation. Other forms of exploitation include organ removal, mixed exploitation in forced labour and sexual
   exploitation, committing crime, begging, pornography (including internet pornography), forced marriages, benefit
   fraud, baby selling, illegal adoption, armed combat and for rituals. United Nations Office on Drugs and Crime, Global
   Report on Trafficking in Persons 2014, www.unodc.org/documents/data-and-analysis/glotip/GLOTIP_2014_full_
   report.pdf, at 33–34 (the data corresponds to the year 2011).
[78] International Agreement for the Suppression of the White Slave Traffic, 18 May 1904, 1 LNTS 83; International
   Convention for the Suppression of the White Slave Traffic, 4 May 1910, 3 LNTS 278.
[79] See generally J. Allain, *The Legal Understanding of Slavery* (Oxford: Oxford University Press, 2012).
[80] Protocol to Prevent, Suppress and Punish Trafficking in Persons, Especially Women and Children, supplementing the
   United Nations Convention against Transnational Organized Crime, 15 November 2000, 2237 UNTS 319.

Human trafficking is usually classified as a transnational crime[81] and is wider in scope than enslavement.[82] When occurring in a transnational context and involving an organized criminal group it captures

the recruitment, transportation, transfer, harboring or receipt of persons, by means of the threat or use of force or other forms of coercion, of abduction, of fraud, of deception, of the abuse of power or of a position of vulnerability or of the giving or receiving of payments or benefits to achieve the consent of a person having control over another person, for the purpose of exploitation.[83]

It focuses on the transactional features (i.e. not only harbouring and receipt, but also recruitment, transportation and transfer),[84] the means of trafficking (e.g. threat or use of force or other forms of coercion, abduction, fraud, deception) and the illegal benefits sought by traffickers, rather than the actual status or condition of the person.

International criminal law has gradually developed anti-slavery law and covered factual types of dependence through a wide interpretation of the concept of enslavement as a crime against humanity.[85] For instance, the ICTY found in a fundamental decision that the existence of enslavement depends on factors or indicia such as the 'control of someone's movement, control of physical environment, psychological control, measures taken to prevent or deter escape, force, threat of force or coercion, duration, assertion of exclusivity, subjection to cruel treatment and abuse, control of sexuality and forced labour'.[86] However, it has largely failed to define 'trafficking' as such as an international crime.

Prosecuting trafficking as a crime against humanity has gained fresh attention in the context of migrant-related crimes. Smuggling and trafficking has become an important element of the mass movement of people. One of the tragedies of such crimes is that they are often overlooked or viewed as tolerable evil because they are less spectacular than conflict-related offences.[87] Many crimes against migrants and refugees remain critically under-investigated, although they involve instances of 'aggravated smuggling', including homicides, torture or rape.[88]

In the ICC context, the inclusion of trafficking as a crime was contested. The Women's Caucus for Gender Justice suggested that trafficking be defined as a separate crime in the Rome Statute. It sought criminalization beyond the exercise of

---

[81] C. Hall and C. Stahn, 'Article 7', in O. Triffterer and K. Ambos, *The Rome Statute of the International Criminal Court: A Commentary* (München, Oxford and Baden-Baden: C. H. Beck, Hart and Nomos, 2016), at 262.

[82] Palermo Protocol, Art. 3 (a).

[83] Ibid.

[84] It covers the recruitment, transportation, transfer, harbouring or receipt of persons.

[85] H. Van der Wilt, 'Trafficking in Human Beings, Enslavement Crimes Against Humanity: Unravelling the Concepts' (2014) 13 *Chinese Journal of International Law* 297–334; N. Siller, 'Modern Slavery: Does International Law Distinguish between Slavery, Enslavement and Trafficking?' (2016) 14 *JICJ* 405.

[86] *Prosecutor* v. *Kunarac*, Judgment, IT-96–23 &-IT-96–23/1-A, 12 June 2002, paras. 118–119.

[87] Ibid., para. 1 ('an international crime whose very banality in the eyes of so many makes its tragedy particularly grave and disturbing').

[88] Report of the Special Rapporteur of the Human Rights Council on extrajudicial, summary or arbitrary executions, Unlawful death of refugees and migrants, A/72/335, 15 August 2017, paras. 41 et seq.

ownership. However, the Statute merges enslavement and trafficking in the definition of crimes against humanity. It only captures a part of the broader phenomenon of trafficking in persons. Trafficking is tied to a specific element of enslavement, namely the 'exercise of any or all of the powers attaching to the right of ownership over a person ... in the course of trafficking in persons, in particular women and children'.[89] This merger has caused conceptual confusion[90] and narrows the scope of prosecution.[91] Ownership does not necessarily entail a commercial transaction, but rather relates to the impossibility of the victim changing their condition.[92]

The ICC Prosecutor has collected information 'relating to serious and widespread crimes allegedly committed against migrants attempting to transit through Libya'.[93] The threshold is high. For trafficking to qualify as enslavement, it needs to meet the contextual elements of crimes against humanity. Trafficking must be part of a widespread or systematic attack against the civilian population. A further threshold is the policy element. Trafficking organizations vary greatly in terms of structure, size and capabilities. They can be groups of just two persons who traffic children in a domestic context, loose networks of associates, hierarchically structured groups, or even armed groups and state-like actors, such as IS, which has engaged in trafficking women and children.[94] The ICC definition may capture a partly broader range of 'group' than the UN Convention against Transnational Organized Crime of 2000 (UNTOC), since it is not purpose-related.[95] It does not expressly require a specific economic purpose or a material benefit. The main criterion appears to be related to the impact of the organization, and the types of victimization that it causes. Only a limited number of organizations or networks are likely to meet the required threshold.[96] Groups that carry out isolated or uncoordinated acts would not be covered.

Prosecuting trafficking as a crime poses particular challenges for domestic jurisdictions, since acts often occur in different states. Therefore, states may be unable to prosecute all elements of the offence, or all persons involved. National courts have used several arguments to overcome this limitation. For example, in the *Sneep* case a Dutch court viewed trafficking as a continuous crime, which allowed it to consider elements of the offence that had occurred in other states.[97] A different option was

---

[89] See Art. 7 (2) (c) ICC Statute.

[90] The Protocol on the expansion of the African Court of Justice and Human Rights envisages jurisdiction for its criminal chambers over trafficking in persons per se (Arts. 28A and 28J), alongside enslavement as a crime against humanity (Art. 28C (1) (c) and 2 (c), which is framed in the same terms as the Rome Statute).

[91] See Section 1.3.2.4.1.

[92] *Prosecutor* v. *Katanga*, ICC-01/04–01/07–3436-tENG, Judgment pursuant to Art. 74 of the Statute, 7 March 2014, para. 976 (*Katanga* Trial Judgment).

[93] Statement of ICC Prosecutor to the UNSC on the Situation in Libya, 9 May 2017, para. 25.

[94] Report of the Independent International Commission of Inquiry on the Syrian Arab Republic, 'Rule of Terror: Living under ISIS in Syria', 14 November 2014, paras. 53–55.

[95] United Nations Convention against Transnational Organised Crime, 15 November, 2241 UNTS 507. Art. 2 of the Convention states that an organized criminal group shall 'mean a structured group of three or more persons, existing for a period of time and acting in concert with the aim of committing one or more serious crimes or offences, established in accordance with this Convention, in order to obtain, directly or indirectly, a financial or other material benefit'.

[96] C. Hall and C. Stahn, 'Article 7', in Triffterer and Ambos, *The Rome Statute of the International Criminal Court,* 262.

[97] District Court Utrecht, Judgment, *Sneep*, Case No. 08/963002–07, 11 July 2008, https://ec.europa.eu/anti-trafficking/ sites/antitrafficking/files/the_sneep_case_en_1.pdf. See Van der Wilt, 'Trafficking in Human Beings', 318–319.

pursued by a Colombian court, which argued that because the perpetrators were part of a larger organized criminal group, the actions carried out by each and every one of the members were attributable to all the members of the organization (*Garcia et al.*).[98] If trafficking is prosecuted as the crime against humanity of enslavement, there is a possibility for universal jurisdiction to be invoked.

1.2.3 Terrorism

Terrorism is a third transnational crime with historical roots. Efforts to criminalize terrorism started in the interwar period, after the assassination of King Alexander I of Yugoslavia and the French Foreign Minister by Croatian and Macedonian separatists in October 1934. The rationale was to ban certain forms of political terrorism, namely acts of transnational terrorism committed by non-state actors. The 1937 Convention for the Punishment and Prevention of Terrorism (1937 Convention)[99] defined terrorism as '[c]riminal acts directed against a State and intended or calculated to create a state of terror in the minds of particular persons, or a group of persons or the general public'.[100] This framing avoided addressing the controversial issue of state engagement in terrorism. The Convention required states to criminalize terrorism and other acts.[101] However, it failed to attract enough ratifications. States shared concerns about the broad definition of terrorism and questioned whether punishment would be more effective than cooperation.

Internationally, the prohibition of terrorism developed in a piecemeal fashion, countering specific elements of it rather than defining it in a single international crime.[102] The law was developed in reaction to specific attacks. For instance, in the 1960s and 1970s numerous sectoral antiterrorism treaties were adopted as a response to hijackings and a series of terrorist attacks against diplomats and civilians. In the course of the 1990s it was increasingly recognized that terrorist attacks affect not only states and political processes, but also individual human rights and international peace and security. This led inter alia to the adoption of the Terrorist Bombings Convention by the General Assembly,[103] the Convention for the Suppression of the

---

[98] Criminal Appellate Court of the Supreme Court of Justice, *Garcia et al*, UNODC No.: COL005, 6 March 2008, at www.unodc.org/cld/case-law-doc/criminalgroupcrimetype/col/2008/garcia_et_al.html?lng=en.

[99] Convention for the Punishment and Prevention of Terrorism, 16 November 1937, League of Nations Doc. C.546(I). M.383(I)1937.V (never entered into force). See generally G. Marston, 'Early Attempts to Suppress Terrorism: The Terrorism and International Criminal Court Conventions of 1937' (2002) 73 *British Yearbook of International Law* 291–313. On the parallel efforts to establish an International Court, with jurisdiction over terrorism, see M. O. Hudson, 'The Proposed International Criminal Court' (1938) 32 *AJIL* 549; J. G. Starke, 'The Convention for the Creation of an International Criminal Court' (1938) 19 *British Yearbook of International Law* 216.

[100] 1937 Convention, Art. 1.

[101] Ibid., Arts. 1 (2), 2 (1)–(5).

[102] G. P. Fletcher, 'The Indefinable Concept of Terrorism' (2006) 4 *JICJ* 894; A. Cassese, 'The Multifaceted Criminal Notion of Terrorism in International Law' (2006) 4 *JICJ* 933.

[103] International Convention for the Suppression of Terrorist. Bombings, 15 December 1997, 2149 UNTS 256.

Financing of Terrorism,[104] further Security Council Resolutions and works on a Draft Comprehensive Convention on International Terrorism.[105]

Contemporary counterterrorism law encompasses nearly fifty offences, including crimes against civil aviation and persons; crimes against shipping or continental platforms; crimes involving the use, possession or threatened use of 'bombs' or nuclear materials; and crimes concerning the financing of terrorism. The Convention for the Suppression of the Financing of Terrorism contains a definition that refers to armed conflicts without any mention of a 'freedom fighters' exception. It is thus, as Ben Saul put it, 'no longer unreasonable to speak of a discernible body of "counter-terrorism law", even if such regime may not be as unified, centralized or coherent as some others'.[106] Existing instruments typically contain obligations to criminalize conduct, proscribe proportional penalties and establish jurisdiction. This suggests that terrorist crimes continue to remain mainly 'transnational' offences.

During the Rome conference, states considered the inclusion of terrorism as a separate crime, but could not agree on a generally accepted definition. At the Kampala Review Conference, states rejected the proposal to add terrorism to crimes listed in the Statute, but agreed to suspend jurisdiction until a definition is found.[107] This means that at the ICC, terrorism can only be addressed within the framework of specific war crimes or crimes against humanity, and their respective contextual elements. It implies that mere membership in a terrorist organization or sporadic acts of terrorism are unlikely to be addressed by the ICC.

In 2011, the Special Tribunal for Lebanon sought to define terrorism as an international crime. Drawing from the common elements of terrorism found in domestic legislations, judicial decisions, treaties and UN resolutions, the Appeals Chamber concluded that a customary rule of international law regarding the international crime of terrorism, at least in time of peace, has indeed emerged.[108] It argued that this customary rule requires the following three key elements: the perpetration of a criminal act (such as murder, kidnapping, hostage-taking, arson and so on), or threatening such an act; the intent to spread fear among the population (which would generally entail the creation of public danger) or directly or indirectly coerce a national or international authority to take some action, or to refrain from taking it; and a transnational element of the act.[109] It also noted that 'a customary rule is

---

[104] International Convention for the Suppression of the Financing of Terrorism, 9 December 1999, 2178 UNTS 197.
[105] Draft Comprehensive Convention against International Terrorism, UN Doc. A/59/894, 12 August 2005.
[106] B. Saul, 'Preface' in B. Saul (ed.), *Research Handbook on International Law and Terrorism* (Cheltenham: Edward Elgar Publishing, 2014) x–xi.
[107] On definitional problems, see Fletcher, 'The Undefinable Concept of Terrorism', 894.
[108] See STL-11-01/I. Interlocutory Decision on the Applicable Law: Terrorism, Conspiracy, Homicide, Perpetration, Cumulative Charging, 16 February 2011, para. 85 (STL Interlocutory Appeal Applicable Law). The STL noted that '[c]riminalisation of terrorism has begun at the domestic level, with many countries of the world legislating against terrorist acts and bringing to court those allegedly responsible for such acts. This trend was internationally strengthened by the passing of robust resolutions by the UN General Assembly and Security Council condemning terrorism, and the conclusion of a host of international treaties banning various manifestations of terrorism and enjoining the contracting parties to cooperate for the repression of those manifestations'. Ibid., para. 103.
[109] Ibid., para. 85.

incipient (in *statu nascendi*) which also covers terrorism in time of armed conflict'.[110] It based this argument on the practice of the ICTY and the SCSL, which 'have found, acts of terrorism can constitute war crimes',[111] and state practice concerning the Convention for the Suppression of the Financing of Terrorism, which has been ratified by a 'very high number of States' without reservations.[112]

However, the decision has failed to garner universal support. Definitions of terrorism in regional and domestic instruments vary greatly.[113] The decision has been criticized for not recognizing the differences of definition, including the *actus reus* and *mens rea*.[114] It is questionable whether a general peacetime rule exists.

There are also important policy concerns as to whether it is feasible to recognize a general crime of terrorism. Many governments have used broad definitions of terrorism in order to silence political opposition, stigmatize human rights defenders, target specific religious or ethnic groups, or curtail civil liberties (e.g. freedom of expression, association, assembly and other human rights). Organizations such as Amnesty International or the International Committee of the Red Cross (ICRC) have thus remained critical towards the consolidation of terrorism as an international crime. As the ICRC noted, penalizing terrorism as an international crime may cause frictions with the law of armed conflict.[115] It may discourage compliance by non-state armed groups with the law of armed conflict in civil war,[116] complicate attacks against lawful targets or stifle humanitarian assistance.[117]

In certain cases, terrorism charges may detract from the scope and nature of abuses. In practice, it is often easier for prosecutors to show that an individual is a member of a terrorist organization than to establish the link of the individual to underlying

---

[110] Ibid., para. 107.

[111] Ibid., para. 107.

[112] Ibid., para. 108.

[113] For an attempt of codification, see Art. 2 of the Draft Comprehensive Convention against International Terrorism. It defines terrorism as follows: 'Any person commits an offence within the meaning of the present Convention if that person, by any means, unlawfully and intentionally, causes: (a) Death or serious bodily injury to any person; or (b) Serious damage to public or private property, including a place of public use, a State or government facility, a public transportation system, an infrastructure facility or to the environment; or (c) Damage to property, places, facilities or systems referred to in paragraph1 (b) of the present article resulting or likely to result in major economic loss; when the purpose of the conduct, by its nature or context, is to intimidate a population, or to compel a Government or an international organization to do or to abstain from doing any act.'

[114] B. Saul, 'Legislating from a Radical Hague: The United Nations Special Tribunal for Lebanon Invents and International Crime of Transnational Terrorism' (2001) 24 *Leiden Journal of International Law* 677–700; K. Ambos, 'Judicial Creativity at the Special Tribunal for Lebanon: Is There a Crime of Terrorism under International Law?' (2011) 24 *LJIL* 655, 677; R. Cryer, H. Friman, D. Robinson and E. Wilmshurst, *An Introduction to International Criminal Law and Procedure* (Cambridge: Cambridge University Press, 2014), 341; G. Werle and F. Jessberger, *Principles of International Criminal Law* (Oxford: Oxford University Press, 2014), 48. See also T. Weigend, 'The Universal Terrorist' (2006) 4 *JICJ* 912, 924 (noting that 'many conventions do not require a "political purpose" element').

[115] ICRC, 'International Humanitarian Law and the Challenges of Contemporary Armed Conflicts', 32IC/15/11, October 2005, 20.

[116] States may, for instance, deny that a terrorist group is a party to a non-international armed conflict within the meaning of international humanitarian law.

[117] See ICRC, 'International Humanitarian Law and the Challenges', 20 ('The prohibition of unqualified acts of "material support," "services" and "assistance to" or "association with" terrorist organizations found in certain criminal laws could, in practice, result in the criminalization of the core activities of humanitarian organizations and their personnel that are endeavouring to meet the needs of victims of armed conflicts or situations of violence below the threshold of armed conflict').

international crimes. The use of terrorism charges may be a shortcut, or even undermine efforts to provide a broader accountability strategy for international crimes.[118]
Terrorism thus remains a highly fragmented crime: some dimensions are domestic,
others are transnational, and yet others may be international.[119]

1.3   Core Crimes

'Core crimes' are inherently related to political violence. Their meaning causes a lot of
confusion. Political leaders, military elites or clan leaders are often qualified as 'war
criminals', 'génocidaires' or 'aggressors' in political jargon. But terms such genocide,
crimes against humanity, war crimes or aggression have become terms of art. Each of
these categories of crime has a distinct protected interest and focus.

Historically, all of these crimes were associated with the idea of state involvement.
But their meaning has evolved over time.[120] They cover an increasing number of areas
of 'public' and 'private' criminality. Contemporary definitions include conduct by
non-state entities and modern forms of violence. Today, every individual is bound
under international law not to commit international crimes such as genocide, crimes
against humanity or war crimes, irrespective of whether the individual acts through a
state or non-state actor.

The move towards accountability is characterized by certain key features: a focus
on human atrocity; the diversification of interpretation and legal regimes; a trend to
award specific protection to specific groups, such as women and children, and shifting
conceptions about the dichotomy between civil and political and social, economic and
cultural rights.

Over past decades each of these crimes has been adjusted to fit new contexts
through the practice of international criminal courts and tribunals.

1.3.1   *Genocide*

Genocide is one of the most contested terms in political discourse.[121] It is essentially
an attack upon human diversity. The term was crafted with the Holocaust in mind.
Since then, it has been used in various contexts: the Khmer Rouge regime, Rwanda,
Srebrenica, Darfur, and attacks against the Yezidi community in Iraq.[122] The notion

---

[118] On the German experience, see P. Frank and H. Schneider-Glockzin, 'Terrorismus und Völkerstraftaten im bewaffne-
ten Konflikt'(2017) 1 *Neue Zeitschrift für Strafrecht* 1–7.

[119] See A. Chehtman, 'Terrorism and the Conceptual Divide between International and Transnational Crime', in Van der
Wilt and Paulussen, *Legal Responses*, 107, 126–127.

[120] On the decline of state affiliation, see J. Cerone, 'Much Ado about Non-State Actors: The Vanishing Relevance of State
Affiliation in International Criminal Law' (2008–2009) 10 *San Diego International Law Journal* 335.

[121] See P. Akhavan, *Reducing Genocide to Law* (Cambridge: Cambridge University Press, 2010).

[122] For a comparison of features of genocide, see M. Levene, *The Meaning of Genocide* (London: I. B. Tauris, 2005),
35–89.

is frequently misunderstood. There is stark discrepancy between social perception and legal meaning.[123] Genocide is often referred to as the 'crime of crimes'.[124] The intent to destroy a group makes genocide 'supremely evil'.[125] But depending on the circumstances, crimes against humanity or large-scale war crimes may be no less serious and heinous than genocide.

1.3.1.1 Origin

Genocide was for a long time a crime without name. In 1941, British Prime Minister Winston Churchill said in a radio broadcast: 'We are in the presence of the crime without a name'.[126] Hannah Arendt noted in her letters to Karl Jaspers: 'The Nazi crimes ... explode the limits of the law; and that is precisely what constitutes their monstrousness. For these crimes, no punishment is severe enough ... This guilt, in contrast to all criminal guilt, oversteps and shatters any and all legal systems'.[127] The term was first officially used in 1944 by Polish-Jewish lawyer Raphael Lemkin. It is included in his work *Axis Rule in Occupied Europe*.[128] Lemkin had witnessed the Holocaust. He used the word 'genocide' to capture the destruction of essential foundations of the life of Jews in Eastern Europe. The term is composed of the Greek word '*geno*' (tribe or race) and the Latin verb '*caedere*' (to kill). The essence of genocide is the destruction of the cohesion and moral dignity of these groups as collective entities, as an element of international society. Lemkin referred to destruction in a holistic sense, including destruction of political and social institutions, culture, language, national feelings, religion and economic existence. One of the distinctive features of genocide is that groups are attacked 'for being' rather than 'for doing'.

Lemkin managed to persuade the Prosecution to include it in the Nuremberg indictment – curiously not under Count Four (Crimes Against Humanity), but under Count Three (War Crimes).[129] In the Nuremberg judgment, genocide was not specifically mentioned. The Holocaust was punished under the notion of 'crimes against humanity', which includes persecution and extermination.[130] The absence may be

---

[123] In 1951, the International Court of Justice recognized the broader social significance of genocide. It noted: 'The Convention was manifestly adopted for a purely humanitarian and civilizing purpose. It is indeed difficult to imagine a convention that might have this dual character to a greater degree, since its object on the one hand is to safeguard the very existence of certain human groups and on the other to confirm and endorse the most elementary principles of morality'. ICJ, *Advisory Opinion on Reservations to the Convention on the Prevention and Punishment of the Crime of Genocide*, 1951 ICJ 15, 23

[124] W. A. Schabas, *Genocide in International Law: The Crime of Crimes* (Cambridge: Cambridge University Press, 2009).

[125] D. Amann, 'Group Mentality, Expressivism, and Genocide' (2002) 2 *International Criminal Law Review* 93, 132.

[126] Prime Minister Winston Churchill's broadcast to the world about the meeting with President Roosevelt on 24 August 1941.

[127] Letter to Karl Jaspers, in L. Kohler and H. Saner (eds.), *Hannah Arendt/Karl Jaspers Correspondence 1926–1969* (New York: Harcourt Brace Jovanovich, 1992), 51, 54.

[128] R. Lemkin, *Axis Rule in Occupied Europe* (Washington, DC: Carnegie Endowment for International Peace, 1944).

[129] Nuremberg Trial Proceedings Vol. 1, Indictment: Count Three (A). Nevertheless, the Charter of the International Military Tribunal did not mention genocide as a war crime; see Nuremberg Trial Proceedings Vol. 1, Charter of the International Military Tribunal, Art. 6 (b).

[130] Nuremberg Trial Proceedings Vol. 1, Charter of the International Military Tribunal, Art. 6 (c).

explained by a number of factors, the relatively new nature of the crime and the reluctance to deal with victim groups, rather than individuals.[131]

After Nuremberg, Lemkin campaigned for the universal prohibition of genocide. Only one year after the Nuremberg judgment, the UN General Assembly adopted a resolution in which it 'affirmed' that genocide is a crime under international law.[132] This is unprecedented and speaks to the particular historical significance of genocide. The crime was defined for the first time in the UN Convention on the Prevention and Punishment of the Crime of Genocide.[133] While not exclusively, the framing of the Convention is strongly oriented towards the types of criminalities that occurred during the Holocaust.[134] The legal definition is narrower in scope than the approach advocated by Lemkin.

The Convention is special in several ways. It does not only contain an early reference to the project of international criminal jurisdiction, but includes structures of state responsibility, in addition to individual criminal responsibility. It encompasses a duty of states to prevent genocide, and an express dispute settlement clause related to state responsibility for genocide.

For a long time, however, the Convention was like a 'new car' that did not leave the garage, to follow the famous analogy of Ian Brownlie. Lawyers like Hersch Lauterpacht articulated these scepticisms early on. He argued in 1955 that the Convention is more 'a registration of protest against past misdeeds of individual savagery' than an 'effective instrument of their prevention and repression'.[135] Ironically, the century nearly ended without a conviction for the crime.

The historical contribution of international criminal courts and tribunals is that they brought the concept of genocide to life.[136] The definition of the Convention was reproduced in the Statutes of international criminal courts and tribunals, such as the ad hoc tribunals for the former Yugoslavia[137] and Rwanda,[138] or the ICC.[139] They adjusted the definition to new contexts.

1.3.1.2 Nature of the Crime

The scope of application of genocide is not restricted to leadership criminality. The essence of the crime lies in the attack on specific protected groups of victims.[140] It

---

[131] I. Marchuk, *The Fundamental Concept of Crime in International Criminal Law* (Berlin/Heidelberg: Springer 2014), 88.
[132] See GA Res. 96 (I), UN Doc. GA/Res/96(I), 11 December 1946.
[133] Convention on the Prevention and Punishment of the Crime of Genocide, 9 December 1948, 78 UNTS 1021.
[134] Josef Kunz wrote in 1949: 'Although the present Convention and Lemkin's ideas have been provoked undoubtedly by the persecution of Jews and others by National Socialist Germany, the Convention is not a *lex specialis* like the Nuremberg Charter. The preamble expressly states that 'at all times of history genocide has inflicted great losses on humanity'. See J. L. Kunz, 'The United Nations Convention on Genocide' (1949) 43 *AJIL* 738, 741.
[135] L. Oppenheim, *International Law: A Treatise*, Vol. I, 8th ed. (ed. Hersch Lauterpacht) (London: Longman, 1955), 75.
[136] Rothenberg, 'Let Justice Judge: Genocide as a Living Concept' (2002) 24 *Human Rights Quarterly* 924.
[137] Art. 4, *Updated Statute of the International Criminal Tribunal for the Former Yugoslavia*, S/Res/827 (1993) of 25 May 1993.
[138] Art. 2, *Statute of the International Tribunal for Rwanda*, S/Res/955 (1994) of 8 November 1994.
[139] Art. 6, *Rome Statute of the International Criminal Court*, 1998.
[140] Fletcher argues that 'genocide and hate crimes are punished more severely because they claim two victims, the individual and the group'. See G. P. Fletcher, *Romantics at War: Glory and Guilt in the Age of Terrorism* (Princeton: Princeton University Press, 2002), 66.

combines features of hate crime and state crime.[141] It can only be committed against national, ethnic, racial[142] or religious groups. Other groups, such as political or cultural groups, are not recognized as protected groups per se.[143] Extermination based on political opinion or state-induced social class is thus not covered.[144] This is understandable in light of the historical context. Inclusion of political groups would have opened a Pandora's Box in relation to internal conflicts, and impeded widespread ratification at the time. Protection was limited to groups characterized by a certain degree of stability and permanence.[145] It is sometimes suggested that involuntary identity marks a common feature of protected groups. However, this argument is not entirely convincing. For instance, nationality or religion may be harder to change than political affiliation, but they are not immutable. As David Nersessian has claimed, it is more correct to state that genocide is tied to 'involuntary association': 'The victim has no choice on whether the perpetrator decides he/[she] will be targeted as a member of the victim group'.[146] Genocide is based on what is called 'othering' in the social sciences.[147] It revolves around prejudice and stigma of perpetrators against a group other than their own.

1.3.1.3 Protected Groups

The framing of the protected groups continues to spark controversy.[148] The Genocide Convention was drafted against the background of the experiences of World War II when international law was still rudimentary in its regulation of the internal realm of states. States did not necessarily contemplate all types of genocidal patterns by which leaders target fellow citizens and members of their own societies. In many modern cases, atrocities have involved mass killings by one part of a national group against another group or segment of the same group. In these cases, it becomes difficult to determine whether they are targeted as members of a national group 'as such' (and thus protected),[149] or because of other criteria, such as their status or membership in a political, economic or professional group. This determination has posed dilemmas in

---

[141] J. E. Alvarez, 'Crimes of States/Crimes of Hate: Lessons from Rwanda' (1999) 24 *Yale Journal of International Law* 365.

[142] On difficulties of the concept of race, see C. Lingaas, 'Elephant in the Room: The Uneasy Task of Defining "Racial" in International Criminal Law' (2015) 15 *International Criminal Law Review* 485.

[143] For a discussion, see H. Shneider, 'Political Genocide in Latin America: The Need for Reconsidering the Current Internationally Accepted Definition of Genocide in Light of Spanish and Latin American Jurisprudence' (2010) 25 *American University International Law Review* 314.

[144] M. C. Bassiouni, *Introduction to International Criminal Law: Second Revised Edition* (Leiden: Brill, 2013), at 154.

[145] For a critique, see Schabas, *Genocide in International Law*, 153.

[146] D. L. Nersessian, *Genocide and Political Groups* (Oxford: Oxford University Press, 2010) 65.

[147] A. Holslag, 'The Process of Othering from the "Social Imaginaire" to Physical Acts: an Anthropological Approach' (2015) 9 *Genocide Studies and Prevention* 96. On the criminology of genocide, see N. Rafter, *The Crime of All Crimes: Toward a Criminology of Genocide* (New York: New York University Press, 2016).

[148] Ibid., 21–25.

[149] The ICTR argued that a national group 'is comprised of individuals that share a legal bond based on common citizenship granting them reciprocal rights and obligations'. See *Prosecutor* v. *Akayesu*, Trial Judgment, ICTR-96-4-T, 2 September 1998, paras. 511–515 (*Akayesu* Trial Judgment).

relation to the qualification of the Katyn massacre by the Soviets during World War II[150] or the acts by the Khmer Rouge in Cambodia.

The Katyn killings were directed at members of the Polish intelligentsia. This may be a subgroup of a national group. However, such subgroups are not protected per se. In Cambodia, the majority of victims were members of the Khmer-majority population.[151] These members were targeted because of their belonging to a specific political, professional or economic class. A UN Rapporteur coined the new term 'auto-genocide' to distinguish this type of act by a government against its own people from the acts through which a regime targets a group which is considered as 'other', such as the killing of the Jewish population and people of Slavic origin by Nazi Germany.[152] The Katyn and Cambodian cases can only be qualified as genocide under a broad reading of the protected group requirement, which qualifies certain subgroups as protected parts of national groups (i.e. partial national groups)[153] or gives effective interpretation to the concept of genocide,[154] e.g. by declaring the list of protected groups non-exhaustive[155] or placing the emphasis on the result (destruction of a protected group, 'in whole or in part').

Determination of group identity became a problem in the Rwandan conflict. The Tutsi population did not objectively constitute a group in the definition of the Genocide Convention. They spoke the same language as the Hutu. They shared the same religion. They also had a common cultural identity. The ICTR determined ethnicity in light of the political, social and cultural context.[156] It recognized that collective identities, and in particular ethnicity, are not social facts, but social constructs dependent on perception.[157] The jurisprudence shifted.[158] It moved gradually from an objective understanding of ethnicity[159] towards a combination of objective and subjective elements. It found that '[a]n ethnic group is one whose members share a common language and culture; or, a group which distinguishes itself, as such (self-identification); or, a group identified as such by others, including perpetrators of the

---

[150] M. Sterio, 'Katyn Forest Massacre: Of Genocide, State Lies, and Secrecy' (2012) 44 *Case Western Reserve Journal of International Law* 615.

[151] At the ECCC, genocide charges were brought for crimes by the Khmer Rouge against the Cham group, an ethnic minority within Cambodia, and the Vietnamese minority in case 002/02.

[152] For a discussion of 'auto-genocide', see C. Fournet, *The Crime of Destruction and the Law of Genocide: Their Impact on Collective Memory* (Aldershot: Ashgate, 2007), 49. On Cambodia, see S. Luftglass, 'Crossroads in Cambodia' (2003–2004) 90 *Virginia Law Review* 893, 903.

[153] In the *Scilingo* case, the Spanish national court held in a controversial decision that the 'national group' requirement should be read to include groups within a particular nation. See Audienca Nacional, *Prosecutor* v. *Scilingo*, Judgment, Aranzadi JUR 2005/132318, ILDC 136 (ES 2005), 19 April 2005. For a critical discussion, see C. Tomuschat, 'Issues of Universal Jurisdiction in the Scilingo Case' (2005) 3 *JICJ* 1074–1081; A. Gil Gil, 'The Flaws of the Scilingo Judgment' (2005) 3 *JICJ* 1082–1091.

[154] J. Quigley, 'International Court of Justice as a Forum for Genocide Cases' (2007) 40 *Case Western Reserve Journal of International Law* 243.

[155] Sterio, 'Katyn Forest Massacre', 628.

[156] ICTR, *Prosecutor* v. *Rutaganda*, ICTR-96-3-T, Judgment, 6 December 1999, para. 55.

[157] On imagined collective identities, see B. Anderson, *Imagined Communities: Reflections on the Origin and Spread of Nationalism* (London: Verso, 2006). See also C. Lingaas, 'Imagined Identities: Defining the Racial Group in the Crime of Genocide' (2016) 10 *Genocide Studies and Prevention* 79.

[158] W. Schabas, 'Groups Protected by the Genocide Convention: Conflicting Interpretations from the International Criminal Tribunal for Rwanda' (2000) 6 *ILSA Journal of International & Comparative Law* 375.

[159] *Akayesu* Trial Judgment, para. 513.

crimes (identification by others)'.[160] It therefore considered both perception and self-perception.[161] It recognized Tutsi as a separate ethic group because they were treated as such in official classifications, and perceived themselves as distinct. This interpretation reflected a sentiment in the Security Council, which had mentioned genocide in Resolution 955 (1994), the founding instrument of the tribunal.[162]

Second, the ICTR acknowledged that sexual violence, including rape, can be a means of committing genocide.[163] The Genocide Convention acknowledges that acts such as sterilization or forced procreation may amount to genocide. However, few people assumed that systematic rape may be a means of committing genocide, in the sense of destroying a group. The *Akayesu* Bench found that rape and sexual violence constitute a form of serious bodily or mental harm that leads to physical and biological destruction of Tutsi women, families and their communities.[164] This is also the case where women are raped with the specific intent to impregnate them with children belonging to another group. *Akayesu* thus took an 'intuitive and common-sensical'[165] approach to interpretation that shaped subsequent rulings.

1.3.1.4 Specific Intent

Genocide does not require the actual destruction of a protected group. However, according to the Convention, the enumerated acts must be committed with the 'intent' of the perpetrator to destroy the group in whole or in part' ('specific intent'). It is difficult to prove.[166] Lemkin saw the intent requirement initially as a tool to facilitate the Prosecution's case in cases of emerging patterns of violence, namely before large-scale loss of life occurs. Under international law it turned into an onerous subjective requirement. It must be directed at one of the listed groups 'in whole or in part'.[167]

The ICTY developed many aspects of modern genocide law. It struggled less with the determination of ethnicity or group requirements. Its main innovation lies in the fact that it adjusted the interpretation of genocide to different contexts, in particular killings and destruction carried out against parts of groups in limited geographic areas, such as enclaves and towns. It accepted that genocide is not a 'game of numbers'.

---

[160] ICTR, *Prosecutor* v. *Kayishema and Ruzindana*, ICTR-95 1–T, Judgment, 21 May 1999, para. 98.

[161] Lingaas argues that a pure, subjective understanding conflicts with the principle of legality. See Lingaas, 'Imagined Identities', 101.

[162] SC Res. 955 (1994), preamble, para. 4 ('Expressing once again its grave concern at the reports indicating that genocide and other systematic, widespread and flagrant violations of international humanitarian law have been committed in Rwanda').

[163] See generally B. Van Schaack, 'Engendering Genocide: The Akayesu Case Before the International Criminal Tribunal for Rwanda', in D. R. Hurwitz and M. L. Satterthwaite (eds.), *Human Rights Advocacy Stories* (New York: Foundation Press, 2008), 19.

[164] *Akayesu* Trial Judgment, para. 732 ('Sexual violence was a step in the process of destruction of the tutsi group – destruction of the spirit, of the will to live, and of life itself').

[165] G. Sluiter and A. Zahar, *International Criminal Law* (Oxford: Oxford University Press, 2008), 172.

[166] The ICTR argued that intent is a mental factor that is 'difficult, even impossible, to determine'. See *Akayesu* Trial Judgment, para. 523.

[167] This reading was confirmed by the ad hoc tribunals and two judgments of the International Court of Justice: ICJ, *Application of the Convention on the Prevention and Punishment of the Crime of Genocide* (*Croatia* v. *Serbia*), 3 February 2015, para. 132; ICJ, *Application of the Convention on the Prevention and Punishment of the Crime of Genocide* (*Bosnia and Herzegovina* v. *Serbia*), Judgment of 26 February 2007, para. 187.

1.3.1.4.1 Objective vs. Subjective Interpretation

Practice started with cases against mid- or low-level defenders. The first case, the *Jelisić* case, was a rather odd case. Goran Jelisić was a 23-year-old commander at the Luka camp in Brcko who was partly deranged and presented himself as a 'Serbian Adolf'. He claimed to hate Muslim women and entered a guilty plea for war crimes and crimes against humanity. He failed to acknowledge genocide, however.

The Trial Chamber acknowledged that genocide may exist, even when the exterminatory intent only extends to a limited geographic zone, such as a region or municipality.[168] The main problem was that Jelisić's crimes were not directly part of a broader Bosnian Serb policy to destroy the Bosnian Muslim population in Brčko. The genocide charge thus deviated clearly from the logic of the Holocaust. It was not grounded in objective factors, such as mass killings carried out according to a broader plan or policy. The question was whether the evil intent of a person alone can amount to genocide, even in the absence of a state or institutional policy. This issue goes to the heart of the nature of genocide, namely whether genocide should be predominantly judged by objective or naturalistic features of the crime, or by the evil intent of the perpetrator.[169]

The first approach is more typical in relation to investigation and prosecution. Investigators or prosecutors typically look first to evidence that crimes were committed, and then analyse the relationship of the defendant to the crime. According to this logic, it must first be determined whether genocidal acts have occurred, and then it is assessed whether the person acted with genocidal intent. Such an approach may be grounded in the historic vision of genocide, its exceptional nature and its distinction from crimes against humanity.

The second approach is more unorthodox. According to this approach, the determination of individual criminal responsibility can be supported by objective factors, such as a broader genocidal plan or policy going beyond the individual agent. However, it requires primarily a consideration of the subjective intent of the accused. According to this logic, a single criminal act may amount to genocide if it is carried out with intent to destroy. Technically speaking, such an understanding is not excluded by the plain wording of the convention, although it contrasts with the social understandings of genocide which tend to focus on objective events, rather than criminal intent.

In *Jelisić*, the ICTY leaned towards this second understanding. The Trial Chamber noted that 'it is in fact the *mens rea* which gives genocide its speciality and distinguishes itself from an ordinary crime and other crimes against international humanitarian law'.[170] The Chamber found that such intent could not be proven in the case at hand. However, it held that the Convention does 'not discount the possibility of a lone

---

[168] *Prosecutor* v. *Jelisić*, IT-95-10-T, Judgment, 14 December 1999, para. 82 (*Jelisić* Trial Judgment).
[169] See M. Jarvis and A. Tieger, 'Applying the Genocide Convention at the ICTY' (2016) 14 *JICJ* 857.
[170] *Jelisić* Trial Judgment, para. 66.

individual seeking to destroy a group as such' since 'the drafters of the Convention did not deem the existence of an organisation or a system serving a genocidal objective as a legal ingredient of the crime'.[171] This point was affirmed by the Appeals Chamber, which held that the evidence at hand 'could have provided the basis for a reasonable Chamber to find beyond a reasonable doubt that the respondent had the intent to destroy the Muslim group in Brčko'.[172]

The *Jelisić* case had limited societal relevance. Some may argue it was trivial. But it framed the methodology towards establishing genocide. As Michelle Jarvis and Alan Tieger have noted in their reflection of ICTY case law, 'The question is not whether a particular set of crimes can be labelled in the abstract as genocide but whether the individual accused person is responsible for genocidal acts committed with genocidal intent'.[173] This approach contrasts with the ICC. The Elements of Crimes contain an additional material element which requires that the 'conduct took place in the context of a manifest pattern of similar conduct directed against that group or was conduct that could itself effect such destruction'.[174] This threshold is specific to the ICC. It was introduced to reflect the special gravity of genocide and to avoid isolated hate crimes falling within the ambit of ICC jurisdiction. This restriction was partly a reaction to *Jelisić*. It may be explained by the fact that the ICC has a much wider jurisdictional mandate in terms of situations than the ICTY. It was rejected by the ICTY Appeals Chamber in the *Krstić* case.[175] Rightly understood, the ICC element does not suggest a reversal of the methodology of establishing genocide, but rather a 'realistic' intent test.

In the *Al Bashir* case, this criterion was used to argue that genocide exists only 'when the threat against the existence of the targeted group, or part thereof, becomes concrete and real, as opposed to just being latent or hypothetical'.[176] As noted by Claus Kress, perpetrators may be deemed to act with genocidal intent if their conduct 'forms part of a *realistic collective campaign* directed towards the destruction of a protected group, in whole or in part'.[177]

1.3.1.4.2 Localized Genocide

The wording of the Convention leaves unclear what 'in part' means exactly. A popular reading might suggest that a genocidal policy involves extermination of thousands, if not millions of people. One of the innovations is that the ICTY extended the protective scope of genocide through a dynamic and fluid approach to the construction of

---

[171] Ibid., para. 100.

[172] *Prosecutor v. Jelisić*, IT-95–10-A, Appeal Judgment, 5 July 2001, para. 68.

[173] Jarvis and Tieger, 'Applying the Genocide Convention', 869.

[174] ICC Elements of Crimes, Art. 6.

[175] See *Prosecutor v. Krstić*, Case No. IT-98–33-A, Judgment, 19 April 2004, para. 224 (*Krstić* Appeals Judgment) ('the requirement . . . does not appear in the Genocide Convention and was not mandated by customary international law').

[176] ICC, PTC I, *Prosecutor v. Al Bashir*, Decision on the Prosecution's Application for a Warrant of Arrest against Omar Hassan Ahmad Al Bashir, ICC-02/05–01/09, 4 March 2009, para. 124.

[177] C. Kress, 'The ICC's First Encounter with the Crime of Genocide', in C. Stahn (ed.), *The Law and Practice of the International Criminal Court* (Oxford: Oxford University Press, 2015), 698.

genocidal intent. It ruled that destruction of a part of a group is sufficient if that part is 'emblematic' of the overall group. This interpretation became prominent in the cases relating to Srebrenica which differed from the systematized and massive group destruction that characterized the Holocaust. The key case was *Krstić*. The Appeals Chamber used unusually strong wording. It affirmed the need to call 'the massacre at Srebrenica by its proper name: genocide'.[178]

Krstić made several key contributions to the interpretation of genocide law. It clarified the geographical scope of genocide. *Krstić* accepted the argument that genocide may occur even when the exterminatory intent extends only to a limited geographic zone – something that has been called 'localized genocide'.[179] The size of the Bosnian Muslim population in Srebrenica amounted to approximately forty thousand people prior to its capture by forces of the Army of Republika Srpska (VRS) in 1995. This number constituted only a fraction of the small percentage of the overall Muslim population of Bosnia and Herzegovina at the time. *Krstić* acknowledged expressly that the importance of the Muslim community of Srebrenica 'is not captured solely by its size'.[180]

The Appeals Chamber noted: 'By seeking to eliminate a part of the Bosnian Muslims, the Bosnian Serb forces committed genocide. They targeted for extinction the forty thousand Bosnian Muslims living in Srebrenica, a group which was emblematic of the Bosnian Muslims in general'.[181] This interpretation is compatible with the victim-centred framing of genocide.[182] However, it reduces the concept of genocide to small parts or units of a broader group. It contains at least two logical reductions. It first reduced the Bosnian Muslim population to the Bosnian Muslims in Srebrenica. It then limited the focus on a part of that subgroup, namely the destruction of military-age Bosnian Muslim men. As the Defence has claimed, the intent to destroy was thus effectively related to the destruction of a 'part of a part' of the group of Bosnian Muslims.[183]

The ICTY failed to enter convictions for genocide in other municipalities than Srebrenica. The Prosecution brought genocide charges for crimes committed in 1992. They were, however, more difficult to prove. In the *Mladić* judgment, the majority acknowledged that some physical perpetrators had the intent to destroy part of the protected group of Bosnian Muslims in specific municipalities (e.g. Sanski Most Municipality, Vlasenica, Foča, Kotor Varoš, Foča, Prijedor).[184] Yet it ultimately

---

[178] *Krstić* Appeal Judgment, paras. 37–38. See G. Southwick, 'Srebrenica as Genocide? The Krstić Decision and the Language of the Unspeakable' (2005) 8 *Yale Human Rights and Development Law Journal* 188.

[179] W. Schabas, 'Was Genocide Committed in Bosnia and Herzegovina? First Judgments of the International Criminal Tribunal for the Former Yugoslavia' (2001) 25 *Fordham International Law Journal* 23, 42.

[180] *Krstić* Appeal Judgment, para. 15.

[181] *Krstić* Appeal Judgment, paras. 37–38.

[182] See generally *Kress*, 'The ICC's First Encounter', 669; K. Ambos, 'What Does "Intent to Destroy"' in Genocide Mean?' (2009) 91 *International Review of the Red Cross* 833.

[183] For a critique, see K. Ambos, *Treatise on International Criminal Law, Vol. II; Crimes and Sentencing* (Oxford: Oxford University Press, 2014), 43.

[184] *Prosecutor* v. *Mladić*, IT-09-92-T. Judgment, 22 November 2017, paras. 3513, 3524, 3535.

found that they lacked intent to destroy a 'substantial part of the protected group', since 'the Bosnian Muslims targeted in each individual municipality formed a relatively small part of the Bosnian-Muslim population in the Bosnian-Serb claimed territory or in Bosnia-Herzegovina as a whole'.[185] Unlike in Srebrenica, the majority was unable to conclude that the 'municipalities themselves had a special significance or were emblematic in relation to the protected group as a whole'.[186] The requirement to destroy a 'substantial part' of the protected group is a jurisprudential innovation. It is not included in the text of the Genocide Convention. It marks an attempt to restrict the otherwise wide interpretation of genocide through a quantitative criterion that is difficult to measure.

1.3.1.4.3 Inferred Intent

Intent is particularly hard to establish since it is difficult to 'look into the mind of the perpetrator'. In the case of the Holocaust, such intent could be shown by Nazi documentation. In modern contexts, this has become more difficult. *Krstić* accepted that genocidal intent may be shown through circumstantial evidence. Intent is mostly inferred from circumstances, 'such as the general context, the perpetration of other culpable acts systematically directed against the same group, the scale of atrocities committed, the systematic targeting of victims on account of their membership in a particular group, the repetition of destructive and discriminatory acts, or the existence of a plan or policy'.[187]

Based on historical assumptions, some scholars maintain that genocide requires evidence of a state plan or policy.[188] However, as tribunals have clarified, this is not strictly required by the text. A focus on a state plan or policy would in particular imply that non-state actors cannot commit genocide. This consequence stands in contrast with the protective rationale of the crime. Genocide is not a leadership crime. It is the targeting of protected groups rather than the quality of the agent that characterizes its essence. It would be absurd to assume that a non-state actor, such as ISIS, could not commit genocide.

In the Holocaust and Rwanda, the killing of women and children was used as an argument to support the establishment of genocidal intent. In the context of Srebrenica, the order to kill related only to the destruction of around seven thousand military-age men and boys in Srebrenica. The Prosecution argued that the intent to kill the men and boys was to eliminate the community as a whole. The sense of destruction went further than biological or physical destruction. It claimed that the 'community survives in many cases only in the biological sense, nothing more. It's a community in despair; it's a community clinging to memories; it's a community that is

---

[185] Ibid., para. 3535.

[186] Ibid., para. 3535.

[187] See *Prosecutor* v. *Tolimir*, IT-05-88/2-T, Judgment, 12 December 2012, para. 745.

[188] See generally W. Schabas, 'State Policy as an Element of International Crimes' (2007–2008) 98 *Journal of Criminal Law & Criminology* 953.

lacking leadership; it's a community that's a shadow of what it once was'.[189] The *Krstić* judgment argued that a combination of factors was geared at the destruction of the group. It used three main arguments. First, Bosnian Serb forces could not have failed to know 'that this selective destruction of the group would have a lasting impact upon the entire group'. Their death 'precluded any effective attempt by the Bosnian Muslims to recapture the territory'.[190] Second, 'the Bosnian Serb forces had to be aware of the catastrophic impact that the disappearance of two or three generations of men would have on the survival of a traditionally patriarchal society'.[191] Third, 'the combination of those killings with the forcible transfer of the women, children and elderly would inevitably result in the physical disappearance of the Bosnian Muslim population at Srebrenica'.[192]

This inference of intent was not without critics.[193] For instance, William Schabas argued that this reasoning 'distort[ed] the definition unreasonably'.[194] He argued that the intent to have a 'lasting impact on the group' is not the same as physical destruction, and that there may have been other plausible explanations for the destruction of 7,000 men and boys in Srebrenica.[195]

The *Krstić* finding was criticized for its predominant victimization of Bosnian Muslims in the conflict. Nevertheless it constitutes one of the most important findings in the history of the Balkan wars

Krstić thus marked to some extent a point of no return, both in moral and in legal terms. No other Chamber has called into question the qualification of Srebrenica as genocide.

In 2007, the International Court of Justice showed a great degree of deference on this point to the ICTY in the *Genocide* case. It relied heavily on *Krstić* and found that the 'Court has no reason to depart from the Tribunal's determination that the necessary specific intent (*dolus specialis*) was established'.[196]

The problems became evident again in the *Karadžić* case.[197] The Trial Chamber deduced intent from the inference of knowledge, in particular a 'coded' conversation between Radovan Karadžić and Miroslav Deronjić, the civilian commissioner in Srebrenica. In that conversation Bosnian Muslim male detainees were described as 'goods' which had to be placed inside the warehouses. The Chamber noted that Karadžić was the 'sole person within the Republika Srpska with the power to

---

[189] *Prosecutor* v. *Krstić*, IT-98–33-T, Judgment, 2 August 2001, para. 592 (*Krstić* Trial Judgment).

[190] Ibid., para. 595.

[191] Ibid.

[192] Ibid.

[193] The Appeals Chamber overturned the Trial Chamber's argument that General *Krstic* shared genocidal intent. He was not found guilty as a main perpetrator, but only as an aider or abetter to genocide, since he was aware of intent to commit genocide on the part of some members of the Bosnian Serb Army.

[194] Schabas, 'State Policy as an Element of International Crimes', 47.

[195] Ibid., at 46–47.

[196] ICJ, *Application of the Convention on the Prevention and Punishment of the Crime of Genocide (Bosnia and Herzegovina v. Serbia)*, para. 295.

[197] ICTY, *Prosecutor* v. *Karadžić*, IT-95–5/18-T, Judgment, 24 March 2016 (*Karadžić* Trial Judgment).

intervene to prevent the Bosnian Muslim males from being killed'.[198] It came to the conclusion that the only reasonable inference is that Karadžić knew that Bosnian Muslim males would be killed. It derived his intent from his subsequent involvement in the implementation of the plan.[199] It argued that the 'accused agreed with and therefore did not intervene to halt or hinder the killing aspect of the plan'.[200] There was a double inference: knowledge was inferred from the conversations, and subsequently intent was inferred from the knowledge.[201] Critics have argued that Karadžić might have simply had reason to know that the killings took place, but only intent to carry out ethnic cleansing.[202] Treating the intent to ethnically cleanse an area by forcibly removing a protected group as the intent to destroy a protected group stretches the boundaries of genocide.

1.3.1.4.4 The Knowledge-Based Approach

In doctrine, there are increasing attempts to rethink genocidal intent.[203] An interpretation of genocidal intent which infers the intent to destroy largely from circumstantial evidence, such as elements of a genocidal plan or policy, is de facto not far from the alternative approach, the knowledge-based approach.[204] This approach was discussed as an alternative to the purpose-based approach by the ILC[205] and in the negotiations of the ICC.[206] It is less directly in line with the wording of the Convention. However, it reflects the spirit of the crime. It takes into account critiques that the focus on specific intent makes genocide too individualistic.[207] As Alexander Greenawalt has argued:

[The knowledge-based] approach emphasizes the destructive result of genocidal acts instead of the specific reasons that move particular individuals to perform such acts. It addresses the

---

[198] ICTY, *Prosecutor* v. *Karadzic*, Judgment Summary, at www.icty.org/x/cases/karadzic/tjug/en/160324_judgement_summary.pdf. The coded conversation is portrayed in para. 5805.

[199] See *Karadžić* Trial Judgment, para. 5811.

[200] *Karadžić* Trial Judgment, para. 5830.

[201] See M. Sterio, 'The Karadzic Genocide Conviction: Inferences, Intent and the Necessity to Redefine Genocide' (2017) 31 *Emory International Law Review* 271, 289.

[202] See M. Milanovic, 'ICTY Convicts Radovan Karadzic', at www.ejiltalk.org/icty-convicts-radovan-karadzic/.

[203] H. Vest, 'A Structure-Based Concept of Genocidal Intent' (2007) 5 *JICJ* 781–797; S. Kim, *A Collective Theory of Genocidal Intent* (The Hague: TMC Asser Press, 2016), 13–91; Ambos, *Treatise on International Criminal Law, Vol. II*, 26–31.

[204] A. K. A. Greenawalt, 'Rethinking Genocidal Intent: The Case for a Knowledge-Based Interpretation' (1999) 99 *Columbia Law Review* 2259; A. Gil Gil, *Derecho Penal Internacional: Especial Consideración del Delito de Genocidio* (Madrid: Tecnos, 1999), 259.

[205] The ILC contemplated a distinction between leaders and subordinates in the framing of genocide in the Draft Code of Crimes against the Peace and Security of Mankind (Art. 17). It noted that subordinates require 'a degree of knowledge of the ultimate objective of the criminal conduct rather than knowledge of every detail of a comprehensive plan or policy of genocide'. See Report of the International Law Commission on the Work of Its Forty-Eight Session, May 6–July 26, UN Doc. A/51/10, 1996, 45.

[206] Report of the Ad Hoc Committee on the Establishment of the International Criminal Court, UN Doc. A/50/22, GAOR, 50th Sess., Supp. No. 22, 6 September 1995, para. 62 ('There was a further suggestion to clarify the intent requirement for the crime of genocide by distinguishing between a specific intent requirement for the responsible decision makers or planners and a general-intent or knowledge requirement for the actual perpetrators of genocidal acts. Some delegations felt that it might be useful to elaborate on various aspects of the intent requirement without amending the Convention, including the intent required for the various categories of responsible individual').

[207] J. D. Ohlin, 'The One or the Many' (2015) 9 *Criminal Law & Philosophy* 285, 289 ('Since fundamentally collective acts, like genocide, are only possible with deep collaboration among its members, a purely individualist account fails to explain the group-level dynamics among the individual members. Genocide is a case in point – it isn't just the aggregate of many individuals committing isolated acts of murder').

related problems of subordinate actors and ambiguous goals by unhinging the question of genocidal liability from that of the perpetrator's particular motive or desires with regard to the group as a whole.[208]

According to the knowledge-based approach, it is less relevant whether or not the perpetrator acted with the particular intent to destroy in whole or in part a protected group. Acting in support of a campaign targeting members of a protected group which the alleged perpetrator knows to have a genocidal purpose or manifest effect is enough to attribute criminal responsibility. This approach tends to recognize that mid- and low-level perpetrators who do not necessarily act with the ulterior intent but know of the genocidal campaign, and act in its furtherance, are as dangerous for the existence of the protected group as those who act with purpose. A key example is Adolf Eichmann, who continuously refused to admit specific intent. Some voices therefore suggest that *génocidaires* must have intent in relation to the underlying acts of genocide, while knowledge suffices in relation to the context, i.e. the existence of a broader genocidal campaign.[209] Others differentiate between categories of perpetrators. For instance, Kai Ambos requires genocidal purpose or desire for high-level perpetrators (e.g. intellectual masterminds), but accepts knowledge and contribution to a collective intent to destroy for low-level perpetrators, i.e. those executing genocidal acts.[210]

Critics question whether it is feasible to extend the definition of genocidal intent to capture subordinates.[211] They claim that the knowledge-based approach may blur the distinction to accessorial liability. As the ICC has stated: 'Those others, who are only aware of the genocidal nature of the campaign, but do not share the genocidal intent, can only be held liable as accessories'.[212]

1.3.1.4.5 Intent and Forced Transfer

Typically, there has been a strong emphasis on killing in genocide cases. The *Tolimir* case raised the relationship between physical or biological destruction and forced transfer.[213] In that case, the ICTY Appeals Chamber addressed for the first time the commission of genocide through acts other than killings, in particular forcible transfers of civilians. Tolimir was an assistant commander of the Army of the Republika Srpska with close lines to General Mladić, who was involved in population transfers from Srebrenica and Žepa. He argued that forcible transfer may only constitute genocide if the displaced population is transferred to concentration camps or places of execution. The Trial Chamber found, by majority, that the removal of the Bosnian Muslim civilian population from Žepa, the demolition of their homes and the mosque,

---

[208] Greenawalt, 'Rethinking Genocidal Intent', 2288.

[209] Vest, 'A Structure-Based Concept of Genocidal Intent', 793.

[210] Ambos, *Treatise on International Criminal Law, Vol. II*, 29–30.

[211] See Kim, *A Collective Theory of Genocidal Intent*, 36.

[212] *Prosecutor v. Al Bashir*, Decision on the Prosecution's Application for a Warrant of Arrest against Omar Hassan Ahmed Al Bashir, 4 March 2009, 49, n. 154.

[213] *Prosecutor v. Tolimir*, IT-05–88/2-T, Judgment, 12 December 2012 (*Tolimir* Trial Judgment).

and the killing of three of the most prominent local leaders, amounted to genocide.[214] The Appeals Chamber clarified that forced displacement of a population does not constitute in and of itself a genocidal act. However, it admitted that forcible transfers of civilians could, in theory, lead to conditions of life calculated to bring about the physical destruction of a protected group. Such transfers may not immediately kill the members of the group, but ultimately seek their physical destruction.

The Appeals Chamber held that 'nothing in the Tribunal's jurisprudence or in the Genocide Convention provides that a forcible transfer operation may only support a finding of genocide if the displaced population is transferred to concentration camps or places of execution'.[215] It found that forcible transfer may ensure the physical destruction of the protected group by 'causing serious mental harm or leading to conditions of life calculated to bring about the group's physical destruction, even if the group members are not transferred to places of execution'.[216] It argued that such transfers may 'threaten the physical destruction of the group in whole or in part, because they compromise the ability of the members of the protected group to lead a normal and constructive life'.[217] Thereby it equated the impossibility of leading a normal and constructive life to the threat of being destroyed.

The Appeals Chamber also recognized that expulsions are not necessarily incompatible with genocidal intent, stressing that facts have to be assessed in a holistic fashion. It argued that acts of forcible transfer may provide a basis for inferring the perpetrators' intent to destroy, in combination with other evidence concerning the commission of large-scale killings and discriminatory actions.[218] It accepted that an expulsion may encompass a variety of destructive acts that reflect an intent to destroy a community. The reasoning recognized that genocidal intent may result from non-destructive acts.[219]

This approach stands in a certain tension with the alleged historical assumption[220] that the purpose underlying the prohibition of genocide is the criminalization of conduct that seeks to destroy a protected group either physically or biologically.[221] It was criticized by Judge Antonetti, who argued that genocidal intent can only be

---

[214] Judge Nyambe dissented.

[215] *Prosecutor* v. *Tolimir*, IT-05–88/2-A, Judgment, 6 April 2015, para. 209 (*Tolimir* Appeal Judgment).

[216] Ibid.

[217] Ibid., para. 212.

[218] Ibid., para. 254.

[219] See also *Krstić* Appeal Judgment, Dissenting Opinion of Judge Shahabuddeen, para. 54 ('the intent to destroy the group as a group is capable of being proved by evidence of an intent to cause the non-physical destruction of the group in whole or in part, except in particular cases in which physical destruction is required by the Statute').

[220] For a critique see, E. Novic, 'Physical-Biological or Socio-Cultural "Destruction" in Genocide? Unravelling the Legal Underpinnings of Conflicting Interpretations' (2015) 17 *Journal of Genocide Research* 63, 75 ('the concept of "physical-biological" group destruction was constructed predominantly by the ILC and the ICTY, rather than grounded on solid sources of interpretation').

[221] The ILC has argued that, 'as clearly shown by the [*travaux préparatoires*], the destruction in question is the destruction of a group either by physical or by biological means, not the destruction of the national, linguistic, religious, cultural or other identity of a particular group. The national or religious element and the racial or ethnic element are not taken into consideration in the definition of the word "destruction", which must be taken only in its material sense, its physical or biological sense'. ILC, Report of the International Law Commission on the Work of Its Forty-Eighth Session (1996), 46.

inferred from facts that will cause the physical or biological destruction of a group, rather than the group's expulsion.[222]

1.3.1.5 'Cultural' Genocide

There has been a long debate over the extent to which cultural destruction may amount to genocide.[223] Cultural dimensions play an important role in the determination of genocide. Technically, the *actus reus* of genocide is not confined to killing. Cultural factors, such as social, historical and linguistic features, are often necessary to explain whether a group qualifies as a racial, ethnic, religious or national group. Physical and biological destruction often goes hand in hand with the elimination of cultural features, property or symbols.

Lemkin argued that the definition of genocide should not only cover the physical destruction of a group, or the elimination of its reproductive capacity, but include attacks on its cultural institutions (e.g. systematic destruction of language, religious institutions and objects).[224] Early drafts of the Genocide Convention contained references to 'national-cultural genocide'.[225] However, critics questioned whether the concept of cultural genocide is concise and grave enough to warrant criminalization. For instance, Denmark cautioned that 'it would show a lack of logic and of a sense of proportion to include in the same convention both mass murders in gas chambers and the closing of libraries'.[226] Other states feared that the recognition of cultural genocide would interfere with minority issues. It was thus only covered to a limited extent. The prohibition to impose 'measures intended to prevent births within the group' relates not only to biological destruction, but affects the social structure of the community. The Genocide Convention prohibits forcible transfer of a group's children, partly because the exposure of children to a different culture or language may alter the future existence of the group.[227] The destruction of cultural monuments or similar acts directed against the culture of the group may be used to support

---

[222] *Tolimir* Appeal Judgment, Separate and Partially Dissenting Opinion of Judge Antonetti, 72–73.

[223] See generally, E. Novic, *The Concept of Cultural Genocide* (Oxford: Oxford University Press, 2016); L. Bilsky and R. Klagsbrun, 'The Return of Cultural Genocide?'(2018) 29 *EJIL* 373–396. Russia made a proposal to cover it in the Genocide Convention as follows: 'In this Convention genocide also means any deliberate act committed with the intent to destroy the language, religion or culture of a national, racial or religious group on grounds of national or religious origin, or religious beliefs such as: (a) Prohibiting the use of the language of the group in daily intercourse or in schools or the printing and circulation of publications in the language of the group; (b) destroying or preventing the use of libraries, museums, schools, historical monuments, places of worship or other cultural institutions and objects of the group.' See General Assembly, Agenda Item 32, UN Doc A/766, 5 December 1948, in H. Abtahi and P. Webb, *The Genocide Convention: The Travaux Préparatoires* (Leiden: Brill Nijhoff 2008), 2039.

[224] R. Lemkin, 'Genocide as a Crime under International Law' (1947) 41 *AJIL* 145, 147 ('mass murder does not convey the specific losses to civilization in the form of the cultural contributions which can be made only by groups of people united through national, racial or cultural characteristics').

[225] Abtahi and Webb, *The Genocide Convention*, 234–235.

[226] UNGA, 'Eighty-Third Meeting: Consideration of the Draft Convention on Genocide', 25 October 1948, UN Docs A/C6/SR83 in Abtahi and Webb, *The Genocide Convention*, 1508.

[227] This clause was originally contained in the cultural genocide provision of the draft Genocide Convention. As the ILC noted: 'The forcible transfer of children would have particularly serious consequences for the future viability of a group as such. ... Moreover, the forcible transfer of members of a group, particularly when it involves the separation of family members, could also constitute genocide'. See ILC, Report of the International Law Commission on the Work of Its Forty-Eighth Session, 46.

allegations of physical genocide or persecution as a crime against humanity.[228] The concept of 'cultural' genocide is thus indirectly enshrined in the Convention. It reflects the political constraints of treaty negotiations rather than the nature and social reality of the crime.

Scholars have noted the inherent contradiction in a predominantly physical/biological conception of destruction. It is contradictory to claim that 'a group must have a distinct identity to attract the protection afforded by the Convention but acts which target their cultural heritage (and which render the group distinctive) are not prohibited per se'.[229] Some decisions have highlighted the close interconnection between the underlying acts of genocide and destruction of the group as social collectivity,[230] and offered a counter-reading to the orthodox view that 'cultural' destruction is not covered:

It is not accurate to speak of 'the group' as being amenable to physical or biological destruction. Its members are, of course, physical or biological beings, but the bonds among its members, as well as such aspects of the group as its members' culture and beliefs, are neither physical nor biological. Hence the Genocide Convention's 'intent to destroy' the group cannot sensibly be regarded as reducible to an intent to destroy the group physically or biologically.[231]

1.3.1.6 Words as Bullets

Genocide is the only crime in which incitement is expressly prohibited. The prohibition takes into account that genocide is often spread through mass mobilization. At Nuremberg, Julius Streicher, the editor of an anti-Semitic magazine, was convicted for hate propaganda against Jewish people. His incitement to murder and extermination was qualified as persecution as a crime against humanity.[232] The drafters of the Genocide Convention criminalized public and direct incitement to genocide in order to counter emerging patterns of genocide and take into account the specific risks of incitement of an indeterminate group of persons (e.g. through speeches, radio, press or other media).[233] Public incitement played a critical role in the Rwandan genocide. The

---

[228] *Krstić* Trial Judgment, para. 580.

[229] A. F. Vrdoljak, 'Cultural Heritage in Human Rights and Humanitarian Law', in O. Ben-Naftali (ed.), *International Humanitarian Law and International Human Rights Law* (Oxford: Oxford University Press, 2011), 299

[230] On a 'relational account' of genocide, see C. Powell, 'What do Genocides Kill? A Relational Conception of Genocide' (2007) 9 *Journal of Genocide Research* 527.

[231] *Prosecutor* v. *Krajišnik*, IT-00–39, Judgment, 27 September 2006, para. 854, n. 1701. See also *Prosecutor* v. *Blagojević and Jokić*, IT-02–60-T, Judgment, 17 January 2005, para. 666. ('A group is comprised of its individuals, but also of its history traditions, the relationship between its members, the relationship with other groups, the relationship with the land. The Trial Chamber finds that the physical or biological destruction of the group is the likely outcome of a forcible transfer of the population when this transfer is conducted in such a way that the group can no longer reconstitute itself – particularly when it involves the separation of its members').

[232] On Streicher, see M. Eastwood, *The Nuremberg Trial of Julius Streicher: The Crime of 'Incitement to Genocide'* (Lewiston, NY: Edwin Mellen Press, 2011).

[233] The Russian Delegate stated: 'It was impossible that hundreds of thousands of people should commit so many crimes unless they had been incited to do so … The peoples of the world would indeed be puzzled if … those who incited others to commit the concrete acts of genocide, were to remain unpunished.' Summary Records of the meetings of the Sixth Committee of the General Assembly, 21 September–10 December 1948, Official Records of the General Assembly, statements by Mr Morozov, 241.

ICTR tried the first 'incitement to genocide' cases. It adopted a wide interpretation which distinguishes it from instigation.[234] It relates to speech that is delivered through classical channels (e.g. a loudspeaker, radio or media) to a large and often indeterminate audience.

The first case was *Akayesu*. He was tried for giving a speech that called for the elimination of the 'Inkotanyi' (which was tantamount to Tutsi). It could not be shown that the speech itself triggered genocide, since killings had started elsewhere. The Chamber found that incitement is an 'inchoate crime' which 'must be punished as such, even where such incitement failed to produce the result expected by the perpetrator'.[235] The ICTR defined the essential contours of the crime. It specified that the person who is inciting must have the specific intent to commit genocide, i.e. a 'desire to . . . create a particular state of mind necessary to commit such a crime in the minds' of the recipients.[236] The underlying intended crime does not need to occur for the crime to be shown. Causation is thus not a legal requirement to prove the crime of incitement. The justification for the punishment of incitement lies in preventive purposes and the potential for the communication to cause genocide.[237] Incitement is deemed to involve such a high risk for society that it is punished irrespective of whether genocide occurs.

The ICTR clarified that the 'public' element may be satisfied if it involves 'a call for criminal action to a number of individuals in a public place or to members of the general public'.[238] Directness requires provocation, rather than a 'mere vague or indirect suggestion'.[239] A key factor is the intended impact on the recipient and the intended meaning conveyed. This must be understood in light of the context.

The most paradigmatic case was the Rwandan *Media* case,[240] which concerned the responsibility of news media in the genocide. It involved three defendants who were charged as representatives of different entities: Ferdinand Nahimana, chief executive of *Radio Télévision Libre des Milles Collines* (RTLM, called 'Radio Machete'), which broadcast ethnic stereotypes to promote hatred for the Tutsi population; Hassan Ngeze, the owner and editor of *Kangura* (Wake Others Up!), an inflammatory newspaper that dehumanized Tutsi as cockroaches; and Jean-Bosco Barayagwis, a government minister who provided the political framework for the killing. The decision broke new ground because it held 'a newspaper editor and a broadcast executive criminally accountable not only for the crime of what they said, the crimes their word did'.[241] The Trial Chamber analysed the euphemisms and found that certain, though

---

[234] W. Schabas, 'Hate Speech in Rwanda: The Road to Genocide' (2000) 46 *McGill Law Journal* 141.
[235] *Akayesu* Trial Judgment, para. 562.
[236] Ibid., para. 560.
[237] *Prosecutor* v. *Nahimana, Barayagwiza, & Ngeze*, ICTR 99–52-T, Judgment and Sentence, 3 December 2003, para. 1015 (*Nahimana* Trial Judgment).
[238] *Akayesu* Trial Judgment, para. 556.
[239] Ibid., para. 557.
[240] G. Della Morte, 'De-Mediatizing the Media Case: Elements of a Critical Approach' (2005) 3 *JICJ* 1019.
[241] See C. MacKinnon, 'International Decisions, Prosecutor v. Nahimana, Barayagwiza, & Ngeze' (2004) 98 *AJIL* 325, 328–329.

not all, broadcasts and articles amounted to incitement. It convicted defendants of deploying speech as a weapon. Judge Pillay said to Ferdinand Nahimana: 'Without a firearm, machete or physical weapon, [you] caused the deaths of thousands of innocent civilians'.[242] One of the most delicate aspects of the case was to develop criteria to distinguish between hate speech and incitement. Hate speech is sanctioned in very different ways and to different degrees in countries over the globe.[243] The Trial Chamber determined that hate speech involves the creation of a violent and dehumanizing social environment for specific groups, e.g. through a statement that 'Tutsis are cockroaches'. It specified that incitement requires a calling on the audience (e.g. listeners, readers) to take action against the groups. The jurisprudence used four criteria: purpose, text, context, and the relationship between speaker and subject.[244] The Open Society Justice Initiative argued before the Appeals Chamber that trial judges had blurred the distinction between hate speech and incitement. The Appeals Chamber upheld the incitement convictions but overturned findings on instigation.[245]

Later, the Prosecution charged Simon Bikindi, a famous Rwandan singer, for inciting genocide through anti-Tutsi songs. The indictment focused on three songs that were often broadcast before and during the genocide. He was ultimately convicted for statements that he made, rather than the music performed.[246] The Chamber found no evidence that the three songs themselves constituted 'direct and public incitement to commit genocide per se',[247] or that *Bikindi* played any role in the broadcasting of his songs.[248]

Jurisprudence has failed to develop a full-fledged theory of incitement. New approaches have been suggested in doctrine. Some authorities draw on performative speech act theory to explain incitement as an inchoate crime. For example, Richard Wilson has argued that speech acts can be considered to be criminal acts according to their meaning, force and effects.[249] Susan Benesch has argued that incitement should be limited to speech that has a reasonable possibility of leading to genocide. She has proposed to take into account several criteria, namely authority, power or influence of the speaker over the audience, the disposition and capacity of the intended audience to commit violent acts, the dehumanizing or inflammatory nature of the speech act, the

---

[242] *Nahimana* Trial Judgment, para. 1099.

[243] According to the 'Brandenburg test' developed by the US Supreme Court, speech is not protected if it 'is directed to inciting or producing imminent lawless action and is likely to produce such action'. See US Supreme Court, *Brandenburg* v. *Ohio*, 395 US 444, 447 (1969).

[244] See G. Gordon, 'Formulating a New Atrocity Speech Offense: Incitement to Commit War Crimes' (2012) 43 *Loyola University Chicago Law Journal* 281, 294.

[245] See *Prosecutor* v. *Nahimana, Barayagwiza, & Ngeze*, ICTR 99-52-A, Judgment, 28 November 2007, para. 695 ('The Appeals Chamber considers that the Trial Chamber did not alter the constituent elements of the crime of direct and public incitement to commit genocide in the media context').

[246] The *Prosecutor* v. *Bikindi*, Case No. ICTR-01-72-T, Judgment and Sentence, 2 December 2008, para. 423. See G. S. Gordon, 'Music and Genocide: Harmonizing Coherence, Freedom and Nonviolence in Incitement Law' (2010) 50 *Santa Clara Law Review* 607; J. La Mort, 'The Soundtrack to Genocide: Using Incitement to Genocide in the Bikindi Trial to Protect Free Speech and Uphold the Promise of Never Again' (2010) 4 *Interdisciplinary Journal of Human Rights Law* 43.

[247] *Bikindi* Trial Judgment, para. 421.

[248] Ibid., para. 262.

[249] R. Wilson, 'Inciting Genocide with Words' (2015) 36 *Michigan Journal of International Law* 277, 319

socio-historical context (e.g. risk factors for violence) and the mode of transmission.[250] Such criteria are necessary to refine the blurry distinction between hate speech and incitement beyond the Rwandan paradigm. In contemporary conflicts, incitement occurs through many other forums, such as the internet, social media or Twitter. The rise of new technologies allows everyone to engage in speech and to be heard. New virtual media may be even more inflammatory than print media. Their criminality cannot be assessed solely by the content of speech, but must take into account the dangers that they create.

Other voices even go a step further, by proposing to extend the incitement offence to crimes against humanity[251] and war crimes more broadly.[252] Proponents of this view argue that it is necessary in order to recognize the unique contribution of speech to atrocity in its own right and to increase prevention. Critics claim that such an extension would overcriminalize behaviour and make distinctions in relation to hate speech even more difficult. Other methods, such as information intervention (e.g. radio jamming[253]) or early warning might be better suited to prevent or limit crime than adjudication by courts.

1.3.1.7 Paradoxes of the 'New Law on Genocide'

The 'new law on genocide' involves many paradoxes. The social meaning of genocide exceeds the legal meaning. In popular jargon, the term genocide is frequently overused. The label adds drama and gravity, because of its historical comparison. Many victims feel strongly about the expressive value of genocide. This provides an incentive for prosecutors to bring a genocide charge. Yet in legal terms genocide remains difficult to establish. It typically needs to be built gradually, through a number of cases. International criminal courts and tribunals have tried to operate within the confines of the Genocide Convention, but they have adjusted it to context, and given it a new meaning.

Legal interpretations have not gone so far as to endorse Lemkin's holistic construction of genocide, which included destruction of political and social institutions, culture, language, national feelings, religion or economic existence.[254] However they have not felt constrained by the *travaux preparatoires* or historical context. As Judge Shahabudeen put it: 'If there is inconsistency, the interpretation of the final text of the Convention is too clear to be set aside by the travaux'.[255] Modern interpretations have

---

[250] S. Benesch, 'Vile Crime or Inalienable Right: Defining Incitement to Genocide' (2008) 48 *Vanderbilt Journal of International Law* 485.

[251] Both, the ICTY and the ICYR have recognized that hate speech can serve as the basis of persecution as a crime against humanity. The ICTY limited it to acts directly calling for violence. *Prosecutor* v. *Kordić & Čerkez*, IT-95-14/2-T, Judgment, 26 February 2001.

[252] See G. Gordon, *Atrocity Speech Law* (Cambridge: Cambridge University Press, 2017).

[253] A. C. Dale, 'Countering Hate Messages that Lead to Violence: The United Nations' Chapter VII Authority to Use Radio Jamming to Halt Incendiary Broadcasts' (2001) 11 *Duke Journal of Comparative & International Law* 109.

[254] The ICTY has expressly ruled that the destruction of historical, cultural or religious heritage alone does not suffice to constitute genocide.

[255] *Krstić* Appeal Judgment, Partially Dissenting Opinion of Judge Shahabudeen, para. 52.

shown that some of the boundaries may be less clear-cut than assumed. Genocide is not only about killing, but can be committed in other ways. Individual intent must be assessed in context. Destruction is mostly a process. In reality, physical or biological destruction is often connected to attacks on cultural and religious property or symbols. The two therefore cannot be as neatly distinguished as the law seems to suggest.

The trend to expand genocide remains contested. The 'new law on genocide' seeks to reinforce the prohibition of genocide, and to express its extraordinary nature in legal judgment, in order to bring some sense of closure to historical injustice. However, at the same time it weakens the nature of the underlying norm. It has made the distinction to crimes against humanity more fluid.

Visions on the path forward remain divided. The ICC approach to genocide is narrower than the one taken by the ICTY. The direction in which modern genocide law will develop is still open. Some voices see virtue in maintaining the special nature of genocide as a crime. They contend that there is merit in a narrow legal definition, that genocide needs to remain distinct from other types of mass killings, and that the category of crimes against humanity might be more appropriate to encompass new forms of violence. Others argue that it is counterproductive to frame genocide as an exceptional crime, since it detracts attention from the broad scope of local and global actors involved in genocide[256] and its close linkage to everyday behaviour and structural forms of violence.[257] They claim that the meaning of genocide should be adjusted to new circumstances in order to avoid a growing disconnect between legal definition and public perception.

Some scholars call for substantial revision of the definition of genocide, such as the elimination of the 'as such' requirement[258] or an expanded notion that might encompass ethnic cleansing'[259], 'politicide' (i.e. mass killing of political groups), 'ethnocide' (i.e. destruction of language and culture for purposes of group extermination) or 'gendercide' (i.e. systematic killing of members of a specific sex). Such an approach continues to meet hesitation by states, since it would broaden state obligations, expose governments to claims of state responsibility and extend civil liability for violations. The power of the word 'genocide', and its broader criminological foundation, are thus likely to continue to exceed its legal meaning, despite the important steps taken in the past quarter of a century.

---

[256] See Roberts and McMillan, 'For Criminology in International Criminal Justice', 325 ('Of genocide can be passed off as an inexplicable, unpredictable, exceptional orgy of spontaneous violence, the former colonizers, and the international community as a whole, are seemingly off the hook').

[257] For instance, Alvarez has drawn attention to the involvement of ordinary citizens in genocide and the role of Western powers. See Alvarez, 'Crimes of States/Crimes of Hate: Lessons from Rwanda', 453–458.

[258] Sterio, 'The Karadzic Genocide Conviction', 292, noting that such an approach 'would allow for acts of reprehensible persecution of members of a subgroup within one of the protected groups to constitute genocide'.

[259] M. Sirkin, 'Expanding the Crime of Genocide to Include Ethnic Cleansing: A Return to Established Principles in Light of Contemporary Interpretations' (2010) 33 *Seattle University Law Review* 489.

1.3.2   Crimes against Humanity

The concept of crimes against humanity captures some features of genocide, such as the idea of extermination. Unlike genocide, it is not yet codified in an international convention.[260] Its origin lies in the humanitarian principles governing armed conflict.[261] However, it has close synergies with human rights protection and the development of values of humaneness. It is increasingly regarded as protecting individual legal interests such as liberty, autonomy and human dignity.[262]

Crimes against humanity differ from genocide. While genocide focuses on the collective nature of the victims as a group, crimes against humanity tend to penalize the collective nature of the perpetration of crimes.[263] Crimes against humanity are attacks on civilian populations that are at risk because of their presence in the targeted population. The basic idea is that a crime is no longer simply an ordinary crime under domestic law, but an international crime, where the collective action of an organization causes harm to the civilian population which reaches the threshold of widespread or systematic violence.[264]

1.3.2.1   Origin

The famous 'Martens clause', contained in the preamble of the Hague Convention of 1907, established the principle that belligerents are protected by the 'principles of the law of nations' that flow from 'laws of humanity, and the dictates of public conscience'.[265] Crimes against humanity were codified for the first time in the Charter of the Nuremberg Tribunal. This inclusion marked a significant development in international law. Under traditional international law, the conduct of a state vis-à-vis its own citizens was a matter of internal affairs. Nuremberg broke with this, but it contained an important limitation. Crimes against humanity could not be charged independently of a nexus to other crimes.[266] They had to be linked to war crimes or crimes against peace – that is, warfare. The fact that Nazi crimes were committed as part of an unjust war served as one of the major justifications for Allied jurisdiction.

---

[260] For efforts on a crimes against humanity convention, see L. Sadat (ed.), *Forging a Convention for Crimes Against Humanity* (Cambridge: Cambridge University Press, 2011), as well as the work of the ILC on the topic as of 2014.

[261] See generally M. C. Bassiouni, *Crimes Against Humanity: Historical Evolution and Contemporary Application* (Cambridge: Cambridge University Press, 2011).

[262] See Ambos, *Treatise on International Criminal Law, Vol. II*, 48.

[263] See J. D. Ohlin, 'Organizational Criminality', in E. van Sliedregt and S. Vasiliev, *Pluralism in International Criminal Law* (Oxford: Oxford University Press, 2014), 118.

[264] For a critique of a broad interpretation of crimes against humanity, based on historical and systematic considerations, see Schabas, 'State Policy as an Element of International Crimes', 953.

[265] The Martens Clause is contained in para. 9 of the Preamble of the Convention with Respect to the Laws and Customs of War by Land and its Annex: Regulations Respecting the Laws and Customs of War on Land ('Until a more complete code of the laws of war is issued, the High contracting parties think it right to declare that in cases not included in the Regulations adopted by them, populations and belligerents remain under protection and empire of the principles of international law, as they result from the usages established between civilized nations, from the laws of humanity, and the requirements of public conscience').

[266] See Art. 6 (c) of the IMT Charter ('murder, extermination, enslavement, deportation, and other inhumane acts committed against any civilian population, before or during the war; or persecutions on political, racial or religious grounds in execution of or in connection with any crime within the jurisdiction of the Tribunal').

In the second half of the twentieth century, the concept of crimes against humanity was emancipated from its war-related nexus. The reference to the concept of 'civilians' in the definition of the crime is reminiscent of the historical linkage to war crimes. However, the concept developed more in line with the human rights tradition. It became one of the most dynamic categories of crime. Crimes against humanity were included in the Statutes of major international criminal courts and tribunals, based on their recognition under customary international law.[267] The ICC Statute contains the most comprehensive modern treaty codification.

1.3.2.2 Normative Theories

The criminalization of crimes against humanity occurred in an incremental way. It partly filled gaps in the international and domestic legal systems. The notion covers very different types of crimes that protect different interests. It is difficult to formulate one overarching normative justification. One common denominator is that the underlying crime must concern a bigger community interest, i.e. 'humanity'. This notion is very undetermined and elastic. Crimes against humanity are to some extent a 'chameleonic crime that can change color over time, since it does not possess an unambiguous conceptual character'.[268] There are competing normative theories to explain their foundation.[269]

1.3.2.2.1 Attack on Humanity and Humanness

According to the first theory, crimes against humanity are international crimes because they present an attack on both humanity as a collective and the quality of the individual as human being.[270] Crimes against humanity are prohibited because they target the victim's humanity and common qualities that humans share.[271] This theory is in line with findings that atrocity crimes are often preceded by processes of marginalizing or dehumanizing the identities of others ('othering') in order to justify crimes.[272] David Luban has argued that part of the gravity of the offence stems from the fact that it targets the identity of human beings as political subjects.[273] This element was reflected in the definition of the ICTR, which contained a discrimination

---

[267] See L. Sadat, 'Crimes Against Humanity in the Modern Age' (2013) 107 *AJIL* 334.

[268] L. van den Herik and E. van Sliedregt, 'Removing or Reincarnating the Policy Requirement of Crimes Against Humanity: An Introductory Note' (2010) 23 LJIL 825.

[269] For a discussion, see M. M. deGuzman, 'Crimes Against Humanity', in W. A. Schabas and N. Bernaz (eds.), *Routledge Handbook of International Criminal Law* (Routledge 2011), 121; C. Jalloh, 'What Makes a Crime Against Humanity a Crime Against Humanity?' (2013) 28 *American University International Law Review* 381.

[270] See generally C. McLeod, 'Towards a Philosophical Account of Crimes Against Humanity' (2010) 21 *EJIL* 281.

[271] Mark Osiel has argued that criminal prosecution strengthens social solidarity since it marks a means through which 'citizens can come to acknowledge the differing views of their fellows'. See M. Osiel, *Mass Atrocity, Collective Memory and the Law* (New Brunswick, NJ: Transaction Publishers, 1997), 22–23, 293.

[272] On 'racial othering', see D. Ferreira Da Silva, 'Many Hundred Thousand Bodies Later: An Analysis of the Legacy of the International Criminal Tribunal for Rwanda', in F. Johns, R. Joyce and S. Pahuja (eds.), *Events: The Force of International Law* (London: Routledge-Cavendish, 2010), 165, 166.

[273] D. Luban, 'A Theory of Crimes Against Humanity' (2004) 29 *Yale Journal of International Law* 85.

requirement in the contextual elements.[274] One critique of this understanding is that it is vague and subject to a metaphysical conundrum on the definition of humanness.[275]

1.3.2.2.2 Threat to International Peace and Security

A second theory relies on the link to international peace and security.[276] It argues that crimes against humanity are international offences since they 'threaten the peace, security and well-being of the world'. This justification is reflected in the Nuremberg and ICTY definitions. It is in line with the rationale to limit the jurisdiction of international courts and tribunals to the most serious crimes. It receives support from the context requirements of crimes against humanity, which relate to magnitude and scale. As the United Nations War Crimes Commission put it, crimes against humanity endanger the international community or shock the conscience of mankind, 'either by their magnitude and savagery or by their large number or by the fact that a similar pattern was applied at different times and places'.[277]

In practice, however, these criteria are applied inconsistently. This theory fails to explain, for instance, why many terrorist attacks, such as the Paris bombings, were qualified as a threat to peace, but not as crimes against humanity.

1.3.2.2.3 Abuse of Power through State or Organizational Policy

A third theory relates the essence of crimes against humanity to the right of individuals to be protected from abuse of power. Crimes against humanity are thus essentially about inversions of power resulting from misuse of authority (e.g. abuses of the monopoly of the use of force, rule of law violations).[278] What forms of power are covered is controversial, however.[279]

The traditional understanding is that crimes against humanity are banned, because they are the result of a state policy that promotes or tolerates such crimes. This theory has a direct nexus to the idea of the responsibility to protect. It grounds crimes against humanity in the idea that states[280] or state-like entities[281] fail in their responsibilities

---

[274] See Art. 3 ICTR Statute ('on national, political, ethnic, racial or religious grounds').

[275] See J. Yovel, 'How Can a Crime Be a Crime Against Humanity? Philosophical Debates Concerning a Useful Concept' (2006) 11 *UCLA Journal of International Law & Foreign Affairs* 39.

[276] See I. Haenen, 'Classifying Acts as Crimes Against Humanity in the Rome Statue of the International Criminal Court' (2013) 14 *German Law Journal* 796, 803. Larry May developed a 'security' and a 'harm' principle to explain crimes against humanity. He argues that crimes against humanity can be justified by the group-based nature of the crimes or their commission through state action. See May, *Crimes Against Humanity* (2005), 86.

[277] United Nations War Crimes Commission, *History of the United Nations War Crimes Commission and the Development of the Laws of War* (London: His Majesty's Stationery Office, 1948), 179.

[278] See R. Vernon, 'What is a Crime Against Humanity?'(2002) 10 *Journal of Political Philosophy* 231, 243–245.

[279] See generally G. Werle and B. Burghardt, 'Do Crimes Against Humanity Require the Participation of a State or a "State-like" Organization?' (2012) 10 *JICJ* 1151; D. Robinson, EJIL Talk! 'Essence of Crimes against Humanity Raised by Challenges at ICC', at www.ejiltalk.org/essence-of-crimes-against-humanity-raised-by-challenges-at-icc/.

[280] M. C. Bassiouni, *The Legislative History of the International Criminal Court: Introduction, Analysis and Integrated Text*, Vol. I (Ardsley, NY: Transnational Publishers, 2005), 151–152.

[281] W. Schabas, *The International Criminal Court: A Commentary to the Rome Statute* (Oxford: Oxford University Press, 2010), 152; Dissenting Opinion by Judge Hans-Peter Kaul to Pre-Trial Chamber II's 'Decision Pursuant to Art. 15 of the Rome Statute on the Authorization of an Investigation into the Situation in the Republic of Kenya', Situation in Kenya ICC-01/09–19, Pre-Trial Chamber II, 31 March 2010, paras. 51–66. See also C. Kreβ, 'On the Outer Limits of

to protect persons under their control. It finds some expression in the ICC Statute which contains an express policy requirement. However, it grounds crimes against humanity too much in the state-oriented focus of human rights law and the idea of elite deviance.

According to modern understandings, the policy element needs to be understood in a wider sense, namely as covering not only action by state or state-like entities, but also other organized entities that direct, instigate or encourage crimes.[282] The view that crimes against humanity require a nexus to a state policy disregards the threats posed by powerful non-state actors. It would imply that an entity cannot commit a crime against humanity without state support. This result contrasts with criminological studies which suggest that the very structure of certain organizations may be 'criminogenic', i.e. conducive to cultures of criminality, by either incentivizing or tolerating violations.[283] This includes not only terrorist or criminal organizations per se, but also political or corporate organizations.

The idea of a strict nexus requirement to state policies has been rejected in modern jurisprudence. It is widely recognized that organizations with de facto control over territories ought to be equated with a state. Most judicial decisions even go a step further. They argue that protection applies in relation to action by non-state actors that are capable of committing a 'widespread or systematic attack', irrespective of a nexus to a state. This wider understanding is in line with the plain text of the Rome Statute, which requires a 'state *or* organizational policy'.[284] It captures inter alia rebel groups or certain terrorist organizations.

The exact criteria differ among Chambers. In a historic decision, the Kenya Authorization Decision, Pre-Trial Chamber II, defined an organization within the meaning of the policy requirement of the ICC Statute as any group that has the capability to perform acts which infringe on basic human values.[285] It further identified a series of relevant, non-exhaustive factors, such as: (i) responsible command, or established hierarchy; (ii) means to carry out a widespread or systematic attack against a civilian population; (iii) control over part of the territory of a state; (iv) having as a primary purpose criminal activities against the civilian population; (v) the articulation, either explicitly or implicitly, of an intention to attack a civilian population; or (vi) being part of a larger group which fulfils some or all of the above-mentioned criteria.[286]

Crimes against Humanity: The Concept of Organization within the Policy Requirement: Some Reflections on the March 2010 ICC Kenya Decision' (2010) 23 *LJIL* 855, 867–871.

[282] On a victim-related justification, see Sadat, 'Crimes Against Humanity in the Modern Age', 371, 375.

[283] See e.g. J. Braithwaite, 'Criminological Theory and Organizational Crime' (1989) 6 *Justice Quarterly* 333–358; M. D. Ermann and R. J. Lundman, 'Deviant Acts by Complex Organizations: Deviance and Social Control at the Organizational Level of Analysis' (1978) 19 *Sociological Quarterly* 55–67.

[284] Art. 7 (2) (a) ICC Statute.

[285] ICC, ICC-01/09–19-Corr, Decision Pursuant to Article 15 of the Rome Statute on the Authorization of an Investigation into the Situation in the Republic of Kenya, 13 March 2010, paras. 90–93 (Kenya Authorization Decision).

[286] Kenya Authorization Decision, para. 93.

In *Katanga*, Trial Chamber II stated that the organization must have 'sufficient resources, means and capacity to bring about the course of conduct or the operation involving the multiple commission of acts referred to in article 7(2)(a) of the Statute'.[287] It defined the organization based on certain generic features: 'capacit[y] . . . for mutual agreement', 'structures or mechanisms . . . to ensure coordination', 'means and resources', and 'membership' necessary to carry out an attack against a civilian population.[288] It thus placed the emphasis on generic structural features, such as capacity, coordination and cohesion, necessary to carry out the attack.[289]

One of the risks of this jurisprudence is that it brings an almost indefinite range of organizations and non-state actors into the scope of application of crimes against humanity and might therefore conflict with the principle of strict construction.[290] The existing theorization is circular. If a showing of the ability to carry out a widespread and systematic attack is all that is required, then the very model becomes superfluous and equivalent to the position that crimes against humanity do not require a policy element at all.[291] Policy cannot simply be inferred from the widespread or systematic nature of the attack. The exact criteria require further specification.

The purpose of the policy element is to distinguish international crimes from ordinary crimes. Most scholars agree that only a limited amount of private criminal organizations come within the ambit of crimes against humanity. This determination cannot be made based on types of criminality (e.g. economic criminality, drug crimes, terrorism etc.). It must be assessed on a case-by-case basis, grounded in the criteria of the policy element.

A first indicator is the size and nature of the organization. For instance, large-scale organizations which operate across borders are more likely to satisfy the rationale than domestic criminal organizations.[292] Individuals units of a broader organization that operates in a decentralized way might be covered by the Kenya Authorization Decision.[293] A second useful criterion is the type of control exercised. For instance, only a limited number of criminal organizations have de facto control over territory. It is reasonable to argue that non-state actors that are bound to abide by international human rights law (e.g. due to effective control) should come within the scope of the policy element. Third, the 'organization' must have the 'primary purpose' of conducting criminal activities against the civilian population.[294]

---

[287] *Katanga* Trial Judgment, para. 1119.
[288] Ibid., paras. 1119–1120.
[289] Ibid., para. 1120.
[290] On concerns, see Kress, 'On the Outer Limits of Crimes against Humanity', 855–873.
[291] See e.g. *Prosecutor* v. *Kunarac, Kovač and Vuković*, IT-96-23/1-A, Appeals Chamber, 12 June 2002, para. 98 (*Kunarac* Appeal Judgment). It held that neither the attack nor the acts of the accused need to be supported by any form of 'policy' or 'plan'.
[292] See S. Wirken and H. Bosdriesz, 'Privatisation and Increasing Complexity of Mass Violence in Mexico and Central America: Exploring Appropriate International Responses', in Van der Wilt and Paulussen, *Legal Responses to Transnational and International Crimes*, 245, 252.
[293] Kenya Authorization Decision, para. 93.
[294] Ibid.

These factors allow for some differentiation between organized crime and crimes against humanity. For instance, drug cartels or human trafficking organizations often use violence for purposes of economic gain. The primary purpose is to benefit from these activities, rather than to target the civilian population.[295] Criminal organizations which carry out attacks to terrorize the civilian population or prompt certain concessions from state authorities may more easily come within the ambit of crimes against humanity.[296] Examples such as the Zeta cartel in Mexico show that the boundaries become fluid when organizations with a criminal purpose target civilians in order to undermine governmental control over a region or area and to expand their activities.[297]

Some fear that crimes against humanity might cover all organized acts that are not random, including acts committed by gangsters, motorcycle gangs or serial killers.[298] This risk is mitigated through these indicators. Such an interpretation would clearly go against the purpose of distinguishing crimes against humanity from domestic crime.

1.3.2.3 Context

Crimes against humanity can be committed in the context of armed conflict and in peacetime. The essential element that distinguishes crimes against humanity from domestic crimes is their context.[299] Crimes against humanity are often related to a social system of oppression and domination. They must be committed as part of a widespread or systematic attack against the civilian population.

The notion of attack is understood in a wide sense. It includes not only the use of armed force, but also any form of mistreatment, including denunciation or discriminatory practices. The civilian population must be the 'primary' object of the attack.[300] This collectivity must share certain distinctive features that mark them as targets of the attack.

An attack is 'widespread' if it is conducted on a large scale and results in a large number of victims.[301] There is no specific numerical threshold. International criminal

---

[295] See S. N. Kalyvas, 'How Civil Wars Help Explain Organized Crime – and How They Do Not' (2015) 59 *Journal of Conflict Resolution* 1517, 1520 ('criminal organizations lack both an ideological profile and an explicit political agenda … Unlike even the most predatory rebel groups, they do not attempt to disguise their profit-oriented motivations behind a political discourse. If anything, they are mainly interested in preserving the political status quo and co-opting existing political institutions rather than subverting them').

[296] See. P. Burns, 'Aspects of Crimes Against Humanity and the International Criminal Court', 11, at https://icclr.law.ubc .ca/wp-content/uploads/2017/08/AspectofCrimesAgainstHumanity.pdf.

[297] See Open Society Justice Initiative, *Undeniable Atrocties: Confronting Crimes against Humanity in Mexico* (New York: Open Society Foundations, 2016), 92–95.

[298] See W. A. Schabas, 'London Riots: Were They Crimes against Humanity?', 15 August 2011, at http:// humanrightsdoctorate.blogspot.nl/2011/08/london-riots-were-they-crimes-against.html.

[299] W. A. Schabas, 'Prosecuting Dr. Strangelove, Goldfinger, and the Joker at the International Criminal Court: Closing the Loopholes' (2010) 23 *LJIL* 847.

[300] *Kunarac* Appeal Judgment, para. 90. This excludes legal attacks on combatants from the scope of crimes against humanity.

[301] *Prosecutor v. Blaškić*, IT-95–14, Judgment, 3 March 2000, para. 206 (*Blaškić* Trial Judgment).

courts and tribunals typically look at factors such as the consequences of the attack upon the targeted population and the number of victims.[302]

'Systematic' refers to the organized nature of the acts of violence, such as the repetition of similar criminal conduct on a regular basis.[303] It can be shown by the existence of a plan involving attacks, or other factors. Indicators are, for instance, the existence of a particular policy or ideology to destroy or weaken a community, discriminatory measures, such as discriminatory laws, measures changing the demography of the population, or the involvement of high-level political and/or military leaders in the establishment of the plan.[304]

However, there are many grey areas. For instance, it remains unclear what type of law enforcement activities are captured by crimes against humanity. A recurrent problem is excessive use of force by police in riot control.[305] It is also controversial to what extent the Prosecution must prove the details of the individual crimes (i.e. the 'trees') that constitute the attack (i.e. the 'forest'). In the *Bemba* case, Judges Morisson and Van den Wyngaert argued that the proof of the 'forest' requires proof of 'the existence of a sufficient number of trees'.[306] Realists counter that it is unrealistic to require the Prosecution to establish direct evidence of hundreds or thousands of crimes to establish the contextual element of crimes against humanity.[307] They would allow establishment of context through proof of a sufficient number of incidents.[308]

1.3.2.4 Crime Typologies and Dynamic Interpretation

Crimes against humanity consist of two types of offences. The first are so-called murder-type offences. Some but not all of them are criminal offences in national legal systems. They are banned internationally because of their cruelty and barbarity. They include murder, extermination, enslavement, deportation or forcible transfer of population, torture, acts of sexual violence or enforced disappearance of persons.

A second type of offences is 'persecution'-related. These may not be criminal or even prohibited in national legal systems. They are typically geared at persecution of a specific group of people on racial, religious or political grounds.[309]

Crimes against humanity overlap partly with domestic offences. Even more than other categories of crimes, they often touch upon sensitive issues regarding values and

---

[302] *Kunarac* Appeal Judgment, para. 95 ('consequences of the attack upon the targeted population, the number of victims, the nature of the acts, the possible participation of officials or authorities or any identifiable patterns of crimes').

[303] Ibid., para. 94.

[304] See e.g. *Blaškić* Trial Judgment, para. 203.

[305] See S. Namewase, *The Use of Excessive Force in Riot Control: Law Enforcement and Crimes against Humanity under the Rome Statute*, PhD thesis, January 2017, http://roar.uel.ac.uk/5899/1/Sylvie%20Namwase.pdf.

[306] *Prosecutor* v. *Bemba*, ICC-01/05-01/08-3636-Anx2, Separate opinion Judge Christine Van den Wyngaert and Judge Howard Morrison, 8 June 2018, para. 60.

[307] *Prosecutor* v. *Gbagbo*, ICC-02/11-01/11-534, Amicus Curiae Observations of Professors Robinson, de Guzman, Jalloh and Cryer, 10 October 2013, para. 42 ('One can be convinced of a "forest" without evidence of the nature and location of particular "trees"').

[308] E.g. *Prosecutor* v. *Gbagbo*, ICC-02/11-01/11-432, Decision adjourning the Hearing on the Confirmation of Charges Pursuant to Article 61(7)(c)(i) of the Rome Statute, 3 June 2013, para. 23.

[309] See generally F. Pocar, 'Persecution as a Crime under International Criminal Law' (2008) 2 *Journal of National Security Law & Policy* 355.

choices in domestic societies and may clash with local customs or gender stereotypes.[310] For example, what qualifies as sexual violence differs according to a given social context. At the Rome Conference, some delegations voiced concern that the Statute might brand certain cultural and religious practices as crimes of sexual or gender violence.[311] Catholic and Arab states were opposed to the criminalization of forced pregnancy, since they feared that it might lead to the legalization of abortion.[312]

Existing crime definitions have captured new patterns of criminality. They have, in particular, been adapted to the privatization of violence. Contemporary interpretations have extended the scope of subjects of international criminal law. They include a broad typology of non-state actors, including militia forces, terrorist groups or other organizations.[313] Crimes against humanity have thus served as a 'gentle civilizer' of modern forms of violence.

1.3.2.4.1 *Modern-Day Slavery and Human Trafficking*

A first example is the approach towards modern forms of slavery and human trafficking. The notion of enslavement captures not only traditional concepts of slavery, such as 'chattel slavery', but various contemporary forms of slavery.[314] It is an umbrella offence that includes slavery, servitude and forced or compulsory labour.[315] The case law of international tribunals has gradually shifted the focus from ownership towards forced labour and other forms of control. For instance, in the *Katanga* case the ICC defined the exercise of ownership as 'the use, enjoyment and disposal of a person who is regarded as property, by placing him or her in a situation of dependence [that deprives the person] of any form of autonomy'.[316] It includes sexual slavery. The main element is not the commercial transaction but the impossibility for the victim to change their condition.[317] The victim's vulnerability and their socio-economic conditions may also be taken into account.

In legal practice, it has been proposed to apply the concept of crimes against humanity to crimes against refugees and migrants.[318] Migrant trafficking schemes often involve torture, ill-treatment or sexual abuse.[319] The wide definition of

---

[310] See K. Campbell, 'The Making of Global Legal Culture and International Criminal Law' (2013) 26 *LJIL* 155.

[311] L. Chappell, 'Women's Rights and Religious Opposition: The Politics of Gender at the International Criminal Court', in Y. Abu-Laban (ed.), *Gendering the Nation State: Canadian and Comparative Perspectives* (Vancouver: University of British Columbia Press, 2008), 139.

[312] C. Steains, 'Gender Issues', in R. Lee (ed.), *The International Criminal Court: The Making of the Rome Statute* (The Hague: Kluwer Law, 1999), 357, 366–367.

[313] Werle and Burghardt argue that the notion of 'organization' covers 'any association of persons with an established structure'. See Werle and Burghardt, 'Crimes Against Humanity', 1151.

[314] *Kunarac* Appeal Judgment, para. 117.

[315] Art. 7 (2) (c) defines the crime of enslavement as 'the exercise of any or all of the powers attaching to the right of ownership over a person and includes the exercise of such power in the course of trafficking in persons, in particular women and children'.

[316] *Katanga* Trial Judgment, para. 975.

[317] Ibid.

[318] See Report of the Special Rapporteur on Torture and Other Cruel, Inhuman or Degrading Treatment or Punishment, A/HRC/37/50, 25 February 2018, paras. 60–64 (2018 Report Special Rapporteur Torture).

[319] Ibid., paras. 30–34.

enslavement covers certain forms of human trafficking. Under the broad interpretation of the notion of 'ownership' adopted by international criminal courts and
tribunals, some forms of acquisition of persons for purposes of exploitation, or even
transaction, might be covered by the concept of crimes against humanity if they cross
the threshold of the policy element.

International criminal courts and tribunals have made it clear that consent of the
victim does not necessarily constitute a bar to criminality. The ICTY clarified that the
very means of exercising control over a person may render consent or free will
impossible. It listed indicators, such as 'the threat or use of force or other forms of
coercion; the fear of violence, deception or false promises; the abuse of power; the
victim's position of vulnerability; detention or captivity, psychological oppression or
socio-economic conditions'.[320]

The same trend is visible in the context of human trafficking. States were conscious
of the risk that defendants might invoke consent as a defence to trafficking (e.g. in the
context of migration or prostitution). The Palermo Protocol specifies expressly that
adult consent to exploitation is irrelevant where any of the prohibited means of
trafficking have been used, including fraud, deception, abuse of power or of a position
of vulnerability, or 'the giving or receiving of payments or benefits to achieve the
consent of a person'.[321] Consent of children is always irrelevant. Despite these
clarifications, the actual application of the principle of irrelevance of consent continues to pose problems in practice, in particular, in relation to more subtle forms of
exploitation. As the UN Office on Drugs and Crime (UNODC) notes:

> Because the means themselves are not clearly defined or delineated in the Trafficking in Persons
> Protocol and in most national laws, there is considerable scope for States to develop and apply
> highly restrictive, exceedingly broad or even contradictory interpretations of particular means:
> from interpretations by which means must be severe enough to vitiate or seriously damage
> consent, to interpretations by which means need not vitiate or even seriously damage consent in
> order to trigger the 'irrelevance of consent' provision.[322]

Violations are not only committed by criminal organizations or private actors, but
may involve different degrees of state complicity or toleration. This delicate link has
been emphasized by the UN Special Rapporteur on Torture. He has called on states
and the ICC to examine potential crimes against humanity against 'millions of
migrants' which may have occurred 'as a direct or indirect consequence of deliberate
State policies and practices of deterrence, criminalization, arrival protection and
refoulement'.[323] Some new mechanisms, such as the Malabo Protocol, provide

---

[320] *Prosecutor* v. *Kunarac, Kovač and Vuković Kunarac*, IT-96-23-T& IT-96-23/1-T, Judgment, 22 February 2001,
para. 542 (*Kunarac* Trial Judgment).
[321] See Palermo Protocol, Art. 3 (b).
[322] UNODC, *The Role of 'Consent' in the Trafficking in Persons Protocol* (Vienna: United Nations Office on Drugs and
Crime, 2014), 10.
[323] 2018 Report Special Rapporteur Torture.

jurisdiction over human trafficking[324] in addition to crimes against humanity. It might evolve into a separate international crime in the future.

1.3.2.4.2 Torture

A second example of the gradual modernization of crimes against humanity is the approach towards torture. Torture is considered an international crime under treaty and customary international law.[325] Its prohibition has been considered to form part of *jus cogens*.[326] International criminal tribunals can punish it in the context of crimes against humanity and war crimes.

Article 1 of the Convention against Torture and Other Cruel, Inhuman or Degrading Treatment or Punishment of 1984 limits torture to circumstances where it is committed 'by or at the instigation of or with the consent or acquiescence of a public official or other person acting in an official capacity'.[327] In the context of international criminal law, the focus has been extended.[328] In *Kunarac*, the ICTY argued that the definition of torture under international criminal law does not necessarily have to match the definition under human rights law. It clarified that the 'characteristic trait' of the offence lies 'in the nature of the act committed rather than in the status of the person who committed it'.[329] It stated that 'acting in an official capacity could constitute an aggravating circumstance when it comes to sentencing, because the official illegitimately used and abused a power which was conferred upon him or her for legitimate purposes'.[330] The *Kunarac* definition made it clear that the presence of a state official or of any other authority-wielding person is not necessary for the commission of torture. This understanding is reflected in the Rome Statute. It prohibits torture irrespective of state involvement. It thus includes non-state actors. The Elements of the Crimes only require that the perpetrator has the victim(s) under custody or control.[331] The ICC definition eliminates the requirement of purpose.

Torture covers contemporary practices which cause severe pain or suffering, such as waterboarding, hooding, sexual violence and threats of torture, as well as techniques that do so if they are used for prolonged periods of time or in combination with other acts, such as sleep deprivation or food deprivation.[332] The ICC Prosecutor listed many

---

[324] See Art. 28J of the Malabo Protocol.

[325] Some authors consider it as one of the most serious transnational crimes. See generally E. De Wet, 'The Prohibition of Torture as an International Norm of jus cogens and Its Implications for National and Customary Law' (2004) 15 *EJIL* 97.

[326] See ICJ, *Questions Relating to the Obligation to Prosecute or Extradite* (*Belgium* v. *Senegal*), 20 July 2012, para. 99.

[327] Convention against Torture and Other Cruel, Inhuman or Degrading Treatment or Punishment, General Assembly Resolution 39/46 of 10 December 1984.

[328] S. Sivakumaran, 'Torture in International Human Rights and International Humanitarian Law: The Actor and the Ad Hoc Tribunals' (2005) 18 *LJIL* 541.

[329] *Kunarac* Trial Judgment, para. 495.

[330] Ibid., para. 494.

[331] Elements of the Crimes, Art. 7 (1) (f).

[332] For a survey, see C. K. Hall and C. Stahn, Art. 7, in Triffterer and Ambos, *Rome Statute of the International Criminal Court*, 269–273.

of the illicit interrogation practices used by CIA agents in the 'war on terror' in its request to authorize an investigation in relation to the situation in Afghanistan.[333]

1.3.2.4.3 Crimes of Sexual and Gender-Based Violence

Third, crimes of sexual and gender-based violence have been developed in an unprecedented fashion through global criminal justice.[334] In warfare, women have often been viewed as 'spoils' of conflict.[335] After World War II, there was considerable uncertainty as to whether sexual and gender-based violence could be prosecuted as a separate substantive crime on its own merits. Sexual violence was largely a blind spot in Nuremberg and Tokyo.[336] The Tokyo trial was silent on sexual slavery suffered by the so-called comfort women, who were used by Japanese forces 'for the purpose of stabilizing soldiers' psychology, encouraging their spirit and protecting them from venereal infections'.[337] Control Council Law No. 10 recognized rape as a crime against humanity. However, the Nuremberg Military Tribunal did not expressly prosecute sexual violence.

Historically, sexual crimes were considered as an attack on the 'honour' of the victim, rather than as a violent physical crime. The Geneva Conventions failed to recognize sexual violence as a grave breach. They qualified rape and other acts of sexual violence as attacks against the 'honour' of women or their personal dignity.[338] This understanding is deeply problematic. As UN reports have noted:

[t]he implication is that 'honour' (or dignity) is something lent to women by men, and that a raped woman is thereby dishonoured … It directly reflects and reinforces the trivialization of such offences … the provisions appear to be more about the role of the 'male warrior' during armed conflict than about recognizing sexual violence as a violation of the rights of women and prohibiting it.[339]

Feminist scholarship has criticized the lack of attention to women's experiences in the conception of international law since the end of the cold war.[340] The ad hoc tribunals have defined gender crimes such as rape[341] and sexual enslavement in a modern fashion.

---

[333] See ICC, Public redacted version of 'Request for Authorisation of an Investigation Pursuant to Article 15', 20 November 2017, ICC-02/17-7-Conf-Exp, ICC-02/17, 20 November 2017, paras. 193–195.

[334] K. D. Askin, *War Crimes Against Women: Prosecution in International War Crimes Tribunals* (Leiden: Martinus Nijhoff, 1997); R. Copelon, 'Gender Crimes as War Crimes: Integrating Crimes Against Women into International Criminal Law' (2000) 46 *McGill Law Journal* 217.

[335] For a differentiated account, see I. Herrmann and D. Palmieri, 'Between Amazons and Sabines: A Historical Approach to Women and War' (2010) 92 *International Review of the Red Cross* 19.

[336] J. Gardam, 'Women and the Law of Armed Conflict: Why the Silence?' (1997) 46 *ICLQ* 55.

[337] United Nations, Preliminary Report Submitted by the Special Rapporteur on Violence against Women, Its Causes and Consequences, UN Doc. E/CN.4/1995/42, 11 November 1994, para. 288.

[338] Art. 27 of the Fourth Geneva Convention IV states that 'women shall be especially protected against any attack on their honour'.

[339] UN, Division for the Advancement of Women, *Women2000: Sexual Violence and Armed Conflict: United Nations Response* (New York: United Nations, 1998).

[340] See e.g. J. Gardam, 'A Feminist Analysis of Certain Aspects of International Humanitarian Law' (1990) 12 *Australian Yearbook of International Law* 265; H. Charlesworth, 'Feminist Methods in International Law' (1999) 93 *AJIL* 379; H. Charlesworth and C. Chinkin, *The Boundaries of International Law: A Feminist Analysis* (Manchester: Manchester University Press, 2000).

[341] Statute of the ICTR, Art. 3 (g).

Akayesu was the first signature case which established an express connection between the use of sexual violence and the political motives underlying identity-based conflict.[342] It marked the first international trial judgment which defined rape and sexual violence[343] and was a hallmark of a new ethos of gender sensitivity. The Prosecution had failed to bring charges relating to sexual violence, partly due to the assumption that victims are unwilling to come forward because of the stigma attached to these crimes, fear, and a presumed lack of sufficient evidence regarding the link between acts of sexual violence and the accused. The Bench moved the Prosecution to include charges for rape as a crime against humanity and inhumane acts in the indictment. The Trial Chamber found *Akayesu* guilty of crimes against humanity of rape and 'other inhumane acts'.[344] It added that '[s]exual violence was an integral part of the process of destruction, specifically targeting Tutsi women and specifically contributing to their destruction and to the destruction of the Tutsi group as a whole'.[345] The Chief Prosecutor of the Special Court for Sierra Leone integrated charges of sexual and gender-based violence into virtually all indictments, including novel paradigms such as 'forced marriages'.[346] At the ICTY, 48 per cent of the indictments contained sexual violence charges.[347] More than thirty persons have been convicted by the ICTY for crimes involving sexual violence. The tribunal conducted inter alia the first international war crimes trial involving charges of sexual violence against men.[348]

The ICC Statute contains one of the most modern and extensive lists of sexual and gender-based violence.[349] It treats sexual violence not merely as a specific form of torture or cruel treatment, but defines the respective offences. It contains a list of crimes that is more modern than most traditional criminal codes, including sexual

---

[342] See generally B. Van Schaack, 'Engendering Genocide: The Akayesu Case Before the International Criminal Tribunal for Rwanda', in D. R. Hurwitz et al. (eds.), *Human Rights Advocacy Stories* (New York: Foundation Press, 2008), 193; C. McKinnon, 'Defining Rape Internationally: A Comment on Akayesu' (2006) 44 *Columbia Journal of Transnational Law* 941.

[343] See K. Askin, 'Sexual Violence in Decisions and Indictments of the Yugoslav and Rwandan Tribunals: Current Status' (1999) 93 *AJIL* 104.

[344] *Akayesu* Trial Judgment, paras. 687–688: 'The Tribunal considers sexual violence, which includes rape, as any act of a sexual nature which is committed on a person under circumstances which are coercive. Sexual violence is not limited to physical invasion of the human body and may include acts which do not involve penetration or even physical contact. ... The Tribunal notes in this context that coercive circumstances need not be evidenced by a show of physical force. Threats, intimidation, extortion and other forms of duress which prey on fear or desperation may constitute coercion, and coercion may be inherent in certain circumstances, such as armed conflict or the military presence were occurring'.

[345] Ibid., para. 731.

[346] See generally C. Aptel, 'Child Slaves and Child Brides' (2016) 14 *JICJ* 305; V. Oosterveld, 'The Gender Jurisprudence of the Special Court for Sierra Leone: Progress in the Revolutionary United Front Judgments' (2011) 44 *Cornell Journal of International Law* 49, 64 et seq.

[347] See ICTY, Crimes of Sexual Violence, In Numbers, at www.icty.org/en/in-focus/crimes-sexualviolence/in-numbers. For a full account, see S. Brammertz and M. Jarvis (eds.), *Prosecuting Conflict-Related Sexual Violence at the ICTY* (Oxford: Oxford University Press, 2016).

[348] ICTY, *Prosecutor* v. *Tadic*, IT-94-1-T, Opinion and Judgment, 7 May 1997. See generally S. Sivakumaran, 'Sexual Violence Against Men in Armed Conflict' (2007) 18 *EJIL* 253.

[349] Sexual and gender-based crimes are included in the list of crimes against humanity and war crimes. Gender is listed as a ground of persecution. The Elements of Crime offer a possibility to consider acts of sexual violence as an element of genocide. For a survey of prosecutorial strategy, see OTP Policy Paper on Sexual and Gender Based Crimes, June 2014, at www.icc-cpi.int/iccdocs/otp/OTP-Policy-Paper-on-Sexual-and-Gender-Based-Crimes-June-2014.pdf.

slavery, enforced prostitution, forced pregnancy, enforced sterilization and other forms of sexual violence.[350] It expressly captures sexual violence against male and female victims[351] and codifies certain forms of reproductive violence[352] (e.g. 'forced pregnancy'[353] or 'enforced sterilization'[354]) for the first time, in addition to sexual violence.[355]

The prosecution of sexual and gender-based violence still faces many challenges,[356] including evidentiary problems. The OTP has experienced difficulties in gathering evidence related to such charges, and linking perpetrators to the crimes. At the ICC, charges failed to be established in the trials of Germain Katanga and Mathieu Ngudjolo.[357] Crimes may easily be regarded as opportunistic crime.

In March 2016, the ICC entered its first conviction relating to sexual violence. Jean-Pierre Bemba, former Congolese vice president, was found guilty for rape as a crime against humanity and as a war crime. The Trial Chamber convicted him due to his failure to prevent or punish such crimes as a military commander.[358] His conviction included the crime of sexual violence perpetrated against men, in this case rape.[359] Bemba was sentenced to eighteen years for rape. On appeal, the conviction was overturned, without detailed consideration of the quality of domestic rape or sexual violence investigations.

Moreover, there are certain deeper concerns regarding the side effects of 'mainstreaming' sexual and gender-based violence in the 'fight against impunity'.[360] International criminal justice and gender discourses, in particular feminist agendas, do not always coincide. Supporters argue that international criminal law may 'transform a legally unacknowledged experience into an acknowledged wrong requiring legal redress'.[361] Critics counter that 'the contemporary international vernacular on sexual violence operates by colonizing gestures of civilizing and saving, delineating who can speak and what can be said about sexual violence in conflict'.[362] The representation of sexual violence in atrocity trials may entrench stereotypes (e.g. the male 'fighter' and

---

[350] On the distinctions, see H. M. Zawati, *Fair Labelling and the Codification of Gender-Based Crimes in the Statutory Laws of the International Criminal Tribunals* (Oxford: Oxford University Press, 2014).

[351] The ICC definition of rape is gender-neutral. See Elements of Crime, Art. 7 (1) (g)-1.

[352] On 'reproductive violence', see Askin, *War Crimes Against Women*, 90–91, 397–403; R. Gray, 'The ICC's First 'Forced Pregnancy' Case in Historical Perspective' (2017) 15 *JICJ* 905.

[353] See Elements of Crime, Art. 7 (1) (g)-4.

[354] Elements of Crime, Art. 7 (1) (g)-5.

[355] On the distinct harms of 'reproductive violence', see Gray, 'The ICC's First "Forced Pregnancy" Case', 907–908.

[356] L. Chappell, *The Politics of Gender Justice at the International Criminal Court: Legacies and Legitimacy* (Oxford: Oxford University Press, 2016).

[357] For a critique, see N. Hayes, '*La lutte continue*: Investigating and Prosecuting Sexual Violence at the ICC', in C. Stahn (ed.), *The Law and Practice of the International Criminal Court* (Oxford: Oxford University Press, 2015), 801.

[358] *Prosecutor* v. *Bemba*, Judgment Pursuant to Article 74 of the Statute, ICC-01/05–01/08, 21 March 2016.

[359] Ibid., para. 100. See generally Sivakumaran, 'Sexual Violence Against Men in Armed Conflict'.

[360] See C. S. Mibenge, *Sex and International Tribunals: The Erasure of Gender from the War Narrative* (Philadelphia: University of Pennsylvania Press, 2013).

[361] V. Oosterveld, 'Evaluating the Special Court for Sierra Leone's Gender Jurisprudence', in C. C. Jalloh (ed.), *The Sierra Leone Special Court and its Legacy: The Impact for Africa and International Criminal Law* (Cambridge: Cambridge University Press, 2013) 234, 235.

[362] C. Mertens and M. Pardy, '"Security" and Its Effects in Eastern Democratic Republic of Congo' (2017) 38 *Third World Quarterly* 956, 971.

the female 'victim') or reduce the complexity of victim identities.[363] The justice lens portrays them predominantly as vulnerable or passive 'victims', rather than as 'survivors' or agents in their community.[364] The criminal trial typically struggles to target the societal norms and stereotypes in societies that facilitate sexual violence. Singling out sexual violence as the definitive experience of women and girls overlooks the broader spectrum of harm to which they may be subject. For instance, in the context of Rwanda, the ICTR portrayed rape mainly as a 'weapon of genocide' used by Hutu against Tutsi women, without engaging with underlying social inequalities.[365] It may also marginalize the experiences of men.[366] As Patricia Sellars has cautioned, 'we often speak in "reductionist" terms, reducing gender to women, and when we refer to gender strategy reducing it to sexual violence committed against women and girls. This is unfortunate. There is room for growth'.[367]

The special treatment of victims of sexual violence may create inequalities among victim populations. For example, the creation of special mobile courts for sexual and gender-based crimes created a novel type of hierarchization which prioritized punishment of sexual violence over the prosecution of murder crimes in the weak national court system.[368] Observers have noted that the special gender-mobile courts entailed a 'brain drain' from local justice institutions, and that the 'political attention on rape as a tactic of war has distracted from a broader investment in ensuring that emergency projects respond to other forms of gender violence or the different needs of women and girls, men and boys'.[369] It is thus important to remain sensitive to the risks that the new focus on sexual violence may entail.

1.3.2.4.4 Enforced Disappearances

Crimes against humanity cover the phenomenon of enforced disappearances.[370] This practice has roots in the practices of the Holocaust. In 1941, German authorities issued the 'Night and Fog' decree which provided a basis for secret detentions of

---

[363] On imagery, see M. Mutua, 'Savages, Victims, and Saviors: The Metaphor of Human Rights' (2001) 42 *Harvard International Law Journal* 201, 204. On feminist critique, see F. N. Aolain, 'Gendered Harms and Their Interface with International Criminal Law' (2014) 16 *International Feminist Journal of Politics* 622; K. Engle, 'Feminism and its (Dis) contents: Criminalizing Wartime Rape' (2005) 99 *AJIL* 778.

[364] For a critique, see P. Scully, 'Vulnerable Women: A Critical Reflection on Human Rights Discourse and Sexual Violence' (2009) 23 *Emory International Law Review* 113; H. Durham and K. O'Byrne, 'The Dialogue of Difference: Gender Perspectives on International Humanitarian Law'(2010) 92 *International Review of the Red Cross* 34.

[365] D. Buss, 'Rethinking Rape as a Weapon of War' (2009) 17 *Feminist Legal Studies* 145–163.

[366] There is still little research as to how sexual violence targets and affects men in particular ways. See C. Dolen, 'Letting Go of the Gender Binary: Charting New Pathways for Humanitarian Interventions on Gender-Based Violence' (2014) 96 *International Review of the Red Cross* 485, 491–492.

[367] P. Viseur Sellers, 'Gender Strategy is Not a Luxury for International Courts' (2009) 17 *American University Journal of Gender, Social Policy and the Law* 301.

[368] See generally Open Society Justice Initiative, *Justice in DRC: Mobile Courts Combat Rape and Impunity in Eastern Congo* (New York: Open Society Foundations, 2013); UNDP, 'Evaluation of UNDP's Support to Mobile Courts in Sierra Leone, the Democratic Republic of Congo, and Somalia', May 2014.

[369] See Y. Douvon, Three Lessons from the Democratic Republic of Congo for the Global Summit to End Sexual Violence in Conflict, 10 June 2014, http://insights.careinternational.org.uk/development-blog/three-lessons-from-drc-for-global-summit-to-end-sexual-violence-in-conflict.

[370] L. Ott, *Enforced Disappearance in International Law* (Cambridge, Antwerp, Portland: Intersentia, 2011).

political enemies.[371] It was geared at seizing control over persons endangering German security in occupied territories 'in the blackness of night' and making them vanish without a trace.[372] It involved acts of arrest, abduction, murder or torture.

Enforced disappearances came to global attention as a human rights problem in the context of Latin American dictatorships of the 1960s. Later, they became a universal phenomenon. They continue to re-occur in contemporary conflicts, such as Syria. They violate a number of human rights, such as the right to life, the right to liberty and security of the person, the right not to be subjected to torture and the right to recognition as a person before the law. The Inter-American Court of Human Rights found in *Velásquez Rodríguez* v *Honduras* that the state's failure to prevent the disappearance, to investigate it and to punish the perpetrators is a violation.[373] In the 1990s, human rights instruments qualified enforced disappearance as a crime against humanity.[374]

The distinguishing characteristic of enforced disappearances lies in the way in which persons are separated from the outside world and deprived of legal protection. As the Working Group on Enforced and Involuntary and Disappearances noted: 'A disappearance is a doubly paralyzing form of suffering: for the victims, frequently tortured and in constant fear for their lives, and for their family members, ignorant of the fate of their loved ones, their emotions alternating between hope and despair, wondering and waiting, sometimes for years, for news that may never come'.[375] The crime is a continuing crime. It starts with the deprivation of liberty and endures 'as long as perpetrators continue to conceal the fate and whereabouts of persons who have disappeared'.[376]

The ILC included the crime in its 1996 Draft Code of Crimes against Peace and Security of Mankind.[377] In 2000, the ICTY found in the *Kupreškić* case that enforced disappearance could be characterized as an 'other inhumane act' under crimes against humanity, although it was not expressly listed in the Statute.[378] The ICC Statute codified it for the first time as a separate crime. The crime consists of two acts: the

---

[371] C. K. Hall and L. v. d. Herik, 'Article 7', in Triffterer and. Ambos, *The Rome Statute of the International Criminal Court*, 226 et seq.

[372] Trials of War Criminals before the Nuremberg Military Tribunals under Control Council Law No. 10: Nuremberg, October 19 October 1946–April 1949, Vol. 3 (Washington, DC: US Government Printing Office, 1951), 75.

[373] Inter-American Court of Human Rights, *Velásquez Rodríguez* vs *Honduras*, Judgment of 29 July 1988, para. 174 (*Velásquez Rodríguez* case).

[374] See UN Declaration on the Protection of All Persons from Enforced Disappearance, A/RES/47/133, 18 December 1992. It was followed by the Inter-American Convention on the Forced Disappearance of Persons, 9 June 1994, OAS Doc OEA/Ser.P/AG/Doc. 3114/94. Both instruments considered enforced disappearances as crimes against humanity.

[375] See United Nations Working Group on Enforced and Involuntary Disappearances, Fact Sheet No. 6 (Rev. 2), Enforced or Involuntary Disappearances (2006), 2.

[376] Art. 17 (1) of the 1992 Declaration.

[377] International Law Commission, *Yearbook of the International Law Commission*, 1996, Vol. II, Part Two, Draft Code of Crimes Against Peace and Security of Mankind, 102.

[378] See ICTY, *Prosecutor v. Kupreskic* et al, Judgment, IT-95-16-T, TC, 14 January 2000, para. 566.

arrest, detention or abduction of a person, and the refusal to acknowledge the deprivation of liberty, or to provide information concerning the fate of the person.[379]

Enforced disappearance has been a typical 'state crime'.[380] It is connected to state action in international human rights instruments. For instance, the Convention for the Protection of All Persons from Enforced Disappearance limits the conduct to 'agents of the State or by persons or groups of persons acting with the authorization, support or acquiescence of the State'.[381]

Very similar types of offences are committed by drug cartels or armed groups. The Rome Statute contains a curious compromise solution. It extends the crime to the conduct of 'political organizations'. This clause is novel. It does appear in other instruments. It is broader than the state, but does not capture all types of private actors. The problem is that the notion 'political' is very broad and fluid. There are different views as to how it should be treated. Some claim that the removal of a person from the protection of the law is tied to the idea of state authority, and that it should be limited to organizations that exercise or replace state functions[382] in order avoid an 'over-privatization of the crime'.[383] Others note that it might capture politically motivated organizations whose purpose is the commission of attacks constituting crimes against humanity.[384] This would be more in line with contemporary readings of crimes against humanity, and reflect the growing role of non-state agents in practices of disappearance.[385] State agents may in any event face responsibility for failure to investigate criminal acts committed by non-state actors.

'Extraordinary renditions', i.e. transfers of detainees around the world without legal process for purposes of detention and interrogation', mark a new form of enforced disappearance.[386] Extraordinary rendition programmes bear various traces of enforced disappearance, such as abduction, imprisonment and concealment of the

---

[379] Art. 7 defines 'enforced disappearance of persons' as 'the arrest, detention or abduction of persons by, or with the authorization, support or acquiescence of, a State or a political organization, followed by a refusal to acknowledge that deprivation of freedom or to give information on the fate or whereabouts of those persons, with the intention of removing them from the protection of the law for a prolonged period of time'. The definition is drawn from the Declaration on the Protection of all Persons from Enforced Disappearance by the UN General Assembly of 1992.

[380] I. Giorgou, 'State Involvement in the Perpetration of Enforced Disappearance and the Rome Statute' (2013) 11 *JICJ* 1001.

[381] International Convention for the Protection of All Persons from Enforced Disappearance, 2716 UNTS 3, 20 December 2006, Art. 2; UN Declaration on Disappearances, Preamble; Inter-American Convention of Human Rights, Art. II.

[382] Giorgou, 'State Involvement', 1020 ('with characteristics similar to the state in terms of structure, purpose and modus operandi'); Ott, *Enforced Disappearance in International Law*, 25 ('Political organizations as phrased in the Rome Statute are not any kind of organizations with political purpose or ambitions, but solely those organizations which replace a State in at least some of its functions').

[383] C. K. Hall and L. v. d. Herik, 'Article 7', in Triffterer and Ambos, *The Rome Statute of the International Criminal Court*, 288.

[384] P. Currat, *Les crimes contre l' humanité dans le Statut de la Cour Pénale Internationale* (Brussels: Bruylant, 2006), 512.

[385] R. Cryer et al., *An Introduction to International Criminal Law and Procedure* (Cambridge: Cambridge University Press, 2014), 260. This view has been confirmed by the UN Human Rights Committee.

[386] D. Weissbrodt and A. Bergquist, 'Extraordinary Rendition: A Human Rights Analysis' (2006) 19 *Harvard Human. Rights Journal* 123; N. Kyriakou, An Affront to the Conscience of Humanity: Enforced Dissapearance in International Human Rights Law, at http://cadmus.eui.eu/bitstream/handle/1814/22700/2012_KYRIAKOU.pdf. See also F. Lau, 'The Treatment of High Value Detainees under the United States' Extraordinary Rendition Program: A Case of Crimes Against Humanity for the International Criminal Court' (2016) 39 *University of South Wales Law Journal* 1261, 1289–1291.

whereabouts of detainees, and intent to remove persons from the protection of the law. Secret detention is typically justified by state secrecy and security reasons. Even US Officials have acknowledged that it is improper to keep suspects '"disappeared" and outside the reach of any justice system'.[387]

1.3.2.4.5 *Apartheid*

The crime of apartheid is somewhat of an anomaly in the list of crimes against humanity. It criminalizes the legitimization of a particular structure, namely a system of oppression and racial discrimination. It has certain synergies with genocide. Like genocide, apartheid is a term of art with a particular stigma and historical heritage, originally connected to the struggle of decolonization. Its criminalization goes back to the cold war era, namely the adoption of the International Convention on the Suppression and Punishment of the Crime of Apartheid (Apartheid Convention) in 1973.

The Convention was targeted at stigmatizing racial discrimination. It specifies that the crime of apartheid 'shall include similar policies and practices of racial segregation and discrimination as practised in southern Africa, and in particular the apartheid regime in South Africa'.[388] The Convention has many innovative features. It contains a reference to criminal responsibility of members of 'organizations' and 'institutions', the exercise of universal jurisdiction based on custody over the accused, and the establishment of an 'international penal tribunal' with jurisdiction over the crime, echoing the Genocide Convention.[389] It marked to some extent a moral point of no return. It made it impossible for the ILC,[390] and later the drafters of the ICC, to ignore the special nature and gravity of apartheid as a crime, although the Apartheid Convention itself received divided support.[391]

In the negotiations on the ICC Statute, it was controversial to what extent apartheid should be recognized as a specific crime.[392] It was not included in the list of war crimes.[393] It overlaps with two other categories of crimes against humanity, namely persecution on racial grounds and other inhumane acts. Its recognition was pushed by delegations from the Southern African Development Community (SADC), including South Africa. Critics claim that its separate criminalization was mainly driven by politics, rather

---

[387] C. Rice, *No Higher Honor. A Memoir of My Years in Washington* (New York: Crown Publishing, 2011), 501–502.

[388] Art. 2, Apartheid Convention.

[389] Art. 5, Apartheid Convention.

[390] Apartheid is included in Art. 20 of the ILC's 1991 Draft Code of Crimes against the Peace and Security of Mankind. Art. 18 (f) of the 1996 final version refers to '[i]nstitutionalized discrimination on racial, ethnic or religious grounds involving the violation of fundamental human rights and freedoms and resulting in seriously disadvantaging a part of the population'.

[391] See C. Tomuschat, 'Crimes Against the Peace and Security of Mankind and the Recalcitrant Third State' (1995) 24 *Israel Yearbook on Human Rights* (1995) 41, 55 ('[t]he fact that the West has consistently rejected the Apartheid Convention proves that a universal opinio iuris is missing).

[392] See generally P. Eden, 'The Role of the Rome Statute in the Criminalization of Apartheid' (2014) 12 *JICJ* 171, 184–185.

[393] P. Eden, 'The Practices of Apartheid as a War Crime: A Critical Analysis' (2013) 16 *Yearbook of International Humanitarian Law* 89–117.

than law.[394] It carries expressive significance, in the sense that it contributes to 'affirmation, exclamation or denunciation', rather than actual enforcement.[395]

The definition of apartheid in ICC Statute differs partly from the Apartheid Convention. Some states voiced concern that the extension of apartheid beyond the South African context might criminalize racist views or policies of radical private actors (e.g. white supremacists).[396] The Statute specifies that apartheid requires conduct committed 'in the context of an institutionalized regime of systematic oppression and domination by one racial group over any other racial group or groups'.[397] The reading of this definition remains contested. Some argue that this framing captures mainly discriminatory practices by a state against members of its own population or polity.[398] This view draws on the analogy to the South African precedent. It implies that the unique stigma and distinction of apartheid from other forms of prohibited discrimination, including persecution, arises from the fact that it is built on 'a state-sanctioned regime of law, policy, and institutions'.[399] Other voices defend a broader interpretation of the concept of an institutionalized regime. They argue that the term 'regime' refers to a 'method or system' of organization and captures 'institutionalized practices by non-state acts, including de facto policies by armed groups'.[400]

Apartheid is framed as a specific intent crime. The perpetrator must commit a prohibited inhumane act, with the intent to 'maintain' such a regime. The crime thus captures mostly the responsibility of leaders and organizers. It may exclude actors that lack governmental control.[401]

The biggest dilemma is to what extent the crime of apartheid can be emancipated from its historical context.[402] The ICC Statute extends the scope beyond the South African context. States have remained reluctant to prosecute apartheid as crime against humanity, despite the wide jurisdictional provisions of the Apartheid Convention. Contemporary scenarios remain contested. The main example where a modern analogy has been made is the situation in the Palestinian Occupied Territories. Palestine has made this argument in its submission to the ICC. It has argued that Israeli policies constitute an institutionalized regime of systematic discrimination that deprives Palestinians of a number of their fundamental human rights.[403] This

---

[394] A. Zahar, 'Apartheid as an International Crime', in A. Cassese (ed.), *Oxford Companion to International Criminal Justice* (Oxford: Oxford University Press, 2009), 245.

[395] R. Clark, 'Crimes against Humanity and the Rome Statute of the International Criminal Court', in M. Politi and G. Nesi (eds.), *The Rome Statute of the International Criminal Court: A Challenge to Impunity* (Aldershot: Ashgate, 2001) 75, 88.

[396] Eden, 'Practices of Apartheid as a War Crime', 97.

[397] Art. 7 (2) ICC Statute.

[398] A. Bultz, 'Redefining Apartheid in International Criminal Law' (2013) 24 *Criminal Law Forum* 205, 225, 229.

[399] J. Dugard and J. Reynolds, 'Apartheid, International Law, and the Occupied Palestinian Territory' (2013) 24 *EJIL* 867, 881.

[400] C. K. Hall, Art. 7, in O. Triffterer, *Rome Statute of the International Criminal Court*, 2nd ed. (München: C. H.Beck/ Hart, Nomos, 2008), 264.

[401] See T. McCormack, 'Crimes against Humanity', in D. McGoldrick, P. Rowe and E. Donnelly (eds.), *The Permanent International Criminal Court: Legal and Policy Issues* (Oxford: Hart Publishing, 2004), 179, 199–200.

[402] C. Lingaas, 'The Crime against Humanity of Apartheid in a Post-Apartheid World' (2015) 2 *Oslo Law Review* 86.

[403] ICC, 'Report on Preliminary Examination Activities 2017', 4 December 2017, para. 63.

argument finds support from some scholars. For instance, John Dugard and John Reynold have argued that 'there are indeed strong grounds to conclude that a system of apartheid has developed in the occupied Palestinian territory'.[404] Opponents criticize this analogy as a 'sensationalist' use of legal concepts in a 'polarized discourse'.[405] They question whether separation is organized along racial lines and draw attention to the particularities of the situation of occupation.[406]

1.3.2.4.6 Persecution

Crimes against humanity encompass persecution. This crime has old roots. It was first qualified as a crime against humanity after the Armenian massacres of 1915. It involves the intentional and severe deprivation of fundamental rights contrary to international law by reason of the identity of the group or collectivity. The ICC Statute differs from the Statutes of the ad hoc tribunals. The discriminatory grounds cover not only political, racial or religious grounds, but also national, ethnic, cultural, gender and 'other grounds that are universally recognized as impermissible under international law'. The definition specifies that the acts must be committed 'in connection' with other acts or crimes within the jurisdiction of the ICC. This requirement was introduced to limit 'sweeping interpretation criminalizing *all* discriminatory practices'.[407] It raises novel questions about the reach of the crime. For instance, discriminatory laws may not by themselves constitute a crime of 'persecution'.

A particular controversial issue is whether persecution might cover discrimination and hate crime on the grounds of sexual orientation and gender identity, i.e. crimes against lesbians, gays, bisexuals and transsexuals (LGBT).[408] This type of discrimination may be traced back to Nazi rule and has become acute in certain contemporary conflicts, such as ISIS attacks on gay people based on biases against homosexuality.[409] The existing definition of gender at the ICC is ambiguous.[410] Neither the Statute nor OTP policy documents refer expressly to 'sexual orientation'. The Statute states that '"gender" refers to the two sexes, male and female, within the context of society. The term "gender" does not indicate any meaning different from the above'.[411] The emphasis on the two sexes, 'male and female', appears to imply that gender refers to

---

[404] Dugard and Reynolds, 'Apartheid, International Law, and the Occupied Palestinian Territory', 912.

[405] Bultz, 'Redefining Apartheid in International Criminal Law', 233.

[406] Y. Zilbershats, 'Apartheid, International Law, and the Occupied Palestinian Territory: A Reply to John Dugard and John Reynolds' (2013) 24 *EJIL* 915, 921–922.

[407] H. von Hebel and D. Robinson, 'Crimes within the Jurisdiction of the Court', in R. S. Lee (ed.) *The International Criminal Court: The Making of the Rome Statute* (The Hague: Kluwer Law International, 1999), 79, 101.

[408] See AMICC, 'LGBT and the International Criminal Court', https://docs.wixstatic.com/ugd/e13974_86535dbba56d43cfbe4d0977839b41da.pdf.

[409] Human Rights and Gender Justice Clinic of the City University of New York, MADRE and Organization of Women's Freedom in Iraq, Communication to the ICC Prosecutor Pursuant to Article 15 of the Rome Statute Requesting a Preliminary Examination into the Situation, Gender-Based Persecution and Torture as Crimes Against Humanity and War Crimes Committed by the Islamic State of Iraq and the Levant (ISIL) in Iraq, 8 November 2017, at www.madre.org/sites/default/files/PDFs/CUNY%20MADRE%20OWFI%20Article%2015%20Communication%20Submission%20Gender%20Crimes%20in%20Iraq%20PDF.pdf.

[410] See V. Oosterveld, 'The Definition of Gender in the Rome Statute of the International Criminal Court: A Step Forward or Back for International Criminal Justice' (2005) 18 *Harvard Human Rights Journal* 55.

[411] Art. 7 (3), ICC Statute.

the biological difference between men and women. This meaning was defended by some delegations, including the Vatican and several religious states and NGOs, which expressed concerns about the inclusion of sexual orientation.[412] The reference to 'the context of society', however, seems to imply that gender is a socially constructed notion, which relates to the social and cultural meanings attached to men's and women's roles in society.[413] Stereotypes and discrimination often arise from societal perceptions about what it means to be 'male and female'. For instance, homosexuals are often discriminated against because of specific social meanings attached to masculinity and femininity and their relationship to sexuality.

According to some voices, discrimination based on sexual orientation and 'gender transgression' thus qualifies as a specific form of gender bias, in particular if it is grounded in perceived departures from assigned gender roles.[414] As Catherine MacKinnon has argued, the ICC gender definition 'does not explicitly encompass gays and lesbians as such, but they are ... covered as women and men, and crimes of discrimination against them as gay or lesbian are often – in my view virtually always – gendered'.[415] These linkages are reflected in the 2014 OTP Policy Paper which states that the gender definition includes 'the social construction of gender and the accompanying roles, behaviors, activities and attributes assigned to women and men, and boys and girls'.[416] It also recognizes that the term must be interpreted in line with international human rights standards,[417] which include efforts to put an end to violence and discrimination based on sexual orientation or gender identity.[418] Several human rights treaty bodies have qualified discrimination based on sexual orientation and gender identity as discrimination based on 'other status'.[419] Even though it is not expressly covered, sexual orientation and gender might thus progressively evolve into a ground of persecution based on gender, or in the long term, into an 'other ground' that is 'universally recognized as impermissible under international law'.[420]

The binary sex-based gender definition of the Statute is subject to critique. The reference to the 'two sexes' makes it difficult to capture 'transgender' identities which

---

[412] For a full account, see V. Oosterveld, 'Constructive Ambiguity and the Meaning of "Gender" for the International Criminal Court' (2014) 16 *International Feminist Journal of Politics* 563, 565–567.

[413] On the tautological nature, see ibid., 567 ('The reference to "the two sexes, male and female" and the final sentence's reference back to these words satisfied the opposing states. The reference to "within the context of society" satisfied the supportive states').

[414] See C. K. Hall, J. Powderly and N. Hayes, 'Article 7' in Triffterer and Ambos, *The Rome Statute of the International Criminal Court*, 293; M. Bohlander, 'Criminalising LGBT Persons under National Criminal Law and Article 7 (i) (h) and (3) of the ICC Statute' (2014) 5 *Global Policy* 401; R. Grey, 'Hate Crime Against Humanity? Persecution on the Grounds of Sexual Orientation under the Rome Statute', at https://beyondthehague.com/2014/02/21/hate-crime-against-humanity-persecution-on-the-grounds-of-sexual-orientation-under-the-rome-statute/.

[415] C. MacKinnon, 'Creating International Law: Gender as Leading Edge' (2013) 36 *Harvard Journal of Law & Gender* 105, 110.

[416] See OTP Policy Paper, para. 15.

[417] Ibid.

[418] Ibid., n. 23. See e.g. the Free and Equal Initiative of OHCHR.

[419] Sexual orientation qualifies as discrimination on the basis of 'other status' under Art. 26 of ICCPR and Art. 2 (2) of ICESCR.

[420] Art. 7 (1) (h) requires 'other grounds' to be 'universally recognized as impermissible under international law'. This sets a very high threshold.

are not 'gender-non-conforming'. This approach is contradictory.[421] It contrasts with the basic premise that conceptions of gender are socially constructed. If the rationale of gender-based persecution is to combat discrimination based on failure to conform to binary gender identities, it is artificial to exclude discrimination against transgender persons who defy these categorizations.

1.3.2.4.7 Other Inhumane Acts

The category of other inhumane acts is a final residual clause that provides leeway to accommodate forms of inhumane treatment that were not expressly prohibited.[422] It rests on the idea that 'however great the care taken in drawing up a list of all the various forms of infliction, it would never be possible to catch up with the imagination of future torturers who wished to satisfy their bestial instincts; and the more specific and complete a list tries to be, the more restrictive it becomes'.[423] There were initial concerns that this clause would absorb an overly broad range of criminal behaviour and run counter to the legality principle. Within the ICC regime, however, the definition is more restrictive than the one used in the Nuremberg and ad hoc tribunals. The inhumane act must be of a 'similar character' to the other acts referred to in Article 7(1), and it must inflict 'great suffering, or serious injury to body or mental or physical health'.[424] These restrictions were inserted to satisfy criticisms of lack of certainty of this crime.

The jurisprudence of the ICC has expressly held that 'this residual category of crimes against humanity must be interpreted conservatively and must not be used to expand uncritically the scope of crimes against humanity'.[425] This suggests that not every human rights violation qualifies as another inhumane act.[426]

One contested example is the practice of 'forced marriage', i.e. patriarchal types of 'bush' marriages by which women and girls are assigned to serve as 'wives' to combatants. The Rome Statute outlaws sexual slavery but does not explicitly prohibit 'forced marriage'. The jurisprudence of the SCSL recognized 'forced marriage' as a crime against humanity in specific contexts. It held that

> while traditionally arranged marriages involving minors violate certain international human rights norms such as the Convention on the Elimination of all Forms of Discrimination against Women (CEDAW), forced marriages which involve the abduction and detention of women and girls and their use for sexual and other purposes is clearly criminal in nature.[427]

---

[421] See Dolen, 'Letting Go of the Gender Binary', 491.
[422] C. Stahn, 'Article 7k' in Triffterer and Ambos, *The Rome Statute of the International Criminal Court*, 235.
[423] See ICTY, *Prosecutor v. Kupreškić et al.,* IT-95-16-T, Judgment, 14 January 2000, para. 563.
[424] Art. 7 (i) (k).
[425] *Prosecutor v. Muthaura, Kenyatta and Ali*, ICC-01/09-02/11, Decision on the Confirmation of Charges Pursuant to Article 61(7)(a) and (b) of the Rome Statute, 23 January 2012, para. 269.
[426] See *Prosecutor v. Katanga and Ngudjolo Chui*, ICC-01/04-01/07-717, Decision on the Confirmation of Charges, 30 September 2008, para. 448 (*Katanga and Chui* Confirmation Decision). See also Ambos, *Treatise on International Criminal Law Vol. II*, 115-116.
[427] SCSL, *Prosecutor v. Brima, Kamara and Kanu*, SCSL-2004-16-A, Judgment, 22 February 2008, para. 194 (*Brima et al.* Appeal Judgment).

In the *Ongwen* case, the Pre-Trial Chamber II of the ICC followed the approach that 'forced marriage' should be considered an inhumane act, rather than sexual slavery,[428] following a previous decision of the SCSL. It noted that 'unlike sexual slavery, forced marriage implies a relationship of exclusivity between the "husband" and "wife", which could lead to disciplinary consequences for breach of this exclusive arrangement and, therefore, is "not predominantly a sexual crime"'.[429] The crime also entails additional harm not of a sexual nature and violates the rights to marry freely and establish a family.[430]

1.3.2.4.8 Merits and Discontents

Crimes against humanity have witnessed a strong degree of 'modernization' and 'privatization'. This enables international criminal courts and tribunals and states to engage with new forms of violence, transformations of conflict and peacetime violations. International definitions are in some respects more 'modern' than domestic approaches. Crime interpretations have a large spillover effect on other accountability agents, such as human rights fact-finding bodies. However, this trend also carries certain risks.

The expanding reach of crimes against humanity makes the boundaries between international and domestic crimes more fluid. There remain valid arguments to distinguish jurisdictional approaches of international criminal tribunals from broader developments.[431] International criminal jurisdictions are typically mandated to deal with particular global challenges, such as crimes that affect peace and security. They are constrained by resource limitations, and particularly geared at addressing types of criminality that states are unable or unwilling to confront. Cynically, the increasing 'privatization' of crimes against humanity may provide a temptation to focus more on violations by non-state actors, rather than state action.[432] In many situations, non-state actors are easier to target. It is more difficult to engage with the conduct of powerful states that fuel violations or cycles of violence. This opens global criminal justice to critique. It is easily seen as a tool by states to target opponents, rather than as an instrument to tame state power.

1.3.3   War Crimes

War crimes are the third and oldest category of atrocity crimes. They are grounded in international humanitarian law, traditionally known as *jus in bello* (the law of war).[433]

---

[428] *Prosecutor* v. *Dominic Ongwen*, ICC-02/04–01/15–422-Red, Decision on the Confirmation of Charges, 23 March 2016, paras. 87 et seq (*Ongwen* Confirmation Decision).

[429] Ibid., para. 93.

[430] Ibid., para. 94.

[431] Kress, 'On the Outer Limits of Crimes against Humanity', 855–873.

[432] F. Mégret, 'Is the ICC Focusing Too Much on Non-State Actors?', in M. M. deGuzman and D. Amann (eds.), *Arcs of Global Justice: Essays in Honour of William A. Schabas* (New York: Oxford University Press 2018).

[433] The origins go back to the just war tradition. See K. Okimoto, *The Distinction and Relationship between Jus ad Bellum and Jus in Bello* (Oxford: Hart, 2011); *Prosecutor* v. *Šainović et al.*, IT-05–87-A, Judgment, 23 January 2014, para. 1662 ('Whether the resort to the use of force is legitimate under international law is a question of *jus ad bellum*, which is distinct from whether the way in which that force was used was legal under international humanitarian law, i.e. *jus in bello*').

It regulates the conduct of parties engaged in an armed conflict and seeks to minimize suffering and harm. It is based on a balancing between military and humanitarian considerations. In armed conflict, certain acts of violence are allowed (lawful)[434] and others prohibited (unlawful). International humanitarian law regulates both lawful and unlawful acts of violence. It needs to reconcile different perspectives: a principled humanitarian commitment 'to prevent or mitigate suffering'[435] and the pragmatic reality of warfare, including choices faced by soldiers in battle.

1.3.3.1 Origin

Historically, international humanitarian law has often been presented as a project of empathy and compassion, with the battle of Solferino as a turning point.[436] However, it has different faces. It is marked by a tension between permissive and prohibitive readings.[437] It is divided into different traditions. The 'Hague law' emerged during the Hague Peace Conferences in 1899 and 1907.[438] It establishes the rights and obligations of belligerents in the conduct of military operations, and limits the means of harming the enemy. It departed from the traditional approach to war according which anything that contributed to victory was permitted. It is permissive in nature, but sets restrictions to warfare. The 'Geneva law'[439] is primarily designed to protect victims of armed conflict and specific categories of persons, such as prisoners of war, detainees, civilians and humanitarian aid workers. A major part of it is contained in the four Geneva Conventions of 1949. Nearly every state in the world has agreed to be bound by them.

Despite its growing global relevance, international humanitarian law continues to be marked by certain frictions.[440] The major ideological differences may be traced back to the controversy between Henri Dunant and Bertha von Suttner before the Hague Peace Conference.[441] Dunant defended the virtues of regulating *jus in bello* in order to constrain evil in war and mitigate the impact of new weapons. Von Suttner claimed that codifying violence weakens the struggle for disarmament and peace, and that is unhelpful to regulate practices that should be prohibited.

This controversy still persists in modern debates. Constructivists view international humanitarian law as an instrument to control the behaviour of belligerents, to protect

---

[434] For instance, the parties are permitted, or at least are not prohibited from, attacking each other's military objectives.

[435] H. Lauterpacht, 'The Problem of the Revision of the Law of War' (1952) 29 *British Yearbook of International Law* 363–364.

[436] For a critical account, see A. Alexander, 'A Short History of International Humanitarian Law' (2015) 26 *EJIL* 109.

[437] See J. Morrow, *Order within Anarchy: The Laws of War as an International Institution* (Cambridge: Cambridge University Press, 2014).

[438] The term derives from the 1899 and 1907 Hague Conventions and relates means and methods of combat. See F. Bugnion, 'Droit de Genève et droit de La Haye' (2001) 83 *International Review of the Red Cross* 901.

[439] The Geneva Law is focused on protection of persons, rather than conduct of hostilities. Ibid.

[440] Alexander, 'A Short History', 113 ('One is the story of the humanization of war and law; the second is a story of imperialism and oppression').

[441] A. Durand, 'The Development of the Idea of Peace in the Thinking of Henry Dunant' (1986) 26 *International Review of the Red Cross* 16–51.

civilians from violence or humanize warfare through law.[442] Sceptics challenge its progressive narratives[443] or caution that it might consolidate war as a legal institution or legitimate violence by failing to prohibit it.[444] Extending international humanitarian law also carries risks, since its standards of targeting and detention are more permissive than human rights law.

Although international humanitarian law and international criminal law are partly autonomous fields with distinct objectives, many of the foundations of the laws of war have been reshaped through criminal adjudication. The interpretation of secondary rules, i.e. war crimes law, provided new impulses for the interpretation of some of the primary rules of international humanitarian law.

International criminal courts and tribunals relied strongly on morality and the humanitarian considerations to advance the law. The Martens clause provided a normative instrument to bridge the gap between 'public conscience' and the law.[445] Judges have combined moral reasoning and dynamic interpretation of the sources of international law to develop the humanitarian foundations of the laws of war. In the *Furundžija* judgment, the ICTY went even so far to argue that 'The essence of the whole corpus of international humanitarian law as well as human rights law lies in the protection of the human dignity of every person, whatever his or her gender ... indeed in modern times it has become of such paramount importance as to permeate the whole body of international law'.[446] Opponents criticized this approach as 'human-rightism' or judicial norm entrepreneurship which blurs the boundaries of humanitarian law.[447]

1.3.3.2 Definition

War crimes are serious violations of international humanitarian law. Many provisions of the Hague or Geneva law fail to specify whether a violation entails criminal responsibility. War crimes law was developed incrementally. Only specific violations of international humanitarian law are criminalized. Early examples may be found in

---

[442] On the 'lesser evil' argument, see J. Dill, 'Should International Law Ensure the Moral Acceptability of War?' (2013) 26 *LJIL* 253, 259.

[443] F. Mégret, 'From "Savages" to "Unlawful Combatants": A Postcolonial Look at International Humanitarian Law's "Other"', in A. Orford (ed.), *International Law and its Others* (Cambridge: Cambridge University Press, 2006), 265.

[444] C. Jochnick and R. Normand, 'The Legitimation of Violence: A Critical History of the Laws of War' (1994) 35 *Harvard International Law Journal* 49; H. Dexter, 'New War, Good War and the War on Terror, Explaining, Excusing and Creating Western Neo-Interventionism' (2007) 38 *Development & Change* 1055, 1067; D. Kennedy, 'Modern War and Modern Law', October 2009, www.law.harvard.edu/faculty/dkennedy/speeches/suffolktalk2009_WarandLaw.htm ('law may do more to legitimate than restrain violence. It may accelerate the vertigo of combat and contribute to the loss of ethical moorings for people on all sides of a conflict').

[445] T. Meron, 'The Martens Clause, Principles of Humanity, and Dictates of Public Conscience' (2000) 94 *AJIL* 78.

[446] *Prosecutor* v. *Furundžija*, IT-95–17/1-T, Judgment, 10 December 1998, para. 183 (*Furundžija* Trial Judgment).

[447] On judicial entrepreneurship, see R. Aloisi and J. Meernik, *Judgment Day: Judicial Decision Making at the International Criminal Tribunals* (New York: Cambridge University Press, 2017), 26–59. See also C. Byron, 'A Blurring of the Boundaries: The Application of International Humanitarian Law by Human Rights Bodies' (2006–2007) 47 *Vanderbilt Journal of International Law* 839.

national criminal codes and military manuals, such as the famous Lieber Code (1863),[448] which contained rules for military conduct in the American Civil War. The Geneva Conventions and its Protocols expressly qualify the so-called grave breaches as 'war crimes'.[449] The term 'grave breaches' is problematic from a conceptual point of view, since it implies a hierarchy, whereby certain violations are considered grave enough to qualify as crimes, whilst others do not.

What constitutes a war crime was largely defined through practice in the twentieth century. After World War I, the Commission on the Responsibilities of War identified a list of thirty-two violations of the laws and customs of war that are subject to prosecution.[450] The Nuremberg Charter included an illustrative list of war crimes, based on key provisions of the 1907 Hague Regulations. Most of the modern contours of war crimes were specified by the jurisprudence of the ad hoc tribunals for the former Yugoslavia and Rwanda. In the 1995 *Tadić* decision, the ICTY gave a rule of thumb: the violation 'must constitute a breach of a rule protecting important values, and the breach must involve grave consequences for the victim'.[451]

1.3.3.3 *Types of Conflicts*

The scope of war crimes has been adjusted to changing patterns of warfare. Historically, international law has focused on interstate violence. The traditional criterion to determine the applicability of the law of war was the existence of a 'state of war'.[452] The Geneva Conventions tied the applicability to the wider concept of armed conflict. The essential question is whether an armed conflict exists in fact. This is meant to be an objective assessment. The problem is that there exists no general body deciding on the legal qualification of a conflict. Legal practice and jurisprudence have thus a taken a key role.

The understanding as to when an international armed conflict (IAC) exists has expanded over time. The traditional criterion for classification of the nature of the armed conflict is actor-based. An international armed conflict involves the use of armed force between two or more states. As the ICTY noted in the 1999 *Tadić* decision, it can exist in a number of situations:[453]

[i]t is indisputable that an armed conflict is international if it takes place between two or more States. In addition, in case of an internal armed conflict breaking out on the territory of a State, it may become international (or, depending upon the circumstances, be international in

---

[448] See Instructions for the Government of Armies of the United States in the Field, General Orders No. 100, War Department Washington DC, 24 April 1863. See generally T. Meron, 'Francis Lieber's Code and Principles of Humanity' (1998) 36 *Columbia Journal of Transnational Law* 269.

[449] W. Ferdinandusse, 'The Prosecution of Grave Breaches in National Courts' (2009) 7 *JICJ* 723.

[450] Commission on the Responsibility of the Authors of the War and on Enforcement of Penalties (1920) 17 AJIL 95.

[451] *Prosecutor v. Tadić*, IT-94-1-AR72, Decision on the Defence Motion for Interlocutory Appeal on Jurisdiction, 2 October 1995, para. 94 (*Tadić* 1995).

[452] See Q. Wright, 'When Does War Exist?' (1932) 26 *AJIL* 362.

[453] See S. Vité, 'Typology of Armed Conflicts in International Humanitarian Law: Legal Concepts and Actual Situations' (2009) 91 *International Review of the Red Cross* 69.

character alongside an internal armed conflict) if (i) another State intervenes in that conflict through its troops, or alternatively if (ii) some of the participants in the internal armed conflict act on behalf of that other State.[454]

An IAC exists when a foreign army occupies territory belonging to another state. It may also be deemed to exist when states use domestic military groups as proxies in warfare.

International criminal courts and tribunals have adopted a more relaxed test than the International Court of Justice in determining when an armed entity may qualify as a proxy.[455] They have held that a conflict between a state and an armed group can be international if a third state exercises 'overall control' over the organized armed group.[456] A sufficient degree of de facto control is deemed to exist 'when a State (or in the context of an armed conflict, the Party to the conflict) has a role in organising, coordinating or planning the military actions of the military group, in addition to financing, training and equipping or providing operational support to that group'.[457] According to this test, the required degree of state control must thus extend beyond mere logistical support. However, it is not required that the state issues specific orders or directs each individual operation of the proxy.[458] This was inter alia the case in the former Yugoslavia where Serbia was found to exercise 'overall control' over the operations of Bosnian Serb forces in Bosnia and Herzegovina.

Most conflicts today are non-international in nature, or contain grey zones in relation to their qualification.[459] States have traditionally been reluctant to recognize responsibility for violations in civil war, since they considered this an 'internal matter'. Common Article 3 to the 1949 Conventions regulates minimum standards (a 'mini'-convention) for non-international armed conflict (NIAC), especially civil wars. It was largely accepted, though, that the law of war crimes does not cover internal armed conflict. Additional Protocol II to the Geneva Convention, which specifically addresses the protection of victims in non-international armed conflict, does not contain any crimes. The legendary 1995 *Tadić* decision broke this distinction. It noted:

elementary considerations of humanity and common sense make it preposterous that the use by States of weapons prohibited in armed conflicts between themselves be allowed when States try to put down rebellion by their own nationals on their own territory. What is inhumane,

---

[454] *Prosecutor* v. *Tadić*, Case No. IT-94–1-A, Judgment, 15 July 1999, para 84 (*Tadić* 1999).

[455] The ICJ adopted an 'effective control' test in *Nicaragua* in the context of state responsibility. See ICJ, *Case Concerning Military and Paramilitary Activities in and Against Nicaragua* (*Nicaragua* v. *U.S.*) (Merits), 1986 ICJ Reports 14. In the *Genocide* case, the ICJ acknowledged that the criterion of 'overall control' may be 'applicable and suitable' as a means of determining whether or not an armed conflict is international in the context of individual criminal responsibility. See ICJ, *Application of the Convention on the Prevention and Punishment of the Crime of Genocide*, 26 February 2007, para 404. See A. Cassese, 'The Nicaragua and Tadic Tests Revisited in Light of the ICJ Judgment on Genocide in Bosnia' (2007) 18 *EJIL* 649

[456] See *Prosecutor* v. *Lubanga*, ICC-01/04–01/06, Judgment pursuant to Art. 74 of the Statute, 14 March 2012, para. 541 (*Lubanga* Trial Judgment); *Katanga* Trial Judgment, paras. 1178 and 1215, building on *Tadić* 1999, para. 137.

[457] See *Tadić* 1999, para. 137.

[458] *Tadić* 1999, para. 137.

[459] See ICRC, Opinion paper, 'How Is the Term "Armed Conflict" Defined in International Humanitarian Law?', March 2008, at www.icrc.org/eng/assets/files/other/opinion-paper-armed-conflict.pdf.

and consequently proscribed, in international wars, cannot but be inhumane and inadmissible in civil strife.[460]

This provided leeway for the ICTY to draw on the law of IAC to develop the much more rudimentary law on NIAC. At the time, this was a controversial move since states that drafted and ratified the Geneva Conventions had not necessarily envisioned such a result.[461] However, in 1998 this ruling was taken into account in the drafting of the ICC Statute which contains an extensive list of war crimes concerning both categories of conflict. It is thus now widely accepted that serious infringements of the international humanitarian law of non-international armed conflicts may also be regarded as amounting to war crimes proper.

The distinction between IACs and NIACs matters from the perspective of accountability.[462] The list of war crimes has typically been more extensive in the context of international armed conflict. Moreover, the regime differs in relation to combat immunity. In international armed conflict, parties to a conflict cannot be prosecuted for their engagement in conflict, unless they violate the law. In non-international armed conflict, there is no 'combatant' or 'prisoner of war' status.[463] States were reluctant to extend combatant immunity to armed groups, in order to avoid insurgency and legitimation of armed force inside states. This creates a paradox from a compliance perspective. Armed groups face the risk of prosecution under domestic law, even if they comply with international humanitarian law.

In practice, the rigid distinction between the two regimes is increasingly under challenge. In many cases, the classification itself poses difficulties in light of the increasing hybridization of warfare,[464] including 'spillover' effects of conflicts, the involvement of multinational armed forces on the side of a party to a conflict, and the transformation of conflicts over time. In many situations, different types of conflict may coexist at the same time. For instance, in both the former Yugoslavia and the DRC, an international and a non-international armed conflict coexisted. Tribunals have specified that the applicable legal regime must be determined in light of the relationship of actors involved, such as the status of parties to the conflict, their mode of intervention[465] and the possible coexistence of two types of conflict.[466] Some voices

---

[460] *Tadić* 1995, para. 119.
[461] Chinese Judge Li criticized the *Tadić* approach as 'an unwarranted assumption of legislative power' in his 1995 Separate Opinion. *Tadić* 1995 Interlocutory Appeal, Separate Opinion, Judge Li, para. 13.
[462] See R. Bartels, 'Timelines, Borderlines and Conflicts' (2009) 91 *International Review of the Red Cross* 36.
[463] As the ICTC explains: 'A non-state party … has no right under domestic law to take up arms and engage in hostilities against the armed forces of a government adversary (the essence of combatant status), nor can it expect to be granted immunity from prosecution for attacks against military targets (the essence of combatant privilege).' See ICRC, 'International Humanitarian Law and the Challenges of Contemporary Armed Conflicts', 50.
[464] See G. S. Corn, 'Hamdan, Lebanon, and the Regulation of Hostilities: The Need to Recognize a Hybrid Category of Armed Conflict' (2007) 40 *Vanderbilt Journal of Transnational Law* 305; R. S. Schöndorf, 'Extra-State Armed Conflicts: Is There a Need for a New Legal Regime?' (2004) 37 *NYU Journal of International Law and Politics* 1.
[465] *Katanga* Trial Judgment, para. 1182.
[466] *Katanga* Trial Judgment, para. 1174,

in doctrine have called for a single and unified definition of armed conflict in order to avoid the fragmentation of regimes and to alleviate classification dilemmas.[467]

A controversial question is to what extent the classification of conflicts can be extended beyond the categories of IAC and NIAC. Some voices have called for an extension of NIAC ('transnational armed conflict') to capture situations where an armed group wages conflict against a state across multiple territories. This approach is based on the view that international humanitarian law relates essentially to the conduct of armed hostilities and their effects on individuals, rather than territorial boundaries.[468] According to this view, the nexus to an armed conflict, i.e. NIAC, is decisive. For instance, the US has argued that where a global armed group, such as al-Qaeda, engages in armed hostilities with a state, this conflict label remains applicable to members of the group, irrespective of where they go (transnational NIAC).[469] This theory implies that the conflict follows the movement of persons and that those who directly participate in hostilities may be targeted on the basis of international humanitarian law in non-belligerent states.

The ICRC has remained critical towards the recognition of a 'global battlefield'. It argued that this theory might unduly expand the application of the rules governing the conduct of hostilities to the detriment of the law on use of force in law enforcement, in particular human rights law.[470] The risk of a territorially unbounded reading of international humanitarian law is that it might incentive extraterritorial uses of force and status-based targeting of individuals.

1.3.3.4 Actors and Threshold

Most modern conflicts involve a large range of actors: classical state agents, paramilitary forces, non-state armed groups, private military contractors and accessories to conflict. The scope of war crimes law takes this into account. It extends beyond traditional armies. Common Article 3 to the 1949 Geneva Conventions specifies that 'each Party to the conflict' is bound. This clause confirms that armed non-state actors have a set of international obligations. Modern war crimes law reflects this understanding. It applies not only to interstate violence and conflicts between a government and armed groups, but also to conflicts between two or more organized armed groups that fight against each other.

---

[467] J. G. Stewart, 'Towards a Single Definition of Armed Conflict in International Humanitarian Law: A Critique of Internationalized Armed Conflict' (2003) 85 *International Review of the Red Cross* 328–333; E. Crawford, 'Unequal before the Law: The Case for the Elimination of the Distinction between International and Non-International Armed Conflict' (2007) 20 *LJIL* 441.

[468] For a discussion, see N. Lubell and N. Derejko, 'A Global Battlefied? Drones and the Geographical Scope of Armed Conflict' (2013) 11 *JICJ* 65.

[469] For a discussion, see L. Blank, 'Defining the Battlefield in Contemporary Conflict and Counter-Terrorism: Understanding the Parameters of the Zone of Combat' (2010) 39 *Georgia Journal of International Law* 1.

[470] ICRC, 'International Humanitarian Law and the Challenges', 15. On extraterritorial application, see M. Milanovic, *Extraterritorial Application of Human Rights Treaties: Law, Principles and Policy* (Oxford: Oxford University Press, 2011).

The qualification of the nature of the armed conflict does not depend on the subjective assessment of the parties. It is linked to the degree of hostilities between armed forces and the intensity of conflict. Most authorities argue that in cases of a NIAC, the armed violence needs to be of sufficient intensity to make it distinguishable from sporadic acts of violence and internal disturbances.[471] Armed violence that does not meet the requisite degree of intensity and organization is governed by international standards and domestic law applying to law enforcement operations. The application of the threshold poses dilemmas in relation to the activity of organized criminal groups (e.g. drug-related violence). They were traditionally excluded from the application of NIAC in order not to recognize their status.

According to the 1995 *Tadić* definition, the main test is whether there is 'protracted' armed violence. It involves two requirements. The first is the intensity of the hostilities.[472] This can be shown by factors such as the gravity and repeated nature of attacks, the collective nature of hostilities, their temporal and territorial scope, including displacement of a large number of people, and/or international reactions. It does not need to entail massive loss of life.[473] The second requirement is the organizational element, i.e. the capacity to carry out attacks.[474] It does not require the same degree of organization as a conventional military force. Indicators are: the organization and structure of the non-state actor; the issuance of orders, internal regulations, political statements and communiqués; the ability to coordinate action between individual units; the use of uniforms or other insignia, the provision of training, the application of disciplinary rules and the ability to recruit new members.

This wide definition of the notion of armed conflict has enabled international criminal courts and tribunals to respond to the growing privatization of warfare. Crimes committed between armed groups have inter alia been prosecuted in the context of the civil war in Sierra Leone, the Balkans conflict and ICC situations, such as the Ituri conflict. This extension increases the protection of civilians. But it also poses new questions in relation to the standards that non-public authorities (e.g. non-state armed groups) are expected to abide by, for instance in relation to detention.[475] Detention by armed groups has become a routine activity in conflict. NIAC lacks an analogous regime to the law of occupation, i.e. an ordering framework to constrain power and define duties in relation to law and order in cases where armed groups exercise effective control over territory. States have remained reluctant to recognize

---

[471] According to a different view, the intensity of violence is not a precondition for the existence of a NIAC. It suffices that an organized armed group has the capacity to sustain military operations. See A. Ahmad Haque, 'Triggers and Thresholds of Non-International Armed Conflict', *Just Security*, 29 September 2016, www.justsecurity.org/33222/triggers-thresholds-non-international-armed-conflict/.

[472] *Tadić* 1995, para. 70.

[473] See *Prosecutor* v. *Boškoski*, IT-04-82-T, Judgment, 10 July 2008, paras. 244 and 249.

[474] See e.g. *Prosecutor* v. *Limaj et al.*, IT-03-66-T, Judgment, 20 November 2005, paras 83–179.

[475] The traditional argument is that armed groups are not entitled to establish courts and try people. But this logic is increasingly under challenge. See D. Casalin, 'Taking Prisoners: Reviewing the International Humanitarian Law Grounds for Deprivation of Liberty by Armed Opposition Groups' (2011) 93 *International Review of the Red Cross* 743; S. Sivakumaran, 'Courts of Armed Opposition: Fair Trials or Summary Justice?' (2009) 7 *JIC* 489.

the authority of armed groups to detain individuals, since this might impede criminal-ization of detention under domestic law.[476]

1.3.3.5 Nexus to Armed Conflict

In a situation of armed conflict, many criminal acts are committed. One of the key prerequisites of a war crime is that the crime is connected to the armed conflict. This requirement serves to distinguish war crimes from ordinary offences. For instance, there is no reason why crimes committed by certain civilians not taking part in hostilities against other civilians should automatically qualify as war crimes. As the ICTY Appeals Chamber noted that '[w]hat ultimately distinguishes a war crime from a purely domestic offence is that a war crime is shaped by or dependent upon the environment – the armed conflict – in which it is committed'.[477] The armed conflict does not necessarily need to have been causal to the commission of the crime, but it must 'at a minimum, have played a substantial part in the perpetrator's ability to commit it'.[478] Factors that indicate a nexus are the status of the perpetrator as combatant, the fact that the act is committed against a member of the opposing party to the conflict, the civilian nature of victims, the nexus of the act to a military and/or conflict related purpose, and/or its commission in an official capacity.

The ICC Statute contains an additional element. It specifies that the ICC has jurisdiction 'in particular' when war crimes are 'committed as part of a plan or policy or as part of a large-scale commission of crimes'.[479] This element is not required under customary international law.

1.3.3.6 Types of War Crimes

The large majority of war crimes can be traced back to the violation of certain fundamental principles of international humanitarian law. They are grounded in the protection of persons and property.

1.3.3.6.1 Protection of Non-Combatants

A first fundamental principle is the principle of protection of non-combatants. It requires parties to an armed conflict to treat civilians, prisoners of war and wounded or sick former combatants humanely. Killing of combatants may be allowed in armed conflict. But it is a war crime to commit certain offences – such as killing, torture, rape, inhuman treatment or biological, medical or scientific experiments – against protected persons.

---

[476] For a challenge of this argument, see S. Murray, 'Non-State Armed Groups, Detention Authority in Non-International Armed Conflict, and the Coherence of International Law: Searching for a Way Forward' (2017) 30 *LJIL* 435, 456; A. Clapham, 'Detention by Armed Groups under International Law' (2017) 93 *International Law Studies* 1.
[477] *Kunarac* Appeal Judgment, para. 58.
[478] Ibid.
[479] See Art. 8, ICC Statute.

The ad hoc tribunals were pioneering in recognizing rape as a violation of the Laws and Customs of War and as a basis of torture under the Geneva Conventions.[480] Property of non-combatants is protected. As in context of crimes against humanity, the protection of persons from sexual and gender-based violence has been strengthened over past decades. There is a growing consensus that sexual and gender-based crimes cannot be justified in armed conflict. In the case against *Bosco Ntaganda*, the ICC adopted a new approach towards the war crimes of rape and sexual slavery. The Pre-Trial Chamber of the ICC recognized that crimes of sexual violence committed against child soldiers by members of their own military force can constitute war crimes.[481] It deviated from a ruling by SCSL which had found that the 'law of international armed conflict was never intended to criminalise acts of violence committed by one member of an armed group against another, such conduct remaining first and foremost the province of the criminal law of the State of the armed group concerned and human rights law'.[482] The ICC argued that 'to hold that children under the age of 15 years lose the protection afforded to them by IHL merely by joining an armed group, whether as a result of coercion or other circumstances, would contradict the very rationale underlying the protection afforded to such children against recruitment and use in hostilities'.[483] The Trial Chamber confirmed that the minimum protection afforded by Article 3 Common to the four Geneva Conventions is independent of the affiliation to an opponent.[484] It argued that rape or sexual slavery could never result in any military advantage,[485] and that 'there is never a justification to engage in sexual violence against any person; irrespective of whether or not this person may be liable to be targeted and killed under international humanitarian law'.[486]

This idea of 'intra-party protection'[487] deviates from a purely reciprocity-based understanding of obligations under international humanitarian law. The Defence qualified it as judicial activism. The Appeals Chamber upheld the view that protection under international humanitarian law goes beyond inter-party relationships.[488] It found that 'international humanitarian law does not contain a general rule that categorically excludes members of an armed group from protection against crimes

---

[480] R. Dixon, 'Rape as a Crime in International Humanitarian Law: Where to from Here?' (2002) 13 *EJIL* 697.

[481] *Prosecutor* v. *Ntaganda*, ICC-01/04–02/06–309, Decision Pursuant to Art. 61 (7) (a) and (b) of the Rome Statute on the Charges of the Prosecutor Against Bosco Ntaganda, 9 June 2014 (*Ntaganda* Confirmation Decision).

[482] See SCSL, *Prosecutor* v. *Sesay, Kallon, Gbao*, SCSL-04-15- T, Trial Chamber, 2 March 2009, para. 1453. For a discussion, see T. Rodenhäuser, 'Squaring the Circle? Prosecuting Sexual Violence against Child Soldiers by their Own Forces' (2016) 14 *JICJ* 171.

[483] *Ntaganda* Confirmation Decision, para. 78.

[484] *Prosecutor* v. *Ntaganda*, ICC-01/04–02/06), Decision on the Defence's challenge to the jurisdiction of the Court in respect of Counts 6 and 9, 9 October 2015, para. 25 (*Ntaganda* Trial Decision).

[485] The Chamber concluded that the prohibition of rape is not only a rule of customary international law but has also attained *jus cogens* status under international law. *Ntaganda* Trial Decision, para. 51.

[486] *Ntaganda* Trial Decision, para. 49.

[487] See S. Sivakumaran, *Law of Non-International Armed Conflict* (Oxford: Oxford University Press, 2012), 246–249.

[488] See J. K. Kleffner, 'Friend or Foe? On the Protective Reach of the Law of Armed Conflict', in M. Matthee, B. Toebes and M. Bras (eds.), *Armed Conflict and International Law: In Search of the Human Face: Liber Amicorum in Memory of Avril McDonald* (The Hague: Asser Press, 2013), 285–303.

committed by members of the same armed group'.[489] This interpretation is in line with the understanding of Common Article 3 as a 'minimum yardstick' in all armed conflicts.[490] The key issue is thus the existence of a nexus with the armed conflict, rather than the status of the victim. The Appeals Chamber clarified that 'any undue expansion of the reach of the law of war crimes can be effectively prevented by a rigorous application of the nexus requirement'.[491]

1.3.3.6.2 Principle of Distinction

A second key principle is the principle of distinction. It relates to targeting. It requires parties to a conflict at all times to distinguish between civilians and combatants. Attacks may be directed only against combatants and military objects. They must not be directed against civilians or civilian objects, such as churches, hospitals or private residences that are not used for military purposes. A good example is the war crime of attacking civilians. It is a crime of conduct. It is completed by the mere launching of an attack against a civilian population or individual civilians. It does not require death, injury or damage. It is further prohibited to carry out reprisals against civilians and the civilian population.[492] The jurisprudence has prioritized protection and standards of humanity over military necessity. This narrative is reflected in the *Kupreškić* case, in which the ICTY found that a 'slow but profound transformation of humanitarian law under the pervasive influence of human rights has occurred', as a result of which 'belligerent reprisals against civilians and fundamental rights of human beings are absolutely inconsistent legal concepts'.[493]

A key problem is that the notions of 'civilian' or 'combatant' are normative concepts that continue to be adapted and specified, sometimes with particular interests in mind.[494] Civilians are persons who are not members of state armed forces or organized armed groups of a party to the conflict.[495] Parties to a conflict are required to take feasible precautions to determine whether a person qualifies as a civilian. Civilians lose their immunity from direct attack, however, when and 'for such time as they take a direct part in hostilities'. This distinction poses considerable difficulties. The term 'direct participation' contains many grey areas. The ICRC has provided an interpretive Guidance which relies on three requirements (threshold of harm, direct

---

[489] *Prosecutor* v. *Ntaganda*, ICC-01/04–02/06 OA5, Judgment on the appeal of Mr Ntaganda against the 'Second decision on the Defence's challenge to the jurisdiction of the Court in respect of Counts 6 and 9', 15 June 2017, para. 63 (*Ntaganda* Appeal Decision).

[490] ICJ, *Case concerning Military and Paramilitary Activities in and against Nicaragua (Nicaragua* v. *United States of America)*, 27 June 1986, Judgment, para. 218.

[491] *Ntaganda* Appeal Decision, para. 68.

[492] On the prohibition of reprisals, see S. Darcy, 'The Evolution of the Law of Belligerent Reprisals' (2003) 175 *Military Law Review* 184.

[493] *Kupreškić* Trial Judgment, para. 529.

[494] H. Kinsella, *The Image before the Weapon: A Critical History of the Distinction between Combatant and Civilian* (Ithaca: Cornell University Press, Ithaca, 2011), 196.

[495] See Art. 50 AP I. In the context of non-international armed conflict, organized armed groups are deemed to consist of individuals whose continuous function it is to take a direct part in hostilities ('continuous combat function').

causation and belligerent nexus) to permit a reliable distinction.[496] In case of doubt, the person in question must be presumed to be protected against direct attack.

The ICC Statute also expressly prohibits attacks on humanitarian assistance and peacekeeping missions, as long as they are entitled to civilian protection.[497] Such attacks have increased in past decades. The criminalization of these attacks is of crucial significance for modern peace operations and providers of humanitarian assistance in conflict settings. It has been charged as a war crime in Sierra Leone, and later by the ICC in relation to Darfur and Georgia.[498] The problem of the crime is that peace operations do not fit neatly into the combatant/civilian divide. They were traditionally equated to civilians since they were authorized to use force only in cases of self-defence. This qualification has become more difficult in light of the rise of 'robust' mandates involving broader authorization to use force. The SCSL adopted a wide reading of protection. It implied that peace operations as such do not lose protection if they use force to overcome resistance against the enforcement of the mandate.[499] This approach has been criticized from the perspective of the 'equal application' of international humanitarian law, since it 'creates a double standard, under which peacekeepers can use offensive, including lethal force and have it counted as self-defence as long as it is within the mandate, whereas a rebel forces' reply to the armed force, even during an immediate exchange of fire, would qualify as the crime of attacking peacekeepers'.[500] Critics argue that the assessment of loss of protection should be based on a functional assessment of activities and personnel.[501]

Special protection attaches to buildings dedicated to religion, education, art, science or charitable purposes or historic monuments. They may not be intentionally targeted, unless they become a legitimate military objective. A key example is the protection of cultural property.[502] Prosecutors have brought charges in relation to destruction of historic sites, such as the Old Town of Dubrovnic and Timbuktu in Mali.

Destruction of cultural property often has a strong symbolic meaning. As a witness before the ICTY put it: 'There's messages that are being sent when sacral buildings are being damaged and destroyed. One part of the message is "we don't respect you, we

---

[496] Interpretive Guidance on the Notion of Direct Participation in Hostilities under International Humanitarian Law, adopted by the Assembly of the International Committee of the Red Cross on 26 February 2009, in (2008) 90 *International Review of the Red Cross* 991–1047. According to the ICRC, a specific act must fulfil the following cumulative criteria in order to qualify as direct participation in hostilities: '1. The act must be likely to adversely affect the military operations or military capacity of a party to an armed conflict or, alternatively, to inflict death, injury, or destruction on persons or objects protected against direct attack (*threshold of harm*), and 2. There must be a direct causal link between the act and the harm likely to result either from that act, or from a coordinated military operation of which that act constitutes an integral part (*direct causation*), and 3. The act must be specifically designed to directly cause the required threshold of harm in support of a party to the conflict and to the detriment of another (*belligerent nexus*)'.

[497] Arts. 8 (2) (b) (iii) and 8 (2) (e) (iii), ICC Statute.

[498] See generally M. A. Bangura, 'Prosecuting the Crime of Attack on Peacekeepers: A Prosecutor's Challenge' (2010) 23 *LJIL* 165.

[499] *Prosecutor* v. *Sesay, Kallon, and Gbao*, SCSL-04-15-T, Judgment, 2 March 2009, para. 228.

[500] M. Pacholska, '(Il)legality of Killing Peacekeepers' (2015) 13 *JICJ* 43, 69.

[501] Ibid., 71–72.

[502] The 1954 Hague Convention for the Protection of Cultural Property in the Event of Armed Conflict and its Protocols (1954 and 1999) define the condition under which individual criminal responsibility may be imposed.

don't respect your system of belied, we don't respect your culture or psychology". Another one is "we don't want you"'.[503] In the context of Dubrovnik, destruction and damage to cultural property was charged in connection with harm to civilians.[504] In the *Al Mahdi* decision,[505] the ICC examined the destruction of cultural property in Timbuktu. The decision marks new ground because it did not require a link to human casualties. It reflects the idea that intentional attacks against cultural property relate not only to affected communities but to the whole of humanity.

The Prosecution argued in its opening remarks that 'history itself ... is at peril through such attacks'.[506] Timbuktu 'played an essential role in the expansion of Islam; it was the cradle of education, a place of enlightenment for generations of students, attracting many scholars'.[507]

The *Al Mahdi* judgment confirmed this theory. It stressed the fact that 'the targeted buildings were not only religious buildings, but had also a symbolic emotional value for the inhabitants of Timbuktu',[508] that 'all the sites but one were UNESCO World Heritage sites', and that the 'destruction does not only affect the direct victims of the crimes, namely the faithful and inhabitants of Timbuktu, but also people throughout Mali and the international community'.[509] The ICC thus adopted a broader vision of culture that incorporates immaterial dimensions. Judges also highlighted that the destruction of 'property' – no matter how culturally significant – is less grave than crimes committed against individuals. The Chamber thus confirmed a certain hierarchy of crimes.[510]

A crime which illustrates the tensions of modern war crimes law like no other is the crime of pillage, i.e. the appropriation of public or private property without consent of the owner.[511] Pillaging property is an old crime. It was originally conceived as a property crime.[512] The Hague Regulations outlawed it in order to ban plundering and looting of villages and towns in armed conflict. It breaks with the old idea that plundering of enemy property is justified as a punitive measure or a means to settle debts arising out of war. It prevents captors from gaining title over private and public

---

[503] *Prosecutor* v. *Brdanin*, IT-99–36, Statement Expert Witness Colin Kaiser, 27 May 2003.
[504] *Prosecutor* v. *Štrugar*, IT-01–42-T, Judgment, 31 January 2005.
[505] *Prosecutor* v. *Al Mahdi*, ICC-01/12–01/15, Judgment and Sentence, 27 September 2016 (*Al Mahdi* Trial Judgment).
[506] Statement of the Prosecutor of the International Criminal Court, Fatou Bensouda, at the opening of Trial in the case against Mr Ahmad Al-Faqi Al Mahdi, 22 August 2016, www.icc-cpi.int/Pages/item.aspx?name=otp-stat-al-mahdi-160822.
[507] Ibid.
[508] Ibid., para. 79.
[509] Ibid., para. 80
[510] Ibid., para. 77. The judgment received mixed reactions. William Schabas has argued that the crime lacked a sufficient nexus to the armed conflict in Mali and that Al Mahdi was convicted for a crime that he did not commit. See W. A. Schabas, 'Al Mahdi Has Been Convicted of a Crime He Did Not Commit' (2017) 49 *Case Western Reserve Journal of International Law* 75.
[511] See L. van den Herik and D. Dam-de Jong, 'Revitalizing the Antique War Crime of Pillage: The Potential and Pitfalls of Using International Criminal Law to Address Illegal Resource Exploitation During Armed Conflict' (2011) 15 *Criminal Law Forum* 237.
[512] See M. Lundberg, 'The Plunder of Natural Resources During War: A War Crime?' (2008) 39 *Georgetown Journal of International Law* 495, 502 ('fundamentally economic and property-based crime').

property. This approach has been labelled as the 'episodic theory' of pillage, based on its close nexus to theft and conflict.[513]

In the aftermath of World War II, the concept was extended to more systemic forms of plunder and appropriation of property under occupation. In the industrial cases, the post-Nuremberg military tribunals relied on the prohibition of pillage to sanction the purchase of confiscated assets or stolen property by German companies during occupation.[514] The ICTY confirmed the interpretation that the crime applies to organized and 'systematic exploitation' of property of protected persons.[515] This understanding implies that 'theft' can occur in complex and slower forms. It covers more systemic and institutionalized forms of unlawful appropriation of property. Some authors argue that it captures more types of illicit behaviour, including the taking of property under the guise of 'legitimate business' or purchase of conflict commodities by private actors who were not involved in the original appropriation of property ('corporate theory').[516] This expanded understanding views pillaging not only as a property crime, but as instrument to curb trade of illicitly captured property. It has been increasingly invoked to counter critiques that international criminal law fails to address the complicity of corporations or businesses in the pillaging of conflict-related resources.[517]

Today it is widely accepted that the concept of pillage applies not only to personal property (e.g. goods, livestock, money), but also to the appropriation of natural resources, even outside occupations.[518] In the *Congo* v *Uganda* case, the ICJ held Uganda responsible for failing to take adequate measures to prevent the 'looting, plundering and exploitation' of DRC's natural resources.[519] The ICC Statute prohibits pillage in IAC and NIAC.[520] It thus has some relevance for modern resource-based conflicts in which ownership over resources serves as an incentive for violence or as an instrument to finance conflict. There are, however, clear limitations to its use as a tool for banning conflict-related economic crime.

Many of the elements of the crime remain unclear. The ICC Statute refers to pillage of a 'town or place'. Pillaging requires appropriation without consent of the owner. Ownership is often defined by national law. This makes it difficult to capture government actors who exploit natural resources to fund conflict or maintain power, i.e. through remission of concessions to third parties.[521] The ICC Elements contain a

---

[513] P. Keenan, 'Conflict Minerals and the Law of Pillage' (2014) 14 *Chicago Journal of International Law* 524, 535.

[514] In the context of IG Farben, prosecutors used the term 'spoliation'.

[515] *Prosecutor* v. *Delalić, Mucić and Delić*, IT-96-21-T, Judgment, 16 November 1998, para. 590 (*Čelebići* Trial Judgment).

[516] See. J. Stewart, *Corporate War Crimes: Prosecuting the Pillage of Natural Resources* (New York: Open Society Institute, 2011), 33–37. On this 'corporate theory', see Keenan, 'Conflict Minerals and the Law of Pillage', 538.

[517] See M. McGregor, 'Ending Corporate Impunity: How to Really Curb the Pillaging of Natural Resources' (2009) 42 *Case Western Reserve Journal of International Law* 469.

[518] See D. Dam-de Jong, *International Law and Governance of Natural Resources in Conflict and Post-Conflict Situations* (Cambridge: Cambridge University Press, 2015), 220–221.

[519] ICJ, *Armed Activities on the Territory of the Congo (DRC* v. *Uganda)*, Judgment, 19 December 2005, para. 246.

[520] See Art. 8 (2) (b) (xvi) and (2) (e) (v).

[521] Dam de-Jong argues that the clause may capture misappropriations by public officials 'in view of the fact that natural resources belong to the State and not its representatives'. Dam de-Jong, *International Law and Governance of Natural*

contested 'personal enrichment' requirement,[522] according to which the perpetrator must intend to appropriate property 'for private or personal use'.[523] It suggests that considerations of military necessity may be invoked to justify conduct. The personal enrichment clause leaves significant leeway to justify exploitation by reference to wide political or public policy goals. For instance, armed groups may argue that they exploit natural resources to finance legitimate acts of resistance against other state power or other armed factions.[524] In light of these difficulties, prosecutors have been reluctant to bring charges for plundering natural resources. For example, the SCSL failed to charge Charles Taylor for exploiting timber and other natural resources in the conflict in Sierra Leone. The ICC has refrained from charging appropriation of natural resources in the Congo (e.g. mines) as pillage.[525]

The Malabo Protocol seeks to avoid the risk of overinflating the content of the crime of pillage by adopting a new approach. Instead of relying on war crimes law, it defines 'illegal exploitation of natural resources' as a novel international crime.[526] The definition relies on the Protocol against the Natural Exploitation of Natural Resources, adopted by the International Conference on the Great Lakes Region on 30 November 2006, which mandates states to criminalize the conclusion of certain agreements relating to natural resources, exploitation of resources without consent of the state, as well as norms and standards of the certification process.[527] The Malabo Protocol turns violations into criminal offences that were originally not meant to trigger individual criminal responsibility. It limits the scope of violations to acts 'of a serious nature affecting the stability of a State, region or the [African] Union'.[528] However, the existing definition lacks precision, clearly goes far beyond the existing status quo and carries the risk of overcriminalization. Even an exploitation of natural resources that fails to comply with 'norms relating to the protection of the environment or the security of the people and staff' is qualified as a crime.[529]

1.3.3.6.3 Principle of Proportionality

A third fundamental principle under international humanitarian law is the principle of proportionality. It prohibits an attack on a military objective if such an attack may be

---

Resources, 221. However this argument becomes weak in cases where officials represent the state, or where state authority is fragile.

[522] For a critique, see *Prosecutor* v. *Brima, Kamara and Kanu*, SCSL-04—16-T, Judgment, 20 June 2007, para. 754 (*Brima et al.* Trial Judgment) ('the requirement of "private or personal use" is unduly restrictive and ought not to be an element of pillage'). See also Stewart, *Corporate War Crimes*, 20–22.

[523] ICC Elements of Crime Art. 8 (2) (b) (xvi) and (2) (e) (v).

[524] See O. Radics and C. Bruch, 'The Law of Pillage, Conflict Resources and Jus Post Bellum', in C. Stahn, J. Iverson and J. Easterday (eds.), *Environmental Protection and Transitions from Conflict to Peace* (Oxford: Oxford University Press, 2017), 143, 151.

[525] For a critique, see Keenan, 'Conflict Minerals and the Law of Pillage', 555 et seq.

[526] Art. 28L *bis* Malabo Protocol.

[527] International Conference on the Great Lakes Region. Protocol against the Natural Exploitation of Natural Resources, 30 November 2006, at https://ungreatlakes.unmissions.org/sites/default/files/icglr_protocol_against_the_illegal_exploit ation_of_natural_resources.pdf.

[528] See chapeau of Art. 28L *bis* Malabo Protocol.

[529] Art. 28L *bis* (f). Malabo Protocol.

expected to cause excessive collateral damage (such as loss of civilian life, injury to civilians, damage to civilian objects) in relation to the concrete and direct military advantage anticipated. An attack constitutes a war crime if it is carried out with the knowledge that the probable consequence will be to kill civilians or destroy civilian objects in violation of the principle of proportionality. The ICTY found that 'in case of repeated attacks, all or most of them falling within the grey area between indisputable legality and unlawfulness, it might be warranted to conclude that the cumulative effect of such acts entails that they may not be in keeping with international law'.[530]

These assessments are problematic. Proportionality is phrased in a prospective manner. It involves elements of precaution, adequacy and necessity. It is difficult for a reasonable observer to assess an attack ex post without full knowledge of the circumstances at the time. Assessments depend heavily on circumstantial evidence. The law fails to specify the dilemma of how human life and military advantage can be balanced against each other.[531] As has been aptly noted: 'A committed pacifist and an "ends justifies the means" militarist may both argue their cases using the language of the proportionality balancing test, referring to good faith and other interpretative tools in so doing, but it is scarcely believable that they will reach the same legal conclusions'.[532] In the ICC context, the proportionality principle is extended to attacks causing 'widespread, long-term and severe damage to the natural environment'.[533] This criminalization is notable, since it protects the environment as such, irrespective of human casualty. However, the notions underlying this threshold are vague, and open to conflicting understandings by interpreters.[534]

A recurring problem is the use of human shields in combat. It is an abuse of the legal protection awarded to civilians. The Rome Statute criminalizes the use of human shields in international armed conflict.[535] It arguably applies also in non-international armed conflict. Involuntary human shields cannot be said to lose their protection. It is more controversial under what circumstances 'voluntary human shields' may be said to participate directly in hostilities. Some claim that persons who persist in shielding despite adequate warning lose their protection as civilians and should be excluded from the proportionality assessment.[536] Others stress that voluntary human shields

---

[530] ICTY, Final Report to the Prosecutor by the Committee Established to Review the NATO Bombing Campaign against the Federal Republic of Yugoslavia, 13 June 2000, 52.

[531] See generally Y. Dinstein, 'Collateral Damage and the Principle of Proportionality', in D. Wippman and M. Evangelista (eds.), *New Wars, New Laws?: Applying the Laws of War in 21st Century Conflicts* (Ardsley: Transnational Publishers, 2005), 211–224.

[532] R. P. Barnidge, 'The Principle of Proportionality under International Humanitarian Law and Operation Cast Lead' in W. C. Banks (ed.), *New Battlefields/Old Laws: Critical Debates on Asymmetric Warfare* (New York: Columbia University Press) 171, 178.

[533] See Art. 8 (2) (b) (iv) ICC Statute.

[534] K. Hulme, *War-Torn Environment: Interpreting the Legal Threshold* (Leiden: Brill, 2004), 92–96.

[535] Art. 8 (2) (xxiii) criminalizes 'the presence of a civilian or other protected person to render certain points, areas or military forces immune from military operations'.

[536] A. Rubinstein and Y. Roznai, 'Human Shields in Modern Armed Conflicts: The Need for a Proportionate Proportionality' (2011) 22 *Stanford Law & Policy Review*, 93, 115; J.-F. Queguiner, 'Precautions Under the Law Governing the Conduct of Hostilities' (2006) 88 *International Review of the Red Cross* 793, 817. This was also the position of the Israeli Supreme Court in the 'targeted killings' case, HCJ 769/02 *Public Committee Against Torture v. Israel*, Judgment, 13 December 2006, para. 36 ('Certainly, if [human shields] are doing so because they were forced to do so by terrorists,

should retain their immunity from direct attack and may not be entirely disregarded in the proportionality principle, since their subjective intentions are difficult to determine and their contribution is indirect.[537] In case of doubt, a presumption in favour of involuntary shielding should apply.[538]

1.3.3.6.4 Restriction of Means and Methods of Warfare

The fourth fundamental principle is the prohibition on employing weapons, ammunition, materials and methods of warfare of a nature to cause superfluous injury and unnecessary suffering to members of the armed forces and civilians who directly participate in hostilities.

A classical prohibited means of warfare is the use of weapons that cause unnecessary suffering. Certain types of weapons are banned per se. They include poison and poisoned weapons, including gases and other devices, such as bullets which expand or flatten in the human body.

Biological weapons, i.e. living mechanisms intended to cause disease or death, and chemical weapons, i.e. chemical substances with toxic effects, are widely banned under international treaty law[539] and customary law.[540] The specific danger of these types of weapons lies in the fact that they do not discriminate between civilians and combatants, cause grievous suffering among the population, may cause considerable fear or make spaces uninhabitable for a long time. The ad hoc tribunals have recognized that their use would constitute a war crime under customary law,[541] but their use was not explicitly listed as a war crime in the ICC.

The provisions on prohibited weapons in the ICC Statute are deficient. In the negotiations, it was proposed to include an explicit prohibition of chemical and biological weapons.[542] However, states opted for an express general prohibition of weapons that that are 'of a nature to cause superfluous injury or unnecessary suffering'. It was implied that there would be a list of prohibited weapons. Such a list

---

those innocent civilians are not to be seen as taking a direct part in the hostilities. They themselves are victims of terrorism. However, if they do so of their own free will, out of support for the terrorist organization, they should be seen as persons taking a direct part in hostilities').

[537] R. Lyall, 'Voluntary Human Shields, Direct Participation in Hostilities and the International Humanitarian Law Obligations of States' (2008) 9 *Melbourne Journal of International Law* 313, 333–334.

[538] M. N. Schmitt, 'Human Shields in International Humanitarian Law' (2009) 47 *Columbia Journal of Transnational Law* 292, 336–337.

[539] The Chemical Weapons Convention prohibits, unequivocally, the use of chemical weapons by anyone in any circumstances.

[540] ICRC, Customary International Law, Rule 74. The Chemical Weapons Convention mandates states parties to criminalize offences; it requires that states parties enact penal legislation prohibiting natural and legal persons under their jurisdiction from developing, producing, acquiring, stockpiling, retaining, transferring, using or engaging in military preparations to use chemical weapons. See Art. VII, Chemical Weapons Convention. It remains less clear to what extent individual criminal responsibility extends to acts such as developing, producing, acquiring, stockpiling or transferring chemical weapons.

[541] *Tadić* 1995, para. 499.

[542] It included bacteriological (biological) agents or toxins for hostile purposes or in armed conflict and chemical weapons as defined in and prohibited by the 1993 Convention on the Prohibition of the Development, Production, Stockpiling and Use of Chemical Weapons and on Their Destruction. See generally A. Alamuddin and P. Webb, 'Expanding Jurisdiction Over War Crimes under Article 8 of the ICC Statute' (2010) 8 *JICJ* 1219.

was never agreed.[543] Inclusion of biological and chemical weapons was barred by the lack of agreement on nuclear weapons.[544] The ICC Statute remained largely an unfinished document in relation to prohibited weapons. There is thus a deep irony. While certain types of conventional weapons are expressly outlawed, some of the most harmful and indiscriminate types of weapons (i.e. weapons of mass destruction) are left aside.[545] Gaps were only filled partially through amendments.

The Rome Statute prohibits the employment of 'asphyxiating, poisonous or other gases, and all analogous liquids, materials or devices' in both international and non-international armed conflicts.[546] Poisonous weapons include gases, substances or devices that cause death or serious harm through their asphyxiating or toxic properties.[547] Originally, the prohibition applied only to international armed conflicts. In 2010, an amendment was adopted to extend it to non-international armed conflicts.[548] This provision covers a variety of chemical weapons.[549]

In 2017, the list of weapons was again extended. The Assembly of States Parties agreed on an amendment that criminalizes the use of biological and toxin weapons, weapons injuring with undetectable X-ray fragments, and laser weapons causing permanent blindness in IAC and NIAC.[550] It failed to include landmines. This piecemeal approach towards the extension of weapon provisions raised concerns. For instance, Germany noted:

We fear that these amendments could trigger a practice of routinely amending the Statute every time new weapons or weapons categories are developed or used. And we worry that this could lead to a more fragmented Rome Statute ... Such a fragmented regime is not conducive to the work of the court, nor does it support efforts towards universality.[551]

The use of chemicals has gained some attention in case law. It is clear that the use of chemical weapons may violate general war crimes[552] or crimes against humanity prohibitions,[553] based on the consequences that they cause. In the *Anfal* case, the Iraqi High Tribunal interpreted the use of chemical weapons as evidence that a

---

[543] At the Kampala Review Conference, Belgium proposed to include chemical weapons, biological weapons, anti-personnel land mines, blinding laser weapons and cluster munitions. This initiative failed to garner sufficient support.

[544] P. Kirsch and D. Robinson, 'Reaching Agreement at the Rome Conference', in A. Cassese et al. (eds.), *The Rome Statute of the International Criminal Court: A Commentary* (Oxford: Oxford University Press, 2002), 79, 80.

[545] W. Schabas, *An Introduction to the International Criminal Court* (Cambridge: Cambridge University Press, 2017), 124.

[546] Arts 8(2)(b)(xviii) and 8(2)(d)(xiv) of the ICC Statute.

[547] See Elements of Crimes, Art. 8 (2) (b) (xvii).

[548] Art. 8 (2) (e) (xiv), Rome Statute of the International Criminal Court; see also J. Goldblat, 'The Biological Weapons Convention – An Overview' (1997) 318 *International Review of the Red Cross* 251.

[549] See M. Cottier and D. Krivanek, 'Article 8', in Triffterer and Ambos, *Rome Statute of the International Criminal Court*, 459–465. It remains contested under what circumstances use of chemical for purposes of riot control would be covered.

[550] Resolution ICC-ASP/16/Res.4., adopted at the 12th plenary meeting, on 14 December 2017, by consensus.

[551] ASP/16, Explanation of the German position on Art. 8, paras. 4 and 5.

[552] It may for instance, satisfy the requirements of the war crime of killing, the war crime of inhumane treatment (causing severe physical or mental pain or suffering), the war crime of wilfully causing great suffering, or the war crime of intentionally attacking civilians.

[553] It may constitute murder, torture or 'other inhumane act', inflicting great suffering or serious injury to body or to mental or physical health.

genocidal act occurred.[554] In the Netherlands, businessman Frans van Anraat was convicted as an accessory to war crimes for selling the chemical thiodiglycol to Saddam Hussein's government from 1984 until 1988.[555] The European Court of Human Rights upheld the ruling, arguing that the use of chemical weapons in warfare constitutes a crime under customary international law.[556] The prohibition on the use of chemical weapons is thus developing into a crime under customary international law.[557]

Punishment of the use of chemical weapons has become a significant bone of contention in the conflict in Syria. The United Nations Joint Investigative Mechanism, established under Resolution 2235 (2015) has found evidence that both Syrian armed forces and ISIS have used toxic substances (e.g. chlorine, sulphur, mustard) as a weapon in conflict.[558] The ICC has not been seized of the matter, due to the lack of agreement on a Security Council referral. However, several bodies have confirmed that use of chemical weapons constitutes a war crime. For instance, the UN Commission of Inquiry has stated expressly that '[t]he use of chemical weapons is prohibited in all circumstances under customary international humanitarian law and is a war crime under the Rome Statute of the International Criminal Court'.[559]

Accountability for use of nuclear weapons is a further dilemma. Nuclear weapons are not expressly marked as a prohibited weapon category under the Rome Statute. Certain African, Latin American and Asian states pushed for their inclusion. Nuclear powers remained opposed, partly due to concerns over the customary nature of the prohibition and the nexus to disarmament strategies. For instance, France declared that war crimes should only be read to include conventional weapons, and not nuclear weapons.[560] Their actual use would, as the International Court of Justice put it, 'generally be contrary to the rules of international law applicable in armed conflict,

---

[554] Iraqi High Tribunal, Second Criminal Court Baghdad – Iraq Ref. No. 1/C Second/2006, 24 June 2007. It found Ali Hassan al-Majid ('Chemical Ali') guilty of genocide attacks against the Kurds. Judges argued that the perpetrators were well aware of the consequences of using chemical weapons which do not differentiate between civilians and fighters.

[555] H. van der Wilt, 'Genocide v. War Crimes in the Van Anraat Appeal' (2009) 7 *JICJ* 557.

[556] ECtHR, *Van Anraat* v. *The Netherlands*, Appl. No. 65389/09, Decision as to Admissibility, 6 July 2010. It stated that customary international law prohibits the use of mustard gas as a weapon of war in an international conflict (para. 92). It held that same is true for use of mustard gas as a weapon of war in non-international armed conflict (para. 94). It concluded that there is 'a rule of customary international law prohibiting the use of chemical weapons by States against civilian populations within their own territory'.

[557] Numerous states have included provisions criminalizing the development, production, acquisition, retention, transfer or use of chemical weapons in their national implementing legislation to the Chemical Weapons Convention or penal codes. E.g. Argentina, Armenia, Australia, Belarus, Belgium, Bosnia and Herzegovina, Brazil, Bulgaria, Burundi, Canada, Congo, Croatia, Denmark, Fiji, Finland, France, Germany, Greece, Hungary, Iraq, Kazakhstan, Liberia, Netherlands, New Zealand, Norway, Peru, Poland, Republic of Korea, Romania, Russia, Senegal, Singapore, South Africa, Spain, Sri Lanka, Sweden, Ukraine, UK, Uruguay. See ICRC Study on Customary International Humanitarian Law, Rule 74, relating practice.

[558] UN, 'Security Council Considers Fourth Report by Joint Investigative Mechanism', 27 October 2016, at www.un.org/press/en/2016/dc3668.doc.htm.

[559] Commission of Inquiry, Eighth Report, A/HRC/27/60, 13 August 2014, para. 117; Fifth Report, A/HRC/23/58, 4 June 2013, para. 136.

[560] See generally A. Golden Bersagel, 'Use of Nuclear Weapons as an International Crime and the Rome Statute of the International Criminal Court', in G. Nystuen, S. Casey-Maslen and A. Golden Bersagel, *Nuclear Weapons under International Law* (Cambridge: Cambridge University Press, 2014), 221–244.

and in particular the principles and rules of humanitarian law'.[561] Like other types of weapons of mass destruction, use of nuclear weapons would likely satisfy the requirements of other war crimes provisions, such as the war crime of inhumane treatment (causing severe physical or mental pain or suffering), wilfully causing great suffering or intentionally attacking civilians.

The number of prohibited methods of warfare has increased in past decades. A prominent example is the use of terror to intimidate the civilian population. Terrorism is specifically prohibited by the Fourth Geneva Convention[562] and Additional Protocol I,[563] which seek to prevent parties to an armed conflict terrorizing civilians under their control through collective punishments. Additional Protocol I[564] and Additional Protocol II[565] specifically prohibit acts of terrorism in the conduct of hostilities, namely threats of violence with the primary purpose to spread terror among the civilian population. In the *Galić* case, the ICTY found that this prohibition is binding not only as treaty law, but also under customary law.[566] This criminalization is not merely a by-product of counterterrorism approaches in the aftermath of 9/11, but an indication of changing approaches towards warfare.[567] It was initially criticized as a progressive development of the law[568] and is not explicitly included in the ICC Statute.

A recent addition to the prohibited methods of warfare is the use of child soldiers. This phenomenon has arisen in many contemporary conflicts.[569] The crime has a dual foundation. It is grounded in human rights law, namely the protection of children against abduction and abuse, and prohibitions under international humanitarian law against integrating children under fifteen into armed forces or groups, and using them in hostilities. There was no express criminalization. The crime came to life before the SCSL. In the case against Hinga Norman, leader of the Civil Defence Forces (CDF), the Defence challenged that it formed part of customary law at the time of the acts charged in the indictment. The SCSL relied on a far-reaching interpretation of sources to establish its existence as a crime. It argued that 'the overwhelming majority of states … did not practice recruitment of children under 15 according to their national laws [or had] criminalized such behavior prior to 1996 [through administrative or

---

[561] ICJ, *Legality of the Threat or Use of Nuclear Weapons*, Advisory Opinion, 8 July 1996, para. 105 (E).

[562] Art. 33 of GC IV. The prohibition aims to protect civilians who find themselves in the power of an adversary in an international armed conflict.

[563] Art. 4 (2) (d). The prohibition relates to persons not or no longer participating directly in hostilities who similarly find themselves in the power of an adversary in a non-international armed conflict.

[564] Art. 51 (2).

[565] Art. 13 (2).

[566] *Prosecutor* v. *Galić*, IT-98-29-A Judgment, 30 November 2006, para. 86.

[567] See M. Glasius, 'Terror, Terrorizing, Terrorism: Instilling Fear as a Crime in the Cases of Radovan Karadzic and Charles Taylor', in D. Zarkov and M. Glasius (eds.), *Narratives of Justice In and Out of the Courtroom: Former Yugoslavia and Beyond* (Berlin: Springer, 2014), 45–61.

[568] See *Prosecutor* v. *Galić*, Separate and Partially Dissenting Opinion of Judge Schomburg, para. 22 ('one cannot conscientiously base a conviction in criminal matters on a "continuing trend of nations criminalising terror as a method of warfare" or on a "trend in prohibiting terror [. . .] continued after 1992"').

[569] Drumbl, *Reimagining Child Soldiers*.

criminal law]'.[570] The ICC Statute expressly defined it as a war crime in international and non-international armed conflict in 1998. At the ICC, it formed the basis of the *Lubanga* case.[571] The crime poses particular challenges for investigation and prosecution in light of its dual foundation.[572]

International criminal courts and tribunals have given a broad interpretation to the crime in order to increase the protection of children in armed conflict. The prohibition on using children under fifteen in hostilities is not limited to combat operations, but also includes support activities such as 'carrying loads for the fighting faction, finding and/or acquiring food, ammunition or equipment, acting as decoys, carrying messages, making trails or finding routes, manning checkpoints or acting as human shields'.[573] In *Lubanga*, the ICC Trial Chamber decided that the 'decisive factor … in deciding if an "indirect" role is to be treated as active participation in hostilities is whether the support provided by the child to the combatants exposed him or her to real danger as a potential target'.[574] Judge Odio Benito even argued that children who experience sexual violence by members of armed groups may be deemed to actively participate in hostilities.[575] This human rights-friendly interpretation was meant to extend protection. However, it went against the principle of strict construction and stood in contrast to the direct participation in hostilities test under international humanitarian law, according to which persons 'directly' participating in hostilities lose protection from direct attack and become a legitimate potential target. The 'risk-based test' was rightly reversed by the Appeals Chamber, which required a 'link between the activity for which the child is used and the combat in which the armed force or group of the perpetrator is engaged'.[576]

One of the critiques of war crimes prosecutions is that they provide a narrow lens on child soldiering as a phenomenon. They emphasize the victimhood of child soldiers and practices of recruitment of children and use in hostilities, while blending out issues relating to rehabilitation, reintegration and reconciliation.[577]

1.3.3.6.5 Mental Elements

The required mental elements of war crimes may differ in terms of their thresholds. The ICC sets a relatively high *mens rea* standard. It states that, unless otherwise provided, intent in relation to consequence exists only if the person 'means to cause

---

[570] *Prosecutor v. Norman*, SCSL 2004–14-AR-72E, 31 May 2004, Decision on Preliminary Motion Based on Lack of Jurisdiction (Child Recruitment), para. 51.

[571] On the *Lubanga* trial, see J. Freedman, *A Conviction In Question: The First Trial at the International Criminal Court* (Toronto: University of Toronto Press, 2017).

[572] Child soldiers are often victims and perpetrators at the same time. See Section 4.3.5.

[573] *Brima et al.* Trial Judgment, para. 737.

[574] *Lubanga Trial Judgment*, para. 628.

[575] *Lubanga Trial Judgment*, Separate and Dissenting Opinion of Judge Odio Benito, paras. 15–21.

[576] *Prosecutor v. Lubanga*, 01/04–01/06 A 5, Judgment on the appeal of Mr Thomas Lubanga Dyilo against his conviction, 1 December 2014, para. 340 (*Lubanga* Appeal Judgment).

[577] I. Derluyn, W. Vandenhole, S. Parmentier and C. Mels, 'Victims and/or Perpetrators? Towards an Interdisciplinary Dialogue on Child Soldiers' (2015) 15 *International Health and Human Rights* (2015) 1, 10.

that consequence or is aware that it will occur in the ordinary course of events'.[578] It is often difficult to determine the scope of criminal responsibility in cases where military actors do not mean to target civilians. Violations may trigger criminal responsibility where an attack is carried out with the purpose of killing civilians or destroying civilian objects, or with the knowledge that the probable consequence will be to kill civilians or destroy civilian objects in violation of the principle of distinction. ICC jurisprudence suggests that this includes cases where there is 'virtual certainty' that unjustified civilian casualties would occur.[579] This may cover scenarios where civilian deaths, injury and property damage occur as a result of carelessness, poor equipment or mistaken targeting information, or where attacks continue to be launched despite knowledge of prior civilian deaths and injury.

1.3.3.6.6 Merits and Discontents

War crimes law has been significantly shaped by the practice of international criminal courts and tribunals. These courts brought international laws out of theory into the courtroom. In this process, humanitarian considerations have moved into the foreground. Norms were not merely applied through a criminal lens, but often construed based on moral or social values. New crimes have been identified. Jurisprudence has attached new social meaning to certain types of conflicts and violations. Former ICTY President Theodor Meron has gently called this the 'humanization of warfare'.[580]

However, these transformations also raise certain criticism. International criminal courts and tribunals reason primarily through the lens of accountability. Human rights considerations and protection of victims are often in the foreground. The humanitarian tradition, particularly military perspectives, are less well reflected. This poses epistemic dilemmas. International criminal courts and tribunals have been geared at establishing a global set of rules. They might not always be fully aware of the humanitarian implications of their rulings, including their impact on the battlefield. International criminal law may thus easily establish a 'parallel' legal reality. It might be necessary to increase the role of experts or *amicus curiae* in relation to aspects of humanitarian law and practice.[581]

Although international criminal law has significantly contributed to the development of the law on NIAC, it may at times trigger unintended consequences which could reduce protection under international humanitarian law. It needs to be assessed more carefully to what extent it is feasible to transpose considerations related to traditional armed forces to non-state armed groups. Setting overly high standards might weaken the normative impact of the law.

---

[578] See Art. 30.

[579] *Lubanga* Appeal, para. 447 ('the standard for the foreseeability of events is virtual certainty').

[580] T. Meron, 'The Humanization of Humanitarian Law' (2000) 94 *AJIL* 239.

[581] On the ICRC, see C. Stahn, 'Between Constructive Engagement, Collusion and Critical Distance: The ICRC and the Development of International Criminal Law' (2016) 15 *Chinese Journal of International Law* 139–166.

One shadow side of the turn to accountability is the growing unpredictability of legal standards and regimes. The ICC Statute is not in all aspects an authoritative account of the current state of law. It is complemented by prohibitions under customary law. This makes it difficult for actors to foresee and apply the law. As Charles Garraway has noted:

If States find that customary law is being used to 'raise the bar' so that requirements are being imposed which States would not be prepared to accept at the conference table on grounds of practicality, then the whole structure of customary law, as providing a foundation for treaty law and underpinning the legal system, may be cast in doubt.[582]

Many of the profound transformations articulated in the courtroom are only slowly trickling down into state practice and realpolitik.

1.3.4 The Crime of Aggression

Aggression is one of the most controversial crimes in international criminal law.[583] Like war crimes, aggression is inherently related to armed violence. Aggression involves not a criminal violation of the *jus in bello*, however, but a criminalization of certain forms of recourse to force, i.e. *jus ad bellum*. It thereby strengthens the trend towards a *jus contra bellum* in the international legal order,[584] namely the restriction of the use of armed force in international relations.

The nature of the crime differs partly from other crimes in that aggression is more diffuse and collective.[585] It can be theorized in at least three ways: as a crime against state sovereignty; as a crime against peace and security; and as a crime against certain collective (e.g. right to self-determination) and individual rights.[586] Traditionally, it has been closely geared at protecting human security, state interests ('sovereignty', 'territorial integrity', 'political independence', self-determination), and the

---

[582] See C. Garraway, 'War Crimes', in E. Wilmshurst and S. Breau (eds.), *Perspectives on the ICRC Study on Customary Law International Humanitarian Law* (Cambridge: Cambridge University Press 2007), 377, 397.

[583] See A. Paulus, 'Second Thoughts on the Crime of Aggression' (2009) 20 *EJIL* 1117; C. Kreß, 'Time for Decision: Some Thoughts on the Immediate Future of the Crime of Aggression: A Reply to Andreas Paulus' (2009) 20 *EJIL* 1129; M. J. Glennon, 'The Blank-Prose Crime of Aggression' (2010) 35 *Yale Journal of International Law* 71; N. Weisbord, 'Prosecuting Aggression' (2008) 49 *Harvard International Law Journal* 161; R. Heinsch, 'The Crime of Aggression After Kampala: Success or Burden for the Future?' (2010) 2 *Göttingen Journal of International Law* 713. For a full account, see C. Kreß and Stefan Barriga (eds.), *The Crime of Aggression: A Commentary* (Cambridge: Cambridge University Press, 2017); L. Sadat (ed.), *Seeking Accountability for the Unlawful Use of Force* (New York: Cambridge University Press, 2018).

[584] See O. Corten, *The Law Against War* (Oxford: Hart Publishing, 2010).

[585] See Q. Wright, 'The Law of the Nuremberg Trial' (1947) *AJIL* 38 ('Though aggressive war may result in larger losses of life, property and social values than any other crime, yet the relationship of the acts constituting the crime to such losses is less close than in the case of crime against humanity. The latter implies acts indicating a direct responsibility for large-scale homicide, enslavement or deportation of innocent civilians. The initiation of aggressive war, on the other hand, implies only declarations or other acts of political or group leadership').

[586] See also F. Mégret, 'What is the Specific Evil of Aggression?', in Kreß and Barriga, *The Crime of Aggression*, 1398.

preservation of peace more generally, i.e. the absence of the unlawful use of armed force.[587] However, some voices suggest that aggression might also criminalize unjustified killing and suffering without justification. According to this broader reading, aggression would complement gaps left by other core crimes, namely the protection of the right to life of combatants and collateral civilians.[588] The idea of individual criminal responsibility is closely linked to unlawful state action in international relations. An individual cannot incur responsibility in the absence of an act of aggression under international law.[589] This makes investigations and prosecutions particularly sensitive.

Although aggression counts among the earliest crimes prosecuted by international tribunals, it has faced significant acceptance problems. Its criminalization has been strongly supported by certain regional blocs (e.g. the non-aligned movement) and smaller states, as part of a broader stance against intervention.[590] However, it has been opposed or viewed with considerable criticism by major powers, including permanent members of the Security Council. The cause of aggression had a smaller lobby in civil society. NGOs have shown less interest in the cause of criminalizing aggression than in other core crimes. Efforts were made to frame the right to peace as a human right, but aggression was not primarily perceived as a humanitarian or a human rights issue.

The difficulties are related to a range of factors: the relatively abstract nature of the protected interests (e.g. sovereignty, peace), the highly political nature of findings on aggression, ambiguities in the law, the overlap with powers of the Security Council, limited state practice and general concerns about the role of the ICC. Most significantly, there is a deeper clash of culture. Dealing with violations of the use of force often requires diplomacy, mediation and de-escalation and appeasement strategies. In situations of ongoing violations, these objectives do not sit well with the accusatorial adversarial nature of criminal proceedings. Codification marks, to some extent, an attempt to criminalize 'the war effort itself'.[591] It connects international criminal law even more than other crimes with not only an accountability-related, but a pacific agenda. It is thus no surprise that regulation has been hard to achieve and is shaped by ambiguities and compromises.[592]

---

[587] Protected interests include stability, security, sovereignty and human rights. See M. Drumbl, 'The Push to Criminalize Aggression: Something Lost Amid the Gains?' (2009) 41 *Case Western Reserve Journal of International Law* 291, 306–307, 313, 318.

[588] See T. Dannenbaum, 'Why Have We Criminalized Aggressive War?' (2017) 126 *Yale Law Journal* 1242, 1274.

[589] As Jens David Ohlin put it: 'The underlying norm is violated by the collective action of the state, and the individual's contribution to that collective effort is then criminalized by the Rome Statute'. See Ohlin, 'Organizational Criminality', 107, 118.

[590] P. Wilson, *Aggression, Crime and International Security* (London and New York: Rouledge, 2009), 95.

[591] Drumbl, 'The Push to Criminalize Aggression', 312, n. 62.

[592] C. Stahn, 'The "End", the "Beginning of the End" or the "End of the Beginning"? Introducing Debates and Voices on the Definition of "Aggression"' (2010) 23 *LJIL* 876.

1.3.4.1 Origin

The crime of aggression has a troubled past. In most historical cases, it has been prosecuted after the fact.[593] This has raised challenges in relation to the *nullum crimen sine lege* principle.

After World War I, the Allied powers created the Commission on the Responsibility of the Authors of the War and Enforcement of Penalties.[594] The majority of the Commission found that, although reproved by public conscience and condemned by history, 'a war of aggression could not be considered an act that violated positive law'. Consequently, the Commission held that 'no criminal charge can be made against the responsible authorities or individuals, and notably the ex-Kaiser'.[595] The Treaty of Versailles provided for the accountability of Kaiser Wilhelm II for his 'supreme offence against international morality and the sanctity of treaties',[596] before a special tribunal that will decide based on 'the highest motives of international policy ... the highest obligations of international undertakings and ... international morality'.[597] Ultimately, the trial did not take place because the Netherlands failed to surrender the Kaiser since crimes against peace did not exist under the Dutch law at the time. In 1928, the Kellogg–Briand Pact outlawed war as a means to settle disputes between states.[598] However, the Pact did not provide for international criminal responsibility of those who resorted to war as an instrument of their national policy.

After World War II, opinions remained divided. Some countries were of the view that the aggression was criminal, whilst others maintained it was not. At the London Conference, in July 1945, the US changed its position,[599] favouring the criminalization of aggression.[600] The crime of aggression was included in the Charter of the International Military Tribunal in Nuremberg, and reproduced almost identically in the Charter of the International Military Tribunal for the Far East.

---

[593] On the history of crimes against peace, see K. Sellars, *Crimes against Peace and International Law* (Cambridge: Cambridge University Press, 2013); K. Sellars, 'Imperfect Justice at Nuremberg and Tokyo' (2010) 21 *European Journal of International Law* 1085.

[594] See generally, K. Sellars, 'Delegitimizing Aggression: First Steps and False Starts after World War I' (2012) 10 *JICJ* 7–40.

[595] Commission on the Responsibility of the Authors of the War and Enforcement of Penalties, *Report to the Preliminary Conference*, 29 March 1919, reprinted in (1920) 14 *AJIL* 95, 118.

[596] Treaty of Versailles, Art. 227. On the background, see W. Schabas, *The Trial of the Kaiser* (Oxford: Oxford University Press, 2018).

[597] Ibid.

[598] Art. 1 of the Pact of Paris of 27 August 1928 states: 'The High Contracting Parties solemnly declare, in the names of their respective peoples, that they condemn recourse to war for the solution of international controversies and renounce it as an instrument of national policy in their relations with one another.' For a discussion, see O. A. Hathaway and S. J. Shapiro, *The Internationalists: How a Radical Plan to Outlaw War Remade the World* (New York: Simon and Schuster, 2017.)

[599] R. Cryer and N. Boister, *The Tokyo International Military Tribunal: A Reappraisal* (Oxford: Oxford University Press, 2008), at 116.

[600] This change of perspective was inspired by the statement of Robert H. Jackson of 6 June 1945: 'We relied upon the Kellogg–Briand Pact and made it the cornerstone of our national policy. We neglected our armaments and our war machine in reliance on it. All violations of it, wherever started, menace our peace as we have now good reasons to know. An attack on the foundations of international relations cannot be regarded as anything less than a crime against the international community which may properly vindicate the integrity of its fundamental compacts by punishing aggressors. We therefore propose to charge that a war of aggression is a crime, and that modern International Law has abolished the defense that those who incite or wage it are engaged in legitimate business.' See R. Jackson, 'Trial of War Criminals', Dept of State Pub 2420 (Washington: US Government Printing Office, 1945), 1–12.

Historically, aggression has been labelled as a 'crime against peace' and described as the 'mother of all crimes'[601] – a connotation that has become slightly anachronistic. The judgment of the IMT considered it as 'the supreme international crime differing only from other war crimes in that it contains within itself the accumulated evil of the whole'.[602] At Tokyo, judges were less unanimous. Judges Pal and Röling dissented in relation to charges relating to aggression.

During the cold war, aggression fell into abeyance. Progress was hampered by competing visions about the legality of the use of force. State practice remained rare. The UN General Assembly adopted Resolution 3314 in 1974, in order to guide the practice of the Security Council in relation to findings on aggression. The Resolution remained minimal in relation to individual criminal responsibility, however. It simply reconfirms the Nuremberg holding that a 'war of aggression' constitutes a crime of aggression.[603]

In the 1990s, i.e. the heroic phase of international criminal justice, states remained divided over the feasibility of approximating aggression to other core crimes. The finding that the crime of aggression constitutes the 'crime of crimes' has become open to challenge with the new jurisprudence of the ad hoc tribunals on genocide and crimes against humanity. In the ICC Statute, aggression was to some extent 'still-born'.[604] It was symbolically included in Article 5 of the Rome Statute, but its exercise of jurisdiction remained pending on the formulation of a novel definition. Years of debates and negotiations were devoted to its clarification in the framework of the Preparatory Commission for the International Criminal Court and the Special Working Group on the Crime of Aggression. At the Kampala Review Conference, states reached agreement on a definition of the crime and the conditions under which the Court can exercise jurisdiction. The final product is marked by compromise and concession.[605]

1.3.4.2 Jurisdictional Dilemmas

Prosecuting aggression poses serious jurisdictional dilemmas. Domestic jurisdiction over aggression is often less developed than in relation to other core crimes.[606] Although some jurisdictions have incorporated or updated domestic definitions of

---

[601] See B. Ferencz, 'The Illegal Use of Armed Force as A Crime Against Humanity' (2015) 2 *Journal on the Use of Force and International Law* 187, 189.

[602] Nuremberg Judgment, *Trial of the Major War Criminals Before the International Military Tribunal*, Vol. I, 186 (1947).

[603] Art. 6 of GA Res. 3314 (1974).

[604] D. Scheffer, 'The Complex Crime of Aggression under the Rome Statute' (2010) 23 *LJIL* 897.

[605] C. Kreß and L. von Holtzendorff, 'The Kampala Compromise on the Crime of Aggression' (2010) 8 *JICJ* 117.

[606] Many states criminalize aggression as a violation against national security interests, such as the use of armed force against the national sovereignty or territorial integrity of a state. But only a limited number of states have implemented the crime of aggression more broadly as a crime under international law. Sometimes definitions are more restrictive than the Kampala definition, by referring to war of aggression rather than an act of aggression. Some argue that jurisdiction should be limited to the nationality and territoriality principle, whilst others claim that states have discretion to assert universal jurisdiction.

the crime,[607] the exercise of domestic jurisdiction is at best an exception. Typically domestic jurisdiction is limited to the territoriality and active nationality principles. Domestic investigations and prosecutions of foreign officials face challenges in relation to state immunity and possibly sovereignty objections,[608] since acts of aggression involve not only individual conduct, but also acts of a state. This reduces the prospects of domestic enforcement. The ICC is, if at all, not only an option of last resort, but often the only forum available.

The jurisdiction of the Court is highly fragmented. As David Scheffer put it:

The Prosecutor will need to maintain a map of the world in the office with an updated set of colored pins stuck on countries' territories indicating the current coverage ... for the crime of aggression globally. There will be differently colored pins on different categories of states parties (those volunteering to be covered by the crime of aggression, those covered by a Security Council resolution, those ratifying the aggression amendments but declaring non-acceptance, those that never ratified or accepted the aggression amendments, and those that withdrew declarations of non-acceptance) and non-party states (those that are covered by a Security Council resolution or have filed a Rome Statute Article 12(3) declaration that invites investigation of ... the crime of aggression ... on its territory).[609]

The new formula that enables the jurisdiction of the Court is a very 'creative development' of the amendment procedure.[610] It treats aggression essentially as a 'new crime', rather than a crime that is already under the jurisdiction of the Court[611] and subject to automatic jurisdiction.[612]

ICC jurisdiction is limited in the case of a state referral or *proprio motu* proceedings. The Court cannot exercise jurisdiction over persons of states which are not party to the Rome Statute or have not accepted the aggression amendment. In these circumstances, exercise of jurisdiction over aggression is tied to the prospect of a Security Council referral.[613] This is atypical regarding the other crimes, for which the

---

[607] A. Reisinger Coracini, 'Evaluating Domestic Legislation on the Customary Crime of Aggression under the Rome Statute's Complementarily Regime', in C. Stahn and L. van den Herik (eds.), *Future Perspectives on International Criminal Justice* (The Hague: TMC Asser Press, 2010) 725.

[608] The ILC initially challenged the possibility of determinations by a domestic court on the basis of the *par inparem imperium non habet* doctrine. This doctrine prohibits states to sit in judgment over other states. Similarly, the 'act of state' doctrine has been invoked to deny domestic courts the capacity to exercise jurisdiction over acts carried out by a state in the exercise of its sovereign powers. But it is questionable whether these doctrines deprive a victim state from the possibility to hold domestic trials for aggression. See N. Strapatsas, 'Complementarity and Aggression: A Ticking Time Bomb?', in Stahn and van den Herik, *Future Perspectives*, 450, 552–460. It seems perverse to argue that acts of aggression, which are prohibited under international law, are manifestations of the sovereign powers of states and ought to be barred from any domestic prosecution.

[609] D. Scheffer, 'The Complex Crime of Aggression under the Rome Statute' (2010) 23 *LJIL* 897, 904.

[610] Art. 121 (5).

[611] Art. 5 (1).

[612] Art. 12 (1).

[613] This follows from a comparison of Art. 15 *bis* and Art. 15 *ter*, which contains no opt-out option, or the exclusion in relation to non-state parties. See also para. 2 of the Understanding on 'Referrals by the Security Council', which states, 'It is understood that the Court shall exercise jurisdiction over the crime of aggression on the basis of a Security Council referral in accordance with article 13, paragraph (b), of the Statute, irrespective of whether the State concerned has accepted the Court's jurisdiction in this regard'.

jurisdiction of the Court is not so limited.[614] Nationals of states parties which have used the opt-out option for aggression[615] are barred from ICC investigation and prosecution if they commit aggression against another state party.

The second specificity relates to the territorial jurisdiction of the ICC. States parties do not enjoy protection by the ICC against crimes of aggression committed by non-state parties against them (i.e. on their territory),[616] although they enjoy such protection for other categories of crimes.[617] This limitation of territorial jurisdiction over the crime of aggression is a negotiated concession to non-state parties, which might otherwise be subject to greater accountability than states parties. Finally, in a compromise during the activation decision, the Assembly limited the Court's jurisdiction to states parties that have ratified the aggression amendment.[618] After activation, the jurisdictional regime for aggression is thus '(more) stringent (than desirable)'[619] and a marked deviation from the general territorial jurisdiction of the ICC under Article 12.

In the light of these restrictions, ICC jurisdiction remains highly fragmented. Some states have an interest in ratifying the amendments for purposes of protection against acts of aggression. Other states might not ratify the amendment at all, or do so with or without opt-out. Technically, the option of a Security Council referral is the most straightforward route to facilitate the exercise of ICC jurisdiction. Yet this prospect remains rather exceptional, given the existing record.

1.3.4.3   Definitional Dilemmas

The definition of aggression has been subject to considerable debate. The scope of application of aggression has become broader, with shifts from classical notions of interstate warfare to more diverse forms of illegal use of force. One of the particularities of aggression is that the action of the individual is criminalized only by virtue of the relationship to the collective element, i.e. state action. The offence requires two types of acts: an act of aggression by a state and an act of an individual.[620] The definition is simultaneously modern and conservative.

1.3.4.3.1   State Act of Aggression

Aggression is usually defined as the most serious and dangerous form of illegal use of force by a state against the sovereignty, territorial integrity or political independence

---

[614] For a defence see D. Akande, 'Prosecuting Aggression: The Consent Problem and the Role of the Security Council', Working Paper, Oxford Institute for Ethics, Law and Armed Conflict, May 2010, at www.elac.ox.ac.uk/downloads/dapo%20akande%20working%20paper%20may%202010.pdf.

[615] Art. 15 *bis* (4)

[616] Art. 8 *bis* (5).

[617] Art. 12 (2).

[618] Resolution ICC-ASP/16/Res.5, adopted at the 13th plenary meeting, on 14 December 2017, para. 2. See C. Kreß, 'On the Activation of ICC Jurisdiction over the Crime of Aggression' (2018) 16 *JICJ* 1–17.

[619] Kreß, 'On the Activation of ICC Jurisdiction over the Crime of Aggression', 17.

[620] See Resolution RC/Res. 6, 11 June 2010, Art. 8 *bis*, at www.icc-cpi.int/iccdocs/asp_docs/Resolutions/RC-Res.6-ENG.pdf.

of another state.[621] For a long time, there has been 'little clarity ... between aggressive acts which are criminal and those which are not'.[622]

The Kampala definition extends individual criminal responsibility from the traditional concept of 'war of aggression' to 'acts of aggression' under Resolution 3314. This is a seismic shift beyond Nuremberg and Tokyo, since the list of acts in Resolution 3314 was not meant to serve as a basis for criminalization. Types of aggression may vary from mere violations of sovereignty (e.g. targeted air strikes) to full-fledged interventions with on-site presence or other unlawful uses of force. In some cases, these acts may involve high civilian casualties or loss of life and disturb peace and security. In others, they may cause limited human damage, or even be exercised with the intent to protect peace and security or human rights.

The definition of the act of aggression is limited by several factors. The crime of aggression requires an act which 'by its character, gravity and scale' constitutes 'a manifest violation of the Charter'.[623] These factors distinguish the crime of aggression from general violations of the prohibition of the use of force. The criminal prohibition of aggression is narrower than the prohibition of the use of force under the UN Charter. Not every illegal use of force entails individual criminal responsibility for aggression. This logic is in line with the construction of other crimes, which confine criminalization to serious violations of underlying norms (e.g. human rights protection, international humanitarian law).

There are a few examples of classical interstate violence which clearly cross the threshold. They include the Iraqi attack against Kuwait in 1990 or annexations. Other cases, such as the Kosovo intervention or the 2003 intervention in Iraq might qualify as unlawful uses of force,[624] but are more difficult to assess from the perspective of the crime of aggression, in light of the complexity of argument in relation to illegality. Such interventions may formally violate state sovereignty, but they raise more complex justificatory dilemmas in relation to peace as a protected interest, or violation of human rights through aggression. The Kampala qualifier sends a message of caution towards the criminalization of uses of force that are subject to substantive legal controversy under the law on recourse to force. The difficult task of the ICC is to determine which grey areas are included and excluded by the crime of aggression.

The concept of aggression also remains state-centric. This is reflected in the nexus of the leadership requirement to state action and the definition of the term 'act of aggression' ('use of armed force by a state'). Modern forms of aggression carried out by non-state actors, such as terrorist organizations, liberation movements or other non-state entities, are excluded.[625] This might be explained by the fact that there are

[621] See GA Resolution 3314 of 14 December 1974.
[622] S. Murphy, 'Aggression, Legitimacy and the International Criminal Court' (2009) 20 *EJIL* 1147, 1150.
[623] Art. 8 *bis* (1).
[624] On Kosovo, see N. Rodley and B. Cali, 'Kosovo Revisited: Humanitarian Intervention on the Fault Lines of International Law' (2007) 7 *Human Rights Law Review* 275. On Iraq, see C. Stahn, 'Enforcement of the Collective Will After Iraq' (2003) 97 *AJIL* 804–823.
[625] For a critique, see A. Cassese, 'On Some Problematic Aspects of the Crime of Aggression' (2007) 20 *LJIL* 841, 846.

sufficient rules under international law that offer protection against violations by non-state actors. The main controversy is under what circumstances use of force by non-state actors can be attributed to a state, for instance due to the exercise of de facto authority or control over such forces.[626]

1.3.4.3.2 Individual Act

The Kampala definition defines aggression as a leadership crime. This has a certain protective quality. It limits the possible perpetrators to those who are in a 'position effectively to exercise control over or to direct the political or military action of a state'. This marks a partial deviation from post-World War II practice which adopted a more flexible 'shape or influence' test in trials against industrial companies (e.g. I. G. Farben, Krupp).[627] The new test takes into account de facto relationships of control. Private actors such as security contractors, business or religious leaders might technically satisfy this requirement. The threshold is high, however, since it requires effective control over state action. One critique of the 'direction and control' requirement is that it presupposes a model of bureaucratic organization, hierarchy and chain of command that may be outdated or hard to establish in the context of collective command structures or multinational operations.

The crime supposes that an act of aggression is committed.[628] Yet once this is shown, the scope of criminalization is rather wide. There might even be risk of over-criminalization, caused by the interaction between planning, preparation and initiation and the general prohibition of attempt under the ICC Statute.[629] If preparation, planning and initiation are read in conjunction with the attempt provision, even attempted preparatory acts, such as attempted preparation, planning or initiation, are covered.

1.3.4.4 Implications

The main significance of the decision to activate ICC jurisdiction over the crime of aggression lies not so much in the expansion of ICC enforcement, but rather in the modern articulation of the crime, and its systemic impact and implications for interstate relations. As Alex Whiting has rightly stated, the Kampala compromise will shape discourse on the criminalization of aggression, irrespective of whether the ICC has actual cases. It is likely to 'force policymakers, military leaders, civil society, journalists, educators, and citizens to pay more attention to the question of the legality

---

[626] International criminal tribunals have relied on the 'overall control' test governing attribution of conduct. See Section 1.3.3.3.

[627] This position is evident in decisions which held that industrialists and foreign political or military leaders could be perpetrators of the crime of aggression. See K. J. Heller, 'Retreat from Nuremberg: The Leadership Requirement in the Crime of Aggression' (2007) 18 *EJIL* 477.

[628] Art. 8 *bis* (2) and Element 3 of the Elements of Crime.

[629] Art. 25 (3) (f). See K. Ambos, 'The Crime of Aggression after Kampala' (2010) 63 *German Yearbook of International Law* 463, 495.

of war, and more specifically to the responsibility of individuals for wars that are illegal'.[630] The ICC definition provided much-needed clarity to the definition of aggression. It can no longer be reasonably argued that the crime of aggression lacks specificity. Challenges in relation to legal clarity do not arise from the definition of the crime, but from ambiguities in the underlying law governing the legality of the use of force.

The Kampala compromise, with its novel criminalization, marks a partial deviation from previous aggression models, not only through its definition, but through its normative embedding. In the ICC context, aggression is no longer merely an abstract violation of the law that exposes conflicting state interests. It is embedded in a broader procedural framework that involves different constituencies (e.g. states, civil society, victims) and independent prosecutorial powers. In this context, it becomes more a global crime than a state sovereignty crime.

Aggression can take multiple forms. It can be a full-fledged war, an intervention or a surgical strike. Victims vary in this context. In some cases aggression entails a violation of state rights or self-determination. In other cases it involves a broader range of victims, including persons harmed or killed through aggressive acts.

The Kampala process, with its definition of the crime of aggression, will undoubtedly influence debates on the legality of the use of force, even in the absence of actual cases. It removes aggression partly from the realm of policy, and places it more firmly on the 'radar screen' of domestic legislators, prosecutors and judges. This is a fundamental step towards greater accountability of political and military elites and compliance (i.e. by threat and internalization). It partly reconnects contemporary criminal law to its past.

The definition of the crime poses the 'hard' questions of when and under what circumstances intervention would fall under the label of aggression.[631] Some critics fear that it may discourage military intervention.[632] Calls to define aggression as a specific intent crime, based on aggressive intent or purpose (i.e. with the aim of occupation, subjugation or annexation) were not successful.[633] The language of criminal law might thus ultimately strengthen the prohibition of the use of force.

At Kampala, the US delegation lobbied in favour of an Understanding[634] that explicitly excluded 'humanitarian intervention'. It stated:

---

[630] A. Whiting, 'Crime of Aggression Activated at the ICC: Does it Matter?', *Just Security*, 19 December 2017, at www .justsecurity.org/49859/crime-aggression-activated-icc-matter/.

[631] See generally M. E. O'Connell and M. Niyazmatov, 'What is Aggression? Comparing Jus ad Bellum and the ICC Statute' (2012) 10 *JICJ* 189; for a critical appraisal, see S. D. Murphy, 'Aggression, Legitimacy and the International Criminal Court' (2009) 20 *EJIL* 1147; W. Schabas, 'Attacking Syria? This Is the Crime of Aggression', at http:// humanrightsdoctorate.blogspot.nl/2013/08/attacking-syria-this-is-crime-of.html.

[632] See H. Hongju Koh and T. F. Buchwald, 'The Crime of Aggression: The United States Perspective' (2015) 109 *AJIL* 257.

[633] For discussion, see K. Ambos, 'The Crime of Aggression after Kampala' (2010) 53 *German Yearbook of International Law* 463–509.

[634] On the Understandings, see C. Kress, S. Barriga, L. Grover and L. von Holtzendorff, 'Negotiating the Understandings on the Crime of Aggression', in S. Barriga and C. Kress (eds.), *The Travaux Préparatoires of the Crime of Aggression* (Cambridge: Cambridge University Press, 2012) 81–97; K. J. Heller, 'The Uncertain Legal Status of the Aggression Understandings' (2012) 10 *JICJ* 229.

It is understood that, for purposes of the Statute, an act cannot be considered to be a manifest violation of the United Nations Charter unless it would be objectively evident to any State conducting itself in the matter in accordance with normal practice and in good faith, and thus an act undertaken in connection with an effort to prevent the commission of any of the crimes contained in Articles 6, 7 or 8 of the Statute would not constitute an act of aggression.[635]

This Understanding failed to gain support. The mere rejection does not imply that 'humanitarian intervention' is intended to come within the ambit of aggression, but it makes the assessment considerably more difficult.

Legally, there are various possibilities to argue that specific types of 'humanitarian interventions' do not qualify as aggression. Both their 'character' and their impact ('consequences') might be used to distinguish them from other types of intervention.[636] Moreover, arguments relating to the degree of legality might come into play, especially if 'gravity' is understood as a normative criterion, i.e. as one relating to the scope of the breach of law, as argued by some.[637] However, it is equally clear from the Kampala compromise that mere motivation or 'good intention' is clearly not enough. The fact that a state claims to act in 'good faith', i.e. for humanitarian purposes or to remedy a breach of a fundamental norm, would not per se exclude it from the scope of application of the Kampala amendments. Similar considerations will apply in relation to other disputed uses of force, such as preventive self-defence.[638]

The potential exercise of jurisdiction over aggression is likely to transform the role of the ICC in the institutional landscape. Evaluating state action is not new per se for an institution like the ICC. The Court is mandated to examine state 'policy' in the context of crimes against humanity, or a 'plan or policy' in the context of war crimes. The examination of the justification of the use of force, though, coupled with a substantive qualifier ('manifest violation of the Charter of the United Nations'), will pose new challenges. There is a risk that cases will focus more on disputes over the legality of the use of force than on links between crime patterns and facts. Aggression draws the ICC into terrain that was previously predominantly occupied by the ICJ and political organs of the United Nations. The ICC (i.e. the Prosecutor and judges) will bear a greater burden in evaluating the legality of state action under international law, and to refine nuances that are otherwise hardly litigated.

It is open to question how well the ICC is equipped to engage with the political dimensions inherent in crimes of aggression. The drafters sought to mitigate the risk of politicization through additional control of the full Pre-Trial division, in cases of *proprio motu* action. This formal requirement will not save the Court from

---

[635] See 2010 Non-Paper by the United States, in S. Barriga and C. Kreß, *Crime of Aggression Library* (Cambridge: Cambridge University Press, 2012), 751–752.

[636] For such an argument, see B. van Schaack, 'The Crime of Aggression and Humanitarian Intervention on Behalf of Women' (2011) 11 *International Criminal Law Review* 491.

[637] See J. L. Root, 'First, Do No Harm – Interpreting the Crime of Aggression to Exclude Humanitarian Intervention', at http://works.bepress.com/joshua_root/1/.

[638] See A. Zimmermann and E. Freiburg, 'Art. 8 bis', in Triffterer and Ambos, *Rome Statute of the International Criminal Court*, 599–601.

engagement with politics and the delicate semantics of warfare. Every step that the Court takes in this field will be closely monitored and ascribed with meaning. Action might be criticized as judicial or prosecutorial overreach, even at its earliest stages, i.e. preliminary examination. Inaction might be interpreted as implicit endorsement.

Aggression raises complex issues in relation to the individualization of responsibility and harm. Aggression is primarily tied to collective state action. It is thus more difficult to determine to what extent the individual should account for the cause and the consequences of aggression. In many cases of aggression, the typical victim is a 'state'. This raises novel issues in relation to victim participation and reparation. States might use ICC jurisdiction over aggression as a surrogate forum for interstate reparation. This may ultimately run against the purpose and mandate of the Court.

Finally, the activation of aggression is likely to create new expectations that the ICC may struggle to fulfil. Given its limited jurisdiction, it might to have to explain why it is not acting in relation to aggression. It is thus no surprise that voices remain divided over the prospects of investigating and prosecuting aggression.

1.4   Sidelined Crimes

Over past decades, most efforts have been invested in strengthening accountability for 'core crimes'. Other crimes have been sidelined in the criminalization process. They include economic crimes and crimes against the environment. These types of criminality often have a direct nexus to atrocity violence and/or global effects. They may cross multiple jurisdictions, sometimes even to a greater extent than core crimes. One of the future challenges of international criminal law is to address criminality at the periphery or even outside the traditional scope of crisis situations.

1.4.1   Organized Economic Crime

A first example is the connection between core crimes and organized economic crime. Conflict and organized crime are often interrelated. Economic crime is often a driver or a consequence of atrocity crime. As noted in scholarship, 'Criminal activities are not a simple sideshow of civil wars, but a key activity of many rebel organizations'.[639] Armed groups may use organized crime to finance activities. At the same time, the very existence of violence or conflict may provide a platform for increased organized economic crime. Core crimes and other crimes, such as corruption and other organized criminal activities, must be addressed simultaneously in order to build peace.[640]

---

[639] Kalyvas, 'How Civil Wars Help Explain Organized Crime', 1521–1522.
[640] S. Brammertz, 'The Connection between War Crimes, Corruption, Financing Terrorism and Organized Crime', International Association of Prosecutors, 17th Annual Conference and General Meeting, 1 November 2012.

International criminal law continues to be driven by a division between 'core crimes' and transnational treaty crime.[641] Organized economic crimes, such as corruption, money laundering or drug trafficking, fall into the second category. They are grounded in treaty-based obligations that apply between states and impose suppression obligations on domestic jurisdictions. The authority to penalize is grounded in national law. Obligations are enforced indirectly, namely through state structures or channels of cooperation.[642] The offence is deemed to break the law of a particular state, or several jurisdictions, but the perpetrator is not treated as an 'international criminal'.

States have sought to address these offences mainly through the obligation to extradite or prosecute. International efforts to find a concerted response to international organized crime have intensified over the past decades, in light of its global complexity, its macro-economic dimensions, its impediment to sustainable development or its nexus to terrorism. Examples are the OECD Convention on Combating Bribery of Foreign Public Officials in International Business Transactions (1997),[643] the UN Convention Against Corruption (2003)[644] and the UN Convention against Transnational Organized Crime (2001),[645] including its two protocols on trafficking and smuggling of persons.[646] The offences (e.g. corruption, bribery, money laundering) are not formally labelled as 'international crimes', but they may affect broader societal interests, such as protection from exploitation, oppression or abuse of power.

The idea that certain types of organized economic crime may entail individual criminal responsibility and should be addressed by international criminal jurisdiction was already suggested by the UN in 1989. The UN General Assembly asked the ILC to establish an 'international criminal court or other international criminal trial mechanism with jurisdiction over persons alleged to have committed crimes ... including persons engaged in illicit trafficking in narcotic drugs across national frontiers'.[647] The ILC included crimes involving illicit traffic in narcotic drugs and psychotropic substances 'with an international dimension' into the list of treaty crimes in its proposal for an international criminal court.[648]

---

[641] R. Clark, 'Treaty Crimes', in W. A. Schabas, *The Cambridge Companion to International Criminal Law* (Cambridge: Cambridge University Press, 2015), 214 *et seq.*

[642] See N. Boister, 'Transnational Criminal Law?' (2003) 14 *EJIL* 953, 962.

[643] The Convention is reprinted in (1998) 37 *ILM* 1.

[644] UN Convention against Corruption, opened for signature 31 October 2003, 2349 UNTS 41.

[645] UN Convention against Transnational Organised Crime, adopted 15 November 2000, 2225 UNTS 209.

[646] Protocol against the Smuggling of Migrants by Land, Sea and Air, supplementing the United Nations Convention against Transnational Organised Crime, adopted 15 November 2000, 2241 UNTS 507 and Protocol to Prevent, Suppress and Punish Trafficking in Persons, Especially Women and Children, supplementing the United Nations Convention against Transnational Organised Crime, adopted 15 November 2000, 2237 UNTS 319.

[647] UN General Assembly, International Criminal Responsibility of Individuals and Entities Engaged in Illicit Trafficking in Narcotic Drugs across National Frontiers and Other Transnational Criminal Activities, A/RES/44/39, 4 December 1989.

[648] See Art. 20 (e) of theDraft Statute for an International Criminal Court, adopted by the International Law Commission at its forty-sixth session, in 1994, referring to Art. 3 (1) of the United Nations Convention against Illicit Traffic in Narcotic Drugs and Psychotropic Substances of 20 December 1988.

In the context of the negotiations of the Rome Statute, Caribbean states and others pleaded for the inclusion of transnational crimes into the jurisdiction of the Court.[649] They argued that organized traffic has a destabilizing effect on states and might cause inability in domestic jurisdictions, in particular in connection with corruption.[650] The close nexus between conflict and the illicit drug industry has been illustrated by the conflicts in Colombia, Afghanistan or Mexico. At Rome, this proposal was rejected on a number of grounds, including concerns about the treaty-based (rather than customary) nature of the crime, the high number of offences[651] and sovereignty concerns.[652] The compromise was to consider these crimes at a future review conference.[653]

Since then, the debate has shifted away from seeking reform of ICC jurisdiction. It is increasingly acknowledged that transnational economic crimes, such as illicit enrichment, money laundering or corruption, may substantiate crimes against humanity, or constitute a means to commit crimes against humanity.[654] New attention has been devoted to alternative avenues. Certain instruments combine jurisdiction over core crimes with economic offences. A curious example is the Malabo Protocol. It outlaws inter alia grand-scale corruption[655], money laundering or exploitation of natural resources, but minimizes the effects of these provisions on the highest public officials through a sweeping immunity clause for senior state officials.[656]

Some voices in doctrine have suggested the establishment of a separate treaty-based court for transnational offences, with jurisdiction to provide institutional support to states in their domestic prosecutions of transnational crimes, or to receive cases referred by states.[657] In December 2017, Latin American experts drafted a 'Draft Statute of the Criminal Court for Latin America and the Caribbean against Transnational Organized Crime' (COPLA), which would be open to Caribbean and Latin American signatories of the UN Convention against Transnational Organized Crime.[658] It covers UNTOC crimes, drug trafficking, money laundering, transnational bribery and illicit trade in cultural artefacts and is meant to be complementary to national jurisdiction, similar to the admissibility regime of the ICC.

---

[649] E.g. Jamaica, Trinidad and Tobago, Barbados, Costa Roca, Guyana.

[650] On the proposal, see P. Robinson, 'The Missing Crimes', in A. Cassese et al. (eds.), *The Rome Statute of the International Criminal Court: A Commentary* (Oxford: Oxford University Press, 2002), 497, 504.

[651] It was argued that states are more effective at trying transnational crime.

[652] N. Boister, 'The Exclusion of Treaty Crimes from the Jurisdiction of the Proposed International Criminal Court: Law, Pragmatism, Politics' (1998) 3 *Journal of Conflict and Security Law* 27; N. Boister, 'Treaty Crimes, International Criminal Court?' (2009) 12 *New Criminal Law Review* 341; A. Schloenhardt, 'Transnational Organised Crime and the International Criminal Court: Developments and Debates' (2005) 24 *University of Queensland Law Journal* 93.

[653] See Resolution E, contained in the Final Act of the Rome Conference which notes that 'the international trafficking of illicit drugs is a very serious crime, sometimes destabilizing the political and social and economic order in States'.

[654] I. Bantekas, 'Corruption as an International Crime and Crime against Humanity' (2006) 4 *JICJ* 466.

[655] See Art. 28 I ('acts of corruption if they are of a serious nature affecting the stability of a state, region or the Union').

[656] Art. 46A *bis*.

[657] N. Boister, 'International Tribunals for Transnational Crimes: Towards a Transnational Criminal Court?' (2012) 23 *Criminal Law Forum* 295, 312.

[658] R. Currie and J. Leon, 'COPLA: A Transnational Criminal Court for Latin America & the Caribbean', 22 January 2018, at https://ssrn.com/abstract=3106855.

1.4.2   Crimes against the Environment

A second example is crimes against the environment.[659] International criminal law has been strongly centred on human protection. The environment has received little attention. There is no international treaty that defines environmental crimes as international crimes. International criminal courts and tribunals have considered environmental harm at best indirectly, i.e. through the lens of core crimes. This is to some extent a paradox. Environmental crimes may have large and transboundary ramifications which affect peace and security or harm the well-being of future generations. As Frédéric Mégret has noted

gravest crimes against the environment belong to this category of global crimes *par excellence* because they are ubiquitous in their materialization and potentially catastrophic in their impact ... Inflicting grave harm on the environment might be the modern-day equivalent of piracy, either because it actually occurs on the High Seas or because, even as it occurs concretely on the territory of a particular state, its impact is global.[660]

Crimes against the environment involve a wide spectrum of offences. In past decades there has been a strong movement to strengthen protection through a transnational approach, i.e. the development of the concept of transnational environmental crimes.[661] These crimes include illegal trade in wildlife, timber and fish stocks, pollutants and waste. They are often driven by large financial incentives, low detection rates and limited enforcement. They have received attention from a transnational perspective, since they cause harm to the environment, may affect health, security and governance, and often have links to violence or corruption. Yet they are often considered as 'victimless' crimes.

Environmental crime does not rank highly in law enforcement strategies. Criminalization still remains mainly within the scope of national jurisdictions. There are no universal 'green crime' agreements. International law contains a number of multilateral environmental agreements, such as the 1973 Convention on International Trade in Endangered Species of Wild Fauna and Flora,[662] the 1989 Basel Convention on the Control of Transboundary Movements of Hazardous Wastes and their Disposal[663] and the 1987 Montreal Protocol relating to trade of ozone-depleting substances.[664] Only the Basel Convention contains references to illegality and criminalization. The

---

[659] The ILC formulated a 'working definition' of the environment which 'includes natural resources, both abiotic and biotic, such as air, water, soil, fauna and flora and the interaction between the same factors, and the characteristic of their landscape'. See ILC, Draft principles on the allocation of loss in the case of transboundary harm arising out of hazardous activities, with commentaries, 2006, Draft principle 2 (b), at http://legal.un.org/ilc/texts/instruments/english/commentaries/9_10_2006.pdf.

[660] F. Mégret, 'The Problem of an International Criminal Law of the Environment' (2011) 36 *Columbia Journal of Environmental Law* 195, 241.

[661] L. Elliott and W. H. Schaedla, *Handbook of Transnational Environmental Crime* (Cheltenham: Elgar, 2016).

[662] Convention on International Trade in Endangered Species of Wild Fauna and Flora, 3 March 1973, 993 UNTS 243.

[663] Basel Convention on the Control of Transboundary Movements of Hazardous Wastes and Their Disposal, 22 March 1989, 1673 UNTS 57.

[664] The Protocol seeks to control the production, consumption and trade of ozone-depleting substances. Montreal Protocol on Substances that Deplete the Ozone Layer, 16 September 1987, 152 UNTS 3.

other conventions remain focused on control, rather than criminal sanction. Member states have the choice to criminalize relevant activities, or to introduce administrative or civil law sanctions, in order to express the illicit nature of conduct.

In international criminal law protection from environmental harm is largely mediated through core crimes. Crimes against the environment are not recognized as a separate category of crime. There were some attempts to brand environmental crime as international crime. In the early phases of the draft articles on state responsibility, the ILC considered massive pollution of the atmosphere or the sea as a breach of an international obligation that could be seen as a state crime.[665] But this notion was later dropped. In the context of the preparation of the Draft Code for an International Criminal Court, the ILC considered the inclusion of the 'crime of willful and severe damage to the environment'. Ultimately, however, the proposal was not retained. The ICC Statute criminalized environmental damage as a war crime in international armed conflict.[666] An argument can be made that the crime should also be extended to non-international armed conflicts.

In recent years, several scholars have argued for stronger criminalization. Some voices have suggested drawing parallels between environmental damage and the concept of genocide. They have advocated for an 'ecocide'[667] or 'geocide' treaty.[668] Others have suggested a new offence that reflects serious damage to the environment[669] or contemplated the idea of an international environmental court.[670] The Office of the Prosecutor of the ICC has stated that it considers the impact of 'crimes that are committed by means of, or that result in, inter alia, the destruction of the environment, the illegal exploitation of natural resources or the illegal dispossession of land'.[671]

---

[665] Draft Articles on Responsibility of States for Internationally Wrongful Acts, adopted by the Commission at its fifty-third session in 2001 (Final Outcome) (International Law Commission) UN Doc. A/56/10, 43.

[666] P. Sharp, 'Prospects for Environmental Liability in the International Criminal Court' (1999) 18 *Virginia Environmental Law Journal* 217.

[667] Ecocide is 'the extensive destruction, damage to or loss of ecosystem(s) of a given territory, whether by human agency or by other causes, to such an extent that peaceful enjoyment by the inhabitants of that territory has been severely diminished'.

[668] L. A. Teclaff, 'Beyond Restoration: The Case of Ecocide' (1994) 34 *Natural Resources Journal* 933; M. A. Gray, 'The International Crime of Ecocide' (1995) 26 *California Western International Law Journal* 215, 258; Berat, 'Defending the Right to a Healthy Environment: Toward a Crime of Geocide in International Law' (1993) 11 *Boston University International Law Journal* 328.

[669] R. McLaughlin, 'Improving Compliance: Making Non-State International Actors Responsible for Environmental Crimes' (2000) 11 *Colorado Journal of International Environmental Law and Policy* 377, 396. 'For the purpose of this Statute, "environmental crimes" means the intentional or reckless commission by an individual or individuals, regardless of the status of the act under any applicable domestic regulation, of any of the following acts: (a) directly causing large scale or serious pollution of the: 1. sea; 2. atmosphere; 3. [other relevant sites/mediums of pollution]; or (b) conducting an activity, the widespread harmful effects of which should have been contemplated by a reasonably prudent individual; or (c) breaching an obligation within the established framework of international law, the observance of which is recognized as essential for the protection of the environment; or (d) aiding or abetting any of the above acts'.

[670] S. D. Murphy, 'Does the World Need a New International Environmental Court?' (2000) 32 *George Washington Journal of International Law & Economics* 333.

[671] ICC, OTP Policy Paper on Case Selection and Prioritisation, 15 September 2016, para. 42, at www.icc-cpi.int/itemsDocuments/20160915_OTP-Policy_Case-Selection_Eng.pdf.

Such initiatives are guided by laudable intentions. Criminalizing environmental crimes as international crimes has a strong expressive effect as to their gravity. It also shifts the focus more strongly towards prevention. International criminal law is likely to embrace new types of environmental offences in the future. However, there are certain caveats. The notion of 'environment' itself is very broad. International criminal law remains a device of exception. It cannot cover all forms of environmental harm, nor is it the best instrument to remedy harm.[672] International criminal law remains largely anthropocentric, and its goals, remedies and conceptions of victimhood do not necessarily coincide with 'those of environmental preservation'.[673] Its role will thus remain limited.[674]

1.4.3   Famine-Related Crimes

A third example of sidelined crimes are famine-related crimes. Statistically, hunger costs more lives than atrocity crimes.[675] In public perception, famine has long been considered a problem that is the result of natural circumstances and which should be addressed through development aid rather than international law. This paradigm is gradually shifting. Famine can be caused in many ways through human behaviour, such as through the denial of humanitarian aid, attacks on humanitarian food convoys, use of starvation as a weapon of war or state policies that drive populations into famine. It often leads to internal displacement movements or forced migration. There are many historical examples. For instance, in 2008 the European Parliament qualified, the Holodomor, i.e. Stalin's artificial famine in Ukraine in the 1930s, as 'an appalling crime against the Ukrainian people, and against humanity'.[676]

Famine and starvation played an important role in the atrocities committed by the Khmer Rouge regime.[677] In Somalia, Al-Shabaab, an Islamic insurgent group, has been associated with crimes against humanity for preventing Somalis from entering

---

[672] There is still considerable debate as to whether criminal sanctions are an appropriate form of responsibility for environmental damage at all. C. Byung-Sun, 'Emergence of an International Environmental Criminal Law?' (2000–2002) 19 *UCLA Journal of Environmental Law and Policy* 11.

[673] See E. Cusato, 'Beyond Symbolism: Problems and Prospects with Prosecuting Environmental Destruction before the ICC' (2017) 15 *JICJ* 491, 506.

[674] T. Smith, 'Creating a Framework for the Prosecution of Environmental Crimes in International Criminal Law', in W. A. Schabas, Y. McDermott and N. Hayes (eds.), *The Ashgate Research Companion to International Criminal Law Critical, Perspectives* (Abingdon: Routledge, 2013).

[675] A. de Waal, *Famine Crimes: Politics and the Disaster Relief Industry in Africa* (Bloomington, IN: Indiana University Press, 1998); A. de Waal, *Mass Starvation: The History and Future of Famine* (Chichester: John Wiley and Sons Ltd., 2018).

[676] European Parliament resolution of 23 October 2008 on the commemoration of the Holodomor, the Ukraine artificial famine (1932–1933), DoC. P6 TA(2008)0523, para. 1. The Holodomor was not qualified as genocide, since Ukrainians were not targeted because of their nationality as such. See generally M. Dolot, *Execution by Hunger: The Hidden Holocaust* (New York: Norton, 1987).

[677] R. C. DeFalco, 'Accounting for Famine at the Extraordinary Chambers in the Courts of Cambodia: The Crimes Against Humanity of Extermination, Inhumane Acts and Persecution' (2011) 5 *International Journal of Transitional Justice* 142.

refugee camps and blocking access to vital humanitarian assistance.[678] Accountability is gaining greater attention. In 2017, Hilal Elver, the UN Special Rapporteur on the right to food, stressed in her Report to the General Assembly that '[c]ontrary to popular belief, casualties resulting directly from combat usually make up only a small proportion of deaths in conflict zones, with most individuals in fact perishing from hunger and disease'.[679] She argued for 'formal recognition of famine as a crime', in order to 'impede the tendency of Governments to hide behind a curtain of natural disasters and state sovereignty to use hunger as a ... weapon'.[680]

The existing legal framework is scattered. Famine-related crimes are not regulated in a separate offence. The notion is too diverse. The term used in criminal contexts is 'starvation'. It does not relate to a status or condition of famine as such, but rather harmful action that persons inflict on each other. It is addressed in a piecemeal fashion in the architecture of atrocity crime.

Starvation qualifies as a war crime, if it is used as a method in warfare.[681] The ICC Statute only regulates it in the context of international armed conflict.[682] However, there is widespread agreement that it should also be prohibited in non-international armed conflict.[683] Starvation may be an instrument to commit genocide, it if is carried with the specific intent to destroy a protected group.[684] For instance, it may be a method of 'inflicting on the group conditions of life calculated to bring about its physical destruction'.[685] It can also constitute crimes against humanity. The most pertinent label is extermination. It includes 'the intentional infliction of conditions of life, inter alia the deprivation of access to food and medicine, calculated to bring about the destruction of the population'.[686] It is wider than genocide since protection does not require targeting of a specific group. Starvation or deprivation of food can also qualify as persecution or 'other inhumane act' (e.g. based on trauma, stress, health implications).[687] For instance, in the *Duch* case the ECCC convicted the accused for starvation as other inhumane act, based on his acknowledgement 'that the deprivation of adequate and sufficient food was deliberate and meant to debilitate

---

[678] D. Kearney, 'Food Deprivations as Crimes Against Humanity' (2013) 46 *NYU Journal of International Law & Politics* 253, 276 ('Its actions combined more traditional forms of persecution (physically arresting their countrymen who were in search of food) with reckless pursuit of policies that brought about widespread death and suffering (evicting aid organizations in the face of ongoing drought)').

[679] Interim report of the Special Rapporteur on the right to food, A/72/188, 21 July 2017, para. 9.

[680] Ibid., para. 92.

[681] S. Hutter, *Starvation as a Weapon* (Leiden: Brill/Nijhoff, 2015).

[682] Art. 8 (2) (b) (xxv), ICC Statute ('[i]ntentionally using starvation of civilians as a method of warfare by depriving them of objects indispensable to their survival').

[683] Mass enforced starvation is prohibited under common Art. 3 to the Geneva Conventions.

[684] *Akayesu* Trial Judgment, paras. 505–506; and *Prosecutor* v. *Kayishema and Ruzindana*, ICTR-95-1-A, Judgement, 1 June 2001, paras. 114–117.

[685] See *Prosecutor* v. *Kayishema*, ICTR-95-1-T, Judgement, 21 May 1999, 116. See L. DeFalco, 'Conceptualizing Famine as a Subject of International Criminal Justice: Towards A Modality-Based Approach' (2017) 38 *University of Pennsylvania Journal of International Law* 1113, 1132–1133.

[686] Art. 7 (2) (b) ICC Statute.

[687] See DeFalco, 'Conceptualizing Famine', 1173–1175.

the detainees in order to maintain control over the prison population, prevent riots and facilitate the generation of confessions'.[688]

The existing law covers deliberate acts of starvation during peacetime and armed conflict, but there are several shortcomings and loopholes. From a legal viewpoint, famine is mostly seen as a method of 'harm production'.[689] It remains difficult to hold states and non-state actors accountable for famine-related crimes. Most cases involving food violations have related to imprisoned populations. Proving extermination or genocidal intent is challenging since starvation is often a slow process with multiple contributory factors. Crimes against humanity may be committed through omission, but require a policy. In the ICC context, the Elements of Crime clarify that such a policy 'cannot be inferred solely from the absence of governmental or organizational action', but requires a 'deliberate failure to take action which is consciously aimed at encouraging' crimes.[690] Recklessness is not sufficient as a mental element of perpetration.[691] There is thus a certain gap: 'the international community has never called for an international criminal trial against government officials or non-State actors for creating, inflicting or prolonging famine, in part because of the legal and political complexities surrounding charges of criminality'.[692]

There are different views on how to move forward. Some voices call for the specification of famine-related crimes. For example, David Marcus has argued that 'Those who deliberately or recklessly starve their own citizens through systematic human rights violations commit crimes against humanity and should no longer go unpunished'.[693] The UN Special Rapporteur on the Right to Food has echoed this view. She has pleaded for a new 'binding agreement' that includes 'prohibitions associated with famine and starvation',[694] in order to incentive prosecutions for famine-related crimes. She has suggested that famine should become 'a crime if there is sufficient evidence of an intentional or reckless effort to block certain groups from access to food under conditions of conflict or hardship'.[695] The virtue of this approach is that it would provide greater visibility to the link between conflict and food security. Alternatives to the recognition of an independent crime include lowering the *mens rea* standard for existing crimes,[696] and an express clarification of the war crimes prohibition in non-international conflict.

Others scholars are more reserved. They question whether criminal law is the right instrument to counter some of the underlying food security problems, such as the blocking of humanitarian assistance or reckless agro-economic policies of

---

[688] *Co-Prosecutor* v. *K. Guek Eav alias Duch*, Case No. 001/18–07–2007/ECCC/TC, Judgment, 26 July 2010, para. 269 (*Duch* Trial Judgment).
[689] DeFalco, 'Conceptualizing Famine', 1187.
[690] See Elements of Crime, Art. 7, n. 6.
[691] Art. 30 ICC Statute.
[692] Interim report of the Special Rapporteur, para. 85.
[693] D. Marcus, 'Famine Crimes in International Law' (2003) 97 *AJIL* 245, 248.
[694] Interim report of the Special Rapporteur, para. 92.
[695] Ibid., para. 86.
[696] Marcus, 'Famine Crimes', 275.

governments. They argue that greater criminalization may have counterproductive effects, since it may make humanitarian work more difficult.[697] More effort should be invested in prevention and broader domestic accountability to affected populations.

1.4.4 Trends and Critiques

Approaches towards international crimes have evolved significantly since the first steps of international criminal law in the late eighteenth and early nineteenth centuries. Modern international criminal law covers both the 'public' and 'private' sides of violence. It has been able to develop in a dynamic way, since it protects different interests: state interests, the autonomy and dignity of individuals and group rights.

International criminal law reinvigorates the idea that economic, social and cultural rights are not necessarily a 'weaker' category of rights.[698] Substantial aspects of economic, social and cultural rights (e.g. housing, food, health, water, work, education) are not only aspirational goals or 'luxury goods', but relevant to both context (contextual elements of crimes) and existing crime definitions, and thus open to criminal sanction. Certain types of violations have been addressed indirectly in charges and judgments, in particular in relation to property-related crimes (e.g. pillaging, attacks on cultural property), discrimination-based offences (e.g. persecution, genocide) or prohibited movements of persons.[699] However, this normative expansion also causes certain concerns and discontents.

International criminal law navigates between progression and normative overreach. The law on crimes, such as genocide, crimes against humanity, war crimes, as well as aggression or terrorism, has taken on fundamental new features over the past two decades. The boundaries of crimes were developed to brand novel features of criminality, express condemnation in relation to violations or 'stigmatize the crimes themselves'.[700] Yet crucial junctures, which have been shaped by jurisprudence, such as the dividing line between genocide and ethnic cleansing, the policy element of crimes against humanity, the scope of criminalization in non-international armed conflict, the distinction between aggression and modalities of the use of force, or the contours of terrorism as international crime in peacetime, continue to meet objections by states or in practice. There is a certain gap between normative ambition and reality.

International criminal law is in some respects more 'progressive' than classical human rights law. In many contemporary conflicts, violence does not emanate from state power, but from non-state armed groups that challenge state authority,

---

[697] A. De Wal, 'Ending Mass Atrocity and Ending Famine' (2015) 386 *The Lancet* 1528, 1529.

[698] L. van den Herik, 'Economic, Social, and Cultural Rights – International Criminal Law's Blind Spot?', in E. Riedel et al. (ed.), *Economic, Social, and Cultural Rights: Contemporary Issues and Challenges* (Oxford: Oxford University Press, 2014), 343–366.

[699] See E. Schmid, *Taking Economic, Social and Cultural Rights Seriously in International Criminal Law* (Cambridge: Cambridge University Press, 2015).

[700] F. Mégret, 'Practices of Stigmatization' (2013) 76 *Law and Contemporary Problems* 287, 305.

governance and territorial control through externally backed force and popular appeal. International criminal law has recognized that non-state actors may face accountability under all three types of core crimes. A non-state armed group might, for instance, face accountability for action, such as destruction of cultural heritage or omissions (e.g. denial of access to humanitarian assistance). Members of organized groups may be held accountable for violations of labour conditions (e.g. slavery and forced labour). However, there is a deeper question of how far criminal responsibility for specific types of violations can be extended to non-state actors based on their authority and control over persons. This is partly new territory. It poses novel normative challenges, including fears of overstretching the realm of criminal law. As rightly observed by Kai Ambos: 'there is clearly a difference between a State's obligation under international law to guarantee the rule of law and protect its citizens and a similar (emerging) duty of a non-state actor'.[701]

Existing crimes are strongly focused on human atrocity. This focus coincides with the rising protection of the individual under international law, and modern doctrines, such as the protection of civilians or the responsibility to protect.[702] Yet it also creates certain frictions and exclusions. The language and the labels used by international criminal law frame a broader view as to how conflict and violence are portrayed. Mass atrocities are seen as the 'worst offences'. Non-human-related interests, such as the protection of the environment, are only indirectly protected or marginalized. As rightly highlighted by critics, the 'atrocity crime' lens focuses on 'the local' predominantly as a site of conflict, evil and violence.[703] This creates a particular stigma that may perpetuate sentiments of inferiority and exclusion. The focus on atrocity crimes places the emphasis on 'extraordinary criminality'. It marginalizes forms of modern violence that are a 'by-product of global social and economic structures'[704] or 'slower'[705] or long-term forms of injustice, such as apartheid[706] or colonial injustices.[707]

In the 1980s, ILC Special Rapporteur Doudou Thiam defended a broader definition of the concept of international crimes ('crimes that assail sacred values or principles of civilization')[708] and proposed to include colonialism, i.e. the

---

[701] See also, Ambos, *Treatise on International Criminal Law, Vol. II*, 47.

[702] See paras. 138 and 139 of the World Summit Outcome Document, UNGA Res. 60/1 of 24 October 2005, UN Doc A/RES/60/1.

[703] See generally K. Clarke, *Fictions of Justice: The International Criminal Court and the Challenge of Legal Pluralism in Sub-Saharan Africa* (New York: Cambridge University Press, 2009); R. Byrne, 'Drawing the Missing Map: What Socio-legal Research Can Offer to International Criminal Trial Practice' (2013) 26 *LJIL* 991; J. Rowen and J. Hagan, 'Using Social Science to Frame International Crimes' (2014) 10 *Journal of International Law and International Relations* 92.

[704] I. Kalpouzos and I. Mann, 'Banal Crimes Against Humanity: The Case of Asylum Seekers in Greece' (2015) 16 *Melbourne Journal of International Law* 1.

[705] See R. Nixon, *Slow Violence and the Environmentalism of the Poor* (Cambridge, MA: Harvard University Press, 2011), 11.

[706] On apartheid, see Section 1.3.2.4.5.

[707] Burgis-Kasthala, 'Scholarship as Dialogue?', 936 ('need for a deep appreciation of the DRC's colonial history not simply as an artefact of the past, but as an ongoing aspect of the present and the future').

[708] See ILC, First Report on Draft Code of Offences Against the Peace and Security of Mankind, UN Doc. A/CN.4/364, 18 March 1983, para. 34.

establishment or maintenance by force of colonial domination, as an international crime in the Draft Code of Offences against the Peace and Security of Mankind.[709] This proposal met fierce resistance by Western powers, paired with a certain sense of denial. For instance, the UK argued in 1993 that '"colonial domination" and "alien domination" do not possess the requisite legal content necessary for inclusion in a code of crimes and have no foundation in international criminal law. "Colonial domination" is . . . an outmoded concept redolent of the political attitudes of another era'.[710] It remains doubtful whether existing crime structures are capable of grasping the structural nature of violence[711] that is behind the label of atrocity crimes. Such structural forms of violence are more difficult to portray in the form of the criminal trial. The contextual elements of crime seek to capture the evil nature through organizational (plan/policy), quantitative (number of victims) or qualitative factors (gravity, scale). However, certain forms of violations are difficult to describe in these categories. The failure to capture them has detrimental consequences. It may present a distorted picture of responsibility for violations and mask broader causes, such as the more distant contributions of international agents, corporations or economic institutions to the crimes. Ultimately, there is a risk that internationalism contributes to a wider worldview, in which structural injustices like economic inequality come to be seen as regular and normal, while violent effects are regarded as a problem.

All core crimes are informed by different bodies of law: human rights law, humanitarian law and classical criminal law. These individual bodies of law have distinct and sometimes conflicting rationales. The scope and direction given to the crime depends on the tradition from which it is approached. The dynamic interpretation of crimes is driven by human rights-centred approaches, such as the famous *Tadic* dictum that a '[a] State-sovereignty-oriented approach has been gradually supplanted by a human-being-oriented approach'.[712] The fact that the human rights tradition and the humanitarian tradition differ, and that a rights-based based approach does not always offer more protection, is sometimes disregarded.

There is a strong trend to promote the protection of certain groups, traditionally seen as more 'vulnerable', such as women, children and the elderly. These persons have been specifically targeted in strategies of war. The development of core crimes has alleviated certain blind-spots. Rape and sexual violence was long viewed as an inevitable by-product of warfare. Modern jurisprudence has made it clear that sexual

---

[709] Ibid., para. 44. See also Sixth report on the Draft Code of Crimes Against the Peace and Security of Mankind, by Mr. Doudou Thiam, Special Rapporteur, *Yearbook of the International Law Commission*: 1988, Vol. II(1), A/CN.4/411 and Corr. 1 & 2, para. 40 ('The subjection of a people to colonial domination is thus now considered, albeit very belatedly, as a crime against the peace and security of mankind. The only problem that arises is a problem of formulation').

[710] See ILC, *Yearbook of the International Law Commission*, 1993, Vol. II(1), Draft code of crimes against the peace and security of mankind, Comments and observations received from Governments, A/CN.4/448 and Add. 1, 101.

[711] The notion goes back to sociologist Johan Galtung. See J. Galtung, 'Violence, Peace, and Peace Research' (1969) 6 *Journal of Peace Research* 167, 171. It includes harm, including injustice and inequity, that results from social structures and is perpetuated through institutions and everyday experiences. See generally P. Farmer, 'An Anthropology of Structural Violence' (2004) 45 *Current Anthropology* 305.

[712] *Tadić* 1995, para. 97.

and gender-based violence can be prosecuted as a war crime, a crime against humanity and genocide, and that a perpetrator cannot take advantage of a coercive environment to invoke consent. However, for these groups, the focus on victimhood and 'vulnerability' may also have negative side effects. It nurtures certain narratives that may reinforce harmful stereotypes of women as powerless and lacking in agency. It might further create artificial discrepancies in relation to victims of similar violations perpetrated during peacetime.

It remains difficult to establish that the exercise of international criminal jurisdiction has an immediate impact on ongoing conflict. In many instances, the most important effect of justice intervention may lie in the 'shadow of a ruling', namely its broader expressive value, and the signals that it might send for future developments.[713]

---

[713] Aloisi and Meernik, *Judgment Day*, 113–151.

2

Individual and Collective Responsibility

The role of international criminal law is inherently linked to the recognition of the individual as subject of international law. Human rights law typically focuses on individuals as holders of rights. Criminal law approaches the individual mainly as a bearer of duties. This focus is grounded in the idea of the moral culpability of the actor. The assignment of responsibility and, in particular, the award of a sanction must be tied to personal culpability.

The concept of individual criminal responsibility has become a core foundation of the identity of international criminal law as a normative project.[1] It is to some extent an instrument to counter dilemmas of collective punishment or 'guilt by association'.[2] A key structural dilemma is that individualization contrasts with the collective nature of violence.[3] This tension is far more pronounced in atrocity trials than in classical criminal trials. It was addressed in the historical debate between Karl Jaspers and Hannah Arendt in the aftermath of the Holocaust.[4] Jaspers argued that '[i]t is nonsensical to charge a whole people with a crime. The criminal is always the individual'.[5] Arendt supported the individual character of guilt, claiming that 'where all, or almost all, are guilty, nobody is'.[6]

Legal approaches regarding the relationship between individual and collective criminal responsibility have developed over time. There are, at least three, different macro-perspectives. They depend on particular visions of the role of the individuals in relation to atrocity crime.

---

[1] Mark Drumbl speaks of 'iconic status'. See M. Drumbl, 'Accountability for System Criminality' (2010) 8 *Santa Clara Journal of International Law* 373, 377.

[2] See Q. Wright, 'International Law and Guilt by Association' (1949) 43 *AJIL* 746.

[3] E. van Sliedregt, *Criminal Responsibility in International Law* (Oxford: Oxford University Press, 2012); M. Drumbl, 'Collective Violence and Individual Punishment: The Criminality of Mass Atrocity' (2005) 99 *N.W.L. Rev.* 539; T. Franck, 'Individual Criminal Liability and Collective Civil Responsibility: Do They Reinforce or Contradict One Another' (2007) 6 *Washington University Global Studies Law Review* 567.

[4] H. Arendt and K. Jaspers, *Hannah Arendt/Karl Jaspers Correspondence 1926–1969*, in L. Kohler and H. Saner (eds.) and R. Kimber and R. Kimber (trans.) (New York: Harcourt Brace and Company, 1992).

[5] K. Jaspers, 'The Question of German Guilt', in N. J. Kritz (ed.), *Transitional Justice: How Emerging Democracies Reckon with Former Regimes, Volume I: General Considerations* (Washington: United States Institute of Peace, 1995), 157, 163.

[6] H. Arendt, *Eichmann in Jerusalem: A Report on the Banality of Evil* (London: Penguin, 2006), 278.

One school sees the individual predominantly as part of a collective structure. George Fletcher has called this the 'romantic' view.[7] It is based on the belief that international crimes 'express the actions and the implicit guilt of entire people'.[8] This position regards individuals as subjects that are inherently shaped by their affiliation to collective structures, such as the nation-state. It relies on the premise that macro-criminality results from an abuse of collective organizational structures that exceed the individual.[9] It views individuals as part of a broader structure, or even as instruments of states or criminal organizations. It links accountability of individuals closely to collective responsibility schemes, including state responsibility.

A second approach starts from a different point of departure. It views the individual as an absolute subject, i.e. as an end in itself. Standing in the tradition of liberalism, it grounds responsibility in the choice and autonomous decision-making powers of individuals as rational and self-determined agents.[10] It acknowledges that individuals may dominate state or structures and use this power as an instrument to commit crimes, based on beliefs or ideologies.[11] Viewing crimes predominantly as an individual rather than a public affair, it is radical in the sense that it holds an individual accountable for a crime in its totality. The prosecution of individuals serves indirectly as a means to ensure accountability for the crimes of the 'state'.

Modern approaches, including criminological studies, place greater emphasis on context.[12] They view individuals as social agents that are driven by certain roles or pressures, such as extraordinary circumstances or the interplay between individual dispositions and context. They acknowledge that international crimes are often embedded in social norms or political and social structures that facilitate violations. Such a vision offers a more nuanced account of the interplay between individualization and collectivization. It helps to assess more critically where it is feasible to individualize, and where it is appropriate to collectivize responsibility.[13]

---

[7] G. Fletcher, *Romantics at War: Glory and Guilt in the Age of Terrorism* (Princeton and Oxford: Princeton University Press, 2002); G. P. Fletcher, 'The Storrs Lectures: Liberals and Romantics at War: The Problem of Collective Guilt' (2002) 111 *Yale Law Journal* 1499.

[8] Fletcher, 'The Storrs Lectures', 1512.

[9] Throughout the twentieth century, many of the worst crimes have been committed within or through state structures. See Schabas, 'State Policy as an Another (2007) 6 *Washington University Global Studies Law Review* 567.

[10] On the individual as 'absolute subject', see F. Mégret, 'Les angles morts de la responsabilité pénale individuelle en droit international' (2013) 71 *Revue interdisciplinaire d'études juridiques* 83, 96.

[11] See L. Backer, 'The Fuhrer Principle of International Law: Individual Responsibility and Collective Punishment' (2003) 21 *Penn State International Law Review* 509.

[12] See F. Neubacher, 'How Can It Happen that Horrendous State Crimes are Perpetrated? An Overview of Criminological Theories' (2006) 4 *JICJ* 787; J. E. Waller, 'The Ordinariness of Extraordinary Evil: the Making of Perpetrators of Collective Violence', in A. Smeulers (ed.), *Collective Violence and International Criminal Justice: An Interdisciplinary Approach* (Antwerp: Intersentia 2010), 19.

[13] M. Osiel, 'Choosing Among Alternative Responses to Mass Atrocity: Between the Individual and the Collectivity', *Ethics & International Affairs* (2013) 71, 18 September 2015, at www.ethicsandinternationalaffairs.org/2015/choosing-among-alternative-responses-mass-atrocity-individual-collectivity/; B. Hola, 'Sentencing at the ICTY: Doing Justice to Complex Realities of International Crimes?', *Humanity*, 4 July 2017, at http://humanityjournal.org/wp-content/uploads/2017/07/02.-Hola-Sentencing-at-the-ICTY.pdf.

2.1   Individualization of Responsibility

The current focus on individualization can only be understood from the past. Historically, the individual was mediated through the state or the abstract concept of humanity. The very idea that individuals hold obligations under international law was recognized long before World War II. The Treaty of Versailles implied that the violation of international law might give rise to individual responsibility. But the main idea was to hold states accountable for violations committed by their agents.[14] This limited the prospects of enforcement. International criminal law emerged partly as a reaction to the shortcomings of state responsibility.[15]

2.1.1   *The Nuremberg Mantra and Its Consequences*

Individual responsibility evolved at a time when states were the main subjects of international law. Traditionally, the criminal responsibility of individuals was mainly deemed to fall within the internal sphere of states. Some early defenders of international criminal justice argued for the idea that international criminal law should relate to states. For instance, in the 1930s, Romanian jurist Vespasien Pella claimed that states are capable of committing international crimes.[16] However, the idea of punishing states contrasted with the concept of their sovereign equality. States preferred to retain liberty to address systemic crimes through political processes rather than formal legal channels.[17] The focus shifted on to the individual, since states themselves could not be prosecuted. The Nuremberg judgment marked a tipping point. It affirmed the capacity of individuals to commit crimes and, most fundamentally, the distinction between the responsibility of states and the responsibility of individuals. Defendants submitted that responsibility should be ascribed to the state, since 'international law is concerned with the actions of sovereign States, and provides no punishment for individuals'.[18] The Nuremberg judgment rejected the claim that individuals can hide behind the state, or other organizational structures. It held that '[c]rimes against international law are committed by men, not by abstract entities, and only by punishing individuals who commit such crimes can the provisions of international law be enforced'.[19] This famous dictum affirmed that individuals are subjects, not just objects, of international law. It pierced the veil of sovereignty. At the time, this had political significance. It mitigated criticisms of victor's justice; made it easier to justify criminal trials, by avoiding notions of collective guilt; and had

---

[14] For an early exploration, H. Kelsen, 'Collective and Individual Responsibility in International Law with Particular Regard to the Punishment of War Criminals'(1943) 31 *California Law Review* 530.

[15] It is to some extent a counter-concept to state responsibility. See Mégret, 'Les angles morts', 85.

[16] V. Pella, 'La repression des crimes contra la personalité de l'Etat' (1930) 33 *Recueil des Cours*, 821–822.

[17] M. Koskenniemi, 'Solidarity Measures: State Responsibility as a New International Order?' (2002) 72 *British Yearbook of International Law* 337.

[18] IMT Judgment (1947) 41 AJIL 172, 220

[19] Ibid., 221.

fundamental repercussions for the framing of modern crime structures. It made it clear that individuals cannot hide behind collective structures or other networks, since they bear direct individual criminal responsibility under international law.

The Nuremberg judgment took a pragmatic approach in relation to the broader responsibility of organizations. It acknowledged the criminal nature of the leadership activities of certain organizations, such as the Nazi Party, the Gestapo, the SD (Sicherheitsdienst) and the SS (Schutzstaffen), and identified the individuals that were part of these entities. It noted that the 'definition should exclude persons who had no knowledge of the criminal purposes or acts of the organization and those who were drafted by the State for membership, unless they were personally implicated'.[20] Non-state actors, such as corporations, were not defined as criminal organizations.

In the aftermath, international criminal law has become hostile to the idea of punishing organizations as such. As Gerry Simpson noted, there has been a strong temptation to assume that '[o]nly individualized justice could ensure the relevance and meaningfulness of international law. Abstract entities were out, flesh and blood human beings were in'.[21] The idea that a state would bear criminal responsibility as a legal person ('state crimes') was rejected by the International Law Commission in the drafting of the Articles on State Responsibility,[22] and later by the ICTY[23] and the ICJ.[24] State criminality retains value as a criminological concept,[25] but it is widely accepted today that only individuals can be accused of international crimes. States may violate legal obligations but such violations are not criminal in nature. State liability is predominantly civil. It is typically expressed in terms of state responsibility and reparations,[26] while responsibility of individuals is expressed in terms of punishment.[27]

The principle of corporate liability was largely phased out at the international level.[28] Technically, it is possible to hold juridical persons accountable for crimes.

---

[20] Ibid., 251.

[21] G. Simpson, *Law, War and Crime: War Crime Trials and the Reinvention of International Law* (Cambridge: Polity Press, 2007), 56–57.

[22] See generally N. Jorgenson, *The Responsibility of States for International Crimes* (Oxford: Oxford University Press, 2000).

[23] The ICTY held that 'under present international law it is clear that states, by definition, cannot be the subject of criminal sanctions akin to those provided for in national criminal system'. See *Prosecutor* v. *Blaškić*, IT-95–14-AR 108, Judgment on the Request of the Republic of Croatia for Review of the Decision of Trial Chamber II of 18 July 1997, 29 October 1997, 25.

[24] ICJ, *Application of the Convention on the Prevention and Punishment of the Crime of Genocide*, 26 February 2007, para. 170 (obligations 'are not of a criminal nature').

[25] P. Green and T. Ward, *State Crime: Governments, Violence and Corruption* (London: Pluto Press, 2004); P. Green and T. Ward, 'Understanding State Crime', in A. Liebling, S. Maruna and L. McAra (eds.), *The Oxford Handbook of Criminology* (Oxford: Oxford University Press, 2017), 438.

[26] E. Wyler and L. A. Castellanos-Jankiewicz, 'State Responsibility and International Crimes', in W. Schabas and R. Bernaz (eds.), *Routledge Handbook of International Criminal Law* (London: Routledge, 2007), 385–404.

[27] This separation of individual criminal responsibility and state responsibility is expressly enshrined in Art. 25 ICC Statute.

[28] For a discussion on corporate international criminal liability, see R. C. Slye, 'Corporations, Veils and International Criminal Liability' (2008) 33 *Brooklyn Journal of International Law* 955–973; D. Stoichkova, *Towards Corporate Liability in International Criminal Law* (Antwerpen: Intersentia, 2010). See also C. Stahn, 'Liberals vs. Romantics: Challenges of an Emerging Corporate International Criminal Law' (2018) 50 *Case Western Reserve Journal of International Law*, 91–125.

There is a growing trend to hold corporations accountable as legal persons in domestic jurisdictions.[29] However, on the international level, it is mostly individuals, rather than companies as abstract persons that can be held criminally liable for complicity in international crimes.[30] In the aftermath of World War II, German industrial agents, such as IG Farben, Krupp or Flick faced charges for complicity in war crimes, crimes against humanity and aggression in trials under Control Council Law No. 10. Tribunals did not try corporations as such. The *IG Farben* judgment[31] stated that:

the corporate defendant, Farben, is not before the bar of this Tribunal and cannot be subjected to criminal penalties ... corporations act through individuals and, under the conception of personal individual guilt ... the prosecution ... must establish ... that an individual defendant was either a participant in the illegal act or that, being aware thereof, he authorized or approved it.[32]

Defendants were charged symbolically as company leaders and individuals to demonstrate the economic power behind Nazi atrocities.

Corporate complicity in crime is a recurring phenomenon.[33] For example, the Truth and Reconciliation Commission in South Africa acknowledged that '[b]usiness was central to the economy that sustained the South African state during the apartheid years [and that] [c]ertain businesses, ... were involved in helping to design and implement apartheid policies'.[34] Despite a trend in human rights law to enhance the accountability of corporations, most international criminal courts or tribunals established after World War II lacked the authority to try legal persons.[35] Corporate criminal responsibility was discussed in the context of the ICC. France made a proposal to extend individual criminal responsibility to juridical persons, including corporations, in cases where individuals commit crimes 'on behalf of and with the explicit consent' of a juridical person, and 'in the course of its activities'.[36] This construction addressed the traditional objection that abstract entities cannot form a *mens rea*, but the proposal was not included in the ICC Statute[37] due to differences concerning criminal liability of corporations in domestic systems and time constraints.

---

[29] Many jurisdictions allow for corporate criminal responsibility, either in general or for specific offences. Other countries (e.g. Italy, Germany, Ukraine) remain more sceptical of the concept and resort to administrative offences or penalty to address wrongdoing. For a critique of corporate criminal responsibility, see V. S. Khanna, 'Corporate Criminal Liability: What Purpose Does It Serve?' (1996) 109 *Harvard Law Review* 1477–1534; J. Hasnas, 'The Centenary of a Mistake: One Hundred Years of Corporate Criminal Liability' (2009) 46 *American Criminal Law Review* 1329.

[30] For a defence, see H. van der Wilt, 'Corporate Criminal Responsibility for International Crimes: Exploring the Possibilities' (2013) 12 *Chinese Journal of International Law* 43.

[31] See F. Jessberger, 'On the Origins of Individual Criminal responsibility under International Law for Business Activity: IG Farben on Trial' (2010) 8 *JICJ* 783.

[32] Trial of Carl Krauch and Twenty-Two Others (I.G. Farben Trial), United States Military Tribunal, Nuremberg, 14 August 1947–29 July 1948, *Law Reports of Trials of War Criminals* (UNWCC), Volume X (His Majesty's Stationary Office 1949), 52.

[33] See W. Huisman and E. van Sliedregt, 'Rogue Traders: Dutch Businessmen, International Crimes and Corporate Complicity' (2010) 8 *JICJ* 803, 807 et seq.

[34] Truth and Reconciliation Commission of South Africa Report, Vol. V, para. 156.

[35] Steven R. Ratner, 'Corporations and Human Rights: A Theory of Legal Responsibility' (2001) 111 *Yale Law Journal* 443.

[36] Working Paper on Art. 23, paras. 5–6, A/Conf.183/C.1/WGGP/L.5/Rev.2, 3 July 1998.

[37] Art. 25 ICC Statute.

Shifts from a naturalistic to a more sociological vision of crime make it possible to argue that corporations can perpetrate crimes.[38] The idea that crimes against international law can be committed by 'abstract legal entities' was only reconsidered recently. In 2014, the Special Tribunal for Lebanon (STL) extended the scope of liability to a corporation, based on the interpretation of Lebanese law.[39] It held that '[c]orporate criminal liability is on the verge of attaining, at the very least, the status of a general principle of law applicable under international law'.[40] The decision received mixed reactions. Some have welcomed it as a step in the right direction, namely as 'a foundation for further development of liability of corporate entities in international criminal law'.[41] Others have decried it as a novel incarnation for international criminal law's 'dream factory'.[42]

The only judicial instrument which recognizes criminal responsibility of corporations expressly in relation to international crimes is the Malabo Protocol. It extends the jurisdiction of the proposed African Court of Justice and Human and Peoples Rights to 'legal persons, with the exception of States'.[43] This has potentially far-reaching implications, since it foresees an organizational model of liability[44] and might be applied to economic crimes, including corruption and the illicit exploitation of natural resources. However, it fails to define the concept of 'legal person', or the applicable penalties. It is also questionable whether a regional approach does justice to the global nature of corporate involvement in international crime.

---

[38] D. Vaughan, 'Criminology and the Sociology of Organizations: Analogy, Comparative Social Organization, and General Theory' (2002) 37 *Crime, Law and Social Change* 117.

[39] STL, *Prosecutor* v. *New TV S.A.L. and Al Khayat*, STL-14–05/PT/AP/AR126.1, Decision on Interlocutory Appeal Concerning Personal Jurisdiction in Contempt Proceedings, 2 October 2014. For a discussion, see N. Bernaz, 'Corporate Criminal Liability under International Law' (2015) 13 *JICJ* 313.

[40] *Prosecutor* v. *New TV S.A.L. and Al Khayat*, para. 67.

[41] Karlijn Van der Voort, Contempt Case against Lebanese Journalists at the STL, 30 April 2014, at http://lebanontribunal .blogspot.nl/2014/04/contempt-case-against-lebanese_30.html.

[42] D. Jacobs, 'The Dream Factory Strikes Again: the Special Tribunal for Lebanon recognizes International Criminal Corporate Liability', 28 April 2010, at https://dovjacobs.com/2014/04/28/the-dream-factory-strikes-again-the-special-tribunal-for-lebanon-recognizes-international-criminal-corporate-liability/.

[43] See generally J. Kyriakakis, 'Corporations before International Criminal Courts: Implications for the International Criminal Justice Project' (2017) 30 *LJIL* 221. Art. 46 C Malabo Protocol on 'Corporate Criminal liability' reads:

  1. For the purpose of this Statute, the Court shall have jurisdiction over legal persons, with the exception of States.
  2. Corporate intention to commit an offence may be established by proof that it was the policy of the corporation to do the act which constituted the offence.
  3. A policy may be attributed to a corporation where it provides the most reasonable explanation of the conduct of that corporation.
  4. Corporate knowledge of the commission of an offence may be established by proof that the actual or constructive knowledge of the relevant information was possessed within the corporation.
  5. Knowledge may be possessed within a corporation even though the relevant information is divided between corporate personnel.
  6. The criminal responsibility of legal persons shall not exclude the criminal responsibility of natural persons who are perpetrators or accomplices in the same crimes.

[44] Responsibility may be tied to the corporate policies, such as lack of proper organization or control of a corporate culture that facilitates violations. See Art. 46 C Malabo Protocol.

The limited recognition of corporate criminal responsibility in international criminal law[45] creates a striking contradiction. The idea that 'companies cannot commit offences' (*societas delinquere non potest*) is a relict of the past.[46] Individual corporate agents can be held accountable for business involvement in crime, but in the absence of corporate penalties (e.g. fines, sanctions) companies as such may be able to retain the profits of their activities. The exclusion of 'abstract entities' from responsibility is thus under challenge in the area of corporate responsibility.[47] Extending responsibility makes sense from a criminological point of view, since business agents are even more likely than other perpetrators of international crimes to consider risks of criminal prosecution in their cost–benefit analysis.[48]

The ILC Draft Articles on Crimes against Humanity contain a compromise solution. They do not make corporate criminal responsibility mandatory, but they include a provision on legal persons in light of the 'the potential involvement of legal persons in acts committed as part of a widespread or systematic attack directed against a civilian population'.[49] It states that

[s]ubject to the provisions of its national law, each State shall take measures, where appropriate, to establish the liability of legal persons for the offences referred to in this draft article. Subject to the legal principles of the State, such liability of legal persons may be criminal, civil or administrative.[50]

This leaves states the option to choose among criminal, civil or administrative responsibility.

2.1.2 Justifications

Conceptually, the principle of individual criminal responsibility was mainly developed in reaction to fears of collective responsibility. Individualization of wrongdoing makes it possible to render retributive justice and to introduce incentives for deterrence. It seeks to prevent formal assignment of blame or guilt to collectivities, such as entire

---

[45] There are seventeen multilateral international instruments with provisions on corporate criminal liability, including the UN Convention against Against Transnational Organized Crime. See B. Swart, 'International Trends towards Establishing Some Form of Punishment for Corporations' (2008) 6 *JICJ* 947, 951.

[46] In the nineteenth century, the concept of corporate criminal liability was rejected, due to inability of legal persons to form a *mens rea* or to be subject of punishment. For a discussion, see A. Clapham, 'Extending International Criminal Law beyond the Individual to Corporations and Armed Opposition Groups' (2008) 6 *J. Int'l Crim. Just.* 899, 926. On the obligations of corporations under international law, see V. Nerlich, 'Core Crimes and Transnational Business Corporations' (2010) 8 *JICJ* 895.

[47] See Van der Wilt, 'Corporate Criminal Responsibility', 77 ('Crimes against international law can be committed by abstract legal entities, provided that they act in tandem with men').

[48] Kyriakakis, 'Corporations before International Criminal Courts', 237. See also B. Fisse and J. Braithwaite, *The Impact of Publicity on Corporate Offenders* (Albany: State University of New York Press, 1983).

[49] See, ILC, Report of the International Law Commission', GAOR 71st Session, Suppl. No. 10. UN Doc A/71/10 (2016), 264.

[50] See Art. 5 (7), ibid., 248. The language is based on Art. 3 (4) of the Optional Protocol to the Convention on the Rights of the Child on the sale of children, child prostitution and child pornography, adopted by General Assembly Resolution A/RES/54/263 of 25 May 2000, entered into force on 18 January 2002.

nations, societies or whole ethnic and religious groups. This rationale was invoked by the ICTY, in particular, to justify investigations and prosecutions against individuals. It treated international criminal justice as an instrument to mitigate feelings of resentment, hatred and frustration. This is vividly illustrated by the words of former ICTY President Antonio Cassese in his first report to the Security Council in 1994:

Far from being a vehicle for revenge, [the tribunal] is a tool for promoting reconciliation and restoring true peace. If responsibility for the appalling crimes perpetrated in the former Yugoslavia is not attributed to individuals, then whole ethnic and religious groups will be held accountable for these crimes and branded as criminal. In other words, 'collective responsibility' – a primitive and archaic concept – will gain the upper hand; eventually whole groups will be held guilty of massacres, torture, rape, ethnic cleansing, the wanton destruction of cities and villages.[51]

There has been reluctance to punish individuals for membership in organizations as such.[52] At Nuremberg, the International Military Tribunal could have taken a broader approach towards the criminal responsibility of organizations.[53] This would have enabled the prosecution of large numbers of mid- or low-level perpetrators for Nazi crimes. However, such mass proceedings were not carried out. Greater emphasis was placed on de-nazification and re-education. The branding of organizations as criminal thus had mainly expressive purposes. In later contexts, criminality for membership in a criminal organization was no longer seriously contemplated, except in the context of counterterrorism.[54] The ad hoc tribunals and the ICC applied an individualized assessment in relation to organizational responsibility, because of their limited capacity and their intended focus on leadership responsibility.

2.1.3   Limitations

Individualization of wrongdoing has many limitations.[55] It assumes that collective criminality can be translated into individual guilt and responsibility. This process is often more difficult than anticipated. An exclusively individualist approach fails to take into account the group dynamics of crime, including the relations among individual members. Mass criminality is often both individual and collective. Some crimes

---

[51] See Annual Report of the International Tribunal for the Prosecution of Persons Responsible for Serious Violations of International Humanitarian Law Committed in the Territory of the Former Yugoslavia since 1991, A/49/342, S/1994/1007, 29 August 1994, para. 16, at www.icty.org/x/file/About/Reports%20and%20Publications/AnnualReports/annual_report_1994_en.pdf.

[52] J. Bush, 'The Prehistory of Corporations and Conspiracy in International Criminal Law: What Nuremberg Really Said' (2009) 109 *Columbia Law Review* 1094–1242.

[53] According to Art. 9, 'the Tribunal could declare, at the trial of any individual member of any group or organization and in connection with any act of which the individual may be convicted, that the group or organization of which the individual was a member was a criminal organization'. On the practice, see N. H. B. Jorgensen, 'Criminality of Organizations', in A. Nollkaemper and H. van der Wilt (eds.), *System Criminality in International Law* (Cambridge: Cambridge University Press, 2009), 201, 204.

[54] See J. D. Ohlin, 'The One or the Many' (2015) 9 *Criminal Law and Philosophy* 285–299.

[55] See G. Fletcher, 'Liberals and Romantics at War: The Problem of Collective Guilt' (2002) 111 *Yale Law Journal* 1499; G. Simpson, 'Men and Abstract Entities: Individual Responsibility and Collective Guilt', in Nollkaemper and Van der Wilt, *System Criminality in International Law*, 88.

may be committed with popular or even democratic support. A full translation of collective conduct into individual responsibility causes complex problems in relation to the knowledge and understanding of collective criminality, causality and determination of blame.[56] The fact that an individual takes part in collective violence does not necessarily mean that this person should be responsible for every act committed within the collective structure.

Individualizing responsibility raises difficulties in relation to fairness and proportionality. The collective and individual dimensions of agency overlap.[57]As George Fletcher has argued, international crimes are often 'deeds that by their very nature are committed by groups and typically against individuals and members of groups'.[58] International crimes rely heavily on contextual elements, such as collective plans or policies or contexts of oppression. There is often only a fine line between holding an individual responsible for a specific act amounting to a crime and responsibility for a whole category of criminality (i.e. war crimes, crimes against humanity, genocide) as such. An individual charged with international crimes may easily become a 'scapegoat' for collective action or face excessive stigmatization. This conflict is particularly pressing in the context of the crime of aggression, where individual criminal responsibility is inherently linked to collective state action. It is thus important to identify the degree to which the individual may be held accountable for its own acts and the acts of the collectivity. Sentencing considerations and reparation are often the only means in the criminal process to relate individual criminal responsibility back to the collective dimensions of crime.

There may also be knowledge deficits and different social understandings in relation to facts and events.[59] The situational context is difficult to reconstruct. The very nature of violence may be at odds with conventional notions of culpability. It may be hard to translate into legal labels of responsibility. Organized attempts to eradicate the concept of the human being test the limits of the law. The very process of determining guilt may exceed the categories of law and its capacity to express harm.

Finally, a predominant focus on individualization may have certain exculpatory effects. One of the flip sides of a strict focus on individualized guilt in institutional responses is that it may implicitly lead to the exculpation of wider society or 'contribute to a myth of collective innocence'.[60] Martti Koskenniemi has cautioned that 'individualization not only narrows historical inquiry and downplays the role of the

---

[56] See C. Steer, *Translating Guilt: Identifying Leadership Liability for Mass Atrocity Crimes* (The Hague: TMC Asser Press 2017), 12–17.

[57] See J. D. Ohlin, 'Group Think: The Law of Conspiracy and Collective Reason' (2007) 98 *Journal of Criminal Law and Criminology* 147.

[58] Fletcher, 'The Storrs Lectures', 1499.

[59] As Immi Tallgren notes, 'by focusing on individual responsibility, criminal law reduces the perspective of the phenomenon to make it easier for the eye. Thereby it reduces the complexity and scale of multiple responsibilities to a mere background'. See Tallgren, 'Sense and Sensibility', 594.

[60] See L. Fletcher and H. Weinstein, 'Violence and Social Repair: Rethinking the Contribution of Justice to Reconciliation' (2002) 24 *Human Rights Quarterly* 573 at 580. Some authorities have argued that the Nuremburg trials provided almost a 'collective amnesty' for the rest of the German people. M. Fulbrook, *German National Identity after the Holocaust* (Cambridge: Polity, 1999), 51.

state but it also may even serve as an alibi for the population at large to relieve itself from responsibility'.[61] It may privilege punishment of individuals over inquiry into the causes of atrocity.[62]

In light of these tensions, individual criminal responsibility has been characterized as a 'wolf in sheep's clothes'.[63] Many scholars have argued that responses to international crimes should not focus exclusively on criminal trials but remain open to certain other mechanisms that locate and ascribe collective responsibility, such as truth commissions or public inquiries.[64] For instance, for purposes of historical clarification or condemnation of a wider 'culture of impunity' underlying crimes, it is necessary to situate crime within a broader framework of social and political analysis.

Most of the acts that trigger individual responsibility imply a state duty to prosecute. The ICJ has made it clear in the *Genocide* case that the Genocide Convention entails state duties of repression and prevention that go beyond the territorial state and may entail a duty to provide reparation.[65] The obligation to punish individuals can be read as a specific form of reparation due by the state. The Inter-American Court on Human Rights has developed a rich jurisprudence on measures that states should provide to avoid repetition of system criminality.[66] Individualization and collective responsibility are thus not mutually exclusive but interrelated. The focus shifts, depending on the orientation of the response.[67] There is a tendency to individualize the wrongdoer for purposes of retribution and deterrence, while collective orientations prevail in approaches towards compensation, security sector reform or transitional justice.

---

[61] Koskenniemi, *Between Impunity and Show Trials*, 14. See also C. Backer, 'The Fuhrer Principle of International Law: Individual Responsibility and Collective Punishment' (2003) 21 *Penn State International Law Review* 509

[62] For a critique, see C. Nielsen, 'From Nuremberg to The Hague: The Civilizing Mission of International Criminal Law' (2008) 14 *Auckland University Law Review* 81 at 99.

[63] L. Fletcher, 'A Wolf in Sheep's Clothing: Transitional Justice and the Effacement of State Accountability for International Crimes' (2016) 39 *Fordham International Law Journal* 447.

[64] See Drumbl, *Atrocity, Punishment and International Law*, 181–209.

[65] ICJ, *Application of the Convention on the Prevention and Punishment of the Crime of Genocide*, 26 February 2007, para. 430.

[66] See *Velásquez Rodríguez* case, para. 166. For a survey, see A. Mayer-Rieckh, 'Guarantees of Non-Recurrence: An Approximation' (2017) 39 *Human Rights Quarterly* 416. Relevant guarantees of non-repetition include: '(a) Ensuring effective civilian control of military and security forces; (b) Ensuring that all civilian and military proceedings abide by international standards of due process, fairness and impartiality; (c) Strengthening the independence of the judiciary; (d) Protecting persons in the legal, medical and health-care professions, the media and other related professions, and human rights defenders; (e) Providing, on a priority and continued basis, human rights and international humanitarian law education to all sectors of society and training for law enforcement officials as well as military and security forces; (f) Promoting the observance of codes of conduct and ethical norms, in particular international standards, by public servants, including law enforcement, correctional, media, medical, psychological, social service and military personnel, as well as by economic enterprises; (g) Promoting mechanisms for preventing and monitoring social conflicts and their resolution; (h) Reviewing and reforming laws contributing to or allowing gross violations of international human rights law and serious violations of international humanitarian law'. See Basic Principles and Guidelines on the Right to a Remedy and Reparation for Victims of Gross Violations of International Human Rights Law and Serious Violations of International Humanitarian Law, adopted and proclaimed by General Assembly resolution 60/147 of 16 December 2005, para. 23.

[67] Osiel, 'Choosing Among Alternative Responses'.

2.2   System Criminality

International criminal justice differs from domestic systems in relation to the nature of the violence it deals with.[68] Domestic systems are typically concerned with 'interpersonal violence'. International crimes have a collective dimension.[69] These crimes can hardly be committed by one perpetrator alone. Some criminologists speak of macro-criminality.[70] They require a network and a multilayered decision-making structure, which serves as a force multiplier. Crimes are often committed through formal or informal networks that exercise pressure on their members. Some persons – the immediate perpetrators – actually commit crimes directly. Other persons organize and plan the criminal operation. Others may hold overall leadership and command, or serve as intellectual masterminds. Still others may simply facilitate the commission of the crime.[71]

Macro-crimes often do not involve a homogenous collectivity, but different smaller groups or sub-entities that are instrumental for the commission of crimes. They include leaders, bureaucrats or specialized agents. They are driven by distinct factors, such as ideology,[72] obedience or group conformity. Some members may develop plans or ideologies to justify action, while others may rationalize and normalize behaviour, or act as opportunists. Through this interaction, acts may gradually appear to become compliant with accepted social norms, rather than deviant in that context.

In her study on *Eichmann in Jerusalem*, Hannah Arendt came to the conclusion that some of the most atrocious crimes in the Holocaust were not committed by psychopaths, but rather by ordinary persons in the pursuit of their alleged duties. This thesis was confirmed by experiences in other contexts, such as Cambodia, Rwanda or the former Yugoslavia.[73] According to this theory, it 'is not personal pathology or an anomic state of affairs but rather normal people and group structures and dynamics – including socialization and conformity to the dominant norms of the moment – through which individuals are brought to participate in crimes against humanity, and ... other forms of crime as well'.[74] Modern criminology has refined criteria to explain macro-criminality through group affiliations and belief systems. Factors include societal strain, which causes suspicion, fear or anxiety; 'us versus them' group affiliations with low intergroup social solidarity; processes of socialization through

---

[68] S. Harrendorf, 'How Can Criminology Contribute to an Explanation of International Crimes?' (2014) 12 *JICJ* 231–252.

[69] See Nollkaemper and Van der Wilt, *System Criminality in International Law*, 1, referring to 'system criminality' whereby 'international crimes – notably crimes against humanity, genocide and war crimes – are often caused by collective entities in which the individual authors of these acts are embedded'.

[70] See H. Jäger, *Makrokriminalität: Studien zur Kriminologie kollektiver Gewalt* (Frankfurt: Suhrkamp, 1989).

[71] A classical example is genocide. A genocidal plan or policy cannot be implemented without structural support, even if the perpetrator is at the top of a state or private organization. It is further driven by certain other situational dynamics, such as feelings of superiority, tension and fear. On violence through emotional dominance, see R. Collins, *Violence: A Micro-Sociological Theory* (Princeton: Princeton University Press, 2008).

[72] On ideology, see Alvarez, 'Destructive Beliefs', 213–231.

[73] See F. Chalk and K. Jonassohn (eds.), *The History and Sociology of Genocide: Analyses and Case Studies* (New Haven: Yale University Press, 1990); R. Gellately and B. Kiernan (eds.), *The Specter of Genocide: Mass Murder in Historical Perspective* (Cambridge: Cambridge University Press, 2003).

[74] D. Maier-Katkin, D. P. Mears and T. J. Bernard, 'Towards a Criminology of Crimes against Humanity' (2009) 13 *Theoretical Criminology* 227, 247.

conformity within group affiliations become a primary rationale; group structure and dynamics which facilitate subordination to authority and acceptance of social roles; belief systems that dehumanize the 'other' and legitimize violence for the sake of a higher order; and gratification systems that diminish self-control. The argument implies that, depending on context, some 'people become war criminals the same way others become war heroes'.[75] Alette Smeulers has gone so far as to identify certain archetypes of perpetrators. She distinguishes at least nine different types of perpetrators: '(1) the criminal mastermind; (2) the careerist; (3) the profiteer; (4) the fanatic; (5) the devoted warrior; (6) the professional; (7) the criminal and sadist; (8) the follower; and (9) the compromised perpetrator'.[76]

2.2.1   Collective Nature

The threat of many international crimes emanates from the fact they are committed in a collective way that requires multiple forms of human interaction. It involves different levels of responsibility: leadership actors who exercise control through decision-making power; agents who plan, organize or manage the implementation, for instance by determining actors involved in the crime and modalities and means of action; and those who execute the crime.[77] These structures exist in state-organized crime and some non-state actors. Leadership actors may play a greater role in the deliberative aspects of collective criminality, while others may hold greater control over the execution of individual crimes.

Understanding how this type of criminality works is a complex process. International criminal investigations must first link all of the pieces of the puzzle together in order to understand the crimes and the collective nature of agency. This requires an understanding of the functioning of organizational and power structures. Then the bits and pieces must be deconstructed. It must be determined which individual forms of agency and control contributed to the collective outcome. Charges and prosecutions must be individualized in order to reflect the individual culpability and individual contribution to the crime. This involves delicate policy choices and selectivity dilemmas.

The degree of culpability does not depend on the physical proximity to the crime, or the execution of the crime by one's own conduct, but the structural relationship to the crime. The most serious violations may be committed by those who possess and wield political power, or orchestrate the violations. They may be far from the actual scene of

---

[75] Ibid., 244.
[76] See A. Smeulers, 'Perpetrators of International Crimes: Towards a Typology', in Smeulers and Haveman, *Supranational Criminology*, 233–265. See also Harrendorf, 'How Can Criminology Contribute', 246–248.
[77] On this typology, see Ambos, *Treatise on International Criminal Law, Vol. I*, 178; H. Vest, *Völkerrechtsverbrecher Verfolgen: Ein Abgestuftes Mehrebenenmodell Systemischer Tatherrschaft* (Bern: Stämpfli, 2011).

the crime. A good example is the case of Adolf Eichmann.[78] Eichmann organized the deportation of the Jewish population, but he was not directly involved in any act of murder. Most would agree that this organizational element carries a particularly high degree of blameworthiness because of its contribution to the context of other crimes.

Jurisprudence has made it clear that distance from the place of commission does not absolve the perpetrator from responsibility. For instance, in *Tadić*, the ICTY held specifically that 'the moral gravity of [acts of] participation is often no less – or indeed no different – from that of those actually carrying out the act in question'.[79]

2.2.2 Role of Hierarchies

The scope of blameworthiness may be linked to structures of hierarchy. The ICC has given an indication in *Katanga and Ngudjolo Chui*. It held that 'the higher in rank or the farther detached the mastermind is from the perpetrator, the greater that person's responsibility will be'.[80] The problem with this assertion is that it relies strongly on classical chains of hierarchy. Reality is often more complex. Non-state actors in particular, or companies, do not necessarily operate in classical military or bureaucratic structures. Decision-making powers are often decentralized. Top-down leadership is replaced by more flexible or egalitarian structures. Areas of responsibility may be less formalized. Authority may be delegated, shared or transferred and thus more difficult to establish. Subunits or specialized groups may hold independent decision-making power or play an instrumental role in management. As noted by Mark Osiel, there is a danger that international criminal courts and tribunals rely partly on fiction in order bring the reality in line with legal concepts.[81] In such contexts, the level of culpability may be less dependent on hierarchy. Blameworthiness is attached rather to the role that the individual shared.

2.2.3 Power and Obedience

A typical problem of international criminal justice is that certain crimes may not be perceived as criminal conduct, since they form part of everyday experience. As Smeulers put it, they involve 'ordinary persons in extraordinary circumstances'.[82] Crimes are rooted in relationships of power. They are part of group dynamics, conformity pressures and reward schemes that create incentives to follow and 'obey'. Studies have shown that affiliation or identification with a collectivity diffuses

---

[78] On Eichmann, see E. Lipstadt, *The Eichmann Trial* (New York: Nextbook Schocken, 2011); W. Schabas, 'The Contribution of the Eichmann Trial to International Law' (2013) 26 *LJIL* 667.
[79] *Tadić* 1999, para. 191.
[80] *Katanga and Chui* Confirmation Decision, para. 503.
[81] M. Osiel, 'The Banality of Good: Aligning Incentives Against Mass Atrocity' (2005) 105 *Colombia Law Review* 1751.
[82] See A. Smeulers, 'Punishing the Enemies of All Mankind' (2008) 21 *LJIL* 971, 973.

responsibility and may enable individuals to commit wrongs that they would not commit individually.[83] The individual motives of perpetrators to commit atrocities differ. But moral deliberation and the sense of personal responsibility may be affected by collective dynamics, command structures and gradual routine. A prominent theory is that of 'crimes of obedience', which was originally developed in behavioural science, including the Milgram[84] and Zimbardo experiments.[85] It is useful to explain the concept of international crimes. It relies on the insight that many crimes result from rule orientation (obedience to authority), role orientation (e.g. identification with certain professional roles as leader, commander etc., group conformity pressure) and/or shifting value orientation.

2.2.3.1 Rule Orientation

The most classical examples of obedience are cases in which individuals are part of a chain of authority and submit to some form of sanction in case of non-obedience.[86] Such structures are common in military and paramilitary groups, governmental bureaucracies and business structures. Obedience is related to rule orientation and the lack of power of the perpetrator. Orders and commands may limit the sense of individual responsibility for actions or the choice to act in accordance with the law. Criminality is gradually perceived as an adherence to the norm. International criminal justice seeks to counter such types of obedience through crime prohibitions and the concept of superior orders, which constrains the possibility to invoke commands and orders as a justification for action. Some scholars have even argued that disobedience and encouragement of civil courage is one of the express rationales of international criminal law: soldiers, civil servants or other persons exercising control are deemed to question orders and disobey authority that conflicts with international criminal law.[87]

2.2.3.2 Role Orientation

A second type of cases relate to role models and practices of professionalization. Not every person blindly follows orders and commands. For instance, Holocaust studies demonstrate that many perpetrators had the opportunity to refuse orders without fear of death or imprisonment.[88] In many instances, the pressure to 'obey' does not result from chains of authority, but from the identification of the perpetrator with a specific

---

[83] G. Lewy, *Perpetrators: The World of the Holocaust Killers* (Oxford: Oxford University Press, 2017).

[84] S. Milgram, *Obedience to Authority: An Experimental View* (New York: Harper & Row, 1974). The experiments were in part inspired by Arendt's conception of evil as banal.

[85] P. G. Zimbardo, *The Lucifer Effect: Understanding How Good People Turn Evil* (New York: Random House, 2008).

[86] For a discussion, see O. S. Liwerant, 'Mass Murder – Discussing Criminological Perspectives' (2007) 5 *JICJ* 917–939.

[87] See B. Leebaw, 'Justice and the Faithless: The Demand for Disobedience in International Criminal Law' (2018) 24 *European Journal of International Relations* 344–366; V. Reuss, 'Zivilcourage als Strafzweck des Völkerstrafrechts? Betroffenenbelange aus teleologischer Perspektive' (2012) 45 *Kritische Justiz* 241–260.

[88] See F. Neubacher, *Kriminologische Grundlagen einer internationalen Strafgerichtsbarkeit* (Tübingen: Mohr Siebeck, 2005), 225–229. For a discussion, see also A. Fenigstein, 'Were Obedience Pressures a Factor in the Holocaust?' (1998) 20 *Analyse & Kritik* 54–73; D. R. Mandel, 'The Obedience Alibi: Milgram's Account of the Holocaust Reconsidered' (1998) 20 *Analyse & Kritik* 74–94.

role or a shared identity. Institutional role models, actions of others, fear of embarrassment and power over others may affect the perception as to what is right and wrong. International criminal justice counters this type of criminality through leadership accountability and expressivism. It further delegitimates role models through concepts such as superior responsibility, which assign responsibility for failure to abide by certain professional standards.[89]

2.2.3.3 Value Reorientation

Finally, some crimes are 'crimes of conviction'. In these cases, obedience is oriented towards a reorientation of values. This reorientation is stimulated by factors such as ideological considerations (i.e. belief in the nobility of the enterprise), lack of personal responsibility and practices of neutralization, i.e. justification of crime through factors such as the dehumanization of victims, the diffusion of responsibility or extralegal norms and values.[90] These cases are most difficult to address through individual criminal responsibility, since the appeal of criminal norms has been supplanted by a different value system. A restoration of 'the rule' requires a deconstruction of the context in which the perpetrator operates.

2.3   Leadership Accountability

Perpetrators of international crimes can be found at all levels, from the president or prime minister down to district governors or mayors of cities and towns. Individual criminal responsibility applies in principle equally to all, irrespective of the rank or level of authority that a person holds. Everyone – from the head of state to soldiers of the lowest rank –can be prosecuted for international crimes.

At Nuremberg, significant attention was devoted to establishing leadership accountability. As Justice Robert Jackson put it: 'The common sense of mankind demands that law shall not stop with the petty crimes by little people. It must also reach men who possess themselves of great power and make deliberate and concerted use of it to set in motion evils which leave no home … untouched'.[91] Leadership accountability was thus presented as an equality argument. However, equal prosecution is often impossible in light of the sheer number of crimes and perpetrators. Typically, international criminal courts and tribunals must choose. They tend to concentrate on 'leadership' accountability, involving the 'masterminds' or the

---

[89] On superior responsibility, see Section 2.4.2.
[90] See G. Sykes and D. Matza, 'Techniques of Neutralization: A Theory of Delinquency' (1957) 22 *American Sociological Review* 664; S. Cohen, *States of Denial: Knowing about Atrocities and Suffering* (Cambridge: Polity Press, 2001), Harrendorf, 'How Can Criminology Contribute', 249–251.
[91] Opening statement by Robert H. Jackson, in *Trial of the Major War Criminals before the International Military Tribunal*, Vol. 2 (1947), 99.

intellectual authors of crime, and/or the leadership of different actors involved in a conflict.[92] The choice is influenced by a number of factors, such as the contribution of a specific entity to the crimes, the degree of individual responsibility, the potential preventive effect of charges and/or operational constraints.

The focus on leadership accountability has merits and downsides. Targeting elites has a strong symbolic effect. It may disrupt existing power structures that facilitated the crime, and may also bestow a sense of equality between victims and perpetrators. It also has negative effects, however.

The equality argument can be turned around. International criminal law may have become too obsessed with leadership accountability. The role of bystanders, companies and other drivers of conflict has been largely ignored in international practice.[93] Immediate victims of crime often wish to see their neighbour tried as much as they seek accountability for core leaders. The costs of failure are high. Going after the leadership requires significant evidence. A 'failed' trial may easily derail the legitimacy of a justice process. Moreover, there is a risk that individuals are punished to set an example, rather than for their own wrongdoing. One of the most inherent challenges of international criminal law is to spread responsibility more equally, and to encompass not only leaders, but those who fuel conflict.[94]

2.4   Modes of Liability

International criminal justice operates on the general premise that several persons can bear individual responsibility for the same crime. Individual responsibility is indivisible in the sense that a perpetrator may be held accountable for a crime even if others have contributed to it. The focus is on the fault of the individual and their nexus to the crime.

International criminal law has developed sophisticated legal models to link perpetrators and crimes. They are geared at capturing the specificities of mass atrocity violence. There is no shortage of theories to hold actors accountable, but fairness warrants that the contribution of the defendant is adequately labelled and qualified.[95] Judges must determine the basis for conviction which provides the most accurate description of the defendant's participation in a crime.

---

[92] H. Olasolo, *The Criminal Responsibility of Senior Political and Military Leaders as Principals to International Crimes* (Oxford: Hart, 2009).

[93] Some attention to this deficit is devoted in the 2016 Policy Paper of the ICC Office of the Prosecutor on Case Selection and Prioritisation. The OTP argues that in its consideration of gravity, it 'will give particular consideration to prosecuting Rome Statute crimes that are committed by means of, or that result in, *inter alia*, the destruction of the environment, the illegal exploitation of natural resources or the illegal dispossession of land'. See OTP, Policy Paper on Case Selection and Prioritisation, 15 September 2016, para. 41.

[94] See L. Fletcher, 'From Indifference to Engagement: Bystanders and International Criminal Justice' (2005) 26 *Michigan Journal of International Law* 1013.

[95] D. Guilfoyle, 'Responsibility for Collective Atrocities: Fair Labelling and Approaches to Commission in International Criminal Law' (2011) 64 *Current Legal Problems* 255.

Approaches towards liability differ across jurisdictions.[96] Romano-Germanic systems typically rely on a differentiation between principals and accessories. Principals face responsibility for a crime of their own (as rapist, murderer etc.), while accessories contribute to the crime of another. In common law systems this distinction is less pronounced, since accessories may be treated 'as if they had actually perpetrated the crime'.[97] Common sense appears to suggest that, in a functional sense, principals are more blameworthy, and therefore carry higher degrees of responsibility than accomplices who assisted the principal, because of their own role in relation to the crime and their moral choice. As the ICTY held in *Tadić*, convicting participants in a common plan to commit an international crime 'only as an aider and abettor might understate the degree of their criminal responsibility'.[98]

In certain cases, however, indirect perpetrators or accessories may be more responsible for crimes than principals in terms of their causal contribution to the crime. Moreover, there is no express sentencing provision in international criminal justice which would require a more lenient sentence for an accessory than a principal. Ordinary concepts of criminal law may have to be adjusted in the context of international crimes.

2.4.1 Collective vs. Individual Responsibility as Perpetrator

The dilemma of allocating responsibility beyond the physical perpetrator has led to an expansion of theories of commission liability, and other forms of liability. It is controversial under what circumstances an individual who is physically and structurally distant from the direct commission of a crime may be held accountable as a perpetrator for collective forms of action.

A lot of intellectual effort has been invested to clarify the concept of joint perpetration. There has been a strong trend to hold senior leaders accountable as co-perpetrators, rather than under other forms of liability, i.e. as planner, instigator, aiders and abettors or superiors. There are two main theories. One theory, joint criminal enterprise (JCE),[99] emphasizes the subjective element of crimes, namely the intention or agreement to take part in a criminal enterprise. The second theory stresses objective elements, namely the control over the crime.[100] Both theories ascribe the crime to the perpetrator, even though it may have been brought about collectively.

---

[96] See N. Lacey, *In Search of Criminal Responsibility: Ideas, Interests, and Institutions* (Oxford: Oxford University Press, 2016).

[97] Guilfoyle, 'Responsibility for Collective Atrocities', 261.

[98] See *Tadić* 1999, para. 192.

[99] See generally S. Powles 'Joint Criminal Enterprise: Criminal Liability by Prosecutorial Ingenuity and Judicial Creativity?' (2004) 2 *JICJ* 606; V. Haan, 'The Development of the Concept of Joint Criminal Enterprise at the International Criminal Tribunal for the Former Yugoslavia' (2005) 5 *International Criminal Law Review* 167; E. van Sliedregt, 'Joint Criminal Enterprise as a Pathway to Convicting Individuals for Genocide' (2007) 5 *JICJ* 184; H. van der Wilt, 'Joint Criminal Enterprise: Possibilities and Limitations' (2007) 5 *JICJ* 91.

[100] See J. Ohlin, E. van Sliedregt and T. Weigend, 'Assessing the Control Theory' (2013) 26 *LJIL* 725; N. Jain, 'The Control Theory of Perpetration in International Criminal Law' (2011) 12 *Chicago Journal of International Law* 159.

2.4.1.1 *Joint Criminal Enterprise*

Mass atrocities typically require collective organization and division of labour. As the late Judge Antonio Cassese argued, the JCE doctrine was meant to enable international courts to establish responsibility for the masterminds of mass atrocities.[101] Its main advantage is that it accommodates the risks posed by non-hierarchical structures of power and diverse contributions to international crimes, covering a wide range of contributions to crimes that go beyond classical forms of domination or control. It relies essentially on the intellectual design, namely the contribution to a common plan or purpose, as the foundation of responsibility. It does not require express articulation, but ties responsibility to participation in a criminal enterprise. This focus extends responsibility to mid- and high-ranking political and military leaders that lack immediate control over the crime, but contribute to it, through coordination or participation in the collective enterprise.

This theory has some contested and some uncontested elements. The uncontested example is attribution of liability in the framework of a functional division of criminal tasks. For instance, if multiple individuals acting with a common purpose embark on criminal activity (i.e. to kill someone), and all of them share that criminal intent, it is reasonable to hold all of them accountable for the result, even though their individual contribution to that result may differ (so-called JCE 1).[102] A similar logic applies if that functional division is carried out in a large systemic setting. If several persons run an organized system of ill-treatment, such as a concentration camp, or a detention centre where persons are mistreated, and each of the members shares the purpose to further this criminal activity, all of them may be held accountable (so-called JCE II).[103]

It is more controversial to what extent a person may be held accountable for consequences that were not directly part of a criminal plan but occurred as a 'natural and foreseeable consequence' of the criminal enterprise (so-called JCE III) if the person willingly took that risk.[104] JCE II has been justified on grounds of public policy, namely: 'the need to protect society against persons who band together to take part in criminal enterprises and, whilst not sharing the criminal intent of those participants who intend to commit more serious crimes outside the common enterprise'.[105] Such a form of collective attribution raises problems in relation to personal culpability (*nullum crimen sine culpa*). It fails to distinguish coincidental from coordinated action. The defendant may easily be held accountable as a perpetrator of a crime, although the corresponding *mens rea* is absent. As a consequence, it has been rightly argued that JCE III should not be applied in relation to specific-intent crimes.[106]

---

[101] A. Cassese, 'The Proper Limits of Individual Responsibility under the Doctrine of Joint Criminal Enterprise' (2007) 5 *JICJ* 109.
[102] *Tadić* 1999, para. 196 et seq.
[103] Ibid., para. 202 et seq.
[104] Ibid., para. 204 et seq.
[105] STL, Interlocutory Appeal Applicable Law, para. 245.
[106] The Appeals Chamber at the STL clarified that an accused cannot be found guilty of international crimes that require special intent, such as genocide and terrorism, under JCE III. See STL, Interlocutory Appeal Applicable Law, para. 249.

Under classical JCE cases, common plan or purpose was inferred by criteria such as an organized structure (e.g. specialized military units with a criminal purpose) or proximity to the scene of the crime (e.g. shooting of prisoners of war). The modern reading of JCE is more undetermined. Conviction depends essentially on the formulation of the criminal enterprise. The more broadly the JCE is formulated, the more likely it is that the defendant will be convicted for some type of contribution to that criminal purpose. JCE easily becomes a tool to 'just convict' them all.[107] A major criticism is that it places 'big' and 'little fish' under one umbrella of perpetration. It blurs the line to accessorial liability by making it harder to become an accessory than a participant in a JCE. In practice, JCE thus dealt less with leadership responsibility than contribution to the realization of a common criminal plan.

JCE III was repeatedly invoked in the jurisprudence of the ad hoc tribunals[108] and the SCSL, but rejected by the ECCC. The ECCC openly questioned whether the World War II authorities and Italian cases cited by *Tadić* supported the customary nature.[109] None of the twelve Nazi trials conducted under Control Council Law No. 10 adopted the concept of liability for foreseeable acts.[110] It is therefore questionable to what extent JCE III reflects 'customary law'. The continued affirmation of its customary nature by tribunals itself does not suffice to turn it into custom.

2.4.1.2 The Control Theory

A second theory bases responsibility on various forms of control.[111] Its advantage lies in the fact that it ties responsibility to objective factors such as contribution and control over the act. It seeks to avoid that defendants are blamed for the collective context in which they operate, rather than their individual culpability.

The control theory was developed in German criminal law doctrine after World War II to hold Nazi leaders accountable for atrocities committed in networks of

---

[107] See M. Elewa Badar, '"Just Convict Everyone!" – Joint Perpetration: From Tadić to Stakić and Back Again' (2006) 6 *International Criminal Law Review* 293. Critically also M. Sassòli and L. M. Olson, 'The Judgment of the ICTY Appeals Chamber on the Merits in the Tadic Case' (2000) 839 *International Review of the Red Cross* 739; J. D. Ohlin, 'Three Conceptual Problems with the Doctrine of Joint Criminal Enterprise' (2007) 5 *JICJ* 69; K. Ambos, 'Joint Criminal Enterprise and Command Responsibility' (2007) 5 *JICJ* 159, 174; A. M. Danner and J. S. Martinez, 'Guilty Associations: Joint Criminal Enterprise, Command Responsibility and the Development of International Criminal Law' (2005) 9 *California Law Review* 150. A counter-argument is that that the lesser degree of culpability should 'be taken into account at the sentencing stage'. STL, Interlocutory Appeal Applicable Law, para. 245.

[108] At least four JCE III convictions have been upheld on appeal: *Tadić*, *Krstić*, *Stakić* and *Martić*.

[109] ECCC, *Prosecutor v. Chea, Sary, Thirith, and Samphan*, 002/19–09–2007-ECCC-OCIJ, Decision on the Appeals Against the Co-Investigating Judges Order on Joint Criminal Enterprise, 20 May 2010, paras. 79–82. See L. Marsh and M. Ramsden, 'Joint Criminal Enterprise: Cambodia's Reply to Tadić' (2011) 11 *International Criminal Law Review* 137.

[110] L. Yanev, 'The Theory of Joint Criminal Enterprise at the ECCC: A Difficult Relationship', in S. Meisenberg and I. Stegmiller (eds.), *The Extraordinary Chambers in the Courts of Cambodia* (The Hague: TMC Asser Press, 2016), 203, 253.

[111] Jain, 'The Control Theory of Perpetration in International Criminal Law' 158. An ICTY Trial Chamber sought to introduce the doctrine of indirect co-perpetration as an alternative to JCE. *Prosecutor v. Stakić*, IT-92–24-T, Judgment, 31 July 2003, paras. 440–441. But it was overruled on appeal.

power.[112] It has seen a revival in international criminal justice in certain domestic cases and ICC jurisprudence.[113]

2.4.1.2.1 Control over the Crime

The framing of modes of liability under the ICC Statute[114] draws on influences of the Romano-Germanic tradition, Anglo-American law (e.g. 'common purpose') and international jurisprudence, as well as certain constructive ambiguities. In *Lubanga*, the ICC grounded co-perpetration 'in the principle of the division of essential tasks for the purpose of committing a crime'.[115] It related responsibility as a perpetrator to the essential nature of the contribution, namely 'the power to frustrate the commission of the crime'. It stated:

> [W]hen the objective elements of an offence are carried out by a plurality of persons acting within the framework of a common plan, only those to whom essential tasks have been assigned – and who, consequently, have the power to frustrate the commission of the crime by not performing their tasks – can be said to have joint control over the crime.[116]

This theory captures perpetrators who control or mastermind crimes, although they are removed from the scene of the crime and do not personally perform any of the acts required by the offence. But it excludes responsibility for participants whose contribution in a collective enterprise is non-essential for the commission of the crime.

This theory is more favourable towards defendants in terms of 'fair labelling'. But it remains entrenched in the idea that criminality results mainly from abuse of power and hierarchy, rather than role orientation and/or value orientation. It is limited in its perception of social reality. It analyses human interaction in collective networks primarily in terms of relationships of domination/subordination. Critics have noted that it may limit the prospects of prosecuting less ordered or controlled forms of violence, such as sexual violence,[117] since it focuses responsibility on those who 'conceived the crime, oversaw its preparation at different hierarchical levels, and controlled its performance and execution'.[118]

2.4.1.2.2 Organizational Control

The 'control over the crime' theory struggles to deal with certain decentralized authority and collaboration. For instance, in *Katanga* and *Ngudjolo* the two defendants could only commit offences through joint action of forces under their

---

[112] C. Roxin, *Täterschaft und Tatherrschaft*, 1st ed. (Berlin: De Gruyter, 1963).
[113] Ohlin et al., 'Assessing the Control-Theory'. For a critique, see J. G. Stewart, 'The End of Modes of Liability for International Crimes' (2012) 25 *LJIL* 165.
[114] G. Werle, 'Individual Criminal Responsibility in Article 25 of the ICC Statute' (2007) 5 *JICJ* 953.
[115] *Prosecutor* v. *Lubanga*, ICC-01/04–01/06, Decision on the confirmation of charges, 29 January 2007, para. 342.
[116] *Lubanga* Trial Judgment, para. 989.
[117] S. Sacouto, 'The Impact of the Appeals Chamber Decision in Bemba: Impunity for Sexual and Gender-Based Crimes?', International Justice Monitor, 22 June 2018, at www.ijmonitor.org/2018/06/the-impact-of-the-appeals-chamber-decision-in-bemba-impunity-for-sexual-and-gender-based-crimes/.
[118] *Katanga* Trial Judgment, para. 1412.

command.[119] This typology was not captured by the strict *Lubanga* conception of perpetration.

The ICC relied on a variation of the control theory to establish liability as a perpetrator. It confirmed that individuals can be held accountable as indirect perpetrators (*'Täter hinter dem Täter'*) for crimes executed by others by virtue of the systemic pressures.[120] Indirect perpetration is typically tied to control over the 'will' of another person. The ICC adopted the concept of organizational control (*Organisationsherrschaft*)[121] originally conceived by German scholar Claus Roxin.[122] This doctrine takes into account dangers that may arise from the use of disciplined organizations for criminal ends. It failed to gain ground in the jurisprudence of the ad hoc tribunals and the STL. The ICC held that perpetrators may commit crimes through functional authority over organizations under their control. It extended the scope of the doctrine from governmental structures (e.g. Nazi administration) to contemporary networks of criminality.[123] This construction marks one of the most far-reaching cases of development of core concepts of modes of liability based on German scholarly doctrine.[124]

The organizational control doctrine is grounded in the idea of abuse of power in the functioning of an organization. It recognizes that organizational control may compensate for the lack of immediate control by superiors over executive agents in hierarchy-based power structures. Liability is linked to functionalist considerations, i.e. the nature and internal systemic dynamics of the organization,[125] and actual control and authority (*'réelle autorité'*) over the events leading to the crime.[126] Organizational control may arise from factors such as 'quasi-automatic' compliance with orders inside the organization leading to their execution,[127] and the fungible nature ('inter-changeability')[128] of the members of the organization in the execution of crimes.

The ICC combined these different types of liability, namely co-perpetration and perpetration through an organization.[129] This implies that leaders may not only be

---

[119] *Katanga and Chui* Confirmation Decision, para. 498.

[120] See generally T. Weigend, 'Indirect Perpetration', in Stahn, *Law and Practice of the International Criminal Court*, 538; G. Werle and B. Burghardt, 'Indirect Perpetration: A Perfect Fit for International Prosecution of Armchair Killers?' (2011) 9 *JICJ* 85 Critics claim that 'perpetration cannot be indirect'. See Guilfole, 'Responsibility for Collective Atrocities', 279.

[121] For a full discussion, see Ambos, *Treatise on International Criminal Law, Vol. I*, 114–118.

[122] C. Roxin, 'Crimes as Part of Organized Power Structures' (2011) 9 *JICJ* 191–205, translated and reprinted from 'Straftaten im Rahmen organisatorischer Machtapparate' (1963) *Goltdammer's Archiv für Strafrecht* 193–207.

[123] See *Katanga* Trial Judgment, para. 1410 ('this type of structure … is not … inconsistent with the very varied manifestations of modern-day group criminality wherever it arises. It cannot be reduced solely to bureaucracies akin to those of Third Reich Germany and which lie at the root of the theory').

[124] For a discussion, see T. Weigend, 'Perpetration through an Organization: The Unexpected Career of a German Legal Concept' (2011) 9 *JICJ* 91; K. Ambos, 'A Workshop, a Symposium and the Katanga Trial Judgment of 7 March 2014' (2014) 12 *JICJ* 219, 227–228.

[125] *Katanga* Trial Judgment, para. 1410.

[126] Ibid., para. 1412.

[127] See on this also *Katanga and Ngudjolo Chui* Confirmation Decision, paras. 515 et seq.

[128] *Katanga* Trial Judgment, para. 1408.

[129] See *Katanga and Chui* Confirmation Decision, para. 492 ('through a combination of individual responsibility for committing crimes through other persons together with the mutual attribution among the co-perpetrators at the senior level, a mode of liability arises which allows the Court to assess the blame worthiness of "senior Leaders" adequately').

responsible for the criminal conduct of organizations under their command, but also for crimes committed by organizational structures headed by their collaborators. For instance, leader X can be held accountable for crimes committed by agents under the control of leader Y, although leader X lacks such control. The result is not very far from the doctrine of joint criminal enterprise.[130] This mutual attribution of liability across different lines of authority or command covers a wide spectrum of criminality. It makes it easier for the Prosecution to establish links between leadership authority and crimes of lower-ranking perpetrators.

2.4.2   Other Forms of Liability

International criminal law foresees a number of other modes of liability that complement commission liability. In most cases, the dilemma is not how to establish a link to the crime, but to identify the proper one.

There are various forms of participation, including soliciting or inducing the commission of a crime, aiding or abetting, or common-purpose liability. This type of liability raises difficult questions in relation to the feasible scope of criminalization. For instance, it remains controversial to what extent financial assistance or other types of assistance provided by external actors to parties to a conflict or to civilians come within the scope of criminal liability if they are carried out with the aim of relieving suffering. The tendency has been to constrain legal constructs, rather than to broaden them.[131]

The scope of aiding and abetting liability has been subject to significant dispute. The main question has been whether it requires that the accomplice had the purpose or desire to facilitate the underlying offence. The SCSL ruled that the *mens rea* for aiding and abetting requires only knowledge and not purpose, namely that 'the accused knew that his acts would assist the commission of the crime by the perpetrator or that he was aware of the substantial likelihood that his acts would assist the commission of a crime by the perpetrator'.[132] The ad hoc tribunals have struggled to identify the relevant test. In *Perišić*, the Appeals Chamber upheld a 'specific direction' test.[133] It held that 'assistance from one army to another army's war efforts is insufficient, in itself, to trigger individual criminal liability for individual aid providers absent proof that the relevant assistance was specifically directed towards

---

For a discussion, see N. Jain, 'Individual Responsibility for Mass Atrocity: In Search of a Concept of Perpetration' (2013) 61 *American Journal of Comparative Law* 831, 870.

[130] S. Manacorda and C. Meloni, 'Indirect Perpetration versus Joint Criminal Enterprise: Concurring Approaches in the Practice of International Criminal Law?' (2011) 9 *JICJ* 151.

[131] For a discussion, see N. Jain, *Perpetrators and Accessories in International Criminal Law* (Oxford: Hart, 2014); M. Aksenova, *Complicity in International Criminal Law* (Oxford: Hart, 2016).

[132] *Brima et al.* Appeal Judgment, paras. 242–243.

[133] *Prosecutor* v. *Perišić*, IT-04–81-A, Judgment, 28 February 2013, para. 36 (Perišić Appeal Judgment). For a critique, see A. Coco and T. Gal, 'Losing Direction: The ICTY Appeals Chamber's Controversial Approach to Aiding and Abetting in Perišić' (2014) 12 *JICJ* 345.

criminal activities'.[134] It introduced a distinction between acts that are 'geographically or otherwise proximate to' the crimes of principal perpetrators, and acts that are 'remote'.[135] It acquitted Perišić because it could not be established that he aided and abetted the Army of the Republika Srpska with the specific aim of helping the group to commit crimes. This test was partly driven by the desire to leave powerful states some flexibility to be involved in future conflicts, without fearing risks of criminalization.[136] It was criticized by the Appeals Chamber of the SCSL in the *Taylor* judgment[137] and in a dissent by Judge Liu. He stated:

Given that specific direction has not been applied in past cases with any rigor, to insist on such a requirement now effectively raises the threshold for aiding and abetting liability. This shift risks undermining the very purpose of aiding and abetting liability by allowing those responsible for knowingly facilitating the most grievous crimes to evade responsibility for their acts.[138]

The requirement that the accused's assistance must be specifically directed towards the criminal conduct was later reversed by a different Appeals Chamber in *Šainović*.[139] It found that *Perišić* had erred in finding that specific direction was a part of customary international law.[140] This has important consequences for practice. State agents or other actors which provide assistance to another state or non-state armed group might be held accountable for war crimes even if they do not have the express intent or purpose to promote such crimes.

The ICC Statute is peculiar in this respect. It sets a high threshold for aiding and abetting liability that is unique to the jurisdictional regime of the ICC and not necessarily reflective of customary international law. It must be shown that the contribution was made 'for the purpose of facilitating the commission' of a crime.[141] Furthermore, ICC practice has required substantial assistance to the crime.[142] This typically excludes lawful types of assistance and/or contributions that, by their nature, could equally have contributed to a legitimate purpose. For instance, contributions by humanitarian organizations to evacuations would be excluded.

---

[134] *Perišić* Appeal Judgment, para. 72.
[135] Ibid., para. 38.
[136] See C. B. Eby, 'Aid "Specifically Directed" to Facilitate War Crimes: The ICTY's Anomalous Actus Reus Standard for Aiding and Abetting' (2015) 14 *Chicago Journal of International Law* 256, 280.
[137] *Prosecutor* v. *Taylor*, SCSL-03–01-A, Judgment, 26 September 2013, para. 477 ('the ICTY Appeals Chamber's jurisprudence does not contain a clear, detailed analysis of the authorities supporting the conclusion that specific direction is an element of the *actus reus* of aiding and abetting liability under customary international law').
[138] *Perišić* Appeal Judgment, Partially Dissenting Opinion of Judge Liu, para. 3.
[139] *Prosecutor* v. *Šainović et al.*, IT-05–87-A, Judgment, 23 January 2014 (*Šainović et al.* Appeal Judgment).
[140] *Šainović et al.* Appeal Judgment, paras. 1617, 1650 (rejecting 'the approach adopted in the *Perišić* Appeal Judgement as it is in direct and material conflict with the prevailing jurisprudence on the *actus reus* of aiding and abetting liability and with customary international law').
[141] Rome Statute, Art. 25 (3) (c). The implications of this qualifier is contested. Some argue that it requires shared intent between accessory and principal. Others claim that a certain degree of knowledge is sufficient to establish the purpose requirement since it is related to the consequences of a person's conduct.
[142] *Prosecutor* v. *Mbarushimana*, ICC-01/04–01/10. Decision on the Confirmation of Charges, 16 December 2011, para. 279 (*Mbarushimana* Confirmation Decision).

The ICC Statute encompasses a different form of accessory liability: common purpose liability. It is 'akin to JCE'.[143] It captures responsibility for any other contribution made to a crime by a 'group of persons acting with a common purpose' that is 'made in the knowledge of the intention of the group to commit the crime'. This liability is so broad that judges have voluntarily constrained it to 'significant' contributions.[144] James Stewart has rightly referred to this as an 'overdetermination problem' of international criminal justice.[145] This threshold requirement was introduced to prevent 'every landlord, every grocer, every utility provider, every secretary, every janitor or even every taxpayer who does anything which contributes to a group committing international crimes' coming within the ambit of Article 25 (3) (d).[146]

International criminal law lacks a separate provision for financial complicity in international crimes. The only express provision is in the Terrorist Financing Convention. It prohibits the provision or collection of funds with the intent to commit an 'act of terrorism', or assist another to do so, as a separate offence, irrespective of whether the funds were actually used to carry out such an act (inchoate offence).[147]

All major legal instruments contain a mode of liability that is unique to international criminal justice: superior responsibility.[148] This liability is based on the idea that failure to prevent criminal action by a person in a position of authority creates a serious danger. It has a dual basis. It is related to the idea of dereliction of duty which is a crime in many military codes, and complicity in the crimes of subordinates. Its legal nature has been disputed. Some argue that it is mainly a form of liability for omission, rather than a form of participation in the crimes of others.[149] Others regard it as a *sui generis* type of responsibility.[150] It contains elements of omission and imputed liability. Superiors must answer for crimes of subordinates if they culpably violate duties of control.

In many contemporary contexts, military or administrative authority is highly decentralized. A superior cannot be deemed to know every detail of the operation of subordinates. The essence of the concept was described as follows at Nuremberg:

Criminality does not attach to every individual in this chain of command from that fact alone. There must be a personal dereliction. That can occur only where the act is directly traceable to him or where his failure to properly supervise his subordinates constitutes criminal negligence

---

[143] J. D. Ohlin, 'Joint Criminal Confusion' (2009) 12 *New Criminal Law Review* 406.

[144] *Mbarushimana* Confirmation Decision, para. 285.

[145] See J. Stewart, 'Overdetermined Atrocities' (2012) 10 *JICJ* 1189–1218.

[146] *Mbarushimana* Confirmation Decision, para. 277.

[147] Art. 2 of the Terrorist Financing Convention.

[148] G. Mettraux, *The Law of Command Responsibility* (Oxford: Oxford University Press, 2009); V. Nerlich, 'Superior Responsibility under Article 28 ICC Statute' (2007) 5 *JICJ* 665.

[149] For instance, the ICTY has argued that under superior responsibility, 'an accused is not charged with the crimes of his subordinates but with the failure to carry out his duty as a superior to exercise control'. See *Prosecutor* v. *Krnojelac*, IT-97-25-A, Judgment, 17 September 2003, para. 171. See also *Prosecutor* v. *Oric*, IT-03-68-A, Judgment, 3 July 2008, Declaration of Judge Shahabuddeen, para. 24.

[150] See *Prosecutor* v. *Bemba*, ICC-01/05-01/08, Judgment Pursuant to Article 74 of the Statute, 21 March 2016, para. 174 (*Bemba* Trial Judgment).

on his part. In the latter case it must be a personal neglect amounting to a wanton, immoral disregard of the action of his subordinates amounting to acquiescence.[151]

The advantage of this doctrine is that it provides a basis for accountability in cases where there is a lack of evidence of direct responsibility of the superior (e.g. lack of direct orders). However, it poses dilemmas in relation to the 'actor's own personal culpability', in particular in cases where superiors are held responsible for negligent failure.[152] A famous illustration is the case against General Tomoyuki Yamashita, the commander of the Japanese Army in the Philippines, before US Courts. *Yamashita* had partly lost control over his troops in World War II. The majority of the US Supreme Court held that a military commander has an 'affirmative duty to take such measures as were within his power and appropriate in the circumstances to protect prisoners of war and the civilian population'.[153] It grounded this duty in the 'purpose to protect civilian populations and prisoners of war from brutality' and excesses.[154] This wide interpretation came close to strict liability for crimes of subordinates. The minority argued that *Yamashita* was convicted for 'the crime of inefficiency in controlling [his] troops'.[155]

Subsequent case law has restricted the 'shadow' of the *Yamahita* doctrine.[156] For instance, the ICTY has repeatedly stated that a superior is only criminally responsible 'if information was available to him which would have put him on notice of offences committed by subordinates'[157] and that '[n]eglect of a duty to acquire such knowledge' is not an offence per se,[158] but only punishable if it amounts to a failure to take necessary and reasonable measures to prevent or to punish.[159] It also clarified that superior responsibility 'does not mean that the commander shares the same responsibility as the subordinates who committed the crimes'.[160] Accordingly, a 'commander is responsible not as though he had committed the crime himself, but his responsibility is considered in proportion to the gravity of the offences committed'.[161] The scope of application of the concept was extended over time. Historically, it was mostly applied in classical army contexts. For instance, the Tokyo Tribunal held Prime Minister Hideki Tojo and Foreign Minister Mamoru Shigemitsu liable for omissions to prevent or punish the criminal acts of the Japanese troops. At the time, the conviction of

---

[151] *United States* v. *Wilhelm von Leeb et al.* (High Command Case), United States Military Tribunal sitting in Nuremberg, reprinted in *Law Reports of Trials of War Criminals, Selected and Prepared by the United Nations War Crimes Commission*, Vol. XII (London: HMSO, 1949), 74–76.

[152] M. Damaška, 'The Shadow Side of Command Responsibility' (2001) 49 *American Journal of Comparative Law* 445, 456.

[153] US Supreme Court, *In re Yamashita*, Judgment, 4 February 1946, (1946) 327 US 1, 16.

[154] Ibid., 15.

[155] Ibid., 35.

[156] See J. Martinez, 'Understanding Mens Rea in Command Responsibility: From Yamashita to Blaškić and Beyond' (2007) 5 *JICJ* 638, 641; I. Bantekas, 'The Contemporary Law of Superior Responsibility' (1999) 93 *AJIL* 573, 594.

[157] *Prosecutor* v. *Delalić, Mucić and Delić*, IT-96-21-A, Judgment, 20 February 2001, para. 241 (*Čelebići* Appeal Judgment).

[158] *Čelebići* Appeal Judgment, para. 226.

[159] *Prosecutor* v. *Blaškić*, IT-95-14-A, Judgment, 29 July 2004, para. 62.

[160] *Prosecutor* v. *Halilović*, IT-01-48-T, Judgment, 16 November 2005, para. 54.

[161] Ibid.

civilian superiors remained controversial.[162] In modern jurisprudence, the concept was gradually extended since boundaries between civilian and military persons are often fluid in conflict. The SCSL made clear that superior responsibility is applicable to structures of authority in 'irregular armies or rebel groups'.[163] The ad hoc tribunals specified that it covers civilian superiors acting in military settings. In the *Čelebići* case, the ICTY applied the doctrine to commanders of prison camps who detained combatants and civilians. It argued that superior responsibility attaches to 'individuals in non-military positions of superior authority'[164] 'to the extent that they exercise *a degree of control over their subordinates which is similar to that of military commanders*'.[165] It argued that the criterion is whether the civilian superior has the 'material ability to prevent and punish the commission of these offences'.[166] This captures civilian leaders and public officials who lead military or paramilitary forces or ministers with authority over security forces.

The limits of the *Čelebići* doctrine were tested by the SCSL in a case against Allieu Kondewa,[167] the high priest and spiritual master of the Civil Defence Forces. In this case, doctrines of control grounded in 'rational, Western, civilized modernity' clashed with 'mysticism, a symbol of pre-colonial African primitivism'.[168] Kondewa's authority exceeded classical notions of control. The Trial Chamber noted:

The Kamajors believed in the mystical powers of the initiators, especially Kondewa, and that the process of the initiation and immunisation would make them 'bullet-proof'. The Kamajors looked up to Kondewa and admired the man with such powers. They believed that he was capable of transferring his powers to them to protect them. Because of the mystical powers Kondewa possessed, he had command over the Kamajors from every part of the country. No Kamajor would go to war without Kondewa's blessing.[169]

It was questionable whether 'Kondewa's *de jure* status as High Priest of the CDF' gave him a sufficient degree of effective control to meet the threshold of superior responsibility. Kondewa was never at the war front itself. The Chamber denied that mystical powers alone were sufficient to establish a superior–subordinate relationship, since it could not be shown that Kondewa had the 'power to decide who should be

---

[162] See Y. Ronen, 'Superior Responsibility of Civilians for International Crimes Committed in Civilian Settings' (2010) 43 *Vanderbilt Journal of Transnational Law* 313, 322.

[163] See *Brima et al.* Trial Judgment, para. 787.

[164] *Čelebići* Trial Judgment, para. 363.

[165] Ibid., para. 378. For a much wider understanding, see *Prosecutor* v. *Aleksovski*, IT-95-14/1-T, Judgment, 15 June 1999, para. 78 ('Although the power to sanction is the indissociable corollary of the power to issue orders within the military hierarchy, it does not apply to the civilian authorities. It cannot be expected that a civilian authority will have disciplinary power over his subordinate equivalent to that of the military authorities in an analogous command position').

[166] *Čelebići* Trial Judgment, para. 378.

[167] *Prosecutor* v. *Fonfana and Kondewa*, SCSL-04-14-T, Judgment, 2 August 2007 (*Fonfana and Kondewa* Trial Judgment). See generally H. van der Wilt, 'Command Responsibility in the Jungle: Some Reflections on the Elements of Effective Command and Control', in C. Jalloh (ed.), *The Sierra Leone Special Court and its Legacy* (Cambridge: Cambridge University Press, 2014), 144.

[168] R. Provost, 'Magic and Modernity in Tintin au Congo (1930) and the Sierra Leone Special Court' (2012) 16 *Law Text Culture* 183, 199.

[169] *Fonfana and Kondewa* Trial Judgment, para. 346.

deployed to go to the war front'.[170] However, it derived superior responsibility from his de facto status as a superior in the district, which granted him 'legal and material ability to issue orders'.[171] The findings were criticized by Judge King on appeal. He noted:

> Without remarking the novelty of its finding, the Appeals Chamber Majority Opinion, for the first time in the history of international criminal law, has concluded that a civilian Sierra Leonean juju man or witch doctor, who practised fetish, had never been a soldier, had never before been engaged in combat, but was a farmer and a so-called herbalist, who had never before smelt military service can be held to be a commander of subordinates in a bush and guerilla conflict in Sierra Leone, 'by virtue' of his reputed superstitious, mystical, supernatural, and suchlike fictional and fantasy powers.[172]

The concept of superior responsibility was extended to purely civilian settings by the ICTR. In a contested judgment, the Rwanda tribunal convicted the leader of a tea factory for failure to prevent crimes, since he exercised legal and financial control over his employees.[173] This reasoning expanded the scope of application from professional duties in classical disciplinary structures to labour relations or corporate hierarchies (e.g. the power of a superior to terminate contracts or sanction misbehaviour during working hours). It went too far since it implied that company managers may face criminal responsibility for mere managerial failures. As Alexander Zahar has rightly argued: 'it cannot be that all business managers stand liable to be convicted for international crimes perpetrated by their employees for the sole reason that they were only linked to them through commonplace ties of labour'.[174] The ICC Statute contemplates responsibility of military and civilian superiors. It is controversial what types of superior–subordinate relationships in the civilian field are covered. Conceptually, it may be justified to capture certain organizations that are engaged in activities that involve the risk of international crimes (e.g. terrorist groups, criminal networks, illicit business activities).[175] However, extending the duties of civilians too far may be counterproductive since it may overstretch responsibilities of individuals for crimes of others, or even encourage 'private justice'. As rightly acknowledged, it would be absurd to hold the director of a dance group responsible as a superior for failing to prevent crimes by its members.[176]

In *Bemba*, the ICC has adopted a cautious approach in relation to military commanders and non-linear relationships of authority. The Trial Chamber held that

---

[170] Ibid., para. 806.
[171] Ibid., para. 868.
[172] *Prosecutor* v. *Fofana and Kondewa*, SCSL-04-14-A-829, Judgment, 28 May 2008 (*Fofana and Kondewa* Appeal Judgment), Partially Dissenting Opinion of Justice George Gelaga King, para. 69.
[173] *Prosecutor* v. *Alfred Musema*, ICTR-96-13-T, Judgment and Sentence, 27 January 2000, para. 880. For a critique, see A. Zahar, 'Command Responsibility of Civilian Superiors for Genocide' (2001) 14 *LJIL*, 591, 602–603; C. Aptel and J. A. Williamson, 'A Commentary on the Musema Judgment' (2000) 6 *Melbourne Journal of International Law* 131.
[174] Zahar, 'Command Responsibility of Civilian Superiors', 602.
[175] See Ronen, 'Superior Responsibility of Civilians', 353.
[176] *Prosecutor* v. *Bikindi*, ICTR-01-72-T, Judgment, 2 December 2008, para. 412.

'"effective control" requires that the commander have the material ability to prevent or repress the commission of the crimes or to submit the matter to the competent authorities. Any lower degree of control, such as the ability to exercise influence – even substantial influence – over the forces who committed the crimes, would be insufficient to establish command responsibility'.[177] It also clarified that mere participation 'of particular forces in joint combat operations is not sufficient in itself to establish that a commander had effective control over all of the different units participating in the operation'.[178] This finding is important in relation to individual responsibility in multinational combat operations. The Appeals Chamber acquitted *Bemba*, in a dramatic turn away from *Yamashita*. The majority noted that superior responsibility is not meant to establish 'a form of strict liability'. It accepted that judges may have to show a degree of deference in judging behaviour, since '[c]-ommanders are allowed to make a cost/benefit analysis when deciding which measures to take, bearing in mind their overall responsibility to prevent and repress crimes committed by their subordinates'.[179]

The decision triggered a vivid debate on the scope of leadership accountability. Judges Morrison and Van den Wyngaert questioned whether persons in 'high leadership positions' necessarily bear 'the highest levels of moral and legal culpability' in light of differentiated spheres of competence and authority of commanders within structures of shared responsibility.[180] Critics noted that this approach 'turns much of international criminal law theory on its head'[181] and might reduce the prospects of holding senior commanders accountable for crimes of sexual violence. As noted by Judge Chile Eboe-Osuji, 'geographic remoteness' does not necessarily 'insulate' a commander from criminal responsibility, but serves as a criterion to determine whether the commander took the necessary and reasonable measures to prevent and punish the crime.[182]

It is contested to what extent superior responsibility requires a stricter causality test at the ICC than the ad hoc tribunals. The text of the Statute suggests that the crimes of subordinates must occur as 'a result of [the commander's] failure to exercise control properly over such forces'. However, the reading of this requirement depends on whether command responsibility is interpreted as a form of participation in the crime of others or as a duty of responsible command. As rightly argued in *Bemba*, it cannot be understood in the sense of a *strict conditio sine qua* non test, but at best as a contribution to risk.

---

[177] *Bemba* Trial Judgment, para. 183.
[178] Ibid., para. 185.
[179] *Prosecutor* v. *Bemba*, Judgment on the appeal of Mr Jean-Pierre Bemba Gombo against Trial Chamber III's 'Judgment Pursuant to Article 74 of the Statute', ICC-01/05-01/08 A, 8 June 2018, para. 170.
[180] Paras. 35, and 36 ('what the law expects from commanders depends on where they find themselves on the hierarchical ladder').
[181] L. Sadat, 'Fiddling While Rome Burns? The Appeals Chamber's Curious Decision in Prosecutor v. Jean-Pierre Bemba Gombo', *EJIL* Talk, 12 June 2018, at www.ejiltalk.org/fiddling-while-rome-burns-the-appeals-chambers-curious-decision-in-prosecutor-v-jean-pierre-bemba-gombo/.
[182] *Prosecutor* v. *Bemba*, Concurring Separate Opinion of Judge Eboe-Osuji, ICC-01/05-01/08-3636-Anx3, 14 July 2018, para. 258.

2.4.3 Challenges

Individual criminal responsibility has become one of the principal justifications of international criminal law. The focus on the individual and on individual culpability marks a core part of its identity and distinction. It reaffirms that individuals are responsible agents and not only 'cogs' in a machine, and reflects the ambition to attribute blame and restore moral order. Attribution of individual criminal responsibility and the collective nature of crimes remain in constant friction, however.[183] The old dogma that 'crimes against international law are committed by men, not by abstract entities' is open to challenge.[184] As Jens David Ohlin has adequately put it, the law mediates between 'seemingly conflicting *desiderata* ', namely 'recognizing that most atrocities are performed by irreducibly collective endeavours, yet convicting individuals solely for their individual participation in these collective projects'.[185] International criminal law recognizes collective agency in some areas but not others. The contextual elements of crimes, such as aggression, genocide, crimes against humanity or war crimes, are to a large extent based on the assumption that crimes are committed through collectivities and that organizations may exercise agency. However, individualization of blameworthiness prevails in the determination of criminal responsibility. Guilt is individual.[186] The principle of individual culpability warrants that individuals are punished for their own wrongdoing, rather than the wrongdoing of others.

The construction of modes of liability reflects an attempt to draw a balance between individual and collective dimensions of responsibility. It recognizes that organizations are rational agents. The control theory even concedes that individuals can commit crimes through organizations. However, the concept of collective guilt hangs like a sword over international criminal justice. There is reluctance to accept that organizations themselves can commit crimes. The concept of JCE has been criticized for establishing 'guilt by association'.[187]

One of the criticisms is that existing law disregards the collective dynamics of agency. As Kirsten Ainley has argued, international criminal law 'misses much of the significance of the societal nature of the person – the effect of social roles; the non-rational behaviour impelled by human social instincts; the enabling function of groups'.[188] Some scholars suggest this tension be addressed through greater differentiation among the nature of collective entities. In decentralist and pluralist organizational structures it may be more feasible to hold individuals accountable for their own

---

[183] Drumbl, *Atrocity, Punishment, and International Law*, 39.

[184] For a critique of the Nuremberg dictum as 'half truth', see R. Jennings, 'The Pinochet Extradition Case in the English Courts', in L. Boisson de Chazournes and V. Gowlland-Debbas (eds.), *The International Legal System in Quest of Equity and Universality. Liber Amicorum George Abi-Saab* (The Hague: Martinus Nijhoff, 2001), 693.

[185] Ohlin, 'Organizational Criminality', 117.

[186] See H. Arendt, *Responsibility and Judgment* (New York: Schocken Books, 2003), 28–29 ('There is no such thing as collective guilt or collective innocence; guilt and innocence make sense only if applied to individuals').

[187] Danner and Martinez, 'Guilty Associations', 75.

[188] See K. Ainley, 'Responsibility for Atrocity: Individual Criminal Agency and the International Criminal Court', in J. Parry (ed.), *Evil, Law and the State: Perspectives on State Power and Violence* (Amsterdam and New York: Rodopi, 2006), 143, 155.

individual contributions.[189] Others argue that international criminal law should devote greater attention to the collective forms of responsibility, e.g. the responsibility of organizations and juridical persons as such.[190] Yet others argue that collective agency may in some instances be a mitigating factor since perpetrators of international crime typically act in the service of certain role models, as state representatives, members of formal or informal armed forces, or other collectives.[191]

The principle of individual criminal responsibility must thus be applied with caution. International criminal law provides a 'vocabulary to structure and understand international political violence',[192] but it struggles to articulate legal forms that express the collective nature of criminal action and still individualize blame.[193] The fact that international crimes are often committed in conformity with locally accepted norms, rather than in defiance of them, requires a holistic perspective on responsibility. Both collective and individual lenses are needed.

2.5   Grounds Excluding Criminal Responsibility

The idea of individual responsibility is inherently connected to the ability of the individual to act differently. In specific circumstances, legal systems may condone or excuse what is formally required by law. For instance, in domestic law it is widely accepted that lack of choice in relation to conduct (e.g. inability to avoid the crime, unavailability of other options)[194] or the lack of capacity of the agent[195] to comply with the law may reduce or eliminate culpability. International criminal law allows a number of grounds excluding criminal responsibility.[196] They challenge the clear division of the law between bad and evil. They acknowledge that punishment is only justified if the underlying act is unwarranted and the offender blameworthy. The framing of such grounds poses particular challenges in light of the collective nature of system criminality, the context of violence, and the focus of international criminal justice on leadership responsibility.

---

[189] Steer, *Translating Guilt*, 13, 18.

[190] For pleas in favour of corporate criminal responsibility, see R. C. Slye, 'Corporations, Veils, and International Criminal Liability' (2008) 33 *Brooklyn Journal of International Law* 955, 961; C. Kaeb, 'The Shifting Sands of Corporate Liability under International Criminal Law' (2016) 49 *George Washington International Law Review* 351. On moral agency of collective entities, see T. Erskine, 'Kicking Bodies and Damning Souls: The Danger of Harming "Innocent" Individuals while Punishing "Delinquent" States' (2010) 24 *Ethics and International Affairs* 261–285.

[191] For instance, George Fletcher has argued for mitigation of individual punishment in case of atrocities committed by collectives. See Fletcher, 'The Storrs Lectures', 1543.

[192] Ainley, 'Responsibility for Atrocity', 157.

[193] See S. Ashenden, 'The Persistence of Collective Guilt' (2014) 43 *Economy and Society* 55–82.

[194] On the choice theory, see C. Finkelstein, 'Excuses and Dispositions in Criminal Law' (2002) 6 *Buffalo Criminal Law Review* 317.

[195] On the capacity theory, see V. Tadros, *Criminal Responsibility* (Oxford: Oxford University Press, 2005), 9, 45.

[196] See generally S. Darcy, 'Defences to International Crimes', in W. A. Schabas and N. Bernaz (eds.), *Handbook of International Criminal Law* (London: Routledge 2011), 231–245; K. Ambos, 'Defences in International Criminal Law', in B. S. Brown (ed.), *Research Handbook on International Criminal Law* (Cheltenham: Elgar 2011); M. Scaliotti, 'Defences Before the International Criminal Court: Substantive Grounds for Excluding Criminal Responsibility – Part I' (2001) 1 *International Criminal Law Review* 111; G. A. Knoops, *Defenses in Contemporary International Criminal Law*, 2nd ed. (Leiden: Brill, 2008).

2.5.1 Context

Acknowledging grounds excluding individual accountability stands in tension with the normative ambition to end impunity and promote a culture of accountability.[197] International crimes are systemic, organized and stretched out over time. This makes it difficult to justify or excuse them, morally or on legal grounds. Grounds excluding criminal responsibility have played a more limited role in international criminal law than in traditional domestic law. In practice, they have only been invoked in exceptional cases. International criminal practice has been mostly concerned with top- or mid-level perpetrators. These defendants preferred to challenge the basis for conviction, rather than providing justifications or excuses for their behaviour. In many cases, those charged influenced the underlying policies or acts leading to the commission of crimes. This makes it difficult to rely on coercive factors.[198] The cognitive and volitional elements of criminal responsibility, namely knowledge and appreciation of wrongfulness by offenders, are more difficult to evaluate in light of the context.[199]

As Antonio Cassese has cautioned: 'law is based on what society can reasonably expect of its members. It should not set intractable standards of behaviour which require mankind to perform acts of martyrdom, and brand as criminal any behaviour falling below those standards'.[200] One of the particular characteristics of atrocity crime is that it is often in conformity with the local rules or expectations, rather than in defiance of them.[201] What may be 'abnormal' to an outside observer may appear 'normal' in the respective context. As Mark Drumbl has argued, participating in atrocity may often be 'a matter of obeying official authority' rather than discarding it,[202] because it is legalized, implicitly endorsed or rationalized through peer pressure.

2.5.2 Approaches

In contemporary practice, defences have been interpreted narrowly, in light of the nature of crimes.[203] Limited space has been provided to the recognition of the context in the determination of defences, due to the 'extraordinary' nature of international crimes and their impact on global community interests. If permitted at all, defences are most likely to succeed in relation to war crimes.

---

[197] See A. Eser, 'Grounds Excluding Criminal Responsibility', in Triffterer and Ambos, *Rome Statute of the International Criminal Court*, 1132.

[198] See Ambos, *Treatise on International Criminal Law, Vol. I*, 360 ['t]he general structure of the defence ... implies, on a factual level, pressure or coercion from "top to bottom"'. In other words, the people at the top cannot invoke duress because they cannot be coerced').

[199] I. Xavier, 'The Incongruity of the Rome Statute Insanity Defence and International Crime' (2016) 14 *JICJ* 793, 798.

[200] ICTY, *Prosecutor v. Erdemović*, IT-96-22-A, Judgment, 7 October 1997, Separate and Dissenting Opinion of Judge Cassese, para. 47. (*Erdemović* Appeal Judgment).

[201] Drumbl, *Atrocity, Punishment, and International Law*, 8.

[202] Ibid., 24.

[203] The Nuremberg judgment found: '[s]uperior orders, even to a soldier, cannot be considered in mitigation when crimes as shocking and extensive have been committed consciously, ruthlessly and without military excuse or justification', in (1947) 41 *AJIL* 283.

Historically, defendants have raised different types of arguments, namely that they have acted based on orders or instructions from others, that they were forced by circumstances, or that the conduct was necessary for military purposes.[204] These grounds have been restricted over time. The Nuremberg Charter and the Statutes of the ad hoc tribunals contained an absolute liability rule in relation to superior orders: an order is no defence, but at best a mitigating factor in punishment, irrespective of the nature of the crime.[205] Military necessity was formulated as an element of specific crimes in statutory instruments, rather than a defence of its own. The argument that violations may be justified in retaliation for breaches of the law by others has been discarded in light of the non-reciprocal nature of the obligations.[206] Other defences were developed based on general principles of law.

Approaches diverge among legal systems. In common law systems, the notion of defences refers to a broader set of grounds that a defendant may invoke in order to avoid liability.[207] Many Romano-Germanic systems distinguish between justifications which exclude wrongfulness of conduct and excuses which negate the blameworthiness of wrongful action.[208] The ICC Statute marked the first attempt to reconcile these different traditions and to formulate a framework related to international crimes specifically. It avoids taking a stance in this doctrinal debate by using the broad notion of 'grounds excluding criminal responsibility'. It expressly lists different two types of grounds.

A first set of grounds excludes responsibility due to the deficits in the ability of the offender to act autonomously, namely lack of mental capacity, and intoxication. These grounds relate to the individual qualities of the person concerned. A second category of grounds relates to the act of the individual, and the circumstances under which this act is committed. They include self-defence and duress. All of these grounds impede the freedom of choice of the person and mental elements of crimes, such as knowledge or intent. The Statute is formulated in a hybrid way.[209] It does not formally specify whether a recognized ground qualifies as a bar to responsibility, a justification or an excuse. Rather, the determination of the consequences was left to the judges.

---

[204] *Law Report of Trials of War Criminals*, Vol. XIV, XV (London: His Majesty's Stationery Office, 1949), 156.

[205] As Zahar and Sluiter have noted: 'Persons accused before the tribunals are senior military or civilian leaders, or, if low-ranking, they are accused of very serious crimes. In neither case can they have been unaware of the illegal nature of the orders resulting in the alleged crimes. If they did perform the acts they are accused of pursuant to orders, then they (or any reasonable person in their position) would have realized that the orders were illegal'. A. Zahar and G. Sluiter, *International Criminal Law: A Critical Introduction* (Oxford: Oxford University Press, 2007) 425.

[206] *Prosecutor* v. *Kupreškić et al.*, IT-95-16-T, Judgment, 14 January 2000, para. 517 (*Kupreškić et al.* Trial Judgment).

[207] For a discussion, see G. P. Fletcher, *The Grammar of Criminal Law: American, Comparative, and International*, Vol. I: Foundations (Oxford: Oxford University Press, 2007), 46.

[208] See generally, H. van der Wilt, 'Justifications and Excuses in International Criminal Law: An Assessment of the Case-Law of the ICTY', in B. Swart, A. Zahar and G. Sluiter (eds.), *The Legacy of the International Criminal Tribunal for the Former Yugoslavia* (Oxford: Oxford University Press, 2011), 275; M. Joyce, 'Duress: From Nuremberg to the International Criminal Court, Finding the Balance Between Justification and Excuse' (2015) 28 *LJIL* 623–642; B. Krebs, 'Justification and Excuse in Article 31 (1) of the Rome Statute' (2010) 2 *Cambridge Journal of International and Comparative Law* 382–410.

[209] Fletcher has argued that, in classifying defences, 'the [analytical] model of the common law prevails in the design of the substantive law applicable in the ICC'. See Fletcher, *Grammar of Criminal Law, Vol. I*, 46.

2.5.3 Mental Capacity

Lack of mental capacity is a widely recognized ground excluding criminal responsibility. It is based in cognitive or volitional defects that exclude or limit the culpability of defendants. This defence is of limited relevance in the international context, since courts are unlikely to try perpetrators who are not fit to stand trial due to a serious mental defect. In Nuremberg, Hitler's deputy Rudolf Hess invoked insanity as a defence in Nuremberg but failed to be exculpated. The ICC Statute formulates a high standard in relation to mental capacity. The test is whether a defendant suffers from a mental disease or defect, and whether this defect destroys the ability of the person to appreciate the unlawfulness of the conduct or the capacity to conform to the law.[210] The main question is thus whether the offender loses the ability to distinguish between right and wrong.

This framing is problematic, since atrocity crimes are often conformist rather than deviant.[211] It implies that a person must be 'one hundred per cent insane when he committed the acts, otherwise he will be regarded as mentally sane'.[212] This 'all or nothing' requirement poses particular difficulties in relation to child soldiers who may suffer from brainwashing or indoctrination at an early age.[213] The indoctrination may alter the perception of what is normal in relation to a reasonable adolescent or impede the ability to question choices. For instance, indoctrination may prevent the ability of a child soldier to develop an adequate moral standard. A partial destruction is not reflected by the provision. Diminished capacity is only a mitigating factor in punishment.[214]

2.5.4 Intoxication

Intoxication is a second defence related to a person's capacity. During World War II and in the Vietnam War, amphetamines and other drugs were used by regular forces for purposes of stimulation, reward or relaxation.[215] In modern conflicts, the presence of intoxicated fighters is a recurrent phenomenon. For instance, in Rwanda Hutu fighters received drugs obtained from looted pharmacies as a reward for committing atrocities against Tutsi. In the Sierra Leonean civil war, warring factions used alcohol and drugs to control child soldiers or enhance their brutality in combat.

---

[210] In 2006, the ICTY held that Vladmi Kovačević did not 'have the capacity to enter a plea and to stand trial, without prejudice to any future criminal proceedings against him should his mental condition change'. *Prosecutor* v. *Kovačević*, IT -01-42/2-I, Public Version of the Decision on Accused's Fitness to Enter a Plea and Stand Trial, 12 April 2006, para. 50.

[211] Xavier, 'The Incongruity of the Rome Statute Insanity Defence', 802.

[212] S. Janssen, 'Mental Condition Defences in Supranational Criminal Law' (2004) 4 *International Criminal Law Review* 83, 85.

[213] See M. A. Thomas, 'Malice Supplies the Age? Assessing the Culpability of Adolescent Soldiers' (2013) 44 *California Western International Law Journal* 1; E. K. Baines, 'Complex Political Perpetrators: Reflections on Dominic Ongwen' (2009) 47 *The Journal of Modern African Studies* 170.

[214] Rule 145 (2) (a) (i).

[215] P. Rexton Kan, *Drugs in Contemporary Warfare* (Dulles, VA: Potomac Books, 2009).

Due to social differences and the nature of international crimes, it is controversial to what extent intoxication may exclude criminal responsibility. In many common law countries, intoxication is not recognized as a full defence. Many Islamic countries argued that use of alcohol or drugs should be an aggravating rather than a mitigating factor in punishment.[216] An ICTY Trial Chamber held that, 'in contexts where violence is the norm and weapons are carried, intentionally consuming drugs or alcohol constitutes an aggravating rather than a mitigating factor'.[217] The ICC Statute reduces the scope of the defence to cases in which the defendant lost the capacity to act as an autonomous person. It excludes cases in which agents become voluntarily intoxicated in order to avoid criminal responsibility.

The practical relevance of the defence is limited. Intoxication may be relevant to isolated acts, for instance where soldiers commit crimes under the influence of drugs or alcohol, but in the context of leadership responsibility this provision is somewhat bizarre.[218] It is hard to establish in relation to the orchestration, planning and implementation of collective mass atrocity crime.

2.5.5   Self-Defence

Self-defence is a permitted defence in nearly all legal systems.[219] In many circumstances, it is viewed as a justification, i.e. as a ground for eliminating the wrongful nature of the act, rather than as a factor excluding the culpability of the defendant.[220] It requires certain adjustments in the context of international crimes.

There is a tension between individual and collective agency. When arguing self-defence, many defendants have conflated the individual circumstances of their action (individual self-defence) with broader justifications related to the use of force in international relations, including the inherent right of states to self-defence under international law. For instance, Radovan Karadžić and Biljana Plavšić, the former President of the Republika Srpska, have tried to justify their actions before the ICTY on the ground that the war against Croats and Muslims was 'a matter of survival and self-defence'.[221] Similar arguments have been raised before the ICTR to justify the killing of Tutsi.[222] The Special Court for Sierra Leone found in a controversial ruling, which was later overturned on appeal,[223] that 'acting in defence of constitutionality by

---

[216] K. Ambos, 'Others Grounds for Excluding Criminal Responsibility', in A. Cassese, P. Gaeta and J. Jones (eds.), *The Rome Statute of the International Criminal Court: A Commentary, Vol. I* (Oxford: Oxford University Press, 2002), 951, 1020, 1029–1031.

[217] *Prosecutor v. Kvočka et al.*, IT-98–30/1/T, Judgment, 2 November 2001, para. 706.

[218] See W. Schabas, 'The General Principles of the Rome Statute' (1998) 6 *European Journal of Crime, Criminal Law and Criminal Justice* 400, 423.

[219] J Ohlin, 'Self-Defence', in A. Cassese (ed.), *The Oxford Companion to International Criminal Justice* (Oxford: Oxford University Press, 2009), 506.

[220] Krebs, 'Justification and Excuse', 398.

[221] *Prosecutor v. Plavšić*, IT-00–39 and 40/1-S, Sentencing Judgment, 27 February 2003, para. 72.

[222] *Prosecutor v. Kayishema and Ruzindana*, ICTR-95–1-A, Judgment, 1 June 2001 para 145; *Prosecutor v. Bagilishema*, ICTR-95–1A-T, Judgment, 7 June 2001, para 883.

[223] *Fofana and Kondewa* Appeal Judgment, paras. 523, 534.

engaging in a struggle or a fight that was geared towards the restoration of the ousted democratically elected Government of President Kabbah' marks a mitigating factor.[224]

International jurisprudence[225] has made it clear that involvement 'in a defensive operation conducted by forces' does not per se constitute a ground for excluding criminal responsibility. Thus, a person involved in such an operation cannot claim self-defence because the state or entity involved acts in self-defence or for a just cause. Rather, the argument of self-defence must be grounded in the action of the offender. This assessment is independent of the consideration of the legality or illegality of the collective action, which must be judged under general rules of international law (e.g. *jus ad bellum*).

There are different philosophical justifications of self-defence. In many legal systems it is accepted that self-defence requires an imminent and unlawful use of force which creates a danger for a protected interest, and a reasonable and proportionate reaction to avert the danger. It is controversial to what extent self-defence can be invoked to protect property interests and thus prioritize property over protection of life.[226] Such an approach is hard to justify in relation to the defence of international crimes. The ICC Statute recognizes such a possibility in relation to war crimes, based on proposals by the US and Israel. It is limited to property that is essential for the survival of the person or another person or for accomplishing a military mission. This aspect of the definition has been subject to severe criticism.[227] It is difficult to imagine what kind of property interests might justify the perpetration of war crimes, such as attacks against civilians, use of prohibited weapons, torture or attacks on protected sites, without violating the proportionality principle. Moreover, the provision seems to imply that there is a hierarchy of crimes according to which war crimes are less severe than other crimes. This is a problematic assumption.

2.5.6   *Duress*

The defence of duress is one of the most debated grounds excluding responsibility. It seeks to accommodate pressures that offenders face when acting under compulsion or coercion. The central question is to what extent criminal law should condemn behaviour that is the result of irresistible coercion or lack of choice. Some of the dilemmas, such as the taking of life to avoid a greater or equal personal harm, go to the very limits of the law.[228] They involve different, and sometimes conflicting, narratives in relation to the conduct of offenders.

---

[224] *Prosecutor v. Fofana and Kondewa*, SCSL-04-14-T, Sentencing Judgment, 9 October 2007, para. 86.
[225] *Prosecutor v. Kordić and Čerkez*, IT-95-14/2-T, Judgment, 26 February 2001, para. 452.
[226] See Ambos, *Treatise on International Criminal Law, Vol. I*, 340–341.
[227] A. Cassese, 'The Statute of International Criminal Court: Some Preliminary Reflections' (1999) 10 *EJIL* 144, 154.
[228] R. E. Brooks, 'Law in the Heart of Darkness: Atrocity & Duress' (2003) 43 *Virginia Journal of International Law* 861; T. Weigend, 'Kill or Be Killed: Another Look at Erdemovic' (2012) 10 *JICJ* 1219.

Duress is recognized as a defence in many national systems. Common law accepts it as a defence, except in cases of the most serious crimes, such as murder, treason or sexual assault. A typical limit is the prohibition to weigh life against life. A victim cannot be demanded by law to give up their life for the life of another, even if this would save a greater number of others or benefit a greater good of society.[229]

In the context of international criminal law, duress is often invoked in conjunction with superior orders. A classical example is an order by a superior to a combatant to commit offences under threat of life. However, the defence also applies to other threats and circumstances that pose a 'choice of evil'. One of the fundamental difficulties is to assess what can be reasonably expected of the offender in such circumstances, and whether it was impossible for the agent to comply with the commands of the law.

The treatment of duress has been contested in international practice.[230] It was accepted in the aftermath of World War II, although the Nuremberg Charter excluded the defence of superior orders. In the *Einsatzgruppen* case, the US Military Tribunal held that 'there is no law which requires that an innocent man must forfeit his life or suffer serious harm in order to avoid committing a crime which he condemns ... No Court will punish a man who, with a loaded pistol at his head, is compelled to pull a lethal lever'.[231] This finding contrasts with the position that duress cannot be defence to murder.

The ICTY faced the problem in the famous *Erdemović* case. The case illustrated the difficulties of judging human behaviour in extraordinary circumstances. *Erdemović* was part of a firing squad which was given orders to kill Muslim men. He shot around seventy prisoners. At trial, *Erdemović* entered a guilty plea, but declared:

Your honour, I had to do this. If I had refused, I would have been killed together with the victims. When I refused, they told me: If you are sorry for them, stand up, line up with them and we will kill you too. I am not sorry for myself but for my family, my wife and son who then had nine months, and I could not refuse because then they would have killed me.[232]

The majority of the Appeals Chamber held 'that duress does not afford a complete defence to a soldier charged with a crime against humanity and/or a war crime involving the killing of innocent human beings'.[233] It found that duress could only be considered as a mitigating circumstance. The majority relied on the professional environment, and the element of choice exercised before the act to justify the conclusion. It argued that duress should not be recognized as a ground excluding criminal

---

[229] *R.* v. *Dudley and Stephens* [1881–5] 14 QBD 273 DC, All ER.

[230] B. J. Risacher, 'No Excuse: the Failure of the ICC's Article 31 "Duress" Definition' (2014) 89 *Notre Dame Law Review* 1403; S. J Heim, 'The Applicability of the Duress Defence to the Killing of Innocent Persons' (2013) 46 *Cornell International Law Journal* 165–190.

[231] *US* v. *Otto Ohlendorf et al.* ('Einsatzgruppen case'), Trials of War Criminals before the Nuremberg Military Tribunals under Control Council Law No. 10, Vol. IV (Washington: United States Government Printing Office, 1951), 480.

[232] *Prosecutor* v. *Erdemović*, IT-96-22-Tbis, Sentencing Judgment, 5 March 1998, para. 14 (*Erdemović* Sentencing Judgment).

[233] *Erdemović* Appeal Judgment, para. 21.

responsibility if the defendant chose to become a member of a unit, organization or group that carried out actions contrary to international criminal law. According to this view, the blameworthiness of the action lies in the fact that the defendant failed to stand up against group dynamics or illegal practices.[234] The argument implies that soldiers, and others with a special duty, can be expected to show a higher level of resistance to coercion.[235] The reasoning emphasizes that the defendant retains an element of choice, that the act of killing trespasses the boundaries of the law, and that victims remain entitled to defend themselves against the taking of life.

The majority advocated an absolute moral standard. It noted:

If national law denies recognition of duress as a defense in respect of the killing of innocent persons, international criminal law can do no less than match that policy since it deals with murders often of far greater magnitude. If national law denies duress as a defense even in a case in which a single innocent life is extinguished due to action under duress, international law, in our view, cannot admit duress in cases which involve the slaughter of innocent human beings on a large scale.[236]

Judge Cassese took issue with this understanding in his dissent. He argued that duress must be considered on a case-by-case basis, regardless of whether the case involved the killing of innocent civilians or not.[237] He argued that ordinary persons, or even soldiers or members of police forces, are too weak to disobey an order that threatens their own lives. Members of such units or organizations may face higher levels of threat and risk than 'ordinary' persons, but they are not necessarily equipped to counter all types of unlawful behaviour by their superiors, or other members of such collectivities.[238] Cassese claimed that the blameworthiness of behaviour should be assessed in the individual context. His argument suggests that the 'real' criminals are those who allowed such circumstances to occur, namely the masterminds of the crimes, rather than those who execute.

Cassese pointed, in particular, to the fact that the detainees would have been killed, at most a few minutes later, by other soldiers even if *Erdemović* had behaved as a hero and refused to kill. He argued that a conviction as a criminal is unjust and unreasonable in circumstances where 'the accused can do nothing to save the victims by laying down his own life'.[239] In such cases, it would be unfeasible to demand that the defendant should have behaved differently.

---

[234] *Erdemović* Appeal Judgment, Joint Separate Opinion of Judge McDonald and Judge Vohrah, para. 84 ('we are of the view that soldiers or combatants are expected to exercise fortitude and a greater degree of resistance to a threat than civilians, at least when it is their own lives which are being threatened. Soldiers, by the very nature of their occupation, must have envisaged the possibility of violent death in pursuance of the cause for which they fight').

[235] For a discussion, see L. E. Chiesa, 'Duress, Demanding Heroism, and Proportionality' (2008) 41 *Vanderbilt Journal of Transnational Law* 741; V. Epps, 'The Soldier's Obligation to Die when Ordered to Shoot Civilians or Face Death Himself' (2003) 37 *New England Law Review* 987.

[236] *Erdemović* Appeal Judgment, Joint Separate Opinion of Judge McDonald and Judge Vohrah, para. 75.

[237] *Erdemović* Appeal Judgment, Separate and Dissenting Opinion of Judge Cassese, paras. 12 and 50.

[238] See Weigend, 'Kill or Be Killed', 1236.

[239] *Erdemović* Appeal Judgment, Separate and Dissenting Opinion of Judge Cassese, para. 48.

This argument is defensible from a rational point of view, but problematic in moral terms since it relies on speculation that the lives of the victims were indeed doomed. It implies a deep ethical problem, namely if a human being is entitled to judge whether a remaining life span is so negligible that it can be disregarded. This dilemma arises in other scenarios, for instance when state agents have to decide whether it is possible to shoot down a hijacked passenger plane in order to avert harm. The German Constitutional Court has rejected the possibility of quantification of life in such circumstances. It has denied duress, based on the ground that the life and dignity of the abducted passengers ought to be respected by law, irrespective of the length of their life span.[240]

The ICC Statute is a tribute to Cassese's argument. It recognizes duress not only as a mitigating factor, but as a potential defence for all crimes in the jurisdiction of the Court. Mixing national traditions, it differs from previous approaches in several ways. It combines two different concepts, namely necessity, which is based on the choice of a lesser evil in conflicting circumstances ('lesser evil defence'), and duress, which is based on lack of choice.[241] The Statute is more permissive than certain domestic legal systems, allowing duress as a defence for killing of civilians. It ties proportionality, at the same time, to a subjectively framed balancing requirement. Duress is excluded if the defendant intended 'to cause a greater harm than the one sought to be avoided'.[242] This allows a defence in situations in which the defendant takes a life to save another. This approach is difficult to reconcile with the theory that international crimes bear a special degree of gravity. One critique is that it prioritizes the defendant's weaknesses and fallible human nature over the physical welfare of victims. Conceptually, such claims of duress in situations of exception can at best be understood as exemptions from personal responsibility.[243] Self-induced risks may exclude the possibility to invoke duress.

A test case for the approach towards defences has been the *Ongwen* case before the ICC.[244] Dominic Ongwen was abducted as a child soldier at an early age by the LRA, where he gradually assumed a position of leadership as commander. He was charged with crimes committed after the age of eighteen at the ICC. The Defence argued that the abduction and structures inside the LRA exposed Ongwen to a kind of institutionalized duress, since he had been brainwashed and forced to live under duress since the age of nine. The Pre-Trial Chamber rejected this claim. It argued that the circumstances of Ongwen's stay in the LRA were not fully beyond his control. It feared that recognition of such types of indoctrination might provide 'blanket immunity' to members of all types of criminal organizations with brutal systems of discipline

---

[240] Judgment of the Federal Constitutional Court of 15 February 2006, 1 BvR 357/05, 115 Entscheidungen des Bundesverfassungsgerichts (2006) 118, at 158.

[241] On the distinction in national law, see Ambos, *Treatise on International Criminal Law, Vol. I*, 342–348.

[242] See Art. 31 (1) (c) ICC Statute.

[243] Ambos, 'Defences in International Criminal Law', 317.

[244] See *Ongwen* Confirmation Decision; N. Grossman, 'Rehabilitation or Revenge: Prosecuting Child Soldiers for Human Rights Violations' (2007) 38 *Georgetown Journal of International Law* 323.

in cases where such membership is not voluntary.[245] The Chamber found that the law does not recognize such a type of institutionalized duress. Threats must be imminent and eliminate choice. The Judges noted that Ongwen could have chosen not to rise in the hierarchy of the LRA, and that he had the choice to avoid rape and reduce the brutality of sexual abuse.[246] Brainwashing and coercive indoctrination alone do not suffice.

This argument highlighted criminal law's 'discomfort with the victim–perpetrator' divide.[247] In *Lubanga*, child soldiers were presented as 'victims' who are incapable of making responsible choices and suffer lasting damage beyond their childhood, due to institutionalized collective pressures. In *Ongwen*, the argument was turned around. The focus was placed on Ongwen's agency as an adult. Ongwen was deemed to retain an element of choice, despite his traumatic childhood and limited ability to develop an ordinary sense of morality which makes him responsible under the law. The Chamber suggested that such circumstances might be better reflected through a mitigation of sentence, which is expressly recognized in 'circumstances falling short of . . . duress'.[248] According to a different logic, brainwashing or coercive indoctrination could be recognized as a new hybrid, or at least as a partial defence, if they were inflicted through coercive means and part of a comprehensive strategy to indoctrinate the defendant.

2.5.7   Superior Order

The conflict between individual agency and collective pressures is most visible in relation to the defence of superior order.[249] The concept of superior order has its origin in military law. It implies that individuals may in principle not invoke obedience to orders to escape guilt, except in very limited circumstances. This principle is key to the individualization of responsibility. It makes it clear that command structures as such do not have an exculpatory effect. This rationale was explained by the US Military Courts in the *High Command* Case. It stated that it cannot be permitted that a 'dictator, absolute though he may be, shall be the scapegoat on whom the sins of all his governmental and military subordinates are wished; and that, when he is driven into a bunker and presumably destroyed, all the sins and guilt of his subordinates shall be considered to have been destroyed with him'.[250] Historically, superior

---

[245] *Ongwen* Confirmation Decision, para. 153.

[246] Ibid., paras. 66 et seq.

[247] M. Drumbl, 'Victims who Victimise' (2016) 4 *London Review of International Law* 217, 242.

[248] Rule 145 (2) (a) (i).

[249] See generally Y. Dinstein, *The Defence of 'Obedience to Superior Orders' in International Law* (Leiden: Sitjhoff, 1965); L. C. Green, *Superior Orders in National and International Law* (Leiden: Sijthoff, 1976); P. Gaeta, 'The Defence of Superior Orders: The Statute of the International Criminal Court versus Customary International Law' (1999) 10 *EJIL* 172.

[250] *US* v. *Wilhelm von Leeb et al.* (High Command Trial), United States Military Tribunal sitting in Nuremberg, Trials of War Criminals before the Nuremberg Military Tribunal under Control Council Law No. 10, Vol. XI, 71–72

order has often been invoked, but it has rarely succeeded. Both the Nuremberg tribunals and the ad hoc tribunals have discarded superior order as a ground excluding criminal responsibility for international crimes. Its scope as a mitigating factor was limited. For instance, in *Erdemović* the ICTY Trial Chamber acknowledged that the relevance as a mitigating factor would depend on the rank of the defendant. It found that 'the precedent setting value of the judgment in this respect is diminished for low ranking accused'.[251] This approach implies that soldiers and fighters ought to be viewed as rational and reflective agents that have a duty to challenge criminal orders.

The ICC Statute applies the concept of superior order to military and civilian contexts. It draws a balance between an absolute liability approach and duties of obedience. It acknowledges that superior order may relieve a defendant from criminal responsibility if the person was 'under a legal obligation to obey orders of the Government or the superior in question', '[t]he order was not manifestly unlawful', and the defendant did not know 'that the order was unlawful'.[252] De facto, this defence applies only to war crimes and aggression, since orders to commit genocide or crimes against humanity are deemed to be 'manifestly unlawful' under the Statute.

This distinction may be explained by the fact that the relevant legal hierarchies exist predominantly in military and paramilitary command structures. However, it remains questionable on substance. In light of the seriousness of all international crimes, it is difficult to argue that an order to commit war crimes or aggression would not be manifestly unlawful. The differentiation produces artificial results in cases where war crimes or acts of aggression coincide with crimes against humanity. It runs against the aim to strengthen critical self-reflection in the application of international humanitarian law or the law on the use of forces. Relevant errors might be better captured by the defence of mistake of fact,[253] or mistake of law.[254]

2.5.8   Other Grounds

The list of defences is not conclusive. The Rome Statute allows the ICC to accept other defences,[255] but such claims will succeed only rarely.[256] Recognizing a new defence is subject to a high threshold. It must be grounded in the sources of law applicable before the Court.[257] In the practice of the ad hoc tribunals, defences have

---

[251] *Erdemović* Sentencing Judgment, para. 51.

[252] Art. 33 (1) ICC Statute.

[253] The ICC Statute allows for the defence of the mistake of fact if it negates the mental element required by the crime.

[254] Cryer argues that Art. 33 is 'actually an expansion of the mistake of law defence'. See R. Cryer, 'Superior Scholarship on Superior Orders' (2011) 9 *JICJ* 959, 971. Mistakes of law may occur if the defendant considers the conduct as lawful due to an incorrect legal assessment. But the threshold is high. In *Lubanga*, the Pre-Trial Chamber held that such a defence can only succeed if the defendant does not realize the social significance or everyday meaning of a normative objective element of the crime. See *Lubanga* Confirmation Decision, para. 316.

[255] Art. 31 (3).

[256] P. Krug, 'The Emerging Mental Incapacity Defense in International Criminal Law: Some Initial Questions of Implementation' (2000) 94 *AJIL* 317, 319.

[257] Art. 21 ICC Statute.

been derived from general principles of law.[258] Such an identification poses severe methodological challenges, since it requires significant inductive and comparative analysis of domestic legal systems.[259] Courts often lack the time to carry out comparative analysis of major legal systems, or are selective in their choice. More often than not, the method risks one being of creation, rather than discovery.[260]

2.6 Merits and Critiques

The development of international criminal law is marked by irony. The law has focused on the crystallization of the principle of individual criminal responsibility and theories to hold perpetrators accountable for collective forms of violence. This is widely hailed as one of the major achievements of the twentieth century. Individual criminal responsibility sends an important message that individuals retain a certain degree of choice and freedom to behave differently. There are, however, also darker sides.

International criminal law seeks to justify itself through universalist ideas, drawn from multiple systems. Yet many of the essential doctrines are Western in origin. Fundamental bases of the allocation of responsibility are modelled after Western-style bureaucracies or military organizations. Existing practices struggle to find an equilibrium between the individual and the collective dimensions of macro-criminality. In certain ways, the tide might have shifted too much to the individual.

Criminal conduct is typically a result of complex factors. Some of these can be related to individual responsibility. Others are grounded in broader contextual or collective factors. In many cases, it is arbitrary to focus solely on a few individuals. Individual criminal responsibility needs to be complemented by certain collective forms of responsibility. International criminal law claims to contribute to the prevention of revenge and lawlessness. This is impossible without broader accountability strategies. Engagement with the concurrent role and responsibility of states is necessary in order to ensure non-repetition of crimes, or to assign responsibility for the totality of the harm caused through mass atrocity crime. The narrow framing of the responsibility of legal persons, including corporations, is under challenge. More attention needs to be given to the role of bystanders who, though not directly involved, provide the breeding ground for violations.

The legal framework remains somewhat detached from social reality.[261] International criminal courts and tribunals have developed ample theories and legal

---

[258] For a pragmatic approach, *Erdemović* Appeal Judgment, Joint Separate Opinion of Judge McDonald and Judge Vohrah, para. 57 ('our approach will necessarily not involve a direct comparison of the specific rules of each of the world's legal systems, but will instead involve a survey of those jurisdictions whose jurisprudence is, as a practical matter, accessible to us in an effort to discern a general trend, policy or principle underlying the concrete rules of that jurisdiction').

[259] S. N. Jain, 'Judicial Lawmaking and General Principles of Law in International Criminal Law' (2016) 57 *Harvard International Law Journal* 111, 133 et seq.

[260] See Zahar and Sluter, *International Criminal Law*, 92–105.

[261] On the risks, see G. Anders, 'Testifying about Uncivilised Events: Problematic Representations of Africa in the Trial against Charles Taylor' (2011) 24 *LJIL* 937.

concepts to explain participation in crimes. However, few attempts have been made to relate such constructs to deeper analysis of behavioural patterns and group dynamics in conflict. Many authority structures in civil wars tend to be less hierarchical or formal than in traditional warfare. They may rely on social or patrimonial links or client–agent relations.[262] Classical ideas of military command and control, developed in post-World War II jurisprudence, do not always offer a proper fit. As noted in scholarship, there is a certain sociological disconnect:

> In Africa ... well-drilled hierarchies of this nature are a rarity. Over the past forty years many African governments, armies and guerrilla movements have found it tremendously difficult to create stable organisations, and authority relations tend to be informal and fluid instead ... While it is not impossible that superiors in such networks should have the 'material ability to prevent or punish' the crimes of their subordinates, as the superior responsibility doctrine demands, it is much less likely than in a Western context.[263]

Discourses shift according to convenience. For instance, the LRA was initially branded as a criminal organization governed by religious or irrational factors, such as the Ten Commandments and Joseph Kony's spiritual influence and control. This narrative mobilized international pressure. In the course of ICC proceedings, the focus shifted. The OTP presented the LRA as an organized rebel movement, with a classical structure of command and a political agenda. These two narratives do not easily coincide.[264]

International criminal courts and tribunals rely rarely on scientific insights from non-legal fields.[265] Insights from social sciences are typically limited to evidence, sentencing or reparation. Organizational theories have been established largely without study of the criminological specificities of atrocity contexts, including reasons why perpetrators engage in such crimes. In Rwanda or Sierra Leone, courts developed a type of 'legal anthropology' in order to understand power structures at the local level or to give meaning to collective concepts such as ethnicity or race.[266] Some grounds excluding criminal responsibility are artificial (e.g. intoxication) or tied to a separation between perpetrators and victims (e.g. mental capacity, duress) that may not always be as clear-cut as assumed.[267] This creates discrepancies between law and reality. It makes international criminal law vulnerable to critiques of artificial decontextualization or overstretching the limits of the law.

---

[262] See I. Bantekas, 'The Anthropological Dimension of International Crimes and international criminal justice', in Bantekas and Mylonaki, *Criminological Approaches to International Criminal Law*, 240, 256.

[263] See T. Kelsall, 'International Criminal Justice and Non-Western Cultures', 12 April 2010, Oxford Transitional Justice Research Working Paper Series, at www.law.ox.ac.uk/sites/files/oxlaw/kelsall_internationalcriminaljustice_final1.pdf.

[264] See A. Branch, 'Rupturing Official Histories in the Trial of Dominic Ongwen', *Justice in Conflict*, 13 April 2016, https://justiceinconflict.org/2016/04/13/rupturing-official-histories-in-the-trial-of-dominic-ongwen/.

[265] I. Bantekas, 'Introduction: An Interdisciplinary Criminology of International Criminal Law', in Bantekas and Mylonaki, *Criminological Approaches to International Criminal Law*, 2–5.

[266] Ibid., 262.

[267] On the role of trauma and the victim–perpetrator divide, see S. Mohamed, 'Of Monsters and Men: Perpetrator Trauma and Mass Atrocity' (2015) 115 *Columbia Law Review* 1157.

3

The Global Institutional Architecture

Institutions have played a key role in framing the history of international criminal justice. International criminal law has struggled to become recognized as a field of law. Even more than other fields, its normative justification (i.e. universality, punishment[1]), is linked to the idea of enforcement.[2] This has led to a strong emphasis on institution building. Initially, there was a conception that 'an international criminal jurisdiction is inconceivable because the state as such cannot be a subject of criminal law and cannot be held criminally responsible'.[3] The turn to global institutions over the past century has reversed this claim. It was influenced by the rise of international organizations and other actors under international law in the course of the twentieth century.[4]

For a long time, the ideal of international justice has gravitated around the idea that an international criminal court would be the centre of a global justice architecture, with others at the periphery.[5] The Genocide Convention contained an early reference to an international criminal tribunal.[6] The work in the UN started in the 1950s. The idea of a global criminal court played a central role in the work of the International Law Commission and NGOs. The very project was associated with dreams for a new world order. The adoption of the ICC Statute in 1998 was celebrated by some as a 'constitutional' moment for the international legal order.[7] However, the tide is

---

[1] In that sense, international criminal courts and tribunals differ from classical human rights institutions. See R. Rastan, 'Comment on Victor's Justice & the Viability of Ex Ante Standards' (2010) 43 *John Marshall Law Review* 569.

[2] F. Mégret, 'The Anxieties of International Criminal Justice' (2016) 29 *LJIL* 197, 200.

[3] V. V. Pella, 'Towards an International Criminal Court' (1950) 44 *AJIL* 37, 40.

[4] The diversification of domestic and international institutions in the field of international criminal justice is symptomatic of the move towards institutionalism in international law more generally. See e.g. D. Kennedy, 'The Move to Institutions' (1987) 8 *Cardozo Law Review* 841–988; J. Charney, 'Is International Law Threatened by Multiple International Tribunals?' (1998) 271 *Recueil des cours* 101; B. Kingsbury, 'Is the Proliferation of International Courts and Tribunals a Systemic Problem?' (1999) 31 *New York University Journal of International Law and Politics* 679.

[5] On global judicialization, see B. Kingsbury, 'International Courts: Uneven Judicialization in Global Order', in J. Crawford and M. Koskenniemi (eds.), *Cambridge Companion to International Law* (Cambridge: Cambridge University Press, 2012), 203–227.

[6] The General Assembly invited the International Law Commission to 'study the desirability and possibility of establishing an international judicial organ for the trial of persons charged with genocide or other crimes'.

[7] L. Sadat, *The International Criminal Court and the Transformation of International Law: Justice for the New Millennium* (New York: Transnational, 2002), 103.

turning. There is a new sense of realism, if not scepticism about the future of international criminal jurisdiction.[8] International criminal justice institutions have been facing increased 'backlash'.[9] There is a certain paradigm shift. Domestic, hybrid, regional or local responses are gaining more attention in light of the limitations of international criminal jurisdiction. There is a strong trend to search for situation-specific responses. This has led to a hybridization of forms. Formal criminal justice is complemented by quasi-judicial bodies or alternatives to classical prosecution and punishment. International criminal justice thus requires to some extent a new account of its foundations.

3.1   The Turn to Global Justice Institutions

The institutional history of international criminal justice is mostly told through the focus on international criminal courts and tribunals. Images of Nuremberg, Tokyo or Hague justice, and their echoes, dominate stories about the genesis of international criminal justice.[10] It is often overlooked that many important impulses emanated from earlier initiatives going back to the interwar period or earlier. As Mark Lewis has shown, international criminal law is not only the product of state negotiation or UN institutional design, but closely linked to the initiatives of professional groups, informal networks or private individuals.[11] Much of its social fabric has grown through the interaction with different disciplines, fields of law (e.g. human rights law, international humanitarian law and public international law) and their professional communities.

3.1.1   A Brief Intellectual History

Calls for the creation of a centralized jurisdiction go back to the early Red Cross moment. Gustave Moynier proposed the creation of an international tribunal to deal with violations of the laws of war in 1872.[12] Moynier and his compatriots felt that a treaty-based judicial mechanism was necessary to promote compliance with rules of

---

[8] See e.g. C. M. Bassiouni, 'The ICC – Qui Vadis?' (2006) 4 *JICJ* 421; D. Luban, 'After the Honeymoon, Reflections on the Current State of International Criminal Justice' (2013) 11 *JICJ* 505; De Vos, Kendall and Stahn, *Contested Justice*; Schwöbel, *Critical Approaches to International Criminal Law*.

[9] On 'backlash' as a broader phenomenon, see K. J. Alter, J. T. Gathii and L. R. Helfer, 'Backlash against International Courts in West, East and Southern Africa: Causes and Consequences' (2016) 27 *EJIL* 293; L. R. Helfer and A. E. Showalter, 'Opposing International Justice: Kenya's Integrated Backlash Strategy Against the ICC' (2017) 17 *International Criminal Law Review* 1.

[10] On geography images, see D. Koller, '. . . and New York and The Hague and Tokyo and Geneva and Nuremberg and . . .: The Geographies of International Law' (2012) 23 *EJIL* 97.

[11] M. Lewis, *The Birth of the New Justice: The Internationalization of Crime and Punishment, 1919–1950* (Oxford University Press, 2014). For a similar account of international humanitarian law, see Alexander, 'A Short History of International Humanitarian Law', 136–137.

[12] G. Moynier, Draft Convention for the Establishment of an International Judicial Body Suitable for the Prevention and Punishment of Violations of the Geneva Convention, Geneva, 1872. For a discussion, see C. K. Hall, 'The First Proposal for a Permanent International Criminal Court' (1998) 322 *International Review of the Red Cross* 57.

humanitarian law. It was 'the first serious effort to draft a statute for a permanent international criminal court'.[13]

This idea was taken up in the interwar period. Several expert bodies proposed the development of a permanent international criminal jurisdiction.[14] Baron Edouard Descamps, a member the League of Nations Advisory Committee of Jurists, and Vespasien Pella, a Romanian diplomat who worked with the Association Internationale de Droit Pénal (AIDP) advocated for the creation of an international criminal court that could try 'crimes against the international order' as well as transnational offences.[15] The International Law Association suggested the creation of an international criminal tribunal under the auspices of the Permanent Court of International Justice, but the proposal was too advanced at the time.[16]

The League of Nations remained sceptical towards a global mechanism, and preferred to tackle specific problems (e.g. terrorism). International criminal law was still largely understood as a body of law that regulates conflicts of law between jurisdictions ('international penal law').[17] States feared that international criminal jurisdiction might conflict with the 'right' of individuals to be tried under domestic law and the immunity of heads of state, or present an impediment to peaceful settlement of disputes.[18] Although scholars such as Hersch Lauterpacht began to regard international criminal law as a potential means to strip away the sovereign veil of the state and to establish the international criminal responsibility of individuals,[19] the idea that international criminal law would be a law applicable by international courts and tribunals was still hypothetical.

Throughout the first half of the twentieth century, states sought to minimize interference with domestic sovereignty. During World War II, individuals such as Raphael Lemkin and Lauterpacht relied on the networks established during the 1920s to support post-war justice. The London International Assembly, chaired by the Belgian lawyer Marcel De Baer, proposed a statute for an international criminal court in October 1943.[20] However, international criminal courts and tribunals were initially created to deal with particular situations.

An early example is the often overlooked UN War Crimes Commission (1943–1948). It was established by the Wartime United Nations[21] to facilitate effective domestic investigations and prosecutions of atrocity crime committed during World War II and

---

[13] Hall, 'The First Proposal', 65.

[14] They include the Committee of Jurists of the League of Nations, as well as the International Association of Penal Law and the International Law Association.

[15] Lewis, *The Birth of the New Justice*, 79.

[16] Historical Survey of the Question of International Criminal Jurisdiction, UN Doc. A/CN.4/7, 12.

[17] E. Wise, 'Prolegomenon to the Principles of International Criminal Law' (1970) 16 *New York Law Forum* 562.

[18] See generally L. Sadat, 'The Proposed Permanent International Criminal Court: An Appraisal' (1996) 29 *Cornell International Law Journal* 665, 672.

[19] See M. Koskenniemi, 'Hersch Lauterpacht and the Development of International Criminal Law' (2004) 2 *JICJ* 810.

[20] Draft Convention for the Creation of an International Criminal Court, Drafted by the Chairman and amended by the Commission, in *The Punishment of War Criminals, Recommendations of the London International Assembly* (London International Assembly October 1943) 18–29.

[21] On the 'wartime history' of the UN, see D. Plesch, *America, Hitler and the UN: How the Allies Won World War II and Forged Peace* (London and New York: I. B. Tauris, 2011); D. Plesch and T. G. Weiss, *Wartime History and the Future United Nations: Past as Prelude?* (London: Routledge, 2014).

to avoid a repetition of the failure of the Leipzig trials after World War I.[22] The Commission marked a decentralized and cooperation-oriented justice model that introduced an unparalleled degree of intergovernmental cooperation between major powers (including the US, India and China) in terms of geographical spread and sharing of knowledge. Based on initiatives by De Baer and Herbert Pell, the US representative on the Commission, the United Nations War Crimes Commission (UNWCC) even advocated the creation of a treaty-based 'United Nations War Crimes Court'.[23] Governments of the Allied Powers preferred military courts, since they did not require burdensome treaty negotiations and were considered to be an effective interim solution to try certain war criminals. This led to the creation of the Nuremberg Tribunal (1945–1946) and the Tokyo Tribunal (1946–1948), and the post-Nuremberg trials.

In 1947, Donnedieu de Vabres, the French judge at Nuremberg and representative on the UN General Assembly's Committee on the Progressive Development of International Law and its Codification, proposed the establishment of an international criminal court.[24]

During this period, the ICRC also stepped up its commitment to international criminal law. It proposed a set of innovations that were of key importance for the regime of the Conventions. It pushed for an express obligation of state parties to enact 'provisions for the repression' of 'any breach of the Convention' through 'criminal penalties or appropriate disciplinary measures'.[25] It suggested punishing grave breaches of the Convention 'as crimes against the law of nations by the tribunals of any of the High Contracting Parties or by any international jurisdiction, the competence of which has been recognized by them'.[26] In its explanation of the proposal, the ICRC noted that this regime 'may be described as a first step towards the introduction of penal legislation of an international character, since it defines as crimes "sui generis" offences known in ordinary parlance as "war crimes"'.[27] In the second half of the twentieth century,[28] the rise of the Cold War and communism became more pressing prerogatives. The idea of international criminal law as a global project was mainly promoted by a small group of international lawyers who sought to develop

---

[22] The UNWCC examined 8,178 cases and listed nearly 37,000 persons as offenders of crime in four years. See The United Nations War Crimes Commission (ed.), *History of the United Nations War Crimes Commission and the Development of Laws of War* (London: His Majesty's Stationary Office, 1948), Chapter 15, at 484. See generally E. Schwelb, 'The United Nations War Crimes Commission' (1946) 23 *British Yearbook of International Law* 363; D. Plesch, *Human Rights after Hitler The Lost History of Prosecuting Axis War Crimes* (Washington, DC: Georgetown University Press, 2017).

[23] See Draft Convention for the Establishment of a United Nations War Crimes Court, C. 50(1) (30 September 1944). For a discussion, see W. Schabas, 'The United Nations War Crimes Commission's Proposal For An International Criminal Court' (2014) 25 *Criminal Law Forum* 171–189.

[24] Memorandum submitted by the delegate of France, Draft Proposal for the Establishment of an International Court of Criminal Jurisdiction, UN Doc. A/AC.10/21 (1947).

[25] ICRC, Remarks and Proposals submitted by the International Committee of the Red Cross: Documents for the Consideration of Governments Invited by the Swiss Federal Council to Attend the Diplomatic Conference at Geneva (21 April 1949) (Geneva: ICRC, 1949), at 18, proposed Art. 39.

[26] Ibid., proposed Art. 40.

[27] Ibid., at 20.

[28] For discussion, see C. Stahn, 'Complementarity and Cooperative Justice Ahead of Their Time? The United Nations War Crimes Commission, Fact-Finding and Evidence' (2014) 25 *Criminal Law Forum* 223.

international criminal justice beyond the World War II paradigm (e.g. Benjamin Ferencz, Cherif Bassiouni, Edward Wise).

In the 1990s, the end of the Cold War and ideals of a new world order provided an opportunity for re-engagement with the project of international criminal justice. The International Law Commission provided some intellectual grounding, through its Draft Statute of an International Criminal Court (1994)[29] and a Draft Code of Crimes against the Peace and Security of Mankind (1996).[30] The growing establishment of criminal institutions was supported by a strong anti-impunity agenda driven by the human rights movement.[31] These factors opened the space for negotiations on the ICC as a global court. The agreement was made possible by the alliance of a group of around sixty like-minded states with a strong commitment to core principles, the strong pressure by NGOs and historical precedents, including the footprints of the ad hoc tribunals. The contemporary institutional architecture is more than ever driven by networks, NGOs and circles of professionals.[32]

3.1.2 Changing Justifications

The history of international criminal institutions is to some extent a history of crisis.[33] There is no linear line of progression.[34] Institutions emerged through trial and error, and social construction[35] 'before, during and after the existence of actual institutions of international criminal justice'.[36]

---

[29] ILC, Draft Statute for an International Criminal Court (1994), in Report of the International Law Commission on the Work of its Forty-Sixth Session, UN GAOR, 49th Sess., Supp. No. 10, UN Doc. A/49/10, paras. 23–91. See J. Crawford, 'The ILC adopts a Statute for an International Criminal Court' (1995) 89 *AJIL* 404.

[30] ILC, Draft Code of Crimes against the Peace and Security of Mankind, in Report of the International Law Commission on the Work of its Forty-Eighth Session, UN GAOR, 51st Sess., Supp. No. 10, UN Doc. A/51/10 (1996), 93. For a critique, see J. Allain and J. Jones, 'A Patchwork of Norms: A Commentary on the 1996 Draft Code of Crimes Against Peace and Security of Mankind' (1997) 8 *EJIL* 100.

[31] See generally M. Glasius, *The International Criminal Court: a Global Civil Society Achievement* (London: Routledge, 2006); H. Haddad, 'Judicial Institution Builders: NGOs and International Human Rights Courts' (2012) 11 *Journal of Human Rights* 126.

[32] There are many new types of investigative, prosecutorial or judicial networks that engage with each other in an informal or a formal way. Much of the professional know-how of the field is shared by a group of individuals that works inside international criminal courts and tribunals or NGOs, or moves across institutions. See E. Baylis, 'Tribunal-Hopping with the Post-Conflict Justice Junkies' (2008) 10 *Oregon Review of International Law* 361; M. J. Christensen, 'Crafting and Promoting International Crimes: A Controversy among Professionals of Core-Crimes and Anti-Corruption' (2017) 30 *LJIL* 501; K. Lohne, 'Global Civil Society, the ICC, and Legitimacy in International Criminal Justice', in N. Hayashi and C. M. Bailliet (eds.), *The Legitimacy of International Criminal Tribunals* (Cambridge: Cambridge University Press, 2017), 449.

[33] S. Katzenstein, 'In the Shadow of Crisis: The Creation of International Courts in the Twentieth Century' (2014) 55 *Harvard International Law Journal* 151. For a critique of the crisis narrative of international law, see H. Charlesworth, 'International Law: A Discipline of Crisis' (2002) 65 *Modern Law Review* 377.

[34] Simpson, 'Linear Law', 159; K. Tiba, 'What Caused the Multiplicity of International Courts and Tribunals' (2006) 10 *Gonzaga Journal of International Law* 202.

[35] See K. Clarke, 'International Justice and the Politics of Sentimentality', in K. Clarke, A. Knottnerus and E. de Volder, *Africa and the ICC* (Cambridge: Cambridge University Press, 2016), 78, 99 ('the history of international criminal law is better seen as a product of affective imaginaries by which social location and embodied logic shape the making of judicial meanings').

[36] See Mégret, 'International Criminal Justice as a Juridical Field', 12.

A common explanation for the turn to global institutions is the idea that domestic jurisdictions affected by international crime lack the will or capacity to investigate or prosecute.[37] The creation of international structures was supported in contexts where domestic authorities were unable to try perpetrators (e.g. due to security conditions, lack of legal or institutional capacity, or enforcement constraints) or were not deemed sufficiently legitimate and independent to conduct trials and prosecutions.

This rationale was inherent in calls for a 'special tribunal' to try the German Emperor under the Versailles Treaty,[38] early proposals for an International Criminal Court in the era of the League Nations,[39] and was later formulated at Nuremberg.[40] The Allied Powers created the tribunal jointly, although any of them could have exercised jurisdiction on their own. However, jurisdictional grounds alone does not suffice to explain post-war justice in the aftermath of World War II. Nuremberg or Tokyo underlined faith in the idea of restoring order and civilization through law, and they had a re-educative ambition. They expressed a broader moral response to war and atrocity that had to be made at the time and in these circumstances. Unity was tied to the image of the common enemy and a particular conception of evil, caused by the horrors of World War II. Their framework and mandate was shaped by a context of military defeat and occupation. As critics claim, prosecutions remained limited, since 'political expediency and the West's desire to get on with the reconstruction of Europe and Germany appeared to have militated against the prosecution of more offenders'.[41] Rationales diversified in the second half of the twentieth century, with the growth of multilateral structures, changing approaches towards sovereignty and the development of human rights frameworks. International criminal justice has seen an astounding revival, after the silence of the Cold War, the fall of communism and the revitalization of the collective security system.[42] States and international organizations have viewed international criminal justice more generally as an emergency tool, namely an instrument to respond to particular crises. This managerial vision was driven by the political transformation of the 1990s. It can be explained by different factors: the wish to respond to the Rwandan genocide and the Yugoslav crisis at the doorstep of Europe, the rise of global media which exposed atrocities, advocacy by non-governmental organizations, and undoubtedly certain feelings of shame or neglect regarding the failure to prevent crises (e.g. ignorance of information, failure of the

---

[37] For instance, Bert Röling argued in 1960 that international judges should try international offences because 'they are violations … of international law'. B. V. A. Röling, 'The Law of War and the National Jurisdiction since 1945', in *Hague Academy of International Law, Collected Courses, 1960-II* (Leiden: A. W. Sijthoff, 1961), 354.

[38] Treaty of Peace with Germany, 28 June 1919, Art. 227. The tribunal was supposed to be international in character, with judges appointed by the United States, Great Britain, France, Italy and Japan.

[39] Convention for the Creation of an International Criminal Court, opened for signature 16 November 1937, League of Nations Official Journal Spec. Supp. 156 (1938).

[40] See Moscow Declaration, 1 November 1943 and London Agreement, 8 August 1945, 28 UNTS 279.

[41] M. Mutua, 'Never Again: Questioning the Yugoslav and Rwanda Tribunals' (1997) 11 *Temple International and Comparative Law Journal* 167, 172.

[42] On the gap between the Holocaust and the birth of the modern human rights movement, see S. Moyn, *Last Utopia: Human Rights in History* (Cambridge, MA: Harvard University Press, 2010).

'peace-keeping' model, complicity).[43] International criminal justice institutions were not only established for retributive purposes, namely to punish crimes. They became to some extent 'fire brigades' to respond to certain types of conflicts and typologies of crimes, and were more closely related to the idea of establishing societal peace.

In this 'heroic phase' of international criminal justice, institutional orientations have shifted. Institutional development has quickly moved from domestic to universal approaches and embraced new forms of verticality. Institutions such as the ad hoc tribunals, the SCSL or the ECCC were established, since there was not sufficient trust in purely domestic justice responses. The ad hoc tribunals for the former Yugoslavia and Rwanda were vested with primacy over domestic jurisdiction. There was a strong sense that international criminal justice is not only a mechanism to fill justice gaps at the domestic level, but in certain circumstances a means to strengthen domestic justice.

The trend to address accountability through courts was reinforced by certain institutional dynamics. The establishment of a judicial mechanism turned into a convenient and manageable option to respond to macro-crimes. International actors replicated or improved features of earlier institutions. Karen Alter has called this multiplication through 'emulation'.[44] For instance, the US viewed the ad hoc tribunals for the Balkans and Rwanda as 'echoes' of Nuremberg.[45] The UN developed a whole matrix of hybrid or internationalized mechanisms in different contexts, such as Sierra Leone, Cambodia, Kosovo, East Timor, Lebanon or Guatemala.

The establishment of the ICC marked an attempt to create a broader system of justice. The main novelty of the Rome Statute is that it institutionalizes a new form of shared responsibility between domestic and international jurisdiction. This is reflected in the principle of complementarity.[46] It reflects the idea that domestic justice systems have the primary responsibility in the pursuit of accountability. The image of the 'unwilling or unable State'[47] was formally born to justify this new type of permanent justice. It became the embodiment of the turn to a new accountability order, in which international criminal justice can co-exist with state power. States vested the Court with the authority to exercise jurisdiction where they do not act, or are unable or unwilling to do so.[48]

---

[43] On 'shame' as a factor underlying creation of the ad hoc tribunals, see Mutua, 'Never Again', 173. For a response, see P. Rosenblum, 'Save the Tribunals; Salvage the Movement, a Response to Makau Mutua' (1997) 11 *Temple International and Comparative Law Journal* 189.

[44] K. J. Alter, 'The Multiplication of International Courts and Tribunals after the End of the Cold War', in C. Romano et al. (eds.), *The Oxford Handbook of International Adjudication* (Oxford: Oxford University Press, 2013, 63, 63–89.

[45] At the adoption of the ICTY Statute, Madeleine Albright noted: 'There is an echo in this chamber today. The Nuremberg principles have been reaffirmed ... The lesson that we are all accountable to international law may finally have taken hold in our collective memory'. See D. L. Bethlehem and M. Weller (eds.), *The Yugoslav Crisis on International Law: Part I, General Issues* (Cambridge: Cambridge University Press, 1997), 204.

[46] See generally C. Stahn and M. El Zeidy (eds.), *The International Criminal Court and Complementarity: From Theory to Practice* (Cambridge: Cambridge University Press, 2011).

[47] For a critique, see N. Tzouvala, 'TWAIL and the "Unwilling or Unable" Doctrine, Continuities, and Ruptures' (2016) 109 *AJIL Unbound* 266.

[48] See Art. 17 ICC Statute.

3.2 Critiques

Throughout history, the development of global criminal institutions has given rise to various types of critiques. Traditionally, states objected to the idea of international criminal jurisdiction, since they feared that this would unduly interfere with their internal affairs.[49] In recent years, the argument that international criminal justice poses a threat to sovereignty has lost some of its force.[50] The telos of sovereignty is changing. It is more widely accepted that sovereignty and international criminal jurisdiction are not incompatible per se. Sovereignty is grounded in individual rights[51] and linked to duties.[52] In many cases, international criminal law actually serves as an extension of sovereignty. It may even empower state jurisdiction.

In contemporary discourse, other critiques have moved to the forefront. International criminal courts and tribunals have faced a growing number of political and socio-legal critiques that question their validity and identity. Some of them are novel, others are old.

3.2.1 Victor's Justice

The most classical critique is victor's justice. This argument goes back to the aftermath of World War II. In 1944, Hersch Lauterpacht argued that 'it is probably unavoidable that the right of punishing war criminals should be unilaterally assumed by the victor'.[53] Both the Nuremberg[54] and Tokyo tribunals[55] were heavily dominated by US influence.[56] They targeted a particular category of persons, namely the vanquished enemy. The main purpose was, as Chief Prosecutor Robert Jackson put, it to 'stay the hand of vengeance and voluntarily submit their captive enemies to the judgment of the law'.[57] This framing may be partly explained by the strong focus of both tribunals on aggressive war. It exposed them to critiques of victor's justice.[58] For

---

[49] See e.g. F. Mégret, 'Epilogue to an Endless Debate: The International Criminal Court's Third Party Jurisdiction and the Looming Revolution of International Law' (2001) 13 *EJIL* 247. For instance, states invoked the sovereignty argument in ICC treaty negotiations when they did not agree on an issue.

[50] See R. Cryer, 'International Criminal Law vs State Sovereignty: Another Round?' (2006) 16 *EJIL* 979, 983–988.

[51] See A. Peters, 'Humanity as the A and Ω of Sovereignty' (2009) 20 *EJIL* 513; C. Stahn, 'Responsibility to Protect: Political Rhetoric or Emerging Legal Norm?'(2007) 101 *AJIL* 99, 111.

[52] See F. Deng et al., *Sovereignty as Responsibility: Conflict Management in Africa* (Washington: Brookings Institution Press, 1996); earlier H. Grotius (trans. R. D. Magoffin), *De Mare Liberum*, Ch. V (Oxford: Oxford University Press, 1916) (1609); H. Grotius (trans. F. W. Kelsey), *De Jure Belli Ac Pacis*, Bk. II, Ch. 2 (Oxford: Clarendon Press, 1925) (1625); see generally H. Lauterpacht, 'The Grotian Tradition in International Law' (1946) 23 *British Yearbook of International Law* 1, 27.

[53] H. Lauterpacht, 'The Law of Nations and the Punishment of War Crimes' (1944) 21 *British Yearbook of International Law* 58.

[54] D. A. Blumenthal and T. L. H. McCormack (eds.) *The Legacy of Nuremberg: Civilising Influence or Institutionalized Vengeance?* (Leiden: Brill, 2008).

[55] D. Zolo, *Victors' Justice: From Nuremberg to Baghdad* (London: Verso, 2009).

[56] On Nuremberg as 'an expression of a peculiarly American legal sensibility', see K. Anderson, 'Nuremberg Sensibility: Telford Taylor's Memoir of the Nuremberg Trials' (1994) 7 *Harvard Human Rights Journal* 281, 289.

[57] R. H. Jackson, Opening Statement before the IMT, Trial of the Major War Criminals before the International Military Tribunal Vol. II Proceedings, 14 November 1945–30 November 1945 (Nuremberg: IMT, 1947), at 99.

[58] See R. Minear, *Victor's Justice: The Tokyo War Crimes Trial* (Princeton: Princeton University Press, 2016).

instance, violations of the Allied Powers, such as the bombing of Dresden or the attacks on Hiroshima and Nagasaki, were ignored.[59] The two tribunals marked a new way 'to talk about' accountability. The moral justification remained ambivalent. The naissance of international trials masked a bitter irony. While pushing for the trial of new international crimes in the name of humanity, 'the adjudicating states either condoned (or practiced as official policy) their own versions of racial mythologies: Britain and France violently put down demands for independence in "their" colonies in Africa and Asia while the United States denied its citizens of African descent basic human rights'.[60] In contemporary practice, such double standards continue to exist.[61] Technically, it is possible to investigate and prosecute international crimes during ongoing violations, i.e. before victory or defeat of a specific party. But in many cases actual efforts have only started after the end of conflict. This means that they are de facto shaped by the political realities of the post-conflict order.[62] There is a risk that only 'losers' of a conflict will face prosecution.[63] Some formal safeguards have been put in place to mitigate victor's justice critiques. In modern tribunals, jurisdictional frameworks and procedures have been adjusted to provide a more objective focus on atrocities. A key justification of the turn to global justice institutions is their alleged impartiality. It requires investigations and prosecution to be even-handed.[64] Modern institutions typically look into particular situations of crisis that are defined in territorial and personal terms. For instance, the ICTY and the ICTR were vested with the mandate to investigate crimes committed on the territory of the former Yugoslavia and Rwanda. Some states claimed expressly that they should be no victor's tribunals.[65] Mandates relating to specific incidents or singular events (such as the 'Hariri killing' in Lebanon) or the prosecution of specific groups have become more suspect. The ICC is required to act in relation to specific 'situations'.[66] The Court expressly rejected a group-based definition of the 'situation' in Uganda.[67] This approach seeks to preserve the objectivity of investigations and prosecutions and to

---

[59] For a critique, see O. Yasuaki, 'The Tokyo Trial: Between Law and Politics', in H. Chihiro, *The Tokyo War Crimes Trial* (Tokyo: Kōdansha, 1986), 45–52.

[60] Mutua, 'Never Again', 171.

[61] W. Schabas, 'Victor's Justice: Selecting "Situations" at the International Criminal Court' (2010) 43 *John Marshall Law Review* 535.

[62] For an argument that international criminal law is virtually always de facto victor's justice, see D. Luban, 'The Legacies of Nuremberg', in Mettraux, *Perspectives on the Nuremberg Trial*, 658.

[63] M. Damaška, 'What Is the Point of International Criminal Justice?' (2008) 83 *Chicago–Kent Law Review*, 329, 361.

[64] Art. 54 (1) of the Rome Statute.

[65] See the statement of Madeleine Albright at the adoption of SC Res. 827, S/PV.3217, 25 May 1993, 12 ('This will be no victors' tribunal. The only victor that will prevail in this endeavour is the truth'). See also the statement of the Russian representative ('for the first time in history, it is not the victors who are judging the vanquished, but the entire international community that, through the Tribunal, will be passing sentence on those who are grossly violating not only the norms of international law but even quite simply our human concepts of morality and humanity'). Ibid., 44.

[66] Rome Statute, Arts. 13 and 14.

[67] The ICC interpreted the referral of the 'situation concerning the Lord's Resistance Army' as a referral concerning the 'situation in Uganda'. Similarly, IS as an 'organization' as such cannot form the object of a 'situation' under the ICC Statute. See C. Stahn, 'Why the ICC Should Be Cautious to Use the Islamic State to Get Out of Africa: Part 1' in *Ejil: Talk!*, 3 December 2014, available at swww.ejiltalk.org/why-the-icc-should-be-cautious-to-use-the-islamic-state-to-get-out-of-africa-part-1/.

prevent one-sided action. However, in practice, international criminal courts and tribunals easily become the object of politics or tactics of 'lawfare'.[68] For instance, self-referrals to the ICC may be used as a tool to continue 'war by other means'.[69]

Impartiality often clashes with selectivity.[70] Only a handful of incidents can be investigated and prosecuted. At the Yugoslavia and Sierra Leone tribunals, prosecutors have been eager to issue indictments against all sides of the conflict. Arguments of 'victor's justice' never full fully disappeared, however, since they cannot be reduced to law.[71] Other situations have revealed open contradictions. For instance, in Rwanda and Uganda prosecutors have only sought indictments against suspects from one side of an armed conflict although suspects from the other sides were implicated in grave atrocities. In Iraq, the Security Council endorsed the establishment of an investigative team to support domestic efforts to 'hold ISIL (Da'esh) accountable ... for acts that may amount to war crimes, crimes against humanity and genocide committed by the terrorist group ISIL (Da'esh) in Iraq',[72] while remaining silent on abuses by Iraqi and other forces.[73] This is sometimes referred to as a 'new' type of 'victor's justice'.[74] It causes challenges to the legitimacy of international institutions. As Victor Peskin has argued, 'The danger is not only that the courts ... perpetuate impunity instead of full accountability. The danger also lies in the prospect that the courts' prosecutions and judgments will be regarded in some quarters (especially in the West) as providing the official and definitive history of the wars in question'.[75]

3.2.2   Imperial Justice

A second critique relates to the interplay between power and inequality.[76] This tension was prominently raised at the Tokyo trial. In his monumental dissent, Radhabinod Pal, the Indian judge on the tribunal, branded the trial as an imperial project by Allied

---

[68] One example is the dispute over the surrender of heads of states with the African Union. It prompted the Assembly of States Parties to amend Rules 68 and 134 quarter of the Rules of Procedure and Evidence on presence at trial of head of states and government, in order to ease tensions with Kenya. It marked in essence diplomacy-led lawmaking for one specific case that might come to haunt the ICC in other contexts.

[69] P. Menon, 'Self-Referring to the International Criminal Court: A Continuation of War by Other Means' (2016) 109 *AJIL Unbound* 260; R. Petit (2010) 'Lawfare and International Tribunals: A Question of Definition? A Reaction on the Creation of the "Khmer Rouge Tribunal"' (2010) 43 *Case Western Reserve Journal of International Law* 189.

[70] R. Cryer, *Prosecuting International Crimes: Selectivity and the International Criminal Law Regime* (Cambridge: Cambridge University Press, 2005).

[71] J. Meernick, 'Victors' Justice or the Law? Judging and Punishing at the International Criminal Tribunal for the Former Yugoslavia (2003) 47 *Journal of Conflict Resolution* 140.

[72] See SC Resolution 2379 of 21 September 2017, para. 2.

[73] For a critique, see Human Rights Watch, 'Flawed Justice: Accountability for ISIS Crimes in Iraq', 5 December 2017.

[74] W. A. Schabas, 'Victor's Justice: Selecting "Situations" at the International Criminal Court' (2010) 43 *John Marshall Law Review*, 535.

[75] V. Peskin, 'Beyond Victor's Justice? The Challenge of Prosecuting the Winners at the International Criminal Tribunals for the Former Yugoslavia and Rwanda' (2016) 4 *Journal of Human Rights* 213, 229.

[76] See generally E. Jouannete 'Universalism and Imperialism: The True-False Paradox of International Law' (2007) 18 *EJIL* 379; F. Cowell, 'Inherent Imperialism' (2017) 15 *JICJ* 667.

Powers[77], geared at creating 'an international legal community in their own image'.[78] Pal claimed that the domination and colonial practices of Western powers by the late nineteenth century should be considered before passing judgment on Japan's responsibility for acts of aggressive war.[79] He noted: 'any interest which the Western powers may now have in the Eastern Hemisphere was acquired mostly through armed violence during this period and none of these wars perhaps would stand the test of being "just war"'.[80] He argued that international criminal justice was marked by imperialism since it maintained a political status quo that reinforced inequality and domination. At the time, Pal was heavily criticized for his stance. Some blamed him for providing impunity to war criminals. Others offered more nuanced critiques. For instance, Judge Röling criticized Pal for neglecting the progress that had been made.[81] He argued that Pal's approach is understandable 'if we look at the past, but not when we look at the future'.[82] However, Pal's argument never fully disappeared.

The ICTY was criticized for institutionalizing a global narrative of the conflict in the Balkans that is dominated by the US and Europe.[83] President Slobodan Milošević raised this critique in his defence strategy before the ICTY. He claimed that the ICTY was an instrument of war, rather than an instrument of peace, because of its alignment with Western power politics.[84] During the ICC negotiations, some members of the non-aligned movement expressed concerns that Security Council influence would 'taint' ICC judicial independence.

African states used this argument in their critique of the ICC. They argued that the ICC is an instrument of Western politics or an impediment to regional solutions. Rwandan President Kagame even went so far as to claim that the ICC 'has been put in place only for African countries, only for poor countries' and that 'Rwanda cannot be part of colonialism, slavery and imperialism'.[85]

In recent years, TWAIL scholars have formulated broader structural critiques that draw attention to (post-)colonial continuities,[86] asymmetric power relations and the

---

[77] Pal argued that the tribunal would be an 'ideological cloak, intended to disguise the vested interests of the interstate sphere and . . . serve as a first line for their defence'. See IMTFE, *Dissentient Judgment of Justice Pal* (Tokyo: Kokusho-Kankokai, 1999), 117.

[78] E. Kopelman, 'Ideology and International Law: The Dissent of the Indian Justice at the Tokyo War Crimes Trial' (1991) 23 *New York University Journal of International Law and Politics* 373, 375.

[79] *Dissentient Judgment of Judge Pal*, 36.

[80] Ibid.

[81] B. Röling and A. Cassese (eds.), *The Tokyo Trial and Beyond* (Oxford; Polity Press, 1993). On Röling, see N. Schrijver, 'B. V. A. Röling: A Pioneer in the Pursuit of Justice and Peace in an Expanded World' (2010) 8 *Journal of International Criminal Justice* 1071.

[82] See C. Hosoya et al. (eds.), *The Tokyo War Crimes Trial: An International Symposium* (Tokyo: Kodansha International, 1986), 153.

[83] B. Žohar, 'Misrepresentation of the Bosnian War by Western Media' (2012) 3 *Journal of Comparative Research in Anthropology and Sociology* 97–110.

[84] J. Graubart and L. Varadarajan, 'Taking Milosevic Seriously: Imperialism, Law and the Politics of Global Justice' (2013) 27 *International Relations* 439.

[85] 'Rwandan President says ICC Targeting African Countries', *Sudan Tribune*, 1 August 2008, at www.sudantribune.com/spip.php?article28103.

[86] A. Anghie, 'The Evolution of International Law: Colonial and Postcolonial Realities' (2006) 27 *Third World Quarterly* 739; B. Rajagopal, *International Law from Below: Development, Social Movements and Third World Resistance* (Cambridge: Cambridge University Press, 2003)

potential inequalities that international criminal law can create.[87] For example, Mahmoud Mamdani has argued that international criminal justice is part of a new 'international humanitarian order'[88] in which there is a worrying emphasis 'on big powers as enforcers of justice internationally' and a thin conception of justice.[89] Both the role of the Security Council and the framing of the complementarity regime have been criticized for institutionalizing sovereign inequality, perpetuating external dominance or entrenching images of saviour and state failure.[90]

In legal discourse, such critiques are often regarded with suspicion because they transcend legal argument and are driven by specific strategic or political interests. The 'imperial' analogy is often abused.[91] International criminal law is in many ways an antidote to classical imperial or colonial forms of domination and subordination. It is to some extent a success of the power of small states in international law. However, it raises equality and justice dilemmas that cannot merely be swept aside. They do not arise in the form of traditional hierarchies or emancipatory claims relating to all spectrums of life ('mission civilisatrice'),[92] but in a novel and more subtle way.[93] Some scholars have called this 'inherent imperialism'.[94]

Self-interest has played a crucial role in the turn to global institutions. Many tribunals were created out of moral convenience. For instance, the establishment of the ICTY was initially branded as 'an act of tokenism by the world community ... that would give the appearance of moral concern'.[95] Some members of the Global South claim that they never had a fully free choice when adhering to international justice instruments. Their choice was rather like the 'Agree' button on the Microsoft Terms and Conditions in relation to software updates,[96] in light of economic and aid

---

[87] Reynolds and Xavier, 'The Dark Corners of the World', 962–969; Anghie and Chimni, 'Third World Approaches to International Law and Individual Responsibility', 91.

[88] M. Mamdani, 'New Humanitarian Order', at www.thenation.com/article/new-humanitarian-order/.

[89] R. Schuerch, *The International Criminal Court at the Mercy of Powerful States* (The Hague: TMC Asser Press, 2017).

[90] Cowell, 'Inherent Imperialism', 677; C. Nielsen, 'From Nuremberg to The Hague: The Civilizing Mission of International Criminal Law' (2008) 14 *Auckland University Law Review* 81. For a critique of the 'failing state' imagery, see C. Call, 'The Fallacy of the "Failed State"' (2008) 29 *Third World Quarterly* (2008) 1491.

[91] On the vulnerability of such critiques, see D. Crane, 'White Man's Justice: Applying International Justice after Regional Third World Conflicts' (2006) 27 *Cardozo Law Review* 1683, 1686 ('African leaders can easily manipulate popular thinking by loudly declaring that the justice being imposed (and threatening the status quo or a leader's power) is "white man's justice," playing upon the fears of colonialism as a way of excusing the rampant corruption and impunity that is Africa, particularly West Africa'). See also B. J. Cannon, D. R. Pkalya and B. Maragia; 'The International Criminal Court and Africa: Contextualizing the Anti-ICC Narrative' (2016) 2 *African Journal of International Criminal Justice* 1.

[92] B Bowden, *The Empire of Civilization: The Evolution of an Imperial Idea* (Chicago: University of Chicago Press, 2009).

[93] It reflects a certain democratization in international relations. It empowers the role of individuals as holders of rights against oppression. See Report of the Special Rapporteur on the Promotion of Truth, Justice, Reparation and Guarantees of Non-recurrence, A/HRC/21/46, 9 August 2012, para. 30.

[94] Cowell, 'Inherent Imperialism', 669, arguing that that inherent imperialism is 'predicated on the domination of weaker states and the diminution of their sovereign decision-making capacities'.

[95] G. Bass, *Stay the Hand of Vengeance* (Princeton, NJ: Princeton University Press, 2000), 203.

[96] On this image of constraints relating to consent, see J. Weiler, 'The Geology of International Law: Governance, Democracy and Legitimacy'(2005) 64 *Zeitschrift für ausländisches öffentliches Recht und Völkerrecht* 547, 557.

conditionalities and the emergence of a 'rule of law economy'.[97] The ICC has struggled to bring 'hard cases' that threaten powerful states.[98]

As Martti Koskeniemi has argued, 'criminalization of international politics ... also strengthens the hand of those who are in a position to determine what acts count as "crimes"'.[99] International criminal courts and tribunals are part of a broader network of power. They exercise different forms of authority in relation to states, other organizations, individuals or groups: coercive and physical powers over individuals, formal and informal institutional powers (e.g. rule-making and decision-making power), and certain forms of social power.[100] The exercise of their powers may create certain forms of hierarchy or fuel inequality, inadvertently or based on pressure from global networks (e.g. multilateral diplomacy, NGOs). For example, international criminal courts and tribunals may produce new subjects and fix meanings through the qualification of conflicts and crimes, or the branding of individuals as 'perpetrators' or 'victims'. The focus on atrocity crime may turn the attention more to states in crisis, rather than stable societies. Concepts such as 'leadership responsibility' or 'gravity' thresholds in international criminal jurisdiction tend to marginalize the influence of economic and political policies of Western leaders and corporations on conflict.[101]

3.2.3 Globalization Critiques

A third line of critique questions the political economy and global orientation of international criminal justice.[102] There are fears that the turn to global institutions creates discrepancies between 'ordinary' justice and elitist international justice regimes.[103]

International criminal courts and tribunals are vulnerable to critiques of technocratization or bureaucratization, i.e. the application of standardized or self-serving decision-making processes or forms of organization to societal problems. Critics argue that the invocation of universal standards, and their enforcement, may empower a global justice industry rather than grassroots-driven approaches.[104] The operation of

---

[97] Clarke, *Fictions of Justice*, 81.

[98] See W. A. Schabas, 'The Banality of International Justice' (2013) 11 *JICJ* 545.

[99] Koskenniemi, 'Hersch Lauterpacht and the Development of International Criminal Law', 825.

[100] Power involves 'the production, in and through social relations, of effects that shape the capacities of actors to determine their circumstances and fate. See M. Barnett and R. Duvall, 'Power in International Politics' (2005) 59 *International Organization* 39.

[101] Schabas, 'Banality of International Justice', 549–550.

[102] See S. Nouwen and W. Werner, 'Doing Justice to the Political: The International Criminal Court in Uganda and Sudan' (2010) 21 *EJIL* 941; S. Kendall, 'Commodifying Global Justice: Economies of Accountability at the International Criminal Court' (2015) 13 *JICJ* 113.

[103] This argument draws on critiques voiced in relation to humanitarian work more generally. See D. Kennedy, *The Dark Sides of Virtue: Reassessing International Humanitarism* (Princeton, NJ: Princeton University Press, 2004).

[104] See C. Schwöbel, 'The Market and Marketing Culture of International Criminal Law', in Schwöbel, *Critical Approaches*, 264–275; Dixon and Tenove, 'International Criminal Justice as a Transnational Field', 393.

justice institutions may create structural dependencies and new forms of international 'ownership', including ownership over narratives and knowledge.

Judgments and decisions are often based on restricted input and geared at social elites.[105] There is an entire circle of global justice professionals who move from one crisis to the next, without deeper or long-term structural embedding in the conflict situation.[106] This 'professionalization' has certain disempowering effects. It creates risks that knowledge and expertise relating to the adjudication of international crimes develop mostly internationally, rather than domestically or locally.[107] There are fears that international justice operates as a frame to 'divide and judge the world'.[108] As Sarah Nouwen has shown in her study on the effects of the ICC, international justice becomes ambivalent if domestic actors simply imitate the normative and procedural universe of the ICC.[109]

Concerns relating to the efficiency and effects of global criminal institutions have prompted a search for alternatives. Instead of seeing a greater degree of homogeneity and centralization, international criminal law is becoming more pluralist. Hybridity is witnessing a revival due to the desire to connect justice more directly to affected populations. New regional initiatives are emerging in response to the selectivity and governance critiques of global institutions.[110]

3.2.4   Socio-Legal Critiques

Socio-legal studies have drawn attention to the limits of legalism,[111] and some deeper ethical dilemmas that affect the justification, scientific grounding and working methods of international criminal justice. Global justice institutions derive empathy and support from the idea of humanitarian crisis, but the adjudication of atrocity may entail a presentation of crisis, evil or 'otherness' that bears traces of alienation or fiction.

International criminal trials involve inquiries into cultures and societies that are often foreign to judges or prosecutors. The judicial process relies on certain social ideal types (i.e. ideas of organization, formation of plan and policy, use of command)

---

[105] The sheer amount of documents makes it hard to follow cases. Vocabulary and procedures are highly technical. Decisions are more geared towards global audiences, rather than victims or societies affected by crime. Their outcome is shaped by institutional practices and automatisms that detract attention from social context. See U. Baxi, 'Postcolonial Legality', in H. Schwarz and S. Ray (eds.), *A Companion to Postcolonial Studies* (Oxford: Blackwell, 2000) 540, 551–552; M. Barnett, 'Humanitarianism as Scholarly Vocation', in M. Barnett and T. Weiss (eds.), *Humanitarianism in Question: Politics, Power, Ethics* (Ithaca: Cornell University Press, 2008), 235, 255; Kennedy, *Dark Sides*, 26–28.

[106] Baylis, 'Tribunal-Hopping with the Post-Conflict Justice Junkies', 361.

[107] For democratization of access to information, see M. Bergsmo, *Complementarity and the Challenges of Equality and Empowerment*, FICHL Policy Brief Series No. 8 (2011), 3–4.

[108] See D. Otto, 'Subalternity and International Law: The Problems of Global Community and the Incommensurability of Difference', in E.-D. Smith and P. Fitzpatrick (eds.), *Laws of the Postcolonial* (Ann Arbor: University of Michigan Press, 1999), 145–180.

[109] S. Nouwen, *Complementarity in the Line of Fire* (Cambridge: Cambridge University Press, 2013), 413.

[110] See Section 3.4.

[111] See J. N. Shklar, *Legalism: Law, Morals, and Political Trials* (Cambridge, MA: Harvard University Press, 1986).

to categorize violence. This representation may not always offer a proper fit to social reality. International criminal courts and tribunals or foreign courts may treat fundamental socio-legal or anthropological questions (e.g. determinations of victimhood, group characterizations) as matters of 'common knowledge', rather than testing them through scientific inquiry.[112] The underlying picture is often constructed through mediated knowledge, i.e. information from states, NGOs or international organizations that have a normative interest in the use of specific labels and their connotations. This process opens international criminal justice to critiques of 'orientalization'.[113] As anthropologist Kamari Clarke has shown, global justice may create artificial representations.[114] The individual is not regarded as a subject as it is, but rather trimmed to fit certain roles or ideal types. There is, in particular, a strong tendency to rely on archetypes of victimhood. The 'victim' becomes to some extent a 'universalized victim' that is emblematic of the harm and suffering caused to the international community as a whole.

The investigation and prosecution of crimes by global institutions involves a certain degree of voyeurism (i.e. viewing the drama of others), and exhibitionist features. This creates ethical dilemmas. Critics point out that harm is to some extent instrumentalized. A crisis situation may easily become a laboratory for justice. NGOs and investigators use the suffering and harm of others for self-serving purposes.[115] This phenomenon has been cynically referred to as 'stealing the pain of others'.[116]

3.3   Paradoxes

International criminal institutions are marked by multiple paradoxes.[117] There is a strong discrepancy between reality and expectation. Global criminal institutions face broad, if not impossible, mandates. They are meant to be normative, formal and detached arbiters of justice, but at the same time efficient managers and social problem solvers. Their governance structures involves different organs that do not necessarily speak with one voice. Whatever courts do is subject to some form of critique, or contestation. International criminal law is marked by intractable

---

[112] See I. Bantekas, 'The Anthropological Dimension of International Crimes and International Criminal Justice', in Bantekas and Mylonaki, *Criminological Approaches to International Criminal Law*, 240, 253.

[113] This critique is related to the work of Edward Said, who was instrumental in the study of 'Orientalism'. E. W. Said, *Orientalism; Western Conceptions of the Orient* (New York: Vintage, 1978). European societies represented notions of modernity, rationality, morality and lawfulness, while others were expressly or implicitly branded as premodern, irrational, immoral and lawless. In the legal field, this approach has gained relevance in the study of legal transplants, and their impacts ('legal orientalism'). T. Ruskola, *Legal Orientalism: China, the United States, and Modern Law* (Cambridge, MA: Harvard University Press, 2013).

[114] See K. Clarke, 'The Rule of Law Through Its Economies of Appearances: The Making of the African Warlord' (2011) 18 *Indiana Journal of Global Legal Studies* 7; Clarke, *Fictions of Justice*, 105–109.

[115] See T. Madlingozi, 'On Transitional Justice Entrepreneurs and the Production of Victims' (2010) 2 *Journal of Human Rights Practice* 208.

[116] S. H. Razack, 'Stealing the Pain of Others: Reflections on Canadian Humanitarian Responses' (2007) 29 *Review of Education, Pedagogy, and Cultural Studies* 375.

[117] See e.g. L. Vinjamuri, 'International Criminal Court and the Paradox of Authority' (2016) 79 *Law and Contemporary Problems* (2016) 275.

relationships or tensions. Darryl Robinson has framed this as 'inescapable dyads'. For 'any position' that international criminal courts and tribunals take, 'one or more powerful criticisms can inevitably be advanced'.[118]

In practice, it is important to distinguish the functions of the institution as a whole from the objectives of specific proceedings. Institutions are often vested with certain broad objectives, such as deterrence, elucidation of facts or justice for victims. Procedures have a more limited function. They give effect to rights, or pursue specific rationales, such as determining guilt or innocence or revealing a 'legal' rather than a broader 'historical truth'.[119]

3.3.1   Goal Ambiguity

The mandates of international criminal courts and tribunals are marked by a considerable degree of 'goal ambiguity'.[120] In the 1990s, international criminal institutions were associated with lofty and partly overambitious goals. In his 2004 report on the 'Rule of Law and Transitional Justice in Conflict and Post-Conflict Societies', the UN Secretary-General outlined a list of broadly defined goals. They include: retribution (i.e. bringing responsible perpetrators to justice), ending violations and preventing their recurrence, 'securing justice and dignity for victims', establishing 'a record of past events', promoting national 'reconciliation', 're-establishing the rule of law', and contributing to the 'restoration of peace'.[121] The framing and application of these goals remains controversial.[122]

There is a clash between a security-oriented, a human rights-based and a more traditional criminal justice-oriented reading of mandates.[123] For example, some suggest that the mandate of international courts should remain restricted to classical criminal justice aims.[124] Others concede that domestic criminal law goals may require adjustment in an international context, or that there might be modest space for broader 'transformative' goals.[125]

---

[118] D. Robinson, 'Inescapable Dyads: Why the International Criminal Court Cannot Win' (2015) 28 *LJIL* 323.

[119] S. Zappalá, *Human Rights in International Criminal Proceedings* (Oxford: Oxford University Press, 2003), 16.

[120] On 'goal ambiguity' as a problem, see Y. Shany, 'Assessing the Effectiveness of International Courts: A Goal-Based Approach' (2012) 106 *AJIL* 225, 233.

[121] See *Report of the Secretary-General on the Rule of Law and Transitional Justice in Conflict and Post-Conflict Societies*, UN Doc S/2004.616, 23 August 2004, para. 38.

[122] The prioritization of goals may shift gradually over time in line with the progression of the mandate of the relevant institution. For instance, the ICTY started as a deterrence-based and retributive justice mechanism. However, with the adoption of the 'completion' strategy, the focus shifted to a greater extent towards local empowerment.

[123] See with respect to the ICC, G. P. Fletcher and J. D. Ohlin, 'The ICC: Two Courts in One?' (2006) 4 *JICJ* 428, at 428–433.

[124] See e.g. O-Gon Kwon, 'The Challenge of an International Criminal Trial as Seen from the Bench' (2007) 7 *JICJ* 360, 372–373; I. Bonomy, 'The Reality of Conducting a War Crimes Trial' (2007) 7 *JICJ* 348, 353.

[125] See generally E. Daly, 'Transformative Justice: Charting a Path to Reconciliation' (2002) 12 *International Legal Perspectives* 73.

3.3.1.1 Prevention and Deterrence

There is considerable uncertainty as to whether and how international criminal institutions affect prevention and deterrence.[126] Some voices claim that 'acting to prevent before the fact, as opposed to acting to punish after the fact' should be the 'primary technique of international law for dealing with mass murder'.[127] The actual contribution of international criminal justice to the prevention of crime is strongly grounded in faith and belief.[128]

Deterrence relates to the 'ability of a legal system to discourage or prevent certain conduct through threats of punishment or other expression of disapproval'.[129] The very argument that international criminal proceedings deter potential abusers is based on speculation. The logic of deterrence relies on a hypothesis, namely a threat created through the certainty, severity or speed of punishment, and its alleged perception by the defendant. Specific deterrence relies on the fiction that lawyers can 'read the mind' of perpetrators and that rational cost–benefit calculations determine the behaviour of defendants. General deterrence relies on the broader demonstration effect of criminal justice and changes in the perception of costs/risks more generally. Both theories entail a great degree of uncertainty, i.e. faith in the logic of the model of deterrence.[130]

Deterrence stemming from the enforcement of laws is tied to two factors: the likelihood of punishment and its severity. These two factors are problematic in the context of international criminal justice. The 'certainty of punishment' is compromised by the selectivity of international criminal justice.[131] The severity of punishment is contested in light of sentencing practice.[132] Proponents point towards greater 'compliance rates' with human rights decisions/monitoring or a correlation between 'justice' threats and crime statistics in individual situations.[133] However, there are many counterfactuals. Ideology-driven perpetrators may not perceive the exercise of international criminal justice as a sanction, but as a publicity tool, or a reward, compared to national penalties. For instance, when LRA leader Joseph Kony was tracked down in Garamba Park in the Congo, he claimed not to understand ICC charges, since he

---

[126] J. Ku and J. Nzelibe, 'Do International Criminal Tribunals Deter or Exacerbate Humanitarian Atrocities?' (2006) 84 *Washington University Law Review* 777; D. Wippman, 'Atrocities, Deterrence, and the Limits of International Justice (1999) 23 *Fordham Journal of International Law* 473, 488; P. Akhavan, 'Beyond Impunity: Can International Criminal Justice Prevent Future Atrocities?' (2001) 95 *AJIL* 7, 31; J. Schense and L. Carter, *Two Steps Forward, One Step Back: The Deterrent Effect of International Criminal Tribunals* (Brussels: Torkel Opsahl Academic EPublisher, 2017).

[127] W. M. Reisman, 'Acting Before Victims Become Victims: Preventing and Arresting Mass Murder' (2008) 40 *Case Western Reserve Journal of International Law* 57, at 59.

[128] M, Aukerman, 'Extraordinary Evil, Ordinary Crime: A Framework for Understanding Transitional Justice' (2002) 15 *Harvard Human Rights Journal* 39; K. Cronin-Furman, 'Managing Expectations. International Criminal Trials and the Prospects for Deterrence of Mass Atrocity' (2013) 7 *International Journal of Transitional Justice* 434.

[129] See P. Akhavan, 'Justice in The Hague, Peace in the Former Yugoslavia? A Commentary on the United Nations War Crimes Tribunal' (1999) 20 *Human Rights Quarterly* 737, 741.

[130] See Tallgren, 'Sensibility and Sense', 570–579.

[131] See J. Mendez, 'Justice and Prevention', in Stahn and El Zeidy, *The International Criminal; Court and Complementarity*, 33, 35.

[132] See Section 5.1.4.

[133] E.g. Sikkink, 'Justice Cascade', 162 et seq.

did not believe that it was possible to draw a distinction between innocent 'civilians' and legitimate targets in the conflict in Northern Uganda.

Hardly any empirical study has managed to demonstrate deterrent impact credibly and to trace clear patterns of causation and weigh intermediate causes. For example, the Open Justice Initiative struggled to reach reliable conclusions about the ICTY's general deterrent impact. It stated:

[W]e know some things with sobering certainty: as has often been noted, the creation of the ICTY did not by itself end atrocities in the Balkans. The 1995 genocide in Srebrenica occurred two years after the ICTY was created, while atrocities in Kosovo surged during 1998–99 ... The July 1995 genocide in Srebrenica occurred at a time when the ICTY was in its institutional infancy.[134]

Schense and Carter conclude their comparative study of the ICTY, ICTR, SCSL and ICC with the finding that

[i]t is ... problematic to attempt to measure or correlate deterrence with the work of international criminal courts ... there are too many actors and too many variables to find a direct or even an indirect effect conclusively ... the perceptions of deterrence or lack of deterrence ... are more identifiable and useful in evaluating the impact of international Tribunals.[135]

The main impact of the threat of prosecution lies in its normative appeal and its communicative functions. International investigations and prosecutions may provide awareness of atrocities, limit the choices of conflict entrepreneurs or stimulate accountability measures at the domestic level. As Hyeran Jo and Beth Simmons have shown, prosecutions may increase social pressures and the leverage for accountability among agents that are concerned about their international legitimacy.[136] Yet ultimately deterrence requires a fuller spectrum of measures, ranging from diplomacy, political pressures and sanctions to threats of punishment.[137]

3.3.1.2 Incapacitation

A second point of contestation is the ability of international criminal courts and tribunals to promote political change. Proponents of a security-related reading of mandates argue that international criminal justice may contribute to peace by challenging political authority. However, it remains contested to what extent public condemnation of atrocities and the demonstration of wrongfulness of actions can help to delegitimize former political elites. There are some positive examples. For instance, Radovan Karadžić was prevented from participating in the 1995 Dayton

---

[134] D. Orentlicher, *Shrinking the Space for Denial: The Impact of the ICTY in Serbia* (New York: Open Society Justice Initiative, 2008), 16; D. Orentlicher, *Some Kind of Justice: The ICTY's Impact in Bosnia and Serbia* (Oxford: Oxford University Press, 2018).

[135] Schense and Carter, *Two Steps Forward, One Step Back*, 337.

[136] H. Jo and B. A. Simmons, 'Can the International Criminal Court Deter Atrocity?' (2016) 70 *International Organization* 443.

[137] N. Grono and A. de Courcy Wheeler, 'The Deterrent Effect of the ICC on the Commission of International Crimes by Government Leaders', in Stahn, *Law and Practice of the International Criminal Court*, 1225, 1240.

Peace Talks because of the indictment brought against him by the ICTY. The ICC has called on states to 'eliminate non-essential contacts with individuals subject to an arrest warrant issued by the Court . . ., contribute to the marginalization of fugitives and take steps to prevent that aid and funds meant for humanitarian purposes or peace talks are diverted for the benefit of persons subject to an arrest warrant'.[138] The overarching goal, though, namely to de-legitimize elites or remove them from power, typically exceeds the judicial power of courts.

It is risky to speculate on specific political effects of criminal charges or trials. In the ICC context, many charges have failed to produce the desired effects. For instance, Sudanese President Al-Bashir has faced restrictions in his travel to some ICC states parties, but has managed to retain power domestically, despite genocide charges.[139] The ICC Prosecutor sought to constrain electoral violence in Africa through the Kenyan cases.[140] Yet Uhuru Kenyatta and William Ruto were elected president and deputy president in the 2013 Kenyan elections, although charges against them were confirmed by the ICC at the time.[141] They used the ICC charges in the campaign, in order to present themselves as 'victims'.[142]

A similar paradox is visible in the former Yugoslavia. Prominent defendants such as Slobodan Milošević or Vojislav Šešelj continued to be regarded as national 'heroes', despite international criminal proceedings. They used the trials as a platform to portray themselves as martyrs, presenting 'Serbs as the ultimate victim group'.[143] In this way, they turned the trials from 'individual' into 'national' trials.

3.3.1.3 Historical Clarification

There is a rich debate among experts on to what extent international criminal trials contribute to history and memory.[144] The duty to seek the truth is inherent in the mandate of judges and sometimes an express prosecutorial duty. However, the relationship between judicial fact-finding and historical clarification remains contested. According to some voices, providing a historical record is not a purpose but at best a useful by-product of judicial work. Robert Storey, the executive trial counsel at Nuremberg, and Hannah Arendt have argued that '[t]he purpose of the trial is to

---

[138] OTP, Prosecutorial Strategy 2009–2012, para. 48.

[139] See L. Smith-van Lin, 'Non-Compliance and Law and Politics of State Cooperation: Lessons from the Al Bashir and Kenyatta Cases', in O. Bekou and D. Birkett (eds.), *Cooperation and the International Criminal Court* (Leiden: Brill/ Nijhoff, 2016) 114.

[140] T. Obel Hansen and C. Sriram 'Fighting for Justice (and Survival): Kenyan Civil Society Accountability Strategies and Their Enemies' (2015) 9 *International Journal of Transitional Justice* 407.

[141] The charges against Kenyatta and Ruto were confirmed in 2012. Kenyatta hired a British PR firm, BTP Advisers, to improve his public image and delegitimize ICC trials.

[142] See R. Warah, *War Crimes: How Warlords, Politicians, Foreign Governments and Aid Agencies Conspired To Create A Failed State In Somalia* (Bloomington: AuthorHouse, 2014) 118.

[143] On the narratives, see I. Steflja, 'The Production of the War Criminal Cult: Radovan Karadžić and Vojislav Šešelj at The Hague' (2018) 46 *Nationalities Papers* 52, 61.

[144] R. A. Wilson, *Writing History in International Trials* (Cambridge: Cambridge UniversityPress, 2011); R. A. Wilson, 'Judging History: The Historical Record of the International Criminal Tribunal for the Former Yugoslavia' (2005) 27 *Human Rights Quarterly* 908.

render justice, and nothing else; even the noblest ulterior purposes – "the making of a record …" – can only detract from the law's main business: to weigh the charges brought against the accused, to render judgment and to mete out due punishment'.[145] According to this line of argument, history should be left to truth and reconciliation commissions, rather than to criminal courts.

Other scholars argue that trials in themselves produce a living record that has historical significance. For instance, Lawrence Douglas has argued in his study of the *Eichmann* and *Demjanjuk* trials (*The Memory of Judgment*) that judicial proceedings can mark a tribute to history and memory, in light of their specific set-up and orchestration.[146] The question is thus not whether proceedings contribute to history, but rather how they do it. Proponents of this position claim that international criminal proceedings may render certain facts less contestable through publicity and testing of evidence. Yet it would go too far to equate judicial fact-finding with accurate historiography or even a broader 'truth-finding' procedure.

Historical and judicial fact-finding differ in their aims and methodologies. International criminal proceedings are mainly aimed at individualizing roles and attributing responsibility. They seek to reduce the complexity of violence to a 'manageable narrative' through sampling facts, legal abstraction and tangible lines of causation.[147] Historical fact-finding takes a broader angle at determining causes and effects and provides greater leeway to admit complexity in reasoning or uncertainty. Historical 'fact-finding' is thus not a primary objective of international criminal proceedings.[148]

3.3.1.4 Reconciliation

In past decades, there has been a strong trend to argue that the purposes of trials reach beyond retribution and vengeance.[149] The prospect of reconciliation is often mentioned as a potential rationale. However, it is questionable to what extent reconciliation should be framed as a goal of international criminal justice per se.[150] The notion itself is ambiguous. It extends beyond the victim–offender relationship that forms part of the criminal trial. It involves interpersonal forgiveness and collective dimensions, including community-based, societal or national reconciliation. It contains certain retrospective elements, such as understanding the past, healing or undoing of wrong,

---

[145] Arendt, *Eichmann in Jerusalem*, 253.

[146] See L. Douglas, *The Memory of Judgment: Making Law and History in the Trials of the Holocaust* (New Haven: Yale University Press, 2001). Douglas makes a powerful argument that the Eichmann and Demjanjuk trials, as well as the trials of Klaus Barbie and Holocaust denier Ernst Zundel, were aimed to do justice both to the defendants and to the history and memory of the Holocaust.

[147] Akhavan, 'Beyond Impunity', 30.

[148] See also Damaška, 'What Is the Point of International Criminal Justice?', 338 ('The best that can be expected … is to provide fragmentary material as a scaffolding for subsequent historical research').

[149] See M. Minow, *Between Vengeance and Forgiveness* (Boston: Beacon Press, 1998); First Annual Report ICTY, UN Doc A/49/342; S/1994/1007, 29 August 1994, paras. 15 and 16.

[150] D. Orentlicher, *Shrinking the Space for Denial*, 58; J. Clark, *International Trials and Reconciliation: Assessing the Impact of the International Criminal Tribunal for the former Yugoslavia* (London: Routledge 2014).

as well as prospective elements (e.g. social repair). It is both a goal, i.e. an ideal state to strive for,[151] and a process 'through which a society moves from a divided past to a shared future'.[152]

The experiences in the Balkans, Latin America and Africa have shown that healing and forgiveness are culturally bound processes that are rooted in local cultures, and start at the level of the individual or community-based structures.[153] The acceptance and internalization of facts are deeply dependent on media or local politics. The presentation of facts alone does not suffice to foster acceptance of truths. Such acceptance is often tied to subjective factors, and narratives. For instance, even a perfectly run trial might fail to reconcile tensions among victim groups, since the perception of reality is heavily shaped by certain emotional or rational factors (e.g. prior attitudes, beliefs, narratives) that impede engagement with other views.[154]

Social science research indicates that reconciliation is linked to cognitive and affective change, grounded in social interaction (e.g. positive experience with the 'other') and a relationship of recognition and trust.[155] It is not linked to the acceptance of a 'single truth' or narrative, but grounded in the acceptance or toleration of conflicting points of view. It lives from the ability to respect the 'other' and tolerate difference, despite opposite or conflicting views of events and facts.[156] This is not something that the criminal trial as such can be expected to establish. The liberal criminal trial may require respect for the will of those who do not want to forgive. Certain acts may simply be beyond forgiveness.

Forgiveness often requires more than a mere apology or generic acknowledgement of responsibility. In the early ICTY practice, guilty pleas were used as a means of reconciling punishment with acknowledgment of wrong or apology.[157] Such admissions of guilt cannot be taken at face value. For instance, in 2003 Biljana Plavšić entered a guilty plea before the tribunal. This move was initially heralded as a significant step towards the advancement of reconciliation,[158] but after sentencing she retracted her guilty plea and expression of remorse. This experience highlights the fragility of negotiated justice. If an apology is offered in return for sentence leniency, it might not necessarily benefit reconciliation.

---

[151] Aiken defines it as 'the act of creating or rebuilding friendship and harmony between rival sides after resolution of a conflict, or transforming the relations between rival sides from hostility and resentment to friendly and harmonious relations'. See N. T. Aiken, *Identity, Reconciliation and Transitional Justice: Overcoming Intractability in Divided Societies* (London: Routledge 2014), 18.

[152] D. Bloomfield, T. Barns and L. Huyse, *Reconciliation after Conflict: A Handbook* (Stockholm: International Institute for Democracy and Electoral Assistance, 2003), 12.

[153] E. Stover and H. Weinstein, *My Neighbour, My Enemy* (Cambridge: Cambridge University Press, 2004).

[154] On the ICTY, see M. Milanović, 'The Impact of the ICTY on the Former Yugoslavia: An Anticipatory Postmortem' (2016) 110 AJIL 233.

[155] See Aiken, *Identity, Reconciliation and Transitional Justice*, 20.

[156] See D. A. Crocker, 'Democracy and Punishment: Punishment, Reconciliation, and Democratic Deliberation' (2002) 5 *Buffalo Criminal Law Review* 509–549.

[157] J. Clark, 'Plea Bargaining at the ICTY: Guilty Pleas and Reconciliation' (2009) 20 *EJIL* 415.

[158] See D. Saxon, 'Exporting Justice: Perceptions of the ICTY Among the Serbian, Croatian, and Muslim Communities in the Former Yugoslavia' (2005) 4 *Journal of Human Rights* 559–572.

Similar concerns have been raised at the ICC in the context of the apology of Germain Katanga. Katanga's remorse was offered after the sentencing judgment, and before the decision on appeal.[159] It caused resentment among victims, since it was perceived as a trade-off for the discontinuance of the appeal.[160] Many experts, therefore, rightly argue that the role and impact of international trials on reconciliation is a modest one.[161] The ICTY acknowledged openly in its last report that 'the Tribunal has not been able to provide justice to victims as fast as the international community, or indeed the Tribunal itself, would have wished'.[162]

3.3.1.5 Building Domestic Capacity

In past decades, the idea of capacity building has gained increased attention in justice strategies.[163] The concept has its origin in development assistance. It is associated with knowledge transfer, sharing of information, evidence and expertise, or division of labour or institutional reform. The concept itself is somewhat misleading. The idea that international justice can create 'domestic capacity' has a certain patronizing quality. It evokes parallels with notions of emancipation in colonial discourse. It suggests that domestic societies need to conform to international narratives and structural measures in order to gain 'ownership' over justice.

The experiences are mixed.[164] In certain cases, such as Rwanda or the former Yugoslavia, international criminal justice had positive transformative effects, for instance in relation to domestic reform of the judicial sector or detention practices.[165] There also questionable examples however. Practice in some of the first ICC situations (e.g. Uganda, DRC) has shown that investment in national capacity may produce artificial or counterproductive side effects.

---

[159] On the link between the expression of remorse and the discontinuation of the appeal, see *Prosecutor v. Katanga*, ICC-01/04–01/07, Notice of Discontinuance of the Prosecution's Appeal against the Article 74 Judgment of Conviction of Trial Chamber II dated 7 March 2014 in relation to Germain Katanga, 25 June 2014, para 2. See generally C. Stahn, 'Justice Delivered or Justice Denied? The Legacy of the Katanga Judgment' (2014) 12 *JICJ* 809.

[160] The Legal Presentative of Victims criticized that the apology was offered after sentencing and in the context of the abandoning of the appeals. *Prosecutor v. Katanga*, ICC-01/04–01/07, Observations des victimes sur le désistement d'appel du Procureur contre le jugement concernant G. Katanga, 26 June 2014.

[161] L. E. Fletcher and H. M. Weinstein, 'Violence and Social Repair: Rethinking the Contribution of Justice to Reconciliation' (2002) 24 *Human Rights Quarterly* 573; V. Peskin, *International Justice in Rwanda and the Balkans* (Cambridge: Cambridge University Press, 2008), 243 et seq.; D. Mendelhoff, 'Truth-Seeking, Truth Telling, and Postconflict Peacebuilding: Curb the Enthusiasm?' (2004) 6 *International Studies Review* 355.

[162] Assessment and Report of Judge Carmel Agius, President of the ICTY, provided to the Security Council pursuant to paragraph 6 of Security Council Resolution 1534 (2004), S/2017/1001, 29 November 2017, para. 62. Ibid., Annex II, Final Report of the Prosecutor, para. 179 ('the denial of crimes and the glorification of convicted war criminals have become immense challenges preventing real reconciliation and stability in the region').

[163] See generally E. Baylis, 'Reassessing the Role of International Criminal Law: Rebuilding National Courts Through Transnational Networks' (2009) 50 *Boston College Law Review* 1; J. Stromseth, 'Justice on the Ground: Can International Criminal Courts Strengthen Domestic Rule of Law in Post-Conflict Societies?' (2009) 1 *Hague Journal on the Rule of Law* 87.

[164] A. Chehtman, 'Developing Local Capacity for War Crimes Trials: Insights from BiH, Sierra Leone, and Colombia' (2013) 49 *Stanford Journal of International Law* 297.

[165] On the ICTR, see A. Dieng, 'Capacity-Building Efforts of the ICTR: A Different Kind of Legacy' (2011) 9 *Northwestern Journal of International Human Rights* 403; S. Kendall and S. Nouwen, 'Toward an Ethos of Modesty at the International Criminal Tribunal for Rwanda' (2016) 110 *AJIL* 212, 224–226.

ICC action has encouraged the direct application of statutory principles by domestic military courts (DRC)[166] or the creation of specialized crime units (Uganda).[167] However, the ability to strengthen domestic investigation and prosecution depends to a large extent on structural factors and institutional dynamics. Technical assistance, such as transfer of knowledge and skills or the provision of supplies and infrastructure, alone do not suffice.[168] External incentives and pressure for quick solutions may encourage domestic responses that satisfy international audiences but remain exceptional in the local context, or detract from other needs of ordinary justice. If states strengthen domestic systems primarily for the sake of satisfying international agendas, reform efforts may lack sustainability or create artificial legal transplants.[169]

3.3.1.6 Expressivism

Some of the unique strengths of international criminal courts and tribunals lie in their expressivist features.[170] Expressivist theories stress the function of criminal law to articulate and reinforce social norms by signalling 'societal reproach'[171] for the violation of norms. As Bert Röling and the late Judge Antonio Cassese have stressed, 'the principal purpose and function of criminal law ... is not that occasionally a criminal should be sentenced. The very function of criminal law is to strengthen and fortify moral opinions'.[172] Expressivism can be partly traced back to the Nuremberg trials, which were associated with the idea that judicial proceedings are a key instrument in transforming society in post-war Germany.[173] Today, this approach is as relevant as ever in international criminal justice.[174] International criminal justice is not the solution to all accountability problems, nor is international criminal justice in itself suited to 'solve' or fix deeper societal divides. What trials and

---

[166] P. Labuda, 'Applying and "Misapplying" the Rome Statute in the Democratic Republic of the Congo', in De Vos, Kendall and Stahn, *Contested Justice*, 408.

[167] The International Crimes Division in Uganda was initially deemed to be part of the comprehensive peace agreement with the LRA, but has rebranded itself 'as a court of complementarity' in relation to the ICC. See generally K. S. Kihika and M. Regué, *Pursuing Accountability for Serious Crimes in Uganda's Courts*, ICTJ Briefing, January 2015, at www.ictj.org/sites/default/files/ICTJ-Briefing-Uganda-Kwoyelo-2015.pdf.

[168] A. Chehtman and R. Mackenzie, *Capacity Development in International Criminal Justice: A Mapping Exercise of Existing Practice* (London, DOMAC, 2009), 22.

[169] On legal transplants and colonization, see B. S. Cohen, *Colonialism and Its Forms of Knowledge* (Princeton, NJ: Princeton University Press, 2006), 58–75.

[170] See Aloisi and Meernik, *Judgment Day*, 113 et seq.

[171] D. M. Amann, 'Group Mentality, Expressivism, and Genocide' (2002) 2 *International Criminal Law Review* 120.

[172] See Remarks by the Late President Cassese, Hearing of 16 February 2011, available at www.stl-tsl.org/en/media/press-releases/summary-of-president-cassese-s-speech?print=1&tmpl=component. For an analysis of Röling's role, see L. van den Herik, 'The Dutch Engagement with the Project of International Criminal Justice' (2010) 57 *Netherlands International Law Review* 303, 311.

[173] See Jackson, Opening Statement before the IMT, Trial of the Major War Criminals before the International Military Tribunal Vol. II Proceedings, 14 November 1945–30 November 1945, 98–99 ('They have so identified themselves with the philosophies they conceived and with the forces they directed that any tenderness to them is a victory and an encouragement to all the evils which are attached to their names').

[174] On expressivist theory and affirmation of faith in the rule of law, see H. van der Wilt, 'Why International Criminal Lawyers Should Read Mirjan Damaska', in C. Stahn and L. van den Herik (eds.), *Future Perspectives on International Criminal Justice* (The Hague: TMS Asser Press, 2010), 44, 99.

institutions signify may sometimes be more important than who they try or what conviction they achieve.[175]

Expressivist rationales are useful to understand some of the strengths and limits of global criminal justice institutions. For example, international criminal courts cannot merely be judged by their number of cases or the severity of punishment. Expressive theories offer a framework to understand how a comparatively limited system of justice (e.g. in terms of arrest, prosecutions or punishment) may be socially significant. Like supreme courts or other highest judiciaries in a domestic system, their strength and virtue may lie in their ability to disapprove criminal conduct, 'send messages', shape debates and discourse, and influence the generation and perception of norms.[176] More than other mechanisms, they are able to express social disapproval of a particular form of behaviour because of their global reach' and 'audience'.[177] Their legal decisions thus have strong normative authority, even if they suffer from non-compliance.

3.3.2   *Multiple Roles and Identities*

A second paradox of international criminal courts and tribunals is their multifaceted identity. To the outside world, they often appear as 'one' unitary entity or one voice. However, they are complex agents with different identities and voices. The institutions as such involve multiple organs with different responsibilities, such as the Prosecution, the judiciary, the Presidency, the Registry or in some cases the Defence. These different organs share distinct interests and may speak with different voices.

The role of international criminal courts and tribunals goes far beyond punishment. They are multiple courts in one.[178] Their core function is criminal, namely to adjudicate crimes and try perpetrators, but their mandates may encompass certain dispute settlement functions. For instance, legal disputes over jurisdiction or cooperation may involve interstate litigation. The criminal function is complemented by certain 'civil' functions. For example, proceedings relating to reparation primarily oppose victims and perpetrators.[179] The protection of witnesses and victims involves security-related functions.

Global justice institutions are not only legal agents, but social actors. They are employers, service providers, negotiators and communicative agencies. International

---

[175] J. Subotic, *Hijacked Justice: Domestic Appropriation of International Norms*, www.du.edu/korbel/hrhw/workingpapers/2005/28-subotic-2005.pdf. On symbolism, see M. Aksenova, 'Symbolism as a Constraint on International Criminal Law' (2017) 30 *LJIL* 475.

[176] T. Meijers and M. Glasius, 'Trials as Messages of Justice: What Should Be Expected of International Criminal Courts?' (2016) 30 *Ethics and International Affairs* 431.

[177] See S. Ivković and J. Hagan, *Reclaiming Justice* (Oxford: Oxford University Press, 2011), 153; Koskenniemi, 'Between Impunity and Show Trials', 11.

[178] F. Jessberger and J. Geneuss, 'The Many Faces of the International Criminal Court' (2012) 10 *Journal of International Criminal Justice* 1081; G. P. Fletcher and J. D. Ohlin, 'The ICC: Two Courts in One?' (2006) 4 *Journal of International Criminal Justice* 428.

[179] See C. Stahn, 'Reparative Justice after the Lubanga Appeal Judgment' (2015) 13 *JICJ* 801.

criminal justice entails different forms of politics: diplomacy, judicial politics. Politics plays a role in the creation of tribunals, the appointment of prosecutors, the funding of operations and the closure of mandates. Many operational decisions require policy choices, in relation to context, arrest, charging policy or security assessments. The main question is thus not whether justice has political features and ramifications, but rather how it engages with them.[180]

The governance structures differ from domestic contexts. National institutions operate in a context where executive power is subject to judicial scrutiny. In international law, the idea of separation of powers is less developed. Executive and legislative powers are often vested in states. International criminal courts and tribunals navigate between judicial independence and stakeholder dependency. They aspire to be independent from the influence of states, but they depend on these same entities, or on other international institutions (e.g. the UN) to receive budgets and cooperation.

A typical criticism of international criminal justice institutions is their alleged lack of accountability. For example, courts are sometimes described as bureaucratic institutions that are 'accountable to no single government'.[181] This critique is partially misguided. International criminal courts require different accountability mechanisms than domestic entities.[182] They are not formally accountable to local populations or single states. They serve a broader constituency. Although they may be subject to less formal channels of control than domestic courts, they are in reality exposed to a greater degree of scrutiny and informal checks and balances than their domestic counterparts, due to their global function, their diverse interlocutors and their operational and funding constraints.[183] As Marlies Glasius has argued, a high degree of scrutiny arises through certain communicative relationships, such as 'accessibility, self-justification, and encouragement of debate'.[184]

In practice, accountability structures differ considerably across institutions. The ad hoc tribunals enjoyed a relatively high degree of independence from their creating body.[185] The situation is different in relation to hybrid mechanisms. They are de facto highly dependent on domestic systems. The ICC Assembly of States Parties strengthened accountability ex post by developing an independent oversight mechanism.[186]

---

[180] M. J. Struett, 'Why the International Criminal Court Must Pretend to Ignore Politics' (2012) 26 *Ethics & International Affairs* 83–92.

[181] See P. McNerney, 'The International Criminal Court: Issues for Consideration by the United States Senate' (2001) 64 *Law & Contemporary Problems* 181, 185–186, 191.

[182] On accountability of Truth Commissions, see C. Tomuschat, 'Between National and International Law: Guatemala's Historical Clarification Commission', in V. Götz, P. Selmer and R. Wolfrum (eds.), *Liber Amicorum Günther Jaenicke* (Heidelberg: Springer, 1998), 991.

[183] On accountability, see A. M. Danner, 'Enhancing the Legitimacy and Accountability of Prosecutorial Discretion at the International Criminal Court' (2003) 97 *AJIL* 510; J. Turner, 'Accountability of International Prosecutors', in Stahn, *Law and Practice of the International Criminal Court*, 382.

[184] See M. Glasius, 'Do International Criminal Courts Require Democratic Legitimacy?' (2012) 23 *EJIL* 43, 64.

[185] Regarding the independence of the ICTY, see J. E. Alvarez, 'Nuremberg Revisited: The Tadic Case' (1996) 7 *EJIL* 245.

[186] Establishment of an independent oversight mechanism, ICC-ASP/8/Res.1. On the complex relationship between the Court and the ASP, see J. O'Donohue, 'The ICC and the ASP', in Stahn, *Law and Practice of the International Criminal Court*, 136.

3.4   Justice Models

The existing institutional architecture encompasses at least four major dimensions: domestic, international, hybrid and regional justice. Traditionally, domestic and international justice have been at the centre. However, over the past two decades many new and hybrid formats have emerged. They are complemented by multiple quasi-judicial or informal justice mechanisms.

3.4.1   Domestic Enforcement

States are the main point of entry for the exercise of criminal jurisdiction, and ultimately the guardians of accountability in the long term.[187] They are under an obligation to investigate and prosecute offences under human rights law, international humanitarian law and international criminal law.[188] This duty is in line with the conception of sovereignty as responsibility.

The landscape of domestic justice is diverse. The advantage of domestic jurisdiction is that it captures a wide spectrum of offences and offenders, including medium and lower level perpetrators and bystanders. States enjoy different types of jurisdiction: prescriptive jurisdiction, which concerns the authority to establish rules of behaviour regulating conduct, adjudicative jurisdiction, which entails the power to subject individuals and other subjects to legal proceedings, and enforcement jurisdiction, which involves the power to enforce the law and sanction non-compliance.[189]

The possibility to investigate and prosecute international crimes depends on jurisdictional reach.[190] Classical international law contains four titles: territoriality which allows a state to exercise jurisdiction if at least one of the constitutive elements of the crime has taken place in its territory;[191] active nationality which covers acts committed by persons having the nationality of the forum state); passive nationality which enables to exercise jurisdiction over acts committed against nationals of the forum state; and universal jurisdiction which involves assertion of jurisdiction over offences regardless of the place where they were committed and the nationalities of the

---

[187] M. Bergsmo, M. Harlem and N. Hayashi (eds.), *Importing Core International Crimes in National Law* (Oslo: Torkel Opsahl Academic EPublisher, 2010); E. King, 'Big Fish, Small Ponds: International Crimes in National Courts' (2015) 90 *Indiana Law Journal* 829; R. Michaels, 'Global Problems in Domestic Courts', in S. Muller, S. Zouridis, M. Frishman and L. Kistemaker, *The Law of the Future and The Future of Law* (Oslo: Torkel Opsahl Academic EPublisher, 2011), 165.

[188] The Geneva Conventions of 1949 require states to establish universal jurisdiction over the grave breaches defined in these Conventions. See generally C. Tomuschat, 'The Duty to Prosecute International Crimes Committed by Individuals', in H.-J. Cremer and H. Steinberger (eds.), *Tradition und Weltoffenheit des Rechts* (Heidelberg: Springer, 2002), 315.

[189] See C. Ryngaert, 'The Concept of Jurisdiction in International Law', in A. Orakhelashvili (ed.), *Research Handbook on Jurisdiction and Immunities in International Law* (Cheltenham: Elgar, 2015) 50, 54 et seq.

[190] See generally S. Macedo, *Universal Jurisdiction: National Courts and the. Prosecution of Serious Crimes Under International Law* (Philadelphia, University of Pennsylvania Press, 2004).

[191] Art. 3 of the 1935 Harvard Draft Convention on Jurisdiction with Respect to Crime recognizes that a state may properly exercise jurisdiction 'with respect to any crime committed in whole or in part within its territory [including] . . . (a) Any participation outside its territory in a crime committed in whole or in part within its territory'. See 'Draft Convention on Jurisdiction with Respect to Crime (Harvard Draft Convention)', (1935) 29 *AJIL* 439.

perpetrator or of the victims.[192] According to the 'effects doctrine', states are able to exercise jurisdiction in cases where conduct takes place abroad but produces substantial, direct and foreseeable effects within their territory.[193]

Domestic courts are generally free to apply their own domestic norms, subject to universally applicable standards and limitations to domestic discretion. It is typically argued that states should, at a minimum, have legislation allowing them to exercise territorial jurisdiction over international crimes and extraterritorial jurisdiction over its nationals who commit crimes abroad.[194] The scope of universal jurisdiction is more contested.[195]

Universal jurisdiction is widely recognized as the jurisdictional title for crimes such as piracy, war crimes,[196] genocide, crimes against humanity or terrorism. It is based on a powerful idea: A crime should not cease to be punishable once a perpetrator crosses national boundaries. Famous cases, such as *Eichmann*,[197] *Pinochet*[198] or *Habré*,[199] have

---

[192] In some cases, domestic courts act as legal agents of international entities. For instance, the ICC Pre-Trial Chamber has held that 'when cooperating with the ICC and therefore acting on its behalf, States Parties are instruments for the enforcement of the jus puniendi of the international community whose exercise has been entrusted to this court when States have failed to prosecute those responsible for the crimes within its jurisdiction'. See ICC, ICC-02/05–01/09, Decision Pursuant to Article 87 (7) of the Statute on the Failure by the Republic of Malawi to Comply with the Cooperation Requests Issued by the Court with Respect to the Arrest and Surrender of Omar Hassan Ahmad Al-Bashir, 12 December 2011, para. 46.

[193] Section 403(2) of the (Third) US Restatement of Foreign Relations Law. See also O'Keefe, *International Criminal Law*, 16.

[194] This duty is based on the close nexus of territoriality and nationality to national sovereignty. Treaty-based duties to prosecute are inter alia contained in the Geneva Conventions and Additional Protocol I, the Genocide Convention, the Convention against Torture and the Convention against Enforced Disappearances. As Cockayne notes, 'territoriality remains the central basis for criminal jurisdiction … [in part because] most other forms of jurisdiction are relatively impractical and inefficient'. J. Cockayne, 'On the Cosmopolitization of Criminal Jurisdiction' (2005) 3 *JICJ* 515, 522.

[195] See generally, E. Kontorovich, 'The Inefficiency of Universal Jurisdiction' (2007) 1 *University of Illinois Law Review* 389; G. Abi-Saab, 'The Proper Role of Universal Jurisdiction' (2003) 1 *JICJ* 596; A. Cassese, 'Is the Bell Tolling for Universality? A Plea for a Sensible Notion of Universal Jurisdiction' (2003) 1 *JICJ* 589; A. J. Colangelo, 'The Legal Limits of Universal Jurisdiction' (2006) 47 *Virginia Journal of International Law* 149.

[196] On the limited level of implementation, see R. van Elst, 'Implementing Universal Jurisdiction over Grave Breaches of the Geneva Conventions' (2000) 13 *LJIL* 815.

[197] In *Eichmann*, universal jurisdiction was applied since Israel did not exist as a state at the time of the commission of crimes. See Israeli Supreme Court, *Attorney General* v. *Adolf Eichmann*, Criminal Appeal 336/61, Judgment, 29 May 1962, para. 12 ('Not only are all the crimes attributed to the Appellant of an international character, but they are crimes whose evil and murderous effects were so widespread as to shake the stability of the international community to its very foundations. The State of Israel, therefore, was entitled, pursuant to the principle of universal jurisdiction, and acting in the capacity of guardian of international law and agents for its enforcement, to try the Appellant. This being the case, it is immaterial that the State of Israel did not exist at the time the offences were committed'). Arguments relating to universal jurisdiction were mixed with the passive personality principle, i.e. crimes committed against the Jewish people.

[198] Lord Browne-Wilkinson noted: '[T]he Torture Convention did provide what was missing: a worldwide universal jurisdiction'. *R* v. *Bow Street Metropolitan Stipendiary Magistrate, ex parte Pinochet Ugarte* (Pinochet III) (2000) 1 AC 147, 204–205); N. Roth-Arriaza, 'The Pinochet Precedent and Universal Jurisdiction' (2001) 35 *New England Law Review* 311; R. C. Power, 'Pinochet and the Uncertain Globalization of Criminal Law' (2007) 39 *George Washington International Law Review* 89; N. Roht-Arriaza, *The Pinochet Effect: Transnational Justice in the Age of Human Rights* (University of Pennsylvania Press, Philadelphia 2005).

[199] Actions were brought under Belgium's universal jurisdiction law and the Court of Justice of the Economic Community of West African States (ECOWAS), before Senegal agreed to create the Extraordinary African Chambers in Senegalese Courts. See S. Marks, 'The Hissène Habré Case: The Law and Politics of Universal Jurisdiction', in Macedo, *Universal Jurisdiction*, 132. See generally R. Brody and H. Duffy, 'Prosecuting Torture Universally: Hissene Habre, Africa's Pinochet?', in H. Fischer, C. Kress and S. R. Lüder (eds.), *International and National Prosecution of Crimes Under International Law: Current Developments* (Berlin: Berlin Verlag Arno Spitz, 2001, 823; E. Cimiotta, 'The First Steps of the Extraordinary African Chambers: A New Mixed Criminal Tribunal?' (2015) 13 *JICJ* 177.

been tried under universal jurisdiction.[200] Universal jurisdiction has an important role for enforcement. States may legally issue a warrant of arrest against a suspect who committed crimes on the territory of another state. However, they are not allowed to enforce their criminal law on the territory of another state without that state's consent.[201] There are different views on the scope of universal jurisdiction and the formulation of a link between the act of crime, the defendants and the victims.

In practice, universal jurisdiction has for a time been 'a project of well-developed democracies', i.e. European states and members of the Commonwealth.[202] Some jurisdictions (e.g. Belgium[203], Spain[204]) have allowed the exercise of universal jurisdiction without a concrete nexus of the affected state to the perpetrator or the crimes ('absolute universal jurisdiction'). Such wide articulations of universal jurisdiction have been criticized on policy grounds, such as artificial representations of community interests, delocalization of justice, encouragement of *in absentia* proceedings,[205] risks of forum shopping by victims[206] or fairness concerns.[207] For instance, Belgium originally had a universal jurisdiction law which allowed prosecutions of crimes in the absence of custody over the perpetrators. It led to the initiation of proceedings against prominent leaders, such as Yasser Arafat, Fidel Castro, Ariel Sharon[208] or George Bush. The application of the law caused political controversy. The African Union issued a declaration condemning the use of universal jurisdiction by Western powers.[209] In 2000, Congo challenged the issuance of a warrant for the arrest of its foreign minister, Yerodia Ndombasi, as an 'exercise of excessive universal jurisdiction' by Belgium before the ICJ.[210] The Court remained divided over the limits of universal jurisdiction.[211]

---

[200] See generally W. Kaleck, 'From Pinochet to Rumsfeld: Universal Jurisdiction in Europe 1998–2008' (2009) 30 *Michigan Journal of International Law* 927.

[201] See R. O'Keefe, 'Universal Jurisdiction:Clarifying the Concept' (2004) 2 *JICJ* 735,740–741.

[202] See M. Langer, 'The Diplomacy of Universal Jurisdiction: The Political Branches and the Transnational Prosecution of International Crimes' (2011) 105 *AJIL* 1, 47.

[203] See Act Regarding Grave Breaches of International Humanitarian Law, in (1999) 38 ILM 918, 921. The law did not require a link between Belgium, the offence, and the offender. For a critique, see S. R. Ratner, 'Belgium's War Crimes Statute: a Postmortem' (2003) 97 *AJIL* 888.

[204] M. Jouet, 'Spain's Expanded Universal Jurisdiction to Prosecute Human Rights Abuses in Latin America, China, and Beyond' (2006–2007) 35 *Georgia Journal of International and Comparative Law* 495.

[205] R. Rabinovitch, 'Universal Jurisdiction in Absentia' (2004–2005) 28 *Fordham International Law Journal* 500; A. J. Colangelo, 'The New Universal Jurisdiction: in Absentia Signaling over Clearly Defined Crimes' (2005) 36 *Georgetown Journal of International Law* 537.

[206] L. Sriram, 'Externalizing Justice through Universal Jurisdiction: Problems and Prospects' (2001) 12 *Finnish Yearbook of International Law* 47.

[207] G. P. Fletcher, 'Against Universal Jurisdiction' (2003) 1 *JICJ* 580.

[208] J. Borneman (ed.), *The Case of Ariel Sharon and the Fate of Universal Jurisdiction* (Princeton: Princeton Institute for International and Regional Studies 2004).

[209] H. van der Wilt, 'Universal Jurisdiction under Attack: An Assessment of African Misgivings towards International Criminal Justice as Administered by Western States' (2011) 9 *JICJ* 1043.

[210] ICJ, *Arrest Warrant* Case, para. 42.

[211] Some judges found that the Court 'ought ... to have found that the Belgian judge was wrong in holding himself competent to prosecute Yerodia Ndombasi by relying on a universal jurisdiction incompatible with international law'. See Separate Opinion of President Guillaume, para. 17. Others argued that such an exercise of universal jurisdiction 'is not precluded under international law'. See Joint Separate Opinion of Higgins, para. 65. See also Dissenting Opinion of Judge Van den Wyngaert, para. 56 ('It may be politically inconvenient to have such a wide jurisdiction because it is not conducive to international relations and national public opinion may not approve of trials against foreigners for crimes committed abroad. This does not, however, make such trials illegal under international law').

Some of the concerns against universal jurisdiction have been overstated. Its limits and risks depend on the scope of executive power and the level of control of prosecutorial discretion in domestic systems.[212] In light of political critiques and the inability to cope with the potentially wide scope of cases, states have become more reluctant in recent years to assert universal jurisdiction. Belgium and Spain have restricted their wide jurisdiction laws.[213]

There is a trend to limit universal jurisdiction to cases where the perpetrator is in the custody of the host state, or where the territorial state or the state of the nationality of the offender is either unwilling or unable to act. In Europe, Germany, Sweden and Norway retain a relatively wide (i.e. 'pure') concept of universal jurisdiction in theory. The breadth of jurisdiction is mitigated by the wide scope of prosecutorial discretion to decide whether or not to initiate an investigation.[214] For instance, in 2005 the German Federal Prosecutor declined to open an investigation against former US Defence Minister Donald Rumsfeld relating to torture in Iraq, on the ground that US authorities were investigating the situation.[215] Subsidiarity is required by law in countries such as Belgium, Spain or Switzerland, or applied in judicial doctrine (e.g. Austria) or prosecutorial discretion (e.g. United Kingdom, Denmark, Norway, Sweden). The purpose of introducing complementarity in interstate relations (so-called horizontal complementarity) is to encourage genuine domestic proceedings in the state best suited to address crimes, and to avoid overly broad assertions of universal jurisdiction.[216] The problem with this approach is that domestic prosecutors face difficulties to gain reliable information on investigations in other states, or to monitor the progress of such proceedings. It may thus ultimately lead to less accountability.

A new approach towards universal jurisdiction was taken by Finnish courts in the *Bazaramba* case, the first genocide trial in Finland. The case involved a Rwandan pastor, Francois Bazaramba, who spread anti-Tutsi propaganda and incited killings and burning of homes during the Rwandan genocide. Finland refused to extradite Bazaramba to Rwanda due to fair trial concerns. Finnish courts conducted universal jurisdiction proceedings for genocide, crimes against humanity and war crimes

---

[212] Langer, 'The Diplomacy of Universal Jurisdiction', 45–47.

[213] L. Reydams, 'Belgium Reneges on Universality: The 5 August 2003 Act on Grave Breaches of International Humanitarian Law' (2003) 1 *JICJ* 679; R. A. Alija, 'The 2014 Reform of Universal Jurisdiction in Spain. From All to Nothing' (2014) 13 *ZIS* 717.

[214] Neither Germany, nor Sweden allow trials *in absentia*. Under Art. 153 (2) (f) of the German Code of Criminal Procedure, Prosecutors may decide not to pursue proceedings in cases where 'no German is suspected of having committed the crime; the offence was not committed against a German; no suspect is, or is expected to be, resident in Germany; the offence is being prosecuted by an international court of justice or by a country on whose territory the offence was committed, a citizen of which is either suspected of the offence, or suffered injury as a result of the offence'.

[215] K. Ambos, 'International Core Crimes, Universal Jurisdiction and § 153f of the German Criminal Procedure Code: A Commentary on the Decisions of the Federal Prosecutor General and the Stuttgart Higher Regional Court in the Abu Ghraib/Rumsfeld Case' (2007) 18 *Criminal Law Forum* 43.

[216] Certain authors suggest that the concept should be formulated by the Assembly of States Parties of the ICC. See L. Burens, 'Universal Jurisdiction Meets Complementarity: An Approach towards a Desirable Future Codification of Horizontal Complementarity between the Member States of the International Criminal Court' (2016) 27 *Criminal Law Forum* 75, 79–80.

relating to a massacre in the municipality of Nyakizu. The Helsinki Court of Appeal held some *in situ* hearings in Rwanda and in Zambia, in order to hear witnesses residing outside Finland.[217] The defendant followed local proceedings via video-link from Finland. In this way, the proceedings mitigated some of the traditional concerns relating to the delocalization of universal jurisdiction.

Crime definitions vary significantly across jurisdictions. They might be adjusted to address specific political and social domestic contexts.[218] States may either rely on definitions under existing international law, or adjust the definitions to the domestic setting, or combine the two methods. The approaches differ between monist systems, according to which international treaty provisions may become part of domestic law without implementing legislation, and dualist systems, which require implementing legislation to give a treaty legal force.[219] For instance, in monist systems, implementation may clarify or refine provisions in line with the principle of legality. In dualist systems, it may be necessary to render them applicable before domestic courts.

Deviations from international law definitions may become critical when they undermine the *rationale* or the essence of international crimes. Such a test was formulated by the European Court of Human Rights in the *Jorgić* case.[220] The Court noted that domestic jurisdictions may determine the concept of genocide under domestic law, provided that the domestic interpretation is consistent with the essence of the offence and could have been foreseen by the defendant.[221] One key factor is the contextual element of international crimes.[222] Modes of liability and procedural law, by contrast, are largely particular to a specific domestic system. This provides greater room to rely on equivalent domestic principles.[223] According to comparative studies, the majority of states maintain the application of national laws on general principles of criminal responsibility, in particular modes of liability. Only a minority creates a specialized regime.[224]

Over the past decades, many important cases have been litigated domestically.[225] There has been a whole range of underreported domestic trials in the aftermath of World War II.[226] Classical cases are the trials against Klaus Barbie, the former head

---

[217] See Porvoo District Court, Judgment, R 09/404, 11 June 2010, at www.internationalcrimesdatabase.org/upload/ICD/ Upload973/Bazaramba%20Judgment%20-%20part%20B.pdf.

[218] J. I. Turner, 'Nationalizing International Criminal Law' (2005) 41 *Stanford Journal of International Law* 1.

[219] J. G. Stark, 'Monism and Dualism in the Theory of International Law' (1936) 17 *British Yearbook of International Law* 66.

[220] ECtHR, *Jorgić* v. *Germany*, Appl. No. 74613/01, Judgment, 12 July 2007.

[221] Ibid., paras. 101, 114.

[222] K. Doherty and T. McCormack, 'Complementarity as a Catalyst for Comprehensive Domestic Penal Legislation' (1999) 5 *UC Davis Journal of International Law and Policy* 147, 166–167.

[223] R. Rastan, 'Situation and Case: Defining the Parameters', in Stahn and El Zeidy, *The International Criminal Court and Complementarity*, 421.

[224] H. Sato, 'Modes of International Criminal Justice and General Principles of Criminal Responsibility' (2012) 4 *Göttingen Journal of International Law* 765, 772.

[225] On the Holocaust cases, see S. Landsman, *Crimes of the Holocaust: The Law Confronts Hard Cases* (Philadelphia: University of Pennsylvania Press, 2005).

[226] F. Borch, *Military Trials of War Criminals in the Netherlands East Indies 1946–1949* (Oxford: Oxford University Press, 2017); G. Fitzpatrick, T. McCormack and N. Morris (eds.), *Australia's War Crimes Trials 1945–51* (Leiden: Brill/ Nijhoff, 2016); K. Sellars (ed.), *Trials for International Crimes in Asia* (Cambridge: Cambridge University Press, 2015); K. J. Heller and G. Simpson (eds.), *The Hidden Histories of War Crimes Trials* (Oxford: Oxford University Press, 2013).

of the Gestapo in Lyon,[227] or the *Finta* case in Canada.[228] There is a growing number of domestic investigations and prosecutions. In the past two decades, more than thirty countries have conducted international crimes cases, involving more than 10,000 perpetrators.[229] Famous examples are the trials against former dictator Alberto Fujimuro[230] in Peru and against Rios Montt in Guatemala.[231] National jurisdictions have exercised extraterritorial jurisdiction in relation to international crimes committed in Afghanistan, Iraq, Mauritania, Uganda, Rwanda, Sierra Leone, the Democratic Republic of Congo, Chad, Argentina, the former Yugoslavia and Syria.[232]

The investigation and prosecution of atrocity crimes is often more complex and cost-intensive than ordinary crimes. Many states have thus adopted specialized laws or prosecution units at the domestic level to investigate and prosecute international crimes.[233] This trend is not only visible in the Western world,[234] but also in a variety of transitional contexts. For example, Colombia has created specialized units for contextual analysis of criminal conduct. The Ugandan High Court has created an International Crimes Division as a product of the Juba peace negotiations. Such initiatives may strengthen the options for enforcement.[235]

Many contemporary studies acknowledge that the quality of national investigations and prosecutions is key for the success of international criminal justice.[236] Some scholars predict that 'the future of international law is domestic'[237] and that international criminal law enforcement will effectively migrate from international tribunals to national courts.[238] One of the most convincing reasons in favour of national justice

---

[227] J.-O. Viout 'The Klaus Barbie Trial and Crimes against Humanity' (1999) 3 *Hofstra Law & Policy Symposium* 155.

[228] Supreme Court of Canada, *R. v. Imre Finta*, Judgment, 24 March 1994; J. H. Bello and I. Cotler, 'Regina v. Finta' (1996) 90 *AJIL* 460.

[229] J. Rikhof, 'Fewer Places to Hide? The Impact of Domestic War Crimes Prosecutions on International Impunity' (2009) 20 *Criminal Law Forum* 1, 51.

[230] K. Ambos, 'The Fujimori Judgment: A President's Responsibility for Crimes Against Humanity as Indirect Perpetrator by Virtue of an Organized Power Apparatus' (2011) 9 *JICJ* 137–158.

[231] S. Kemp, 'Guatemala Prosecutes former President Ríos Montt: New Perspectives on Genocide and Domestic Criminal Justice' (2014) 12 *ICJ* 133.

[232] Rikhof, 'Fewer Places to Hide?', 1.

[233] See Human Rights Watch, 'The Long Arm of Justice: Lessons from Specialized War Crimes Units in France, Germany, and the Netherlands', 16 September 2014, at www.hrw.org/sites/default/files/reports/IJ0914_ForUpload.pdf.

[234] For example Belgium, Canada, Denmark, The Netherlands, Norway and Sweden have established special units to investigate and prosecute international crimes.

[235] ICC member states may be divided in least four categories of states: a number of states define core crimes in their legislation in identical terms to the Rome Statute. Other states use broader definitions than the ICC Statute. Again others have more restrictive definitions. Finally, some have not taken any action with respect to definition or implementation. See J. Terracino, 'National Implementation of ICC Crimes: Impact on National Jurisdictions and the ICC' (2007) 5 *JICJ* 421.

[236] ICTJ, *Handbook on Complementarity* (New York: ICTJ, 2016), www.ictj.org/complementarity-icc/; Bergsmo, Harlem and Hayashi, *Importing Core International Crimes in National Law*.

[237] A.-M. Slaughter and W. Burke-White, 'The Future of International Law is Domestic (or, the European Way of Law)' (2006) 47 *Harvard International Law Journal* 327–352.

[238] W. Burke-White, 'A Community of Courts: Towards a System of International Criminal Law Enforcement' (2002) 24 *Michigan Journal of International Law* 1–100. This view is reflected in the statement of the first ICC Prosecutor, who argued that the 'absence of trials' before the ICC 'as a consequence of the regular functioning of national institutions, would be a major success'. See Election of the Prosecutor, Statement by Mr Luis Moreno-Ocampo, New York, 22 April 2003, ICC-OTP-20030502-10.

is its potential lasting effect on the local judiciary and victims. Domestic prosecutions also have disadvantages, however.

Within national jurisdictions, the investigation and prosecution of international crimes often competes with other priorities, such as domestic organized crime, drug criminality or terrorism. Collecting evidence or hearing witnesses relating to crimes committed abroad, or in post- or actual conflict situations, is a challenge for domestic prosecutors and courts. Asylum seekers or refugees located in prosecuting states might be unwilling to provide statements, due to fear, mistrust in foreign state or police structures, or a general lack of knowledge about domestic proceedings.[239] Funding for atrocity trials is limited. In light of this political reality, enforcement remains uneven. Investigations and prosecutions are often an option of last resort that competes with other, more immediate concerns.

The scope of domestic jurisdiction may influence the approach towards accountability, and provide a limited perspective on the underlying atrocities. For instance, German, Dutch, Swedish and Spanish prosecutors have initiated a new set of investigations and prosecutions in relation to crimes in Syria. They only capture a small fraction of atrocities against civilians, since they are focused on terrorism or foreign fighters.[240] Terrorist offences are often easier to prosecute than core crimes since they only require proof of the link between the individual and the terrorist organization, rather than poof of the direct connection between the individuals and crimes.[241] However, terrorism charges may not reflect the nature of international crimes, and send a message that governments care mostly about the domestic threats. In the Syrian context, initial national trials have mostly concerned low-level members of ISIS or the Syrian government.[242] Moreover, key crimes such as use of chemical weapons, destruction of cultural property or forcible transfer of civilians may only play a marginal role in domestic cases.

Most domestic systems contain statutory limitations (e.g. time limits for prosecution). If applicable they may lead to impunity for serious crimes. National provisions on the non-applicability of statutory limitations for international crimes remain 'quite divergent'.[243] Both the UN and the Council of Europe have therefore adopted conventions which render statutory limitations inapplicable to genocide, crimes against humanity and war crimes.[244]

Further bars to investigation and prosecution may arise from the non-retroactivity of domestic legislation. Approaches towards the strictness of the principle of legality

---

[239] See Human Rights Watch, '"These are the Crimes we are Fleeing": Justice for Syria in Swedish and German Courts', 3 October 2017.
[240] Ibid.
[241] Ibid.
[242] Ibid.
[243] R. Kok, *Statutory Limitations in International Criminal Law* (The Hague: TMC Asser Press, 2007), 9.
[244] Convention on the Non-Applicability of Statutory Limitations to War Crimes and Crimes Against Humanity, adopted by General Assembly Resolution 2391 (XXIII) of 26 November 1968, 754 UNTS 73; European Convention on the Non-Applicability of Statutory Limitations to Crimes against Humanity and War Crimes, Strasbourg, 25 January 1974.

in domestic jurisdictions differ.[245] This may influence the choice of jurisdiction. For instance, in 2010 the Court of Justice of the Economic Community of West African States (ECOWAS) found that the international crimes legislation adopted by Senegal in 2007 to prosecute Hissène Habré for, among others, crimes against humanity committed in Chad twenty years before violated the principle of legality, specifically the principle against non-retroactivity of criminal law. The Court held that such crimes could be prosecuted only by a hybrid tribunal.[246]

3.4.2   *International Criminal Jurisdiction*

International criminal jurisdiction is to some extent a counter-model to domestic justice. It derives its authority from an international legal instrument or act. International criminal jurisdictions have been established on the basis of a variety of sources: through domestic consent, UN resolutions or multilateral treaties. Often several sources are combined.

Legally, there are different theories to justify international jurisdiction. According to one theory, international jurisdiction derives from state authority, namely state consent and typically an act of delegation.[247] It involves two elements: the power of the affected state to exercise jurisdiction, and a delegation of that power to an international entity. This theory is in line with a state-based vision of international criminal law.

According to a second theory, i.e. a universalistic view, jurisdiction is not derived from the territorial or national jurisdiction of a specific state,[248] but based on a *jus puniendi*,[249] i.e. respect for the rights of citizens and human dignity. This theory relies on the premise that states exercise jurisdiction as trustees on behalf of individuals and humanity who are victims of crimes.[250] It grounds the normative justification in an implied social contract through which individuals accept punishment 'in exchange for the state's duty to protect its members'.[251] It implies that international criminal jurisdiction may reach beyond the criminal jurisdiction of individual states.

---

[245] K. Gallant, *The Principle of Legality in International and Comparative Law* (Cambridge: Cambridge University Press, 2009).

[246] The ECOWAS Court found that Habré could only be tried by an 'special or ad hoc procedure of an international character'. Court of Justice of the Economic Community of States of West Africa, *Hissène Habré* v. *Republic of Senegal*, ECW/CCJ/JUD/06/10, Judgment, 18 November 2010, para. 61. See V. Spiga, 'Non-retroactivity of Criminal Law: A New Chapter in the Hissene Habre Saga' (2011) 9 *JICJ* 5.

[247] See generally S. Wallerstein, 'Delegation of Powers and Authority in International Criminal Law' (2015) 9 *Criminal Law and Philosophy* 123.

[248] On the 'universalistic view', see Y. Shany, 'In Defence of Functional Interpretation of Article 12(3) of the Rome Statute' (2010) 8 *JICJ* 329, 331.

[249] See Ambos, 'Punishment without a Sovereign?', 293.

[250] International crimes are crimes against local society and the international legal order. See Aukerman, 'Extraordinary Evil, Ordinary Crime', 39, 46. In particular, the exercise of universal jurisdiction is based on the idea that states act as trustees of humankind based on the nature, i.e. the gravity of the crime.

[251] Bassiouni, *Introduction to International Criminal Law*, 914.

3.4.2.1   Ad Hoc Justice

International criminal jurisdictions were initially established on an ad hoc basis. They vary greatly in form and design.

The post-World War II tribunals had a close nexus to occupation. The Nuremberg tribunal was essentially a multinational jurisdiction.[252] It derived authority from the London agreement, which was signed by representatives of the United States, the United Kingdom, France and the Soviet Union, and the unconditional surrender of Germany.[253] It was meant to fill a sovereignty gap left by the absence of German state structures. The Tokyo Tribunal was grounded on the Japanese Declaration of Surrender and a proclamation signed by General Douglas MacArthur, Supreme Commander for the Allied Powers,[254] which contained the Charter of the tribunal as an annex. Both tribunals thus stand primarily as precedent in terms of crystallizing law, rather than institutional design.

Most institutions established in the second half of the twentieth century have been created in connection with international organizations, and most notably the UN.

The ad hoc tribunals for the former Yugoslavia and Rwanda deviated from earlier precedents. They were established by the UN Security Council under Chapter VII of the United Nations Charter. This marked a crucial moment for the emancipation of international criminal justice from domestic jurisdiction. They shared many unique features based on their authority derived from Chapter VII. The Statutes were *sui generis* legal instruments 'resembling a treaty'.[255] They were vested with primacy over domestic jurisdiction and the power to oblige states to cooperate (vertical cooperation).[256] These supranational features allowed them to substitute or override classical state power. They were composed entirely of United Nations selected judges, prosecutors and staff.

The legal framework contrasted with political reality. There was initially strong scepticism as to whether the tribunals would get off the ground.[257] The ICTY lacked support from players in the region. It was feared that it would remain powerless and unable to carry out arrests. The ICTR was created without the support of the Rwandan Unity government. Rwanda voiced concerns about the scope of temporal

---

[252] Michael Scharf has argued that the Nuremberg Tribunal can be conceptualized in different ways, i.e. as an entity acting on behalf of the international community, or as an entity with delegated national jurisdiction of the Allied Powers. See M. Scharf, 'The United States and the International; Criminal Court: The ICC's Jurisdiction over Nationals of Non-Party States: A Critique of the US Position' (2001) 64 *Law and Contemporary Problems* 70, 103–109.

[253] The London Agreement contained a Charter setting out the constitution, jurisdiction and functions of the International Military Tribunal.

[254] Special Proclamation: Establishment of the International Military Tribunal for the Far East, 19 January 1946, in N. Boister and R. Cryer, *Documents on the Tokyo International Military Tribunal, Vol. I* (Oxford: Oxford University Press, 2008), 5.

[255] *Prosecutor* v. *Kanyabashi*, ICTR-96-15-A, Decision on the Defence Motion for Interlocutory Appeal on the Jurisdiction of Trial Chamber I, 3 June 1999, Joint and Separate Opinion of Judge McDonald and Judge Vohrah, para. 15.

[256] The ICTY was created under Resolution 827 of 1993, S/RES/827. The ICTR was established by Resolution 955 of 1994, S/RES/955, Resolutions and main justifications.

[257] See remarks by Madeleine Albright, UN SCOR, 48th Sess. 3217th mtg, S/PV.3217, 25 May 1993, 13 ('Those sceptics – including the war criminals – who deride this Tribunal as being powerless because the suspects may avoid arrest should not be so confident').

jurisdiction and the lack of capital punishment. It argued that the tribunal would only 'appease the conscience of the international community rather than respond to the expectations of the Rwandese people'.[258] It criticized that those 'who devised, planned and organized the genocide' may 'escape capital punishment whereas those who simply carried out their plans would be subjected to the harshness of this sentence'.[259] Cynics claimed that some states never wanted the tribunals to succeed.

Both tribunals faced challenges to their jurisdiction. They used strong arguments to defend their autonomy and independence.[260] At the ICTY, *Tadić* became the signature case. The Appeals Chamber reaffirmed not only the power of the Security Council to create independent and impartial tribunals as instruments of maintaining peace, but also the necessity of primacy over domestic justice. It held:

It would be a travesty of law and a betrayal of the universal need for justice, should the concept of State sovereignty be allowed to be raised successfully against human rights ... when an international tribunal such as the present one is created, it must be endowed with primacy over national courts. Otherwise, human nature being what it is, there would be a perennial danger of international crimes being characterised as 'ordinary crimes', or proceedings being 'designed to shield the accused', or cases not being diligently prosecuted.[261]

In practice, both tribunals have existed far longer than initially expected, namely for over two decades. Both tribunals managed to conduct a significant number of trials, despite political opposition. The ICTR has conducted proceedings against eighty-five accused.[262] The ICTY has managed to secure arrest of all of the 161 persons indicted.

In the course of their operations, the ad hoc tribunals went through roughly similar phases. First, they struggled to get cases. After they secured arrests, many of the complexities became apparent in practice. They had to develop a partly new body of jurisprudence and create their own procedural rules. Courtroom practice highlighted many limitations and challenges. Proceedings took longer than anticipated. The detachment from affected societies became more visible. Both tribunals struggled to respond to calls for local justice, and to counter biases among local populations.[263] When the case load increased, they soon came to be seen as a strain on UN resources. This led to the development of completion strategies and the reinforcement of outreach programmes. Judges created a mechanism to refer mid- or low-level cases back

---

[258] UN SCOR, 49th Sess., 3453d mtg., UN Doc. S/PV.3453, 8 November 1994, 15.

[259] Ibid., 16.

[260] The ICTR relied on arguments made by the Prosecution in the trial against Hans Frank at Nuremberg to deny a conflict with state sovereignty. It stated: 'The principle of State sovereignty which might protect these men is only a mask; this mask removed, the man's responsibility reappears'. *Prosecutor* v. *Kanyabashi*, Decision on the Defence Motion on Jurisdiction, Case No. ICTR-96–15-T, 18 June 1997, para. 34.

[261] *Tadić* 1995, para. 58.

[262] ICTR Key Figures of Cases (September 2016), at http://unictr.unmict.org/en/cases/key-figures-cases.

[263] See e.g. Milanovic, 'The Impact of the ICTY on the Former Yugoslavia', 233, 236–258; M. Klarin, 'The Impact of the ICTY Trials on Public Opinion in the Former Yugoslavia' (2009) 7 *JICJ* 89, 90; L. E. Fletcher, 'From Indifference to Engagement: Bystanders and International Criminal Justice' (2005) 26 *Michigan Journal of International Law* 1013, 1078.

to domestic jurisdictions.[264] In the final phase, they developed legacy strategies to preserve the record and leave a lasting footprint.

During the completion strategy, it became evident that the need for justice does not simply stop with the closure of cases. This prompted the creation of a follow-up tribunal, namely the Mechanism for the International Criminal Tribunals (MICT). Legally, the MICT is not simply an annex of the ad hoc tribunals, but a successor court of its own, established by Security Council Resolution 1996 (2010).[265] It was vested with different residual functions and ad hoc functions, namely the tracing of remaining ICTR fugitives, hearing remaining appeals, holding retrials or conducting contempt cases.

Institutionally, the model of the two ad hoc tribunals has remained an exception. It offers several advantages. It reflects a strong level of international commitment, comes with robust powers to require arrest and transfer of suspects, and ensures the application of a unified legal regime. However, it has suffered from 'tribunal fatigue'. It was suggested in other contexts, such as Somalia, Syria, MH17 or ISIS, but it failed to be adopted, due to the lack of necessary political support and power politics in the Security Council and other considerations, such as budgetary concerns,[266] remoteness from domestic justice and the availability of other mechanisms.

3.4.2.2 The Rome Statute System

The existence of the ad hoc tribunals strengthened the historical momentum for the creation of the ICC, i.e. a permanent and treaty-based court with a global reach. This institutional format has a strong normative appeal. It counters some of the weaknesses of previous justice models. It alleviates the traditional critique that international criminal justice is established ex post. It allows a reaction to ongoing violations, and it may make international criminal justice more predictable, coherent and less partial.

The creation of the Court was highly contested.[267] The ILC presented a proposal of a draft statute in 1994, i.e. shortly after the establishment of the ad hoc tribunals.[268]

---

[264] The Bosnian War Crimes Chamber was partially created to allow the ICTY to transfer cases concerning mid-level perpetrators to domestic courts.

[265] G. McIntyre, 'The International Residual Mechanism and the Legacy of the International Criminal Tribunals for the Former Yugoslavia and Rwanda' (2011) 3 *Göttingen Journal of International Law* 923.

[266] For instance, the UN Secretary-General has argued that a Security Council-created piracy tribunal 'is not likely to be among the most cost-effective [options]. ... [I]t would require premises, and may incur other such costs that a special chamber within a national jurisdiction may not have. In addition, ... it would be required to follow the United Nations common system for staffing and salaries. The total cost would be likely to exceed the costs of a special chamber in a national jurisdiction in the region'. See Report of the Secretary-General on possible options to further the aim of prosecuting and imprisoning persons responsible for acts of piracy and armed robbery at sea off the coast of Somalia, UN Doc S/2010/394, 26 July 2010, para. 101.

[267] On early legal objections, see M. Morris, 'High Crimes and Misperceptions: The ICC and Non-Party States' (2001) 64 *Law and Contemporary Problems* 13; D. Scheffer, 'The United States and the International Criminal Court' (1999) 93 *AJIL* 12; R. Wedgwood, 'The International Criminal Court: An American View' (1999) 10 *EJIL* 93. On reactions, see F. Mégret, 'Epilogue to an Endless Debate: The International Criminal Court's Third Party Jurisdiction and the Looming Revolution of International Law' (2011) 12 *EJIL* 247; D. Akande, 'The Jurisdiction of the International Criminal Court over Nationals of Non-Parties: Legal Basis and Limits' (2003) 1 *JICJ* 618; G. M. Danilenko, 'ICC Statute and Third States', in Cassese, Gaeta and Jones, *The Rome Statute of the International Criminal Court*, 1871.

[268] See ILC Draft Statute for an International Criminal Court (1994).

Many key powers, such as the US, Israel, China, Russia and India, remained reserved towards the idea or viewed it as a potential threat to their sovereign interests.[269] The existence of the ad hoc tribunals had an empowering effect on supporters. Crime provisions, procedures and the broader infrastructure of international criminal law had come to life. State representatives and NGOs could not only rely on historical draft codes or the Nuremberg heritage to negotiate a treaty, but on more recent precedents, and a developing accountability culture.

Two major bones of contention during the negotiations were the powers of the Prosecutor and the possibility to exercise jurisdiction over non-states parties. Both issues were solved through compromise solutions.

Drafters granted the ICC the power to initiate investigations on its own motion and to determine whether it has jurisdiction over crimes committed. This decision has enormous conceptual significance. It means that the authority to investigate and prosecute international crimes is no longer exclusively triggered by states. The Prosecutor is de facto a representative of a broader *jus puniendi* of international society. The main caveat is that *proprio motu* action by the Prosecutor requires additional judicial control, namely authorization by Pre-Trial judges.[270]

ICC jurisdiction is treaty-based. It is in principle limited to crimes committed in states parties or by their nationals.[271] However, there are two exceptions. The Security Council can refer a situation relating to a non-state party, by virtue of its powers under Chapter VII. In this case, the ICC becomes a 'quasi' ad hoc tribunal which does not require consent by the state concerned to exercise jurisdiction.[272] In addition, a non-state party may voluntarily accept the exercise of jurisdiction by declaration, without becoming a party to the ICC Statute.[273]

One of the most innovative feature of the Statute is its more systemic turn to the interaction between international and domestic legal systems. The Statute not only creates a court, it establishes a system of justice.[274] By ratifying the Statute, a state acknowledges that crimes within the jurisdiction of the Court shall, in principle, either be investigated or prosecuted by a domestic jurisdiction or by the Court itself.[275] The ICC enjoys an independent right of assessment (*droit de regard*) over the situation and the choices of justice adopted in the domestic context.

The system of justice that the Rome Statute contemplated is in many ways imperfect. The Statute itself has been applied as a 'gold standard' in many contexts, judicial

---

[269] F. Megret, 'Three Dangers for the International Criminal Court: A Critical Look at a Consensual Project' (2001) 12 *Finnish Yearbook of International Law* 193–247, at 194; L. N. Sadat and S. R. Carden, 'The New International Criminal Court: An Uneasy Revolution' (2000) 88 *Georgetown Law Journal* 381.

[270] Art. 15 (3).

[271] Art. 12 ICC Statute.

[272] Art. 13 (b) ICC Statute.

[273] Art. 12 (3) ICC Statute. See generally C. Stahn, M. El Zeidy and H. Olásolo, 'The International Criminal Court's Ad Hoc Jurisdiction Revisited' (2005) 99 *AJIL* 421.

[274] This is reflected in the preamble in which states express their commitment to 'guarantee lasting respect for and the enforcement of international justice'.

[275] Art. 17 ICC Statute.

and non-judicial settings, inside and outside the ICC,[276] despite its flaws and partial deviations from customary law. However, the ICC as an institution has faced many challenges.

In practice, the ICC has been highly dependent on states. It has strongly relied on state consent to facilitate its operation and increase its impact. It has focused on situations with uncontested jurisdictional titles, based on the referrals of state parties, the Security Council or voluntary acceptances of jurisdiction by non-state parties.[277] Self-referrals were initiated to enhance the prospects of cooperation. Investigations were limited to easy targets: non-Western powers or non-armed groups. This has led to criticisms that the Court is too consensual.[278]

The relationship with the Security Council has been marked by friction and disappointment.[279] The Council effectively used the ICC as a drop box for unsettled human security problems in Darfur and Libya, while providing it with very limited means to succeed. As former ICTY Prosecutor Louise Arbour noted, the two referrals may have served more to 'underscore the Court's impotence' rather than to 'enhance its alleged deterrent effect'.[280]

The Court has struggled for funding. It has witnessed an annual push for 'zero nominal growth' by the Assembly of States Parties, despite a growing number of situations. Costs for Security Council referrals in relation to Darfur and Libya were entirely placed on the Court, despite language contrary to that effect in the Statute.[281] There is to some extent a 'free rider' problem whereby non-parties enjoy some of the advantages of the Court, without bearing the costs of running it.

The experiences in existing situations show clear differences to the ad hoc model. The ICC is virtually part and parcel of justice discourse in almost any conflict situation. It is comparatively wider in its span of situations, but also more selective and thus less deeply involved in the respective context.

Early hopes that the existence of the ICC would reduce the need for other international[282] or internationalized tribunals[283] have proved to be over-optimistic. The existing capacity limits and jurisdictional gaps have yielded calls for additional, and

---

[276] See Schabas, *Unimaginable Atrocities*, 140.

[277] Art. 12 (3).

[278] See inter alia P. Clark, 'Law, Politics and Pragmatism: ICC Case Selection in the Democratic Republic of Congo and Uganda', in P. Clark and N. Waddell (eds.), *Courting Conflict? Peace, Justice and the ICC in Africa* (London: Royal African Society, 2008) 37–47.

[279] See C. Stahn, 'Marital Stress or Grounds for Divorce? Re-Thinking the Relationship Between R2P and International Criminal Justice' (2015) 26 *Criminal Law Forum* 13.

[280] See L. Arbour, 'Doctrines Derailed? Internationalism's Uncertain Future', at www.crisisgroup.org/global/doctrines-derailed-internationalism-s-uncertain-future.

[281] Art. 117. For a critique, see R. Cryer, 'Sudan, Resolution 1593, and International Criminal Justice' (2006) 19 *LJIL* 195.

[282] See M. Bohlander, 'Possible Conflicts of Jurisdiction with the Ad hoc International Tribunals', in Cassese, Gaeta and Jones, *The Rome Statute of the International Criminal Court*, 687, 690 ('[Article 12 (2)] could make the creation of new Ad Hoc Tribunals superfluous').

[283] See e.g. L. Condorelli and T. Boutruche, 'Internationalized Criminal Courts and Tribunals: Are They Necessary?', in C. Romano, A. Nollkaemper and J. Kleffner (eds.), *Internationalized Criminal Courts: Sierra Leone, East Timor, Kosovo, and Cambodia* (Oxford: Oxford University Press, 2004), 427, 435 ('Hence, if there is an ICC that works and that has jurisdiction over the area and perpetrators of future crimes, we will not need to create other ad hoc or internationalized tribunals').

more specialized treaty-based courts. Such mechanisms have been suggested in different fields: counterterrorism, transnational crime and environmental crime.

3.4.3 Hybrid Justice

Hybrid justice is a third approach to deal with international crimes.[284] It is often not a result of 'grand institutional design'[285] but rather a medium to accommodate political tensions.[286] Conceptually, it offers a midway between international and domestic justice. Hybrid structures are often grounded in two types of authority: state authority and international authority.

The term 'hybrid' is not a classical legal term of art. There is not one 'hybrid model'. The concept is elastic. It captures a range of institutional options that integrate domestic and international structures. As Elizabeth Bruch notes: 'A tribunal may be hybrid in its origins (created through domestic and international processes), its mandate (splicing together domestic and international law) or its composition (combining domestic and 'international' members)'.[287] The turn to hybrid justice has gained prominence after the end of the Cold War.[288] A first 'wave' of hybrid and internationalized institutions included the SCSL,[289] the ECCC,[290] the Special Crimes Panels in Kosovo and East Timor, the War Crimes Chamber in Bosnia and Herzegovina and the STL.[291] These mechanisms were created to address accountability dilemmas in specific situations. This trend is witnessing a renaissance, due to critiques and limitations of international criminal jurisdiction and more structural defences of hybridity.[292] Actors such as the UN, the AU and the EU have recognized hybrid justice as a pragmatic and flexible response to international crimes. New hybrid

---

[284] See generally S. Williams, *Hybrid and Internationalised Criminal Tribunals: Selected Jurisdictional Issues* (Oxford: Hart, 2012); Romano, Nollkaemper and Kleffner, *Internationalized Criminal Courts*; S. Nouwen, '"Hybrid Courts": The Hybrid Category of a New Type of International Crimes Courts' (2006) 2 *Utrecht Law Review* 190; E. R. Higonnet, 'Restructuring Hybrid Courts: Local Empowerment and National Criminal Justice Reform' (2006) 23 *Arizona Journal of International and Comparative Law* 347.

[285] L. Dickinson, 'The Promise of Hybrid Courts' (2003) 97 *AJIL* 295, 296.

[286] See H. Hobbs, 'Hybrid Tribunals and the Composition of the Court: In Search of Sociological Legitimacy' (2016) 16 *Chicago Journal of International Law* 482, 491.

[287] E. M. Bruch, 'Hybrid Courts: Examining Hybridity Through a Post-Colonial Lens' (2010) 28 *Boston University International Law Journal* 1, 6.

[288] S. Katzenstein, 'Note, Hybrid Tribunals: Searching for Justice in East Timor' (2003)16 *Harvard Human Rights Journal* 245; Dickinson, 'Promise of Hybrid Courts', 295, P. Kermani Mendez, 'The New Wave of Hybrid Tribunals: A Sophisticated Approach to Enforcing International Humanitarian Law or an Idealistic Solution with Empty Promises' (2009) 20 *Criminal Law Forum* 53–95.

[289] See Jalloh, *The Sierra Leone Special Court and its Legacy*.

[290] S. Meisenberg and I. Stegmiller (eds.), *The Extraordinary Chambers in the Courts of Cambodia: Assessing Their Contribution to International Criminal Law* (New York: Springer, 2016); J. D. Ciorciari and A. Heinde (eds.), *Hybrid Justice: The Extraordinary Chambers in the Courts of Cambodia* (Ann Arbor: University of Michigan Press, 2014).

[291] A. Alamuddin, N. Nabil Jurdi and D. Tolbert (eds.), *The Special Tribunal for Lebanon: Law and Practice* (Oxford: Oxford University Press, 2014).

[292] F. Mégret, 'In Defense of Hybridity: Towards a Representational Theory of International Criminal Justice' (2005) 38 *Cornell International Law Journal* 725, 746–747 ('hybridity might be something profoundly desirable normatively as such'); H. Hobbs, 'Towards a Principled Justification for the Mixed Composition of Hybrid International Criminal Tribunals' (2017) 30 *LJIL* 177–197.

mechanisms include the Special Court in the Central African Republic,[293] the Extra-ordinary African Chambers[294] and the Kosovo Specialist Chambers and Specialist Prosecutor's Office.[295]

Hybrid mechanisms are no longer considered a 'second-best option' to purely international jurisdiction. They rather represent a different approach, with its own strengths and justifications. The 'hybrid' nature captures, in particular, the duality of international criminal law as global and local crime.[296] Hybrid justice is being 'marketed' as a lenient and cost-effective alternative to international justice.[297] However, it is still in a stage of experimentation.[298]

The form of the 'hybrid' is popular since it provides a means to accommodate the difficult 'politics of international criminal justice'.[299] Formally, one can distinguish at least two types of hybrids: hybrid courts, in the narrow sense, and internationalized domestic courts. In practice, however, the design of hybrid institutions is deeply shaped by context and politics. It is thus the lack of uniformity that makes 'hybrid justice' an attractive policy option.

3.4.3.1 Hybrid Courts

Hybrid courts are mixed national–international courts that operate as independent criminal institutions outside the traditional realm of domestic jurisdiction. They are created by an international legal instrument, apply elements of international and domestic law and have a mix of local and foreign judges.

One of the advantages of hybrid courts lies in their interlinkage with the domestic system. 'Justice' is more closely related to the traditions of the domestic legal system and domestic communities.[300] The legal basis is typically formalized in an international instrument, but subject to domestic consent. The incentive for domestic 'buy in' results from the nexus to the domestic system, and the promise of control.

Classical examples of hybridity are the Special Court for Sierra Leone and the Special Tribunal for Lebanon. Internationalization was suggested for a number of

---

[293] P. Labuda, 'The Special Criminal Court in the Central African Republic: Failure or Vindication of Complementarity?' (2017) 15 *JICJ* 175.

[294] S. Williams, 'The Extraordinary African Chambers in the Senegalese Courts: An African Solution to an African Problem?' (2013) 11 *JICJ* 1139–1160.

[295] R. Muharremi, 'The Kosovo Specialist Chambers and Specialist Prosecutor's Office' (2016) 76 *Zeitschrift für ausländisches öffentliches Recht und Völkerrecht* 967; E. Cimiotta, 'The Specialist Chambers and the Specialist Prosecutor's Office in Kosovo: The "Regionalization" of International Criminal Justice in Context' (2016) 14 *JICJ* 53.

[296] Mégret, 'In Defense of Hybridity', 747.

[297] See A. Cassese, 'Report on the Special Court for Sierra Leone', 12 December 2006, 12; D. Cohen, 'Hybrid' Justice in East Timor, Sierra Leone and Cambodia: 'Lessons Learned' and Prospects for the Future' (2007) 43 *Stanford Journal of International Law* 1.

[298] S. Williams, 'Hybrid Tribunals: A Time for Reflection' (2016) 10 *International Journal of Transitional Justice* 538.

[299] P. McAuliffe, 'Hybrid Tribunals at Ten: How International Criminal Justice's Golden Child Became an Orphan' (2011) 7 *Journal of International Law and International Relations*, 1, 22.

[300] F. Dame, 'The Effect of International Criminal Tribunals on Local Judicial Culture: The Superiority of the Hybrid Tribunal' (2015) 24 *Michigan State International Law Review* 211.

reasons: security concerns, and certain perceived deficits of domestic justice, such as an inadequate domestic justice infrastructure, or lack of trust in the judiciary.[301] Their success is mixed.

3.4.3.1.1 Special Court for Sierra Leone

The Special Court for Sierra Leone was established on the basis of a UN-brokered agreement to try those who 'bear the greatest responsibility' in the conflict in Sierra Leone.[302] It was driven by the ambition to consolidate a fragile peace. It had primacy over the domestic courts of Sierra Leone.[303] Domestic courts in Sierra Leone were not sufficiently prepared to take on the challenge of war crimes trials, due to a lack of resources and infrastructure.[304] Ex-combatants from both the rebel Revolutionary United Front (RUF) and the local CDF remained divided over the impartiality of domestic courts.[305] The decision to remove the jurisdiction of the Court from the domestic legal system was guided by the intention to exempt it from the scope of application of the amnesty under the Lomé Peace Accord, which was considered by many as an essential condition for peace, at least domestically.[306]

The SCSL is often presented as 'the most successful of the hybrid tribunals'.[307] It defined itself as an international criminal tribunal with an international mandate. It brought cases against the three major factions in the conflict. It conducted proceedings against twenty-one defendants and developed a successful outreach programme. A key milestone was the proceedings against Charles Taylor.[308] The trial was moved from Freetown to The Hague. The *Taylor* judgment marked the first conviction of a former head of state by an international tribunal after the end of World War II.

However, the SCSL framework also had certain weaknesses.[309] The Court struggled to apply an essentially Western legal framework to local cultures.[310] Conceptions of rights, responsibility and authority structures differed from local structures. Cultural

---

[301] Sloane, 'Expressive Capacity of International Punishment', 49.

[302] See Art. 1 of the Agreement Between the United Nations and the Government of Sierra Leone on the Establishment of a Special Court for Sierra Leone and Art. 1 of the Statute of the Special Court.

[303] See Art. 8 of the Statute of the Special Court for Sierra Leone.

[304] Sources indicate that by June 2002, only five out of fourteen magistrate courts were operational. See *Fourteenth Report of the Secretary-General on the UN Mission in Sierra Leone*, UN Doc. S/2002/679 of 19 June 2002, at 24.

[305] See *Thirteenth Report of the Secretary-General on the UN Mission in Sierra Leone*, UN Doc. S/2002/267 of 14 March 2002, 17.

[306] See Sierra Leone Truth and Reconciliation Commission, Final Report, Part 1, Findings, para. 553 ('The Commission finds that the amnesty clause in the Lomé Agreement was well intentioned and meant to secure peace. The Commission finds that in repudiating the amnesty clause in the Lome Agreement, both the United Nations and the Government of Sierra Leone have sent an unfortunate message to combatants in future wars that they cannot trust peace agreements that contain amnesty clauses').

[307] McAuliffe, 'Hybrid Tribunals at Ten', 6.

[308] *Prosecutor* v. *Taylor*, SCSL-03-01-I-059, Decision on Immunity from Jurisdiction, 31 May 2004 (*Taylor* Immunity Decision).

[309] J. Cockayne, 'The Fraying Shoestring: Rethinking Hybrid War Crimes Tribunals' (2005) 28 *Fordham International Law Journal* 616.

[310] For a critical account, see T. Kelsall, 'Insufficiently Hybrid: Assessing the Special Court for Sierra Leone' (2009) 27 *Law in Context* 132, 149 ('SCSL failed to adapt to the local context in some very significant ways: its political legitimacy was attenuated as soon as it prosecuted members of a popular local militia; its investigations team made routine blunders; the Outreach effort, while laudable, was too little too late; the Court alienated members of the local legal profession; at trial, it failed to get the best out of witnesses, imposed alien laws on a local population, and applied legal doctrines ill-fitted to the nature of local social reality').

differences between the witnesses and Court officials compromised accurate fact-finding. Witness testimony was often inconsistent with past statements. As Nancy Combs has argued, this had multiple causes that go beyond educational differences:

cultures do not attach the same importance to dates, distances, and other objective units of measure as we do in West ... Because Western speech patterns tend to be relatively direct, witnesses who provide indirect, circuitous answers are often thought at best to lack confidence in their perceptions, and at worst to be deceptive ... [B]ecause the trial judges often are not intimately familiar with the culture in question, they are left not knowing what speech signals or demeanor clues should give rise to concern.[311]

The symmetric focus on three defendants of each of the three factions created an 'illusion of equivalency'.[312] Leaders of the CDF continued to be viewed as heroes domestically. Sierra Leonean Judge Bankole Thompson sought to acquit the CDF defendants Fofana and Kondewa of all charges, on the ground that 'fighting for the restoration of democracy and constitutional legitimacy could be rightly perceived as an act both of patriotism and altruism, overwhelmingly compelling disobedience to a supranational regime of prescriptive norms'.[313] The Trial Chamber recognized the contributions of the two accused to peace, and 'the supreme sacrifices that they made to achieve this through a bloody conflict' as a mitigating factor.[314] This argument was overturned by the majority of the Appeal Chamber, which noted that political motives do not serve as a mitigating factor.[315] The two Sierra Leonean judges, Justices King and Kamanda, remained more inclined than their international colleagues to honour the fact that the CDF were fighting to reinstate the democratically elected government.[316]

Support for the Court waned over time. As Antonio Cassese noted:

The intent was laudable but the funding was flawed. The Court's finances were premised on voluntary contributions that have proven to be parsimonious, uncertain, and precarious ... the Special Court has ended up suffering from the same two shortcomings that its founders intended to avoid by establishing a court markedly different from the ad hoc tribunals: excessive length of proceedings and costly nature of the institution.[317]

3.4.3.1.2 *The Special Tribunal for Lebanon*
The Special Tribunal for Lebanon was established with a narrower focus, namely the murder of former Lebanese Prime Minister Rafiq Hariri in a car bomb explosion on

---

[311] N. Combs, 'Fact-Finding Without Facts: A Conversation with Nancy Combs' (2011) 105 *Proceedings of the Annual Meeting of the American Society of International Law* 315, 316.

[312] B. van Schaack, 'The Building Blocks of Hybrid Justice' (2016) 44 *Denver Journal of International Law & Policy* 101, 189.

[313] *Fofana and Kondewa* Trial Judgment, Separate Concurring and Partially Dissenting Opinion of Justice Bankole Thompson, para. 90.

[314] *Fofana and Kondewa* Trial Judgment, para. 514.

[315] *Fofana and Kondewa* Appeal Judgment, para. 535.

[316] *Fofana and Kondewa* Appeal Judgment, Partially Dissenting Opinion of Justice George Gelaga King, para. 93; Partially Dissenting Opinion on Sentencing of Justice Jon Kamanda, para. 15.

[317] A. Cassese, 'Report on the Special Court for Sierra Leone', 12 December 2006, para. 293 and 296.

14 February 2005, and related political attacks. The main rationale was to signal that political assassination cannot go unpunished.[318] A UN-mandated International Independent Investigative Commission concluded that domestic investigations into the bombing were flawed and recommended an independent judicial response.[319] Domestic authorities preferred an international mechanism with a Lebanese 'footprint', namely application of domestic laws and procedures, and mixed judges and prosecutors. The tribunal was meant to be established by an agreement between the United Nations and Lebanon. The agreement was signed by the government, but not ratified by parliament due to opposition from domestic factions.[320] Following a request by the government, the tribunal was thus effectively set in motion by a Security Council Resolution (SC Resolution 1757).[321] Its jurisdiction was not tied to a situation, but rather a set of facts, namely killings between 1 October 2004 and 12 December 2005, and later related killings. This selective focus raises challenges.[322] The focus on the assassination of Rafiq Hariri, and other connected attacks, creates dilemmas of selective justice in relation to other political killings and crimes.[323] It ignores the broader political context of the civil war, the role of Syrian forces and other crimes committed.

The STL is unique and novel as a legal experiment.[324] Unlike the ad hoc tribunals, it is not a subsidiary body of the Security Council.[325] The STL is the first hybrid tribunal with jurisdiction over terrorism. The applicable law is predominantly national in character. Victims were allowed to participate in trial proceedings.[326] The Defence Office was recognized as a separate organ of the tribunal. The tribunal is the first tribunal since Nuremberg that allows trials *in absentia*. This option was included in the Statute based on fears that perpetrators would not be surrendered to the tribunal.[327]

The work of the tribunal has been marked by a strong discrepancy between legal significance and societal context. The contribution of the STL has been mainly symbolic. Its creation was seen by some states as a means to create new institutional

---

[318] McAuliffe, 'Hybrid Tribunals', 30–31.
[319] Report of the International Independent Investigation Commission Established Pursuant to Security Council Resolution 1595 (2005), 19 October 2005, paras. 206–207.
[320] The session on ratification was not convened.
[321] UN Doc. S/RES/1757 (2007), 30 May 2007. See B. Fassbender, 'Reflections on the International Legality of the Special Tribunal for Lebanon' (2007) 5 *JICJ* 1091.
[322] For a critique, see M. Burgis-Kasthala, 'Defining Justice during Transition? International and Domestic Contestations over the Special Tribunal for Lebanon' (2013) 7 *International Journal of Transitional Justice* 497, 507 ('Such limitations suggest that the STL is much more the product of its maker – the UNSC – than other international criminal tribunals').
[323] M. Wierda, H. Nassar and L. Maalouf, 'Early Reflections on Local Perceptions, Legitimacy and Legacy of the Special Tribunal for Lebanon' (2007) 5 *JICJ* 1065, 1072; O. Nashabe, 'The Special Tribunal for Lebanon (STL): Selective Justice & Political Maneuvers' (2012) 1 *International Journal of Criminology and Society* 247, 248.
[324] C. Aptel, 'Some Innovations in the Statute of the Special Tribunal for Lebanon' (2007) 5 *JICJ* 1107.
[325] The STL was financed partly by Lebanon, and partly by contributions from the international community, including the US.
[326] J. de Hemptinne, 'Challenges Raised by Victims' Participation in the Proceedings of the Special Tribunal for Lebanon' (2010) 8 *JICJ* 165.
[327] P. Gaeta, 'Trials In Absentia before the Special Tribunal for Lebanon: To Be (Present) or Not To Be (Present)' (2007) 5 *JICJ* 1165; W. Jordash and T. Parker, 'Incompatibility with International Human Rights Law: Trials in Absentia at the Special Tribunal for Lebanon' (2010) 8 *JICJ* 487.

pathways for the prosecution of terrorism at the international level. It remained largely an experiment in legal engineering. It contributed inter alia to the articulation and development of the law in relation to the definition of terrorism as international crime, the legal responsibility of corporations and privacy in relation to collection of telephone metadata.[328] Its practical significance has remained limited. Its operation was affected by the continuing divide between the Sunni and pro-Western March 14 movement and Hezbollah. Hezbollah remained strongly opposed to the tribunal. The tribunal was unable to secure arrests and had to conduct trials *in absentia*. The Security Council has done little to support cooperation. Thus the actual trial record remains largely virtual. It is questionable whether *in absentia* trials can produce a credible narrative of what happened and who is ultimately responsible.

3.4.3.2 *Internationalized Domestic Courts*

A second type of hybrid justice is the integration of mixed domestic–international courts into the structure of the domestic legal system. Such internationalized courts differ from hybrid courts due to the fact that they lack a separate international legal identity of their own, distinct from the legal personality of the domestic state. They are internationalized domestic institutions, which have jurisdiction over special categories of crime. Internationalized courts apply both domestic and international law. Domestic judges may, under some circumstances overrule international judges.

Early examples are the former United Nations Mission in Kosovo (UNMIK) courts in Kosovo[329] or the Special Crimes Panels in East Timor.[330] They have been followed by a range of other institutions, which differ in relation to establishment, design and legal framework. One of the alleged merits of this type of hybridity is that it is closer to domestic culture and promotes norm internalization and 'capacity building'. The success varies according to context, however.

3.4.3.2.1 *The Extraordinary Chambers in the Courts of Cambodia*
The Extraordinary Chambers in the Courts of Cambodia illustrate the complex dilemmas of this type of hybridity.[331] They were established in 2003 to try crimes committed by senior leaders of the Khmer Rouge during their four-year reign between

---

[328] See *Prosecutor* v. *Ayyash et al.*, STL-11-01/T/AC/AR126.9, Decision on Appeal by Counsel for Mr Oneissi Against the Trial Chamber's Decision on the Legality of the Transfer of Call Data Records Decision on the Legality of the Transfer of Call Data Records, 28 July 2015. The decision concerned the collection of metadata of the entire Lebanese population between 2003 and 2010. It found that the 'the absence of judicial control did not violate any international human rights standard on the right to privacy' (para. 60).

[329] See UNMIK Regulations 2000/6 of 15 February 2000 and 2000/64 of 15 December 2000. For a survey, see J. Cerone and C. Baldwin, 'Explaining and Evaluating the UNMIK Court System', in Romano, Nollkaemper and Kleffner, *Internationalized Criminal Courts*, 44.

[330] See UNTAET Regulation No. 2000/15 of 6 June 2000. For an assessment, see C. Reiger and M. Wierda, *The Serious Crimes Process in Timor-Leste: In Retrospect* (New York: ICTJ, 2006).

[331] See generally C. Sperfeldt, 'From the Margins of Internationalized Criminal Justice: Lessons Learned at the Extraordinary Chambers in the Courts of Cambodia' (2013) 11 *JICJ* 1111; H. B. Jørgensen, *The Elgar Companion to the Extraordinary Chambers in the Courts of Cambodia* (Cheltenham: Edward Elgar, 2018).

1975 and 1979.[332] The exiled Khmer Rouge coalition continued to hold Cambodia's seat in the UN General Assembly until the 1990s. The Chambers were created by an international agreement between the United Nations General Assembly and the government of Cambodia, after years of complex negotiation.[333] The structure is a compromise between conflicting prerogatives. The UN pushed for internationalization in order to ensure a sufficient degree of independence, impartiality and objectivity. Cambodian authorities preferred to retain domestic ownership. The Extraordinary Chambers were thus integrated into the domestic legal order, but internationalized.

The Chambers are composed of a majority of Cambodian judges. They act in concert with international judges who are appointed by the Supreme Court of the Magistracy, upon nomination by the Secretary-General. Every key position at the ECCC is shared by an international and a Cambodian counterpart. The structure involves co-Investigating Judges, co-Prosecutors and co-Civil Party Representatives. A 'super-majority' rule was introduced as a protection against political interference.[334] It requires the vote of at least one international Pre-Trial or Trial judge for a decision to pass. The procedure combines inquisitorial features of Cambodian Law at pre-trial, with common law-oriented adversarial trials, and victim participation as civil parties.[335] It reflects a lack of confidence in the Cambodian justice system.

The ECCC faced concerns about politicization, costs and ageing defendants from the start. Pol Pot and some of his senior leaders had died before the creation of the ECCC. Trials were limited to a few key leaders, including Kaing Guek Eav, alias Duch, the former head of the notorious S-21 interrogation centre (Case 001), Nuon Chea, the main ideologue of the regime, and Khieu Samphan, the former head of state (Case 002). The two cases had a strongly symbolical function. The trial and judgments served mainly as a means to record and preserve the history of the Khmer Rouge regime, and to provide a dialogue between victims and perpetrators.[336] More than 250,000 Cambodians followed the hearings. Over 3,800 victims registered as civil parties in Case 002. The proceedings were associated with the promise to strengthen the independence and impartiality of the Cambodian judicial system. The 'shared' institutional framework was meant to foster this process. However, the two 'faces' of the Chambers, i.e. the national and international, remained divided.[337]

---

[332] See J. Menzel, 'Justice Delayed or Too Late for Justice? The Khmer Rouge Tribunal and the Cambodian "Genocide" 1975–79' (2007) *Journal of Genocide Research* 215. On the evidentiary problems, see M. A. Lejmi, 'Prosecuting Cambodian Genocide: Problems Caused by the Passage of Time Since the Commission of the Alleged Crimes' (2006) 4 *JICJ* 300.

[333] Agreement between the United Nations and the Royal Government of Cambodia Concerning the Prosecution under Cambodian Law of Crimes Committed during the Period of Democratic Kampuchea, 6 June 2003, 2329 UNTS 117.

[334] Williams, *Hybrid and Internationalised Criminal Tribunals*, 130.

[335] S. Vasiliev, 'Trial Process at the ECCC: The Rise and Fall of the Inquisitorial Paradigm in International Criminal Law?', in Meisenberg and Stegmiller, *The Extraordinary Chambers in the Courts of Cambodia*, 389.

[336] For instance, 3,869 civil parties were admitted and participated as a consolidated group in the trial of Case 002-01.

[337] McAuliffe, 'Hybrid Justice', 43.

Proceedings have suffered from allegations of political interference and corruption.[338] The government failed to execute the orders of the international prosecutor to call leading domestic politicians as witnesses. National prosecutors and the Cambodian government opposed investigations concerning three lower-level leaders in cases 003 and 004. Several international co-investigative judges have resigned from office. In 2017, the co-investigative judges considered a 'permanent stay' of these cases, based on fears that the lack of funds or financial uncertainty might threaten the 'judicial independence fairness and the integrity of the proceedings'.[339] The ECCC thus became partly a victim of its political context, donor fatigue and the double-headed staffing structure. It was financed through two channels: voluntary contributions from the international community (in particular Japan), and contributions from the government of Cambodia related to Cambodian staff and infrastructure. Despite these shortcomings, Cambodians were overall positive towards the ECCC.[340] Case 002, which included charges of genocide against the Cham and Vietnamese minorities, was branded as a 'Nuremberg moment' for Cambodia by UN Special Expert David Scheffer.[341]

3.4.3.2.2 Extraordinary African Chambers in Senegal

The Extraordinary African Chambers (EAC) in Senegal are a variation of this approach.[342] They were established in 2012 to prosecute the 'person or persons' most responsible for international crimes committed' under the rule of former President Hissène Habré in Chad between 1982 and 1990, following twenty years of political negotiations and judicial battles. The Chambers mark the first internationalized tribunal that was established with the involvement of the AU. They are a prime example as to how advocacy networks[343] and interaction by civil society, state and global actors may shape accountability.[344]

The creation is a result of external pressure and an error in legal history. Civil society lobbied for more than two decades for a trial of Habré. Some described the case as 'Africa's Pinochet'.[345] The EAC were established as a reaction to a

---

[338] M. Staggs Kelsall, 'Symbolic, Shambolic or Simply Sui Generis? Reflections from the Field on Cambodia's Extraordinary Chambers' (2009) 27 *Law in Context* 154, 170.

[339] ECCC, 004 2 07 09 2009 ECCC OCIJ, Combined Decision on The Impact of the Budgetary Situation on Cases 003, 004, and 004/2 and Related Submissions by the Defence for Yim Tith, 11 August 2017, para. 69.

[340] P. Pham et al., *After the First Trial: A Population-Based Survey on Knowledge and Perceptions of Justice and the Extraordinary Chambers in the Courts of Cambodia* (Berkeley: Human Rights Center, UC Berkeley School of Law, 2011), 26.

[341] G. Wright, 'Khmer Rouge Leaders' Life Terms Upheld', Cambodia Daily, 24 November 2016, at www.cambodiadaily.com/editors-choice/life-sentences-upheld-khmer-rouge-leaders-120914/. See also D. Scheffer, 'What Has Been "Extraordinary" About International Justice in Cambodia?', Speech William & Mary Law School, 25 February 2015, at www.unakrt-online.org/articles/speech-un-special-expert-david-scheffer-what-has-been-%E2%80%98extraordinary%E2%80%99-about-international.

[342] Cimiotta, 'The First Steps of the Extraordinary African Chambers', 177.

[343] M. Keck and K. Sikkink, *Activists beyond Borders: Advocacy Networks in International Politics* (Ithaca, NY: Cornell University Press, 1998).

[344] C. Sperfeldt, 'The Trial against Hissène Habré: Networked Justice and Reparations at the Extraordinary African Chambers' (2017) 21 *International Journal of Human Rights* 1243, 1244.

[345] Brody, 'The Prosecution of Hissène Habré: An "African Pinochet"', 321.

questionable ruling by the ECOWAS Court of Justice which found that the international crimes legislation adopted by Senegal in 2007 to prosecute Habré for crimes committed in Chad violated the principle of legality, specifically the principle against non-retroactivity of criminal law.[346] In July 2012, the ICJ ordered Senegal to try Habré for torture or to extradite him to Belgium.[347] In August 2012, Senegal and the African Union entered into an agreement on the establishment of a new judicial structure within the Senegalese domestic justice.[348] Hybrid justice was thus used as a technique to enable Senegal to exercise universal jurisdiction over crimes committed in Chad.[349]

The Chambers are an internationalized domestic jurisdiction.[350] They deviate from the ECCC structure. Prosecutors and investigative judges were nominated by Senegal's justice minister and appointed by the AU. Judges from Chad were not involved. The Presiding Judges of the Trial and the Appeals Chamber were from another AU country.[351] Ultimately, this construction was based on the premise that the exercise of universal jurisdiction by an internationalized court is less objectionable than its exercise by a single state.

The trial against Habré started on 20 July 2015.[352] On 30 May 2016, Habré was convicted of crimes against humanity, war crimes and torture, including rape and sexual violence.[353] Charges of sexual and gender-based violence were only included late at trial, namely after civil society agents (e.g. Justice Rapid Response) had filed amicus briefs which were then used by the legal representatives of victims in their arguments.[354] The trial was largely hailed as a success.[355] It marked several 'firsts'. It was the first universal jurisdiction case to proceed to trial in Africa. Habré was the first head of state ever to be personally convicted of rape. The Trial Chamber awarded individual reparations to victims, but rejected the request to hold the Chadian government civilly liable.

The EAC approach might easily be seen as a step towards 'African solutions to African problems'.[356] However, it represented a 'political compromise and a solution

---

[346] Spiga, 'Non-retroactivity of Criminal Law', 5.

[347] ICJ, *Questions Relating to the Obligation to Prosecute or Extradite (Belgium v. Senegal)*, Judgment, 20 July 2012, para. 121.

[348] Agreement Between the Government of the Republic of Senegal and the African Union on the Establishment of Extraordinary African Chambers within the Senegalese Judicial System, 22 August 2012.

[349] For a critique, see D. Sharp, 'Prosecutions, Development, and Justice: The Trial of Hissein Habré' (2003) 16 *Harvard Human Rights Journal* 148, 172–173 ('once the international NGOs have either achieved their precedent, run out of money, or lost interest, Chad's victims will be left behind to question whether symbolic justice is worth its steep price').

[350] Statute of the Extraordinary African Chambers within the courts of Senegal created to prosecute international crimes committed in Chad between 7 June 1982 and 1 December 1998, 22 August 2012.

[351] Statute EAC, Art. 11.

[352] M. Fall, 'The Extraordinary African Chambers: The Case of Hissène Habré', in G. Werle, L. Fernandez and M. Vormbaum (eds.), *Africa and the International Criminal Court* (The Hague: TMC Asser Press, 2014), 117–131.

[353] EAC, *Ministère Public* v. *Hissein Habré*, Judgment, 30 May 2016.

[354] See K. Thuy Seelinger, 'The Landmark Trial against Dictator Hissène Habré', *Foreign Affairs*, 16 June 2016.

[355] S. A. E. Høgestøl, 'The Habré Judgment at the Extraordinary African Chambers: A Singular Victory in the Fight Against Impunity' (2016) 34 *Nordic Journal of Human Rights* 147.

[356] S. Williams, 'The Extraordinary African Chambers in the Senegalese Courts: An African Solution to an African Problem?' (2013) 11 *JICJ* 1139.

to a particular impunity problem, rather than a carefully constructed model for transitional justice'.[357] Ironically, the costs are primarily borne by donor countries, such as the Netherlands, the United States, Belgium, Germany and France), and regional bodies, including the EU.

3.4.3.2.3 The Kosovo Specialist Chambers and Prosecutor's Office

The Kosovo Specialist Chambers are another type of internationalized court.[358] They are vested with the jurisdiction to investigate and prosecute transnational and international crimes that have been left aside by the ICTY or preceding EULEX panels in Kosovo, including killings, abductions, illegal detentions, illicit trafficking in human organs and sexual violence committed between 1 January 1998 and 31 December 2000. The creation is a follow-up of a report of the Parliamentary Assembly of the Council of Europe (Marty Report),[359] which found that crimes committed by members of Kosovo Liberation Army (KLA) against the Serbian population and certain Albanian Kosovars had been insufficiently investigated. The report criticized that 'international organisations in place in Kosovo favoured a pragmatic political approach, taking the view that they needed to promote short-term stability at any price, thereby sacrificing some important principles of justice'.[360] In 2011, a Special Investigative Task Force (SITF) was created by the EU. It concluded in 2014 that the crimes were organized and large-scale enough to warrant prosecution, and that there was sufficient evidence to charge KLA members with crimes.[361] EULEX had lost trust on Kosovo. Security concerns and fears of witness intimidation posed obstacles to holding proceedings in Kosovo, where members of the KLA continued to be regarded as war heroes. This led to the creation of a new entity, the Kosovo Specialist Chambers. They encompass two entities, the Specialist Chambers of Kosovo and the Specialist Prosecutor's Office. They were established by a national law, Law No. 05/L-053, following an exchange of letters between the President of Kosovo and the High Representative of the European Union.[362] The legal nature is disputed. According to one view, the Kosovo Specialist Chambers are created based on an international act, namely the exchange of letters between the EU and Kosovo.[363] According to a second

---

[357] Ibid., 1159.
[358] S. Williams, 'The Specialist Chambers of Kosovo: the Limits of Internationalization?' (2016) 14 *JICJ* 25; M. E. Cross, 'Equipping the Specialist Chambers of Kosovo to Try Transnational Crimes: Remarks on Independence and Cooperation' (2016) 14 *JICJ* 73; F. Korenica, A. Zhubi and D. Doli, 'The EU-Engineered Hybrid and International Specialist Court in Kosovo: How "Special" Is It?' (2016) 12 *European Constitutional Law Review* 474.
[359] Council of Europe, Committee on Legal Affairs and Human Rights, 'Inhuman Treatment of People and Illicit Trafficking in Human Organs in Kosovo', AS/Jur (2010) 46, 12 December 2010 ('Marty Report').
[360] Marty Report, para. 10.
[361] Statement of the Chief Prosecutor of the Special Investigative Task Force, 29 July 2014.
[362] This construction was endorsed by a ruling of the Constitutional Court of Kosovo. See Constitutional Court of the Republic of Kosovo, Case No. KO26/15, Assessment of an Amendment to the Constitution of the Republic of Kosovo proposed by the Government of the Republic of Kosovo and referred by the President of the Assembly of the Republic of Kosovo on 9 March 2015 by Letter No. 05–433/DO-318, 15 April 2015.
[363] See Muharremi, 'Kosovo Specialist Chambers and Specialist Prosecutor's Office', 980.

view, they are formally part of the legal order of Kosovo, but highly international-ized.[364] This means that cooperation duties are based on a traditional interstate form of cooperation.

The legal construction is unique. The power to appoint staff has been delegated to the EU as Appointing Authority.[365] In return, the budget is paid by the EU and other contributors. The Kosovo Specialist Chambers are to some extent mixed domestic regional Chambers. They are composed entirely of international rather than domestic judges. In terms of composition and personnel, they are thus international rather than domestic. The applicable law is highly complex due to the broad range of legal sources applicable in the legal order of Kosovo. It includes the highly internationalized Constitution of the Republic of Kosovo, the law on the Specialist Kosovo Chambers and Prosecution's Office as 'lex specialis', 'customary international law', including the case law of the international courts and tribunals, and 'international human rights law'.[366] The modes of liability alone are governed by three different legal orders: the Kosovo Specialist Law, international law and domestic Kosovo law.[367] JCE was not mentioned expressly.

The jurisdiction is framed in a unique way. It is essentially focused on one side of the conflict, namely the KLA. This is novel in the sense that it focuses on accountabil-ity of the 'victors' of the conflict, rather than the 'vanquished'. The Specialist Cham-bers are thus welcomed by Serbia as an instrument to bring justice to Kosovo Serbs. However, they continued to face suspicion of bias by Kosovar Albanians.

One distinctive feature is physical relocation. Previous mixed domestic–inter-national entities were typically located in the domestic country. In this case, they are located in The Hague. This externalization may be explained by security consider-ations, such as potential threats to judges, prosecutors and witnesses.

Another particularity is the replication of domestic structures. The Specialist Chambers are more or less an exact mirroring of domestic justice institutions, not only on one level, but all levels of the Court system: The Basic Court, the Court of Appeals, the Supreme Court and the Constitutional Court.[368] This contrasts with the idea of mixing international and domestic structures, which is typical of hybrid mechanisms. This approach was adopted to protect the Specialist Chambers from control by the Constitutional Court of Kosovo or other domestic entities. One risk of this approach is that it may lead to the development of parallel international struc-tures. The absence of domestic judges has downsides in terms of diversity of expertise and local perception.

---

[364] This view was taken by the Constitutional Court of Kosovo, Case No. KO26/15, para. 59 ('the proposed Specialist Chambers will be established within the unique and independent judicial power that is exercised by courts based on the Constitution).

[365] Assembly of the Republic of Kosovo, Law on Specialist Chambers and Specialist Prosecutor's Office, Law No. 05/L-053, 3 August 2015, Art. 28.

[366] Ibid., Art. 3 (2).

[367] Art. 16 (3). For a survey, see L. Yanev, 'Co-Perpetration Responsibility in the Kosovo Specialist Chambers' (2016) 14 *JICJ* 101, 103–106.

[368] Law No. 05/L-053, Art. 24.1 (a).

3.4.3.2.4 *The Special Criminal Court in the Central African Republic*

The Special Criminal Court in the Central African Republic (CAR) is the first internationalized court created in an ongoing ICC situation.[369] It was established to deal with the political violence following the removal of former President François Bozizé by the Séléka rebel group in March 2013. The existence of the Court is an open recognition that the involvement of the ICC in a conflict situation alone will not suffice to deal with accountability dilemmas. The Special Criminal Court was created as a court within the national legal system of CAR by an organic law on 3 June 2015,[370] based on a recommendation of the Bangui Forum on National Reconciliation.[371] It is a special national court which bears traces of internationalization. The UN Commission of Inquiry on the Central African Republic expressed qualified support for the idea of an internationalized court.[372] The decision to ground the Court in the domestic system was guided by the intent to ensure local input and enhance domestic justice reform more generally.

The Special Criminal Court operates primarily on the basis of domestic law, but has a mixed judicial structure. It bears resemblance with the ECCC. It foresees a carefully crafted balance of power between national and internationally appointed officials, with shifting majorities over four chambers: Pre-Trial Investigation Chamber, Special Indictment Chamber, Trial Chamber and Appeals Chamber. The jurisdiction of the Court is wide. It covers senior, mid- or lower-level perpetrators, irrespective of whether they are members of state or non-state armed groups. The Court's temporal jurisdiction includes not only the 2012–2014 conflict, but also crimes committed since 2003,[373] including Bozizé's coup d'état in 2003. A mapping report issued by United Nations Multidimensional Integrated Stabilization Mission in the Central African Republic (MINUSCA)[374] lists 620 incidents of serious crimes between 2003 and 2015 that might come within the ambit of the mandate.[375] The Court will thus have difficult selectivity choices.

The strong embedding in the domestic legal order is expressed in the formulation of substantive jurisdiction. It comprises 'gross violations of human rights and serious violations of international humanitarian law ... as defined by the Central African Penal Code and by virtue of international law obligations undertaken by the CAR ...

---

[369] Labuda, 'The Special Criminal Court in the Central African Republic', 175.
[370] Organic law on the creation, organization and functioning of the Special Criminal Court, Law No. 15/003, 3 June 2015.
[371] Report of the Secretary-General on the situation in the Central African Republic, S/2015/576, 29 July 2015.
[372] International Commission of Inquiry on the Central African Republic, Final Report, S/2014/928, 22 December 2014, paras. 65–66.
[373] Law No. 15/003, Art. 3.
[374] MINUSCA was mandated by SC Res. 2301 (2016) to 'monitor, help investigate, and report publicly and to the Security Council on violations of international humanitarian law and on violations and abuses of human rights committed throughout the CAR, including undertaking a mapping of such violations and abuses since 2003 to inform efforts to fight impunity'.
[375] See OHCHR, Report of the Mapping Project Documenting Serious Violations of International Human Rights and International Humanitarian Law Committed in the Territory of the Central African Republic Between January 2003 and December 2015, May 2017, at www.ohchr.org/Documents/Countries/CF/Mapping2003-2015/2017CAR_Mapping_Report_EN.pdf.

particularly genocide, crimes against humanity and war crimes'.[376] The domestic definitions differ partially from the ICC crime definitions.[377]

The Special Criminal Court enjoys primacy over ordinary courts. One of the risks of this privileged position is that it may detract from reforms and investments in the ordinary criminal court system. The Organic Law is at the same time deferential to ICC jurisdiction. It provides that the ICC has priority jurisdiction over the Special Criminal Court if the ICC Prosecutor 'is seized of a case entering concurrently in the jurisdiction of the ICC and the Special Criminal Court'.[378] The irony of this provision is that it is more deferential to the ICC than mandated by the Rome Statute. It virtually provides primacy to the ICC over the same cases.[379]

The domestic nature of the Court, and its potentially wide mandate, contrasts with the strong external budgetary dependence. The Organic Law states that the budget falls within 'the responsibility of the international community', and that funds would be provided through 'voluntary contributions, including from MINUSCA and any other sources mandated by the UNSC or the UN, in consultation with the government'.[380]

3.4.3.3 Merits and Critiques

Hybrid justice is clearly in vogue. It is likely that more types of hybrid justice will emerge in the future. Hybrid and internationalized courts enjoy support from civil society since they provide a local face to justice and may have some positive spillover effects in relation to the rule of law. However, each institution is to some extent an experiment of its own. The very model of a hybrid is under contestation.

In practice, hybrid justice is even more than other mechanisms a means to accommodate the political tensions of international criminal justice. It is often a product of intense negotiations between domestic actors and members of the international community. It reflects the idea that 'imperfect justice' may be better than 'no justice'.

Approaches towards the balance between international and domestic judges and corresponding checks and balances vary considerably.[381] Existing experiences indicate that the involvement of international actors alone is not sufficient to protect an institution from political influence, bias and selectivity. The concrete impact of hybrid justice on norm transfer and 'capacity building' is often more limited than assumed. The presence of local judges alone does not automatically provide legitimacy. It needs

---

[376] Law No. 15/003, Art. 3
[377] See D. Musila, 'The Special Criminal Court and Other Options of Accountability in the Central African Republic: Legal and Policy Recommendations', International Nuremberg Principles Academy, Occasional Paper No. 2 (Nuremberg: International Nuremberg Principles, 2016), 15–18.
[378] Law No. 15/003, Art. 37.
[379] See Labuda, 'The Special Criminal Court in the Central African Republic', 183, 193 ('it is irreconcilable with even the widest interpretations of complementarity under Article 17').
[380] Law No. 15/003, Art. 53.
[381] See H. Hobbs, 'Hybrid Tribunals and the Composition of the Court: In Search of Sociological Legitimacy' (2016) 16 *Chicago Journal of International Law* 484.

to be earned. Other criteria, such as specific expertise, diverse backgrounds or gender balance are crucial for the success of hybrid institutions.

One of the weaknesses of hybrid mechanisms is that they often suffer from insufficient resources and a lack of political commitment. Their hybrid nature implies that they may be attacked by both sides, their international and domestic stakeholders. Functions such as outreach or legacy are not considered to be part of the core mandate. These factors are not necessarily failings of the respective institutions, but often a consequence of the difficult political, legal and institutional context in which they operate.

The funding structure makes hybrid courts vulnerable. As the Co-Investigating Judges of the ECCC noted on the verge of collapse of cases 003 and 004 due to budgetary constraints:

despite the existence of modern international criminal tribunals since the early 1990s and recurring complaints across tribunals about funding shortfalls the community of states has yet to establish a reliable funding model that allows courts to function on the international level as they would on the national level under a tax based system and to accommodate the demands of judicial independence in an otherwise overwhelmingly executive driven institutional and political environment.[382]

3.4.4   *Regional Courts*

Regional justice is a fourth accountability approach.[383] The lack of regional criminal courts is one of the striking gaps in the global justice architecture. Regional courts have become an important instrument for the enforcement of human rights.[384] They have been sidelined in international criminal justice however.

3.4.4.1 *The Naissance of Regional Mechanisms*

Initially, the idea of regional justice may have been perceived as a challenge to the proclaimed universality of international criminal law.[385] However, regionalism is increasingly recognized as an asset. It offers a means to balance the mutual benefits and weaknesses of international and domestic justice, and take into account legitimate

---

[382] ECCC, Combined Decision on the Impact of the Budgetary Situation on Cases 003, 004 and 004/2, para. 64.

[383] For a discussion, see W. W. Burke-White, 'Regionalization of International Criminal Law Enforcement: A Preliminary Exploration' (2003) 38 *Texas International Law Journal* 729; W. A. Schabas, 'Regions, Regionalism and International Criminal Law' (2007) 4 *New Zealand Yearbook of International Law* 3; R. Burchill, 'International Criminal Tribunals at the Regional Level: Lessons from International Human Rights Law' (2007) 4 *New Zealand Yearbook of International Law* 25; C. Jalloh, 'Regionalizing International Criminal Law?' (2009) 9 *International Criminal Law Review* 445–499; C. Bhoke Murungu, 'Towards a Criminal Chamber in the African Court of Justice and Human Rights' (2011) 9 *JICJ* 1067; F. Kebede Tiba, 'Regional International Criminal Courts: An Idea Whose Time Has Come?' (2016) 17 *Cardozo Journal of Conflict Resolution* 521.

[384] The European Court of Human Rights was created in 1950. It was followed by the Inter American Court of Human Rights in 1979, the Caribbean Court of Justice in 2001 and the African Court of Human and Peoples' Rights in 2004.

[385] It perpetuates the image of 'geographies of justice' line.

regional or cultural preferences in relation to crimes. As William Burke White has argued: 'In terms of cost, legitimacy, political independence, and judicial reconstruction, regionalization may be a normatively preferable means of enforcing international criminal law. To that extent, regionalization merits attention as a viable part of a system of international criminal law enforcement'.[386] Regionalization depends on a number of structural factors, such as economic incentives, mutual trust and cooperation, and a sense of regional identity. This may explain why regional criminal courts are often suggested, but rarely created. An early example of a regional criminal court is the Caribbean Court of Justice. It is vested with appellate jurisdiction for civil and criminal law matters in the Caribbean region.[387] For a long time, however, the idea did not gain ground in the field of atrocity crimes. Instead, regional human rights courts have taken on a quasi-criminal function in relation to the adjudication of international crimes.[388] They differ from criminal courts in terms of expertise, methodology and judicial culture. They are not well equipped to deal with criminal responsibility, since they lack investigative capacity and focus on state violations.

The creation of a regional criminal court is sensitive from a sovereignty perspective and the parallel competencies of domestic courts. In the 1990s, the Organization of American States (OAS) considered the establishment of a Regional Criminal Court for the Americas, but it failed to be adopted.[389] EU efforts have focused on the creation of a European Public Prosecutor, and the adoption of legal instruments to strengthen criminal enforcement, such as the European Arrest Warrant, the European Evidence Warrant or the Framework Decision on the freezing of property and evidence.[390] Practice has largely moved towards the regionalization of domestic courts, and regional support to hybrid institutions, rather than the development of specialized regional expertise.

3.4.4.2 The Malabo Protocol

The debate has taken a new spin with the initiative of the AU to develop a regional criminal jurisdiction. The US proposed the creation of a regional African criminal court as a counter-model to the Darfur referral by the Security Council.[391] African states turned to regionalism as a result of dissatisfaction with institutions such as the ICC and the Security Council, and the dominance of Western states in justice

---

[386] Burke-White, 'Regionalization of International Criminal Law Enforcement', 730.

[387] D. P. Bernard, 'The Caribbean Court of Justice: A New Judicial Experience' (2010) 37 *International Journal of Legal Information* 219.

[388] For instance, the Inter-American Court of Human Rights has monitored domestic prosecutions in over fifty cases and developed rich case law in relation to the right to truth, forced disappearances, amnesties and reparations. See A. Valeria Huneeus, 'International Criminal Law by Other Means: The Quasi-Criminal Jurisdiction of the Human Rights Courts' (2013) 107 *AJIL* 1.

[389] On the recent COPLA initiative, see Section 1.4.1.

[390] R. Pereira, 'The Regionalization of Criminal Law: The Example of European Criminal Law,' in L. van den Herik and C. Stahn (eds.), *The Diversification and Fragmentation of International Criminal Law* (Leiden: Martinus Nijhoff, 2012).

[391] Schabas, 'Regions, Regionalism and International Criminal Law', 23.

discourse. They first worked within multilateral structures (e.g. the ICC Assembly of States Parties, UN) to change the status quo. After these efforts failed, they adopted the proposal to extend the jurisdiction of the African Court of Justice and Human and People's Rights in 2014. The turn to regionalism was driven by multiple factors: concerns of African leaders over the exercise of universal jurisdiction by certain European countries,[392] the focus of the ICC on African situations, the failure of the Security Council to use its powers under Article 16 of the ICC Statute to suspend ICC investigations and prosecutions against African heads of state[393] and dissatisfaction with the responses of the ICC Assembly of States Parties.

The Malabo Protocol challenges the vision that the ICC should serve as a 'regional Court for Africa'.[394] It envisages the creation of the first ever regional criminal court. It is a double-edged sword. It has certain attractions.[395] It offers an alternative account of international criminal justice that responds to certain valid critiques, such as the neglect of quotidian crimes and economic causes of conflict.[396] The Protocol combines atrocity crimes (aggression, genocide, crimes against humanity, war crimes) with transnational crimes, such as terrorism, money laundering, trafficking in persons, drugs and hazardous wastes. It recognizes corporate criminal responsibility.[397] Some offences, like slavery or illicit exploitation of natural resources, are inherently connected to the continent's troubled history of external intervention. Other crimes, such as the alleged crime of 'unconstitutional change of government',[398] lack universal recognition and might lead to a slippery slope. This new crime is not only considerably vague, but might also stifle resistance against oppressive regimes.[399] The immunity provisions are visibly designed to shield African leaders from investigation and

---

[392] For example, a French Judge indicted nine Rwandese officials. Rwanda claimed that they were entitled to personal immunity. See C. Jalloh, 'Universal Jurisdiction, Universal Prescription? A Preliminary Assessment of the African Union Perspective on Universal Jurisdiction' (2010) 21 *Criminal Law Forum* 1.

[393] A draft resolution invoking Art. 16 was put to a vote on 15 November 2013 by Morocco, Rwanda and Togo but failed to be adopted.

[394] See A. Branch, 'Dominic Ongwen on Trial: The ICC's African Dilemmas' (2017) 11 *International Journal of Transitional Justice* 30, 36–37.

[395] M. Du Plessis, 'Implications of the AU Decision to Give the African Court Jurisdiction Over International Crimes' (2012) Institute for Security Studies, available at https://issafrica.s3.amazonaws.com/site/uploads/Paper235-AfricaCourt.pdf.

[396] M. Sirleaf, 'The African Justice Cascade and the Malabo Protocol' (2017) 11 *International Journal of Transitional Justice* 71.

[397] See L. van den Herik and E. van Sliedregt, 'International Criminal Law and the Malabo Protocol: About Scholarly Reception, Rebellion and Role Models', in S. Dewulf (ed.), *Liber amicorum Chris van den Wyngaert* (Antwerp: Maklu 2018) 511.

[398] According to Art. 28E of the Malabo Protocol, the crime consists of 'committing or ordering to be committed the following acts, with the aim of illegally accessing or maintaining power: a) A putsch or coup d'état against a democratically elected government; b) An intervention by mercenaries to replace a democratically elected government; c) Any replacement of a democratically elected government by the use of armed dissidents or rebels or through political assassination; d) Any refusal by an incumbent government to relinquish power to the winning party or candidate after free, fair and regular elections; e) Any amendment or revision of the Constitution or legal instruments, which is an infringement on the principles of democratic change of government or is inconsistent with the Constitution; f) Any substantial modification to the electoral laws in the last six (6) months before the elections without the consent of the majority of the political actors'.

[399] The crime covers even persons who peacefully exercise their rights. For an analysis, H. van der Wilt, 'Unconstitutional Change of Government: A New Crime within the Jurisdiction of the African Criminal Court' (2017) 30 *LJIL* 967. See G. Kemp and S. Kinyunyu, 'The Crime of Unconstitutional Change of Government', in Werle and Vormbaum, *The African Criminal Court*, 57, 69.

prosecution by the ICC. The Protocol recognizes immunity for 'Any serving AU Head of State or Government, or anybody acting or entitled to act in such capacity, or other senior state officials based on their functions, during their tenure of office'.[400] The provision creates an incentive for office holders to stay in power to avoid prosecution. Critics fear that it might in practice provide a licence for impunity.[401] It puts the AU in direct conflict with the Rome Statute. Regionalization thus has many faces: it can be a blessing, and a curse.

3.4.5 Other Accountability Mechanisms

Formal criminal justice has occupied a central space in the discourse on global justice, due to its immediacy, drama and strong impact on politics. However, accountability extends beyond courts. Classical criminal justice institutions are complemented by a range of other accountability mechanisms that provide a broader perspective on accountability. They include fact-finding bodies, truth commissions or customary local procedures. These mechanisms do not satisfy formal requirements of punishment for international crimes.[402] They may provide a more contextualized or 'local' face to accountability. Their function, purpose and design differs according the individual context.

3.4.5.1 Commissions of Inquiry and Investigative Bodies

Human rights fact-finding plays an important role in relation to accountability. In the 1970s and 1980s, human rights fact-finding was largely dependent on civil society organizations since UN institutional structures were less well developed.[403] The focus of accountability was typically geared at establishing state violations. Since the 1990s, there has been a growing trend towards individualization of fact-finding. The UN has established more than twenty international commissions of inquiry with mandates to investigate serious violations of human rights, international humanitarian law violations or international crimes.[404] These commissions are neither classical fact-finders, nor formal criminal bodies. Their role is not only to establish the facts and circumstances underlying human rights violations, but to provide legal characterizations of

---

[400] Malabo Protocol, Art. 46A *bis*.

[401] L. Oette, 'The African Union High-Level Panel on Darfur: A Precedent for Regional Solutions to the Challenges Facing International Criminal Justice?', in V. Nmehielle (ed.), *Africa and the Future of International Criminal Justice* (The Hague: Eleven International Publishing, 2012) 353, 370–371; M. Sirleaf, 'Regionalism, Regime Complexes and the Crisis in International Criminal Justice' (2016) 54 *Columbia Journal of Transnational Law* 699, 727.

[402] Disciplinary or administrative penalties alone would not satisfy the need for appropriate punishment, particularly in cases of grave violations of human rights. See Human Rights Committee, *Bautista de Arellana* v. *Colombia*, Communication 563/1993, Views of 27 October 1995, para. 8.2.

[403] The United Nations Office of the High Commissioner for Human Rights was established in 1993.

[404] F. D'Alessandra, 'The Accountability Turn in Third Wave Human Rights Fact-Finding' (2017) 33 *Utrecht Journal of International and European Law* 59–76.

facts and to explore possible avenues of responsibility of states and individuals.[405] They are thus a 'softer', and potentially less coercive way of establishing accountability than criminal bodies. They serve as a forum to collect information underlying crimes and violations, or sometimes even as precursor to formal criminal investigation or prosecution.

The work of such commissions is increasingly juridified.[406] Commissions with an accountability mandate may be roughly divided into two groups. Some commissions are 'scoping' commissions. They are geared at tracing patterns of violence in situations and fact-finding per se. They do not necessarily conduct legal or quasi-legal investigations. Their inquiry has a broader focus, namely to signal or warn of human rights violations or identify accountability strategies. They may precede, or follow the establishment of more formal investigative bodies. Classical examples are the UN Mapping Exercises in the DRC and CAR, which were mandated to conduct 'a mapping' of serious human rights and international humanitarian law violations, identify or develop transitional justice mechanisms and propose priority areas for future investigations. This information may be used to contextualize violations and identify accountability strategies.

Other commissions have investigative powers with a focus on criminal responsibility (investigative commissions). They may be mandated to identify not only broad patterns of violations and abuses, but incidents, specific categories of crime or even individual perpetrators of crime.[407] Their findings provide investigative links for formal justice mechanisms or contribute to prevention more broadly, i.e. by providing early-warning data that can alert actors to the risk of atrocity. Examples are the Commission of Experts for the former Yugoslavia and Rwanda, the United Nations International Independent Investigation Commission (UNIIIC), the Commissions of Inquiry for Darfur and Libya, the United Nations Fact Finding Mission on the Gaza Conflict, the International Commission of Inquiry Mandated to Establish the Facts and Circumstances of the Events of 28 September 2009 in Guinea and the UN Commission of Inquiry on the Syrian Arab Republic. The work of some, but not all (Gaza, Syria), of these commissions has been followed by more specific international justice initiatives. Some missions have triggered international investigations and prosecutions (ICTY, Darfur, Lebanon). Others have supported international investigations (ICTR, Libya, Ivory Coast) or preliminary examinations by the ICC (Guinea).

---

[405] See L. van den Herik, 'An Inquiry into the Role of Commissions of Inquiry in International Law: Navigating the Tensions between Fact-Finding and Application of International Law' (2014) 13 *Chinese Journal of International Law* 507.

[406] C. Schwöbel-Patel, 'Commissions of Inquiry: Courting International Criminal Courts and Tribunals', in C. Henderson (ed.), *Commissions of Inquiry: Problems and Prospects* (Oxford: Hart/Bloomsbury, 2017), 145.

[407] For a typology, see C. Stahn and D. Jacobs, 'The Interaction Between Human Rights Fact-Finding and International Criminal Proceedings', in P. Alston and S. Knuckey (eds.), *The Transformation of Human Rights Fact-Finding* (New York: Oxford University Press), 255, 258–259.

These types of commissions occupy a new space in the global justice landscape. They are a quick and less formalized way of responding to violations than courts and tribunals. Their added value lies in the collection of information and material, the preservation of certain sources and materials, the identification of leads for investigation, and the framing of accountability options. However, they often face severe limitations in relation to access to crime sites or information providers, and potential protection of 'witnesses'. Their findings do not carry the same legal authority as formalized judicial proceedings, and are often contested by states opposed to their establishment. Sadly, in some situations, the reports of such commissions may remain the only immediate accountability response to violations.

Overall, there is an increasing tendency to view private or public fact-finding bodies as a precursor to criminal investigations.[408] Some voices seek to extend the naming and shaming functions of commissions, including their role in establishing legal 'responsibility' of individuals for alleged violations. This trend requires careful consideration. One of the major strengths of commissions lies in their non-juridical role, and their ability to engage with politics. It is important not to conflate the role of such commissions with formal criminal mechanisms. The goals and professional cultures of human rights fact-finding differ partly from investigation and prosecution. Commissions apply different standards and methodologies than prosecutors or courts and lack many of the safeguards and protections that formal criminal processes enjoy, such as due process guarantees or judicial scrutiny.[409] Identifying perpetrators stands in a certain tension to the quasi-/non-judicial nature of these bodies. Individualization contrasts with the collective nature of violence that characterizes many types of abuses. Elucidating organizational structures, establishing context or providing 'leads' for formal investigations may be more helpful than providing a list of names for investigation. The establishment of a commission of inquiry should not become an excuse to avoid the more burdensome path of criminal investigation and prosecutions. As scholars have noted, commissions of inquiry might add more usefully to diplomacy and peacemaking by taking some distance to the individualized criminal lens and focusing to a greater extent on socio-economic violations and structural violence.[410]

When engaging with the responsibilities of individuals, it is essential to avoid harm to criminal investigations in the documentation and collection of information for accountability purposes ('no harm principle'). The work of human rights fact-finders may complicate witness statements and evidence gathering by formal criminal bodies. It is thus essential to rely on persons who know how information might be used as evidence in court, and who can minimize the damage to future investigations.

---

[408] Some scholars speak of a 'new sequential model' that could 'become paradigmatic for future cases where politics is blocking the path to justice in conflict'. See C. Fehl and E. Mocková, 'Chasing Justice for Syria', PRIF Spotlight 5/2017, www.hsfk.de/en/service/news/news/chasing-justice-for-syria/.

[409] A. Bisset, 'Commissions of Inquiry and Procedural Fairness', in Henderson, *Commissions of Inquiry: Problems and Prospects*, 309–335

[410] Schwöbel-Patel, 'Commissions of Inquiry', 155.

Commissions of inquiry differ from the more formalized International, Impartial and Independent Mechanism to Assist in the Investigation and Prosecution of Crimes in Syria (IIIM). This Mechanism has a 'quasi-prosecutorial' function. It is vested with formal legal mandate to collect and preserve evidence and prepare files for trials in national and/or international courts, and must abide by international criminal law standards.[411] It is not a criminal jurisdiction per se, with genuine power to issue arrest warrants or prosecute individuals, but rather a connecting point to domestic jurisdictions, including states exercising universal jurisdiction, or a future criminal body.[412] It was initially seen as a political compromise based on the failure to agree on international jurisdiction or a specialized court. However, it fills to some extent a missing link in the accountability landscape between human rights investigations and domestic criminal jurisdiction. Its merit lies in the fact that it 'sees accountability as a responsibility extending across multiple jurisdictions and involving coordination between national and international actors'.[413]

3.4.5.2 Truth Commissions

Truth and reconciliation commissions are a second type of mechanism that sheds a broader light on accountability.[414] They play a crucial role, in particular in post-conflict contexts, where it is not always possible to rely fully on criminal proceedings to counter injustices.[415] Some authorities argue that the establishment of a truth commission is a necessary corollary of a right to truth.[416] Traditionally, such commissions have sometimes been viewed as an alternative to formal criminal justice. In contemporary settings, they serve mostly as a supplement to, rather than as a substitute of criminal investigations and prosecutions.

Many of the Latin American commissions were established after the fall of military dictatorships (e.g. Argentina, Chile, El Salvador and Guatemala) and as part of an active effort to combat impunity after years of silence.[417] As Christian Tomuschat has noted, a decision to establish a truth commission requires 'a fair degree of political maturity of a country': 'truth commissions have always been instruments of a

---

[411] See UN GA Res. A/RES/71/248, 11 January 2017 (International, Impartial and Independent Mechanism to Assist in the Investigation and Prosecution of Persons Responsible for the Most Serious Crimes under International Law Committed in the Syrian Arab Republic since March 2011), para 4. See C. Wenaweser and J. Cockayne, 'Justice for Syria? The International, Impartial and Independent Mechanism and the Emergence of the UN General Assembly in the Realm of International Criminal Justice' (2015) 15 *JICJ* 211.

[412] See Report of the International, Impartial and Independent Mechanism to Assist in the Investigation and Prosecution of Persons Responsible for the Most Serious Crimes under International Law Committed in the Syrian Arab Republic since March 2011, A/72/764, 28 February 2018, para. 7.

[413] Ibid., para. 12.

[414] See generally P. Hayner, *Unspeakable Truths* (New York: Routledge, 2001); P. Hayner, 'Fifteen Truth Commissions 1974 to 1994: A Comparative Study' (1994) 16 *Human Rights Quarterly* 558.

[415] See A. Bisset, *Truth Commissions and Criminal Courts* (Cambridge: Cambridge University Press, 2012); W. A. Schabas and S. Darcy, *Truth Commissions and Courts* (Dordrecht: Kluwer, 2004).

[416] Hayner, *Unspeakable Truths*, 176. Truth has different meanings. It may refer to factual truth, personal truth, or social truth.

[417] N. Roht-Arriaza, 'Truth Commissions and Amnesties in Latin America: The Second Generation' (1998) 92 *American Society of International Law Proceedings* 313.

deliberate policy of compromise. They have not simply been imposed by the winning party after the end of an internal conflict. Rather, the contending parties have generally agreed to have their conduct scrutinized with that of their opponents'.[418] Their goals and functions share multiple synergies with criminal jurisdictions.[419] Some commissions have 'quasi-judicial' powers, such as the power to conduct investigations, take statements, hold public hearings and issue summons to appear and subpoenas.[420] They represent to some extent a 'judicialized' approach to alternative justice. One of their alleged advantages is that they are better equipped than courts to explain the origins and causes of violations and to translate them into a narrative.

There is no uniform formula. Truth commissions differ significantly in terms of their mandate (selective/comprehensive enquiry), powers (fact-finding/quasi-judicial functions), composition (domestic/international or mixed) and functions (public reporting/recommendation vs. reintegration of perpetrators into society). Some commissions have close synergies to commissions of inquiry. Their mandate is geared at identifying state violations (e.g. enforced disappearances) or potential perpetrators. Other commissions place more emphasis on documenting or explaining violations or promoting reconciliation. Truth commission processes can help survivors to create a meaning of atrocities and mitigate feelings of guilt. The delivery of a final report often marks an important symbolic moment for domestic societies. However, follow-up on recommendations has remained a challenge in many contexts.

The South African model has been widely discussed, since it included an amnesty for truth clause. It is often falsely presented as an illustration of the peace versus justice dichotomy. The Commission had the power to grant individuals amnesty for politically motivated offences upon full disclosure of the crimes. But only 10 per cent of the 7,000 persons who applied for amnesties in South Africa were relieved from criminal sanction. The Commission noted in its Final Report that 'the granting of a general amnesty should be resisted' in order to 'avoid a culture of impunity and to entrench the rule of law'.[421] Its strength lies in the fact that it translated 'knowledge into acknowledgment'. However, its record remained unfinished due to a lack of follow-up on compensation and prosecution.

The methodology of the South African model had limits. The Commission acknowledged the 'healing potential of storytelling, of revealing the truth before a respectful audience and to an official body'.[422] Critics have noted that speaking does not automatically translate into healing.[423] Storytelling is only one piece in a broader psychological process and does not necessarily provide closure by itself. Mahmood

---

[418] See C. Tomuschat, 'Clarification Commission in Guatemala' (2001) 23 *Human Rights Quarterly* 233, 235.

[419] Former ICTY President Jorda recognized that a truth commission and the tribunal could perform 'complementary and distinct roles'. See ICTY, 'The ICTY and the Truth and Reconciliation Commission in Bosnia and Herzegovina', 17 May 2001, at www.icty.org/en/press/icty-and-truth-and-reconciliation-commission-bosnia-and-herzegovina.

[420] See C. Stahn, 'Accommodating Individual Criminal Responsibility and National Reconciliation: The UN Truth Commission for East Timor' (2001) 95 *AJIL* 959.

[421] Truth and Reconciliation Commission of South Africa Report, Vol. 5, 29 October 1998, 309.

[422] Ibid., 351.

[423] See B. Hamber, *Transforming Societies after Political Violence* (Dordregt: Springer, 2009), 65.

Mamdani argued that the truth and reconciliation process only provided a 'diminished truth', since it focused on individual victims and perpetrators of gross violations and thereby reduced apartheid from 'a relationship between the state and entire communities to one between the state and individuals',[424] while marginalizing the systemic dimensions and economic injustices of apartheid policies.[425]

Today, it is controversial whether the sole establishment of a truth and reconciliation commission, such as the South African one, would be compatible with a good faith exercise of obligations in relation to international crimes. Human rights courts, such as the Inter-American Court of Human Rights, have stressed the duty to investigate and prosecute systematic and gross human rights violations. In many contemporary contexts, there is a division of labour. Truth and reconciliation commissions operate alongside international or hybrid justice mechanisms. Some violations are treated by truth and reconciliation commissions, while certain categories of crimes remain subject to the option of criminal investigations and prosecutions. Paradigmatic examples are the truth commissions in East Timor[426] and Sierra Leone.[427] They marked an attempt to reconcile the need for reconciliation and forgiveness with criminal responsibility. Colombia adopted a highly complex accountability model, which includes a truth commission, a special approach to criminal responsibility for serious crimes,[428] namely the option of mitigated punishment or alternative forms of sanction in case of confession, and reparation schemes in order to promote peace.[429] It seeks to address peace and justice dilemmas in line with international legal obligations.

The interaction between truth commissions and formal criminal justice mechanisms has caused certain problems in practice (e.g. in relation to access to testimony, witness fatigue and use of records). For instance, in Sierra Leone persons appearing before the Commission could not gain immunity before the Court. The Commission deplored that many victims failed to come forward based on a fear that their information may be turned over to the Court. The SCSL refused to let one of its defendants, Sam Norman Hinga, testify in public to the TRC on his own request.[430] The division of

---

[424] M. Mamdani, 'Amnesty or Impunity? A Preliminary Critique of the Report of the Truth and Reconciliation Commission of South Africa' (2002) 32 *Diacritics* 32, 33–34.

[425] M. Mamdani, 'A Diminished Truth', in W. James and L. de Vijver (eds.), *After the TRC: Reflections on Truth and Reconciliation in South Africa* (Athens, OH: Ohio University Press; Cape Town: David Philip, 2000), 58.

[426] P. Burgess, 'A New Approach to Restorative Justice: East Timor's Community Reconciliation Processes, in N. Roht-Arriaza and J. Mariezcurrena (eds.), *Transitional Justice in the Twenty-First Century: Beyond Truth versus Justice* (Cambridge: Cambridge University Press, 2006), 176; M. Hirst, *An Unfinished Truth: An Analysis of the Commission of Truth and Friendship's Final Report on the 1999 Atrocities in East Timor* (New York: International Centrte for Transitional Justice, 2009).

[427] W. Schabas, 'A Synergistic Relationship: The Sierra Leone Truth and Reconciliation Commission and the Special Court for Sierra Leone' (2004) 15 *Criminal Law Forum* 3; T. Kelsall, 'Truth, Lies, Ritual: Preliminary Reflections on the Truth and Reconciliation Commission in Sierra Leone' (2005) 27 *Human Rights Quarterly* 361.

[428] E.g. crimes against humanity, serious war crimes, hostage taking, kidnapping of civilians, sexual violence.

[429] For a discussion, see C. Josi, 'Accountability in the Colombian Peace Agreement: Are the Proposed Sanctions Contrary to Colombia's International Obligations?' (2017) 46 *Southwestern Law Review* 401.

[430] See *Prosecutor* v. *Hinga Norman*, Case No. SCSL-2003–08-PT, Decision on Appeal by the Truth and Reconciliation Commission for. Sierra Leone and Chief Samuel Hinga Norman JP Against the Decision of His Lordship, Mr Justice. Bankole Thompson Delivered on 30 October 2003 to Deny the TRCs Request to Hold a Public Hearing with Chief

labour caused frustration. The TRC considered the decision as a 'serious blow to the cause of truth and reconciliation in Sierra Leone', causing 'grave and irreparable damage not only to the detainee himself but also to the people of Sierra Leone'.[431] Similar complaints were voiced in East Timor.

The risk of such conflicts is mitigated in the context of the ICC. The ICC tries only a very limited number of offenders in each situation. In case of conflict, the Prosecutor may defer to truth commission proceedings under the interests of justice clause.[432]

3.4.5.3 Alternative Forms of Justice

Many domestic systems have alternative mechanisms of dispute resolution that are carried out locally, according to traditional customs or practices.[433] Local justice is often easily accessible, expeditious and cost-effective, and used to address socio-economic issues, such as property or family issues. It comes in many different forms.[434] Some mechanisms focus more on community-healing, rituals or group reconciliation than on individualization and criminal punishment. Such mechanisms are not necessarily an appropriate forum to try international crimes. However, they serve as a useful supplement to domestic criminal proceedings, or as an alternative to amnesty, geared at promoting healing or societal integration of perpetrators. They may promote non-Western notions of community building, well-being and social justice.[435]

A prominent example is the *gacaca* trials in Rwanda,[436] which involved 260,000 local community judges. *Gacaca* means 'justice on the grass'. This approach was partly a reaction to the mass nature of criminality. The Rwandan government estimated that it would take at least 200 years to complete the trial of genocide-related detainees if the country relied on its conventional court system.[437] Persons who designed or organized the genocide or faced charges of torture or sexual violence (Category I perpetrators) were tried by conventional courts. However, the large

---

Samuel Hinga Norman JP, 28 November 2003; N. Boister, 'Failing to get to the Heart of the Matter in Sierra Leone? The Truth Commission is Denied Unrestricted Access to Chief Hinga Norman' (2004) 2 *JICJ* 1100.

[431] Press Release by the Truth and Reconciliation Commission, 'Special Court Denies Hinga Norman's right (and that of the other detainees) to appear publicly before the TRC, Freetown, Sierra Leone, 01 December 2003', at www .sierraleonetrc.org/images/docs/hinganorman/2003-12-01_FINAL_TRC_PRESS_RELEASE.pdf.

[432] Art. 53 (1) (c) and 2(c) ICC Statute. See generally P. Hayner, *The Peacemaker's Paradox: Pursuing Justice in the Shadow of Conflict* (New York: Rouledge, 2018), Chapter 8 (Interests of Justice); E. B. King, 'Does Justice Always Require Prosecution? The International Criminal Court and Transitional Justice Measures' (2013) 45 *George Washington International Law Review* 85.

[433] See R. Shaw, L. Waldorf and P. Hazan, *Localizing Transitional Justice: Interventions and Priorities after Mass Violence* (Stanford: Stanford University Press, 2010); L. Waldorf, 'Mass Justice for Mass Atrocity: Rethinking Local Justice as Transitional Justice' (2006) 79 *Temple Law Review* 1– 88; K. McEvoy and L. McGregor (eds.), *Transitional Justice From Below* (Portland: Hart Publishing, 2008).

[434] S. G. Gordon, 'Complementarity and Alternative Mechanisms of Justice', in Stahn and El Zeidy, *The International Criminal Court and Complementarity*, 745, 752 et seq.

[435] See T. Allen, *Trial Justice* (London and New York: Zed, 2006), 134 ('there is a balance in the community that cannot be found in the briefcase of the white man').

[436] See P. Clark, *The Gacaca Courts, Post-Genocide Justice and Reconciliation in Rwanda: Justice without Lawyers* (Cambridge: Cambridge Uiniversity Press, 2010).

[437] F-X. Nsanzuwera, 'The Contribution of the ICTR for Rwandans', in A.-M. de Brouwer and A. Smeulers (eds.), *The Elgar Companion to the International Criminal Tribunal for Rwanda* (Cheltenham: Edward Elgar, 2016), 488, 491.

burden of trials, including cases relating to homicide, serious bodily harm or property offences, was transferred to the village level, in order to promote return and reconciliation. The *gacaca* trials were carried out by community leaders in an interactive process that was designed to reconcile offenders with the community. Mass justice through *gacaca* was chosen over a widespread amnesty system or a truth commission, because Rwanda did not want to deviate from the principle of accountability after the genocide.

The format of the trials was initially welcomed by many Rwandans, in particular as an alternative to the remote ICTR or national proceedings. The *gacaca* programme provided an opportunity to alleviate the ethnic boundaries entrenched by conflict, and to accept perpetrators as fellow Rwandans in local communities. Over time, however, it came to be seen more critically, i.e. as hierarchical and state-directed, with perceptions differing from village to village.[438] It raised serious concerns from a fair trial perspective. *Gacaca* was traditionally limited to minor offences. Its extension to serious crimes was a reinvention. It allowed lay members of a local community to impose criminal sanctions on persons suspected of having committed medium-level or even severe crimes. This is difficult to reconcile with the right to be tried by a competent, independent and impartial tribunal by means of procedures established by law. The absence of compensation for judges and the lack of training made them susceptible to bribery and fairness concerns. Community-elected judges tried more than 1.2 million cases.[439] The punishment included reduced penalties as well as community service upon confession and guilty plea. One of the perceived weaknesses of the *gacaca* law was that it excluded crimes committed by soldiers of the ruling party, the Rwandan Patriotic Front (RPF).

Local dispute settlement and reconciliation mechanisms have been used in different forms in other contexts. For instance, the East Timorese Truth Commission involved local leaders in its hearings. They included elements of local dispute resolution (*nahe biti boot*).[440] In Sierra Leone, public truth-telling before the truth commission was complemented by more family and community-oriented reconciliation rituals (*Fambul Tok*).[441] Afghanistan combined informal Afghan justice mechanisms (*Jirga* and *Shura*) with state courts and human rights institutions in its approach to post-conflict justice.[442] The Agreement on Accountability and Reconciliation, signed by the Government of Uganda and the LRA in 2007, envisaged the creation of a War Crimes

---

[438] J. E. Burnet, 'The Injustice of Local Justice: Truth, Reconciliation, and Revenge in Rwanda' (2008) 3 *Genocide Studies and Prevention: An International Journal* 173.

[439] See Human Rights Watch, *Justice Compromised: The Legacy of Rwanda's Community-Based Gacaca Courts*, 31 May 2011, www.hrw.org/report/2011/05/31/justice-compromised/legacy-rwandas-community-based-gacaca-courts.

[440] D. Babo-Soares, 'Nahe Biti: The Philosophy and Process of Grassroots Reconciliation (and Justice) in East Timor' (2004) 5 *The Asia Pacific Journal of Anthropology* 15.

[441] L. Graybill, 'Traditional Practices and Reconciliation in Sierra Leone: The Effectiveness of Fambul Tok' (2010) 3 *Conflict Trends* 41.

[442] See M. Christensen, 'Judicial Reform in Afghanistan: Towards a Holistic Understanding of Legitimacy in Post-Conflict Societies' (2011) 4 *Berkeley Journal of Middle Eastern & Islamic Law* 101, 105.

Division in the High Court, a truth commission and traditional Acholi and non-Acholi rituals.[443]

Local mechanisms should not be romanticized. They may be guided by specific state interests, shield crimes from accountability, reduce atrocities to a local affair, entrench gender divides[444] and create hierarchies that cause new grievances or impede national political justice.[445] They do not alleviate the need for formal justice. However, they may provide an additional face of justice that promotes a fuller account of accountability. As Mark Osiel has rightly noted, where a 'country pursues only a single mode of atrocity response', it may 'over-individualize or over-collectivize its treatment of wrongdoer and victim'.[446] Local justice provides a much-needed safeguard against the standardization and technocratization of accountability through global institutions.

3.5   Systemic Interaction

Making international criminal justice a 'global' project requires a better balance of international and local modalities of justice. A key challenge is the interaction between interrelated layers of justice, i.e. domestic justice, global institutions, hybrid models and regional justice mechanisms.[447] International criminal law contains only rudimentary formal legal principles to guide these relations: complementarity and cooperation.

3.5.1   Complementarity

Complementarity is grounded in the idea that international and domestic institutions have a shared responsibility in investigating and prosecuting international crimes. From a strictly legal perspective, complementarity is a mechanism to organize concurrent jurisdiction between international and domestic jurisdiction. However, its social meaning extends beyond this narrow understanding. Its understanding has evolved significantly over time.

---

[443] E. Baines, 'The Haunting of Alice: Local Approaches to Justice and Reconciliation in Northern Uganda' (2007) 1 *International Journal of Transitional Justice* 91.

[444] For example, in East Timor, women were only marginally represented in the community reconciliation hearings. Traditional rituals may privilege male elders.

[445] For instance, critiques of the *mato oput* ritual in Uganda noted that it is Acholi-focused and trivializes the nature of LRA crimes. See D. Sharp, 'Transitional Justice and "Local" Justice', in C. Lawther, L. Moffett and D. Jacobs (eds.), *Research Handbook on Transitional Justice* (Cheltenham: Edward Elgar, 2016), 142, 154.

[446] Osiel, 'Choosing Among Alternative Responses'.

[447] See generally P. Schiff Berman, *Global Legal Pluralism* (New York: Cambridge University Press, 2012), 152 et seq.

3.5.1.1 Diverse Complementarity Meanings

Complementarity is an old idea.[448] An early version was contemplated in the Draft Convention for the Creation of an International Criminal Court Submitted to the London Assembly in February 1944. It recognized the priority of domestic investigation and prosecution.[449] Later, the ILC introduced the idea of complementarity to enable a future international criminal court to dismiss cases.[450] It granted the Court discretion ('may') to find cases inadmissible that are investigated or prosecuted domestically. In the ad hoc tribunals, complementarity was not originally contemplated. However, judges created a mechanism to refer mid- or low-level cases back to domestic jurisdictions under Rule 11*bis* of the Rules of Procedure and Evidence, as part of the completion strategy to facilitate burden-sharing. The elements are not identical,[451] but are similar to the complementarity test.

A fuller concept of complementarity was developed in the ICC context. It is not only a concession of justice to sovereignty,[452] but the basis of a system of justice with domestic responsibility as a starting point.[453] As the ICC Appeals Chamber noted in *Katanga*, complementarity marks in essence a principle which strikes 'a balance between … the primacy of domestic proceedings' and the goal to 'put an end to impunity'.[454] Complementarity serves different functions. It protects sovereignty, by reaffirming the primary role of states in exercising criminal jurisdiction over international crimes; it promotes effective investigation and prosecution, by encouraging states to make genuine efforts to hold perpetrators accountable in line with their duty to investigate and prosecute crimes; it facilitates a certain division of labour between different layers of jurisdiction, i.e. by resolving conflicts of jurisdiction and limiting cases that come before the ICC; and it stimulates cooperation and sharing of good practices between international and domestic justice actors.

Originally, complementarity was understood in a technical-legal sense, namely as a tool to sort out conflicts of jurisdiction between the ICC and domestic jurisdictions. It differs from jurisdictional filters, such as the principle of subsidiarity or the exhaustion of domestic legal remedies. It means that ICC jurisdiction is only meant to come into

---

[448] In early contexts, such as Nuremberg and Tokyo, the issue had marginal importance since German and Japanese courts either did not function or did not have jurisdiction over international crimes. The ICTY and ICTR were vested with primacy over domestic courts. On the emergence, see M. El Zeidy, 'The Genesis of Complementarity', in Stahn and El Zeidy, *The International Criminal Court and Complementarity*, 71.

[449] The Draft Convention stated: 'As a rule, no case shall be brought before the Court when a domestic Court of any of the United Nations has jurisdiction to try the accused and it is in a position and willing to exercise such jurisdiction'. See UNWCC, Draft Convention of an International Criminal Court Submitted to the London International Assembly (Drafted by M. de Baer and amended by Commission I of the LIA), SC II/2, 14 February 1944, Art. 3 (1).

[450] Art. 35 of the 1994 ILC Draft Statute.

[451] See M. El Zeidy, 'From Primacy to Complementarity and Backwards: (Re)-Visiting Rule 11bis of the Ad Hoc Tribunals' (2008) 57 *ICLQ* 403.

[452] F. Gioia, 'State Sovereignty, Jurisdiction, and "Modern" International Law: The Principle of Complementarity in the International Criminal Court' (2006) 19 *LJIL* 1095, 1096.

[453] M. Ellis, 'The International Criminal Court and Its Implication for Domestic Law and Capacity-Building' (2002) 15 *Florida Journal of International Law* 215, 221.

[454] *Prosecutor* v. *Katanga*, ICC-01/04–01/07–1497, Judgment on the Appeal of Mr. Germain Katanga against the Oral Decision of Trial Chamber II of 12 June 2009 on the Admissibility of the Case, 25 September 2009, para. 85 (*Katanga* Appeal Admissibility).

play where a domestic process is absent or deficient, either because a state lacks the will to carry out proceedings genuinely (e.g. due to a lack of intent to bring the persons concerned to justice), or because it lacks the ability to do so (e.g. due to collapse or unavailability).[455]

According to contemporary theorizations, complementarity is more than an instrument to settle disputes between the ICC and domestic criminal jurisdiction.[456] It is not only a foundation of the ICC, but a broader *leitmotif* of international criminal justice. It was replicated in other global contexts, such as the framing of the 'Responsibility to Protect' doctrine in the 2005 World Summit Outcome Document.[457]

In general, four main understandings may be distinguished. In its narrowest sense, complementarity can be understood as a legal admissibility device for the ICC. William Burke White has called this the 'gateway' function of complementarity.[458] It reaffirms the primary role of states in exercising criminal jurisdiction over international crimes. It organizes concurrent jurisdiction and determines and limits cases that come before the ICC.[459]

According to a second understanding, complementarity is an operational principle of the Rome Statute geared at facilitating effective investigation and prosecution of international crimes.[460] It is often referred to as 'positive complementarity'.[461] Based on this view, complementarity has a number of broader systemic functions, namely (i) to promote effective investigation and prosecution, by encouraging states to make genuine efforts to hold perpetrators accountable in line with their duty to investigate and prosecute crimes; and (ii) to stimulate cooperation and sharing of good practices between international and domestic justice actors.

---

[455] For a critique of the 'slogan' version of complementarity related to inability and unwillingness, see D. Robinson, 'The Mysterious Mysteriousness of Complementarity' (2010) 21 *Criminal Law Forum* 67.

[456] N. N. Jurdi, *The International Criminal Court and National Courts: A Contentious Relationship* (Farnham: Ashgate, 2011), 164–165. The literature includes references to different notions, such as 'classical complementarity', 'positive complementarity', 'negative complementarity', 'proactive complementarity', 'constructive complementarity', 'radical complementarity', 'regional complementarity' or 'horizontal complementarity'.

[457] See para. 139 of the World Summit Outcome Document ('we are prepared to take collective action, in a timely and decisive manner, through the Security Council, in accordance with the Charter, including Chapter VII, on a case-by-case basis and in cooperation with relevant regional organizations as appropriate, should peaceful means be inadequate and national authorities manifestly fail to protect their populations from genocide, war crimes, ethnic cleansing and crimes against humanity'). See generally B. N. Schiff, 'Can the International Criminal Court Contribute to the Responsibility to Protect?' (2016) 30 *International Relations* 298.

[458] W. Burke White, 'Reframing Positive Complementarity: Reflections on the First Decade and Insights from the US Federal Criminal Justice System', in Stahn and El Zeidy, *Complementarity and the International Criminal Court* 341, 360.

[459] This approach (i.e. 'complementarity as admissibility') is grounded in a historic reading of the Rome Statute, the preamble and Art. 17.

[460] It is grounded in certain legal aspects, such as cooperation of the ICC with domestic jurisdictions (Art. 93 (10)) and managerial duties of the Office of the Prosecutor (Art. 54), such as the mandate 'to ensure the effective investigation and prosecution of crimes', as well as prosecutorial discretion in relation to the initiation, timing and focus of ICC action as policy considerations. See C. Stahn, 'Complementarity: A Tale of Two Notions' (2008) 19 *Criminal Law Forum* 87.

[461] The Report of the Bureau on Complementarity defines 'positive complementarity' as 'all activities/actions whereby national jurisdictions are strengthened and enabled to conduct genuine national investigations and trials of crimes included in the Rome Statute'. Assembly of States Parties, Report of the Bureau on Stocktaking: Complementarity, ICC-ASP/8/51, 18 March 2010, para. 16.

According to a third approach, the meaning of complementarity extends beyond the ICC. It refers to a broader complementarity of institutions.[462] For instance, the practice of the ad hoc tribunals to refer cases back to domestic jurisdiction under Rule 11*bis* may be said to constitute a form of quasi-complementarity.[463] It led inter alia to the creation of new domestic mechanisms, such as the Bosnian War Crimes Chamber.

More recently, the term has been applied to describe a set of relationships between other actors, such as the relationship between the ICC and hybrid courts or regional courts. For instance, the Law on Special Criminal Court in the Central African Republic[464] has been said to institute a system of 'reverse complementarity' between the ICC and the Special Criminal Court.[465] It seeks to avoid conflicts arising out of parallel investigations being merely settled by the *ne bis in idem* principle (i.e. first come, first served). The Malabo Protocol on the African Court of Justice and Human and Peoples' Rights embraced the idea of complementarity at the regional level, by envisaging 'complementary jurisdiction' between the African Court and 'national courts', as well as 'the Courts of the Regional Economic Communities'.[466]

Finally, the concept of complementarity comes into play in the relationship between states. It has been referred to as 'horizontal complementarity'.[467] The purpose of introducing complementarity in interstate relations is to encourage genuine domestic proceedings in the state best suited to address crimes, and to avoid overly broad assertions of universal jurisdiction.

3.5.1.2 No One-Size-Fits-All Model

In contemporary discourse, there is a strong discrepancy between legal meaning and policy discourse. NGOs have used complementarity as an argument to promote universalization and a certain homogenization of justice approaches, in particular in relation to implementation of the Rome Statute.[468] There is a tendency to push for replication of the highest international standards, or to make more of the concept than

---

[462] Under the ICC Statute, the notion of complementarity is formally limited to the relations between the ICC and states.

[463] See generally O. Bekou, 'Rule 11 BIS: An Examination of the Process of Referrals to National Courts in ICTY Jurisprudence' (2009) 33 *Fordham International Law Journal* 723; P. McAuliffe, 'Bad Analogy: Why the Divergent Institutional Imperatives of the Ad Hoc Tribunals and the ICC Make the Lessons of Rule 11 bis Inapplicable to the ICC's Complementarity Regime' (2015) 11 *International Organizations Law Review* 345.

[464] Art. 37. The original French text reads: 'Lorsqu'en application du Traité de Rome de la Cour Pénale Internationale ou des accords particuliers liant l'Etat centrafricain à cette juridiction internationale, il est établi que le Procureur de la Cour Pénale Internationale s'est saisi d'un cas entrant concurremment dans la compétence de la Cour Pénale Internationale et de la Coup Pénale Spéciale, la seconde se dessaisit au profit de la première'.

[465] V. Arnould, 'The Uncertain Promise of Hybrid Justice in the Central African Republic' (2015) 14 *Africa Policy Brief* 1, 5.

[466] See Art. 46H of the Malabo Protocol. The provision is modelled after the admissibility regime of the ICC Statute, but lacks any reference to the relationship to the ICC.

[467] See C. Ryngaert, 'Horizontal Complementarity', in Stahn and El Zeidy, *Complementarity and the International Criminal Court*, 855.

[468] Several NGOs have developed comprehensive checklists and manuals for implementation of the ICC Statute. See e.g. the 'Handbook for Implementing the Rome Statute' (Human Rights Watch 2001), the 'Manual for the Ratification and Implementation of the Rome Statute' (International Center for Criminal Law Reform and Criminal Justice Policy 2008), and the 'Updated Checklist for Effective Implementation' (Amnesty International 2010). For a critique, see F. Mégret, 'Too Much of a Good Thing? Implementation and the Uses of Complementarity', in Stahn and El Zeidy, *Complementarity and the International Criminal Court*, 361.

it actually entails. In many instances, domestic jurisdictions, or other mechanisms, simply copy, i.e. cut and paste, Rome Statute definitions, out of convenience.[469] However, rightly understood, complementarity marks in essence an instrument to accommodate legitimate differences and to allow for pluralism and diversity.[470] It does not require uniformity, but at most a certain degree of equivalence between international and domestic justice approaches.[471]

In the ICC context, complementarity is an incentive for states to approximate substantive criminal law in the area of core crimes,[472] rather than an imperative to model national criminal justice systems after the image of the ICC.[473] Many jurisdictions rely on a mix of 'international' and 'ordinary crime' definitions in order to try offences, or they adjust modes of liability to capture the relevant type of criminality. The Statute does not per se oblige states to investigate and prosecute beyond preexisting obligations, nor can the Court compel states to exercise jurisdiction. The Statute encourages processes of approximation indirectly, namely through norm expression, articulation of practices and policy incentives for states to avoid the exercise of ICC jurisdiction.[474] There is, at best, an 'obligation of result' in relation to criminalization. As noted by David Donat Cattin, 'states can do more, but shall do no less, than what the Rome Statute prescribes, so to ensure that crimes against humanity, war crimes and acts of genocide be duly incorporated in the relevant legal order and not left unpunished'.[475] The complementarity assessment of the ICC is process-based.[476] It relates to the assessment of genuineness of domestic justice processes, namely their sincerity and effectiveness, rather than specific outcomes. This framing seeks to avoid the perception that complementarity serves as a value judgement on the overall national justice system.[477] Factors such as fairness or the level of punishment are not judged in the absolute, but only in relation to the respective domestic process. For instance, ICC jurisdiction may be justified in cases where irregularities in procedures (i.e. lack of independence or impartiality) impede investigation or prosecution. However, the ICC Statute does not prescribe minimum or

---

[469] See Eden, 'Role of the Rome Statute in the Criminalization of Apartheid', 189–190.

[470] F. Mégret and M. G. Samson, 'Holding the Line on Complementarity in Libya: The Case for Tolerating Flawed Domestic Trials' (2011) 13 *JICJ* 571, 572.

[471] This was partly reaffirmed by the jurisprudence of the ICC Appeals Chamber in the Libyan cases. It held in the *Al Senussi* Appeal that 'there is no requirement in the Statute for a crime to be prosecuted as an international crime domestically'. *Prosecutor* v. *Gaddafi and Al-Senussi*, ICC-01/11–01/11–565, Judgment on the appeal of Mr Abdullah Al-Senussi against the decision of Pre-Trial Chamber I of 11 October 2013 entitled 'Decision on the admissibility of the case against Abdullah Al-Senussi', 24 July 2014, para. 119 (*Al Senussi* Appeals Judgment).

[472] See H. van der Wilt, 'Equal Standards? On the Dialectics between National Jurisdictions and the International Criminal Court' (2008) 8 *International Criminal Law Review* 229.

[473] Under the Rome Statute, a state might be found to be partially unavailable if its domestic legal system does not contain a legal basis for prosecution of crimes within the jurisdiction of the ICC. See Art. 17 (3) ICC Statute.

[474] Some studies indicate that implementation of the ICC Statute has led to an increase of national prosecutions for international crimes. See Rikhof, 'Fewer Places to Hide', 1, 51.

[475] D. Donat Cattin, 'Approximation or Harmonisation as a Result of Implementation of the Rome Statute', in Van den Herik and Stahn, *Diversification and Fragmentation of International Criminal Law* ', 361, 373.

[476] The process-based approach seeks to preserve the diversity of domestic justice systems. See D. Robinson, 'Three Theories of Complementarity: Charge, Sentence, or Process?' (2012) 53 *Harvard International Law Journal Online* 165.

[477] L. Moreno-Ocampo, 'A Positive Approach to Complementarity: The Impact of the Office of the Prosecutor', in Stahn and El Zeidy, *Complementarity and the International Criminal Court*, 21, 23.

maximum requirements for national proceedings. States remain, in principle, free to determine adequate penalties for crimes.[478]

There are at least two different methodologies to approach complementarity. Their feasibility depends on the respective context. The first one is based on schemes of punishment and reward (i.e. a 'carrot-and-stick' approach).[479] It relies on the premise that states will investigate and prosecute in order to avoid scrutiny by the ICC, or the stigma of being viewed as an ICC situation country. This approach assumes that the initiation or threat of ICC proceedings and the role of the Court as watchdog serves as a catalyst for domestic justice approaches. It reaches its limits in cases in which states do not perceive ICC jurisdiction as a threat, or where they may even prefer the ICC to investigate and prosecute.

The second approach is grounded in consent and cooperation. It shares synergies with rule of law reform and development strategies.[480] It is based on the idea that international criminal justice may serve as a 'gentle incentivizer' of domestic proceedings through cooperation and assistance to states. It relies on the theory that the Court may satisfy its mandate by enabling states to deliver justice in accordance with the Rome Statute.[481] The risk of this method is that it may implicate the Court in negotiating justice, delay the exercise of jurisdiction, or create complicity dilemmas, for instance in relation to the application of the death penalty in domestic settings.[482]

3.5.1.3 Challenges and Critiques of ICC Practice

The idea of complementarity has significant appeal from a systemic perspective. However, it has caused political tensions and unintended side effects in ICC practice. There are at least four structural dilemmas: centre–periphery divides, context sensitivity, imbalances between goals and effects, and sustainability problems.

The ICC has adopted a rather strict approach towards the required degree of symmetry between domestic and ICC action in its complementarity jurisprudence.[483] The Court has ruled that domestic investigations and prosecutions must mirror the ICC case, in terms of persons and incidents covered.[484] This implies that states must

---

[478] The ICC may give preference to proceedings at the domestic level, even though they might actually lead to the imposition of a lower sentence. For a sentence-based approach to complementarity, see K. J. Heller, 'A Sentence-Based Theory of Complementarity' (2012) 53 *Harvard International Law Journal* 202.

[479] See C. Stahn, 'Taking Complementarity Seriously', in Stahn and El Zeidy, *Complementarity and the International Criminal Court*, 233, 250.

[480] See R. Rastan, 'Complementarity: Contest or Collaboration?', in M. Bergsmo (ed.), *Complementarity and the Exercise of Universal Jurisdiction for Core International Crimes* (Oslo: Torkel Opsahl Academic EPublisher 2010), 83.

[481] For a study, see E. Witte, *Putting Complementarity into Practice: Domestic Justice for International Crimes in DRC, Uganda, and Kenya* (New York: Open Society Foundations, 2011).

[482] See P. Seils, 'Making Complementarity Work', in Stahn and El Zeidy, *Complementarity and the International Criminal Court*, 989, 1012.

[483] See C. Stahn, 'Admissibility Challenges before the ICC: From Quasi-Primacy to Qualified Deference?', in Stahn, *The Law and Practice of the International Criminal Court*, 228–259.

[484] It held that admissibility requires a 'judicial assessment of whether the case that the State is investigating sufficiently mirrors the one that the Prosecutor is investigating'. See *Prosecutor v. Gaddafi and Al-Senussi*, ICC-01/11–01/11 OA 4, Judgment on the appeal of Libya against the decision of Pre-Trial Chamber I of 31 May 2013 entitled 'Decision on the Admissibility of the Case against Saif Al-Islam Gaddafi', 21 May 2014, para. 73 ('*Gaddafi* Appeal Judgment'); *Al Senussi* Appeals Judgment, para. 119.

adjust their criminal strategy to this focus of inquiry and model their own action after ICC proceedings, in order to be able to challenge admissibility successfully.[485] Complementarity has de facto come close to primacy by other means. The Court has rejected the argument that admissibility should be based on a comparison of the gravity of charges, or the broader scope and reach of investigations and prosecutions.[486] This has led to the curious result that defendants faced a more limited case before the ICC than in the domestic context. It has thus been suggested that the ICC should show a greater level of deference to domestic jurisdictions, and leave states a greater margin of appreciation in relation to prosecutorial policies.[487] Post-colonial critiques stress that the concept of the 'unwilling' or 'unable' state is ambivalent since it allows the ICC to present domestic legal systems as deficient and to brand itself as saviour.[488] There is a certain risk that complementarity approaches and policies divide the world into an accountability universe of the ICC ('us'), and a parallel system of domestic justice ('them').

A second dilemma is context sensitivity. The ICC articulation of complementarity is not necessarily adjusted to the complexities of conflict and post-conflict settings. It is to some extent an 'all or nothing' principle. The time factor is not sufficiently contemplated in the contemporary application of complementarity. As Payam Akhavan has noted: 'The ICC clock tends to run too fast for states emerging from mass-atrocities'.[489] ICC complementarity policies might be under-inclusive in relation to the interests of state in transition.[490] Existing jurisprudence makes it hard for domestic states to take justice into their own hands. They face a 'race for time' dilemma, since the ICC is typically ahead of time and steering the scope, focus and pace of proceedings. This makes it difficult for states to start 'taking investigative steps or prosecuting a case' during admissibility proceedings. For instance, Kenya argued that this approach leaves virtually no prospects for domestic justice, 'since a national jurisdiction may not always have the same evidence available as the Prosecutor and therefore may not be investigating the same suspects as the Court'.[491] Libya submitted that it conflicts with the need to '[empower] national jurisdictions in challenging transitional

---

[485] See R. Rastan, 'What Is a "Case" for the Purpose of the Rome Statute?' (2008) 19 *Criminal Law Forum* 435.

[486] For such an argument, see *Prosecutor* v. *Katanga and Ngudjolo Chui*, ICC-01/04–01/07–949, Motion Challenging the Admissibility of the Case by the Defence of Germain Katanga, Pursuant to Article 19 (2) (a) of the Statute, 11 March 2009, para. 46. It was rejected by the Appeals Chamber in *Katanga* Appeal Admissibility, paras. 75–78.

[487] See Stahn, 'Admissibility Challenges before the ICC', 258; K. Ambos, *Treatise on International Criminal Law, Vol. III* (Oxford: Oxford University Press, 2016), 284.

[488] See N. Sekhon, 'Complementarity and Post-Coloniality' (2013) 27 *Emory International Law Review* 799; Cowell, 'Inherent Imperialism', 677, arguing that describes 'states as lacking control and power, and then creates a legal regime vesting power, and by implication sovereignty, within the ICC').

[489] P. Akhavan, 'Complementarity Conundrums: The ICC Clock in Transitional Times' (2016) 14 *JICJ* 1043–1059.

[490] *Gaddafi* Appeal Judgment, Dissenting Opinion of Judge Anita Ušacka, para. 55. In the Kenyan proceedings, the Court failed to address the question whether the investigative functions of the Truth, Justice and Reconciliation Commission would be a bar to admissibility.

[491] See *Prosecutor* v. *Muthaura, Kenyatta and Ali*, ICC-01/09–02/11 OA, Judgment on the appeal of the Republic of Kenya against the decision of Pre-Trial Chamber II of 30 May 2011 entitled 'Decision on the Application by the Government of Kenya Challenging the Admissibility of the Case Pursuant to Article 19 (2) (b) of the Statute', 30 August 2011, para. 42.

situations'. A strict complementarity jurisprudence might deprive a domestic society of an indigenous process of trial and error.[492]

A third dilemma is the relationship between goals and effects. ICC action had a 'catalytic influence' on domestic jurisdiction. However, the effects produced have not necessarily been those that the Court intended. The focus on 'positive complementarity' (i.e. self-referrals and cooperative complementarity policies) has been at the heart of critique.[493] It has drawn investigations and prosecution more towards non-state actors than government criminality. This risk became evident in relation to Uganda, where the focus on the LRA detracted from governmental crimes. It has resurfaced in the DRC. As Patrick Labuda has observed, one contradiction of ICC complementarity policy is that the OTP may have 'used the Court's limited resources to "chase" rebels, most of whom the Congolese government wants prosecuted domestically anyway'.[494]

In other cases, ICC action has prompted individual and case-related action and response games with domestic jurisdictions which led to duplication of structures. For instance, in the *Gaddafi* case, the ICC and the national government mirrored each other's failures. They were both unable to arrest. The idea of complementarity was thus partly turned on its head. The ICC and domestic jurisdictions shared strengths and weaknesses, rather than complementing each other's capacities. *Katanga* was first tried before the ICC, and has faced re-trial in the DRC.[495] This goes against the idea of effective forum choice.

A final dilemma is sustainability.[496] Existing approaches often reflect a short-term lens on complementarity. They are focused on the here and now, rather than lasting enforcement of international criminal justice. The ICC lacks continuing monitoring structures and a convincing completion strategy for situations. For instance, in the case of *Al-Senussi*, the ICC closed the case after the admissibility challenge. Proceedings were simply left to domestic authorities, without further interaction between the ICC and the Libyan government, or further monitoring. Subsequent changes in the domestic context were ignored. As has been rightly suggested by Priscilla Hayner: '[w]hat may be missing is a process by which the prosecutor could more comfortably evaluate the likely impact and timing of her actions in each different national context

---

[492] For a critique, see *Gaddafi* Appeal Judgment, Dissenting Opinion of Judge Anita Usacka, ICC-01/11–01/1 1-547-Anx2 (OA 4), para. 65.

[493] As pointed out in scholarship: 'If ICC prosecutions are viewed as threatening to the regime, the relationship is likely to change from cooperative to adversarial, thereby denying or restricting access to evidence and witnesses and undermining the very reason why the prosecutor encouraged self-referrals in the first place'. See K. Rodman and P. Booth, 'Manipulated Commitments: The International Criminal Court in Uganda' (2013) 35 *Human Rights Quarterly* 271, 300.

[494] P. Labuda, 'Taking Complementarity Seriously: Why is the International Criminal Court Not Investigating Government Crimes in Congo?', *Opinio Juris*, 28 April 2017, at https://opiniojuris.org/2017/04/28/33093/.

[495] *Prosecutor* v. *Katanga*, ICC-01/04–01/07, Decision Pursuant to Article 108 (1) of the Rome Statute, 7 April 2016, para. 11.

[496] The ICC has associated its own legacy in a situation with factors such as a 'lasting impact on bolstering the rule of law in a particular society, by conducting effective trials to contribute to ending impunity, while also strengthening domestic judicial capacity'. Report of the Court on Complementarity: Completion of ICC Activities in a Situation Country, ICC-ASP/12/32, 15 October 2013, para. 27.

over time'.[497] The very existence of the complementarity principle may require the development of better 'exit strategies' from situations.

Finally, the limits of complementarity as a model have become clearer. The determination of complementarity involves a large degree of discretion, despite its legal articulation. For some crimes, such as aggression, the very idea that domestic jurisdiction should serve as a first port of entry for adjudication is questionable. For other crimes, the existing umbrella, as it has been applied in practice, may be too strict, and warrant a greater degree of flexibility towards domestic jurisdiction.[498]

3.5.1.4 Beyond Complementarity

The idea of complementarity as a broader principle, i.e. in the sense of complementarity of justice responses, is still in its infancy. It requires more flexibility than the formal ICC vision of complementarity enshrined in the ICC Statute.

It is necessary to rely on different justice models in a given atrocity crime context. The ICC may not be the best justice response in a specific situation, nor should it be perceived as superior to other institutions. Its existence does not rule out the case for ad hoc tribunals, nor does it preclude the engagement of additional institutions, such as hybrid courts.[499] Accountability may require tailor-made hybrid mechanisms, domestic justice and alternative forms of justice.

It is illusory to believe that such institutional plurality can be put into neat boxes or rubrics. Proposals have been made to organize justice responses along a division of labour, based on categories of perpetrators, or by distinguishing between crime categories. This is artificial. The jurisdiction of the ICC is not exclusively focused on the 'most responsible' perpetrators, nor should such perpetrators necessarily be tried exclusively through universal institutions. It may be an important signal to entrust domestic or hybrid mechanisms with the power to try the 'most responsible leaders'. It is equally difficult to base a division of labour on a distinction between crime categories. The distinction between international and transnational crimes is increasingly blurred and under challenge.[500]

The interplay of justice responses cannot be regulated in the abstract. It must be determined in the context. Some relations, such as the relationship between the ICC and regional or hybrid courts require further specification (e.g. through protocols or understandings), in order to avoid confrontation and facilitate cooperation. However, the accountability architecture must remain open to legal and non-legal approaches and the limits of criminal law to deal with the nature of atrocity crimes.

---

[497] See P. Hayner, 'Does the ICC Advance the Interests of Justice?', 4 November 2014, at www.opendemocracy.net/openglobalrights/priscilla-hayner/does-icc-advance-interests-of-justice.

[498] See K. Heller, 'Radical Complementarity' (2016)14 *JICJ* 637, 664, arguing that greater weight should be placed on the sincerity of the process, i.e. 'genuine effort to bring a suspect to justice').

[499] The ICC carries out thematic prosecutions or a few emblematic cases in each situation. On the corresponding 'legacy' dilemmas, see E. Evenson and A. Smith, 'Completion, Legacy, and Complementarity at the ICC', in Stahn, *Law and Practice of the International Criminal Court*, 1259.

[500] See Section 1.4.4.

It is thus necessary to think beyond complementarity and identify alternative frames. As Mark Drumbl has suggested, the concept of 'qualified deference' might be better equipped to address these challenges than complementarity. It has several advantages.

Unlike complementarity, [qualified deference] does not search for procedural symmetry between process and liberal criminal procedure, and unlike primacy, [it] does not impose liberal criminal procedure. ... [It] welcomes the fact justice mechanisms may serve purposes other than merely to determine guilt or innocence of the accused (i.e. juridical) and to impose criminal punishment (i.e. to satisfy retributive or deterrent aims).[501]

A second concept may be borrowed from the literature on legal pluralism.[502] It is the principle of 'legitimate difference'. It preserves diversity within convergence.[503] It accommodates a plurality of different, yet equally legitimate approaches within a common texture. The idea of 'legitimate difference' postulates a more open mindset towards 'otherness'. It serves as an incentive to counter unreflected practices of imitation and replication of global approaches under the umbrella of complementarity.

3.5.2   *Cooperation*

Cooperation is a second key element of systemic interaction.[504] It is essential at different stages of international criminal justice, from investigation to the enforcement of sentences. It involves not only arrest and surrender of defendants,[505] but access to information, logistical support, judicial cooperation, operational support, assistance with security or access to places, sites and evidence.[506]

It comes into play at different levels. In interstate relations, cooperation relates to support for criminal proceedings in another state. It is governed by principles of sovereign equality, reciprocity and mutual interests. Cooperation with international criminal courts and tribunals poses distinct challenges. Such courts do 'not make up a judicial branch of a central government' and do 'not possess, *vis-à-vis* organs of

---

[501] M. Drumbl, 'Policy Through Complementarity: The Atrocity Trial as Justice', in Stahn and El Zeidy, *Complementarity and the International Criminal Court*, 197, 224.

[502] W. Burke White, 'International Legal Pluralism' (2004) 25 *Michigan Journal of International Law* 963, E. van Sliedregt and S. Vasiliev, 'Pluralism: A New Framework for International Criminal Justice', in Van Sliedregt and Vasiliev, *Pluralism in International Criminal Law*, 3.

[503] See A. Bianchi, *International Law Theories: An Inquiry into Different Ways of Thinking* (Oxford: Oxford University Press, 2016), 232.

[504] K. Raustiala, 'The Architecture of International Cooperation: Transgovernmental Networks and the Future of International Law' (2002) 43 *Virginia Journal of International Law* 1.

[505] As Louise Arbour put it, initially 'there was only one overwhelming, all-encompassing and ... life-threatening issue for the ICTY as it had been conceived: arrests'. See L. Arbour, 'The Crucial Years' (2004) 2 *JICJ* 396, 397.

[506] See generally G. Sluiter, *International Criminal Adjudication and the Collection of Evidence: Obligations of States* (Antwerp: Intersentia, 2002); D. McClean, *International Co-operation in Civil and Criminal Matters* (Oxford: Oxford University Press, 2012); D. Stroh, 'State Cooperation with the International Criminal Tribunals for the Former Yugoslavia and for Rwanda' (2001) 5 *Max Planck Yearbook of United Nations Law* 249; H.-P. Kaul and C. Kress, 'Jurisdiction and Cooperation in the Statute of the International Criminal Court: Principles and Compromises' (1999) 2 *Yearbook of International Humanitarian Law* 143.

sovereign States, the same powers which accrue to national courts in respect of the administrative, legislative and political organs of the State'.[507] They rely heavily on states and international organizations to receive cooperation in relation to arrest, gathering of evidence or enforcement of sentences.

The system of cooperation has developed significantly in past decades in relation to international crimes. Special legal frameworks or streamlined procedures (e.g. 'transfer' rather than extradition) apply in relation to certain international criminal courts and tribunals. There are more and more judicial spaces where multilateral frameworks supersede bilateral structures or extend beyond the UN model agreements. The 9/11 attacks have strengthened channels of cooperation between states, particularly in the field of tracing, freezing and seizing of assets and exchange of intelligence information.[508] However, in practice, it remains a challenge to obtain political leverage to secure cooperation. The success of cooperation depends largely on the national and international political commitments in the respective context. Often institutional pressures or soft compliance mechanisms (e.g. networks), and action by NGOs before domestic courts, may deliver more tangible results than formal legal procedures.

3.5.2.1 Models of Cooperation

In international law, cooperation regimes have usually been theorized in terms of two categories: interstate cooperation and cooperation with international jurisdictions.[509] The features of these models have been developed by the ICTY Appeals Chamber in *Blaskić*. The Chamber distinguished two different approaches: (i) the classical 'horizontal' relationship between equal sovereign states, in which arrest and transfer is based on 'treaties of judicial cooperation or, if such treaties are not available, on voluntary interstate cooperation';[510] and (ii) a 'vertical' relationship which is based on the supremacy of international jurisdiction and binding powers of cooperation.[511] However, the reality has become more complex.

The ICC system is mid-way between these two models. It is a special multilateral treaty system, which contains vertical features, but maintains some elements of classical extradition schemes (e.g. operation of the rule of speciality, communication on the basis of 'requests', limited direct on-site powers of the Court, execution of requests by the relevant authorities of the requested state, recognition of certain grounds for the postponement or refusal of the execution of requests).[512] This system

---

[507] See ICTY, *Prosecutor* v. *Blaskić*, IT-95–14-AR108bis, Judgment on the Request of the Republic of Croatia for Review of the Decision of Trial Chamber II of 18 July 1997, 29 October 1997, para. 40 (*Blaskić Subpoena* Appeal).

[508] See SC Res. 1373 (2001) of 28 September 2001. For a discussion, see Bassiouni, *Introduction to International Criminal Law*, 515–518.

[509] See B. Swart, 'General Problems', in Cassese, Gaeta and Jones, *The Rome Statute of the International Criminal Court*, 1589, 1590–1592.

[510] See *Blaskić Subpoena* Appeal, para. 47.

[511] Ibid., paras. 47 and 54.

[512] See also Cryer et al., *Introduction to International Criminal Law and Procedure*, 518.

seeks to reconcile the primacy of domestic jurisdiction under the Rome Statute with the commitment and legal duty to prosecute crimes within the jurisdiction of the Court.[513] Hybrid tribunals often fall between the cracks. Their cooperation regime depends on their founding instrument, and their legal nature.

3.5.2.1.1 The Classical Horizontal Regime

Classical 'horizontal' schemes are largely treaty-based. They operate through extradition and mutual legal assistance, specified in bilateral or multilateral agreements. States are unable to enforce their jurisdiction on the territory of other states. This means that they have to rely on international judicial cooperation and extradition to obtain custody over a person for the purpose of prosecution.[514] Basic principles are laid down in the UN Model Treaties on Extradition and Mutual Assistance in Criminal Matters.[515] However, the law of extradition itself has undergone some important changes over the past decades. Traditional models of judicial cooperation and assistance were characterized by the predominance of reciprocity, the recognition of exceptions to extradition (grounds for refusal) and dispute settlement through third party determination.

Historically, a state receiving a request for cooperation has been entitled to invoke various exceptions to extradition, including the 'political offence' exception (grounded inter alia on non-intervention in internal affairs); the 'military offence' exception, constitutional prohibitions of the transfer of nationals and extradition in the case of death penalty or life imprisonment, sovereignty-related grounds for refusal (security, *ordre public* etc.).

Today, the scope of application of reciprocity and the discretion to invoke grounds of exception have been significantly reduced in the area of international crimes. Bilateral approaches and domestic exceptions are difficult to reconcile with the universal nature of such crimes. The crimes which fall within the jurisdiction of the ICC have been recognized by states parties as crimes which 'are of concern to the international community as a whole'.[516] It has become considerably more difficult to deny extradition due to the gradual codification of core crimes and the crystallization of universal jurisdiction.

---

[513] See para. 6 of the preamble of the ICC Statute.

[514] On some occasions, states have simply abducted individuals from the territory of other states (e.g. the Eichmann case). This practice may violate state sovereignty. The ICTY stated in *Nikolić*: 'in clear cases of State involvement in a forced abduction serious questions may arise about respect for the sovereignty of the injured State. This may, in particular, be the case in situations where extradition treaties between the injured State and the forum State have not been properly applied, deliberately circumvented or otherwise violated and where the injured State protests'. See *Prosecutor v. Nikolić*, IT-94-2-PT, Decision on defence motion challenging the exercise of jurisdiction by the Tribunal, 9 October 2002, para. 99 (*Nikolić* Jurisdiction Decision). See also Section 3.5.2.2.2.

[515] Model Treaty on Mutual Assistance in Criminal Matters, 14 December 1990, adopted by General Assembly Resolution 45/117, subsequently amended by General Assembly Resolution 53/112; Model Treaty on Extradition, 14 December 1990, adopted by General Assembly Resolution 45/116, subsequently amended by General Assembly Resolution 52/88.

[516] See para. 4 of the preamble of the ICC Statute and Art. 1.

The scope of application of exceptions has been considerably narrowed. The political offence exception[517] has been excluded for specific crimes, such as genocide, crimes against humanity, torture or war crimes.[518] The duty to extradite or prosecute certain crimes places a higher burden on the requested state.[519] It forces the state of the nationality of the offender to prosecute, when refusing to extradite its own nationals. It has become difficult to justify exclusion of nationals from jurisdiction, since a state can require assurances from another state to ensure compliance with fair trial guarantees.

In certain regional contexts, such as the EU, extradition and judicial cooperation is organized based on the principle of mutual trust.[520] For instance, an EU arrest warrant can be enforced in all member states. It contains express limitations to the dual criminality requirement and the nationality exception for specific categories of crimes, and turns enforcement into a judicial matter which does not require a political decision on extradition.[521] Offences that give rise to surrender without verification of the double criminality requirement include 'crimes within the jurisdiction of the International Criminal Court'.[522] The European Investigation Order simplifies the procedures of judicial authorities to request evidence located in another EU country.[523] The EU also created a special network (the Genocide Network) under the auspices of Eurojust to support better exchange of information and cooperation in relation to core crimes.[524]

3.5.2.1.2 The Vertical Approach
The relationship between the ad hoc tribunals and states differed fundamentally from classical interstate cooperation. The tribunals derived cooperation powers from the

---

[517] This exception emerged in the eighteenth century. It is based on the belief that the alleged political offender might be subjected to an unfair trial in their home country (e.g. due to resistance to anti-democratic political oppression). See generally C. van der Wyngaert, *The Political Offence Exception to Extradition: The Delicate Problem of Balancing the Rights of the Individual and the International Public Order* (Deventer: Kluwer, 1980).

[518] See Art. VII of the Genocide Convention and Art. 1 of the Additional Protocol to the European Convention on Extradition of 15 October 1975 (Crimes against humanity, graves breaches of the Geneva Conventions). See also *Furundžija* Trial Judgment, para. 157 (Torture 'must not be excluded from extradition under any political offence exception').

[519] Judge Yusuf has argued that that existing treaties containing a duty to extradite or prosecute may be divided into two categories: 'clauses that impose an obligation to extradite, and in which prosecution becomes an obligation only after the refusal of extradition; and clauses that impose an obligation to prosecute, with extradition being an option available to the state. See ICJ, *Questions relating to the Duty to Prosecute or Extradite (Belgium v. Senegal)*, Separate Opinion Judge Yusuf, paras. 19–22.

[520] See generally V. Mitsilegas, *EU Criminal Law after Lisbon: Rights, Trust and the Transformation of Justice in Europe* (Oxford: Hart Publishing, 2016).

[521] See Council Framework Decision, European arrest warrant and the surrender procedures between Member States 2002/584/JHA, 13 June 2002. On the nexus to intenational crimes, see L. Vierucci, 'The European Arrest Warrant' (2004) 2 *JICJ* 275.

[522] Council Framework Decision 2002/584/JHA, Art. 2 (2).

[523] See Directive 2014/41/EU of the European Parliament and of the Council of 3 April 2014 regarding the European Investigation Order in criminal matters. See I. Armada, 'The European Investigation Order and the Lack of European Standards for Gathering Evidence: Is a Fundamental Rights-Based Refusal the Solution?' (2015) 6 *New Journal of European Criminal Law* 8.

[524] See Council Decision 2002/494/JHA of 13 June 2002, establishing a European network of contact points in respect of persons responsible for genocide, crimes against humanity and war crimes, as well as Council Decision 2003/335/JHA of 8 May 2003, strengthening investigation and prosecution.

delegated authority of the Security Council. Both entities were vested with the power to issue binding orders.[525] The Appeals Chamber of the ICTY argued that recourse to mandatory cooperation should be preceded by requests for voluntary cooperation as a matter of 'sound policy'.[526] In practice, however, the respective domestic jurisdictions were under a strict duty to cooperate.[527] The Rules of Procedure and Evidence made it clear that specified domestic impediments to transfer (e.g. national extradition provisions) are inapplicable to the tribunal.[528]

The Statute of both tribunals recognized the *ne bis in idem* exception.[529] But the Statutes excluded any discretion in the context of the treatment of competing requests for cooperation. Doubts as to the legality of a request did not provide a unilateral ground of refusal. The respective tribunal was entitled to decide on their merits.[530]

In a landmark judgment in *Blaskić*, the tribunal asserted the power to issue binding orders to private individuals (i.e. not state officials) and compel them to appear in court, produce documents or assist the Court, in cases where 'the authorities of the State or entity concerned' have been requested to comply with a request for assistance, but 'prevent the Tribunal from fulfilling its functions'.[531] This meant that the tribunals could hold private individuals in contempt of court for non-compliance with an order or request.

Non-compliance with the duty to enforce was followed by the possibility of threats and sanctions.[532] However, in practice the success of cooperation resulted not only from robust legal powers, but mostly from other factors, such as indirect political leverage, domestic politics and external pressures.[533]

In the former Yugoslavia, the prospects of cooperation and arrest were significantly enhanced by the involvement of international actors such as the NATO-led Stabilization Force (SFOR) and United Nations Transitional Administration for Eastern Slavonia, Baranja and Western Sirmium (UNTAES) in enforcement activities.[534]

---

[525] See Art. 28 ICTR Statute and Art. 29 ICTY Statute.

[526] See *Blaskić Subpoena* Appeal, para. 31.

[527] See R. Bank, 'Cooperation with the International Criminal Tribunal for the Former Yugoslavia in the Production of Evidence' (2000) 4 *Max Planck Yearbook of United Nations Law* 233, 239–240.

[528] Rule 58 of the ICTY Rules of Procedure and Evidence.

[529] See Art. 10 ICTY Statute.

[530] See G. Sluiter, 'State Cooperation with the ICC', in R. Yepes-Enriquez and L. Tabassi (eds.), *Treaty Enforcement and International Cooperation in Criminal Matters* (The Hague: TMC Asser Press, 2002), 127, 131.

[531] *Blaskić Subpoena* Appeal, para. 55. The Appeals Chamber argued that '[i]t is ... to be assumed that an inherent power to address itself directly to those individuals inures to the advantage of the International Tribunal. Were it not vested with such a power, the International Tribunal would be unable to guarantee a fair trial to persons accused of atrocities in the former Yugoslavia'.

[532] Rule 59 empowered the ICTY to notify the Security Council in case of failure to execute a warrant or transfer order. Rule 61 was introduced into the Rules and Procedure and Evidence, in order to endow the tribunal with the power to issue an international warrant of arrest to all states in case of failure to execute a warrant.

[533] See V. Peskin, *International Justice in Rwanda and the Balkans: Virtual Trials and the Struggle for State Cooperation* (New York: Cambridge University Press, 2008). On civil society networks, see Keck and Sikkink, *Activists Beyond Borders*. On compliance in the ICC context, see E. Hunter, 'Using "Managerial Compliance" to Strengthen the International Criminal Court Cooperation Regime', in Bekou and Birkett, *Cooperation and the International Criminal Court*, 366.

[534] The practice of the Security Council and NATO clarified that the mandate of both entities included powers of arrest. For an analysis, see P. Gaeta, 'Is NATO Authorized or Obliged to Arrest Persons Indicted by the International Criminal Tribunal for the Former Yugoslavia?' (1998) 9 *EJIL* 174.

Srebrenica and the Kosovo War marked turning points in the attitudes of Western powers.[535] Ultimately, pressures by the US, the EU and World Bank, and most importantly the prospect of EU accession and economic progression, were essential driving factors for compliance. This influenced both governmental and societal attitude towards compliance, and facilitated the arrest of all indicted persons in the case of the ICTY.[536] Conditionality policies fell on fertile ground in the Balkans, in light of the disaggregation of state structures and regional incentives. Compliance was more interest-based than norm-based.

In the context of the ICTR, the success of cooperation was heavily influenced by feelings of guilt of Western powers, donor preferences and domestic politics. Compliance by Rwanda may be largely explained by the fact that the dominant genocidal narrative of the tribunal (i.e. the victimization of the Tutsi) coincided largely with governmental interests. When former Chief Prosecutor Carla Del Ponte sought to bring charges against leaders of the Rwandan Patriotic Front (RPF) for three massacres, she encountered fierce resistance from the Kagame government and very limited support from the Security Council.[537] Donors did not link development aid to cooperation in relation to RPF investigations. After Del Ponte's failure to agree on domestic proceedings, the Council decided to separate the mandate of the ICTY and the ICTR Prosecutor.[538] This was an elegant way to end her power to pursue the cases.

3.5.2.1.3 The 'Mixed' ICC Regime

The ICC system combines features of the vertical and the horizontal model.[539] States parties made a collective commitment under Part 9 of the Statute to cooperate with the Court 'in its investigation and prosecution of crimes'. This reduces the 'institutional veil' between the Court and domestic jurisdiction.

The ICC regime shares some of the vertical features of the ad hoc tribunals. The 'distinct nature of the Court' is recognized and reflected in Part 9 of the Statute.[540] Cooperation is not tied to reciprocity. The system relies, in principle, on mandatory state cooperation by way of statutory accession or a Security Council Resolution.[541]

---

[535] Richard Goldstone initially deplored the 'lack of will on the part of the leading Western states to support and enforce the orders of the tribunal'. See R. J. Goldstone, 'Bringing War Criminals to Justice in Ongoing War', in J. Moore (ed.), *Hard Choices: Moral Dilemmas in Humanitarian Intervention* (Lanham, MD: Rowman & Littlefield, 1998), 195, 202.

[536] The EU made accession talks dependent on arrest of persons indicted by the ICTY. Serbian authorities adopted an action plan to arrest *Mladić* when the EU suspended discussions.

[537] See V. Peskin, 'Victor's Justice Revisited: Rwandan Patriotic Front Crimes and the Prosecutorial Endgame at the ICTR', in S. Straus and L. Waldorf (eds.), *Remaking Rwanda: State Building and Human Rights after Mass Violence* (Madison: University of Wisconsin Press, 2011), 173–183.

[538] On 28 August 2003, the Security Council amended Art. 15 of the Statute of the ICTR. See SC Resolution 1503 of 28 August 2003. The tribunal had its own prosecutor since 15 September 2003.

[539] See generally R. Rastan, 'The Responsibility to Enforce: Connecting Justice with Unity', in C. Stahn and G. Sluiter, *The Emerging Practice of the International Criminal Court* (Leiden: Martinus Nijhoff, 2009), 163.

[540] See Art. 91 (2) (c).

[541] This is illustrated by the respective obligations to cooperate under Arts. 86 ('general obligation to cooperate' by state parties), 87 (5) (request for cooperation to non-states parties) and 89 (1) (obligation of states parties to 'comply with requests for arrest and surrender').

States parties are obliged under the statute to cooperate with respect to requests for arrest and surrender and other forms of assistance. Non-state parties or international organizations may agree to enter into a cooperation relationship[542] The Statute does not recognize exceptions to the duty to cooperate in relation to arrest and surrender. Grounds of refusal are exceptional, limited to other forms of cooperation and assistance, and subject to procedural constraints, such as consultation or postponement clauses. The Court has the final authority to adjudicate a dispute over cooperation with a state party. Nevertheless, the ICC system differs in a number of respects from classical verticalism.

The most important difference to the ad hoc tribunals is that the ICC relies to a larger extent on coordination with domestic authorities. The obligation to cooperate is governed by two legal regimes: Part 9 of the Rome Statute and relevant 'procedure[s] under ... national law'.[543] The Court is entitled to 'request' cooperation. However, the execution of such requests depends on modalities under domestic law. Domestic implementing legislation usually determines the effect of such requests in the internal legal order of the requested entity.[544] Requests can only in very limited circumstances (e.g. 'unavailability of any authority or any component of [a state's] judicial system',[545] non-compulsory measures of assistance[546]) be executed directly by the Court on the territory of a state party.[547]

In many tribunals, cooperation is conceived as a one-way street, i.e. cooperation of states with an international jurisdiction. The ICC regime is different. It allows 'reverse cooperation', i.e. cooperation and assistance from the Court to domestic jurisdictions.[548] This option highlights the close connection between complementarity and cooperation. In its own operations, the ICC collects a wealth of evidence and information that goes beyond ICC cases. The ICC has made it clear that 'reverse cooperation' should not be invoked by states as a shield against ICC investigations and prosecutions. It has however shared some material with domestic authorities in the DRC situation in order to facilitate other domestic cases.[549]

Part 9 limits cooperation duties to states. This makes it more difficult to address obligations of cooperation to individuals.[550] However, the ICC had its own *Blaškić*

---

[542] Non-states parties and intergovernmental organizations may enter into a cooperation relationship with the ICC by way of consent. See Art. 87 (5) and (6). In case of a declaration of acceptance of jurisdiction under Art. 12 (3), a non-state party is obliged to cooperate with the Court.

[543] See Arts. 88, 89 (1) and 93 (1).

[544] See generally OTP, *Informal Expert Paper: Fact-Finding and Investigative Functions of the Office of the Prosecutor, including International Cooperation* (2003), at www.legal-tools.org/doc/ba368d/pdf/.

[545] See Art. 57 (3) (d).

[546] See Art. 99 (4).

[547] See on the need for such powers, L. Arbour and M. Bergsmo, 'Conspicuous Absence of Jurisdictional Overreach', in H. van Hebel et al. (eds.), *Reflections on the International Criminal Court* (The Hague: T. M. C. Asser Press, 1999), 137.

[548] See F. Gioia, 'Complementarity and "Reverse Cooperation"', in Stahn and El Zeidy, *The International Criminal Court and Complementarity*, 807.

[549] R. Gallmetzer, 'Prosecuting Persons Doing Business with Armed Groups in Conflict Areas' (2010) 8 *JICJ* 947, 955–956.

[550] See C. Kress and K. Prost, 'Article 86', in Triffterer and Ambos, *The Rome Statute of the International Criminal Court* (2016), 2014–2016.

moment in the Kenya situation. In that context, cooperation was compromised by challenges of witness intimidation and lack of will of domestic authorities. The Appeals Chamber held that 'Trial Chambers have the power to compel the appearance of witnesses before the Court, in the sense of creating a legal obligation for the individual concerned'.[551] The ICC can order states to ensure that witnesses provide evidence from their territory.

In practice, cooperation proved to be highly dependent on domestic political dynamics and international support. In cases where ICC proceedings were triggered by governments in power, targeted rebel groups or coincided with governmental interests (e.g. Uganda, DRC, Ivory Coast), the ICC was able to rely in state cooperation. Some of the arrests and transfers to the Court (e.g. *Lubanga*, *Ntaganda*, *Ongwen*) were facilitated by major powers or the UN. In cases where the ICC challenged ruling political elites, such as in Sudan and Kenya, it failed to get the necessary cooperation and assistance. Not only the affected legal regimes, but a number of states parties failed to abide by their obligation to cooperate, or contested the authority of the ICC. There is thus a deep discrepancy between legal obligation and compliance. As Kenneth Rodman notes:

If . . . investigations target influential state agents in ways that put sovereign cooperation at risk, the United States and European Union are unlikely to act as surrogate enforces, linking aid to compliance, because of the potential costs to traditional national interests in contrast to their willingness to link reconstruction aid and path to EU membership to the willingness of Serbia and Croatia to surrender politically influential suspects to the ICTY, which was valued as a means of marginalizing the ethnic extremists who had destabilized the region.[552]

The Statute includes a system to denounce and sanction failures of cooperation. A failure to cooperate is a breach of an international obligation. The Court can ultimately refer the matter to the Assembly of States Parties[553] or the Security Council which can condemn the behaviour, ask for compliance or even take measures to sanction the violation. However, this system of political control has not functioned effectively. The Court has made multiple findings on non-cooperation in the context of visits by Sudanese President Al-Bashir to ICC states parties, such as Malawi, Chad, the DRC and the Central African Republic, and reported them to the Assembly and the Council. Yet none of them has taken decisive follow-up action. ICC states parties and third states have stayed remarkably silent in relation to findings on non-cooperation. This marks a 'significant blow to the effectiveness of the cooperation

---

[551] The Trial Chamber derived this from Art. 64 (6) (b). See *Prosecutor* v. *Ruto and Sang*, ICC-01/09.01/11 OA 7 OA 8, Judgment on the appeals of William Samoei Ruto and Mr Joshua Arap Sang against the decision of Trial Chamber V (A) of 17 April 2014 entitled 'Decision on Prosecutor's Application for Witness Summonses and resulting Request for State Party Cooperation', 9 October 2014, para. 107.

[552] K. A. Rodman, 'How Politics Shapes the Contributions of Justice: Lessons from the ICTY and the ICTR' (2016) 110 *AJIL Unbound* 234, 238.

[553] The Assembly established guidelines on non-cooperation in an Annex to Resolution ICC-ASP/10/Res. 5, adopted by consensus at the plenary meeting on 21 December 2011. However, there is no consensus on non-judicial sanctions, e.g. exclusion from the Assembly or suspension of the right to vote.

regime ... and the efficacy of the Court itself'.[554] It suggests that the underlying reasoning and approach by the ICC on head of state immunity may not have carried enough justification and moral authority to induce cooperation or diplomatic or other sanctions for non-compliance.

A show case example is South Africa's failure to arrest President Al-Bashir. In May 2017, South Africa provided assurances of non-arrest under a host agreement with the AU, in order to allow Al-Bashir to attend an AU summit in Johannesburg. The ICC reminded South Africa of its duty of arrest under Part 9 in consultations preceding the visit. A domestic NGO, the Southern Africa Litigation Centre, filed a Court motion to compel the government to cause Al-Bashir to be arrested and surrendered to the ICC.[555] The government let Al-Bashir leave the country via a military base. The Supreme Court of Appeal of South Africa found that the government's action was 'inconsistent with South Africa's obligations in terms of the Rome Statute and Section 10 of the Implementation of the Rome Statute of the International Criminal Court Act 27 of 2002'.[556] The Pre-Trial Chamber made it clear in its subsequent decision on non-compliance that mere disagreements of states with a ruling of the ICC do not provide a reason to set aside the authority of the Court.[557] However, it failed to refer South Africa to the ASP or the Security Council, partly as a result of frustration regarding the lack of follow-up by the Council over the 'past 24 meetings ... following the adoption Resolution 1593 (2005)'.[558] This decision is a concession of law to politics. Ultimately, the South African example shows that NGOs and domestic courts are important guardians of compliance with cooperation duties.

3.5.2.2   Gaps and Dilemmas

Despite advances in strengthening legal regimes for cooperation, existing frameworks contain gaps and challenges.

3.5.2.2.1 Gaps in the Legal Framework
The legal framework concerning interstate cooperation in relation to international crimes remains underdeveloped.[559] The ICC Statute is not a framework for cooperation between states as such. The Genocide Convention makes reference to a duty to extradite, but does not make provision for other forms of legal assistance. The duty to extradite or prosecute under the Geneva Convention is limited to 'grave breaches'.

---

[554] See Kress and Prost, 'Article 87', 2042.
[555] *Southern Africa Litigation Centre* v. *Minister of Justice and Constitutional Development & others* [2015] 3 All SA 505 (GP); 2015 (9) BCLR 1108 (GP); 2015 (2) SA 1 (GP).
[556] Supreme Court of Appeal of South Africa, *The Minister of Justice and Constitutional Development* v. *The Southern African Litigation Centre*, Case No. 867/15, [2016] ZASCA 17, 15 March 2016, para. 4.
[557] See *Prosecutor* v. *Al-Bashir*, ICC-02/05-01/09, Decision under Art. 87 (7) of the Rome Statute on the non-compliance by South Africa with the request by the Court for the arrest and surrender of Omar Al-Bashir, 6 July 2017, para. 121 (*Al-Bashir* Non Cooperation Decision).
[558] *Al-Bashir* Non Cooperation Decision, para. 138.
[559] See W. Ferdinandusse, 'Improving Interstate Cooperation for the National Prosecution of International Crimes: Towards a New Treaty?' (2014) 18 *ASIL Insights* 15.

For crimes against humanity, there is no specialized framework.[560] This contrasts with modern conventions in the field of transnational crime (e.g. the UN Convention against Transnational Organized Crime or Corruption) or the Convention on Enforced Disappearance, which have more detailed provisions governing judicial cooperation and legal assistance.[561] The lack of specific treaty provisions for cooperation in relation to core crimes provides an obstacle for certain states to extradite perpetrators or to provide assistance to other states in relation to certain coercive measures, such as search and seizure or telephone intercepts. Several states have proposed a Multilateral Treaty for Mutual Legal Assistance and Extradition in Domestic Prosecution of Atrocity Crimes (crimes of genocide, crimes against humanity and war crimes),[562] in addition to the work of the ILC on Crimes Against Humanity.[563]

Hybrid and internationalized courts do not fit easily into the existing distinction between horizontal and vertical cooperation. They rely, in principle, on voluntary assistance and cooperation by states, since their foundational agreements do not create duties of cooperation for third parties.[564] They are dependent on the Security Council or requests for cooperation issued by the territorial state under its own legal assistance agreements, in order to obtain cooperation by third states. This may complicate accessibility to documents, arrest or detention of persons located in third states and the transfer of indictees. Problems caused by a lack of enforcement powers became apparent in the case of East Timor. The Special Panels for Serious Crimes were set up by a Regulation of UNTAET as part of the domestic legal system of East Timor, without enforcement powers vis-à-vis Indonesia. Indonesia refused voluntary cooperation and withheld assistance to the Serious Crimes Panels. This meant that most Indonesian high-level perpetrators, including top-level army, police and militia commanders, remained beyond the reach of the Panels.[565] In Cambodia, five serving members of the Royal Government refused to comply with summonses to appear and could not be compelled to testify as witnesses. Often, being open and transparent on non-compliance is the only concrete measure that hybrid entities can take.

---

[560] In its Draft Articles on Crimes Against Humanity, the ILC proposed a novel *aut dedere aut judicare* provision (Draft Art. 9), based on the Convention against Enforced Disappearances, and a regime concerning judicial assistance (Draft Art. 13), modelled after Art. 46 of the United Nations Convention against Corruption.

[561] Art. 11 (1) of the Convention against Enforced Disappearances takes into account the option of the state to 'surrender' the person to an international criminal tribunal whose jurisdiction it has recognized.

[562] See International Initiative for Opening Negotiations on a Multilateral Treaty for Mutual Legal Assistance and Extradition in Domestic Prosecution of Atrocity Crimes, Assembly of States Parties to the Rome Statute, XIIth session, 20–28 November 2013, at https://asp.icc-cpi.int/iccdocs/asp_docs/ASP12/GenDeba/ICC-ASP12-GenDeba-Netherlands-Joint-ENG.pdf.

[563] On the relationship, see D. Tladi, 'Complementarity and Cooperation in International Criminal Justice', Institute of Security Studies Paper 277, November 2014, at https://issafrica.s3.amazonaws.com/site/uploads/Paper277V2.pdf.

[564] Art. 17 of the Agreement Between the United Nations and the Government of Sierra Leone limited the obligation to comply with requests for assistance to the government of Sierra Leone. The same approach is reflected in Art. 25 of the Agreement between the United Nations and the Royal Government of Cambodia Concerning the Prosecution under Cambodian Law of Crimes Committed During the Period of Democratic Kampuchea.

[565] See S. de Bertodano, 'Current Developments in Internationalized Courts: East Timor – Justice Denied' (2004) 2 *JICJ* 910, 911.

Cooperation in financial investigations, and the tracing, freezing, seizing and eventual transfer of assets, remains a weak spot.[566] Such measures involve administrative and criminal aspects. They can be taken for different purposes, such as crime control, criminal sanction or civil reparation. The international legal framework is highly fragmented. Legal obligations in connection with criminal activities exist under specific multilateral conventions, such as the Convention against Illicit Traffic in Narcotic Drugs and Psychotropic substances,[567] the UN Convention for the Suppression of the Financing of Terrorism[568] or the Council of Europe Convention on Laundering, Search, Seizure, and Confiscation of the Proceeds from Crime.[569] They are complemented by anti-money-laundering frameworks and financial control regimes (e.g. under Security Council Resolution 1373).[570] The absence of a comprehensive cooperation regime may be explained by different reasons: the different nature and methodologies of criminal and administrative control schemes (e.g. cooperation in penal matters vs. national; financial control or banking regulation), the reluctance of governments and financial institutions to constrain the free movement of capital and persons, and potential concerns against abuse of freezing or seizure of assets by law enforcement authorities.[571]

Procedures for the freezing and seizure of assets provide in theory a very powerful tool to target the wide economic dimensions of international crimes and to address economic impunity. However, in the context of international criminal courts and tribunals, they are underdeveloped. Some authors have rightly referred to the 'short arm of international criminal justice'.[572] In the context of Nuremberg, the US Military Tribunal ordered the forfeiture of the property of German industrial firm Krupp.[573] Yet the penalty was ultimately not implemented. Jens Ohlin has highlighted the paradox: 'Even though confiscation of an industrial fortune gained in part from looting may well have been legally justified – it represented ill-gotten gains from slave labor – confiscation of Krupp's fortune was not legally justified, at least according to US officials, because equally culpable defendants had not suffered the same fate'.[574] The ICC regime foresees three types of measures: precautionary measures taken at the

---

[566] Bassiouni, *Introduction to International Criminal Law*, 511–518; C. Ferstmann, 'Cooperation and the International Criminal Court: The Freezing, Seizing and Transfer of Assets for the Purpose of Reparations', in Bekou and Birkett, *Cooperation and the International Criminal Court*, 227.

[567] Arts. 5 and 7 of the UN Convention against Illicit Traffic in Narcotic Drugs and Psychotropic Substances, 19 December 1988.

[568] Art. 8 of International Convention for the Suppression of the Financing of Terrorism. See generally I. Bantekas, 'The International Law on Terrorist Finance', in B. Saul (ed.), *Research Handbook on International Law and Terrorism* (Cheltenham: Edward Elgar, 2014), 121.

[569] Council of Europe, Convention on Laundering, Search, Seizure and Confiscation of the Proceeds from Crime, 8 November 1990, European Treaty Series, No. 141.

[570] I. Bantekas, 'The International Law of Terrorist Financing' (2003) 97 *AJIL* 316.

[571] See Bassiouni, *Introduction to International Criminal Law*, 511–518.

[572] See M. Galvis Martínez, 'Forfeiture of Assets at the International Criminal Court: The Short Arm of International Criminal Justice' (2014) 12 *JICJ* 193.

[573] US Military Tribunal Nuremberg, *US* v. *Krupp et al.*, Judgment of 31 July 1948. See C. McCarthy, *Reparations and Victims Support in the International Criminal Court* (Cambridge: Cambridge University Press, 2012), 44.

[574] See J. Ohlin, 'Krupp and Others', in A. Cassese (ed.), *Oxford Companion to International Criminal Justice* (Oxford: Oxford University Press, 2009), 780.

early stage of proceedings, i.e. 'protective measures for the purpose of forfeiture, in particular for the ultimate benefit of victims'; post-conviction penalty, i.e. 'forfeiture of proceeds, property and assets derived directly or indirectly from that crime, without prejudice to the rights of bona fide third parties'; and 'forfeiture of property for the purpose of reparations'.[575] The Statute requires states parties to cooperate in the 'identification, tracing and freezing or seizure of proceeds, property and assets and instrumentalities of crimes for the purpose of eventual forfeiture'.[576] A key ambiguity has been to determine whether precautionary measures are limited to property and assets derived directly or indirectly from crime, e.g. benefits procured through the criminal activity of the person or converted assets. The ICC Appeals Chamber has given a broad and victim-friendly interpretation to the Statute. It has found that 'there is no requirement that property and assets subject to a Chamber's request for cooperation ... be derived from or otherwise linked to alleged crimes within the jurisdiction of the Court',[577] since victims would otherwise be unable to obtain protective measures for potential reparations at early stages of the proceedings.[578]

The ICC has sought such cooperation in several cases, such as *Kenyatta* and *Bemba*. In *Bemba*, the ICC managed to secure the freezing of assets of the defendant in Portugal, including several bank accounts, a house and a yacht.[579] In other cases, the Court has faced obstacles. The execution of requests for cooperation is dependent on national legislation. In many national systems, cooperation duties are limited to proceeds and instrumentalities of crime.[580] For instance, Kenya has challenged the idea that duties of states parties extend beyond this narrow focus. Non-states parties have generally no obligation to cooperate with the Court. This poses particular problems where assets or proceeds of crimes are held in two or more states with competing claims. Moreover, the ICC regime is often slower than the UN machinery. The assets of some defendants (e.g. Lubanga, Katanga, members of the Gaddafi regime) have been frozen for different reasons (e.g. breach of an arms embargo) pursuant to Security Council or other sanctions regimes. This may give rise to conflicting priorities. For instance, in the Libyan context some states preferred to devote funds seized from regime members under Security Council sanctions to humanitarian purposes, rather than ICC justice.

---

[575] Rule 99 of the Rules of Procedure and Evidence.

[576] Art. 93 (1) (k).

[577] *Prosecutor* v. [Redacted], ICC-ACRed-01/16, Judgment on the Appeal of the Prosecutor against the decision of [Redacted], 15 February 2016, para. 1, www.legal-tools.org/doc/c01204/pdf/.

[578] Ibid., para. 50.

[579] See *Prosecutor* v. *Bemba*, ICC-RoC85–01/13, Corrigendum to the 'Decision on the Defence application to the Presidency for judicial review of the Registrar's second decision on legal assistance dated 27 February 2014', ICC-RoC85–01/13–21-Conf-Exp, 20 May 2014, 20 May 2014, para. 13. The assets were partly used to pay for Defence costs.

[580] V. Oosterveld, M. Perry and J. McManus, 'The Cooperation of States with the International Criminal Court' (2001–2002) 25 *Fordham International Law Journal* 767.

3.5.2.2.2 Human Rights Dilemmas

Cooperation may raise difficult human rights issues.[581] On several occasions, persons have claimed to have be arrested through irregular methods (e.g. luring, kidnapping and abduction) or in violation of human rights norms. Such practices may violate the individual rights of suspects or the principle of state sovereignty. For instance, Adolf Eichmann was abducted by Israeli special forces in Argentina without state consent. Similarly, Klaus Barbie, head of the Gestapo in Lyon, was smuggled out of Bolivia in a 'disguised extradition' to facilitate trial in France. National courts have occasionally applied the *male captus bene detentus* doctrine,[582] according to which a court can legitimately exercise jurisdiction over an individual even though such a person was brought before the court in an irregular way.[583] International criminal courts and tribunals have been more reserved towards this doctrine and have balanced it against abuse of process considerations. They have accepted that a serious irregularity in arrest may under some circumstances trigger a need to release the person or mitigate the sentence.

The ICTY issued a fundamental ruling in the *Nikolić* case. Dragan Nikolić, a Bosnian Serb commander, claimed to have been abducted by private agents that had no contact to SFOR or the ICTY prior to his transfer. The ICTY found that violations of state sovereignty alone may not provide a ground to decline jurisdiction.[584] However, it acknowledged that abuse of process can be a bar to the exercise of jurisdiction in cases where violations can be attributed to the tribunal. It stated: 'a situation where an accused is very seriously mistreated, maybe even subjected to inhuman, cruel or degrading treatment, or torture, before being handed over to the Tribunal, may constitute a legal impediment to the exercise of jurisdiction over such an accused'.[585] The ICTY retained jurisdiction, because the mistreatment could not be attributed to SFOR or tribunal agents and was not of an 'egregious nature'.[586]

In the *Barayagwiza* case, the ICTR made an open finding on human rights violations. The defendant was kept in provisional custody in Cameroon for over eight

---

[581] See generally K. Zeegers, *International Criminal Tribunals and Human Rights Law: Adherence and Contextualization* (The Hague: TMC Asser Press, 2016).

[582] See C. M. Bassiouni, 'Unlawful Seizures and Irregular Rendition Devices as Alternatives to Extradition' (1973) 7 *Vanderbilt Journal of Transnational Law* 25 (1973); C. Paulussen, *Male Captus Bene Detentus? Surrendering. Suspects to the International Criminal Court* (Antwerp: Intersentia, 2010).

[583] In *Eichmann*, the Israeli courts defended jurisdiction on the ground that the defendant was charged 'crimes of a universal character ... condemned publicly by the civilized world' and that Argentina had 'condoned the violation of her sovereignty and has waived her claims, including that for the return of the appellant'. See Supreme Court of Israel, *Attorney General of Israel* v. *Eichmann* (1962) 36 ILR 277, 306. In the *Barbie* case, the French Court of Cassation argued that 'ordinary extradition rules do not apply' to crimes against humanity. See Court of Cassation, *Fédération Nationale des Déportés et Internés Résistants et Patriotes and Others* v. *Barbie*, Court of Cassation (Criminal Chamber), 6 October 1983, (1988) 78 ILR 125, 128.

[584] *Nikolić* Jurisdiction Decision, para. 104 ('if a violation of State sovereignty had taken place, the Accused should first have been returned to the FRY, whereupon the FRY would have been immediately under the obligation of Article 29 of the Statute to surrender the Accused to the Tribunal').

[585] *Nikolić* Jurisdiction Decision, para. 114.

[586] Ibid., para. 114.

months prior to transfer to the ICTR. The ICTR had limited control over these factors.[587] The Appeals Chamber ruled that the tribunal might decline to exercise jurisdiction in cases where the accused has been victim of 'serious and egregious violations ... [which] would prove detrimental to the court's integrity'.[588] It found that abuse of process may provide an obstacle to trial in two circumstances, namely: '(1)where delay has made a fair trial for the accused impossible; and (2) where in the circumstances of a particular case, proceeding with the trial of the accused would contravene the court's sense of justice, due to the pre-trial impropriety or misconduct'.[589] The Appeals ordered prosecutions to be halted, since a trial of the accused would mark a 'travesty of justice' affecting the 'public confidence in the Tribunal'.[590] When new circumstances regarding the modalities of detention became apparent, the ICTR ultimately failed to release the defendant, but reduced the sentence.

Death penalty issues are a second human rights dilemma. Human rights jurisprudence has made it clear that the imposition of the death penalty may constitute a violation of the right to life or the prohibition on torture and cruel and inhuman treatment. The European Court of Human Rights has famously held that the death penalty may serve as a bar to extradition.[591] The Human Rights Committee has held that states that have abolished the death penalty are obliged 'not to expose a person to the real risk of its application' and must seek assurances of its non-application before deportation or extradition.[592] UN-established courts and the ICC are barred from applying the death penalty. However, they may encounter cooperation problems with domestic courts.

A curious situation arose in Rwanda. Initially mid- and lower-level defendants faced the risk of execution in domestic trials in Rwanda, while high-level perpetrators were exempted from the death penalty before the ICTR. The tribunal was barred from transferring cases back to Rwanda under Rule 11 *bis*, until Rwanda abolished the death penalty.[593]

The ICC faces similar dilemmas.[594] The Rome Statute is not an abolitionist treaty. It states expressly that the Statute is non-prejudicial to the application of national penalties.[595] Under existing human rights jurisprudence on the prohibition of inhuman or degrading treatment or punishment, however, the Court would face

---

[587] W. A. Schabas, 'Barayagwiza v. Prosecutor' (2000) 94 *AJIL* 563.

[588] *Prosecutor* v. *Barayagwiza*, ICTR-97-19-AR72, Decision, 3 November 1999, para. 74.

[589] Ibid., para. 77.

[590] Ibid., para. 112.

[591] See e.g. ECtHR, *Soering* v. *United Kingdom*, Appl. No. 14038/88, Judgment, 7 July 1989, paras. 92 et seq.; *Al Saddoon and Mufdhi* v. *United Kingdom*, Appl. No. 61498/08, Judgment, 2 March 2010, paras. 143–144.

[592] Human Rights Committee, *Roger Judge* v. *Canada*, Communication No. 829/1998, UN Doc. CCPR/C/78/D/829/1998 (2003), para. 10.4 ('For countries that have abolished the death penalty, there is an obligation not to expose a person to the real risk of its application. Thus, they may not remove, either by deportation or extradition, individuals from their jurisdiction if it may be reasonably anticipated that they will be sentenced to death, without ensuring that the death sentence would not be carried out').

[593] Rule 11 *bis* (C) of the Rules of Procedure and Evidence states: 'In determining whether to refer the case in accordance with paragraph (A), the Trial Chamber shall satisfy itself that the accused will receive a fair trial in the courts of the State concerned and that the death penalty will not be imposed or carried out'.

[594] See J. Trahan, 'The International Criminal Court's Libya Case(s): The Need for Consistency with International Human Rights as to Due Process and the Death Penalty' (2017) 17 *International Criminal Law Review* 803.

[595] Art. 80 ICC Statute.

difficulties to transfer a defendant back to a state where the death penalty is practised, after their transfer to the ICC. Similar problems arise in relation to reverse cooperation, i.e. cooperation of the ICC with domestic jurisdictions carrying out the death penalty. The duty to act in accordance with international human rights[596] may be read as prohibition to become complicit in proceedings that lead to imposition of the death penalty. Certain forms of cooperation with domestic investigations and prosecutions may thus be barred. Some even go so far as to argue that the exposure to capital punishment should affect decisions on complementarity, since it 'gives a green light to permitting someone to be exposed to capital punishment, even if no "sending" of the individual is involved'.[597] This reading may overstretch the boundaries of due process considerations under complementarity.

The need for cooperation extends beyond arrest and surrender. National witness protection systems and effective detention facilities are key for the enforcement of international criminal justice. International criminal courts and tribunals have struggled with the treatment of witnesses, release of defendants and post-conviction issues, due to lack of cooperation by states. Relocation of witnesses after testimony is a recurring challenge since it requires state consent and cooperation. Asylum claims by detained witnesses have created a 'catch 22' situation for the ICC in the DRC situation.[598] The Congolese witnesses claimed that they would face retaliation after their return to the DRC since they implicated President Kabila in war crimes. The asylum claim had to be decided by Dutch courts. Dutch courts denied protection in the light of the involvement of witnesses in crime but found that they could not be returned because they would risk an unfair trial or even the death penalty. The European Court of Human Rights found that the Netherlands had no obligation to take custody over the defendants since they remained formally under ICC jurisdiction.[599] The ICC found that it 'cannot serve as an administrative detention unit for asylum seekers'.[600] The witnesses were held in the Court's detention unit for more than two years until the decision on their asylum applications was made. The ICC finally agreed with the Congolese government on a list of 'protective measures' for the witnesses after their transfer to the DRC, namely detention in a secure prison facility guarded by specially trained guards, regular visits and monitoring by ICC personnel, and assurances that the death penalty would not be executed.[601]

---

[596] Art. 21 (3) ICC Statute.

[597] Trahan argues that an 'inadmissibility finding' indirectly facilitates exposure to capital punishment. See Trahan, 'The International Criminal Court's Libya Case(s)', 835.

[598] See G. Sluiter, 'Shared Responsibility in International Criminal Justice: The ICC and Asylum' (2012) 10 *JICJ* 661; J. van Wijk and M. Cupido, 'Testifying Behind Bars: Detained ICC Witnesses and Human Rights Protection', in Stahn, *Law and Practice of the International Criminal Court*, 1084.

[599] ECtHR, *Longa* v. *the Netherlands*, Appl. No. 33917/12, Decision on Admissibility, 9 October 2012. Art. 93 (7) of the ICC Statute formed the basis of the detention.

[600] See *Prosecutor* v. *Ndugjolo Chui*, ICC-01/04.02/12 A, Order on the implementation of the cooperation agreement between the Court and the Democratic Republic of the Congo concluded pursuant Art. 93 (7) of the Statute, 20 January 2014, para. 27.

[601] See *Prosecutor* v. *Katanga and Ndugjolo Chui*, ICC-01/04–01/07, Decision on the Security Situation of witnesses DRC-D02-P-0236, DRC-D02-P-0228 and DRC-D02-P-0350, 24 August 2011, para. 13.

During proceedings, defendants may apply for interim release. Under human rights law, 'deprivation of liberty should be an exception and not the rule'.[602] Due to the seriousness of crimes, and the difficulty to apprehend defendants, international courts and tribunals have been reluctant to grant such release. Early ICTY rules contained a presumption against provisional release, in light of the grave nature of the charges, the risks for international or national forces to apprehend the defendant after release, and the lack of confidence in compliance with assurances by authorities in the former Yugoslavia. According to former Rule 65 (B) release could be ordered 'only in exceptional circumstances'.[603] In 1999, the practice was amended. Judges dropped the 'exceptional circumstances' requirement and allowed release by a Trial Chamber 'if it is satisfied that the accused will appear for trial, and if released, will not pose a danger to any victim, witness or person'.[604] Other tribunals, such as the ICTR or the SCSL, also formally eliminated the threshold of exceptional circumstances. In practice, however, detention remained the rule rather than the exception.[605]

At the ICTY, the test remained hard to show since the burden to establish an entitlement to interim release remained with the defendant. The ICTR failed to grant any requests for interim release, due to the difficulty to obtain assurances from states to return detainees.[606] The SCSL justified continued detention, despite the option of bail, due to the risk of public disorder in Sierra Leone as a result of provisional release.[607] The ICC framework has a more flexible regime.[608] In *Bemba*, Judge Pikis openly criticized the 'assumption that it is for the person to demonstrate that he is entitled to remain free, and not for his accusers to establish the necessity for his detention'.[609] Jurisprudence has clarified that the Prosecutor has the burden to show that detention of the person concerned is necessary. An ICC Pre-Trial Chamber granted release to Jean-Pierre Bemba.[610] The decision was overturned on appeal since conditional release depends on the willingness of a state to accept the person

---

[602] *Prosecutor* v. *Bemba*, ICC-01/05–01/08–475, Decision on the Interim Release of Jean-Pierre Bemba Gombo and Convening Hearings with the Kingdom of Belgium, the Republic of Portugal, the Republic of France, the Federal Republic of Germany, the Italian Republic, and the Republic of South Africa, 14 August 2009, para. 77 (*Bemba* Interim Release Decision).

[603] For a discussion, see M. Fairlie, 'The Precedent of Pretrial Release at the ICTY: A Road Better Left Less Traveled' (2009/2010) 33 *Fordham International Law Journal* 1101, 1129 et seq.

[604] ICTY, Rules of Procedure and Evidence, Rule 65 (B), UN Doc. IT/32/Rev.17, 7 December 1999). The ICTR made a similar amendment in 2003. See ICTR, Rules of Procedure and Evidence, Rule 65(B), UN Doc. ITR/3/Rev.13, 27 May 2003.

[605] For a rejection of this claim, see *Prosecutor* v. *Brdanin & Talić*, IT-99–36 Decision on Motion by Momir Talic for provisional Release, 28 March 2011, para. 17.

[606] See K. de Meester, K. Pitcher, R. Rastan and G. Sluiter, 'Investigation, Coercive Measures, Arrest and Surrender', in G. Sluter. H. Friman, S. Linton, S. Vasiliev and S. Zappala (eds.), *International Criminal Procedure* (Oxford: Oxford University Press, 2013), 171, 327–328.

[607] *Prosecutor* v. *Sesay*, SCSL-04–15-AR65–297, Decision on Appeal against Refusal of Bail, 14 December 2004, para. 36; *Prosecutor* v. *Norman, Fonfana and Kondewa*, SCSL-04–14-T, Fonfana – Decision on Application for Bail under Rule 65, 5 August 2004, paras. 82–84.

[608] See A. Dumbryte, 'Interim Release in the Practice of the ICC', in Stahn, *Law and Practice of the International Criminal Court*, 1077.

[609] See *Prosecutor* v. *Bemba*, ICC-01/05–01/08 OA, Judgment on the appeal of Mr. Jean-Pierre Bemba Gombo against the decision of Pre-Trial Chamber III entitled 'Decision on Application for Interim Release', 16 December 2008, Dissenting opinion of Judge Georghios M. Pikis, para. 36.

[610] *Bemba* Interim Release Decision, para. 69.

concerned and to enforce any conditions specified. The Appeals Chamber found that a Chamber must identify 'a State willing and able to accept the person concerned' before 'a decision on conditional release'.[611] This limits the prospects of success.

3.5.2.2.3 Enforcement of Sentences

The treatment of defendants after trial is one of the blind spots of international criminal justice.[612] Persons convicted by international criminal courts and tribunals mostly serve their sentence in a different forum than the territorial state, due to security reasons or humanitarian concerns relating to the conditions and treatment of prisoners. For instance, persons sentenced by the ICTR, the SCSL or the ICC have been transferred to a third state for purposes of enforcement of sentences, far removed from their relatives. Securing cooperation in relation to the enforcement of sentences is a difficult trade-off. It requires two levels of state consent, agreement of the state with the tribunal on enforcement of sentences, and the willingness of that state to accept a specific defendant. ICTY defendants have been spread out over thirteen European countries. ICTR prisoners were predominantly sent to Mali and Benin. SCSL defendants served their sentence in Arusha or the UK (Charles Taylor). The existing distribution is mostly governed by cost-efficiency and pragmatic considerations that are decided on an ad hoc basis. This may create vast discrepancies prison conditions and difficulties in relation to family visits or rehabilitation of perpetrators. Moreover, any international involvement ends when sentences are served.

As Barbora Hola and Joris van Wijk have argued:

> After their release, the international prisoners simply disappear from the radar of the international community (unless they enter a witness protection programme and cooperate with the tribunals) and there is no supervision of their conduct or any attention paid to their activities. Some go back to their countries of origin and return to political posts they held prior to or during the periods when crimes were committed. Some simply cannot go anywhere since no country is willing to accept them.[613]

Ultimately, cooperation thus depends on a plurality of approaches. It cannot be confined to ad hoc diplomatic pressures, coercive compliance strategies (e.g. aid conditionality) or sanctions (e.g. naming and shaming). It also requires confidence-building and longer-term term measures that allow states to overcome obstacles to cooperation.

---

[611] *Prosecutor v. Bemba*, ICC-01/05-01/08 OA 2, Judgment on the appeal of the Prosecutor against Pre-Trial Chamber II's 'Decision on the Interim Release of Jean-Pierre Bemba Gombo', 2 December 2009, para. 106.

[612] M. M. Penrose, 'Lest We Fail: The Importance of Enforcement in International Criminal Law' (1999–2000) 15 *American University International Law Review* 322–394; R. Mulgrew, 'On the Enforcement of Sentences Imposed by International Courts, Challenges Faced by the Special Court for Sierra Leone' (2009) 7 *JICJ* 373–396.

[613] B. Hola and J. van Wijk, 'Life after Conviction at International Criminal Tribunals: An Empirical Overview' (2014) 12 *JICJ* 109, 131–132.

3.6   Impediments to Enforcement

Investigations and prosecutions may be barred by a number of factors, such as amnesties, immunities, statutes of limitations or restrictions to the temporal scope of jurisdiction (non-retroactivity). The increased recognition of a *jus puniendi* for international crimes has limited the space for invocation of bars to investigation and prosecution. The interpretation of the scope and effect of these bars is under dispute.

The *ne bis in idem* principle, i.e. the right not be tried twice, is generally recognized as a bar to proceedings in domestic jurisdictions. It protects at least three cardinal interests: legal certainty, the proportionality of punishment, and the legal effects of judgments. Its application in the international context remains fragmented. *Ne bis in idem* applies in different variations in the relationship between international criminal courts and tribunals. Its horizontal effect, namely its transnational application across domestic jurisdictions, remains contested.

Immunities and amnesties count among the most contested impediments to international criminal justice. Technically, they constitute procedural bars to the exercise of criminal jurisdiction.[614] Both concepts have developed significantly over time. In certain 'hard' cases they may provide a space to accommodate some of the tensions that the exercise of criminal justice may entail in international relations and domestic politics. The circumstances under which they constitute a bar to the exercise of international criminal justice are limited. Legal disputes are often used as a means to voice broader policy discontents about the effects of international criminal justice.

3.6.1   *Ne bis in idem*

The *ne bis in idem* principle is widely recognized as a procedural bar to prosecution under human rights law and international law. It applies to final judgments in criminal matters. It protects an individual against double prosecution. It pursues several objectives: to encourage diligent prosecution, uphold public confidence in the justice system, and to prevent 'repeated attempts to convict for an alleged offence, . . . thereby subjecting him to embarrassment, expense and ordeal, and compelling him to live in a continuing sense of anxiety and insecurity'.[615] The existing legal regime is marked by a certain degree of contradiction. Human rights considerations demand that individuals enjoy equal protection against double prosecution for the same conduct, irrespective of whether they are prosecuted in their own jurisdiction, by third states or an international jurisdiction.[616] This argument contrasts with the interests of states that

---

[614] They should not be confused with substantive defences to individual criminal responsibility.

[615] *Prosecutor v. Sary*, 002/19–09–2007-ECCC/OCIJ (PTC75), Decision on Ieng Sary's Appeal against the Closing Order, 11 April 2011, para. 142 (*Sary* Appeal Closing Order).

[616] See S. Gless, 'Ne bis in idem in an International and Transnational Criminal Justice Perspective: Paving the way for an Individual Right?', in Van der Wilt and Paulussen, *Legal Responses to Transnational and International Crimes*, 220, 223.

seek to retain domestic jurisdiction in order to accommodate national criminal policies, divergent crime conceptions and/or lack of trust in other systems. In the international context, human rights considerations have been balanced against 'the interest of the international community and victims in ensuring that those responsible for the commission of international crimes are properly prosecuted'.[617] The approach towards *ne bis in idem* depends highly on the context of the respective forum.

3.6.1.1   *International* Ne bis in idem *Protection*

States have generally regulated *ne bis in idem* as a bar to prosecution in the context of treaty regimes or the relationship between domestic and international courts and tribunals. For instance, the Statutes of the ad hoc tribunals, the SCSL, the STL and ICC contain provisions on the impact of national judgments on international proceedings ('upward effect' of *ne bis in idem*), and the reverse scenario ('downward effect'). All frameworks recognize that an international criminal court or tribunal is barred from exercising jurisdiction against an individual who has already been tried for the same acts or conduct.[618] However, the conditions and exceptions vary.

The Statutes of the ad hoc tribunals and the SCSL contained an ordinary crime exception. It allowed these courts to conduct a re-trial in cases in which the underlying acts were characterized as ordinary crimes in domestic proceedings.[619] They were able to re-prosecute a person for the same crime, while national courts were prevented from doing so. This approach implies a certain superiority of international prosecution. The ICC regime grants more leeway to domestic jurisdictions, in light of the principle of complementarity. The main test is not whether an ICC crime label was used, but rather whether proceedings related to the same 'conduct'.

A second limitation is the fraudulent trial exception. A prosecution may not violate *ne bis in idem* if national proceedings were not conducted independently and impartially. This exception derives from human rights jurisprudence which views *ne bis in idem* as an instrument to ensure that states comply with their human rights obligation. For instance, the Inter-American Court of Human Rights held that individuals may not benefit from *ne bis in idem* protection if the proceedings were 'intended to shield the accused party from criminal responsibility', 'were not conducted independently or impartially with due procedural guarantees', or 'there was no real intent to bring those responsible to justice'.[620] The problem is that the relevant test is formulated in different terms in statutory instruments. The ECCC applied this exception to argue that defendant Ieng Sary could face criminal proceedings, although he was convicted in 1979 in an *in absentia* trial by the People's Revolutionary Court. It argued that the trial was flawed from a due process perspective (i.e. lack of impartiality), although it

---

[617] *Sary* Appeal Closing Order, para. 143.
[618] Art. 14 (7) of the ICCPR uses different language. It prohibits trial or punishment for the same offence.
[619] Art. 10 (2) (a) ICTY Statute, Art. 9 (2) (a) ICTR Statute and Art. 9 (2) (a) SCSL Statute.
[620] IACtHR, *Almonacid-Arellan et al.* v. *Chile*, Judgment, 26 September 2006, para. 154.

was guided by the intent to prosecute and convict.[621] This reading is more contested in the ICC context, where the relevance of due process considerations in admissibility assessments is disputed.[622]

It is questionable to what extent the 'downward effect' of ICC trials should bar further domestic trials. The Statute prohibits the ICC from conducting trials in relation to 'conduct' that has been tried domestically, but only protects defendants from domestic re-trial in relation to 'crimes' for 'which that person has already been convicted or acquitted'.[623] That leaves significant leeway for domestic courts to carry out further proceedings. The ICC Presidency validated this approach in *Katanga*, where it allowed a further trial for crimes other than those relating to the Bogoro attack on 24 February 2004.[624]

3.6.1.2 *The Problem of Transnational Application*

A blind spot in *ne bis in idem* protection is its application in interstate relations. International law lacks a general rule requiring states to respect this principle in a transnational context.[625] The ICCPR mandates respect of *ne bis in idem* 'in accordance with the law and penal procedure of each country'.[626] The Human Rights Committee has acknowledged that it prohibits double jeopardy in a given state, but 'does not guarantee *ne bis in idem* with respect to the national jurisdiction of two or more states'.[627] The same limited understanding is reflected in Protocol 7 to the ECHR, which lacks transnational application.[628] In Europe, states have made efforts since the 1970s to give *ne bis in idem* a regional dimension through specific multilateral treaty regulation, including the prohibition of double punishment. The transnational application is inter alia recognized in the Convention Implementing the Schengen Agreement (CISA)[629] and Article of the EU Charter of Fundamental Rights.[630] It might thus be argued that '[i]n the EU, the traditional *ne bis in idem* principle has developed from a domestic legal principle into a transnational human right'.[631] Beyond such specific regional contexts, states have remained reluctant to recognize

---

[621] *Sary* Appeal Closing Order, para. 175.

[622] See K. Heller, 'The Shadow Side of Complementarity; The Effect of Article 17 of the Rome Statute on National Due Process' (2006) 17 *Criminal Law Forum* 255.

[623] Art. 20 (2).

[624] *Prosecutor* v. *Katanga*, ICC-01/04–01/07–3679, Decision Pursuant to Article 108 (1) of the Rome Statute, 7 April 2016, para. 25.

[625] In 1995, the ICTY held that ne bis in idem 'is generally applied so as to cover only a double prosecution within the same State, and has not received broad recognition as a mandatory norm of transnational application'. See *Prosecutor* v. *Tadić*, IT-94-1-T, Decision on Defence Motion on the Principle of Non-Bis-In-Idem, 14 November 1995, para. 19.

[626] Art. 14 (7).

[627] Human Rights Committee, *AP* v. *Italy*, Communication No. 204/1986, CCPR/C/31/D/204/86, para. 7.3.

[628] Art. 4 (1) states: 'No one shall be liable to be tried or punished again in criminal proceedings under the jurisdiction of the same state for an offence for which he has already been finally acquitted or convicted in accordance with the law and penal procedure of that State'.

[629] Convention Implementing the Schengen Agreement of 14 June 1985, Art. 54.

[630] It states: 'No one shall be liable to be tried or punished again in criminal proceedings for an offence for which he or she has already been finally acquitted or convicted within the Union in accordance with the law'.

[631] See J. Vervaele, 'The Transnational Ne bis in idem Principle in the EU: Mutual Recognition and Equivalent Protection of Human Rights' (2005) 1 *Utrecht Law Review* 100, 117.

the transnational effect of *ne bis in idem*. Reasons include the 'race for time' dilemma, i.e. the fact that the state which prosecutes first would bar others from doing the same, and the lack of harmonization of international crimes.

This status quo sits uneasily with idea of an emerging system of justice governing international crimes. If states are encouraged to extend universal jurisdiction, they must also provide greater attention to the implications of such jurisdiction on the protection of persons. Risks of abuse can be taken into account through relevant restrictions (e.g. the fraudulent trial exception). As Sabine Gless has noted, there is a structural imbalance:

[international law] essentially caters to law enforcement needs and rarely takes the position of the individual into account ... if states establish cooperation and use their jus puniendi side-by-side, they must also take individual rights into account, and for instance, provide an interface translating the *ne bis in idem* principle into [transnational criminal law].[632]

The International Association of Penal Law has gone so far as to argue that *ne bis in idem* is a 'human right' that should have international and transnational application.[633]

3.6.2   Immunities

Immunities are common practice in international relations. Their interplay with international criminal law is complex, in particular in relation to the question of what immunity bars criminal proceedings against an official of a state. As the ICJ has noted, immunity is not designed to provide impunity, but to balance competing rationales.[634] The main purpose of immunities is to protect certain official acts carried out by individuals on behalf of the state (functional immunity), or to facilitate the role of certain office holders in international affairs (e.g. heads of states, ministers, diplomats) during their term of office (personal immunity). Functional immunity is conduct-based.[635] It relates to acts carried out in an official function, and excludes acts in a private capacity. One of the rationales of functional immunity is to ensure that wrongful acts are not attributed to agents personally, but rather to the state on whose behalf they act.[636] Functional immunity continues to apply after the individual has ceased to hold public office, since the protection is tied to state conduct. Personal immunity relates to the office or status of a person. It covers acts of persons essential to a state's administration, whether in their personal or official capacity. However, it ceases to apply when individuals lose their representative role.

---

[632] Gless, 'Ne bis in idem', 237.
[633] See International Association of Penal Law, Resolutions adopted by the XVIth International Congress of Penal Law, Budapest, 5–11 September 1999, Section IV B 4.
[634] ICJ, *Arrest Warrant* Case, para. 60.
[635] D. Akande and S. Shah, 'Immunities of State Officials, International Crimes, and Foreign Domestic Courts' (2011) 21 *EJIL* 815, 825.
[636] *Blaškić Subpoena* Appeal, para. 38.

Immunity does not exonerate the person to whom it applies from all criminal responsibility. Immunity does not apply in the state's own jurisdiction; it can be waived, or limited. Overall, there is a tendency among states to diminish the scope of immunity in relation to grave human rights violations and international crimes.[637] The law contains certain grey areas as to what extent there are exceptions to immunity in the relationship between states for certain categories of international crimes, or in relation to certain types of international jurisdictions.

3.6.2.1 Towards an International Crimes Exception in Interstate Relations?

The law on immunity in interstate relations is in flux. It needs to strike a balance between the functioning of mutual interstate relations and the protection of the international legal order. The crucial question is where to draw the line. The Nuremberg judgment implied that state sovereignty does not shield persons from individual responsibility because they act on behalf of a state. The *Pinochet* decision made it clear that former heads of state are not immune from prosecution.[638] *Pinochet* sent a message that international criminal law can target political elites. Criminologists began to observe a 'Pinochet syndrome',[639] whereby heads of states would face the prospects of arrest when travelling abroad. However, it is disputed to what extent there is an international crimes exception. A distinction must be made between functional immunity, which relates to acts carried out on behalf of a state, and personal immunity, which protects the representative function of certain categories of persons.

3.6.2.1.1 Functional Immunity

The argument that a state official can rely on functional immunity in relation to international crimes is conceptually weak. It is contradictory to argue that a state can rely on functional immunity grounded in sovereignty if the very commission of international crimes marks an abuse of sovereignty, which is prohibited by international laws and requires prosecution. This contradiction has been outlined in Nuremberg. The judgment challenged the assumption that state officials are mere instruments of the state. It noted: 'He who violates the laws of war cannot obtain immunity while acting in pursuance of the authority of the State, if the State in authorizing action moves outside its competence under international law'.[640] Several national courts have challenged that functional immunity is a bar to the prosecution of international crimes, such as crimes involving a state element (e.g. enforced

---

[637] ICJ, *Arrest Warrant* Case, Joint Separate Opinion of Judges Higgins, Kooijmans and Buergenthal, para. 75 ('a trend is discernible that in a world which increasingly rejects impunity for the most repugnant offenses the attribution of responsibility and accountability is becoming firmer ... and the availability of immunity as a shield more limited').

[638] House of Lords, *R v. Bow Street Magistrates' Court ex parte Pinochet* (No. 3), 24 March 1999, ILM 38 (1999), 581; J. C. Barker, 'The Future of Former Head of State Immunity after ex parte Pinochet' (1999) 48 *ICLQ* 937; A. Bianchi, 'Immunity versus Human Rights: The Pinochet Case' (1999) 10 *EJIL* 237.

[639] B. Crossette, 'The World; Dictators Face the Pinochet Syndrome', *New York Times*, 22 August 1999, at www.nytimes .com/1999/08/22/weekinreview/the-world-dictators-face-the-pinochet-syndrome.html?_r=0.

[640] Nuremberg Judgment (1947) 41 AJIL 172, 220–221.

disappearance, torture[641]) or war crimes, crimes against humanity or genocide more generally. However, some powerful states affected by allegations of international crimes (e.g. China, France, the US, Russia), continue to rely on the applicability of functional immunity for acting and former officials before foreign courts.[642]

The ICJ has taken a reserved stance in the *Arrest Warrant* case in 2000. In that case, Belgium argued that incumbent foreign ministers do not enjoy immunity from criminal prosecution in relation to international crimes before foreign criminal jurisdictions. The ICJ addressed functional immunity in a confusing *obiter dictum*. The Court noted that prosecution of former state officials is limited to 'acts committed during that period of office in a private capacity'.[643] This might be read to imply that functional immunity serves as a bar to the prosecution of official acts committed during terms of office. The only way to discard immunity would to be to argue that international crimes are acts carried out in a private capacity. This argument is weak, however, since it would disregard the inherent connection between international crimes and state policy (e.g. in the context of aggression, crimes against humanity or genocide).

The ICJ *obiter* marks a clear step back from the rationale of the Nuremberg judgment.[644] The claim that functional immunity can serve as a shield for state-inflicted crime is highly suspicious. If state officials are implicated in crime, immunity easily becomes not only a 'procedural' impediment, but a 'substantive bar' to accountability. Several judges have questioned whether international crimes attract functional immunity. Based on precedents such as *Pinochet* or *Eichmann*, Judges Higgins, Kooijmans and Buergenthal have argued that 'serious international crimes cannot be regarded as official acts because they are neither normal State functions nor functions that a State alone (in contrast to an individual) can perform'.[645] The existing argument carries risks of abuse. As Judge van den Wyngaert has noted, '[m]ale fide Governments could appoint suspects of serious human rights violations to cabinet posts in order to shelter them from prosecution in third States'.[646] The critique of the majority approach in the *Arrest Warrant* case is reflected in the Fifth Report of ILC Special Rapporteur Concepcion Escobar Hernandez on 'Immunity of State officials from foreign criminal jurisdiction' (2016).[647] The report states that

---

[641] See *R* v. *Bow Street Metropolitan Stipendiary Magistrate, ex parte* Pinochet Ugarte (No. 1) [2000] 1 AC 61 (HL) 109 and 111 (Lord Nicholls), 115–16 (Lord Steyn) and 118 (Lord Hoffmann).

[642] See R. O'Keefe, 'An "International Crime" Exception to the Immunity of State Officials from Foreign Criminal Jurisdiction: Not Currently, Not Likely' (2015) 109 *AJIL Unbound* 167, 171. On state practice, see S. Murphy, 'Immunity *Ratione Materiae* of State Officials from Foreign Criminal Jurisdiction: Where is the State Practice in Support of Exceptions?' (2018) 112 *AJIL Unbound* 4–8.

[643] *ICJ, Arrest Warrant Case*, para. 61.

[644] The Nuremberg Tribunal stated expressly: 'The principle of international law which under certain circumstances protects the representatives of a State, cannot be applied to acts which are condemned as criminal by international law. The authors of these acts cannot shelter themselves behind their official position in order to be freed from punishment in appropriate proceedings'. Nuremberg Judgment (1947) 41 AJIL 172, 221.

[645] ICJ, *Arrest Warrant Case*, Joint Separate Opinion of Judges Higgins, Kooijmans, and Buergenthal, para. 85.

[646] ICJ, *Arrest Warrant Case*, Dissenting Opinion of Judge Van den Wyngaert, para. 21.

[647] ILC, Fifth report on immunity of state officials from foreign criminal jurisdiction, by Concepción Escobar Hernández, A/CN.4/701, 14 June 2016 (ILC, Fifth report on immunity of state officials).

[a]lthough varied, the practice [of national courts] reveals a clear trend towards considering the commission of international crimes as a bar to the application of the immunity of State officials from foreign criminal jurisdiction, either because such crimes are not considered official acts, or because they are considered an exception to immunity, owing to their gravity or to the fact that they undermine values and principles recognized by the international community as a whole.[648]

Which types of crimes are covered by this exclusion is disputed. The ICJ has rejected the argument that the existence of a state duty to extradite or prosecute under a multilateral convention alone affects immunities under customary international law.[649] It has also rejected the argument that the potential *jus cogens* nature of a violated norm creates an automatic exception to immunity.[650]

As rightly suggested in doctrine, the granting of functional immunity is incompatible with the object and purposes of instruments that allow extraterritorial jurisdiction over crimes committed in an official capacity.[651] Clear examples are instruments banning torture, enforced disappearance, genocide, war crimes in a non-international armed conflict or crimes against humanity.[652] This approach has been reaffirmed by the Draft Article 7 of the ILC Draft Articles on Immunity of State officials from foreign criminal jurisdiction.[653] It suggests that functional immunity should not apply to these crimes, while remaining ambiguous in relation to the crime of aggression.[654] However, reactions to Draft Article 7 have been reserved. Some have argued that the suggested exclusion remains *de lege ferenda* in light of scant state practice.[655] The future and reception of the article remains uncertain.

3.6.2.1.2 Personal Immunity

It is more difficult to argue that there is an international crime exception in relation to personal immunities. Such immunities are temporary by nature, i.e. restricted to the

---

[648] Ibid., para. 179.

[649] ICJ, *Arrest Warrant Case*, para. 59.

[650] Ibid., para. 78; ICJ, *Jurisdictional Immunities of the State (Germany v. Italy)*, Judgment, 3 February 2012, para. 95.

[651] See Akande and Shah, 'Immunities of State Officials', 841–846.

[652] It is more controversial to what extent this extends to piracy, slavery or terrorism (see Bassiouni, *Introduction to International Criminal Law*, 95), or 'corruption-related crimes' and 'crimes that cause harm to persons, including death and serious injury, or to property' (ILC, Fifth report on immunity of State officials, para. 248). Others remain sceptical whether an international crime exception exists under customary law at all. See O'Keefe, 'International Crime Exception', 168.

[653] See 'Draft Article 7 Crimes in respect of which immunity does not apply'. It reads: '1. Immunity shall not apply in relation to the following crimes: (a) Genocide, crimes against humanity, war crimes, torture and enforced disappearances; (b) Crimes of corruption; (c) Crimes that cause harm to persons, including death and serious injury, or to property, when such crimes are committed in the territory of the forum State and the State official is present in said territory at the time that such crimes are committed'. See ILC, Report of the International Law Commission Sixty-ninth session (1 May–2 June and 3 July–4 August 2017), A/72/10, 164.

[654] ILC, Fifth report on immunity of state officials, para. 222, arguing that 'the crime of aggression must be entrusted primarily to international courts and tribunals, given the political implications it could have for the stability of relations between States; … and there do not appear to be any cases of State practice in which the crime of aggression has been characterized as a limitation or an exception to the exercise of immunity, at either the legislative or the judicial level'.

[655] Murphy, 'Immunity Ratione Materiae of State Officials from Foreign Criminal Jurisdiction', 8; R. van Alebeek, 'The "International Crime" Exception in the ILC Draft Articles on the Immunity of State Officials from Foreign Criminal Jurisdiction: Two Steps Back?' (2018) 112 *AJIL Unbound* 27, 32.

term of office. They have inter alia been recognized in relation to heads of state, heads of government and ministers for foreign affairs. They protect the stability of interstate relations and the sovereign equality of states. For instance, arresting an acting head of state or government in office is a severe interference with the autonomy and independence of a foreign state and might cause political instability or an outbreak of violence.

In the *Arrest Warrant* case, the ICJ clearly rejected the idea of an international crimes exception in relation to personal immunities. It held that immunities of senior state officials before foreign courts are absolute during terms of office.[656] This finding coincides with rulings by domestic courts which have upheld the immunity of acting heads of state from criminal prosecution. For example, even the *Pinochet* decision recognized that a serving head of state cannot be arrested and prosecuted in a foreign state. The ILC noted that 'national courts have generally recognized the immunity of Heads of State, Heads of Government and Ministers for Foreign Affairs in all circumstances, without taking into consideration the possible existence of one of the limitations or exceptions'.[657] It therefore concluded that international crime-related exclusion of immunity 'shall not apply to persons who enjoy immunity ratione personae during their term of office'.[658] This reasoning represents the existing *lex lata*. It seeks to strike a balance between the protection of sovereign equality and the rule of law by allowing the exercise of foreign criminal jurisdiction over senior officials after the end of their function. However, the existing justification has certain weaknesses that require further scrutiny.

First, it is questionable who should be covered by personal immunities to protect state functions. The assessment may differ according to function and context. For instance, ministers do not necessarily impersonate the essential function of the state in the same way as heads of states or governments.

Second, there is a deeper question of whether sovereign equality should bar the exercise of criminal jurisdiction in all circumstances. The recognition of personal immunity in relation to international crimes may have counterproductive side effects. It provides an incentive to stay in office as long as possible, if need be through autocratic methods or political violence. Granting immunity is thus not always the best means to protect sovereign interests.

Moreover, maintaining absolute personal immunity during terms of office is not necessarily conducive to the stability of interstate relations. It may facilitate the continuation of crime, conflict with state duties to prevent crime (e.g. under the Genocide Convention[659]), or frustrate claims of victims relating to access to justice

---

[656] ICJ, *Arrest Warrant Case*, paras. 58, 60, 61.
[657] ILC, Fifth report on immunity of state officials, para. 237.
[658] Ibid., para. 248.
[659] *Al-Bashir* Non Cooperation Decision, Minority Opinion Brichambaut, para. 36: 'Upholding personal immunities in this context would seriously hinder efforts to prevent and suppress genocide and run counter to the object and purpose of the Genocide Convention').

or to reparation.[660] The hard question is thus whether the priority of personal immunity over the *jus puniendi* is always 'a price is worth paying'.[661]

3.6.2.2 An International Court or Tribunal Exception?

In specific instances, immunities are relinquished through international instruments, either through specific multilateral or bilateral agreements, or by other means (e.g. Security Council Resolution). This practice has triggered debate as to whether there is a general immunity exception in relation to international courts or tribunals.

3.6.2.2.1 Conflicting Rulings

The ICTY has confirmed on multiple occasions that there is no immunity for core crimes.[662] The ICJ *Arrest Warrant* judgment marked the beginning of a doctrine of exceptionality in relation to international criminal jurisdiction.[663] The ICJ found in paragraph 61 of the judgment that immunities may not apply in relation to 'to criminal proceedings before certain international criminal courts, where they have jurisdiction', such as the ICTY, the ICTR or the treaty regime of the ICC. In 2004, the Special Court for Sierra Leone relied on paragraph 61 of the *Arrest Warrant* decision to dismiss immunity claims by Charles Taylor, even before his arrest and initial appearance in spring 2006.[664] It argued that the rationales of immunity do not apply in relation to international courts since 'they are not organs of a State but derive their mandate from the international community'.[665] A similar argument was made by the ICC Pre-Trial Chamber in the *Malawi/Chad* decision, which noted that immunity conflicts do not arise in relation to 'international courts and tribunals which are "totally independent of states and subject to strict rules of impartiality"'.[666]

This interpretation misreads paragraph 61 of the ICJ *Arrest Warrant* decision. The ICJ did not necessarily imply an 'international court' exception per se. This notion is far too vague. Rather, the underlying idea is that exceptions to immunity can be created through state consent to founding instruments of courts and tribunals, or through other means, such as Chapter VII resolutions of the Security Council. Formally, it is thus not the nature of the Court, but rather the relinquishment of

---

[660] *Arrest Warrant Case*, Dissenting Opinion of Judge Van den Wyngaert, para. 22 ([v]ictims of such violations bringing legal action against such persons in third States would face the obstacle of immunity from jurisdiction'). See also ILC, Fifth report on immunity of state officials, para. 206 ('applying immunity from jurisdiction in relation to international crimes constitutes a denial of victims' right of access to justice and to obtain reparation for the crimes they have endured').

[661] C. Kreß, 'The International Criminal Court and Immunities under International Law for States Not Party to the Court's Statute', in M. Bergsmo and L. Yan (eds.), *State: Sovereignty and International Criminal Law* (Oslo: Torkel Opsahl Academic EPublisher, 2012), 223, 265; *Arrest Warrant Case*, Dissenting Opinion of Judge Van den Wyngaert, para. 36, arguing that '[i]mmunity should never apply to crimes under international law, neither before international courts nor national courts'.

[662] See *Blaškić Subpoena* Appeal, para. 41; *Furundžija* Trial Judgment, para. 140.

[663] See ICJ, *Arrest Warrant Case*, para. 61.

[664] *Taylor* Immunity Decision, para. 50.

[665] Ibid., para. 51.

[666] *Prosecutor* v. *Al-Bashir*, ICC-02/05–01/09, Decision Pursuant to Article 87 (7) of the Rome Statute on the Failure by the Republic of Malawi to Comply with the Cooperation Requests Issued by the Court with Respect to the Arrest and Surrender of Omar Hassan Ahmad Al-Bashir, 12 December 2011, para. 34 (*Malawi* Cooperation Decision).

immunity through a direct or indirect legal act, that makes immunity inapplicable. This justification is more plausible.

3.6.2.2.2 *The Battle Over Immunities in the ICC Context*

The interpretation of immunity has given rise to significant controversy in the ICC context. Article 27 of the ICC Statute excludes immunity related to official capacity in the relationship between ICC states parties. In the context of proceedings against Al-Bashir, the ICC had to determine to what extent the personal immunity of a head of state of a non-state party serves as a bar to arrest by states parties of the ICC. The problem is that Article 27 does not bind Sudan as a third state. Some states (e.g. South Africa, Jordan) and the AU argued that ICC states parties are not under an obligation to execute the warrant of arrest due to the continuing application of personal immunity in interstate relations. The resolution of the conflict depended on the interpretation of the effect of the Security Council referral on the application of personal immunity. The ICC has offered conflicting interpretations in this respect.

In a first decision, the Pre-Trial Chamber I argued that the referral entails the applicability of all provisions of the ICC Statute to Sudan, including the immunity exception under Article 27.[667] This interpretation relies on the idea that it is unreasonable to expect that the Security Council sought to exempt heads of states from ICC jurisdiction. It implies that states parties face no conflict as to head of state immunity since this immunity is rendered inapplicable in the relationship between ICC states parties and Sudan through the Chapter VII resolution of the Council which renders Article 27 applicable to Sudan as non-state party.[668] This position has been criticized for misreading the nature of the referral.[669]

In a second decision, the *Malawi/Chad* decision, a different Bench ruled that there is no conflict because the alleged tribunal exception under paragraph 61 of the ICJ *Arrest Warrant* decision has crystallized into customary law, also in the relationship to non-state parties to the ICC.[670] This claim is an over-optimistic reading of customary law that stands in contrast to practice. It would imply that immunities of nationals of non-state parties are inapplicable to the ICC in all circumstances, notably also in the

---

[667] *Prosecutor* v. *Al-Bashir*, ICC-02/05–01/09, Decision on the Prosecution's Application for a Warrant of Arrest against Omar Hassan Ahmad Al-Bashir, 4 March 2009, para. 45 ('by referring the Darfur situation to the Court, Pursuant to Article 13 (b) of the Statute, the Security Council of the United Nations has also accepted that the investigation into the said situation, as well as any prosecution arising therefrom, will take place in accordance with the statutory framework provided for in the Statute, the Elements of Crimes and the Rules as a whole'). For such a reading, see D. Akande, 'The Legal Nature of Security Council Referrals to the ICC and its Impact on Al-Bashir's Immunities' (2009) 7 *JICJ* 342; see also Kreβ, 'The International Criminal Court and Immunities', 240–243.

[668] Akande, 'The Legal Nature of Security Council Referrals', 333. See also *Prosecutor* v. *Al-Bashir*, ICC-02/05–01/09, 3 April 2018, Prosecution Response to the Hashemite Kingdom of Jordan's Appeal against the 'Decision under Article 87 (7) of the Rome Statute on the non-compliance by Jordan with the request by the Court for arrest and surrender [of] Omar Al-Bashir', para. 23.

[669] P. Gaeta, 'Does President Al Bashir Enjoy Immunity from Arrest?' (2009) 7 *JICJ* 324 (a 'referral by the Security Council is simply a mechanism envisaged in the Statute to trigger the jurisdiction of the ICC: it does not and cannot turn a state non-party to the Statute into a state party, and it has not turned Sudan into a state party to the Statute').

[670] *Malawi* Cooperation Decision, para. 43 ('[T]he Chamber finds that customary international law creates an exception to Head of State immunity when international Courts seek a Head of State's arrest for the commission of international crimes').

absence of a Security Council referral. It has been rightly criticized for deviating from customary law.[671]

A third decision deviated from the reasoning of the *Malawi/Chad* ruling. It argued that the Security Council referral contained a waiver of the immunity of Al-Bashir.[672] This argument is problematic.[673] A waiver presupposes that immunity applies in relation to the Court in the first place. Moreover, it must normally be expressly declared.[674] The wording of the Resolution is ambiguous. Some Council members contested the view that the Security Council Resolution would abrogate head of state immunity.[675]

This lack of clarity has made the ICC vulnerable to legal critique. South Africa sought further clarification of the relationship between Article 27 and Article 98 of the Statute.[676] The AU called into question the immunity from ICC prosecution for sitting heads of state and other senior government officials.[677]

When Al-Bashir travelled to South Africa in May 2017 to attend an AU summit, the government failed to arrest him. The dispute over South Africa's obligation to arrest resulted in a fourth decision of the Pre-Trial Chamber, which adopted yet another line of reasoning. The majority rejected the waiver argument. It held that Sudan cannot oppose immunity to the ICC since the Security Council referral placed Sudan in a position 'analogous to those of States Parties to the Statute'.[678] It supported this argument by the fact that the Resolution requires Sudan to cooperate fully' with the court, i.e. as if it were a state party.[679] Sudan is thus formally not a state party, but is

---

[671] For instance, the AU and the Arab League have contested that there is an exception in customary international law for personal immunities of Heads of State. *Al-Bashir* Non Cooperation Decision, Minority Opinion Brichambaut, para 89.

[672] *Prosecutor* v. *Al-Bashir*, ICC-02/05–01/09–195, Decision on the Cooperation of the Democratic Republic of the Congo Regarding Omar Al-Bashir's Arrest and Surrender to the Court, 9 April 2014, para. 29 ('the SC implicitly waived the immunities granted to Omar Al-Bashir under international law and attached to his position as a Head of State').

[673] *Al-Bashir* Non Cooperation Decision, para. 96 ('The majority of the Chamber clarifies that, indeed, it sees no such "waiver" in the Security Council resolution, and that, in any case, no such waiver – whether "explicit" or "implicit" – would be necessary').

[674] ILC, Third Report on Immunity of State Officials from Foreign Criminal Jurisdiction, by Roman Anatolevich Kolodkin, Special Rapporteur, A/CN.4/646, para. 55.

[675] See UN Security Council, 7478th Meeting, 29 June 2015, S/PV.7478. For instance, Russia recalled that, 'in addition to the obligation to cooperate with the ICC, the Statute states that parties to the Statute are bound by obligations arising from international legal norms governing the immunity of high-level officials, particularly Heads of States, of States that, like the Sudan, are not party to the Rome Statute'.

[676] See Request by South Africa for the inclusion of a supplementary item in the agenda of the fourteenth session of the Assembly titled 'Application and Implementation of Article 97 and Article 98 of the Rome Statute', ICC-ASP/14/35, 27 October 2015. In its *Al-Bashir* decision in March 2016, the South African Court was unable to hold that 'there is an international crimes exception to the immunity and inviolability that heads of state enjoy when visiting foreign countries and before foreign national Courts'. It grounded the duty of South Africa to arrest in domestic legislation, namely the South African Implementing Legislation of the ICC Statute. This reasoning limits the effectiveness of the ICC regime, since it makes enforcement dependent on domestic law. Supreme Court of Appeal of South Africa, *The Minister of Justice and Constitutional Development* v *The Southern African Litigation Centre*, Case No. 867/15, 15 March 2016, [2016] ZASCA 17.

[677] Art. 46A *bis* of the Protocol on Amendments to the Protocol on the Statute of the African Court of Justice and Human Rights provides: 'No charges shall be commenced or continued before the court against any serving AU Head of State of Government, or anybody acting or entitled to act in such capacity, or other senior state officials based on their functions, during their tenure of office.' See generally R. Pedretti, *Immunity of Heads of State and State Officials for International Crimes* (Leiden: Brill/Nijhoff, 2015).

[678] *Al-Bashir* Non Cooperation Decision, para. 88. It held that the 'effect of a referral is to enable the Court to act in the referred situation, and to do so under the rules according to which it has been designed to act' (para. 86).

[679] Ibid., para. 87. See also Cryer et al., *Introduction to International Criminal Law and Procedure*, 561.

bound by similar obligations by virtue of the Security Council referral. As the majority put it: 'as a result of Security Council Resolution 1593 (2005), the interactions between Sudan and the Court with respect to the Court's exercise of jurisdiction in the situation in Darfur are regulated by the Statute'.[680] Judge Marc Perrin de Brichambaut challenged this reasoning in his minority opinion. He argued that 'the current state of the law does not allow a definite answer to be reached in relation to the question of whether this resolution removes the immunities of Omar Al Bashir'.[681] He questioned whether 'the referral of the Darfur situation to the Court by the UN Security Council rendered Sudan analogous to a State Party', or removed 'the immunities enjoyed by Omar Al-Bashir as a sitting Head of State'.[682] He argued that immunity was lifted by a crime exception in relation to genocide. He claimed that the 'Genocide Convention implicitly removes the immunities of incumbent "constitutionally responsible rulers"'.[683] This justification takes into account the special nature of the Genocide Convention. However, it raises the curious question whether Al-Bashir would enjoy immunity before the ICC in relation to other crimes, such as crimes against humanity or war crimes.[684]

The justifications offered for discarding immunity have thus differed considerably in the ICC context. The reasoning in the majority of decisions suggests that it is too early to postulate a general 'international court' exception in relation to immunities. Immunities may be rendered inapplicable in three ways: through treaty provisions between parties, Chapter VII resolutions of the Security Council or waivers of immunity. Given the conflicting readings, the treatment of immunities of heads of state is likely to remain a contested issue. The most plausible reading in relation to the Al-Bashir dilemma is that the Security Council referral removed immunity from arrest.[685] The Council should, when referring future situations, place an obligation on all states to cooperate with the Court. In this way, obligation to arrest and surrender would flow from the UN Security Council and would, by virtue of Article 103 of the Charter, trump other obligations.

3.6.3   The Amnesty Dilemma

Amnesties have played an important role in the context of international criminal justice. The turn to global norms and institutions is partly a reaction to amnesty laws

---

[680] *Al-Bashir* Non Cooperation Decision, para. 91. See also *Prosecutor* v. *Al-Bashir*, ICC-02/05–01/09, Decision under Art. 87 (7) of the Rome Statute on the non-compliance by Jordan with the request by the Court for the arrest and surrender or Omar Al-Bashir, 11 December 2017, para. 38.

[681] *Al-Bashir* Non Cooperation Decision, Minority Opinion Brichambaut, para. 83.

[682] Ibid., para. 99.

[683] Ibid., para.101.

[684] See D. Jacobs, 'The ICC's Approach to Immunities and Cooperation', in Stahn, *Law and Practice of the International Criminal Court*, 281, 297–298.

[685] See also E. de Wet, 'Referrals to the International Criminal Court Under Chapter VII of the United Nations Charter and the Immunity of Foreign State Officials' (2018) 112 *AJIL Unbound* 33, 37. See also *Prosecutor* v. *Bashir*, Amicus Curiae Observations of Professors Robinson, Cryer, deGuzman, Lafontaine, Oosterveld, and Stahn, ICC-02/05-01/09-362, 18 June 2018, paras. 2–17.

barring state armed forces and their proxies from prosecution. Amnesties continue to be invoked as policy options in state discourse and transitional justice policies. However, they are regarded with a great deal of suspicion in legal practice. They are seen as an impediment to human rights.[686]

International criminal justice discourses focus predominantly on the clash between amnesties and the duty to investigate and prosecute international crimes.[687] The reality is, however, more complex. The law contains grey areas. In some situations, it is impossible to demand full criminal justice and punishment for all crimes or to realize such an ambition in the immediate aftermath of conflict. Formal criminal investigations and prosecutions must be seen in context with other factors, such as state duties to end conflict, truth recovery or guarantees of non-repetition of violations.[688] The evaluation of amnesties thus depends on the type and context of the measure.

3.6.3.1 Notion and Forms of Amnesty

Technically, amnesties are a bar to investigation and prosecution for certain categories of crimes or individuals. The term is derived from the Greek notion 'amnēstia' which means 'forgetfulness' or 'oblivion'.[689] It associates the idea of amnesty with the aim of removing the traces of crimes. In modern practice, the concept of amnesty covers many different measures, ranging from blanket protection for crimes committed during a specific period of time to more nuanced types of amnesty. They can exist *de jure* or de facto.

The strong legal aversion to amnesty emerged in reaction to dubious amnesties granted after military coups in Latin America (e.g. Argentina, Chile, Uruguay, Guatemala, Nicaragua and Peru).[690] These amnesties were largely condemned, modified or set aside by courts years after their passing, in an effort to counter impunity.[691] A paradigmatic passage is the strong statement by the Inter-American Court of Human Rights in *Barrios Altos*:

---

[686] See M. Freeman, *Necessary Evils: Amnesties and the Search for Justice* (Cambridge: Cambridge University Press, 2009), 1.

[687] See A. O'Shea, *Amnesty for Crime in International Law and Practice* (Hague: Kluwer Law International, 2002), D. Orentlicher, 'Settling Accounts: The Duty to Prosecute Human Rights Violations of a Prior Regime' (1991) 100 *Yale Law Journal* 2537, 2548–254.

[688] See T. Hadden, 'Transitional Justice and Amnesties', in Lawther, Moffett and Jacobs, *Research Handbook on Transitional Justice*, 358.

[689] N. Weisman, 'A History and Discussion of Amnesty' (1972) 4 *Columbia Human Rights Law* 520, 529.

[690] See generally D. Cassel, 'Lessons from the Americas: Guidelines for International Response to Amnesties for Atrocities' (1996) 59 *Law and Contemporary Problems* 197.

[691] In 1992, the Inter-American Commission on Human Rights found the amnesties in Argentina and Uruguay were incompatible with the American Convention. See *Alicia Consuelo Herrera et al. v. Argentina; Santos Mendoza et al. v. Uruguay*, cases 10.029, 10.036, 10.145, 10.305, 10.372, 10.373, 10.374, 10.375, Report No. 29/92, 2 October 1992. See also *Garay Hermosilla et al. v. Chile*, case 10.843, Report No. 36/96, 15 October 1996; *Irma Reyes et al. v. Chile*, cases 11.228 et al., Report No. 34/96, 15 October 1996; *Catalán Lincoleo v. Chile*, case 11.771, Report No. 61/01, 16 April 2001; *Las Hojas Massacre Case v. El Salvador*, case 10.287, Report No. 26/92, 24 September 1992; *Ignacio Ellacuría et al. v. El Salvador*, case 10.488, Report No. 136/99, 22 December 1999.

Self-amnesty laws leave victims defenceless and perpetuate impunity and are therefore clearly incompatible with the letter and spirit of the American Convention. These kinds of laws prevent identification of the individuals responsible for human rights violations because they block investigation and access to justice and prevent the victims and their relatives from knowing the truth and receiving appropriate reparation.[692]

However, contemporary practice is more nuanced. Amnesties are a frequent tool of conflict resolution. For instance, the Truth and Reconciliation Commission for Sierra Leone claimed in its Final Report that the RUF would not have signed the Lomé Peace agreement if there had been no option of amnesty or pardon.[693] It stated:

> those who argue that peace cannot be bartered in exchange for justice, under any circumstances, must be prepared to justify the likely prolongation of an armed conflict. Amnesties may be undesirable in many cases … However, amnesties should not be excluded entirely from the mechanisms available to those attempting to negotiate a cessation of hostilities after periods of brutal armed conflict. Disallowing amnesty in all cases would be to deny the reality of violent conflict and the urgent need to bring such strife and suffering to an end.[694]

Amnesties may be seen as an option to pacify conflict or deal with the sheer impossibility of a full criminal justice response. Amnesties can serve as incentives for truth-seeking or accountability.[695] Some use the term 'smart amnesties' to captures measures that are 'designed to facilitate a peaceful transition and reconciliation', while satisfying 'legitimate demands' for 'truth', 'responsibility and repentance'.[696]

Amnesties can be limited to specific events, individuals, types of crimes or organizations, or can be narrowed down in the context of their application. They may be individualized or tied to certain conditions,[697] such as disarmament, acknowledgment of crimes, apology, commitments not to resume violence, community service or reparation to victims. Such conditions are frequently used to balance the duty to investigate and prosecute with conflicting rationales in conflict and post-conflict settings, such as the need to end hostilities, facilitate truth recovery or ensure the non-recurrence of violations. Some forms of amnesties are thus not geared at 'forgetting', but aimed at providing truth recovery or ensuring some form of accountability. They may look towards the future, rather than the past.

---

[692] IACtHR, *Case of Barrios Altos (Chumbipuma Aguirre and others* v. *Peru)*, Judgment, Series C, No. 75, 14 March 2001, para. 41.

[693] Report of the Sierra Leone Truth and Reconciliation Commission, *Witness to Truth* (2004), Vol. 3 B, Chapter 6, para. 10.

[694] Ibid., para. 11.

[695] L. Mallinder, *Amnesty, Human Rights and Political Transitions: Bridging the Peace and Justice Divide* (Oxford: Hart Publishing, 2008).

[696] See A. Kushleyko, 'Accountability v. "Smart Amnesty" in the Transitional Post-conflict Quest for Peace', in N. Szablewska and S.-D. Bachmann (eds.), *Current Issues in Transitional Justice: Towards a More Holistic Approach* (Berlin: Springer, 2014), 31, 34–35.

[697] R. C. Slye, 'The Legitimacy of Amnesties under International Law and General Principles of Anglo-American Law: Is a Legitimate Amnesty Possible?' (2002) 43 *Virginia Journal of International Law* 173, 245–246.

3.6.3.2 *Legal Treatment*

The question to what extent amnesties are prohibited under international law requires nuanced consideration.[698] Not all amnesties are evil. Some of them may have positive and negative effects, or complement other accountability mechanisms. Amnesties that are part of a comprehensive peace settlement, or are adopted in a democratic process, may enjoy a significant degree of political legitimacy. There is virtue in complementing retributive and restorative approaches. As rightly cautioned by Kai Ambos, it is unhelpful to overestimate 'the restorative effect of amnesty and forgiveness' or to underestimate 'the reconciling power of (criminal) justice'.[699]

As to the legal implications, two dimensions need to be distinguished: Whether an entity may enact amnesties under international law (e.g. as part of a peace deal), and to what extent such a measure may bar investigation and prosecution by international criminal courts and tribunals and/or third states.

The first question is governed by general international law. There is no international treaty that explicitly prohibits the granting of amnesty. Amnesty clauses have been included in peace treaties for centuries. Article 6, paragraph 5 of Additional Protocol II to the Geneva Conventions states that '[a]t the end of hostilities, the authorities in power shall endeavour to grant the broadest possible amnesty to persons who have participated in the armed conflict, or those deprived of their liberty for reasons related to the armed conflict'.[700] It allows states, for instance, to grant rebels amnesty for certain acts of warfare, such as killing members of the opposing forces, if they do not amount to war crimes.[701] The ICC Statute does not preclude amnesties as such.[702] Certain forms of amnesties may be 'necessary evils' to ensure short-term peace. Amnesties may be granted for humanitarian reasons, for example to demobilize and reintegrate combatants into their communities or to release prisoners of war and civilian detainees from detention. For instance, in Uganda more than 26,000 fighters have benefited from amnesties.

At the same time, it is widely acknowledged that granting amnesties conflicts with the duty to investigate and prosecute international crimes, such as grave breaches of Geneva Conventions, genocide, torture or enforced disappearances. The United Nations has adopted the policy that 'United Nations officials, including peace negotiators and field office staff, must never encourage or condone amnesties that prevent

---

[698] See e.g. L. Mallinder, 'Amnesties' Challenge to the Global Accountability Norm? Interpreting Regional and International Trends in Amnesty Enactment', in F. Lessa and L. A. Payne, *Amnesty in the Age of Human Rights Accountability: Comparative and International Perspectives* (Cambridge: Cambridge University Press, 2012).

[699] K. Ambos, 'The Legal Framework of Transitional Justice: A Systematic Study with a Special Focus on the Role of the ICC', in K. Ambos et al. (eds.), *Building a Future on Peace and Justice: Studies on Transitional Justice, Peace and Development* (Berlin: Springer, 2009), 19, 26.

[700] The provision applies in non-international armed conflict. It is therefore compatible with the duty to prosecute grave breaches of the Geneva Conventions.

[701] The ICRC reads it as not covering war crimes. See Rule 159 of the Customary Law Study.

[702] See generally, C. Stahn, 'Complementarity, Amnesties and Alternative Forms of Justice: Some Interpretative Guidelines for the International Criminal Court' (2005) 3 *JICJ* 695.

prosecution of those responsible for serious crimes under international law'.[703] However, legal practice is more differentiated.

Several international courts have found that amnesties are inadmissible when they are intended to prevent the investigation and punishment of international crimes. For instance, the Grand Chamber of European Court of Human Rights found in *Marguš* v. *Croatia* that there is '[a] growing tendency in international law to see such amnesties as unacceptable because they are incompatible with the unanimously recognized obligation of States to prosecute and punish grave breaches of fundamental human rights'.[704] Blanket amnesties which absolve individuals of responsibility for genocide, war crimes and crimes against humanity are not permissible under international law. Legal practice from bodies such as the American Court of Human Rights suggests that amnesties should not be granted to persons who have committed grave violations of human rights and international humanitarian law, even beyond 'self-amnesties'.[705] In the *Kwoyelo* case, the Ugandan Supreme Court found that international crimes were not covered by the terms of the Ugandan Amnesty Act, since they did not constitute acts 'in furtherance of rebellion or in the cause of the war'. As Chief Justice Bart Katureebe explained:

> Whereas one may understand civilians being killed in cross-fire or when cities are bombed by aircraft or artillery, as being deaths while one is carrying out acts in furtherance of the war, it is difficult to see how acts of genocide against a given population, or the willful killing of innocent civilians in their homes when there is no military necessity, can be regarded as being in furtherance of the war or rebellion.[706]

Courts have been reluctant to accept an absolute ban on amnesties. When examining the Lomé Peace Agreement, the Special Court for Sierra Leone conceded that 'Sierra Leone may not have breached customary law in granting an amnesty'.[707] The ECCC adopted a similar approach. It noted that 'state practice in relation to other serious international crimes [not prohibited by treaty] is insufficiently uniform to establish an absolute prohibition in relation to them'.[708] Certain national Supreme Courts have upheld amnesty laws because they contribute to the achievement of peace, democracy

---

[703] OHCHR, *Rule of Law Tools for Post-Conflict States: Amnesties* (New York and Geneva: United Nations, 2009), 27.

[704] ECtHR, *Marguš* v. *Croatia*, Appl. No. 4455/10, Judgment, 27 May 2014, para. 139.

[705] IACtHR, *Barrios Altos* v. *Peru*, para. 41; *Case of Gelman* v. *Uruguay*, Judgment, 24 February 2011, para. 229 and 225 ('amnesty provisions, the statute of limitation provisions, and the establishment of exclusions of responsibility that are intended to prevent the investigation and punish those responsible for serious violations to human rights such as torture, summary, extrajudicial, or arbitrary executions, and enforced disappearance are not admissible, all of which are prohibited for contravening irrevocable rights recognized by International Law of Human Rights'). For internal armed conflict, see *Cases of the Massacres of El Mozote and Nearby Places* v. *El Salvador*, Judgment, 25 October 2012, paras. 284–286.

[706] Supreme Court, *Uganda* v. *Thomas Kwoyelo*, Constitutional Appeal No. 01 of 2012, 8 April 2015, 41.

[707] *Prosecutor* v. *Kallon & Kamara*, SCSL-2004–15-AR72(E), SCSL-2004–16-AR72(E), Decision on Challenge to Jurisdiction: Lomé Accord Amnesty, 13 March 2004, para. 84 (*Kallon & Kamara* Amnesty Decision).

[708] *Prosecutor* v. *Nuon Chea et al.*, 002/19–09–2007-ECCC/TC, Decision on Ieng Sary's Rule 89 Preliminary Objections (*Ne Bis In Idem* and Amnesty and Pardon), 3 November 2011, para. 53 (*Nuon Chea* Amnesty Decision).

and reconciliation.[709] The European Court of Human Rights left it open whether it could 'be accepted that amnesties are possible where there are some particular circumstances, such as a reconciliation process and/or a form of compensation to the victims'.[710] As rightly pointed out by Tom Hadden, 'prosecuting authorities must have some discretion to decide how to prioritize their resources' and to ensure that duties can 'in practice be complied with'.[711] Practice suggests that conditional amnesties 'have generally not been invalidated'.[712] They must rather be assessed 'on a case by-case basis, depending on a number of factors, including the process by which the amnesty was enacted, the substance and scope of the amnesty, and whether it provided for any alternative form of accountability'.[713] It is difficult to argue that victims have an absolute right to punishment. In contexts of transition, certain forms of amnesties, adopted by legitimate democratic institutions, might be permissible for specific categories of crimes, if they are subject to conditions, i.e. procedures that include the option of criminal punishment, and provide for alternative sanctions (e.g. suspended sentences, alternative sentences). Some useful policy suggestions are offered by the Belfast Guidelines on Amnesty and Accountability.[714]

The second question concerns the effect of amnesties. Tribunals, such as the SCSL or the ECCC, have made it clear that if an amnesty is granted, it does not affect the exercise of international jurisdiction over individual perpetrators. Thus it may not be applicable to other jurisdictions.

The rationale behind this argument has been formulated by the Special Court for Sierra Leone:

Where jurisdiction is universal, a State cannot deprive another State of its jurisdiction to prosecute the offender by the grant of amnesty. It is for this reason unrealistic to regard as universally effective the grant of amnesty by a State in regard to grave international crimes in which there exists universal jurisdiction. A State cannot bring into oblivion and forgetfulness a crime, such as a crime against international law, which other States are entitled to keep alive and remember.[715]

International criminal courts and tribunals remain entitled to assess and ignore amnesties in relation to individual persons that are investigated or prosecuted for core crimes.[716] Whether such investigations or prosecutions are carried out, however, remains a matter of prosecutorial discretion.

---

[709] For instance, in the AZAPO case, the South African Constitutional Court acknowledged that granting of amnesty is necessary to achieve reconciliation and democratic transition. See *Azanian People's Organisation and Others v. President of the Republic of South Africa and Others*, Case CCT 17/96, Judgment, 27 July 1996, para. 22 (noting that the 'principle that amnesty should, in appropriate circumstances, be accorded to violators of human rights in order to facilitate the consolidation of new democracies was accepted' in other historical contexts).

[710] *Marguš* v. *Croatia*, para. 139.

[711] Hadden, 'Transitional Justice and Amnesties', 370.

[712] *Nuon Chea* Amnesty Decision, para. 52.

[713] Ibid., para. 52.

[714] *Belfast Guidelines on Amnesty and Accountability* (Ulster: Transitional Justice Institute, 2013).

[715] *Kallon & Kamara* Amnesty Decision, para. 67.

[716] The SCSL did not feel bound by the amnesty in Lomé Accord. Similarly, the ECCC found that the 1996 Royal Decree in Cambodia did not constitute an impediment to the exercise of jurisdiction over core crimes. See *Nuon Chea* Amnesty

The ICC Statute allows the Prosecutor not to proceed if criminal action is not in the interests of justice. The ICC Office of the Prosecutor has given a narrow meaning to this clause. It found that there is a 'strong presumption' that 'investigations and prosecutions will be in the interests of justice', and that the interests of justice provision should not be considered as a conflict management tool requiring the Prosecutor to assume the role of a mediator in political negotiations.[717] However, the Prosecution retains wide discretion to determine the timing and scope of justice intervention. It decides when to bring charges, whom to indict, and how to sequence cases. It can thus mitigate conflicts between peace and justice, or leave space for alternative approaches to justice. International criminal courts and tribunals should thus not too easily be presented as an obstacle to peace.

An innovative alternative approach to amnesties was adopted by Colombia. It ruled out amnesty for international crimes but allowed alternative sentences or forms of punishment. The Justice and Peace Law, aimed at demobilizing paramilitary forces, provided room to replace ordinary sentences by alternative sentences, carrying a maximum of eight years of imprisonment, in case of confession of crimes. It relied fully on the judiciary to carry out prosecution and sentencing. This approach facilitated prosecution of some mid- and lower-level paramilitaries, but was criticized for its slowness and failure to promote prosecution of paramilitary leaders.[718] The Comprehensive System for Truth, Justice, Reparation and Non-Repetition, negotiated in the peace talks with the Revolutionary Armed Forces of Colombia (FARC), led to the creation of a Special Jurisdiction for Peace which is designed to target those who are considered to be the most responsible. It foresees sentences of up to eight years, in case of confession of crimes, as well as special modalities to serve sentences (i.e. alternatives to prison), depending on the truth provided (i.e. confession at a preliminary stage), the gravity of conduct, the degree of responsibility and commitment to reparations and non-recurrence. Alternative sanctions include participation in community projects, such as construction work, agricultural projects, removal of explosives). Reduced prison terms may be awarded to persons who belatedly confess crimes.

The Inter-American Court of Human Rights did not fully rule out an approach entailing suspended sentences and softer punishments. The hard question is when a reduction of punishment may turn into an impermissible form of impunity. This assessment is more closely related to the rationales of punishment. The Court determined a number of conditions in the *La Rochela* case. It held:

the punishment which the State assigns to the perpetrator of illicit conduct should be proportional to the rights recognized by law and the culpability with which the perpetrator acted, which in turn should be established as a function of the nature and gravity of the events. The

---

Decision, para. 55 and 54 (noting that '[w]hile the 1996 amnesty may have been a useful negotiation tool in ending the conflict, ... it was unaccompanied by any truth or reconciliation process').

[717] OTP Policy Paper on the Interests of Justice, September 2017, 1, 8.

[718] D. Acosta Arcarazo, R. J. Buchan and R. Ureña, 'Beyond Justice, Beyond Peace? Colombia, the Interests of Justice, and the Limits of International Criminal Law' (2015) 26 *Criminal Law Forum* 291, 295–299.

punishment should be the result of a judgment issued by a judicial authority. Moreover, in identifying the appropriate punishment, the reasons for the punishment should be determined ... Every element which determines the severity of the punishment should correspond to a clearly identifiable objective and be compatible with the Convention.[719]

A rationale, such as promoting disarmament and a negotiated peace process after conflict might constitute a legitimate rationale within the meaning of the Convention.

Such an approach has been defended by Judge Diego Garcia-Sayán in his concurring opinion in the *El Mozote* case. He has argued that in certain transitional contexts (e.g. a negotiated peace process in internal armed conflict), states are unable to comply with all of their obligations and 'must weigh the effect of criminal justice both on the rights of the victims and on the need to end the conflict'.[720] He admitted that

in the difficult exercise of weighing and the complex search for this equilibrium, routes towards alternative or suspended sentences could be designed and implemented; but, without losing sight of the fact that this may vary substantially according to both the degree of responsibility for serious crimes and the extent to which responsibility is acknowledged and information is provided about what happened. This may give rise to important differences between the 'perpetrators' and those who performed functions of high command and gave the orders.[721]

The law is thus not black or white. It contains grey areas in relation to the absolute prohibition of amnesties for international crimes and the appropriate form of punishment. This flexibility is not a weakness, but a strength. It is necessary to reconcile the demand for justice under some circumstances with conflicting prerogatives. The move towards reduced sentences or alternative sanctions, with differing levels of restrictions upon liberty, supervision and obligations, marks a useful departure from the traditional binary between amnesty and classical criminal justice. The question as to whether reduced sentences are found to be compatible with Rome Statute principles by the ICC depends 'upon the particular circumstances of the case' and the approach towards punishment rationales.[722]

3.6.3.3 Pardons

Pardons are more difficult to judge than amnesties. They are not formal impediments to criminal justice. They are not meant to prevent the investigation and prosecution of international crimes as such, within the meaning of the *Barrios Altos* jurisprudence. Pardons are typically granted after criminal proceedings and may follow a partial enforcement of a sentence. They thus relate more directly to the issue of the propor-

---

[719] See IACtHR, *Case of the Rochela Massacre* v. *Colombia*, Judgment, 11 May 2007, para. 196.
[720] IACtHR, *The Massacres of El Mozote and Nearby Places* v. *El Salvador*, Concurring Opinion of Judge Diego Garcia-Sayán, para. 27.
[721] Ibid., para. 30.
[722] For a list of criteria, see remarks of ICC Deputy Prosecutor J. Stewart, 'Transitional Justice in Colombia and the Role of the International Criminal Court', 13 May 2015, 11–12, at www.icc-cpi.int/iccdocs/otp/otp-stat-13-05-2015-eng.pdf.

tionality of punishment. They become critical when they are 'voiding the effects of a conviction'.[723]

Central and South America has witnessed a wave of controversial pardons over past decades, involving state officials, such as former Peruvian President Fujimori. Their assessment depends on the individual circumstances under which they were granted. Some guidance may be derived from factors justifying early release after conviction.[724] In many legal systems, it is accepted that punishment may be attenuated or reduced after a period of term served, based on criteria such as the conduct of defendants, the acceptance of culpability or on humanitarian grounds. In particular, 'humanitarian pardons' (e.g. medical grounds) may not be irreconcilable with the purposes of punishment, since imprisonment may be particularly harsh in case of illness or age. For instance, the UN High Commissioner for Human Rights has argued that, in certain situations 'there may be little justification for many older persons' continued incarceration in the prison system ... Instead, alternative forms of punishment may be preferable'.[725] However, in the context of international crimes, such grounds must be reconciled with the special nature of international crimes, expressivist purposes of punishment and their impact on victims. Based on the practice of international criminal courts and tribunals, substantial enforcement of the sentence is a key factor. As noted in doctrine: 'A pardon for an individual that has served 2/3 of his sentence is more likely to be accepted than one for someone who has only served 1/3'.[726]

3.7   Merits and Critiques

The turn to global justice institutions has been shaped by the tension between idealism and realpolitik.[727] For more than a century, individuals and civil society networks have pushed for thicker accountability structures and a global criminal court. International criminal courts and tribunals were for a long time at the centre of discourse. This vision is gradually changing. It has become clear that accountability requires more multifaceted and pluralist structures.

Some of the 'dark sides' of the turn to international norms and institutions have become apparent. Experiences with international and hybrid justice have shown that international mechanisms cannot be isolated from politics, or even suffer from a lack of political savviness. Mandates have expanded. This has opened international criminal courts and tribunals to broader socio-legal and justice critiques. The link to

---

[723] IACtHR, *Case of Gutiérrez-Soler* v. *Colombia*, Judgment, 12 September 2005, para. 97.

[724] See Section 5.1.6.

[725] See Report of the United Nations High Commissioner for Human Rights, E/2012/51, 20 April 2012, para. 61.

[726] See A. Gurmendi Dunkelberg, 'The Legality of Pardons in Latin America (Part II)', at http://opiniojuris.org/2017/11/17/the-legality-of-pardons-in-latin-america-part-ii/.

[727] See generally C. Tomuschat, *Human Rights: Between Idealism and Realism* (Oxford: Oxford University Press, 2014); S. Bibas and W. Burke-White, 'When Idealism Meets Domestic-Criminal-Procedure Realism' (2010) 59 *Duke Law Journal* 637.

international peace and security has remained fragile. The international community has been good at creating new treaties and new institutions, but less successful in relating universalist approaches to local contexts. It has become apparent that the relinquishment of jurisdiction to international institutions may create human rights vacuums or equality dilemmas for individuals. Funding has remained a constant dilemma.

Many of the effects of international criminal courts and tribunals have turned out to be more complex and diffuse than anticipated. International criminal law is meant to serve as a constraint on state power. In many areas, however, states seek to maintain their authority or retain a degree of flexibility to address conflicting obligations. Paradigm examples are the critiques relating to complementarity in the ICC context or unsettled debates on the law of immunities, the permissible scope of amnesties or the transnational application of the *ne bis in idem* principle. The ICC has been successful in contexts where it operated with the support of governments. It has struggled to pursue cases challenging the authority of recalcitrant regimes (e.g. Sudan, Kenya).

In many instances, the importance of international criminal courts and tribunals lies not only in the production of certain judicial outcomes (i.e. cases, trials, reparation), but in the transformation of certain normative discourses, the creation of common discursive spaces or the initiation of longer-term processes. A key challenge is to inquire more deeply into what justice goals matter for local communities.

Some of the resulting tensions cannot be entirely solved. For instance, a certain degree of selectivity is inherent and unavoidable in a system that deals with investigation and prosecution of system criminality, and defines itself partly through the expression of legal and moral blame and the reaffirmation of global norms. As Gerry Simpson notes: 'each war crimes trial is an exercise in partial justice to the extent that it reminds that the majority of war crimes go unpunished'.[728] Even a perfectly run trial may fail to reconcile tensions among victim groups, since the perception of reality by these groups is heavily shaped by certain emotional or rational factors (e.g. prior attitudes, beliefs, narratives) that impede engagement with other views.[729] However, the negative side effects that arise from these tensions have to be handled more constructively. This requires greater sensitivity to the forms of power and dependencies created through the turn to global criminal institutions, a better grounding of their knowledge and expertise, openness to challenge, and greater sustainability.

Over past decades, the institutional landscape has become more diverse, decentralized and pluralist. Quasi- or non-judicial bodies have gained greater weight. Crimes are increasingly documented by quasi-judicial or even private bodies. International criminal jurisdiction is no longer a counter-model, but increasingly connected to

---

[728] See G. Simpson, 'War Crimes: A Critical Introduction', in T. McCormack and G. Simpson (eds.), *The Law of War Crimes: National and International Approaches* (The Hague: Kluwer, 1997), 1, 8.

[729] On the ICTY, see Milanović, *The Impact of the ICTY on the Former Yugoslavia*, 233.

domestic justice. The model of the ad hoc tribunals has enjoyed waning support. The 'hybrid' emerged as a new form to accommodate justice politics and the shortcomings of international jurisdiction. New regional approaches are emerging. This diversity is both an asset and a challenge from a systemic perspective. It is necessary to determine more thoroughly in what areas dialogue, coordination or consistency is desirable. For example, quasi- or non-judicial bodies should not try to emulate international criminal justice mechanisms. Hybrid or regional courts may bring nuances that global institutions lack.

One of the downsides of the rise of global institutions is that national justice efforts (e.g. universal jurisdiction cases, civil claims) or other accountability mechanisms (e.g. commissions of inquiry) often remain in the 'shadow' of international responses. They are easily perceived as a precursor to an international mechanism or as a follow-up to their activities. This 'shadow' has some positive effects. It may strengthen the leverage of domestic courts, fact-finding bodies or quasi-judicial mechanisms. However, it also has some negative implications. It focuses attention on atrocities and situations that are under international scrutiny, and sidelines frozen, long-standing or forgotten conflicts or less spectacular forms of everyday violence. A more universalist account requires emancipation from the shadow idea.

In justice policies, international criminal justice is too often seen as a quick fix for accountability dilemmas. This vision is misleading. Much of the groundwork needs to done before courts emerge, or after they have left. Legal responses need to be better connected to diplomacy, development or long-term prevention strategies.

4

International Criminal Justice Procedures

The turn to procedures is a rather recent phenomenon. Hans Kelsen argued in 1944 that the '[i]nternationalisation of the legal procedure against war criminals would have the great advantage of making the punishment, to a certain extent, uniform'.[1] For a long time, procedural issues have remained in the shadow of international criminal justice.[2] States placed greater emphasis on the definition of jurisdiction and substantive law than on procedure. The discourse about international criminal justice was largely focused on outcomes, such as punishment or impunity. The success of international criminal justice as a project was tied to these deliverables. Procedure was essentially seen as a means to an end, rather than an end in itself. This limited functional understanding only changed gradually.

Today, it is more widely accepted that procedures are more than a set of technical legal issues.

Modern theorists claim that the justification of international criminal justice does not emanate solely from the authority underlying its creation, but from the central function of proceedings.[3] Functionality is understood in a broader way. International criminal law is partly about norm affirmation. From this perspective, the value of procedures lies not only in outcomes. Procedures are rather part of a process of reshaping societal reality and expressing normative values.[4] To some extent, they allow international justice agents to constitute themselves as a 'moral community'.[5]

This broader vision raises difficult questions about the relationship between criminal procedure and justice. There are competing views. In international criminal law and transitional justice discourse, it is increasingly recognized that the value of

---

[1] Hans Kelsen, *Peace Through Law* (Chapel Hill: The University of North Carolina Press, 1944), 112.

[2] G. S. Gordon, 'Toward an International Criminal Procedure' (2007) 45 *Columbia Journal of Transnational Law* 635, 637.

[3] As David Luban has argued: 'the legitimacy of international tribunals comes not from the shaky political authority that creates them, but from the manifested fairness of their procedures and punishments'. See D. Luban, 'Fairness to Rightness: Jurisdiction, Legality, and the Legitimacy of International Criminal Law', in S. Besson and J. Tasioulas (eds.), *The Philosophy of International Law* (Cambridge: Cambridge University Press, 2010), 569. See also M. Damaska, 'Reflections on Fairness in International Criminal Justice' (2012) 10 *JICJ* 611.

[4] A. Duff, *Trials and Punishment* (Cambridge: Cambridge University Press, 1991), 35.

[5] See F. Mégret, 'In Defense of Hybridity: Towards a Representational Theory of International Criminal Justice' (2005) 38 *Cornell International Law Review*, 725, 742–743.

procedures derives from certain intrinsic qualities of the legal process.[6] International criminal courts and tribunals often define their identity or conception of justice by reference to procedural concepts, such as access to justice, fairness, effectiveness or inclusiveness of procedures. They feature prominently in performance indicators.[7] Supporters of restorative justice view international criminal proceedings more broadly as part and parcel of transitional justice.

Critics of international criminal justice challenge this vision of procedural justice. They point to the weaknesses of the formal nature of law and the binary effects of criminal procedure:

> The logic of a court trial is zero sum: you are either innocent or guilty. This kind of logic ill fits the context of a civil war. Victims and perpetrators in civil wars often trade places in ongoing cycles of violence. No one is wholly innocent and none wholly guilty. Each side has a narrative of victimhood. Victims' justice is the flip side of victors' justice: both demonize the other side and exclude it from participation in the new political order.[8]

A legal process thus remains an unsatisfactory answer to atrocity crimes. Sceptics question the broader socio-pedagogical functions of criminal proceedings or highlight their risks. They argue that international criminal proceedings may easily be perceived as a 'show trial',[9] an undue assertion of authority or power, or as an instrument to reduce justice to law.

4.1   Hybridization of International Criminal Procedure

International criminal procedure is strongly influenced by Western liberal traditions. It is marked by conflicting ideas of liberty. International criminality focuses on human wrongdoing. States are under a duty to investigate and prosecute crimes and provide access to justice. This may require the restriction of individual rights for the purpose of maintaining public order and safety. At the same time, due process requires that individual cannot be deprived of life, liberty or property without appropriate legal procedures and safeguards. These considerations are often in conflict with each other. The criminal process typically involves authoritative elements, since it pits state or broader public interests against the interests of defendants. But it also requires defence of fairness and the individual rights of persons.

---

[6] See J. D. Ohlin, 'Meta-Theory of International Criminal Procedure: Vindicating the Rule of Law' (2009) 14 *UCLA Journal of International Law & Foreign Affairs* 77.

[7] See B. Kotecha, 'The ICC's Office of the Prosecutor and the Limits of Performance Indicators' (2017) 15 *JICJ* 543.

[8] M. Mamdani ,'Beyond Nuremberg: The Historical Significance of the Post-apartheid Transition in South Africa' (2015) 43 *Politics & Society* 61, 80.

[9] A show trial is more focused on the audience rather than the defendant. See generally Koskenniemi, 'Between Impunity and Show Trials', 1; J. Peterson, 'Unpacking Show Trials: Situating the Trial of Saddam Hussein' (2007) 48 *Harvard International Law Journal* 257, 260–269. As Mark Osiel has argued, '[w]hether show trials are defensible depends on what the state intends to show and how it will show it'. See Osiel, *Mass Atrocity, Collective Memory and the Law*, 65.

Structurally, it is important to distinguish the functions of the respective institution from the objectives of specific proceedings. International criminal justice pursues certain macro-objectives, such as retribution (i.e. prosecution and punishment), deterrence, prevention, elucidation of facts, justice for victims or strengthening of domestic jurisdiction. They are optimization commands. Procedures are related to these goals, but they have a more determinate function. They typically give effect to rights, or pursue specific rationales, such as determining guilt or innocence or revealing a 'legal', rather than a broader 'historical truth'.[10] The choice of the type of procedure depends on weighing of macro-goals. For instance, a fair, effective and expeditious trial is necessary to solve a dispute between the parties and inflict 'just deserts' on the defendant. Accurate fact-finding is essential for broader policy rationales, such as crime control, satisfaction to victims or contribution to historical record.

Domestic cultures vary.[11] As Mirjan Damaška has shown in his seminal analysis of criminal justice systems (*Faces of Justice*), there are certain archetypes.[12] In adversarial systems, the legal process is conceived as a contest. It is based on the idea that truths emerge best through the free confrontation of subjective points of view. In inquisitorial systems, the process is more like an inquest. It places greater trust in the assessment of facts by an objective external party. Both systems foresee different roles for judges, prosecutors and defendants. In the adversarial system, the parties dominate the proceedings, from the initiation of proceedings to their termination. They control the evidence. The main aim of proceedings is to decide a conflict between two parties. The judge is an umpire or adjudicator who listens to the arguments and evidence of the parties.

In inquisitorial systems, the collection of evidence is not entirely in the hands of the parties. Judges are more actively seeking the truth in cooperation with the parties. The record may form part of a dossier. The judge controls the trial, may order evidence to be produced, interrogate the accused and witnesses, or become involved in the gathering of evidence[13] The trial is not a 'zero sum' game. The Prosecution is allowed to appeal acquittals.

The two archetypes are abstractions. Each tradition is more complex than its constituent norms, and highly dependent on institutional understandings and social contexts. The pursuit of the traditional goals of criminal justice does not 'provide compelling reasons to prefer either a contest model or an inquest model of the legal proceedings'.[14] Many modern systems contain variations of the two archetypes or

---

[10] On the relationship between law and history, see Wilson, *Writing History in International Trials*, 6–10.

[11] F. Orie, 'Accusatorial v. Inquisitorial Approach in International Criminal Proceedings', in Cassese, Gaeta and Jones, *Rome Statute of the International Criminal Court*, 1439–1497; M. Delmas Marty and J. Spencer (eds.), *European Criminal Procedures* (Cambridge: Cambridge University Press, 2005).

[12] M. Damaška, *The Faces of Justice and State Authority: A Comparative Approach to the Legal Process* (New Haven: Yale University Press, 1986).

[13] M. Langer, 'The Rise of Managerial Judging in International Criminal Law' (2005) 53 *American Journal of Comparative Law* 835.

[14] B. Swart, 'Damaška and the Faces of International Criminal Justice' (2008) 6 *JICJ* 88.

multiple hybrid features.[15] Domestic codes are not necessarily adjusted to the needs of mass atrocity cases.[16]

The procedure of international criminal courts and tribunals continues to be marked by certain clashes between the two traditions. It is in many ways shaped by its own distinct features and policy considerations.[17] International procedures are characterized by a strong focus on transparency, advocacy and certain restorative elements. The existing landscape is characterized by diversity. There is no single set of rules applicable to all international criminal proceedings. Due to the diversity of sources, the divergent definition of the roles of actors (e.g. Prosecution, Judges, victims) in proceedings and the specificities of each procedural regime, there are only a few general principles (i.e. presumption of innocence, independence and impartiality of proceedings, requirement of fairness and expeditiousness). The rules depend to a large degree on choices with regard to the type of process that ought to be applied in the adjudication. There is a 'lex fori' rule. Each international court or tribunal has its own rules of procedure and evidence.[18]

Overall, there is a strong trend towards the hybridization of procedures. Domestic archetypes are adapted. International criminal courts and tribunals seek to learn lessons from other institutions. This process has led to rethinking of the role of actors in the justice process, and many procedural innovations. However, it also carries risks. The success of hybridization depends to a large extent on the role of individuals and institutional cultures within institutions, rather than the law itself. It may create types of procedural pluriformity that come at the expense of fairness and equal treatment of defendants.

4.2   Developments and Trends

International criminal courts and tribunals have been a laboratory for procedural experimentation. Procedural frameworks have developed incrementally. After World War II, few standards were formalized. International criminal proceedings were a novelty that differed essentially from interstate disputes. A traditional weakness has

---

[15] As Damaška argued, 'the venerable frontier between Anglo-American and Continental European criminal procedures has become increasingly ill-marked, open and transgressed'. See M. Damaška, 'Negotiated Justice in International Criminal Courts' (2004) 2 *JICJ* 1018, 1019.

[16] For example, the first trials under the German Code of International Crimes have shown that even well-established legal systems may face challenges in holding domestic trials. European Centre for Constitutional and Human Rights, *Weltrecht in Deutschland? Der Kongo-Kriegsverbrecherprozess: Erstes Verfahren nach dem Völkerstrafgesetzbuch* (Berlin: ECCHR, 2016).

[17] Damaška, 'What is the Point of International Criminal Justice?', 329. As Antonio Cassese put it, 'the philosophy behind international trials is markedly at variance with that underpinning each of those national systems'. See A. Cassese, 'Black Letter Lawyering v. Constructive Interpretation' (2004) 2 *JICJ* 265.

[18] V. Nerlich, 'Daring Diversity: Why There Is Nothing Wrong with "Fragmentation" in International Criminal Procedures' (2013) 26 *LJIL* 777. Protection of witnesses and assessment of the credibility of witnesses are two areas where domestic criminal justice systems may benefit from the experience of international criminal courts and tribunals. See Sluiter, *International Criminal Adjudication and the Collection of Evidence*, 484.

been the 'dramatic disparity between the circumstances of the accusers and of the accused'.[19] Fair trials guarantees were seen as necessary in order not to compromise the integrity of proceedings. In particular, Justice Jackson insisted on the idea of fair trials, rather than public 'show trials'. At Nuremberg, he famously grounded protection of fair trial rights in self-interest: 'To pass these defendants a poisoned chalice is to put it to our own lips as well'.[20]

Defendants were presumed innocent and had a genuine opportunity to defend themselves. However, protections were largely viewed in the context of the historical circumstances. Defendants were granted 'minimum rights essential to a fair trial' in proceedings.[21] There was scepticism towards a reliance on technical rules in proceedings which would allow the 'guilty' to 'benefit from the exceptional circumstances under which war trials are necessarily held, and so escape just punishment'.[22] In the Nuremberg proceedings, the access of Defence Counsel to the archives of the Prosecution was restricted due to the unusual circumstances of the cases and mistrust regarding the Defence.

International criminal procedure in the modern sense emerged after the Cold War. It devotes more structured attention to the rights of the accused and due process of law than its post-war precedents. International criminal law was seen as a new instrument to advance human rights and humanitarian law. Rules of procedure were developed under conditions of urgency. The founding resolutions of the ad hoc tribunals left the elaboration largely in the hands of judges who exercised a quasi-legislative function. The ad hoc tribunals devoted a good part of their judicial activity to the development and adjustment of rules of procedure, in a trial and error process.[23] The Rules were originally largely drafted in analogy to a domestic prosecution system, though they had to be adjusted to the context of international criminal proceedings.

The ad hoc tribunals drew their inspiration largely from adversarial features found in common law. Over time, however, they integrated certain inquisitorial features from the Romano-Germanic tradition into the process in order to accommodate the complex nature of international trials.[24] Some of the alleged benefits of the adversarial procedure turned out to be elusive. For instance, the assumption that an adversarial process is better equipped to protect the interests of the Defence turned out to be problematic. The idea of proceedings as a contest between the defendant and the

---

[19] Robert H. Jackson, Opening Statement for the United States of America, On the Subject of International Military Tribunal No. I (21 November 1945), in *Trial of the Major War Criminals before the International Military Tribunal, Nuremberg 14 November 1945—1 October 1946*, Vol. 2 (1947), 101.

[20] Ibid. For a discussion of the imagery, see H. Christie, 'The Poisoned Chalice: Imperial Justice, Moral Relativism, and the Origins of International Criminal Law' (2010) 72 *University of Pittsburgh Law Review* 361.

[21] At Nuremberg, there was no right to appeal for defendants. The Nuremberg Charter further lacked other due process protections, such as the presumption of innocence, the duty to disclose exculpatory evidence or the right to remain silent.

[22] UNWCC, Information Concerning Human Rights Arising from Trials of War Crimes, UN.Doc. E/CN.4/W.19, 15 May 1948, at 272, 273.

[23] F. Guariglia, 'The Rules of Procedure and Evidence for the International Criminal Court: A New Development in International Adjudication of Individual Criminal Responsibility', in Cassese, Gaeta and Jones, *Rome Statute of the International Criminal Court*, 1111.

[24] D. Mundis, 'From "Common Law" Towards "Civil Law": The Evolution of the ICTY Rules of Procedure and Evidence' (2004) 14 *LJIL* 367–382.

international community caused concerns from the perspective of the principle of equality of arms, and the expectations of victims and domestic societies which followed a different model. The length of proceedings was criticized.[25] As former ICTY Judge Bonomy has noted, some of the aggressive legalist features of the adversarial procedure and practices of plea bargaining sit uneasily with domestic culture or broader societal aims of proceedings: 'The confrontation which is an essential part of the adversarial process tends to antagonize witnesses, with the result that the conflict being explored is revived, this time as a contest between counsel representing the accused on one side and the witness whose sympathies lie naturally with the other'.[26] These shortcomings led to certain adjustments of the adversarial model, i.e. a form of 'tempered adversariality',[27] with many hybrid elements and a more proactive role of the judges in the courtroom.[28] This mix is reflected in the legal instruments of other international and hybrid courts (e.g. SCSL, ECCC), including the procedural framework of the ICC, which is in many respects a construction *sui generis*. It is neither fully common law, nor Romano-Germanic, but a unique attempt to take into account the specific features of international crimes, while ensuring full respect of the rights of defendants. This approach has certain advantages, because it allows procedures to be adjusted to modern developments.[29] It also has disadvantages, since the combination of approaches from different cultures can result in an artificial 'mishmash of the two systems'.[30]

In terms of management of proceedings, international criminal courts and tribunals have generally been reluctant to adopt a 'dossier'-based approach, i.e. to compile a comprehensive case file that sets the framework for proceedings. Such a dossier is common in certain inquisitorial systems (e.g. France, Belgium), but foreign to predominantly adversarial cultures. It enables the judge to have full access to the information of parties and to manage proceedings. The traditional objection against a dossier is that it taints the impartiality of the judge as arbiter of the facts, transforms proceedings into an inquest without orality, reduces the immediacy of trials and limits the rights of the defence. The ideological divide over the feasibility of a 'dossier' has led to the development of complex rules of disclosure regulating the exchange of material and evidence between Prosecution and Defence.

Fairness of proceedings has become a cardinal principle of proceedings.[31] Richard Goldstone, the first ICTY Prosecutor, famously claimed that the success of

---

[25] Zacklin, 'The Failings of the Ad Hoc International Tribunals', 545.

[26] Bonomy, 'The Reality of Conducting a War Crimes Trial', 348, 350.

[27] P. C. Keen, 'Tempered Adversariality: The Judicial Role and Trial Theory in the International Criminal Tribunals' (2004) 17 *LJIL* 767.

[28] On the historical development, see Ambos, *Treatise on International Criminal Law, Vol. III*, 8–44.

[29] As Judge Robinson has argued, 'ultimately the question is not the legal system from which a particular measure or procedure comes, but whether its incorporation in the law of the Tribunal produces a result that is consistent with international standards of fairness'. See P. L. Robinson, 'Rough Edges in the Alignment of Legal Systems in the Proceedings at the ICTY' (2005) 3 *JICJ* 1056.

[30] Bibas and Burke-White, 'When Idealism Meets Domestic-Criminal-Procedure Realism', 695.

[31] It relates to the rights of the defendants, and it is overarching requirement of criminal proceedings. See M. Damaška, 'Reflections on Fairness in International Criminal Justice' (2012) 10 *JICJ* 611.

international courts should not be measured by the 'number of convictions', but by the 'fairness of the trials'.[32] Fairness involves certain procedural dimensions, such as the right to a fair trial, equality of arms, the presumption of innocence, the safety of witnesses and victims, and the ability to present one's case, as well as certain normative considerations, such as coherence and equal and unbiased application of norms and standards to all participants in the process. Key principles of fairness are: transparency, consistency, equality and impartiality.[33]

The problem is that it is an abstract concept that remains in the eye of the beholder. Determining fairness is a balancing act. Courts are constantly torn between different constituencies, such as the rights of the Defence, the interests of the Prosecution, victims and affected states, and different goals of the justice process.[34] The protection of the rights of the accused is often assessed against other considerations, such as expeditious management of the trial or the prohibition to use the courtroom as a platform for propaganda.[35]

One constant friction of procedures is the interplay between criminal procedure and human rights. Criminal procedure is increasingly shaped by human rights instruments, including international fair trial norms.[36] Human rights treaties form metaprinciples for international adjudication.[37] Due process and fair trial guarantees have become a cornerstone of legal frameworks. For instance, the UN insists on a continuing basis that international proceedings must respect internationally recognized standards regarding the rights of the accused at all stages of its proceedings. Some hybrid mechanisms, such as the ECCC, were established based on mistrust of domestic justice standard. However, international criminal justice navigates between two types of liberalism: classical criminal principles which protect the integrity of the criminal process or the interests of defendants (e.g. culpability, fair warning, fair labelling), and human rights provisions which seek to maximize protection for victims of crimes.[38] The balance between these prerogatives is in flux.

Approaches towards the protection of the rights of victims have changed fundamentally over the past decades. Restorative approaches have become an increasingly important feature of criminal procedure, in light of the recognition of rights, such as access to justice and the right to an effective remedy.[39] This has created major shifts in

---

[32] R. J. Goldstone, Address Before the Supreme Court of the United States, 1996 Central European and Eurasian Initiative Leadership Award Dinner (2 October 1996, cited in M. S. Ellis, 'Achieving Justice Before The International War Crimes Tribunal: Challenges For The Defense Counsel' (1997) 7 *Duke Journal Of Comparative & International Law* 519, 526 n. 37.

[33] McDermot, *Fairness in International Criminal Trials*, 6.

[34] The idea of fairness has been extended to other stakeholders on the process, such as the Prosecution, victims or states.

[35] See F. Mégret, 'Beyond Fairness: Understanding the Determinants of International Criminal Procedure' (2009) 14 *UCLA Journal of International Law & Foreign Affairs* 37.

[36] J. D. Jackson, 'The Effect of Human Rights on Criminal Evidentiary Processes: Towards Convergence, Divergence or Realignment?' (2005) 68 *Modern Law Review* (2005) 737–764.

[37] This is most visibly reflected in Art. 21 (3) of the ICC Statute.

[38] See Robinson, 'Identity Crisis', 930–931; S. Zappalà, 'The Rights of Victims v. The Rights of the Accused' (2010) 8 *JICJ* 137, 140.

[39] B. McGonigle-Leyh, *Procedural Justice? Victim Participation in International Criminal Proceedings* (Antwerp: Intersentia, 2011); L. Moffett, *Justice for Victims at the International Criminal Court* (New York: Routledge, 2014).

the criminal procedure of many states, and also in the context of international criminal justice. Victims are no longer simply an object of proceedings, but increasingly are given a voice. This has altered conceptions of procedures. The legitimacy of proceedings is judged not only according to classical fairness and due process considerations. Rather, it is expected that the 'procedure as such and the result ... be acceptable to all parties involved, i.e. in criminal matters to the victim, the perpetrator, and the society'.[40] The adjudication of atrocity crimes is often driven by a number of factors that distinguish them from adjudication of ordinary crimes: their context, their publicity and drama, the stakes of victims, and the broader policy rationales of proceedings that go beyond dispute resolution among competing parties. It is increasingly argued that the process of adjudication as such is an essential element of international trials. For instance, criminal proceedings serve not only to secure retribution or punishment, but to signal that no conduct stands outside the law. Modern theorists have thus developed broader normative accounts of international criminal procedure which look at their diverse functions, and their interplay with broader conceptions of justice.[41] Functions of procedures include culpability determinations, ensuring due process protection, contributing to truth-finding, and allowing structured victim participation, including through eyewitness accounts. Jens David Ohlin has argued that rule of law functions are at the heart of the justification of international criminal procedure.[42] The challenge of these broader normative theories is that they require new methods to ascertain procedure. They require further interdisciplinary inquiry into the social effects and consequences of procedures.

Rules and principles of international criminal procedures require some flexibility and openness towards procedural innovations. Standards cannot be detached from the reality.[43] The gathering of evidence is often difficult in a transnational setting. Translation and equality of arms may pose special challenges. Often, perfection is the enemy of the good. However, there are limits and risks that come with flexibility and broader functionalist considerations. As Darryl Robinson has cautioned: 'human rights liberalism produces a criminal law system that is increasingly authoritarian in its disregard for constraining principles, and risks using the accused as an object in a didactic exercise rather than respecting autonomy and fairness'.[44] Critiques relating to fairness remain a central concern of international criminal justice.

---

[40] C. Safferling, *International Criminal Procedure* (Oxford: Oxford University Press, 2012), 63.

[41] See Mégret, 'Beyond "Fairness"'37; Ambos, *Treatise on International Criminal Law, Vol. III*, 7.

[42] J. D. Ohlin, 'A Meta-Theory of International Criminal Procedure: Vindicating the Rule of Law' (2009) 14 *UCLA Journal of International Law and Foreign Affairs* 77.

[43] D. Groome, 'Re-evaluating the Theoretical Basis and Methodology of International Criminal Trials' (2007) 25 *Penn State International Law Review*', 800–802.

[44] Robinson, 'Identity Crisis', 931.

4.3 Justice Actors

Criminal procedure is a living instrument. It is shaped by the identities of agents, their different responsibilities and the choices they make. To the outside, the process may easily appear like a scripted play, with binary features. The Prosecution initiates and drives proceedings. The Defence represents the interests of suspects and accused. The judiciary tries cases. Victims echo the case against the accused. In reality, the criminal process is more complex. Procedure evolves through different forms of interaction. Courtroom action and advocacy are directed towards multiple constituencies (i.e. the judges, defendants, victims, specific communities or the wider public). Parties and participants to proceedings are not uniform actors, but entities with multiple faces in the justice process. The role and narratives shift according to the proceedings.[45] 'Winning a case' is one of the objectives of the Prosecution, the Defence or victims. However, the justice of the criminal process goes beyond determination of guilt or innocence or 'victory' of the parties. Elucidation of facts, allocation of liability in broader networks of criminality, moral vindication and bestowal of a sense of trust in the law are important rationales that go beyond the immediate interests of parties and participants. Procedural justice is thus defined by various factors other than 'victory' in contest: fidelity to law and facts, openness to contrary positions and narratives, inclusiveness of reasoning, recognition of a sense of humaneness and equality between perpetrator and victims, and certain discursive features, such as interaction between parties and participants and communication with a broader public.

4.3.1 The Prosecution

The Prosecution is typically a hierarchically organized office.[46] It symbolizes like no other actor the public interest in international criminal procedures. It represents multiple interests: the abstract community interest in the pursuit of criminal justice, the interests of persons affected by international crimes, and to some extent also the interests of the Defence. This poses difficult representational dilemmas. The international community is a 'fictive client'. The interests of victims are presented in an abstract, rather than a 'personal' way. The Defence has a natural mistrust against representation of Defence interests (e.g. Prosecution-led collection of exculpatory evidence). In public discourse, formal legal measures gain most attention. However, the role of the Prosecution is more diverse. It encompasses analysis and examination of information, investigation and prosecution. These three functions exist at the domestic and the international level. They differ in form and methodology.

---

[45] Competing parties or participants do not always have opposite interests.

[46] See generally G. Townsend, 'Structure and Management', in L. Reydams, J. Wouters and C. Ryngaert (eds.), *International Prosecutors* (Oxford: Oxford University Press, 2012), 171.

4.3.1.1   Unique Features

International prosecutors are a unique species of justice agents. They hold the 'most political function' in international criminal justice.[47] They have not only judicial, but also certain quasi-judicial or even political functions (e.g. negotiation).[48] Their work is inherently linked to politics due to the political context of crimes, the politics behind institutional engagement and their large degree of choice. Investigating and prosecuting international crimes is to some extent a 'continuation of politics through judicial means'.[49] The Prosecution faces conflicting roles. It is meant to be an impartial agent of justice, but also an effective advocate. It is supposed to act as an officer of the Court, but it also has police and enforcement functions. Securing global enforcement of the law requires diplomacy. This makes prosecutors vulnerable.[50] They are in a constant tension between independence and dependence. They are bound by law, but at the same time enjoy a significant amount of discretion.[51]

Their status differs partly from domestic systems. In common law systems, the Prosecution is typically part of the executive branch of power and is responsible to democratically elected executive officials. In many civil law systems, prosecutors are subject to wider judicial control. On the international plane, these institutional forms of accountability are less developed. International prosecutors are often selected by political bodies. They are typically removed from constraints of democratic accountability and the checks and balances operating within a specific domestic constituency or society. This is not necessarily a deficit, but to some extent inherent in the exercise of international justice. Accountability is more commonly modelled after features and frameworks that are common in the institutional law of international organizations. It involves institutional balance and political control, rather than strict judicial scrutiny.

The struggle for prosecutorial independence has been one of the emancipatory features of international criminal justice. At Nuremberg and Tokyo, prosecutors were representatives of national governments.[52] Government interests influenced proceedings. As Telford Taylor admitted in his memoirs, the list of suspects at Nuremberg was essentially drawn up during the Potsdam Conference.[53] At Tokyo, US General

---

[47] L. Côté, 'Independence and Impartiality', in Reydams, Wouters and Ryngaert, *International Prosecutors*, 319, 321.

[48] On the communicative power of prosecutors, see J. Dobson and S. Stolk, 'The Prosecutor's Important Announcements; the Communication of Moral Authority at the International Criminal Court' (2016) *Law, Culture and the Humanities*, https://doi.org/10.1177/1743872116666466.

[49] L. Reydams, J. Wouters and C. Ryngaert, 'Conclusions', in Reydams, Wouters and Ryngaert, *International Prosecutors*, 926, 928.

[50] See M. Fairlie, 'The Hidden Costs of Strategic Communications for the International Criminal Court' (2016) 51 *Texas International Law Journal* 281.

[51] On prosecutorial discretion, see C. Stahn, 'Judicial Review of Prosecutorial Discretion: On Experiments and Imperfections', in G. Sluiter (ed.), *International Criminal Procedure: Towards a Coherent Body of Law* (London: Cameron May, 2009), 235.

[52] Under the ICC regime, the Prosecutor and the Deputy Prosecutor need not be nationals of a state party. Schabas suggests this measure was a way to give the American government a means to participate in the ICC. See W. A. Schabas, *An Introduction to the International Criminal Court* (Cambridge: Cambridge University Press, 2017), 368 et seq.

[53] T. Taylor, *The Anatomy of the Nuremberg Trials: A Personal Memoir* (New York: Alfred A. Knopf, 1992, 83.

McArthur had a decisive influence on the trial.[54] He gave instructions not to indict the Japanese Emperor, since this might hamper the political reconstruction process in Japan.[55] In the aftermath, states remained for a long time opposed to an international criminal court as a result of fears that an international prosecutor would start cases based on unfiltered evidence by non-governmental organizations. Today, international prosecutors are vested with a considerable degree of independence.[56]

Independence is a prerequisite for effective and impartial investigations and prosecutions. It is reflected in the Statute of most modern international criminal courts and tribunals. It protects prosecutors from external instruction, political accountability and attacks from powerful states. They enjoy three types of independence: institutional independence as an organ,[57] individual independence in the exercise of professional duties, and freedom in decision making.[58] Functionally, their status is thus comparable to that of an international civil servant.

Independence is complemented by a certain margin of discretion. In domestic systems, prosecutors are often duty-bound to investigate and prosecute certain categories of crimes, e.g. under the principle of legality. The main difference between domestic enforcement of criminal law and the international context, as Louise Arbour has pointed out, lies in the 'broad discretionary powers granted to the International Prosecutor in selecting the targets for prosecution'.[59] Discretion enables prosecutors to manage some of the political tensions of the work and defend choices. The precise amount of discretion varies according to the mandate. Prosecutors are generally empowered to decide who will be charged, when and how. Discretion works, as Ronald Dworkin once put it, like 'the hole in a doughnut'.[60] It is surrounded by certain general legal restrictions, including safeguards against arbitrary decision making, but it offers a space for freedom of action within these constraints. The exercise of discretion is often disguised by rhetoric. Prosecutors say they decide on the basis of the law and the evidence. In many circumstances, however, these two factors alone may not suffice to explain the choices.

The prosecutor may have to consider other factors as well in deciding how to proceed. These might include the need to demonstrate the court's viability (for example, by charging at a level

---

[54] He had had the power to 'reduce, approve, or alter any punishments meted out'. See H. P. Bix, *Hirohito and the Making of Modern Japan* (New York: Perennial Harper Collins Publishers, 2000), 592.

[55] Ibid., 545.

[56] S. A. Fernández de Gurmendi, 'The Role of the International Prosecutor', in R. S. Lee (ed.), *The International Criminal Court. The Making of the Rome Statute. Issues, Negotiations, Results* (The Hague: Kluwer Law International, 1999) 175.

[57] See Rome Statute, Art. 42 (1).

[58] Côté, 'Independence and Impartiality', 323–357.

[59] See L. Arbour, 'The Need for an Independent and Effective Prosecutor in the Permanent International Criminal Court' (1999) 17 *Windsor Yearbook of Access to Justice* 217.

[60] R. Dworkin, *Taking Rights Seriously* (Cambridge, MA: Harvard University Press, 1978) 31.

or in a manner that prevents states from simply ignoring the court's orders); its efficacy (by charging persons who may readily be apprehended); its efficiency (by limiting the number of charges, and thereby the length of trials); or its independence (in appropriate circumstances, by charging officials of governments which have referred situations to the court).[61]

A certain margin of appreciation is thus necessary to carry out investigative and prosecutorial functions. Its exercise requires not only respect of the law, but political intelligence. Any decision that the Prosecution takes is subject to criticism from one side or the other. This makes it important to ground practice in consistent and objective prosecutorial policies, transparent decision making and professional diligence.[62] Discretion is curtailed in several ways: through legal norms and institutions, political control (e.g. funding restrictions), judicial review and internal prosecutorial policies or guidelines.

Some critics claim that international prosecutors enjoy too much independence. For instance, Ralph Zacklin has argued that ICTY governance posed accountability problems for the UN due to the 'decentralization of power and accountability, coupled with the need to respect judicial and prosecutorial independence'.[63] Such critiques must be read with a degree of caution. Domestic approaches towards the accountability of prosecutors differ considerably, depending on whether they are elected (e.g. US), part of the executive branch of power or integrated into the judiciary. Similarly, international approaches differ. They encompass ethical guidelines and self-regulation, judicial supervision, disciplinary measures and, most of all, a high degree of informal pressure (e.g. through diplomacy, NGO scrutiny). This exposes prosecutorial practices to significant checks and balances.

Although prosecutorial independence is well accepted in law, it faces considerable constraints in practice. Governments and political bodies, such as the Security Council, can interfere in various ways with prosecutorial independence. Hybrid courts have faced particular challenges. As Luc Côté rightly observes:

Being an 'international' prosecutor is just not enough when confronted with lack of support and resources (East Timor), political interference from state leaders (Cambodia), or the UN executive (Kosovo). In such situations a prosecutor needs more than 'being an international', and individual integrity and impartiality alone are not sufficient; statutory guarantees of independence, respect of the separation of power, and a concrete and indefectible commitment to fighting impunity is required.[64]

---

[61] J. Goldston, 'The International Criminal Court: Justice and Politics', *Open Democracy*, 13 January 2010, at www.opendemocracy.net/james-goldston/international-criminal-court-justice-and-politics.

[62] See M. Varaki, 'Introducing a Fairness-Based Theory of Prosecutorial Legitimacy before the International Criminal Court' (2016) 27 *EJIL* 769.

[63] Zacklin, 'Failings of the Ad Hoc International Tribunals', 543.

[64] Côté, 'Independence and Impartiality', 319, 414.

4.3.1.2 Role and Responsibilities

The role and responsibilities of international prosecutors differ across institutions, based on the underlying procedural regime.[65] Their powers reflect a mix of common law and Romano-Germanic traditions. Generally, they have a double role: They are parties to the legal process and to some extent agents of justice. Prosecutors are typically the 'engine' of proceedings. They start the case.[66] They are master of proceedings (*dominus litis*), and may withdraw the case, either until the start of the trial or throughout proceedings. In addition, they serve as an officer of the Court. The ICTY clarified this in the *Kupreškić* case. It held that:

the Prosecutor of the Tribunal is not, or not only, a Party to adversarial proceedings but is an organ of the Tribunal and an organ of international criminal justice whose object is not simply to secure a conviction but to present the case for the Prosecution, which includes not only inculpatory, but also exculpatory evidence, in order to assist the Chamber to discover the truth in a judicial setting.[67]

As a 'party', prosecutors cannot be required to be 'neutral'. However, they are meant to be 'non-partisan'. This has several implications. Prosecutors must, first of all, respect the presumption of innocence. This means that they are bound to keep an open mind towards the innocence of the defendant throughout proceedings. Second, prosecutors must conduct investigations and prosecutions with the aim of reaching a just verdict. One essential aspect of their role as agents of justice is that they are required to consider not only inculpatory, but also exculpatory evidence.[68] The duty to disclose exculpatory evidence often poses problems in practice, since the understanding of what constitutes exculpatory evidence may contrast with the adversarial goals of the Prosecution. Third, prosecutors must respect the rights of the accused at all times. They must also take into account the interests and circumstances of persons affected by crime, such as victims and witnesses. Ultimately, the Prosecution bears the burden of proving the defendant's guilt beyond reasonable doubt.

During the investigation, prosecutors are allowed to adopt a wide range of coercive and non-coercive measures to obtain evidence. The degree of judicial supervision varies. In the cases of Nuremberg and Tokyo, there was hardly any judicial supervision of prosecutorial action during the early stages of proceedings. In the context of the ICC and the ad hoc tribunals, specific aspects of the investigation are supervised. In the ECCC, investigations are conducted and controlled by an investigative judge.

---

[65] See K. Ambos and S. Bock, 'Procedural Regimes', in Reydams, Wouters and Ryngaert, *International Prosecutors*, 488–541.

[66] See, Art. 42 (1) of the Rome Statute.

[67] *Prosecutor* v. *Kupreškić et al.*, IT-95-16-T, Decision on the Communications between the Parties and their Witness, 21 September 1998, 2, sub. (ii).

[68] Art. 54 of the ICC Statute requires the Prosecutor expressly to establish the truth and investigate incriminating and exculpatory evidence equally.

A key challenge of the role of the Prosecutor is to deal with impartiality, i.e. to demonstrate an independent mindset in prosecutorial action.[69] The reality of selective justice marks, as Pierre Hazan put it, the 'original sin' of international criminal justice.[70] The Prosecution struggles to provide 'equal justice' to victims or to express an 'equivalence of blame' in cases. Impartiality is an approximation. As Luc Côté admits: 'The reality is that no international prosecutor was able to exercise his functions without being accused by one side or another of partiality or lacking independence'.[71] For instance, the ICTR was famously criticized for prosecuting Hutus rather than Tutsis, and failing to indict RPF suspects due to threats of non-collaboration (i.e. a pending witness crisis) and retaliation by the Kagame government.[72] The ICTY faced critique for its controversial decision not to investigate NATO's bombing of Kosovo,[73] and its focus on crimes committed by Serbs, creating allegations of 'partial impartiality'.[74] The SCSL was even-handed in its choice of defendants, but was blamed for prosecuting cases based on membership in groups (AFRC, RUF and CDF) rather than the gravity of crimes.[75] The best defence against such arguments is to explain constraints and choices with reasonable arguments.

It is extremely difficult to challenge selective prosecution judicially. The Prosecution is bound to comply with the principle of equality before the law and the requirement of non-discrimination. However, prosecutors are typically better placed than judges to determine the local realities, the use of prosecutorial resources or enforcement priorities. It is presumed that international prosecutors act sensibly and responsibly. The threshold for a challenge is high. In the *Kabiligi* case, the Defence requested Trial Chamber judges to order an investigation into the airplane crash of President Habyarimana and other senior ministers on 6 April 1994, since this was necessary to understand subsequent massacres in Rwanda. The Chamber argued that the issue was 'one solely for the discretion of the Prosecutor'.[76] In the *Čelebići* case, Landzo, one of the accused, argued that he was arbitrarily charged, since he was 'the only person the Prosecutor's office could find to "represent" the Bosnian Muslims'.[77] The ICTY rejected the claim. It argued that the Defence has the burden to establish that the decision to prosecute is based on an unlawful or improper (including

---

[69] See Côté, 'Independence and Impartiality', 319–415.

[70] See P. Hazan, *Justice in a Time of War* (College Station: Texas A & M University Press, 2004), 37.

[71] Côté, 'Independence and Impartiality', 413–414.

[72] See Peskin, *International Justice in Rwanda and the Balkans*, 190. According to Del Ponte, Kagame noted: 'You are destroying Rwanda, you will disrupt the reconstruction of the nation, stop the investigation . . . we will not allow you to do this'. See C. Del Ponte, *Madame Prosecutor: A Memoir* (New York: Other Press, 2008), 225.

[73] A. Laursen, 'NATO, the War over Kosovo, and the ICTY Investigation' (2002) 17 *American University International Law Review* 765, 813–814.

[74] See E. Bruning, M. Scallon, J. Rudy and J. Whall, 'Partial Impartiality: A Review of Alleged Bias in the International Criminal Tribunal for the Former Yugoslavia' (2016) *Northeastern University Political Review* 5.

[75] According to the Truth Commission, the CDF only committed 6 per cent of the crimes. This 'leaves the number of CDF defendants relatively high'. See F. de Vlaming, 'Selection of Defendants', in Reydams, Wouters and Ryngaert, *International Prosecutors*, 542, 570.

[76] *Prosecutor v. Kabiligi*, ICTR-97–34-I, Decision on the Defence Motion Seeking Supplementary Investigations, 1 June 2000, para. 12.

[77] See *Prosecutor v. Delalić et al.*, Brief of the Appellant, Esad Landzo on Appeal Against Conviction and Sentence, 2 July 1999, 17.

discriminatory) motive, and that the Prosecution failed to prosecute similarly situated persons.[78] This makes it virtually impossible for a Defence claim to succeed.

4.3.2   The Defence

The Defence is a counterpart to the Prosecution. It faces a heavy burden. International courts are viewed as instruments to 'fight impunity'. The Defence needs to counter charges that are associated with the protection of human rights and the values of the international community. Only a limited number of cases are investigated and prosecuted internationally. The rationales for prosecution often reach beyond the individual role of defendants. In light of the selectivity of international criminal justice and the limited resources, an acquittal is easily perceived as a failure.[79] Formally, defendants are presumed to be innocent. In practice, however, the Defence case is often compromised by prejudices and stigmas. Some claim that the Defence faces in reality a 'presumption of guilt' rather than a 'presumption of innocence'.[80] High-level defendants are frequently demonized or pre-judged by the public and in the media before the start of the legal process. For instance, Charles Taylor was branded as a 'criminal' rather than a suspect before his trial.[81] The Defence needs to confront such biases and develop counter-narratives.

4.3.2.1   Roles

The Defence plays a crucial role from a justice perspective. A fair and effective Defence serves not only the defendant,[82] but the interests of the criminal justice system as a whole. It protects the equality of arms between the Prosecution and the Defence and the rights of a defendant to a fair trial, including acquittal in case of innocence and proportional sentencing. The Defence is essential for the integrity of proceedings and the process of truth-finding.[83] Each story has several sides. An effective Defence is necessary to ensure that 'justice is done, and seen to be done'. For the Prosecution, it might be better to lose a weak case than to win it in an unfair manner.

---

[78] *Čelebići* Appeal Judgment, para. 607.

[79] J. Turner, 'Defense Perspectives on Law and Politics in International Criminal Trials' (2007–2008) 48 *Virginia Journal of International Law* 529.

[80] S. Zappalá, 'Presumption of Innocence', in Cassese, *The Oxford Companion to International Criminal Justice*, 457–458.

[81] Former UN Secretary General Annan called Charles Taylor a war 'criminal' after arrest. Defence Counsel Karim Khan complained that this goes against the presumption of innocence. See M. Corder, 'Liberia's Taylor Appears Before Hague Court', Associated Press, 22 July 2006.

[82] B. Elberling, *The Defendant in International Criminal Proceedings: Between Law and Historiography* (Portland: Hart Publishing, 2012)

[83] See generally C. Rohan and G. Zyberi (eds.), *Defense Perspectives on International Criminal Justice* (Cambridge: Cambridge University Press, 2017); M. Hiéramente and P. Schneider (eds.), *The Defence in International Criminal Trials* (Baden-Baden: Nomos, 2016).

The rights of the Defence are not 'merely' human rights guarantees. They are a fundamental element of the fairness of proceedings.[84] They differ according to stages of the proceedings. Defendants benefit from the benefit of the doubt. The ethos of Defence lawyers is not to prejudge or form opinions without knowledge of the facts or the testing of evidence. Formally, the defendant is a suspect until charges have been confirmed by a judge. Suspects enjoy certain human rights protections. For instance, the ICC Statute contains a mini-Charter of rights.[85] It includes the right to be informed prior to being questioned, the right to remain silent, the right not to be compelled to incriminate oneself or confess guilt, the right to be questioned in the presence of counsel, and the right to legal assistance.

After confirmation of the charges, the defendant becomes an accused person. This means that a catalogue of more extensive fair trial guarantees come into play. They include the right to have adequate time and facilities to prepare the defence, the right be tried without undue delay and the right to self-representation.

4.3.2.2 Macro-Challenges

The Defence has a key role during different stages of criminal proceedings: investigation, pre-trial, trial and appeals. It is at a certain disadvantage vis-à-vis the Prosecution.[86] Judges must give a central role to the rights of the Defence at all stages of the proceedings, in order to balance this disparity.

4.3.2.2.1 Equality of Arms

A first obstacle is the lack of material equality between the prosecution and the Defence. The principle of equality of arms is a fundamental prerequisite of an adversarial process.[87] However, the Defence is never at full par with the Prosecution. It needs to confront the Prosecution case, and in certain circumstances submissions by victims. International courts and tribunals have made it clear that equality of arms does not imply equality of means, but at best a certain equivalence.[88] In practice, there are some structural inequalities.

Prosecutors are better equipped to gather evidence on the territory of states. Each prosecutorial team is composed of multiple lawyers, police investigators, analysts and in-house experts, case managers and staff. The Defence comes in quite late, namely when a case hypothesis has been formulated and evidence has been collected by the

---

[84] See McDermott, *Fairness in International Criminal Trials*, 41. See also M. Damaška, 'The Competing Visions of Fairness: The Basic Choice for International CriminalTribunals' (2011) 36 *North Carolina Journal of International Law and Commercial Regulation* 365, 379.

[85] Art. 55 ICC Statute.

[86] S. Kay and B. Swart, 'The Role of the Defence', in Cassese, Gaeta and Jones, *The Rome Statute of the International Criminal Court*, 1421.

[87] See generally M. Fedorova, *The Principle of Equality of Arms in International Criminal Proceedings* (Antwerp: Intersentia 2012); C. C. Jalloh and A. DiBella, 'Equality of Arms in International Criminal Law: Continuing Challenges', in Schabas, McDermott and Hayes, *The Ashgate Research Companion to International Criminal Law*, 251.

[88] *Prosecutor v. Kayishema and Ruzindana*, ICTR-95 1-T, Judgment, 21 May 1999, para. 60; *Prosecutor v. Kordić and Čerkez*, IT-95–14/2-A, Judgment, 17 December 2004, para. 176.

Prosecution. It has fewer opportunities to carry out its own independent investigation. Defence lawyers often face obstruction when they seek to carry out Defence investigations.[89] They struggle to operate in states that are uncooperative, or to receive the protection that is necessary to carry out their functions. They often lack the power to request cooperation from state authorities or to compel witnesses to cooperate. For instance, national authorities in inquisitorial systems may be unfamiliar with providing assistance to Defence investigations, since such investigations are carried by investigative judges in their own jurisdiction. When the Defence starts its own investigation, memories may have been tainted and material documents lost.

4.3.2.2.2 Moving Targets

A second challenge is the large amount of material that the Defence needs to confront.[90] The Prosecution often discloses large amounts of materials and investigative data to the Defence. The materials may be unorganized or provided on a rolling basis. The Prosecution may limit disclosure in the hope of gaining a tactical advantage. This makes it difficult for Defence teams to analyse the evidence supporting the charges. The Prosecution case is often not static, but dynamic. This means that the Defence must to some extent aim at a 'moving target'. It faces the risk that the right to be tried without an undue delay is used as a stick against the defendant.

4.3.2.2.3 Confronting Hearsay or Anonymous Evidence

A third problem is the use of anonymous or hearsay evidence and concealment of sources. According to the presumption of innocence, 'everyone shall be presumed innocent until proved guilty'.[91] Defendant have a right to see and to know the identity of their accusers. It is difficult for the Defence to challenge information in reports that do not clearly identify the sources that they rely upon for the relevant information. The Prosecution has used such information (e.g. press articles, NGO or UN reports) to support narratives about a conflict or to continue to detain a person in custody. International criminal courts and tribunals have not accepted such sources to prove the acts or conduct of the accused.[92] They have however been more flexible than common jurisdictions in allowing hearsay evidence, i.e. second-hand information, while admitting that such evidence has low probative value.[93]

In some cases, prosecutors have used anonymous witness testimony in order to protect witnesses from re-traumatization through confrontation with the accused.

---

[89] See C. Buisman and D. Hopper, 'Defense Investigations and the Collection of Evidence', in Rohan and Zyberi, *Defense Perspectives on International Criminal Justice*, 519.

[90] See M. G. Karnavas, 'The Role of the Defense in the Trial Stage', in Rohan and Zyberi, *Defense Perspectives on International Criminal Justice*, 277, 283.

[91] Art. 66 ICC Statute.

[92] See e.g. Rule 92 *bis* of the Rules of Procedure and Evidence of the SCSL ('a Chamber may, in lieu of oral testimony, admit as evidence in whole or in part, information including written statements and transcripts, that do not go to proof of the acts and conduct of the accused').

[93] *Prosecutor* v. *Gbagbo*, ICC-02/11–01/11, Decision Adjourning the Hearing on the Confirmation of Charges Pursuant to Article 61 (7) (c) (i) of the Rome Statute, 3 June 2013, para. 35.

This practice may conflict with the right of the Defence to examine witnesses and to have adequate time and facilities for the preparation of the Defence. In the *Lubanga* case, the Pre-Trial Chamber refused to allow anonymous victims to add evidence to the Prosecution case, since this would violate the principle prohibiting anonymous accusations.[94]

4.3.2.2.4 *Guilt by Association*

Finally, the Defence often struggles to defend itself against broad theories of liability, such as joint criminal enterprise or command responsibility, and the use of circumstantial evidence. This creates risks of 'guilt by association'.[95] In some cases, judges virtually 'saved' the prosecution case by resorting to circumstantial evidence to enter a conviction. This is problematic.[96] Defendants may have had limited notice of the evidence. Moreover, the conviction may be based on the subjective opinions of judges ('intimate conviction' of the judge), rather than guilt beyond reasonable doubt.

4.3.2.3 *Strategies*

Defendants may invoke specific defences, such as mental disease or defect, self-defence, duress or mistake of fact or law.[97] However, most cases are won on evidentiary grounds. The most effective Defence strategy is often to induce a reasonable doubt in relation to the charges, to challenge Prosecution evidence and to call into question the connection between the defendant and the crime.[98]

The preparation of a successful Defence case starts at pre-trial. The defendant has a right to be tried by a court established by law. Defence teams before the ICTY, the ICTR and the STL have sought to challenge the legality of the establishment of these courts. Some defendants, like former President Slobodan Milošević, have argued that they face 'victor's justice'.[99] All of these challenges have been rejected, however.

The primary object of Defence arguments are the charges by the Prosecution. The defendant has the right to be informed promptly and in detail of the nature, cause and content of the charges. This implies that charges must be specific enough in order to allow an effective defence. In international criminal tribunals, defendants are often

---

[94] *Prosecutor* v. *Lubanga*, ICC-01/04–01/06–462, Decision on the Arrangements for Participation of Victims a/0001/06, a/0002/06, and a/0003/06 at the Confirmation Hearing, 22 September 2006, 7. The Appeals Chamber noted in *Katanga* that if 'anonymous victims wish to participate as individuals at a hearing or to make individual observations they would have to disclose their identities to the parties'. See *Prosecutor* v. *Katanga*, ICC-01/04–02/12–140, Decision on the Participation of Anonymous Victims in the Appeal and on the Maintenance of Deceased Victims on the List, 23 September 2013, para. 19.

[95] See Danner and Martinez, 'Guilty Associations'; J. D. Ohlin, 'Co-Perpetration German Dogmatik or German Invasion?', in Stahn, *Law and Practice of the International Criminal Court*, 519.

[96] *Prosecutor* v. *Katanga*, ICC-01/04–01/07–3436-AnxI, Minority Opinion of Judge Christine Van den Wyngaert, 10 March 2014, para. 313 ('It is thus quite clear that the charges against Germain Katanga under Art. 25 (3) (d) (ii) are a creation of the Majority alone, presumably in order to arrive at a ground for conviction, because none was available under Article 25 (3) (a)').

[97] See Section 2.5.

[98] On defence strategy, see G. G. Smith, 'Developing a Case Theory and a Defense Strategy', in Rohan and Zyberi, *Defense Perspectives on International Criminal Justice*, 385.

[99] See G. Bass, 'Victor's Justice, Selfish Justice' (2002) 69 *Social Research* 1037.

charged with a wide array of counts and alternative modes of liability, since it is difficult to establish who did what to whom, when, where and why. A key aspect of Defence strategy is to develop its own counter-narratives to events or to challenge the role or nexus of the defendant to crimes.

In order to mount an effective defence, the Defence has a right to see and confront the evidence. This right is partly implemented through disclosure of evidence. The Defence strategy typically involves two elements: defence and attack. The Defence may challenge and discredit existing prosecution evidence. In addition, the Defence may carry out an independent investigation, in order to establish its 'own case'. This flows from the right to have adequate time and facilities for the preparation of the defence.[100]

At trial, the Defence has the right to call, examine and confront witnesses. The Court has a duty to assist the Defence in obtaining the attendance of witnesses.

A defence strategy may succeed in many different ways. In *Lubanga*, judges suspended proceedings due to fair trial concerns.[101] In other cases, flaws in the Prosecution case may be so egregious that the case is not admitted to trial. In yet other cases, Defence challenges may force the Prosecution to withdraw charges. This occurred in the case against Kenyan President Kenyatta. In this case, the Trial Chamber terminated the proceedings.[102] However, this was only a partial victory for the Defence. The Chamber did not enter a not guilty verdict, which would bar further prosecution under the *ne bis in idem* principle. It allowed the Prosecution to bring new charges at a later date based on the same or similar factual circumstances.[103]

Finally, some trials lead to a full acquittal.[104] There are numerous examples. The Rwanda tribunal acquitted 14 defendants. At the Yugoslavia tribunal, 19 of 151 accused were acquitted. Famous examples are the Kupreškić brothers, Delalić, Haradinaj and Šešelj. The ICC acquitted its first defendant in 2012: Mathieu Ngudjolo Chui, who was co-charged with Germain Katanga. An acquittal clears the defendants of future charges for the same conduct.

Defendants who are acquitted pay a high price for the time spent in pre-trial and trial detention. They may easily remain an 'international pariah' due to the publicity and stigma of trials.[105] For instance, at the ICTR, some defendants were obliged to remain in detention after acquittal, since they were not able to return home in safety. Acquitted persons have limited prospects of compensation for wrongful arrest or

---

[100] Art. 14 (3) (b) ICCPR.
[101] *Prosecutor* v. *Lubanga*, ICC-01/04–01/06, Decision on the consequences of non-disclosure of exculpatory materials covered by Art. 54 (3), 14 March 2012.
[102] *Prosecutor* v. *Kenyatta*, ICC-01/09–02/11–1005, Decision on the withdrawal of charges against Mr Kenyatta, 13 March 2015.
[103] Ibid., para. 9.
[104] See generally A. Cayley and A. Orenstein, 'Motion for Judgement of Acquittal in the Ad Hoc and Hybrid Tribunals' (2010) 8 *JICJ* 575.
[105] B. Hola and J. van Wijk, 'Acquittals in International Criminal Justice: Pyrrhic Victories?' (2017) 30 *LJIL* 241, 251.

detention.[106] Financial compensation is only awarded in exceptional circumstances. The threshold is high. At the ICC, compensation is only awarded in cases of 'a grave and manifest' miscarriage of justice.[107]

4.3.2.4 Representation

The way in which Defence interests are represented differs from context to context. Suspects and accused have a right to defend themselves in person or through a legal representative. Given the complexity of international criminal proceedings, defendants before international courts and tribunals are represented by counsel or rely on their assistance. They are typically appointed and funded by the tribunal. The right to counsel and to legal assistance is important from the early stages of proceedings.[108] The ICC has established a system to protect Defence interest even before identification of individual suspects or arrest and surrender to the Court. The Court typically appoints ad hoc counsel to represent the general interests of the Defence. It may also provide a duty counsel to assist persons questioned by the Prosecutor. Defence counsel are required to act in the 'best interest of the client' but must not obstruct justice.

Several prominent defendants, such as Slobodan Milošević, Vojislav Šešelj, Radovan Karadžić and Hinga Norman, have decided to represent themselves.[109] This has become a battlefield in Court. For instance, ICTY officials switched off Milošević's microphone when he accused the Yugoslavia tribunal of trying to justify 'NATO war crimes committed in Yugoslavia'.[110] The right to representation is grounded in the defendant's autonomy interests. It is more fully protected in adversarial cultures.[111] Tribunals have made it clear that it is not absolute, but qualified. It must be balanced against certain interests of justice, such as the integrity of the legal process and the need to ensure fair and expeditious proceedings.[112] An unqualified recognition of

---

[106] Art. 85 (3) of the Rome Statute is the only express provision. See generally S. Beresford, 'Redressing the Wrongs of the International Justice System: Compensating for Persons Erroneously Detained, Prosecuted, or Convicted by the Ad Hoc Tribunals' (2002) 96 *AJIL* 628; J. D. Michels, 'Compensating Acquitted Defendants for Detention before International Criminal Courts' (2010) 8 *JICJ* 407.

[107] The mere fact that a defendant was detained and then acquitted does not suffice. An arrest is only unlawful if it is not based on a reasonable suspicion. An acquittal or termination of proceedings triggers compensation only in case of a 'grave and manifest miscarriage of justice'. The ICC Trial Chamber rejected Ngudjolo's request for compensation due to the failure to meet this threshold. See *Prosecutor* v. *Ngudjolo Chui*, ICC-01/04–02/12–301, Decision on the "Requête en indemnisation en application des dispositions de l'article 85(1) et (3) du Statut de Rome", 16 December 2015, para. 69.

[108] See T. Gut, S. Kirsch, D. Mundis and M. Taylor, 'Defence Issues', in Sluiter et al., *International Criminal Procedure*, 1204–1283.

[109] See e.g. N. Jorgensen, 'The Right of the Accused to Self-Representation Before International Criminal Tribunals' (2004) 98 *AJIL* 711, N. Jorgensen, 'The Right of the Accused to Self-Representation Before International Criminal Tribunals: Further Developments' (2005) 99 *AJIL* 663; M. Bohlander, 'A Fool for a Client: Remarks on the Freedom of Choice and Assignment of Counsel at the International Criminal Tribunal for the Former Yugoslavia' (2005) 16 *Criminal Law Forum* 159.

[110] For a discussion, see M. Scharf, 'Chaos in the Courtroom, Controlling Disruptive Defendants and Contumacious Counsel in War Crimes Trials' (2006–2007) *Case Western Reserve Journal of International Law* 155, 166.

[111] *Prosecutor* v. *Milošević*, IT–02–54–T, Reasons for Decision on the Prosecution Motion Concerning Assignment of Counsel, 4 April 2003, para. 21.

[112] See e.g. *Prosecutor* v. *Milošević*, IT-02-54-AR73.7, 'Decision on Interlocutory Appeal of Trial Chamber's Decision on the Assignment of Defence Counsel', 1 November 2004, paras. 12–14 (*Milošević* Counsel Appeal).

self-representation may run counter to the demand for an effective defence (which is key for an adversarial process). It also conflicts with the didactic functions of trials, where defendants use the courtroom as a stage to compromise proceedings.

Limits to self-representation have been gradually developed through case law. Judges have appointed additional legal agents to ensure an effective Defence in cases where defendants disrupted proceedings or suffered from health problems. For instance, in the *Milošević* case, the Chamber appointed an *amicus curiae* 'to assist in the proper determination of the case', due to the accused's refusal to engage counsel, his declining health and the need to ensure a fair trial.[113] This was an emergency measure, which conflicts with the traditional non-partisan role of the 'friend of the court'.[114] In other cases, judges have appointed standby counsel to represent Defence interests. For example, in *Šešelj*, the Chamber noted that the 'Tribunal has a legitimate interest in ensuring that the trial proceeds in a timely manner without interruptions, adjournments or disruption'[115] and ordered the imposition of a counsel, since the defendant used the trial 'as a vehicle for the furtherance of his political beliefs and aspirations' and was in need of legal assistance.[116] At the ICC, defendants have been more reluctant to represent themselves. Judges have the authority to appoint counsel 'in the interests of justice'.[117] This is expressly foreseen in the Regulations of the Court.

The way in which Defence structures are organized differs across institutions. At the ad hoc tribunals, Defence interests were supported by the Registry. The SCSL introduced a special Defence office. In the STL, the Defence is formally recognized as a separate organ of the Tribunal. This institutionalization is guided by the ambition to strengthen the equality of arms.[118] Specific professional organizations have been established to support defence functions before international criminal courts and tribunals. They include the 'Association of Defence Counsel practising before the International Courts and Tribunals', which has been focused on the ad hoc tribunals and its successor mechanism, and the International Criminal Court Bar Association (ICCBA) which has been created in 2016 to facilitate the proficiency and competence of Counsel and to promote professional standards. In practice, ethical dilemmas have

---

[113] *Prosecutor* v. *Milošević*, IT–99–37–PT, Order Inviting Designation of Amicus curiae, 30 August 2001. The Order stated that the amicus curiae would assist the Trial Chamber by: '(a) making any submissions properly open to the accused by way of preliminary or other pre-trial motion; (b) making any submissions or objections to evidence properly open to the accused during the trial proceedings and cross-examining witnesses as appropriate; (c) drawing to the attention of the Trial Chamber any exculpatory or mitigating evidence; and (d) acting in any other way which designated counsel considers appropriate in order to secure a fair trial'. See also *Prosecutor* v. *Milošević*, IT–02–54, Order Concerning Amici Curiae, 11 January 2002.

[114] Judge Shahabuddeen criticized this use of the amicus curiae model. Milošević Counsel Appeal, Separate Opinion of Judge Shahabuddeen, para. 15 ('an amicus curiae is limited to his essential function as a friend of the court, as distinguished from being a friend of the accused. More pertinently, under the system of the Tribunal, he is not legally competent to act as counsel for the accused, and he certainly is not an intervener').

[115] *Prosecutor* v. *Šešelj*, Case No. IT-03–67-PT, Decision on Prosecution's Motion for Order Appointing Counsel to Assist Vojislav Šešelj with his Defence, 9 May 2003, para. 21.

[116] Ibid., para. 22.

[117] See Regulation 76 of the Regulations of the Court.

[118] J. Jones and M. Zgonec-Rozej, 'Rights of Suspects and Accused', in Alamuddin, Jurdi and Tolbert, *The Special Tribunal for Lebanon: Law and Practice*, 177, 191.

arisen in relation to fee-splitting by counsel, influencing of witnesses, and revelation of confidential information.[119]

4.3.2.5 Presence at Trial

One of the most controversial questions is to what extent a trial can be held in the absence of the defendant.[120] The answer differs among courts and domestic legal traditions. The accused must generally be present during the trial. This is part of a fair trial and the right of the accused ('*audi alteram partem*'). The notion of 'trial in absentia' covers a variety of scenarios, ranging from partial absence at trial to a full-fledged absence from criminal proceedings (e.g. due to the fact that the defendant is at large). A partial absence may be justified on grounds such as disruptive behaviour in court or voluntary absence.[121] A complete trial in the absence of the defendant is more contested.[122] Both the Nuremberg Tribunal[123] and the Special Tribunal for Lebanon[124] have held trials in complete absence, since they were unable to secure the appearance of the accused. An express provision allowing *in absentia* trials was included in the STL Statute,[125] since it was feared that Syria would not hand over suspects. A trial *in absentia* may partially serve the interest of victims and the international community. However, it conflicts with the liberal foundations of the justice process and fairness guarantees. The Appeals Chamber of the STL determined that

> in absentia trials are possible only where i) reasonable efforts have been taken to notify the accused personally; ii) the evidence as to notification satisfies the Trial Chamber that the accused actually knew of the proceedings against them; and that iii) it does so with such degree of specificity that the accused's absence means they must have elected not to attend the hearing and therefore have waived their right to be present.[126]

The STL clarified that there 'is no requirement under the Tribunal's Statute or Rules, or under international human rights law that the Chamber must receive positive evidence of the accused's knowledge, or that notification must be carried out officially and in person'.[127] Fairness concerns may be mitigated through the

---

[119] On misconduct, see G. Zyberi, 'Dealing with Professional Misconduct by Defense Counsel during International Criminal Proceedings', in Rohan and Zyberi, *Defense Perspectives on International Criminal Justice*, 109–134.

[120] See P. Gaeta, 'To Be (Present) or Not To Be (Present)' (2007) 5 *JICJ* 1165; W. A. Schabas, 'In Absentia Proceedings before International Criminal Courts', in Sluiter and Vasiliev, *International Criminal Procedure: Towards a Coherent Body of Law*, 339–342.

[121] See M. H. Zakerhossein and A.-M. Brouwer, 'Diverse Approaches to Total and Partial in Absentia Trials by International Criminal Tribunals' (2015) 26 *Criminal Law Forum* 181, 220–213.

[122] Ibid., 223 ('total *in absentia* trials should be prohibited in international criminal law, whereas partial *in absentia* trials can be accepted in certain circumstances').

[123] Art. 12 of the Nuremberg IMT Charter stated that the Tribunal 'shall have the right to take proceedings against a person charged with crimes set out in Article 6 of this Charter in his absence, if he has not been found or if the Tribunal, for any reason, finds it necessary, in the interests of justice, to conduct the hearing in his absence'. Martin Bormann was tried *in absentia* at Nuremberg, since he was not apprehended and there were doubts as to whether or not he has dead.

[124] W. Jordash and T. Parker, 'Trials in Absentia at the Special Tribunal for Lebanon' (2010) 8 *JICJ* 507.

[125] Art. 22 STL Statute.

[126] *Prosecutor* v. *Ayyash*, STL-11–01/PT/AC/AR126.1, Decision on Defence Appeals against Trial Chamber's Decision on Reconsideration of the Trial In Absentia Decision, 1 November 2012, para. 31 (Trial in Absentia Decision).

[127] Ibid., para. 32.

organization of an effective defence. However, the overall value of *in absentia* trials remains doubtful.

There are serious concerns as to judicial economy. Under human rights law, accused who are convicted *in absentia* have the right to be retried, unless defended at trial by counsel of their choosing.[128] A trial *in absentia* is thus constantly under the threat of the right to 'retrial', based on fairness guarantees.[129] This brings not only costs, but remaining uncertainty. Rendering a judgment and penalty that cannot be enforced has limited value from a retributive perspective. It may compromise the credibility of the tribunal or cause frustration among victims.[130]

The ICTY, the ICTR and the ICC follow a stricter regime. They do not allow a trial in absentia, but rather 'a procedure in absentia'.[131] The ad hoc tribunals were able to confirm an indictment *in absentia* under Rule 61.[132] This option was a compromise, namely 'an apology for [the] Tribunal's helplessness'[133] and a tool to enhance pressure for compliance. A similar possibility exists at the ICC. The Pre-Trial Chamber can confirm charges in the absence of a defendant.[134] However, at these institutions it is not permitted to start trial proceedings against accused persons who cannot be apprehended.[135] Trials can only be partially held *in absentia*, namely if an accused disrupts the trial, waives the right to be present or is temporarily excused from presence at trial. Typically, the accused cannot simply refuse to attend trial without a valid reason. Following pressure by the African Union concerning the trial of Kenyan President Kenyatta, and Vice-President Ruto, however, the ICC has allowed absence from trial on a case-by-case basis for accused who appear voluntarily, namely based on a summons to appear. It created a special rule for persons who fulfil 'extraordinary public duties at the highest level'.[136] It makes heads of state 'a little bit less equal' than other accused.

4.3.3 Role of Judges

The role of a judge in an international setting differs partly from domestic systems. Judges in international criminal courts and tribunals are typically professional judges.

---

[128] ECtHR, *Krombach v. France*, Appl. No. 29731/96, Judgment, 13 February 2012, para. 87 ('the authorities have a positive obligation to afford the accused the opportunity to have a complete rehearing of the case in her or her presence'). For a critique, see Gaeta, 'To Be (Present) or Not To Be (Present)', 1170.

[129] Art. 22 (3) of the STL Statute reflects this caveat. It provides that 'in case of conviction in absentia, the accused, if he or she had not designated a defense counsel of his or her choosing, shall have the right to be retried in his or her presence before the Special Tribunal, unless he or she accepts the judgment'.

[130] M. Gardner, 'Reconsidering Trials In Absentia at the Special Tribunal for Lebanon: An Application of the Tribunal's Early Jurisprudence' (2011) 43 *George Washington International Law Review* 134, 135.

[131] *Prosecutor* v. *Ayyash et al.*, Trial In Absentia Decision, para. 37.

[132] On Rule 61, see B. T. Hildreh, 'Hunting the Hunters: The United Nations Unleashes its Latest Weapon in the Fight against Fugitive War Crimes Suspects – Rule 61' (1998) 6 *Tulane Journal of International & Comparative Law* 499.

[133] See *Prosecutor* v. *Rajic*, IT-95-12-TC, Separate Opinion of Judge Sidhwa, Rule 61 Decision, 13 September 1996, para. 7.

[134] See Rule 125 of the ICC Rules of Procedure and Evidence.

[135] See e.g. Art. 61 ICC Statute.

[136] Rule 134 quater of the ICC Rules of Procedure and Evidence.

There are no juries or lay judges. The absence of lay judges may be explained by the legal and factual complexity of cases and the systemic challenges of atrocity trials. Judges are not only arbiters over the Defence and the Prosecution case who evaluate evidence, decide on guilt or innocence, and pass judgment. They are vested with significant managerial powers, or even certain truth-seeking functions.[137]

Often, the first and most difficult task of judges of an international criminal court or tribunal is to adapt to a new legal culture.[138] Judges are shaped by the influence of their domestic legal cultures.[139] There are commonalities shared by legal traditions, particularly with respect to protecting the rights of the accused and the administration of justice.[140] However, there are significant differences when it comes to fact-finding and the power of the bench to scrutinize and dictate evidence. For example, in many common law jurisdictions, the role of the judge is limited to answering questions of law, both substantive and procedural, ensuring the rights of the accused, guaranteeing the proper and efficient administration of justice through their management of the proceedings, and finally determining the appropriate sentence in the event of a finding of guilt beyond all reasonable doubt. In civil law jurisdictions, the Bench has a more proactive role. Judges are fact-finders who enjoy the power to question witnesses, call evidence and ultimately to adjudicate on the guilt of the accused. In the context of international criminal courts and tribunals, judges are required to act as multitaskers. They typically exercise several functions simultaneously: umpire, fact-finder, interpreter of the law, and ultimate administrator of justice.

4.3.3.1 Fact-Finding

Accurate fact-finding is a cornerstone of the criminal process. Judges act as the ultimate adjudicators of fact. There is no jury of peers to which the arguments and evidence submitted by the Prosecution, the Defence and victims are directed. The role of the Prosecution is to persuade the Bench that the evidence meets the required threshold.

In the exercise of their judicial functions, judges are more constrained than historians. Criminal proceedings deal with specific facts and context, rather than the broader history of events. Judges do not collect sources, but rely mostly on material presented to them. They have limited means to map and deconstruct facts. Their

---

[137] Langer, 'Rise of Managerial Judging', 835.

[138] See J. Jackson and Y. M'Boge, 'The Effect of Legal Culture on the Development of International Evidentiary Practice: From the "Robing Room" to the "Melting Pot"' (2013) 26 *LJIL* 947; M. Bohlander, 'Language, Culture, Legal Traditions and International Criminal Justice' (2014) 12 *JICJ* 491. On the ICTY experience, see A. Whiting, 'ICTY as a Laboratory of International Criminal Procedure', in Swart, Zahar and Sluiter, *The Legacy of the International Criminal Tribunal for the Former Yugoslavia*, 83, 87 ('As trials unfolded, common lawyers at the ICTY found themselves admiring features of the civil law system, whose lawyers in turn saw merit in certain common law features. Thus in many cases the procedural solutions and revisions devised at the ICTY were the work of judges, with input from the parties, not acting as theorists seeking to impose an overarching system on the Rules, but rather as participants trying to devise pragmatic solutions to specific challenges that arose in particular cases').

[139] J. Almqvist, 'The Impact of Cultural Diversity on International Criminal Proceedings' (2006) 4 *JICJ* 745.

[140] On compatibility of principles of Islamic law, see M. Badar, 'Islamic Law (Shari'a) and the Jurisdiction of the International Criminal Court' (2011) 24 *LJIL* 411.

vision of events is strongly filtered through legal notions. The structure of the procedure forces them to strive for utmost certainty and to eliminate grey areas.

Due to the impartiality of judges and the resources devoted to the legal process, international criminal courts and tribunals are often considered as an ideal type of judicial fact-finding. However, factors such as the nature of the mass criminality, the focus on specific leadership personalities, or the distance from the scene and context of the crime, pose significant challenges to fact-finding capacity.

International proceedings rely heavily on eyewitness testimony, since there is often no documented record of orders or actions. This practice creates epistemic problems. 'Educational, cultural or linguistic differences' between witnesses and court staff complicate communication and reliability assessments. Judge Patricia Wald put it nicely when she said: 'I know no judge in [an international] tribunal who does not acknowledge that he or she is totally at the mercy of the translator in the courtroom'.[141] Not all testimonial deficiencies are detected or reflected in legal decisions. Nancy Combs, for instance, has reviewed nearly all cases of the SCSL and some ICTY cases. She criticized international criminal courts and tribunals for the use of judicially inexperienced judges and 'Fact-Finding Without Facts'.[142] Her study comes to the astonishing conclusion that 'more than 50 percent of prosecution witnesses appearing in these trials testified in a way that was seriously inconsistent with their pre-trial statements'.[143]

Some of these risks, such as contradictory and inconsistent testimony, are of course inherent in any trial.[144] They can be mitigated through measures such as better on-site investigation, improvement of communication between witnesses and fact-finders in the courtroom, and contempt proceedings sanctioning witness interference. However, the strong predominance of eyewitness testimony, and its proper assessment and contextualization in light of other evidence and undisputed facts, remains a problem. There is a need to diversify the types of evidence.

Moreover, fact-finding through international procedures raises deeper methodological challenges. In devising procedures, international agents have sought to develop a framework that provides the best 'epistemic fit' to international crimes.[145] They have drawn on lessons and practices from other tribunals in order to identify an ideal legal framework. Some have argued for a 'customary international criminal procedural law'.[146] Few efforts have been made to connect principles of an emerging law of

---

[141] P. Wald, 'Running the Trial of the Century: The Nuremberg Legacy' (2006) 7 *Cardozo Law Review* 1559, at 1570–1571.
[142] N. Combs, *Fact-Finding Without Facts: The Uncertain Evidentiary Foundations of International Criminal Convictions* (Cambridge: Cambridge University Press, 2010), 4, 234–235.
[143] Ibid., at 4.
[144] See W. Ferdinandusse, 'Fact-Finding by and about International Criminal Tribunals' (2013) 11 *JICJ* 677.
[145] J. Jackson, 'Finding the Best Epistemic Fit for International Criminal Tribunals' (2009) 7 *JICJ* 17.
[146] *Prosecutor* v. *Ruto and Sang*, Case No. ICC-01/09–01/11–1274-Corr2, Decision on Prosecutor's Application for Witness Summonses and Resulting Request for State Party Cooperation, 17 April 2014, paras. 88–92. This concept is at odds with Art. 21 and general international law. It is more appropriate to refer to 'general principles' in relation to procedure. See L. Van den Herik, 'The Decline of Customary International Law as a Source of International Criminal Law', in C. Bradley (ed.), *Custom's Future: International Law in a Changing World* (New York: Cambridge University Press, 2016), 230–252.

international criminal procedure to the domestic contexts in which they come to apply. There is often a strong disconnect to local context. Both international judges sitting in international or hybrid courts and foreign domestic judges adjudicating international crimes are less familiar with the historical, political and social context of crimes and the culture of defendants, witnesses and victims. Defendants, witnesses and victims may face difficulties adapting to international procedures. As Tim Kelsall has noted:

> Just as most of the jurisprudence used in international criminal trials is Western in origin, so is the procedure ... It is difficult ... to imagine how unnerving international trials must be for many ... witnesses, who find themselves miles from home, in a courtroom of extraordinary grandeur, confronted with robed judges and lawyers who speak a foreign language, and who subject them to highly unusual communicative practices including frequently hostile cross-examination. It is no wonder that getting clear testimony in such circumstances has often proved difficult, a problem compounded in contexts, not uncommon in Africa, where secrecy is prized as a high social ideal, and in which there have developed a repertoire of dissembling rhetorical techniques.[147]

The underlying fact base of trials is often constructed through mediated knowledge, i.e. information from states, NGOs and international organizations that have a normative interest in the use of specific labels and their connotations. At the ICC, these dilemmas became evident in the *Katanga* case.[148] The judgment rested on the theory that Katanga contributed to a campaign by Ngiti fighters to 'wipe out' out the village of Bogoro and its Hema population, since it occupied a strategic position for the Union des patriotes congolais (UPC) in the Ituri conflict.[149] However, key foundations of this theory, such as the concept of 'militia', ethnic foundations and an 'alleged anti-Hema ideology', remained underdeveloped.

The weaknesses were outlined in the Minority Opinion of Judge Christine van den Wyngaert. Van den Wyngaert questioned key categorizations of organizational violence. She argued that the judgment failed to explain 'with any level of precision how the so-called militia of the Ngiti fighters of Walendu-Bindi was structured or how it supposedly operated',[150] or 'how and when the "thousands" of individual members of the Ngiti fighters of Walendu-Bindi would have adopted the alleged common purpose to attack the Hema civilian population'.[151] She claimed that 'so little is known about how, when and by whom most of the crimes against civilians were actually carried out that it is totally impossible to form any opinion about the systematic nature of it'.[152]

---

[147] T. Kelsall, 'International Criminal Justice and Non-Western Cultures', 12 April 2010, Oxford Transitional Justice Research Working Paper Series, at www.law.ox.ac.uk/sites/files/oxlaw/kelsall_internationalcriminaljustice_final1.pdf.
[148] See Stahn, 'Justice Delivered or Justice Denied', 809.
[149] See *Katanga* Trial Judgment.
[150] Minority Opinion of Judge Christine Van den Wyngaert, ICC-01/04–01/07–3436-AnxI, 8 March 2014, para. 205.
[151] Ibid., para. 207.
[152] Ibid., para. 274.

Her critique attacks the trend to present and construe facts through prefabricated legal constructs. Her argument goes to the heart of the limits and risks of global knowledge production in a judicial context:

> it is factually wrong to reduce this case, and especially the reasons of the different Ngiti fighters and commanders for participating in the operation against the UPC, to ethnic fear and/or hatred. Such oversimplification may fit nicely within a particular conception of how certain groups of people behave in certain parts of the world, but I fear it grossly misrepresents reality, which is far more complex. It also implicitly absolves others from responsibility.[153]

Ultimately, reliance on social ideal types might produce narratives of fact that stand in contrast to historical accounts.[154]

4.3.3.2 Interpreting the Law vs. Lawmaking

The judiciary is the guardian of the law. The most classical role of a judge is to apply and interpret the applicable law. Judges have the authority to determine the meaning of legal provisions and their application in individual cases.

A key difficulty of international criminal law is that it encompasses a diversity of provisions: classical penal norms and principles (e.g. crime definitions, modes of liability and general principles of criminal law), institutional provisions, and human rights- or civil liability-oriented rules or principles. Interpretative approaches may differ according to the nature of the respective provision.[155] For instance, certain institutional issues (e.g. cooperation, admissibility) may have to be interpreted by classical principles of public international law (e.g. text, drafter's intent) or the law of international organizations (e.g. inherent powers, effectiveness). Other issues (e.g. determination of individual criminal responsibility) are subject to rules of interpretation of criminal justice, such as strict construction or the prohibition of analogy. Yet other issues (e.g. fair trial rights, rights of victims, reparation) may need to be determined in light of interpretative approaches under human rights law. The choice of the proper interpretative method may depend on the background of judges and cause friction. As William Schabas has noted: 'Judges recruited from the public international law field will lean towards the Vienna Convention, while those who are criminal law practitioners in national legal systems will favour strict construction'.[156] The relationship between legal interpretation and lawmaking is a constant friction in international criminal proceedings. Generally, the judiciary is not meant to serve as a legislative organ. Laws are typically made in a political process that involves broader input, greater transparency and more supervision than judicial deliberations. In international criminal law, however, judges were never simply 'la bouche de la loi'.

---

[153] Ibid., para. 318.
[154] For a critique, see A. Branch, 'International Justice, Local Injustice' (2004) 51 *Dissent* 22.
[155] See generally L. Grover, *Interpreting Crimes in the Rome Statute of the International Criminal Court* (Cambridge: Cambridge University Press, 2014).
[156] W. Schabas, *Introduction to the International Criminal Court* (Cambridge: Cambridge University Press, 2011), 216.

They have played a key role in the development of law, due to the imperfections of the international legal system, their expert authority, peer pressure and subtle influences by NGOs and justice constituencies. They have acted as pioneers and engineers. This role may be partly explained by the rudimentary nature of international criminal law and the strong moral incentive to create accountability systems for atrocity crime.[157]

The statutory instruments of international criminal courts and tribunals are often rudimentary. Sometimes, provisions are kept deliberately 'ambiguous' in order to facilitate political compromise and leave interpretation open to judicial practice ('constructive ambiguity').[158] Specific sources of international criminal law, such as customary law or general principles of law, provide leeway for judicial creativity.[159] The mandate and context of international criminal courts and tribunals, including the absence of a general legislator in international law, create strong policy incentives to adopt a flexible interpretation of the judicial function and to correct imperfections in the law.[160] Judges have used their power to resolve ambiguities or fill certain gaps. As Rosa Roisini and James Meernik have explained:

International judges have gone through a process of 'acculturation'. Over the years, they have identified themselves with a specific group (the international criminal legal community) charged with a mandate (prosecuting violations of humanitarian and human rights law) and in pursuit of a similar interest (leaving a lasting legacy broadly accepted by the international community, states, and political actors to advance human rights) ... with their decisions judges have considerably restructured the social understanding of international crimes.[161]

The degree to which judges resort to judicial creativity differs. There is a spectrum of approaches. In his separate Opinion in *Erdemović*, Judge Cassese provided a principled justification for an 'active' role of the judge in the development of international law. He stated:

national courts operate in a context where the three fundamental functions (law-making, adjudication and law enforcement) are discharged by central organs partaking of the State's direct authority over individuals. That logic cannot be simply transposed onto the international level: there, a different logic imposed by the different position and role of courts must perforce inspire and govern international criminal proceedings.[162]

The main challenge is how to strike a proper balance between the flexibility offered and the limits set by the principle of legality, which implies a right to be tried under pre-existing, foreseeable and sufficiently precise law. The European Court of Human

---

[157] B. van Schaack, 'Nullum Crimen Sine Lege: Judicial Lawmaking at the Intersection of Law and Morals' (2008) 97 *Georgetown Law Journal* 121.

[158] Constructive ambiguity leaves room for future interpretation. See Kress, 'The Procedural Law of the International Criminal Court', 605–606. However, in case of misguided application, 'constructive' ambiguity may also become 'destructive'.

[159] N. Arajärvi, *The Changing Nature of Customary International Law: Methods of Interpreting the Concept of Custom in International Criminal Tribunals* (London: Routledge, 2014).

[160] See generally R. Higgins 'Policy Considerations and the International Judicial Process' (1968) 17 *ICLQ* 67.

[161] See Roisini and Meernik, *Judgment Day*, 56.

[162] *Prosecutor* v. *Erdemović*, Separate and Dissenting Opinion of Judge Cassese, para. 5.

Rights held that 'the Convention cannot be read as outlawing the gradual clarification of the rules of criminal liability through judicial interpretation, provided that the development is consistent with the essence of the offence and could reasonably be foreseen'.[163] The ICTY Appeals Chamber followed this approach. It found that the *nullum crimen* principle 'does not prevent a court, either at the national or at the domestic level, from determining an issue through a process of interpretation and clarification as to the elements of a crime'.[164] In practice, there is often only a thin line between clarification of a rule, progressive development and lawmaking.[165]

Especially in the formative years of international criminal law, judicial bodies have relied, perhaps even more than in other fields, on an extensive interpretation of the judicial mandate and legal constructivism. Judges have been reluctant to accept the idea of a *non liquet*, i.e. the absence or insufficiency of law on a question at hand.[166] They have been eager to solve problems, give precision to norms, or if necessary extend the realm of law. In particular, the ad hoc tribunals have made extensive use of custom to determine the scope and nature of their subject-matter jurisdiction. Both tribunals have applied customary international law as a fallback option for areas not covered by the Statute. They have served as 'customary midwives', and operated 'within, rather than outside, the process of formation of custom'.[167]

Tribunals have broadened the basis of evidence necessary to establish the existence of a customary rule and extended the concept of custom to several areas that are not typically covered by, or associated with, state practice in public international law, or a corresponding *opinio juris*, such as modes of liability or defences (e.g. duress).[168] They have relied on general principles of law to fill gaps in the definition and scope of offences (e.g. rape), or to clarify procedures and sentencing.[169] Some forms of judicial creativity entailed judicial lawmaking, i.e. the creation of new crimes or the broadening of principles of liability (e.g. JCE, superior responsibility). Such judicial activism creates difficult tensions with the principle of legality in the area of substantive criminal law and matters affecting the guilt and innocence of defendants. Some developments have only gained acceptance through subsequent practice, codification or rejection of legal challenges.

Judicial creativity is slightly less problematic in relation to procedural law. Procedures are highly dynamic. Judges require a certain amount of flexibility and discretion in order to exercise their managerial functions. The principle of legality imposes fewer

---

[163] ECtHR, *S.W.* v. *the United Kingdom*, Appl. No. 20166/92, Judgment, 22 November 1995, para. 36. See also ECtHR, *C.R.* v. *the United Kingdom*, Appl. No. 20190/92, Judgment, 22 November 1995, para. 34.

[164] *Prosecutor* v. *Aleksovski*, IT-95–14/1-A, Judgment, 24 March 2000, para. 127.

[165] M. Shahabuddeen, 'Does the Principle of Legality Stand in the Way of Progressive Development of Law?' (2004) 2 *JICJ* 1007.

[166] J. Stone, 'Non Liquet and the Function of Law in the International Community' (1959) 35 *British Yearbook of International Law* 124.

[167] G. Mettraux, *International Crimes and the Ad Hoc Tribunals* (Oxford: Oxford University Press, 2005), 15.

[168] See Herik, 'Decline of Customary Law', 230.

[169] See F. Raimondo, 'General Principles of Law, Judicial Creativity, and the Development of International Criminal Law', in Darcy and Powderly, *Judicial Creativity at the International Criminal Tribunals*, 45–59.

constraints on procedures.[170] Interpretation of procedural law relies to a large extent on context and function.[171] Some areas, such as admissibility of evidence or disclosure, are highly dependent on court practices. The ultimate benchmark is fairness. It may prohibit unfair changes of rules and procedures in the same case, but it does not rule out judicial creativity. Sometimes the absence of procedural law may be more damaging from a fairness perspective than its creation by judges. Due to the incomplete nature of rules of procedure and evidence, judges have almost inevitably been engaged in procedural lawmaking.[172] For instance, the ad hoc tribunals,[173] the SCSL and the Kosovo Specialist Chambers were mandated to adopt their own rules of procedure.

In practice, procedural lawmaking by judges has created dilemmas. It may, first of all, raise challenges in relation to predictability. For example, the ICTY Rules of Procedure and Evidence were amended fifty times since their creation in 1994. This experience suggests that ICTY judges 'actually liked[d] lawmaking, instead of adopting a highly reserved attitude towards it'.[174] Such changes may cause disruption and uncertainty for parties, and ultimately affect their ability to prepare their case. In the ICC context, judges have less space for lawmaking, since the general procedural framework was predetermined by the drafters and cannot be amended by judges.[175] However, individual ICC Chambers have adopted very different procedural approaches in relation to key issues, such as disclosure, victim participation, witness proofing or admissibility of evidence. This meant that defendants faced vastly different practices, depending on the Chamber that adjudicated the case. The Common Practice Manual adopted by judges, which contains 'recommendations'[176] and guidelines reflecting best practices, has been described as a 'return to procedural lawmaking by judges',[177] caused by the absence of amendments by state parties.

A second concern is the creation of artificial legal transplants. The ad hoc tribunals have relied on the doctrine of 'autonomous interpretation' to address this concern. It implies that

---

[170] See S. Vasiliev, 'The Making of International Criminal Law', in C. Brölmann and Y. Radi (eds.), *Research Handbook on the Theory and Practice of International Lawmaking* (Cheltenham: Edward Elgar, 2016), 354, 362.

[171] It depends on factors such as (i) the purposes of the specific procedure, (ii) the specific interests of different parties and participants in proceedings, and (iii) its context, i.e. its link to the object and purpose of the respective institution. They vary across institutions and may evolve over time.

[172] See G. Sluiter, 'Procedural Lawmaking at the International Criminal Tribunals', in Darcy and Powderly, *Judicial Creativity at the International Criminal Tribunals*, 315.

[173] In *Tadić*, the ICTY stated that the Security Council surely expected that '[the Statute] would be supplemented, where advisable, by the rules which the Judges were mandated to adopt, especially for Trials and Appeals'. See *Tadić* 1995, para. 4.

[174] Sluiter, 'Procedural Lawmaking', 324.

[175] For a critique, see D. Hunt, 'The International Criminal Court: High Hopes, "Creative Ambiguity" and an Unfortunate Mistrust in International Judges' (2004) 2 *JICJ* 56.

[176] See *Prosecutor* v. *Gbagbo and Blé Goudé*, ICC-02/11-01/15-369, Judgment on the appeal of Mr Laurent Gbagbo against the decision of Trial Chamber I entitled 'Decision giving notice pursuant to Regulation 55(2) of the Regulations of the Court', 18 December 2015, para. 54.

[177] Y. McDermott, 'The International Criminal Court's Chambers Practice Manual: Towards a Return to Judicial Law Making in International Criminal Procedure?' (2015) 15 *JICJ* 873, 904.

[a]ny time international provisions include notions and terms of art originating in national criminal law, the interpreter must first determine whether these notions or terms are given a totally autonomous significance in the international context, i.e., whether, once transposed onto the international level, they have acquired a new lease of life, absolutely independent of their original meaning. If the result of this inquiry is in the negative, the international judge must satisfy himself whether the transplant onto the international procedure entails for the notion or term an adaptation or adjustment to the characteristic features of international proceedings.[178]

This approach encourages a move towards an independent system of international criminal procedure. It also entails downsides. It creates a danger that international criminal courts and tribunals become increasingly 'self-centred'.

A third concern is the absence of human rights scrutiny. Procedural activism has generated some good rules, but also less good ones. Some rules may be in violation of human rights standards. In domestic systems, such flaws can be corrected. Procedural rules are subject to control of human rights norms and corresponding supervisory or monitoring mechanisms. International criminal courts and tribunals lack such an institutional embedding. They are independent institutions. They are deemed to correct their own shortcomings or violations. They lack an external human rights forum. The joint exercise of judicial and quasi-legislative power may raise account-ability problems. As Göran Sluiter has pointed out, judicial creativity might benefit from stronger input by affected parties and participants, or even independent review in the formulation of rules.[179] A compelling example is the review process of the Rules of Procedure of the Kosovo Specialist Chambers. The Rules were formally adopted by the judges. However, before entering into force they were subject to review by a special Constitutional Court Chamber which examined their compatibility with inter-national human rights, in particular the European Convention on Human Rights.[180] This process led to amendment of several rules.[181]

4.3.3.3 Managerial Functions

A third key function of judges is to ensure a proper administration of justice. This poses special challenges in relation to international crimes which involve complex facts and vast amounts of evidence. More often than not, trials last for a number of years. They consist of hundreds of hours of court sessions, hundreds of items of evidence and dozens of witnesses. For example, in the *Lubanga* case, the Trial

---

[178] *Prosecutor* v. *Erdemović*, Separate and Dissenting Opinion of Judge Cassese, para 6.

[179] Sluiter, 'Procedural Lawmaking', 331.

[180] Specialist Chamber of the Constitutional Court, KSC-CC-PR-2017–01/F00004, Judgment on the Referral of the Rules of Procedure and Evidence Adopted by Plenary on 17 March 2017 to the Specialist Chamber of the Constitutional Court Pursuant to Article 19(5) of Law No. 05/L-053 on Specialist Chambers and Specialist Prosecutor's Office, 26 April 2017; Specialist Chamber of the Constitutional Court, KSC-CC-PR-2017–03/F00006/2, KSC-CC-PR-2017–03, Judgment on the Referral of Revised Rules of the Rules of Procedure and Evidence Adopted by Plenary on 29 May 2017 to the Specialist Chamber of the Constitutional Court Pursuant to Article 19(5) of Law No. 05/L-053 on Specialist Chambers and Specialist Prosecutor's Office, 28 June 2017. See general A. Heinze, 'The Kosovo Specialist Chambers' Rules of Procedure and Evidence: A Diamond Made Under Pressure?' (2017) 15 *JICJ* 985.

[181] Rules 19(3), 31, 32, 33, 35(1)(b) and (c), 35(3), 36(1) and (2), 38(1) and (5), 54(4), and 158(2) of the Rules were initially found inconsistent with the Constitution.

Chamber sat through 204 days of hearings, during which it received evidence from 63 witnesses, and accepted 1,373 items of evidence.[182] The complexity and expansive nature of international criminal proceedings requires strong managerial skills and cooperation between parties.

In many international settings, the procedure was adjusted to allow judges to speed up proceedings, facilitate cooperation and coordination among participants and parties and ensure a fair and effective management of proceedings. This 'managerial' model differs from traditional inquisitorial and adversarial models. As Maximo Langer has argued,

> in this model the judge is no longer the investigator of the inquisitorial system or the umpire of the adversarial system, but an active manager, negotiator and mediator of the case. ... the parties both are conceived not only as zealous advocates of their positions, but also as collaborators with the judge who have the duty to help the judge reduce the court caseload, simplify the case and speed up the procedure.[183]

Under the managerial model, procedure remains dominated by the idea of competition between the case of the Prosecution and the case of the Defence. Judges are not meant to serve as 'accusers'. However, they may take a more active role in setting time limits, facilitating agreement, streamlining charges, limiting the number of witnesses heard, or controlling and expediting cases.

Managerial powers apply at pre-trial and trial. For instance, during pre-trial, judges do not merely serve as a filter for prosecutorial charges or as guardian of civil liberties.[184] They may be involved in organizing disclosure of Prosecution evidence to the Defence and witness protection, including the use of in-court witness protection measures. During the trial, they are mandated to ensure that proceedings are run in a fair, orderly and efficient manner. Parties have less power to dispose of procedural and substantive issues than in a purely adversarial system. Judges might be entitled to intervene in the parties' cases on their own motion or call witnesses they consider relevant, in order to determine the truth.[185]

Judges have further important functions to maintain the authority of courts. They may hold proceedings for offences against the administration of justice.[186] The power to hold contempt cases is inherent in the judicial function.[187] It sanctions conduct such as the giving of false testimony, deliberately presenting false or forged evidence,

---

[182] ICC Press Release, ICC-CPI-20120314-PR776, ICC First verdict: Thomas Lubanga guilty of conscripting and enlisting children under the age of 15 and using them to participate in hostilities, 14 March 2012.

[183] M. Langer, 'The Rise of Managerial Judging in International Criminal Law', UCLA School of Law Research Paper No. 04–19, 18 October 2004, 64–65, at https://papers.ssrn.com/sol3/papers.cfm?abstract_id=606341.

[184] Rome Statute, Art. 61.

[185] See G. Acquaviva, N. Combs, M. Heikkilä, S. Linton, Y. McDermott and S. Vasiliev, 'Trial Process', in Sluiter et al., *International Criminal Procedure*, 489, 578.

[186] G. Sluiter, 'The ICTY and Offences against the Administration of Justice' (2004) 2 *JICJ* 631.

[187] Approaches differ between accusatorial and inquisitorial systems. In adversarial systems, contempt powers are typically part of a 'law of contempt' and subject to the contempt power of the judiciary, which may hold a person in contempt of court and enjoys discretion as to the penalty. In civil law jurisdictions, there is often no distinction between the 'law on contempt' and other criminal offences.

corruptly influencing or tampering with witnesses, or attempting to solicit or bribe an official of the Court. International criminal courts and tribunals are vulnerable to such interference. Tampering with witnesses may impede the discovery of the truth, impede justice to victims and ultimately preclude courts from fulfilling their mandate. In past decades, there have been more than seventy cases relating to contempt of court.[188] The ICC has struggled with witness interference in nearly all of its cases (except *Al Mahdi*).[189] In its first fifteen years, it convicted more persons for obstructing justice than for actual international crimes.

4.3.4   Victims

The role of victims in international criminal proceedings has changed significantly over time. Procedurally, victims are to some extent 'new kids on the block'. Unlike judges, prosecutors and defence counsel, victim participants are no primary players. Their role in the criminal process is limited and subject to the rights of the Defence.[190]

4.3.4.1   The Case for Victim Participation

The role of victims as an independent voice in international prosecutions and trials is relatively new. Victims have traditionally formed part of the constituency of international criminal justice. International criminal courts and tribunals derive political support from reports of gross human rights violations and the plight of victims. They have claimed to exercise justice for, on behalf of, or in the name of victims. However, victims have lacked legal standing of their own for a long time.[191] In the post-World War II trials and the ad hoc tribunals, they were called as witnesses, mostly for the prosecution. They thus served mainly as suppliers of evidence.

The status as witness contains many limitations. Witnesses serve the interests of the Court or the party that calls them. This approach coincides with the conception of cases as contests between two parties. A traditional objection to victim participation has been that it affects the equality of arms between the Prosecution and the Defence. Over past decades, this binary vision has come under challenge.[192] There is a strong moral case to treat victims no longer simply as spectators or objects of trials, but as subjects. This is backed by changing legal practice.

---

[188] N. A. David, 'Contempt of Court: A Digest of the Case Law of Contempt of Court at International Criminal Tribunals and the International Criminal Court' (2015–2016) 44 *Denver Journal of International Law & Policy* 87, 88.

[189] See L. Richardson, 'Offences against the Administration of Justice at the International Criminal Court: Robbing Peter to Pay Paul?' (2017) 15 *JICJ* 741.

[190] Zappalà, 'The Rights of Victims v. the Rights of the Accused', 137.

[191] S. Karstedt, 'From Absence to Presence, From Silence to Voice: Victims in International and Transitional Justice since the Nuremberg Trials' (2010) 17 *International Review of Victimology* 9.

[192] For a victim-oriented approach, see R. Aldana-Pindell, 'An Emerging Universality of Justiciable Victims' Rights in the Criminal Process to Curtail Impunity for State-Sponsored Crimes' (2004) 26 *Human Rights Quarterly* 605; R. Aldana-Pindell, 'In Vindication of Justiciable Victims' Rights to Truth and Justice for State-Sponsored Crimes' (2002) 35 *Vanderbilt Journal of Transnational Law* 1399.

The exclusion of victims contrasts with claims by the victim rights movement. Victim rights advocates have criticized criminal justice systems since the 1960s for sidelining the persons most affected by crimes. They have argued that classical criminal trial formats leave victims voiceless, powerless or even demoralized.[193] Common law jurisdictions have started to grant victims certain procedural rights, such as victim impact statements, as of the 1970s.[194] This trend gained a new momentum with victim-centred human rights instruments and the rise of restorative justice theories. The 1985 Declaration of Basic Principles of Justice for Victims of Crime and Abuse of Power[195] strengthened the rights of victims of domestic criminal law to access to justice and redress for violations. The UN Basic Principles and Guidelines on the Right to a Remedy and Reparation for Victims, which were adopted by consensus in the UN General Assembly, provided mechanisms, modalities and procedures to address 'gross violations of human rights law' and 'serious violations of international humanitarian law'.[196] They were initially meant to provide guidance to states, rather than absolute rights. However, they have been said to form an 'international bill of rights of victims',[197] in particular in transitional justice processes.

Human rights activists have argued that the effective investigation and prosecution of human rights violations requires participation and input by victims and survivors, since they have a story to tell and a right to be heard. Restorative justice theories have challenged the assumption that justice is solely concerned with punishing the perpetrators. Both factors favour a more inclusive conception of justice, which includes restoration of victims' rights and redress.

As of the late 1990s, victim participation was included in the framework of several courts and tribunals: the ICC, the ECCC and the STL. The ICC regime marked an attempt to address concerns of 'secondary victimization' that were raised in the context of the ad hoc tribunals.[198] Many of the theoretical objections against victim participation, such as its alleged incompatibility with the presumption of innocence, or the conflation of victims with a 'second prosecutor', have been discarded. For instance, the UN Basic Principles clarify that a person can be 'considered a victim regardless of whether the perpetrator of the violation is identified, apprehended, prosecuted, or convicted'.[199] There are multiple safeguards to prevent victim

---

[193] E. O'Hara, 'Victim Participation in the Criminal Process' (2005) 13 *Journal of Law & Policy* 229, 234 et seq.

[194] J.-A. Wemmers, 'Where Do They Belong? Giving Victims a Place in the Criminal Justice Process' (2009) 20 *Criminal Law Forum* 395, 398.

[195] General Assembly Resolution 40/34 of 29 November 1985, Annex. It addresses issues such as access to justice, fair treatment, restitution, compensation and assistance.

[196] General Assembly Resolution 60/147 of 16 December 2005, Annex.

[197] See M. Cherif Bassiouni, 'International Recognition of Victims' Rights' (2006) 6 *Human Rights Law Review* 203.

[198] C. Van den Wyngaert, 'Victims before International Criminal Courts: Some Views and Concerns of an ICC Trial Judge' (2012) 44 *Case Western Reserve International Law Journal* 475, 494. At the ICTY, the impact of a crime on a victim's relatives could be taken into account at sentencing. See *Prosecutor* v. *Krnojelac*, IT-97-25-A, Judgment, 17 September 2003, para. 260.

[199] Basic Principles and Guidelines on the Right to a Remedy and Reparation, Principle 9.

submissions presenting the defendant with a 'second accuser'.[200] It is increasingly recognized that victim participation is not per se incompatible with an adversarial process or the rights of defendants.[201] The question is rather how it can be reconciled with these features, and what benefits it offers.

Proponents of victim participation argue that involvement in criminal proceedings serves victims in different ways. Some claim that victim participation is necessary to give legitimacy to international criminal justice.[202] Others stress that victim participation has an important symbolic effect, since it gives trials a human face. Involvement in criminal proceedings may further have a certain therapeutic or empowering effect. It may restore a sense of equality between perpetrator and victims, or even contribute to some form of healing, by recognizing harm and attributing responsibility.[203] As Mariana Pena and Gaelle Carayon have noted: 'Victimhood leads to disempowerment, as the crimes ordinarily put victims in a situation where they lose control and are subject to perpetrators' will. Allowing victims to make decisions for themselves can play a role in reversing that situation'.[204] Yet others claim that victim participation may have certain judicial functions. It may, for instance, assist in truth-finding,[205] provide an alternative account of facts or even a check on prosecutorial perspectives,[206] and/or facilitate reparation claims. It can also have a useful spillover effect on the possibility for victims to seek redress in other forums.

Critics challenge some of these assumptions. They question whether victim participation actually produces the alleged therapeutic or judicial effects[207] and whether the alleged benefits outweigh the costs. As feminist and other critiques have pointed

---

[200] For instance, in the ICC context, victims do not have the full status of a party to proceedings and face restrictions in relation to the ability to lead evidence.

[201] T. van Boven, 'The Position of the Victim in the Statute of the International Criminal Court', in H. von Hebel et al. (eds.), *Reflections on the International Criminal Court: Essays in Honour of Adriaan Bos* (T. M. C. Asser Press, 1999), 77–89, at 87; G. Bitti and H. Friman, 'Participation of Victims in the Proceedings', in R. Lee (ed.), *The International Criminal Court: Elements of Crimes and Rules of Procedure and Evidence* (Ardsley: Transnational Publishers, 2001), 456.

[202] M. Findlay, 'Activating a Victim Constituency in International Criminal Justice' (2009) 3 *International Journal of Transitional Justice* 183, 189 ('International criminal justice has no choice but to move towards a victim constituency if its legitimacy and functional relevance are to be confirmed beyond the authority of legislative instruments and sponsor agencies').

[203] J. de Hemptinne, 'Challenges Raised by Victims' Participation in the Proceedings of the Special Tribunal for Lebanon' (2010) 8 *JICJ* 165, 167. The United Nations Special Rapporteur on the promotion of truth, justice, reparation and guarantees of non-recurrence, Pablo de Greiff, noted: 'Victim participation implies the recognition of victims as rights holders, which is tremendously empowering for them and other'. Report of the Special Rapporteur on the promotion of truth, justice, reparation and guarantees of non-recurrence, A/HRC/27/56 (2014), 27 August 2014, para. 94.

[204] M. Pena and G. Carayon, 'Is the ICC Making the Most of Victim Participation?' (2013) 7 *International Journal for Transitional Justice* 518, 534.

[205] See L. Catani, 'Victims at the International Criminal Court' (2012) 10 *JICJ* 905, 919. For an argument that victims contributed to factual issues and truth-telling in Lubanga and Katanga, see C. H. Wheeler, 'No Longer Just a Victim: The Impact of Victim Participation on Trial Proceedings at the International Criminal Court' (2016) 16 *International Criminal Law Review* 525, 545–546.

[206] C. Jorda and J. de Hemptinne, 'The Status and Role of the Victim', in Cassese, Gaeta and Jones, *The Rome Statute of the International Criminal Court*, 1387.

[207] Some scholars argue that post-war trials 'neither harm individuals' nor ease their emotional and psychological suffering'. See D. Mendeloff, 'Trauma and Vengeance: Assessing the Psychological and Emotional Effects of Post-Conflict Justice' (2009) 31 *Human Rights Quarterly* 593.

out,[208] the very use of the notion of 'victim' itself entails a certain stigma. It evokes a degree of passivity, helplessness and shame that may stand in contrast to the self-perception of affected subjects. Others fear that the rise of victims' rights may overburden criminal courts, prolong trials and leave many victims unsatisfied. Prosecutors share concerns that victim involvement may compromise their ability to convict defendants. Others question the alleged positive effects on victims. Criminal charges and trials are highly selective. This may create implicit hierarchies among victims or fuel resentment and tensions in affected communities.[209] Victim participation may have hidden costs for non-participating victims.[210] Litigation involves large operational costs and a high degree of bureaucratization. Sceptics suggest that resources spent on participation and representation might be better invested in less formal measures that allow victims to rebuild their lives.[211] A nuanced assessment of the merits of victim participation thus requires a broader vision that exceeds the judicial framework and advocacy considerations.

4.3.4.2 Role in Proceedings

The increasing involvement of victims in proceedings poses daunting procedural challenges. Victim participation is still largely an experiment.[212] The way in which victims can participate in proceedings differ.

4.3.4.2.1 Domestic Approaches

Domestic legal systems recognize several ways of victim participation.[213] Many civil law jurisdictions allow for victims to join criminal proceedings as a civil complainant (*partie civile*).[214] This model allows victims to join a criminal case with a civil claim order in order to obtain reparation for damages. A small number of jurisdictions (e.g. Spain) recognize the right of victims to participate in criminal proceedings as a prosecutor.[215] However, this right is often limited to minor offences in which there

---

[208] The concept of vulnerability is deeply engrained in feminist critique. See E. C. Gilson, 'Vulnerability and Victimization: Rethinking Key Concepts' (2016) 42 *Journal of Women in Culture and Society* 71, 72; L. Kelly, *Surviving Sexual Violence* (Cambridge: Polity Press 1988).

[209] E. Haslam and R. Edmunds, 'Victim Participation, Politics and the Construction of Victims at the International Criminal Court: Reflections on Proceedings in Banda and Jerbo'(2013) 14 *Melbourne Journal of International Law* 727; K. McEvoy and K. McConnachie, 'Victimology in Transitional Justice: Victimhood, Innocence and Hierarchy' (2012) 9 *European Journal of Criminology* 527.

[210] See C. P. Trumbull IV, 'The Victims of Victim Participation in International Criminal Proceedings' (2008) 29 *Michigan Journal of International Law* 777, 823 ('forms of victim participation that delay the proceedings or take up prosecutorial resources are most costly for non-participating victims because they limit the number of suspects that the Prosecutor can bring to trial').

[211] Van den Wyngaert, 'Victims before International Criminal Courts', 495–496.

[212] See M. Rauschenbach and D. Scalia, 'Victims and International Criminal Justice: A Vexed Question?' (2008) 870 *International Review of the Red Cross*, 441–459; S. Vasiliev, 'Victim Participation Revisited: What the ICC Is Learning about Itself', in Stahn, *Law and Practice of the International Criminal Court*, 1133, 1138 et seq.

[213] See M. E. Brienen and E. H. Hoegen, *Victims of Crime in 22 European Criminal Justice Systems* (Nijmegen: Wolf Legal Publishers, 2000); A.-M. de Brouwer and M. Heikkilä, 'Victim Issues: Participation, Protection, Reparation and Assistance', in Sluiter et al., *International Criminal Procedure*, 1299, 1341–1343.

[214] McGonigle Leyh, *Procedural Justice*, 79–81.

[215] On the private prosecution model in Spain, see J. Perez Gil, 'Private Interests Seeking Punishment: Prosecution Brought by Private Individuals and Groups in Spain' (2003) 25 *Law & Policy* 151.

is no public interest in prosecution (private prosecution model). Other jurisdictions allow victims to serve as a 'subsidiary prosecutor' in cases where a public prosecutor decides not to initiate proceedings.[216] This allows victims to enjoy powers comparable to public prosecutors. Several civil law systems (e.g. Germany, Austria) allow victims to complement public prosecutors in an auxiliary capacity (auxiliary model).[217] This means that they might submit evidence, suggest questions to be posed to witnesses and the defendant, and comment on statements and evidence submitted in the proceedings. In many common law systems (e.g. United States, New Zealand, Australia, Canada) victims can deliver impact statements at sentencing.[218]

4.3.4.2.2 *International Approaches*

International criminal proceedings are in many ways *sui generis* in terms of their procedural culture, the nature of crimes and the numbers of victims affected. Models such private, subsidiary or auxiliary prosecution by victims are not particularly well suited to trials that involve international community interests, highly complex fact patterns and mass victimization. This has led to the development of differentiated approaches.

Several international treaties mandate states to include provisions on victim participation in domestic law. However, the obligation is typically framed in 'soft' terms in the sense that it is made subject to domestic law.[219] Tailor-made regimes on victim participation have been developed in specific contexts by international criminal courts and tribunals.

At the ECCC, victims were allowed to participate as civil parties.[220] This approach followed the Cambodian system which relied on the French model. According to the civil party model, the main rationale of participation is linked to the civil claim, namely to obtain reparation. Participation had an important symbolic function. It provided an element of humanity to proceedings and allowed for expression of suffering. The Cambodian model posed many challenges, however.[221] Domestic approaches had to be adjusted in order to fit the adjudication of crimes committed decades ago. The Court was only allowed to award collective and symbolic reparations.

Local NGOs were instrumental in collecting submission of civil party applications.[222] The criteria for recognizing civil party status differed. Initially, the concept

---

[216] McGonigle Leyh, *Procedural Justice*, 82.

[217] Brienen and Hoegen, *Victims of Crime in 22 European Criminal Justice Systems*, 28.

[218] McGonigle Leyh, *Procedural Justice*, 84–86.

[219] See Art. 32 (5) of the United Nations Convention against Corruption, Art. 8 of the Optional Protocol to the Convention on the Rights of the Child on the sale of children, child prostitution and child pornography, and Art. 25 (3) of the United Nations Convention against Transnational Organized Crime.

[220] See E. Hoven, 'Civil Party Participation in Trials of Mass Crimes: A Qualitative Study at the Extraordinary Chambers in the Courts of Cambodia' (2014) 12 *JICJ* 81.

[221] R. Killean, 'Procedural Justice in International Criminal Courts: Assessing Civil Parties' Perceptions of Justice at the Extraordinary Chambers in the Courts of Cambodia' (2016) 16 *International Criminal Law Review* 1; M. Elander, 'The Victim's Address: Expressivism and the Victim at the Extraordinary Chambers in the Courts of Cambodia' (2013) 7 *International Journal of Transitional Justice* 91; M. Mohan, 'The Paradox of Victim-Centrism: Victim Participation at the Khmer Rouge Tribunal' (2009) 9 *International Criminal Law Review* 733.

[222] See I. Stegmiller, 'Legal Developments in Civil Party Participation at the Extraordinary Chambers in the Courts of Cambodia' (2014) 27 *LJIL* 465, 474.

of victimhood was tied to crimes within the jurisdiction of the ECCC. During Case 001, it was narrowed to victims with a nexus to charges.[223] This caused discontent and feelings of rejection among certain victims. The scope of victim participation was subject to conflicting interpretations. According to the Internal Rules of the ECCC, civil participation was aimed at 'supporting the Prosecution'.[224] This meant that submissions of victims were subject to ultimate consent of the Prosecution.[225] Victims felt that their participatory rights did not go far enough, while the Prosecution and the Defence claimed that victim participation did not substantially add to the case, or even compromised proceedings.

Judges restricted procedural rights in order to maintain effective proceedings. In the *Duch* case, judges made it clear that victims are not on equal footing with the Prosecution.[226] In a contested decision, the majority limited the right of victims to make submissions on sentencing or to present evidence relating to the character of the defendant, with reference to the civil claim-oriented nature of participation.[227] The decision prompted civil parties to boycott proceedings. Throughout trials, the questioning of witnesses by civil party lawyers posed problems. It caused delays, through repetitive questions and lack of coordination among civil party groups. In Case 002, which concerned leading Khmer Rouge officials, victim participation expanded the realm of the case. Victim interventions prompted the co-prosecutors inter alia to include charges relating to forced marriage and other crimes.[228] The judges introduced strict rules on representation in Court. In light of the high number of victims (nearly 4,000), civil parties were meant to participate in trials as a 'consolidated group'. This meant that they did not share their views through their own civil party lawyer, but through lead co-lawyers, who had the primary responsibility to represent the consolidated group. Observers have questioned as to whether the civil party model expanded the experiences of victims significantly beyond the ad hoc tribunals[229] and allowed them to make a meaningful contribution to the trial.[230]

---

[223] Internal Rules were revised on 9 February 2010. For the implications, see *Duch* Trial Judgment, paras. 647–649.

[224] Rule 23, para. 1 lit. a.

[225] See S. SaCouto, 'Victim Participation at the International Criminal Court and the Extraordinary Chambers in the Courts of Cambodia: A Feminist Project' (2012) 18 *Michigan Journal of Gender and Law* 297, 339.

[226] *Prosecutor* v. *Kaing Guek Eav*, 001/18–07–2007/ECCC/TC, Decision on Civil Party Co-Lawyers' Joint Request for a Ruling on the Standing of Civil Party lawyers to Make Submissions on Sentencing and Directions Concerning the Questioning of the Accused, Experts and Witnesses Testifying on Character, 9 October 2009, para. 25.

[227] Ibid., para. 26 ('their role within the trial must not, in effect, transform them into additional prosecutors'), para. 40 ('Civil Parties may not make submissions on or recommendations concerning Sentencing'), and para. 44.

[228] *Prosecutor* v. *Nuon Chea et al.*, Case No. 002/19–09–2007-ECCC-OCIJ, Order on Request for Investigative Action Concerning Forced Marriages and Forced Sexual Relations, 18 December 2009. See also L. Nguyen and C. Sperfeld, 'Victim Participation and Minorities: Ethnic Vietnamese Civil Parties at the Extraordinary Chambers in the Courts of Cambodia' (2014) 14 *Macquarie Law Journal* 97.

[229] See Sacouto, 'Victim Participation', 350 ('in light of the recent restrictions on victim participation, particularly in cases where large numbers of victims are expected to participate, it is not at all clear that victims will be able to communicate a richer, more nuanced picture of their experiences than they were able to in the context of the ad hoc tribunals or the SCSL').

[230] For a moderately optimistic account, see E. Stover, M. Balthazard and A. Koenig, 'Confronting Duch: Civil Party Participation in Case 001 at the Extraordinary Chambers in the Courts of Cambodia' (2011) 93 *International Review of the Red Cross* 503, 540 et seq.

The ICC and the STL followed a different model that goes beyond the civil party idea. It allows victims to act as autonomous participants in criminal proceedings. Under this model, the idea of participation is less directly connected to reparations.

The ICC Statute set new ways of conceptualizing victim participation. It marks the first international codification of the rights of victims in international criminal proceedings. It is based on the premise that victims can contribute to prosecutions and trials in many different ways beyond providing testimony.[231] The Statute acknowledges that the interests of victims may not coincide with those of the Prosecution. It grants victims an autonomous role as participants in proceedings which allows them to contribute to proceedings from the early stages of the legal process, and separately at the reparations stage. Unlike the Prosecution, victims intervene in a personal capacity.

The ICC framework includes specific participatory rights, which entitle victims to intervene,[232] as well as a general participatory regime which contains multiple qualifiers.[233] Mapping out a novel system has been a challenge. The Statute seeks to strike a balance between three different objectives: preserving the role of the Prosecutor as 'master of proceedings', ensuring effective victim participation, and safeguarding the rights of the Defence. Judges have tried to mitigate the risks of increased victim participation through close judicial scrutiny. However, victim participation has polarized opinion like hardly any other issue.[234]

One of the innovative features of victim participation at the ICC is that it redefines the relationship to prosecutorial powers. The ICC Statute differs from domestic models. Victims are not meant to serve as second prosecutors, but they serve to some extent as a check on prosecutorial practices. The Statute takes into account that victims may not have the same vision of the case as prosecutors. Victims are not only allowed to submit information to the Prosecution. They may complement the information provided by the Prosecutor in proceedings. This is particularly important during the framing of the scope of proceedings. The Statute allows victims expressly to make representations to the Chamber[235] when the Prosecutor seeks authorization to open an investigation *proprio motu*. Victim representatives have made submissions on the scope of situations and the relevant crime base in relation to the opening of investigations in the situation in Kenya, in Côte d'Ivoire and in Afghanistan.[236]

---

[231] L. Moffett, 'Meaningful and Effective? Considering Victims' Interests Through Participation at the International Criminal Court' (2015) 26 *Criminal Law Forum* 255.

[232] See e.g. Art. 53 (3) and 19 (3) of the ICC Statute. See generally C. Stahn, H. Olásolo and K. Gibson, 'Participation of Victims in Pre-Trial Proceedings of the ICC' (2006) 4 *JICJ* 219.

[233] Art. 68 (3).

[234] C. Chung, 'Victims' Participation at the International Criminal Court: Are Concessions of the Court Clouding the Promise?' (2008) 6 *Northwestern Journal of International Human Rights* 459.

[235] See Art. 15 (3) ICC Statute.

[236] See Situation in the Islamic Republic of Afghanistan, ICC-02/17–29, Final Consolidated Registry Report on Victims' Representations Pursuant to the Pre-Trial Chamber's Order ICC-02/17-6 of 9 November 2017, 20 February 2018, Annex 1.

Representations of victims at this stage serve to enable the Chamber to 'reach its *own* conclusions with regard to the Request presented by the Prosecutor'.[237]

Victims also have a voice when the Prosecutor takes a decision not to investigate or prosecute. They do not enjoy independent standing to initiate judicial review. However, they can take part in the judicial review of negative prosecutorial decisions whenever such proceedings are triggered by other actors (e.g. states, judges).[238] Victim representatives have exercised this power inter alia in the context of the Israeli raid on civilian ships of the Gaza Freedom Flotilla (Flotilla incident). They argued that the Prosecution adopted too narrow an understanding of the gravity of crimes and urged the Prosecutor to reconsider the decision not to investigate.[239]

Victims are also entitled to make observations on jurisdiction and admissibility of cases.[240] This right may be explained by the interests of victims in the general outcome of proceedings. If proceedings fail due to lack of jurisdiction or admissibility, the legal process as such or options of reparation may be frustrated.

The clarification of general participation rights has caused significant controversy. The relevant clause, Article 68 (3), is both an innovation and a masterpiece of ambiguity and compromise.[241] It was in part borrowed from the 1985 UN Declaration of Principles of Justice for Victims of Crime and Abuse of Power, which is relates to victim participation in judicial and administrative processes at the domestic level.[242] It states that victims shall be permitted to present views and concerns whenever their personal interests are affected. This right can be exercised at the procedural stages determined appropriate (for instance, the confirmation of charges), and in a manner consistent with the rights of the accused and a fair and impartial trial. The scope of participation has had to be clarified through case law. It has been challenged by the Prosecution and the Defence. Both parties remained reserved regarding the rights of victims.[243]

A key problem of the ICC regime is the 'juridification' of victimhood, and its exclusionary processes and effects.[244] As Sara Kendall and Sarah Nouwen have shown, the systemic structure of the ICC system, including its distinction between situation- and case-related proceedings, makes the Court vulnerable to critiques of

---

[237] See Situation in Georgia, ICC-01/15–12, Decision on the Prosecutor's request for authorization of an investigation, 27 January 2016, Separate Opinion of Judge Péter Kovács, para. 19.

[238] Art. 53 (3) ICC Statute.

[239] Office of Public Counsel for Victims, ICC-01/13–27-Conf, Observations on behalf of victims in the proceedings for the review of the Prosecutor's decision not to initiate an investigation, 23 June 2015, paras. 154 et seq.

[240] See Rome Statute, Art. 19 (3).

[241] See S. Vasiliev, 'Article 68 (3) and Personal Interests of Victims in the Emerging Practice of the ICC', in Stahn and Sluiter, *Emerging Practice of the International Criminal Court*, 635, 651–653.

[242] See Declaration of Basic Principles of Justice for Victims of Crime and Abuse of Power, UN GA Res. 40/34, 29 November 1985, para. 6 (b) ('The responsiveness of judicial and administrative processes to the needs of victims should be facilitated by: . . . Allowing the views and concerns of victims to be presented and considered at appropriate stages of the proceedings where their personal interests are affected, without prejudice to the accused and consistent with the relevant national criminal justice system').

[243] On the OTP position, see OTP, Policy Paper on Victims' Participation, April 2010.

[244] Kendall and Nouwen, 'Representational Practices at the International Criminal Court', 243, referring to a 'pyramid of legally "relevant" victims'.

hierarchizing victims. It virtually creates three different classes of victims: a broader category of victims whose general victimhood is testified in abstract terms, such as victims of situation-related violence; victims of the case whose status is individualized; and victims entitled to reparation as a result of harm suffered through the actions of the convicted person. In particular, situation-related victims tend to drop off the radar screen the more the case advances. The Appeals Chamber has made it clear that victims do not have a 'general right' to participate at the investigation stage.[245] They can only participate in proceedings during investigations where such a right is provided for and if their personal interests are affected. ICC Chambers have ruled early on that the scope of participation in case-related proceedings is linked to the charges of the prosecution.[246] This implies that only few victims of a specific conflict situation may actually enjoy the benefits of participation. Reparation is only granted to victims who suffered harm from crimes of perpetrators who have been convicted. There are thus to some extent real victims, Court-created victims and invisible victims.

The determination of the label of 'victim' is the result of a complex process, controlled by different agents. As victimologists have pointed out: 'Becoming a victim ... is a social process that starts with a criminal offence but also requires a cognitive decision by the person(s) against whom it is directed to see themselves as, and assume the status of, victims as part of their strategy for coping with it'.[247] The ICC has put in place a multilayered system of seeking applications through which individuals agree to be recognized as 'victims'. It ranges from general public notifications and call for submissions to active use of intermediaries (e.g. NGOs) to convey information and provide assistance with application. The process bears traces of 'victim entreneurship', in the sense that it actively encourages individuals to take on the identity and status of victim of international crimes.

The generic definition of victims in the ICC Rules of Procedure and Evidence is broad. It includes individuals and certain organizations or institutions that have 'suffered harm as a result of the commission of any crime within the jurisdiction of the Court', including certain indirect victims who suffered loss, injury or damage as a result of the harm caused to direct victims.[248] Due to the sheer number of applicants, the ICC has had to experiment with vetting procedures. The numbers of victim applications vary greatly, running from a few hundred up to several thousand per

---

[245] Situation in the DRC, ICC-01/04 OA4 OA5 OA6, Judgment on victim participation in the investigation stage of the proceedings in the appeal of the OPCD against the decision of Pre-Trial Chamber I of 7 December 2007 and in the appeals of the OPCD and the Prosecutor against the decision of Pre-Trial, 19 December 2008, para. 58 ('victims cannot be granted procedural status of victim entitling them to participate generally in the investigation'). In an unprecedented decision, the Pre-Trial Chamber extended outreach and communication to preliminary examinations in the situation in Palestine, arguing that 'victims ... have the right to provide information to, receive information from and communicate with the Court, regardless and independently from judicial proceedings, including during the preliminary examination stage'. See Situation in the State of Palestine, Decision on Information and Outreach for the Victims of the Situation, ICC-01/18-2, 13 July 2018, para. 10.

[246] *Prosecutor* v. *Lubanga*, ICC-01/04–01/06–1432, Judgment on the Appeals of the Prosecutor and the Defence against Trial Chamber I's Decision on Victims' Participation of 18 January 2008, 11 July 2008, para. 108 (*Lubanga* Appeal Victim Participation).

[247] J. Dignan, *Understanding Victims and Restorative Justice* (Maidenhead: Open University Press, 2005), 30.

[248] Rule 85 of the ICC Rules of Procedure and Evidence.

case. The ICC had to develop appropriate methods. It has applied no fewer than five different models at pre-trial and trial, before seeking to harmonize approaches.

The ICC started with an individual application model, according to which each application had to be considered individually by judges.[249] This model led to severe backlogs. In several cases, the Registry was unable to comply with orders to transmit files, and Chambers were not able to decide on applications.[250]

These delays prompted a reform of the application process. In the *Gbagbo* case, the Pre-Trial Chamber tested a different model.[251] It suggested a partly collective application process, which allowed each victim to file an individual application, but recorded information relating to crimes or incidents in a collective fashion, i.e. via affected groups.[252] Victims' applications were thus determined collectively, before an individual decision. This procedure contrasted with the individualized nature of applications, warranted by Rule 89 of the ICC Rules of Procedure and Evidence. The group-related application process poses difficulties for individual victims (e.g. victims of sexual and gender-based crimes) who may face stigmatization from other members of the same group by virtue of the exposure of their individual harm.

In the Kenya situation, Trial Chamber V suggested a novel differentiated model which combined the two schemes.[253] The Chamber held that victims who seek to present their views and concerns individually before the Chamber should follow the individualized procedure under Rule 89 of the Rules, while other victims, who sought to participate without appearing before the Chamber, should be permitted to present their views and concerns without such scrutiny. This approach continued to raise legal concerns, since it gave an interpretation to Article 68 (3) which conflicted with Rule 89 of the Rules since it bypassed 'individual assessment by the Chamber' in relation to 'the second category' of victims.[254]

A fourth approach (*Ntaganda* pre-trial model) returned to the individualized assessment and facilitated the application process, but outsourced decision-making power to the Registry.[255]

The *Ntaganda* Trial Chamber preserved the power of judges to take decisions, but distinguished among different victim groups: i.e. (i) applicants who clearly qualify as victims (Group A); (ii) applicants who clearly do not qualify as victims (Group B); and (c) applicants for whom the Registry could not make a clear determination for

---

[249] On the procedure, see Rule 89.
[250] For instance, in the *Bemba* and *Lubanga* trials and the *Mbarushimana* confirmation process, the Registry was not able to comply with obligations.
[251] *Prosecutor* v. *Gbagbo*, ICC-02/11–01/11, Decision on Issues Related to the Victims' Application Process, 6 February 2012.
[252] Ibid., para. 10 et seq.
[253] *Prosecutor* v. *Ruto and Sang*, ICC-01/09–01/11, Decision on Victim's Representation and Participation, 3 October 2012 (*Ruto and Sang* Participation Decision); *Prosecutor* v. *Mathaura and Kenyatta*, ICC-01/09–02/11–498, Decision on Victims' Representation and Participation, 3 October 2012.
[254] *Ruto and Sang* Participation Decision, para 25.
[255] *Prosecutor* v. *Ntaganda*, ICC-01/04–02/06–54, Decision Requesting the Victims Participation and Reparations Section to Submit Observations, 26 April 2013, paras. 3 and 5. The Chamber simplified the information required under Rule 89. See *Prosecutor* v. *Ntaganda*, ICC-01/04–02/06–67, Decision Establishing Principles on the Victim's Application Process, 28 May 2013, paras. 20–21.

any reason (Group C).[256] This meant that the treatment of victim applications, and their corresponding participatory rights, diverged across Chambers. In 2016, judges agreed on a common approach in the practice manual, which requires the Chamber to take decisions on individual applications only where the Defence or the Prosecution object to the Registry's assessment of the application.[257]

The scope of participatory rights was subject to intense litigation. Adherents of an adversarial tradition remained sceptical towards the possibility of victim representatives presenting independent evidence relating to the guilt and innocence of defendants. Proponents of a more inquisitorial model were inclined to allow victims' legal representatives to present evidence on the guilt or innocence. The Appeals Chamber opted for a compromise solution, in a split majority decision. It granted victims the right to tender evidence and to call their own witnesses.[258] However, it did not recognize a right of victims 'to tell their story and have their story heard by the Judges'.[259] It decided that such rights are mediated and subject to judicial scrutiny, since they are ultimately grounded in the judicial prerogative to ascertain the truth.[260] This decision was criticized by both sides, namely for overinflating victims' rights by the Prosecution, and for overly constraining victim participation by victim representatives.

Observers of the ICC have remained divided as to what extent victim participation has added to the content of trials. Advocates of victim participation stress that victims have made important contributions to proceedings and managed to bring the Court closer to 'the reality on the ground'.[261] They claim that victim participation has facilitated a better understanding of the local context of testimony and crimes. For instance, in the *Bemba* and *Lubanga* cases, victim participation arguably assisted judges in understanding local languages and habits.[262] In *Lubanga*, victim representatives pushed the Prosecution to extend charges to sexual offences, which was later heeded in other cases. In *Ruto and Sang* and the *Kenyatta* case, victims presented their views on the possibility of holding parts of the proceedings *in situ*, and on the absence of the accused during the proceedings. In *Katanga*, victims tendered five pieces of evidence and called two witnesses. In the judgment, the Trial Chamber relied on the evidence of the two victims who had testified on the Bogoro attack based on a request of the legal representatives. The costs of legal representation are limited, since victims are typically represented collectively.

---

[256] See *Prosecutor v. Ntaganda*, ICC-/01/04–02/06–449, Decision on Victims' Participation in Trial Proceedings, 6 February 2015, para. 24.

[257] See *Chamber Practice Manual*, February 2016, 20–22, at www.icc-cpi.int/iccdocs/other/Chambers_practice_manual–FEBRUARY_2016.pdf.

[258] *Lubanga* Appeal Victim Participation, para. 94.

[259] See *Prosecutor v. Ntaganda*, ICC-01/04–02/06, Public redacted version of 'Response on behalf of Mr Ntaganda to 'Request by the Common Legal Representative of the Victims of the Attacks for leave to present evidence and victims' views and concerns', 28 February 2017, para. 19.

[260] Art. 69 (3), *Lubanga* Appeal Victim Participation, para. 95.

[261] FIDH, 'Five Myths about Victim Participation in ICC Proceedings', December 2014, 15.

[262] Ibid., 15.

Sceptics doubt whether the benefits of victim participation are proportional to the investment in time and resources, and the hidden operational costs. They claim that the merits of participation are mainly symbolic and likely to cause disappointment among victim groups, rather than a sense of closure. As Judge van den Wyngaert has argued:

Victims have vested enormous hopes in the ICC, which, through its outreach programs, has created immense expectations. Many resources have gone into fees, salaries and expenses, which are in sharp contrast with the resources that will eventually be available to pay for reparations. If it should appear that both participation in the trials and reparations are more symbolic than real, a different kind of frustration may emerge.[263]

Overall, the contribution of victim participation to ICC proceedings has been modest. As the International Federation for Human Rights has noted:

Essentially, the role of victims is one of filling in gaps . . . Legal representatives may identify and highlight gaps in the way the evidence is presented or in the factual or legal interpretation. Another way of filling in gaps is to present a different perspective (the victims') or communicating concerns that victims may have in respect to issues being decided upon by the Court.[264]

Victim participation at the ICC is thus highly aspirational. One risk is that it may do more to promote the legitimacy of the ICC than to respond to the actual concerns and expectation of victims.[265]

The system of victim participation at the STL has been inspired by the ICC system.[266] The Statute of the STL contains a reproduction of Article 68 of the ICC Statute.[267] It gives victims a voice that exceeds their status as a civil party under Lebanese law. Victims are vested with the right to present evidence at trial,[268] on the condition that it does not simply '"double-up" the Prosecution evidence',[269] to examine and cross-examine witnesses[270] and make submissions on the impact of the crimes. However, their rights were restricted through the Rules of Procedure and Evidence. The Rules limit the notion of victims to persons who 'suffered physical, material or mental harm as a direct result of a terrorist attack'.[271] Victims can exercise these powers only after confirmation of an indictment,[272] and based on the authorization of the judges. They are precluded from making observations on the sentence.[273] The STL

---

[263] Van den Wyngaert, 'Victims before International Criminal Courts', 494–495.

[264] FIDH, 'Five Myths', 9.

[265] On the lived experience, see R. Hodzić, 'Living the Legacy of Mass Atrocities: Victims' Perspectives on War Crimes Trials' (2010) 8 *JICJ* 113.

[266] See de Hemptinne, 'Challenges Raised by Victims' Participation in the Proceedings of the Special Tribunal for Lebanon', 165.

[267] Art. 17 STL Statute.

[268] Rule 146.

[269] *Prosecutor* v. *Ayyash et al.*, Decision on the Legal Representatives of Victims' Application to Call Evidence, Schedule the Presentation of Evidence and Directions on Disclosure Obligations, STL-11–01/T/TC, 31 July 2017, para. 71.

[270] Rule 87 (B).

[271] Rule 2 of the STL Rules of Procedure and Evidence.

[272] Rule 87 (A).

[273] Rule 87 (C).

lacks the power to order reparations. Victims must pursue compensation claims through Lebanese civil courts.[274]

On a global scale, the turn towards victim participation is difficult to reverse. Victim participation symbolizes the need to treat victims with dignity and respect. It gives persons affected by crime an opportunity to discuss proceedings, provide their views and have their concerns considered. This moral imperative is hard to dispute. There are lots of myths about both the pros and the cons of victim participation that require further attention. The Prosecution, the Defence and the judges exercise roles that go beyond their individual interests. They are guardians of the fairness and integrity of the criminal process as a whole, and part of the truth-finding process. Victims have an equally important role. However, their rights must be reconciled with the protection of the rights of the Defence, and other interests. The narrow format of the legal process contrasts with the willingness of victims to express harm and tell their story.

The ICC Statute is not necessarily a blueprint for other contexts. It needs to be assessed more thoroughly regarding to what extent human rights entitlements, such as the right to be informed, the right to truth and the right to reparations, can be successfully transposed to criminal proceedings. Human rights principles and concepts cannot be simply applied, but may require a process of translation to the context of criminal proceedings. The line between gathering social support for justice and causing disappointment in local communities is very thin.[275]

Victim participation increases victim visibility. However, the broader question as to how recognition of victimhood is produced and how criminal procedures reflect victimization is only gradually gaining attention.[276] Perspectives from critical victimology suggest that 'concepts such as "victim" and "victimization" ... are both malleable and far from universal ... the image of "the victim" is capable of being invoked and sometimes even manipulated or exploited, whether to serve the interests of victims per se, particular groups of victims or even other objectives'.[277] Victimhood is a socially produced status. The determination of victimhood in criminal proceedings involves power and control over persons, and whose voices are heard. One of the dangers of the turn to victim participation is that it reduces complex victim identities[278] and forms of victimization to universal atrocity crime labels that dominate public perception. Norwegian criminologist Nils Christie has developed the concept of

---

[274] See Art. 25 STL Statute.
[275] S. Robins, 'Failing Victims? The Limits of Transitional Justice in Addressing the Needs of Victims of Violations' (2017) 9 *Human Rights and International Legal Discourse* 41; B. Zhang, 'Recognising the Limits of Victims' Participation: A Comparative Examination of the Victim Participation Schemes at the ECCC and ICC', in Meisenberg and Stegmiller, *The Extraordinary Chambers in the Courts of Cambodia*, 515.
[276] R. Killean, 'Constructing Victimhood at the Khmer Rouge Tribunal: Visibility, Selectivity and Participation' (2018) 24 *International Review of Victimology* 273–296.
[277] Dignan, *Understanding Victims and Restorative Justice*, 35.
[278] J. Bernath, 'Complex Political Victims in the Aftermath of Mass Atrocity: Reflections on the Khmer Rouge Tribunal in Cambodia (2015) 10 *International Journal of Transitional Justice* 46.

'the ideal victim'[279] to identify stereotypes in the presentation of victimhood in domestic crime. International criminal law may easily produce new global stereotypes (e.g. in relation to women, children, victims of sexual and gender-based violence etc.),[280] create political hierarchies among victims or marginalize those who do not receive attention.

4.3.5   Victims vs. Perpetrators: The Child Soldier Dilemma

The lines between victims and perpetrators are often porous in atrocity crime situations. The criminal trial tends to be framed in binary categories: guilt and innocence, capacity and incapacity, adult or child, victim and perpetrator. The child soldier dilemma does not fit neatly into these categories.[281] Child soldiers are used in conflicts worldwide.[282] In many cases, they are victims of human rights violations. Recruiting children under fifteen into forces or armed groups is a war crime.[283] Yet child soldiers often perpetrate horrific atrocities. Their victims find little comfort in the fact that child soldiers are themselves victims. There are competing attitudes towards the criminal responsibility of child soldiers: a victim-oriented and an accountability-oriented narrative.[284]

4.3.5.1   The Victim Narrative

The predominant narrative in international law is that child soldiers are victims that deserve protection. Children have a special status under international law. Article 3 of the Convention on the Rights of the Child states that 'the best interests of the child' shall be a primary consideration 'in all actions concerning children'.[285] Recruitment, enlistment and use of children under the age of fifteen in hostilities is a crime against children. Sexual slavery of children is expressly criminalized. To date, no child has

---

[279] Christie described the 'ideal victim' as an elderly lady who is robbed by an adult male drug abuser, while on her way to help her sick sister. See N. Christie, 'The Ideal Victim', in E. A. Fattah (ed.), *From Crime Policy to Victim Policy* (London: Palgrave Macmillan, 1986), 17.

[280] J. van Wijk, 'Who Is the "Little Old Lady" of International Crimes? Nils Christie Concept of the Ideal Victim Reinterpreted' (2013) 19 *International Review of Victimology* 159–179.

[281] See M. Drumbl, 'Child Soldiers and Clicktivism: Justice, Myths, and Prevention (2012) 4 *Journal of Human Rights Practice* 481; Drumbl, *Reimagining Child Soldiers*; M. Happold, *Child Soldiers in International Law* (Manchester: Manchester University Press, 2005).

[282] Involvement of children in conflict cuts across sexes. The ways in which children enter conflict and what they do differs greatly. Some children enter conflicts voluntarily, driven by ambition, patriotism or the promise of opportunity. Others are recruited through violence or threats. Often, shortage of troops is used as an argument by commanders. However, there are other factors. Children are attractive fighters since they are obedient, easy to manipulate and open to dangerous assignments. See *Lubanga* Judgment, para. 851; *Ongwen* Confirmation Decision, para. 142. Some of them have strong incentives, since membership in armed forces gives them power and prestige.

[283] The role of children typically varies according the child's age, gender and abilities. Some child soldiers are used as sex slaves. Others serve as combatants, leaders or guards or play support roles. On child recruitment as war crime, see Section 1.3.3.6.4.

[284] B. Ursini, 'Prosecuting Child Soldiers: The Call for an International Minimum Age of Criminal Responsibility' (2015) 89 *St. John's Law Review* 1023; F. Leveau, 'Liability of Child Soldiers Under International Criminal Law' (2013) 4 *Osgoode Hall Review of Law and Policy* 36.

[285] Convention of the Rights of the Child, GA Res. 44/25, 20 November 1989, Art. 3.1.

been charged in an international tribunal for war crimes or atrocities. The Principles and Guidelines on Children Associated with Armed Forces or Armed Groups (Paris Principles) state expressly that child soldiers who commit crimes should be 'considered primarily as victims of offences against international law; not only as perpetrators'.[286] This reading is confirmed by the ICC Statute. Article 26 states that the Court shall have no jurisdiction over any person 'who was under the age of 18 at the time of the alleged commission of the crime'.[287] This provides a strong indication against prosecution of crimes committed by child soldiers under the age of eighteen by international courts and tribunals. The SCSL had jurisdiction to prosecute children of fifteen years and older. However, it decided not to use this prerogative in prosecutorial policy.[288]

There are many arguments to support this approach. Recruitment, enlistment and use of children in hostilities is per se against the best interests of the child. Both the Special Court for Sierra Leone and the ICC in *Lubanga* have made it clear that the perpetrator cannot rely on the consent of the child as an affirmative defence to child soldier charges.[289] The main responsibility for participation in conflict lies typically with armed forces or groups that enlist, recruit or accept children, rather than the children themselves. Children should not be prosecuted for their membership in armed forces or groups.

Second, child soldiers often suffer from specific psychological and mental health conditions. The experience of acts of violence and the continued embedding in group structures can hamper children's development and their ability to function as children. Some do not fully understand their acts at the time of the commission of crimes, or lack the necessary *mens rea*. It is doubtful to what extent they can appreciate the contextual elements of international crimes and form intent for complex offences.

Third, it is difficult to determine a clear-cut age limit in relation to criminal responsibility. The minimum age of criminal responsibility varies from country to country. International criminal law lacks a differentiated juvenile justice system that is typically applied in domestic settings. Persons under the age of fifteen are not legally allowed to join armed forces. It would be contradictory to charge them for acts committed in this context. Child soldiers aged between fifteen and eighteen may have a greater capacity to make independent choices. However, there are doubts as to what extent they act entirely voluntarily and are in control of their actions. This is very

---

[286] UNICEF, *The Paris Principles. Principles and Guidelines on Children Associated With Armed Forces or Armed Groups*, February 2007, Principle 3.6.

[287] Art. 26 ICC Statute.

[288] As former Prosecutor David Crane explained: 'It would have been impractical to prosecute even particularly violent children because there were so many. Further, it was imperative that the prosecution seriously consider the clear intent of the UN Security Council and the drafters of the Statute creating the Court to prosecute those and only those who bore the greatest responsibility – those who aided and abetted; created and sustained the conflict; and planned, ordered, or directed the atrocities. No child did this in Sierra Leone'. See D. Crane 'Prosecuting Children in Times of Conflict: The West African Experience' (2008) 15 *Human Rights Brief* 11, 15.

[289] *Prosecutor v. Brima, Kamara and Kanu*, SCSL-04-16-T, Sentencing Judgment, 19 July 2007, para. 735; *Fofana and Kondewa* Appeal Judgment, para.140; *Lubanga* Trial Judgment, paras. 610–618.

difficult to assess, in particular when capacity needs to be assessed retrospectively – sometimes years after crimes were committed.

Finally, formal criminal prosecution might not be the best way to deal with accountability. Certain alternatives to criminal proceedings, such as restorative justice mechanisms and social rehabilitation, might be better suited to the needs of child soldiers than traditional means of punishment.

4.3.5.2 *The Accountability Narrative*

At the same time, it is unhelpful to portray all child soldiers simply as victims. Treating child soldiers per se as infants that are incapable of making responsible choices oversimplifies their autonomy and complex identities. As Mark Drumbl has argued, they often have a margin of discretion, with 'the ability to act, the ability not to act, and the ability to do other than what he or she actually had done'.[290]

Not all child soldiers have been abducted. Some fight for what they see as a legitimate political cause. Certain children aged between fifteen and eighteen might be able to appreciate the wrongfulness of their acts. Many legal systems allow differentiations in the treatment of responsibility, according to age. For instance, the Convention on the Rights of the Child does not expressly exclude criminal prosecution of children.[291] In many countries, this responsibility is determined on an individual basis, based on the psychological development of the child.

Moreover, accountability may serve both the child and the interests of long-term peace. As noted in scholarship, 'in practice, the portrayal of child soldiers as victims often turns out to be counterproductive in reintegrating them into their communities, and in coming to terms themselves with what they have done'.[292] The absence of accountability might encourage the use of children to commit atrocities.

Prosecuting child soldiers can be both a tragedy and a necessary evil. There is an emerging consensus that children below the age of eighteen should not be prosecuted for war crimes and crimes against humanity by international courts. However, this does not mean that there are no options for accountability.

4.3.5.3 *Bridging the Divide*

There are at least three ways to break the strict victim/perpetrator divide. One approach is to hold child soldiers accountable in ways other than criminal prosecutions, for instance by using transitional justice mechanisms, such as truth and reconciliation commissions. This approach is in line with the Convention of the Rights of the Child which encourages states to pursue alternatives to judicial proceedings for children.[293]

---

[290] Drumbl, *Reimagining Child Soldiers*, 98.
[291] See Art. 40.
[292] Derluyn, Vandenhole, Parmentier and Mels, 'Victims and/or Perpetrators?', 4.
[293] See Convention on the Rights of the Child, Art. 37.

A second approach is to try child soldiers before domestic courts, but subject to international standards for juvenile justice. Such prosecutions may not present the best way to ensure the interest of the child and should thus be a last resort. Special measures may have to be put in place to protect the 'well-being' of the juvenile.

A third approach is to hold child soldiers accountable internationally for crimes that were committed by them as adults, namely after the age of eighteen. This last approach was taken by the ICC in the *Ongwen* case.[294]

The criminal system typically offers two avenues to accommodate their dual status as victimizer and victim. Child soldiers can, first of all, invoke certain grounds excluding criminal responsibility.[295] Second, they can benefit from mitigating circumstances that reduce the sentence. For instance, the ICC framework requires judges to take into account 'the individual circumstances of the convicted person', including circumstances falling short of duress.[296] In this way, the traumatic childhood and conditions of child soldiers can be taken into account without precluding responsibility or prospects of reparation for victims.

In domestic systems, they may benefit from alternative sentences. International criminal justice is underdeveloped in this regard. It lacks special measures for juvenile justice and sentencing.

4.3.6 *Witnesses*

Witnesses lack an autonomous status in international criminal proceedings. Yet they are key to the success of proceedings.[297] For instance, at the ICTY more than 4,650 witnesses have testified since 1996.[298] Hardly any case in an international forum succeeds without their participation.[299] Witnesses to some extent form the 'Achilles heel' of international and domestic proceedings for international crimes. The parties rely heavily on their testimony.

The types of witnesses differ. Some are victims or survivors ('victim witnesses'), who are asked to testify about crimes or harms they suffered and help establish the crime base. They are essential to provide a first-hand account of crimes.[300] Others are

---

[294] See the justification by Prosecutor Bensouda: 'We are not here to deny that Mr. Ongwen was a victim in his youth. [. . .] This Court will not decide his goodness or badness, nor whether he deserves sympathy, but whether he is guilty of the serious crimes committed as an adult, with which he stands charged'). See Statement of the Prosecutor of the International Criminal Court, Fatou Bensouda, at the opening of trial in the case against Dominic Ongwen, 6 December 2016, at www.icc-cpi.int/Pages/item.aspx?name=2016-12-06-otp-stat-ongwen.

[295] See Section 2.5.

[296] See Rule 145 (2) (a).

[297] See E. Stover, *The Witnesses* (Philadelphia: University of Pennsylvania Press, 2005); S. Ntube Ngane, *The Position of Witnesses before the International Criminal Court* (Leiden: Martinus Nijhoff/Brill, 2015).

[298] See ICTY, *Echoes of Testimony: A Pilot Study into the Long-Term Impact of Bearing Witness before the ICTY*, June 2016; K. Lynn King and J. Meernik, *The Witness Experience: Testimony at the ICTY and Its Impact* (New York: Cambridge University Press, 2017).

[299] Former ICTY Judge Wald called them 'precious commodities'. See P. Wald, 'Dealing with Witnesses in War Crime Trials: Lessons from the Yugoslav Tribunal' (2002) 5 *Yale Human Rights and Development Journal* 217, 238.

[300] For an analysis, see M.-B. Dembour and E. Haslam, 'Silencing Hearings? Victim-Witnesses at War Crimes Trials' (2004) 15 *EJIL* 151.

'insider witnesses'[301] who may provide insights into the inner functioning of organizations or criminal networks (e.g. plans, orders, policies).[302] They are necessary to establish the link of the defendant to the crimes, including proof of modes of liability.[303] Obtaining insider witnesses is difficult, since such witnesses may be involved in crime and face special security threats in case of testimony. They may demand assurances of non-prosecution by the OTP prior to testimony, or at least seek mitigated sentences through a guilty plea. For instance, at the ICTY, the Prosecution was only able to target higher-level offenders after it had access to insider witnesses and clarified the procedure for plea agreements.[304] The ICC has attempted to attract cooperation by insider witnesses (e.g. middle-ranking officers) by emphasizing that it would focus prosecution on the most responsible leaders.[305] However, such assurances do not bar insider witnesses from prosecution before domestic courts.

Other witnesses are expert witnesses. They are typically professionals who may be called to testify on context, specific issues (e.g. demographics, forensics) or other matters that are beyond the knowledge of the Court.

The treatment of witnesses depends on the underlying procedural model. In the adversarial system, witnesses are more commonly viewed as witnesses of the parties. This means that they are predominantly called by parties and divided into Prosecution and Defence witnesses. In inquisitorial systems, witnesses are more closely related to the truth-finding process of proceedings and are 'witnesses of the Court'.[306] This implies that they may be called by judges and have a less partisan role in proceedings. For instance, the ad hoc tribunals have held that witnesses become 'witnesses of justice' after taking the solemn declaration.[307]

The evaluation of testimony by crime base or insider witnesses often poses delicate problems. Witnesses who have suffered from crimes can hardly be expected to be neutral. They may have a general interest in seeking punishment, which is unrelated to the individual culpability of the defendant at trial. At the ICTY, nearly two-thirds of all witnesses were called by the Prosecution. Defence counsel sometimes complain

---

[301] An insider witness is 'a person who may have worked closely with an accused, and who will typically be able to give valuable testimony to the conduct of the accused'. See M. B. Harmon and F. Gaynor, 'Prosecuting Massive Crimes with Primitive Tools: Three Difficulties Encountered by Prosecutors in International Criminal Proceedings' (2004) 2 *JICJ* 403, 408.

[302] See generally G. Chlevickaite and B. Hola, 'Empirical Study of Insider Witnesses' Assessments at the International Criminal Court' (2016) 16 *International Criminal Law Review* 673.

[303] For instance, the Taylor trial, thirty out of ninety-one Prosecution witnesses were insiders who testified about the nexus of the defendant to the RUF. See generally S. Stepakoff, G. Shawn Reynolds, S. Charters and N. Henry, 'Why Testify? Witnesses' Motivations for Giving Evidence in a War Crimes Tribunal in Sierra Leone' (2014) 8 *International Journal of Transitional Justice* 426–451.

[304] See C. Del Ponte, 'Investigation and Prosecution of Large-scale Crimes at the International Level: The Experience of the ICTY' (2006) 4 *JICJ* 539, 545.

[305] C. Mahoney, *The Justice Sector Afterthought: Witness Protection in Africa* (Pretoria: Institute for Security Studies, 2010), 33.

[306] See e.g. *Prosecutor* v. *Lubanga*, ICC-01/04–01/06–679, Decision on the Practices of Witness Familiarisation and Witness Proofing, 8 November 2006, para. 26.

[307] See *Prosecutor* v. *Kupreškić et al.*, IT-96–16, Decision on Communications Between the Parties and Their Witnesses, 21 September 1998; *Prosecutor* v. *Jelisić*, IT-95–10-T), Decision on Communication Between Parties and Witnesses, 11 December 1998.

that defence witnesses are treated less courteously or with a greater degree of suspicion than prosecution witnesses.

Eyewitnesses are often most reliable. However, their memories may be transformed by group testimony, i.e. discussions with others that reshape memories and narratives. It is important to understand not only what witnesses experienced, but also what led them to see events in this way. International criminal courts and tribunals have relied on a number of indicators to assess the veracity of the testimony. They include: knowledge of the facts, time span between the event and testimony, internal consistency of the testimony, its coherence with other evidence, personal interests affecting the motivation to tell the truth, as well as demeanour, conduct and character.[308] In certain cases, the answers need to be 'decoded'.

Live testimony is the rule.[309] However, tribunals have increasingly accepted the possibility of testimony via video-link. This is important if witnesses are unable to attend proceedings or face security risks. It allows judges to assess the body language, demeanour or credibility of witnesses, while alleviating the need to compel witnesses to testify against their will in Court. Video-link testimony requires a safe location that is conducive to giving testimony, and must be compatible with the rights of parties, including the right of the defendant to examine or have examined witnesses against them.

Special rules have been developed to facilitate testimony regarding sexual and gender-based crimes and avert the traumas of secondary victimization through questioning in Court. The ad hoc tribunals and the SCSL have inter alia relied on written statements, prior transcripts and judicial notice in order to reduce examination and cross-examination of victims of sexual violence.[310] For instance, a witness statement or a part of it may be accepted in writing without having to examine it. In case of examination, the Prosecution may discuss with the Defence whether questioning needs to go into the details of the sexual offence, or whether points can be conceded. Victim consent is deemed to be vitiated or disallowed as a defence in relation to sexual and gender-based crimes if the victim has been subject to coercive circumstances, such as violence, duress, detention or other forms of oppression.[311] Where consent is raised as an argument, it must be discussed in session closed to the public (i.e. *in camera*). It is also prohibited to draw negative inferences from prior or subsequent sexual conduct. For instance, in the conflict in Sierra Leone, the SCSL refused to derive consent from continued sexual relations between 'bush wives' and their presumed 'husbands'.[312]

---

[308] T. Kelsall, *Culture under Cross-Examination* (New York: Cambridge University Press, 2012), 183.

[309] See e.g. Art. 69 (2) of the ICC Statute.

[310] *Prosecutor* v. *Karemera, Ngirumpatse and Nzizorera*, ICTR-98-44-T, Decision on Prosecution Motion for Admission of Evidence of Rape and Sexual Assault Pursuant to Rule 92 *bis* of the Rules and Order for Reduction of Prosecution Witness List, 11 December 2006, para. 3.

[311] See Rule 70 of the ICC RPE, Rule 96 of the ICTR RPE.

[312] *Brima et al.* Trial Judgment, Partly Dissenting Opinion of Judge Doherty, para. 48.

A controversial issue has been the practice of 'witness proofing', i.e. the preparation of witnesses before testimony.[313] The ad hoc tribunals have allowed substantive preparation of witnesses for trial, i.e. conversations between the Prosecution or the Defence and a witness prior to testimony, comparison of projected testimony with earlier statements, or clarification of deficiencies or differences in recollection. Witness preparation was justified by pragmatic concerns, such as the weaknesses of human memory, the long periods of time between original statement and testimony, and the objective of facilitating 'accurate, complete, orderly and efficient presentation of the evidence in the trial'.[314] For parties, such preparation may be important to 'win' the case. However, it contains grey areas between effective and undue preparation and may pose ethical dilemmas. The more witnesses are interviewed by different persons, the more they become influenced or 'contaminated'. The ICC has criticized 'witness proofing' based on fears that pre-testimonial contacts with witnesses might comprom- ise the integrity of evidence. In the *Lubanga* case, the Trial Chamber, presided by British Judge Fulford, decided that it is permitted to refresh memory, but prohibited to discuss the content of the witness statement or any exhibits in court, since this could lead to a distortion of the truth ('rehearsal of in-court testimony') and diminish the spontaneous nature of testimony.[315] This line of reasoning was questioned by Trial V in the Kenya cases.[316] It claimed that spontaneity of testimony is often a fiction when victims come to trial. It argued that risks of undue witness coaching may be mitigated by 'transparency', i.e. a witness preparation protocol regulating duty of disclosure and video-recording, and effective 'use of cross-examination'. The problem with this approach is compliance control. The sanctions in case of violations remain unclear.

There are several limitations to testimony. The defendant may choose to provide testimony, but cannot be ordered to do so based on the right against self- incrimination. This testimonial privilege protects the 'person charged' against improper compulsion by public authorities. Conflicts of interests may arise if a defendant is compelled to testify as a witness against another accused. In such cases, any self-incriminating information emerging during testimony against the other accused cannot be used directly or indirectly in the case against the defendant.[317]

---

[313] See W. Jordash, 'The Practice of "Witness Proofing" in International Criminal Tribunals: Why the International Criminal Court Should Prohibit the Practice' (2009) 22 *LJIL* 501; K. Ambos, '"Witness Proofing" Before the ICC: Neither Legally Admissible nor Necessary', in Stahn and Sluiter, *The Emerging Practice of the International Criminal Court*, 599.

[314] *Prosecutor v. Limaj and others*, IT-03-66-T, Decision on Defence Motion on Prosecution Practice of 'Proofing' Witnesses, 10 December 2004, para. 2.

[315] *Prosecutor v. Lubanga*, ICC-01/04-01/06. Decision Regarding the Practices Used to Prepare and Familiarise Witnesses for Giving Testimony at Trial, 30 November 2007, paras. 51-52.

[316] *Prosecutor v. Muthaura and Kenyatta*, ICC-01/09-02/11, Decision on Witness Preparation, para. 47 ('Chamber considers that the risk can be adequately addressed by appropriate safeguards'), *Prosecutor v. Ruto and Sang*, ICC-01/09-01/11, Decision on witness preparation, 2 January 2013, para. 43.

[317] *Prosecutor v. Karadžić*, IT-9S-S/18-AR73.11, Decision on Appeal Against the Decision on the Accused's Motion to Subpoena Zdravko Tolimir, 13 November 2013, para. 45.

The defendant is protected against anonymous witness testimony. Partial anonymity (e.g. voice or face distortion, use of pseudonyms) may be necessary and allowed as a protective measure to safeguard a witness from intimidation. For instance, in the *Lubanga* trial the ICC used face and voice distortion for the testimony of alleged child soldiers.[318] Absolute anonymity is more problematic.[319] Human rights jurisprudence has sought to balance witness security with fairness considerations. It has failed to establish a categorical ban, but clarified that a conviction cannot be based solely or decisively on anonymous statements.[320]

Appearing as witness in public criminal trials may clash with the work and mandates of specific professional groups or organizations. Some of them enjoy testimonial privileges. One key example is the ICRC.[321] It often has privileged access to parties in conflict, including detention facilities, due to its trustworthiness and confidentiality restrictions. It has traditionally objected to allowing delegates to testify in proceedings or share confidential information, since its humanitarian mandate depends on impartiality, neutrality and confidentiality. This privilege is protected.[322]

Similar tensions arise in relation to journalists, who are often eyewitnesses at crime scenes. Compelling war journalists to testify may compromise their perceived objectivity, access to information and security.[323] A prominent example is the case of former *Washington Post* journalist Jonathan Randal, who was asked to testify before the ICTY by the Prosecution since he had interviewed an ICTY accused (Radoslav Brđanin) and written an article on ethnic cleansing that the OTP sought to introduce into evidence. Randal challenged the subpoena and was supported by a large group of media organizations that defended the right to freedom of expression and the freedom of the press. The ICTY Appeals Chamber recognized that journalists enjoy no absolute, but a qualified privilege. It argued that a journalist may only be compelled to testify if the 'evidence has a direct and important value in determining a core issue in the case'[324] and if there is no reasonable alternative to receive the evidence from

---

[318] *Prosecutor* v. *Lubanga*, ICC-01/04–01/06-T-227-Red-ENG, Transcript, 14 January 2010, 6, line 22; 7, line 2, at www .icc-cpi.int/iccdocs/doc/doc1392937.pdf.

[319] See M. Kurth, 'Anonymous Witnesses before the International Criminal Court: Due Process in Dire Straits', Stahn and Sluiter, *The Emerging Practice of the International Criminal Court*, 615, 634.

[320] ECtHR, *Sapunarescu* v. *Germany*, Application No. 22007/03, Decision as to the Admissibility of Application, 11 September 2006, paras. 32–33.

[321] G. Rona, 'The ICRC Privilege Not to Testify: Confidentiality in Action' (2002) 84 *International Review of the Red Cross* 845.

[322] See *Prosecutor* v. *Simić*, IT-95-9, Decision on the Prosecution Motion under Rule 73 for a Ruling Concerning the Testimony of a Witness, 27 July 1999, para. 73. Hudge Hunt argued that the ICTY should have the final say in the balancing of competing public interests (i.e. justice v. confidentiality), in particular in cases where non-disclosure might relate to exculpatory evidence. Ibid., Separate Opinion Judge Hunt, paras. 29–32. See also Rule 74 of the ICC Rules of Procedure and Evidence. An absolute protection of the ICRC is contained in Rule 164 of the STL Rules of Procedure and Evidence.

[323] S. Jones, 'Compelling War Correspondents to Testify: A Prerogative of International Criminal Tribunals?' (2006) 15 *Dalhousie Journal of Legal Studies* 133; M. A. Fairlie, 'Evidentiary Privilege of Journalist Reporting in Area of Armed Conflict' (2004) 98 *AJIL* 805; K. Buchanan, 'Freedom of Expression and International Criminal Law: An Analysis of the Decision to Create a Testimonial Privilege for Journalists' (2004) 35 *Victoria University of Wellington Law Review* 609.

[324] *Prosecutor* v. *Brđanin and Talić*, IT-99-36-AR73.9, Decision on Interlocutory Appeal, 11 December 2002, para. 48.

another source.[325] In the *Taylor* case, the SCSL extended the same test to the protection of confidential sources.[326] Ultimately, journalistic privilege might thus be set aside by a countervailing public interest, in cases in 'where the identification of the source is necessary either to prove guilt, or to prove a reasonable doubt about guilt'.[327] This test does not entirely satisfy the needs of journalists for whom protection of confidential sources is essential. They might remain unwilling to disclose confidential sources (e.g. whistle-blowers) even if they risk fines.

Securing witness protection is a continuing challenge in international criminal justice, due to lack of enforcement powers, dependency on national authorities and risks of leaking information.[328] Witnesses may need formal police or ad hoc protection to be able to provide statements or appear for testimony. In Court, they may be safeguarded through protective measures. After testimony, they may require special protective measures, and in some cases inclusion in a witness protection programme with relocation or identity change. Relocation of witnesses requires state consent and cooperation. One critical gap across international criminal courts and tribunals is the limited number of relocation agreements with states.[329] Many witnesses are unwilling to speak to the Prosecution unless they know how they will be protected or whether they are eligible for relocation arrangements. Negotiating such arrangements after testimony can take more than a year.

4.3.7   Other Actors

International criminal proceedings often address issues that go far beyond those of the primary parties to the case. The Rules of Procedure and Evidence of international criminal courts and tribunals allow some flexibility to accommodate such concerns. They allow certain other agents to intervene in proceedings, either as of right, on invitation by the Bench, or on their own motion, subject to leave by judges.

4.3.7.1 Role of States

One chronic tension is the role of states in proceedings. International criminal proceedings are centred on individuals. They are meant to be independent of the influence of states. However, the crimes adjudicated have a strong connection to state duties and affect the identity of collectivities. Judgments and decisions of international

---

[325] Ibid., para. 49.

[326] *Prosecutor* v. *Taylor*, SCSL-03-1-T, Decision on the Defence Motion for the Disclosure of the Identity of a Confidential 'Source' Raised During Cross Examination of TF1-355, 6 March 2009, paras. 30-33.

[327] *Prosecutor* v. *Brima et al.*, SCSL-04-16-AR73, Decision on Prosecution Appeal Against Decision on Oral Application for Witness TF1-150 to Testify Without Being Compelled to Answer Questions on Grounds of Confidentiality, 26 May 2006, Separate and Concurring Opinion of Hon. Justice Geoffrey Robertson, QC, para. 33.

[328] See M. Eikel, 'Witness Protection Measures at the International Criminal Court: Legal Framework and Emerging Practice' (2012) 23 *Criminal Law Forum* 97.

[329] It has been difficult to obtain relocation agreements. On the low number, see A.-A. Bertrand and N. Schauder, 'Practical Cooperation Challenges Faced by the Registry', in Bekou and Birkett, *Cooperation and the International Criminal Court*, 152, 175.

criminal courts and tribunals profoundly shape the law and influence the practice of domestic courts. Existing procedures do not pay sufficient attention to this interrelation. States have a right to intervene in relation to specific issues that directly affect them, such as challenges to jurisdiction or admissibility or cooperation.[330] In specific circumstances, states may have a right to seek a review of a decision[331] or to appeal.[332] They are rarely given a voice beyond such matters, however.

For example, Croatia sought to challenge this status quo in the *Gotovina* case, in which Generals Ante Gotovina and Mladen Markać and leaders of the Croatian government were listed as members of a joint criminal enterprise. Croatia argued that criminal trials affect state interests that are different from those of accused individuals. It submitted that a state 'should have "at least" a limited right to intervene and explain its interest' if it is 'found to have participated in a crime by reason of actions taken by individual members of that state's government'.[333] The ICTY rejected a general right of states 'to intervene or file statements of interest in judicial proceedings'.[334] It found that such an extension would 'expand the Tribunal's jurisdiction beyond the limits set in the Statute and detract from the Tribunal's focus on individual criminal responsibility'.[335]

This limited focus may create legitimacy problems, in particular in relation to state-based crimes.[336] As Mirjan Damaška has noted:

Charges of international crime often criminalize state policy, so that the government and if democratically elected, large segments of the population – feels it is itself on trial . . . convictions obtained without the state's input are likely to be perceived by many persons in the affected state as an attribution of criminality without the possibility of defense.[337]

States may seek to intervene as *amicus curiae*, i.e. as friends of the Court. This possibility is foreseen in the procedure of many international criminal courts and tribunals.[338] However, it has its inherent limitations. *Amicus* submissions are subject to leave by a court, in principle limited to matters of law, and are meant to be filed by neutral informers, rather than affected stakeholders. States have rarely used this

---

[330] See Regulations 109 and 109 of the ICC Regulations.
[331] Art. 53 ICC Statute.
[332] See e.g. Rule 108 *bis* of the ICTY Rules of Procedure and Evidence.
[333] *Prosecutor* v. *Gotovina and Markać*, Decision on Motion to Intervene and Statement of Interest by the Republic of Croatia, 8 February 2008, para. 9.
[334] Ibid., para. 14.
[335] Ibid., para. 15.
[336] On the need to involve states in relation to adjudication on aggression, see Section 1.3.4.
[337] See M. Damaška, 'Should National and International Justice be Subjected to the Same Evaluative Framework?', in Sluiter et al., *International Criminal Procedure*, 1418, 1422.
[338] The ad hoc tribunals, the SCSL, STL and ICC allow states to seek permission to file amicus briefs. See e.g. Rule 103 of the ICC Rules and Rule 74 of the ICTY Rules ('[a] Chamber may, if it considers it desirable for the proper determination of the case, invite or grant leave to a State, organization or person to appear before it and make submissions on any issue specified by the Chamber').

opportunity.[339] Attempts to use the *amicus curiae* status to defend the state or state officials have been rejected.[340]

4.3.7.2   Civil Society Interventions

Civil society actors have strongly influenced international criminal proceedings. The *amicus* procedure has served as an important channel for civil society actors to shape choices.[341] The rules provide judges with a broad discretion to admit *amicus curiae* briefs where this is 'desirable for the proper determination' of the case. In principle, *amici curiae* are deemed to serve the general interest of the Court. It has been increasingly accepted that the *amicus* status does not require full impartiality, however, since the filing party often has 'strong interests in or views on the subject matter before the court'.[342]

In criminal proceedings, the added value of external input needs to be balanced against other considerations, such as the efficiency of proceedings, fairness and impartiality as well as judicial expertise. The value of partisan advocacy through amicus briefs remains contested. Supporters claim that it contributes to a 'democratization' of trials since it gives civil society a voice in proceedings and widens the perspective on issues at stake. Critics note that *amicus* briefs may instrumentalize the judicial process for policy purposes or prolong proceedings, if they reach beyond the issues before the Court. They argue that courts should not be 'fishing for friends', since legal disputes should be solved primarily through party submissions or judicial deliberations.[343]

The initiation of *amicus* procedures differs. In some cases, submissions are invited by judges.

Both the ad hoc tribunals, and hybrid courts have sought submissions in relation to controversial issues or legal grey areas. For instance, in *Blaškić*, the ICTY invited *amicus* submissions on the power of a judge of a Trial Chamber to issue a subpoena to a state and officials of a state.[344] The SCSL has sought submissions from academics and NGOs on disputed legal issues, such as the immunity of Charles Taylor, the war

---

[339] At the ICTY, interested states have been invited to make submissions as *amicus curiae* in the case of deferral of cases to domestic jurisdictions. See e.g. *Prosecutor* v. *Karadžić et al.*, IT-95-5/18, Decision in the Matter of a Proposal for a Formal Request for Deferral, 16 May 1995.

[340] The Appeals Chamber denied application to intervene in *Prosecutor* v. *Gotovina* et al., IT-06-90-A, Decision on Motion to Intervene and Statement of Interest by the Republic of Croatia, 8 February 2012. See also, *Prosecutor* v. *Gotovina et al.*, IT-06-90-AR108 *bis*.1, Decision on Prosecution's Motion to Strike Request for Review Under Rule 108 *bis*, 13 December 2006.

[341] S. Williams and H. Woolaver, 'The Role of the Amicus Curiae in International Criminal Tribunals' (2006) 6 *International Criminal Law Review* 151.

[342] *Prosecutor* v. *Bagosora*, ICTR-96-7, Decision on the Amicus Curiae Application by the Government of the Kingdom of Belgium, 6 June 1998, 3.

[343] The ICC held that it would need to 'resort to amicus curiae observations only on an exceptional basis, when it is of the view that such observations providing specific expertise are needed'. See *Prosecutor* v. *Ruto, Kosgey and Sang*, ICC-01/09-01/11-84, Decision on the 'Request for Leave to Submit Amicus Curiae Observations Pursuant to Rule 103 of the Rules of Procedure and Evidence', 12 May 2011, para. 8.

[344] *Prosecutor* v. *Blaškić*, IT-95-14, Order Submitting the Matter to Trial Chamber II and Inviting Amicus Curiae, 14 March 1997.

crime of recruitment of children, the prohibition of amnesties, or the testimonial privilege of journalists. The ECCC invited *amicus* briefs on the application of JCE as a mode of liability before the ECCC for crimes committed during the period of 1975–1979 which led to an in-depth review of the doctrine.[345] The STL invited NGOs and academic institutions to submit briefs on terrorism as an international crime, before its contested Appeals Chamber decision.[346] The ICC made a controversial use of the *amicus* procedure in the Darfur situation. It invited briefs by external parties to put pressure on the Prosecutor to act.

In other cases, *amicus* briefs are unsolicited. Both NGOs and academics have actively used the possibility to seek leave to file briefs. For instance, Amnesty International appeared as *amicus curiae* in the *Pinochet* case. At the ICTR, NGOs had a significant impact on the treatment of sexual violence in the *Akayesu* case.[347] The Coalition for Women's Human Rights in Conflict Situations requested the Prosecutor to include charges of sexual violence in the indictment, based on the testimony of witnesses and the findings of a Human Rights Watch Report (*Shattered Lives*).[348] This prompted a change in prosecutorial strategy. The Trial Chamber recognized expressly in the judgment that the 'interest shown in this issue by non-governmental organizations' is 'indicative of public concern over the historical exclusion of rape and other forms of sexual violence from the investigation and prosecution of war crimes'.[349] This precedent opened a whole line of submissions on sexual and gender-based violence at other courts. For instance, at the ICC, NGOs filed briefs in relation to sexual and gender-based violence and reparations.

The impact of *amicus* briefs is difficult to measure. Some courts have adopted guidelines for the submission of briefs; others lack precision. Generally, *amicus* submissions are most useful if they address novel or underdeveloped legal questions, provide specialized knowledge on issues of fact or law that are not easily accessible to the Court, or extend the argument beyond the views of parties to proceedings.[350] In some circumstances, they may have served as a substitute for the voices of victims in the courtroom. The reception varies. In some instances, judges have explicitly adopted the conclusions made by the *amicus* and referenced briefs. For example, the SCSL and

---

[345] See e.g. K. Ambos, 'Amicus Curiae Brief in the Matter of the Co-Prosecutors' Appeal of the Closing Order Against Kaing Guek Eav "Duch" Dated 8 August 2008' (2009) 20 *Criminal Law Forum* 353.

[346] *Prosecutor* v. *Ayyash et al.*, STL-11–01/I, Interlocutory Decision on the Applicable Law: Terrorism, Conspiracy, Homicide, Perpetration, Cumulative Charging, 16 February 2016, STL Interlocutory Appeal Applicable Law, para. 2. The critical brief by Ben Saul was filed after the deadline. It is printed in (2011) 22 *Criminal Law Forum* 365–388.

[347] See generally Van Schaack, 'Engendering Genocide', 193; C. MacKinnon, 'Defining Rape Internationally: A Comment on Akayesu' (2006) 44 *Columbia Journal of Transnational Law* 941.

[348] See Human Rights Watch, *Shattered Lives: Sexual Violence During the Rwanda Genocide and Its Aftermath* (New York: Human Rights Watch, 1996); Coalition for Women's Human Rights in Conflict Situations, 'Amicus Brief Respecting Amendment of the Indictment and Supplementation of the Evidence to Ensure the Prosecution of Rape and Other Sexual Violence within the Competence of the Tribunal', at www.iccwomen.org/publications/briefs/docs/Prosecutor_v_Akayesu_ICTR.pdf.

[349] *Akayesu* Trial Judgment, para. 417.

[350] See L. E. Carter, M. S. Ellis and C. Jalloh, 'NGO Intervention in Court Proceedings through Amicus Curiae Briefs', in L. E. Carter, M. S. Ellis and C. Jalloh, *The International Criminal Court in an Effective Global Justice System* (Cheltenham: Elgar 2016), 264, 327–330.

the ECCC have intensively used briefs to develop reasoning on key legal debates.[351] The ICTR, ICTY and the ICC, which are more closely embedded in the institutionalized environment of the UN or the Assembly of States Parties, have been more reserved. References to briefs are less frequent.

Amicus briefs can be important instruments to help develop the law and correct biases. Civil society actors often hold unique expert knowledge, and have time and resources that courts lack. Their submissions can strengthen the frame of criminal proceedings in contour, colour and contrast. However, civil society intervention also poses risks. Some NGOs may use *amicus* briefs to enforce agendas on courts, or to gain recognition. One risk is that they pretend to act on behalf of others, while advancing their own causes. Civil society briefs may further create imbalances in relation to the perspectives provided. For instance, military perspectives on international humanitarian law, or state perspectives on general issues of public international law, tend to be underrepresented in proceedings. NGO *amicus* submissions have oriented international criminal law more strongly towards human rights agendas. In contemporary practice, NGO efforts are strongly geared at international criminal courts and tribunals, due to their visibility. With the gradual shift of gravity from the international to the domestic realm, it is becoming ever more pressing to gear *amicus* activities more closely to national accountability mechanisms which may lack experience in relation to trials.

4.4   The Justice Process

International criminal proceedings are highly complex. They typically take several years. To the outside, the justice process is often portrayed as a unitary undertaking. The focus is on judgments, trials and sentences. In reality, however, rendering justice is a more diffuse and pluralistic process. It involves different stages: a preliminary phase, investigations, pre-trial, trial and, as the case may be, appeals and reparations. Each of these stages has different functions, and involves different strategic choices. The modalities vary across courts and tribunals.

The type of justice that proceedings convey differs according to the relevant type of proceedings. For instance, the preliminary phase and investigations entail crucial decisions about allocation of resources and selection of situations and cases. They expose dilemmas of selective justice. Pre-trial proceedings filter strengths and weaknesses of the Prosecution case and prepare trials. The trial as such has many faces. While criminal punishment is deeply retributive, the legal process as such may have certain restorative or expressivist features. Reparations in turn serve to express or

---

[351] The ECCC even used legal argument in one *amicus* brief, without making proper reference to it. See Carter, Ellis and Jalloh, 'NGO Intervention in Court Proceedings', 268.

remedy harm. The protection of the rights of defendants, and fairness more generally, is a central interest that runs through these proceedings from beginning to end.

The features of each stage of proceedings differ according to institutional design, and balances between inquisitorial or accusatorial cultures. Mostly, they do not follow a pure inquisitorial or a pure adversarial model, but contain many *sui generis* features adjusted to context.[352]

4.4.1   The Pre-Investigative Phase

Proceedings start with the submission and collection of material and information, the determination of jurisdiction, and internal analysis by the Prosecutor. This pre-investigative phase is of key importance, but critically underdefined in international criminal justice.[353]

4.4.1.1 Functions

In domestic systems, national prosecutors have a significant degree of control over initiation of proceedings. Many preliminary steps remain confidential. In the international context, the reality is different. Prosecutors operate in an environment where every step is closely watched. They are highly dependent on external information providers, who may have an interest in publicity. From the very start of proceedings, they may face obstacles in relation to the exercise of jurisdiction over international crimes or attempts to undermine their authority.

In the history of international law, the functioning and working methods of the pre-investigative phase have received very limited attention.[354] Preliminary proceedings were essentially deemed to be within the discretion of the Prosecution in the Nuremberg and Tokyo Charters, the Statutes of the ad hoc tribunals, the SCSL and the STL. They did not make an explicit distinction between preliminary activities and investigation. The rules of the ECCC are more closely aligned to the inquisitorial tradition. They distinguish between the 'preliminary investigation', which is run by the two co-prosecutors, and the 'judicial investigation', which is run by investigating judges.[355] The ICC Statute uses the term preliminary examination. It refers roughly to a phase that is 'not yet an investigation', but a 'sort of pre-investigation carried out by the Prosecutor'.[356] It serves to determine whether there is a reasonable basis to initiate an investigation. This requires an initial assessment of information received, analysis of

---

[352] See e.g. Kress, 'The Procedural Law of the International Criminal Court', 603.

[353] See Ambos, *Treatise on International Criminal Law*, Vol. III, 335–342; I. Stegmiller, *The Pre-Investigation Stage of the ICC: Criteria for Situation Selection* (Berlin: Duncker & Humblot, 2011).

[354] See also H. Fujiwara and S. Parmentier, 'Investigations', in Yeydams, Wouters and Ryngaert, *International Prosecutors*, 572, 594–596.

[355] See ECCC Internal Rules, Rule 50, entitled 'Preliminary Investigations', and Rule 55 dealing with 'judicial investigation'.

[356] G. Turone, 'Powers and Duties of the Prosecutor', in Cassese, Gaeta and Jones, *The Rome Statute of the International Criminal Court*, 1146.

legal criteria, such as jurisdiction or admissibility, and a final determination that there is sufficient ground to open an investigation.

In theory, there are two different approaches towards pre-investigative activities.[357] According to one model, they have a minimalist function, namely to provide a gateway to investigations. This vision is in line with the classical criminal function of international courts and tribunals. It is illustrated by the lack of international regulation in statutory frameworks. According to a second model (i.e. a consequentialist approach), pre-investigative activities may have a certain virtue as such, irrespective of whether they lead to investigations. This approach is more controversial and closer to the human rights tradition. It implies that such activities may serve a number of other rationales than facilitating investigations and prosecutions, such as atrocity alert, deterrence or catalysing proceedings by other accountability actors, such as domestic jurisdictions. This second approach has been adopted by the ICC.

Preliminary examinations have had an unexpected career at the Court.[358] The ICC Prosecutor virtually carved out a new type of procedure that navigates between internal analysis, atrocity alert and monitoring of situations.[359] Preliminary examinations have become one of the most important activities of the Court. No other document raises as much excitement and fear among states than the annual report on preliminary examinations by the OTP. It is comparable to country monitoring under human rights mechanisms. It publicly lists situations of inquiry, and contains analysis of jurisdictional requirements, the gravity of crimes, and domestic accountability approaches. The list has included many hot spots of crisis (e.g. Israel–Palestine conflict, Burundi) or situations where the ICC has been trapped for years (e.g. Colombia). Three situations (Afghanistan, UK/Iraq and Ukraine) have involved permanent members of the Security Council. Being on the list involves a 'naming and shaming' effect that is akin to being qualified as a Chapter VII situation country by the UN. The ICC Prosecutor has used the threat of opening investigations and its discretion as leverage to seek to deter the escalation of violence, put perpetrators on notice, or spur domestic justice policies. This policy was meant to protect the ICC from selectivity critiques, including its lack of attention to Big Powers and its strong focus on Africa. However, it goes against some of the orthodox mantras of international criminal justice, such as its alleged distance from politics, its preference for certainty and predictability, and its reliance on formal channels of justice.

---

[357] On the two models, see C. Stahn, 'Damned If You Do, Damned If You Don't: Challenges and Critiques of Preliminary Examinations at the ICC' (2017) 15 *JICJ* 413, 417–420.

[358] See generally D. Bosco, 'Discretion and State Influence at the International Criminal Court: The Prosecutor's Preliminary Examinations' (2017) 111 *AJIL* 395; C. Stone, 'Widening the Impact of the International Criminal Court: The Prosecutor's Preliminary Examinations in the Larger System of International Criminal Justice', in M. Minow, C. True-Frost and A. Whiting (eds.), *The First Global Prosecutor: Promise and Constraints* (University of Michigan Press, 2015), 287; F. Guariglia and E. Rogier, 'The Selection of Situations and Cases by the OTP of the ICC', in Stahn, *The Law and Practice of the International Criminal Court*, 350, 354–356.

[359] OTP, Policy Paper on Preliminary Examinations, November 2013, at www.icc-cpi.int/iccdocs/otp/otp-policy_paper_preliminary_examinations_2013-eng.pdf.

Preliminary examinations have been compared to the 'functions carried out by UN mandated international commissions of inquiry, established prior to the constitution of certain other international tribunals'.[360] This analogy reflects the limited amount of formal power held by the Prosecution. During preliminary examination, the ICC cannot apply coercive investigative measures or rely on Part 9 of the Statute to compel states to cooperate.[361] It relies on external communications, open source material and voluntary witness statements. However, the real strength of preliminary examinations lies in their strong 'soft power'. The mere announcement of violations, media alerts, the publicity of analysis, and the subsequent public pressure serve as powerful incentives for compliance. Preliminary examinations have a key function from a justice perspective. They contribute to prevention of violations and reaffirmation of norms. They pre-shape choices as to who should be investigated and prosecuted internationally. Moreover, they may send important signals about the type of crimes or atrocities that international criminal justice cares about.

4.4.1.2 Dilemmas

The conduct of pre-investigative steps involves many routine activities that remain hidden to the public eye. Yet it has also revealed some of the fundamental justice dilemmas that international criminal proceedings face.

One of the most controversial actions at the ICTY was the decision not to initiate investigations into possible crimes committed by NATO during the Kosovo bombing campaign in 1999, including attacks on Serbian TV and radio stations and the Chinese Embassy.[362] Documentation showed that 495 civilians were killed and 820 civilians were wounded during the campaign. NATO was criticized for waging a 'zero casualty' campaign by flying airplanes at heights that made it impossible for them to properly distinguish between military and civilian objects on the ground. Louise Arbour established an expert committee to assess whether there was a sufficient basis to proceed with an investigation. The Committee concluded that there was no evidence of genocide or crimes against humanity and recommended not starting investigations in relation to potential war crimes. The reasoning was controversial. The Committee concluded that: 'In all cases, either the law is not sufficiently clear or investigations are unlikely to result in the acquisition of sufficient evidence to substantiate charges against high level accused or against lower accused for particularly heinous offences'.[363] These conclusions were shaky. The tribunal did not refrain from

---

[360] Meester, Pitcher, Rastan and Sluiter, 'Investigation, Coercive Measures, Arrest and Surrender', 181.

[361] Part 9 of the Statute applies to investigations and prosecutions.

[362] For a critique, see A.-S. Massa, 'NATO's Intervention in Kosovo and the Decision of the Prosecutor of the International Criminal Tribunal for the Former Yugoslavia Not to Investigate: An Abusive Exercise of Prosecutorial Discretion' (2006) 24 *Berkeley Journal of International Law* 610.

[363] Final Report to the Prosecutor by the Committee Established to Review the NATO Bombing Campaign Against the Federal Republic of Yugoslavia, 13 June 2000, para. 90, in (2000) 39 ILM 1257.

clarifying the law in other contexts.[364] The reasoning implied that the OTP should not even seek to start investigations because it was unlikely to receive support and evidence from NATO. This logic is difficult to explain. The opening of investigations might have allowed the ICTY to get more specific evidence from individuals and information on specific incidents. The outcome created the impression that the OTP took potential NATO offences less seriously than other crimes.

The ICC faced a similar dilemma in relation to the Iraq war. In 2006, the OTP declined to open an investigation regarding war crimes committed by members of UK armed forces in detention centres in Iraq. It used a questionable methodology. It found that 'there was a reasonable basis to believe that crimes within the jurisdiction of the Court had been committed, namely wilful killing and inhuman treatment'.[365] However, it argued that the 'number of potential victims of crimes within the jurisdiction of the Court in this situation – 4 to 12 victims of wilful killing and a limited number of victims of inhuman treatment – was of a different order than the number of victims found in other situations under investigation or analysis by the Office'.[366] This comparative gravity analysis across situations is problematic. As William Schabas has noted, it is like comparing 'apples' and 'oranges'.[367] Each situation must be considered on its own merits. The analysis gave a quantitative dimension to the analysis of the gravity of criminality that stands at odds with broader normative considerations. In public perception, images of torture, such as those at Abu Ghraib, and the lack of discipline to prevent such violations, count among some of the most atrocious violations, even if they were limited in number. The gravity requirement is elastic and cannot be simply reduced to numeric figures.

Certain situations might deserve investigation because of the cruelty of crimes or their grave impact. The 2006 Iraq decision faced critique for its incoherence and implicit shielding of 'Big Powers'. It led to further NGO submissions, and a reopening of the preliminary examination in 2014.[368] The quantitative approach was later reversed in practice, when the OTP opened an investigation into an attack against peacekeepers in Sudan, despite a low number of victims.[369]

Today, it is recognized that gravity requires consideration of certain 'quantitative' and 'qualitative' elements, including (i) the scale of the crimes, which refers, inter alia, to the number of direct and indirect victims and the damage caused by the crime, (ii)

---

[364] N. Ronzitti, 'Is the Non Liquet of the Final Report by the Committee Established to Review the NATO Bombing Campaign Against the Federal Republic of Yugoslavia Acceptable?' (2000) 82 *International Review of the Red Cross* 1017, 1020.

[365] OTP, Communication Concerning the Situation in Iraq, 9 February 2006, 8.

[366] Ibid., 9.

[367] W. A. Schabas, 'Prosecutorial Discretion v. Judicial Activism at the International Criminal Court' (2008) 6 *JICJ* 731, 741–747.

[368] See ICC, 'Prosecutor of the International Criminal Court, Fatou Bensouda, Re-opens the Preliminary Examination of the Situation in Iraq', 14 May 2014.

[369] *Prosecutor v. Abu Garda*, ICC-02/05-02/09-243-Red, Decision on the Confirmation of Charges, 8 February 2010), para. 33 (*Abu Garda* Confirmation Decision).

the nature of the crimes, (iii) their manner of commission; and (iv) their impact, which includes their consequence for the local or international community.[370]

Existing OTP practice faces a 'width vs. depth' dilemma. The ICC has opened many preliminary examinations, including some that have largely gone unnoticed (e.g. the war crimes allegations in relation to two incidents against South Korean warships in the Yellow Sea). Three preliminary examinations have been closed without a decision to investigate (Honduras, South Korea and Venezuela). Ultimately dealing with fewer situations, but doing them in depth, may be more promising than covering a wide spectrum of situations with only a few cases.

Some preliminary examinations have taken too long (e.g. Colombia, Georgia), without proper explanation or development of a clear hypothesis.[371] It has thus been suggested that time limits for the duration of preliminary examinations be developed. For instance, Pre-Trial Chamber III argued that the OTP has a duty to decide within a reasonable time whether or not to proceed to investigation, regardless of the complexity of the situation.[372] The OTP has refused to recognize any hard time limits. The 2013 OTP Policy Paper only contains a non-committal list of factors for the termination of preliminary examinations, including 'the availability of information, the nature, scale and frequency of the crimes, and the existence of national responses in respect of alleged crimes'.[373] It is necessary to develop internal benchmarks and better channels of communication where situations are pending for years, and, most of all, a sustainable 'exit strategy' from preliminary examinations. States like Colombia, Mexico and the UK have rightly claimed that there should be clearer criteria as to when a situation is de-listed.[374]

The ICC has struggled to find a proper balance between confidentiality and transparency. The OTP has placed considerable emphasis on transparency as a principle. It generally makes preliminary examinations public. The initial assessment of information on alleged crimes received from information providers under Article 15 (Phase 1)[375] is made public if there is considerable interest or a large number of communications. Such publicity is in line with the public nature of criminal proceedings. However, it also has costs. Going public may compromise access to victims and witnesses, complicate dialogue with states or even raise due process concerns if it

---

[370] Policy Paper on Preliminary Examinations, paras. 61 et seq.
[371] On Colombia, P. Seils, 'Making Complementarity Work: Maximizing the Limited Role of the Prosecutor', in Stahn and El Zeidy, *The International Criminal Court and Complementarity*, 989, 1010–1011.
[372] The Statute does not contain an express time limit. However, a number of provisions of the Statute and the Rules contain a 'reasonable time' standard as well other related standards such as 'without delay', 'promptly' or 'in an expeditious manner' in relation to the exercise of their functions by the different organs of the Court.
[373] Policy Paper on Preliminary Examinations, para. 89.
[374] The Strategic Plan 2016–2018 contains a commitment to develop 'cooperation activities and networks related to preliminary examinations', further enhance 'complementarity at the preliminary examination stage', and continue to 'increase the transparency of and public information on preliminary examinations'. OTP, Strategic Plan 2016–2018, para. 54.
[375] The framework involves four phases. Phase 1, which involves the initial assessment of all information on alleged crimes received under Art. 15, Phase 2, which relates to the examination of jurisdictional requirements, Phase 3 which focuses on analysis of the admissibility of potential cases in terms of complementarity and gravity, and Phase 4 which looks at the interests of justice requirement. See Policy Paper on Preliminary Examinations, paras. 78–83.

implicates individual suspects. Existing approaches may benefit from lessons learned in the field of humanitarian action. For instance, the ICRC applies a phased approach to highlight violations. It starts with confidential dialogue, and gradually moves up to techniques of mobilization and finally denunciation of violations.[376] Certain controversial legal issues, such as the nature of the qualification of the armed conflict and the scope of jurisdiction over specific offences (e.g. Israeli settlements, CIA interrogation techniques), need to be explained better if they are publicly analysed in reports.

4.4.2   Investigation

Investigations are critical to understand facts and shape cases. The purpose of the investigation is to identify, collect and process information in order to establish whether crimes have been committed, by whom and why. The main challenge is not only to collect and analyse evidence, but to set it into context.

4.4.2.1   Comparative Foundations

Criminal investigations differ from human rights inquiries.[377] Human rights inquiries are geared at establishing the context of violations and, where feasible, identifying individuals in order to illustrate certain patterns of violations or promote changes in policy. Criminal investigations are primarily aimed at identifying evidence to hold individuals accountable before a court of law. This implies that they are subject to different safeguards and standards of proof.[378] Criminal investigators are not only meant to establish facts, but are subject to formalized requirements. They are bound by professional duties, are required to disclose evidence, may be called to testify about investigative methods, and must balance their mandate against the rights of the Defence, as well as victims and witnesses.

Criminal inquiries often start with an examination of open-source materials. Several international criminal courts and tribunal could rely on a pool of information and material collected by international fact-finding bodies. Such information may provide useful leads for an investigation. For instance, witness statements can be of use for investigations, if the providers agree for the information to be shared with criminal investigators. However, the record and fact base collected through human rights fact-finding does not alleviate the need for an independent criminal investigation, since methodologies, focus and standards of proof differ.

The way in which criminal investigations are organized differs across legal systems. In inquisitorial systems, the investigation is often structured as a non-partisan inquiry

---

[376] On the ICRC approach, see 'The International Committee of the Red Cross's (ICRC's) confidential approach' (2012), at www.icrc.org/eng/assets/files/review/2012/irrc-887-confidentiality.pdf.

[377] A. Babington-Ashaye, A. Comrie and A. Adeniran, *International Criminal Investigations* (The Hague: Eleven Pub, 2018).

[378] Jujiwara and Parmentier, 'Investigations', 572, 580–581.

into facts. Prosecutors are bound by the principle of objectivity which requires them to investigate exonerating and exculpatory facts and circumstances. Some systems (e.g. France, Belgium, Spain, the Netherlands) entrust the investigations of serious crimes to an investigative magistrate who may carry out investigative tasks and interview witnesses.[379] This model is based on the idea that the impartiality of the investigation may be secured best through the role of state officials. There is only 'one case'.[380] The role of the Defence is limited. It can ask the Prosecution of the investigative magistrate to interview witnesses or carry out other investigative tasks.

Adversarial systems operate on different premises. Investigations are run by the parties, and thus to a greater extent guided by self-interest. There are two cases, the Prosecution case and the Defence case. Parties are deemed to collect their own evidence, and thus are vested with investigative tools. The investigation is often led by the police. Prosecutors have a limited role. The Defence may conduct its own investigation.[381] This model is guided by the ideal of the equality of parties, but requires significant resources.[382]

International criminal investigations differ from domestic investigative structures. International criminal courts and tribunals lack police officers. Institutionally, the Prosecutor is typically in charge of the investigation. The judicial role is usually limited. Pre-trial judges may have a certain role to assist parties in preparing their respective cases (e.g. at the STL and the ICC). However, the idea to entrust an investigative magistrate with investigative authority has enjoyed limited support. In many domestic systems, the role of investigating judges has been declining.[383] In the international context, it has only been practised in the Cambodian context, where co-investigating judges are in charge of investigations and formulations of indictments, following the initiation of investigations and prosecutions by the co-prosecutors.

The alleged advantage of an investigative judge model lies in its impartiality. It ensures that no facts are hidden. It seeks to protect Defence interests against imbalances with the Prosecution. The downsides may outweigh the merits, however. The Cambodian experience has been criticized for decreasing rather increasing the equality of arms. The co-investigating judges prohibited the Defence from carrying out its own investigation.[384] They faced difficulties living up to their duty to actively search for

---

[379] See generally M. Ploscowe, 'Investigating Magistrate (Juge D'Instruction) in European Criminal Procedure' (1935) 33 *Michigan Law Review* 1010; B. Elsner, B. Aubusson de Cavarlay and P. Smit, 'The Examining Magistrate's Function and Involvement in Investigative Matters' (2008) 14 *European Journal on Criminal Policy and Research* 225.

[380] See Ambos, *Treatise on International Criminal Law, Vol. III*, 2.

[381] At the ECCC, the Defence cannot undertake its own investigation, but must request the Co-Investigating Judges to undertake investigative acts.

[382] See C. Schuon, *International Criminal Procedure: A Clash of Legal Cultures* (The Hague: TMC Asser Press, 2010), 263.

[383] In Germany, Portugal and Italy, Investigative Judges were abolished as a result of procedural reforms. In countries like France or Belgium, they only deal with a small minority of cases.

[384] Letter from the Office of Co-Investigating Judges to the NUON Chea Defence re: Response to your letter dated 20 December 2007 concerning the conduct of the judicial investigation, 10 January 2008, A110/1, ERN: 00157729–00157730, para 2 ('Before this Court, the power to conduct judicial investigations is assigned solely to the two independent Co-Investigating Judges and not to the parties. There is no provision which authorizes the parties to accomplish investigative action in place of the Co-Investigating Judges, as may be the case in other procedural systems').

exculpatory evidence. Defence counsel challenged the fairness of the ECCC model, since it placed the Defence in an unequal position vis-à-vis the co-prosecutors, leaned towards the investigation of inculpatory evidence and offered them less access to material.[385] The Defence failed to develop trust in the work of the Co-Investigating Judges. The experience left doubts over whether an inquisitorial system is better equipped than an adversarial model to protect the rights of the Defence in relation to the investigation of international crimes. The Defence remained vulnerable since Investigating Judges were unable to conduct an exhaustive investigation. The investigative model has at least two weaknesses. It may increase the confidential nature of investigations and result in less presentation of evidence. The *Sary* Defence team concluded that by following the 'principle of sufficiency' of evidence (rather than a broader duty to ascertain the truth), 'the Office of the Co-investigating Judges is acting like a common law prosecutor but doing so with the power of a French investigating judge. This leaves Mr. Ieng Sary facing the worst of both the common law and civil law systems with neither of the built-in protections inherent in both systems'.[386] At the ICC, the idea of an investigative judge has been discussed.[387] However, drafters opted for a slimmer model of judicial involvement. The Prosecutor remains the master of proceedings. Pre-trial judges do not take part in the investigation or contribute to the preparation of investigative case files. They are thus not 'investigative judges'.[388] They merely exercise certain powers of review. For instance, the Prosecution must seek authorization to initiate an investigation if it acts on its own motion, i.e. without a state or a Security Council referral.[389] Authorization is required for certain enforcement measures. In special circumstances (e.g. unique investigative opportunities), Pre-trial judges may exercise powers in relation to the preservation of evidence.[390]

4.4.2.2 Macro-Challenges

The Prosecution typically gathers evidence in relation to three elements: the so-called crime base, which includes events and persons, the context and the linkage of the perpetrator to the crime. This poses particular operational challenges in the context of international crimes.

---

[385] Letter from Nuon Chea Defence Team, Re: Lack of Confidence in the Judicial Investigation, 15 October 2009. On deficiencies in relation to the investigation of exculpatory evidence, see *Prosecutor* v. *Chea et al.* 002/19–09–2007-ECCC-OCIJ, Joint Defence Request for Investigative Action to Seek Exculpatory Evidence in the Shared Materials Drive, 20 April 2009, para 19.

[386] *Prosecutor* v. *Sary*, Case No. 002/19–09–2007, Ieng Sary's Appeal against the Co-Investigating Judges' Order Denying the Joint Defence Request for Investigative Action to Seek Exculpatory Evidence in the Share Material Drive, 24 July 2009, para. 10.

[387] For a discussion, see J. de Hemptinne, 'The Creation of Investigating Chambers at the International Criminal Court: An Option Worth Pursuing?' (2007) 5 *JICJ* 402, 416, arguing that it is 'unlikely' that the idea of investigative Chambers at the ICC 'would generate any enthusiasm among states, which would look unfavourably to the idea of assigning all investigative functions to independent chambers, especially considering that this solution would require the adoption of many new provisions'.

[388] Ambos, *Treatise on International Criminal Law, Vol. III*, 2, 100.

[389] Art. 15 ICC Statute.

[390] Arts. 56 and 57 ICC Statute.

The links to crimes are often widely dispersed across different jurisdictions. Investigators may lack direct access to the territory or legal space of crimes.[391] On-site investigations require the consent of the country concerned to enter, take statements and carry out surveillance measures. Investigators may face security risks or hostility from national authorities or certain local communities. In certain cases, investigations may have to be delayed until a conflict ends.

The crime base can be very large, involving multiple geographic areas, hundreds of individual crime scenes, and many events and actors. It is impossible to investigate and prosecute all alleged crimes. Certain categories of crimes, such as sexual and gender-based crimes, require specific investigative methods.[392] Analysts and investigators must make choices as to what to prioritize. Often certain incidents are used as a sample in order to demonstrate a broader pattern of crimes or victimization.

Establishing context or lines of authority may be more important than determining who committed the physical crime. Prosecutors must understand the 'big picture' in order to formulate a narrative and case strategy. They may have to analyse the conduct of actors involved in conflict and the role of third parties, including financial streams. Maintaining impartiality is often problematic, in light of the nature of violations and the suffering caused in conflict.[393]

Establishing linkages is one of the biggest challenges. It requires prosecutors to reconstruct authority structures, decision-making processes and exchanges of information and orders before and after the crime. International investigators can be more easily identified as outsiders than local investigators. It may thus be feasible to develop mixed investigation teams.

4.4.2.3 Building Cases

Building a criminal case is a multi-stage process. Massive human rights violations can be shown by documentation, video and audio recordings, witness statements, maps or forensic information. Transforming material into a criminal case is a more complex undertaking. It requires several steps: collection and analysis of material, investigation and the formation of a case theory. It involves document collection and analysis, collection of crime base and linkage-witness statements, as well as identification of individual suspects.[394] The process may be roughly divided into different stages.

---

[391] For instance, in the investigation in Georgia, the ICC was able to draw in support from the Georgian side but has not received cooperation from Russia or South Ossetia.

[392] M. Marcus, 'Investigation of Sexual and Gender-Based Violence under International Criminal Law', in A. de Brouwer, C. Ku, R. Römkens and L. van den Herik (eds), *Sexual Violence as an International Crime: Interdisciplinary Approaches* (Antwerp: Intersentia 2013), 211.

[393] Hannah Arendt famously argues that the case against Eichmann was 'built on what the Jews had suffered, not on what Eichmann had done'. See H. Arendt, *Eichmann in Jerusalem: A Report on the Banality of Evil* (New York: Penguin, 1992), 6.

[394] M. Bergsmo and W. H. Wiley, 'Human Rights Professionals and the Criminal Investigation and Prosecution of Core International Crimes', in Norwegian Center for Human Rights, *Manual on Human Rights Monitoring: An Introduction for Human Rights Field Officers* (Oslo; Norwegian Center for Human Rights, 2010).

The first step is to provide a fact base, i.e. to establish what actually happened. Prosecutors receive a lot of information from different providers, such as states, NGOs, intelligence agencies, individuals, or specialized bodies, such as fact-finding bodies. They are complemented by open source information, such as public reports, national or local media, videos or social media, and other sources, including but not limited to Facebook, Twitter and YouTube. In the first phase, investigators often cast the net widely, by trying to capture as much evidence as possible about events.

In a second stage, investigators analyse the evidence in order to develop theories of events and to identify potential suspects.[395] The relevant 'raw material' is often overwhelming in quantity. It needs to be processed into evidence. This requires analysis, verification, processing and testing. Only information and material that is relevant, credible, accurate and reliable can be used as evidence in court. For instance, open source information may be used to establish the time or location of events, but it needs to be verified. It must be shown that documents or digital evidence (e.g. videos) are genuine and that its content are valid. Information and material that is authentic and verified needs to be tested in relation to its reliability. Not only witness testimony, but also documents or data can be unreliable. For instance, a description of a fact may lack a sufficient degree of reliability if it is based on hearsay or anonymous sources.

In a third stage, investigators deepen the collection of evidence to pursue concrete lines of inquiry, eliminate doubt in relation to hypotheses and meet relevant burdens of proof.[396] This requires close coordination between investigators and prosecutors, who need to rely on evidence at trial. It culminates in the building of a case, including more detailed identification of the crime base and modes of liability.

There are two main types of evidence, direct or circumstantial evidence. Some information may provide direct evidence of a crime. Most evidence, however, is circumstantial. This means that it provides bits and pieces of information that tell a broader story, if they are seen in context with other elements.[397]

Whenever evidence is collected, it is important to track the origin and possession of information and evidence, i.e. the 'the chain of custody'.[398] It serves to demonstrate that no one interfered with the evidence. It is important to record: what was collected or provided, who collected or received it, where it was collected or received, when it was collected or received. Without demonstration of a chain of custody, evidence may not be useable in court.

The analytic methods differ and might change in the course of the investigation. Investigations rely on a combination of inductive and deductive methods. For instance, crime-based evidence is often induced from facts and information. Linkage

---

[395] Groome speaks about 'discovering the case'. D. Groome, 'Evidence in Cases of Mass Criminality', in Bantekas and Mylonaki, *Criminological Approaches to International Criminal Law*, 117, 122.

[396] Some use the expression 'exploring the case'. Groome, 'Evidence in Cases of Mass Criminality', 122.

[397] A good example is the Srebrenica investigation. The massacre was reconstructed through forensic evidence, together with other circumstantial factors that proved the modalities and location of killings.

[398] *ICTY Manual on Developed Practices* (Turin: UNICRI, 2009), 28.

evidence, however, is more commonly deduced from organizational structures and contexts. Investigators navigate between these two techniques.

Throughout the investigation, the collection of evidence is closely interrelated with analysis. Prosecutors must collect enough evidence to build a reliable case. But the issue of how much and what type of evidence is needed depends on the formulation of a charging theory. It involves the identification of suspects, the formulation of specific charges, and the identification of modes of liability. This theory is gradually refined throughout the investigation. It is connected to different factors, such as context-related evidence, victim-related evidence (e.g. scope and intensity of victimization), perpetrator-related evidence (e.g. conduct of the accused, modes of liability), and punishment-related evidence (e.g. mitigating or aggravating factors).[399]

4.4.2.4 Gathering Evidence

The conditions for taking evidence are often poor in the case of international crimes. This is why international criminal courts and tribunals typically rely on a combination of different forms of evidence: documentary evidence, witness evidence, physical and other forms of evidence. They require expertise in different professional fields, such as law, social sciences, forensics, psychology or languages.

4.4.2.4.1 Types of Evidence

Documentary evidence is of key importance for framing a case. It has had significant impact in trials. For instance, the Nuremberg tribunal completed its operation in a relatively short period of time because it was able to rely on documentary evidence and was geared at a limited number of offenders.[400] In other contexts, this is more difficult since leaders do not leave a paper trail. For instance, senior leaders or military commanders rarely document illegal orders or details relating to the implementation of crimes, or may use coded messages. This makes it difficult to prove plans or policies. Details need to be assembled through different bits and pieces. For instance the ICTY relied on very different sources to build its cases.[401] In some instances, it was able to retrieve records of internal meetings, police reports, combat reports, speeches and interviews that provided an account of events and agents involved in crime. In other cases, it relied on transcripts of intercepted telephone or radio communications. For example, the ICTY used intercepted coded conversations in the *Krstić* and the *Karadžić* cases to establish the intent to kill the Bosnian Muslim men in Srebrenica.[402] It also used diaries to support witness testimony. The ICC relied heavily on intercepts

---

[399] See Jujiwara and Parmentier, 'Investigations', 586–587.
[400] The Nuremberg judgment noted: 'Much of the evidence presented to the Tribunal on behalf of the Prosecution was documentary evidence, captured by the Allied armies in German army headquarters, Government buildings, and elsewhere. Some of the documents were found in salt mines, buried in the ground, hidden behind false walls and in other places thought to be secure from discovery. The case, therefore, against the defendants rests in a large measure on documents of their own making, the authenticity of which has not been challenged except in one or two cases', (1947) 41 AJIL 172, 174.
[401] Del Ponte, 'Investigation and Prosecution of Large-scale Crimes', 553–555.
[402] On inferred intent of *Karadžić*, see Section 1.3.1.4.3.

of LRA communications in its arrest warrants against members of the LRA leadership.[403] Reports from sources such as NGOs, human rights bodies or governments must be read with caution, since they are typically prepared to establish a historical record of events or to influence the actions of policymakers, rather than to make a case at trial.

Witness testimony is a second, traditional type of evidence. It has enormous importance due to the strongly adversarial nature of international criminal proceedings. For instance, the mass killings in Rwanda were mainly demonstrated through witness testimony. It is vulnerable, since it comes with all the strengths but also the risks of human interaction. At the ICTY, expert witnesses were called to assess military aspects of crimes, including targeting decisions (dual use facilities) or proportionality determinations (e.g. collateral damage).

Physical evidence is a third major category of evidence. It includes forensic evidence and physical objects collected at the crime scene. Forensic evidence played an essential role in reconstructing events at Srebrenica.[404] Investigators faced difficulties tracing crimes, since bodies had been moved from Srebrenica to secondary graves. Investigators used aerial footage of the region to identify sites of mass graves.[405] They were able to show that bodies been moved with the help of forensic investigations. The exhumations established not only the number of victims, but also the time (e.g. through watches found) and manner of the killings (e.g. based on blindfolds recovered from graves), as well as the targeting of boys and military aged men. Together, these findings helped to develop a narrative of events, including the underlying intent of perpetrators.

Finally, digital and audio evidence has a long history. For instance, in the Nuremberg trials, the main breakthrough for the Prosecution was a presentation of a documentary at trial which showed the conditions in concentration camps. It had a significant impact on defendants. Hermann Göring reportedly said: 'It was such a great afternoon [...] and then they showed that awful film, and it just spoiled everything[406] At the ICTY, the Prosecution used video footage of BBC interviews with Serbian leaders (e.g. *Death of Yugoslavia*) as evidence. A particularly crucial piece in the eyes of public opinion was the shocking video which showed members of the Scorpions paramilitary unit executing men and boys from Srebrenica in Trnovo.[407] The video was presented at trial, but not admitted as evidence since it

---

[403] The OTP received the recordings from the Uganda People's Defence Forces and the Uganda Police Force. In the *Ongwen* case, the OTP requested the Chamber 'to recognise as formally submitted 2,507 items of evidence related to the interception of LRA radio communications by the Ugandan government'. See *Prosecutor* v. *Ongwen*, ICC-02/04–01/15, 'Prosecution's formal submission of intercept evidence via the "bar table"', 28 October 2016, para. 1.

[404] See I. Delpla, X. Bougarel and J.-L. Fournel, *Investigating Srebrenica: Institutions, Facts, Responsibilities* (New York: Berghahn Books, 2012).

[405] *Tolimir* Trial Judgment, paras. 65, 67–68, 70, 435, 454, 457, 459, 478, 561, 564; *Krstić* Trial Judgment, paras. 114, 223, 229, 230, 238, 250, 253, 258.

[406] R. Conot, *Justice at Nuremberg* (New York: Harper & Row, 1983), 149.

[407] See V. Petrovic, 'A Crack in the Wall of Denial: The Scorpions Video in and out of the Courtroom', in D. Zarkov and M. Glasius (eds.), *Narratives of Justice In and Out of the Courtroom* (Berlin: Springer, 2014), 89–109.

lacked a direct nexus to the defendants. The ICTR relied on radio announcements, which called for the persecution of Tutsis.[408] At the ICC, video footage was critical in the *Lubanga* case. The OTP sought to demonstrate that Lubanga used children under the age of fifteen in forces under his control based on video evidence and accompanying testimony by protected witnesses. The Trial Chamber took the video clips into account in its evidentiary assessment, including the assessment of the age of child soldiers.[409]

A novel approach was taken at the STL.[410] In the *Ayyash et al.* case, the OTP relied on 'raw data' of mobile telephone communications and messenger services to establish that the defendants formed a network to carry out the attack against Hariri.[411] It collected raw data from 'every mobile phone call made and text message sent in Lebanon between 2003 and 2010'.[412] Such evidence raises difficult issues in relation to its probative value. Its authenticity and reliability as evidence needs to be established through source identity information, expert testimony, or other sources of evidence. It may be necessary to have a witness present the digital evidence to a judge. The Defence must be given an opportunity to examine the source and content. This became a problem in the disclosure process before the STL. The Defence argued that it was not able to provide an effective defence since it was unable to validate and verify the raw data call records received by the OTP.[413]

Investigators can also draw on a larger pool of new methods and technologies to trace evidence, including remote sensing, satellite imagery and cyber-investigations. Such technologies are crucial since they enable investigators to collect information without having to gain access to the territory. They may help to establish a sequence of events or connections between perpetrators and crimes. The ICC used such technology inter alia in the Darfur situation. It relied on satellite images to show the civilian use of a peacekeeping site at Haskanita in the *Abu Garda* case.[414] Special cyber-investigation protocols are developed to ensure that digital evidence is gathered in a sound way.

---

[408] *Prosecutor* v. *Rutaganda*, ICTR-96-3-T, Judgment, 13 February 1996, paras 357, 370.

[409] The Appeals Chamber upheld the Trial Chamber assessment by majority. See *Lubanga* Appeals Judgment, paras 222–223.

[410] The ICC relied on call data records in the *Bemba et al.* case to show the efforts of the defendant to influence witnesses. See *Prosecutor* v. *Bemba* et al, ICC-01/05–01/13–1905-Red, Public Redacted Version of 'Prosecution's Closing Brief', 10 June 2016, paras. 21, 43.

[411] *Prosecutor* v. *Ayyash et al.*, STL-11-0 1/PT /PTJ, Public Redacted Version of 'Decision on Issues Related to the Inspection Room and Call Data Records' dated 18 June 2013, 19 September 2013, para. 4.

[412] *Prosecutor* v. *Ayyash et al.*, STL-11–01/T/AC/AR126.9, Decision on Appeal by Counsel for Mr Oneissi against the Trial Chamber's Decision on the Legality of the Transfer of Call Data, 28 July 2015, paras 3–4. The OTP traced data of billions of calls and text messages. See *Prosecutor* v. *Ayyash et al.*, STL-11-0 1/PT /PTJ, 20140116_STL-11–01_T_T29_OFF_PUB_EN, Transcript, 16 January 2014, p. 48, lines 12–13.

[413] See *Prosecutor* v. *Ayyash et al.*, STL-11–01/PT-PTJ, Public Redacted Version of 'Annex A to Defence Office Internal Memorandum Regarding Call Data Records' Filed 31 January 2013 – Corrected Version, 19 September 2013, paras. 27–28.

[414] *Abu Garda* Confirmation Decision, fn. 62.

4.4.2.4.2 Challenges of New Technologies

One of the biggest challenges of the use of new technologies is the treatment of open source information, i.e. the reliance on data collected from publicly available sources, for purposes of criminal investigation.[415] This type of information facilitates investigations, because it does not require the OTP to seek cooperation through state structures. Reliance on open sources is not an entirely new phenomenon. Open source information is often at the start of the initiation of investigations.[416] During the criminal investigation it is used as a springboard to provide leads for the investigation, or to corroborate other types of evidence, such as witness testimony or as circumstantial evidence. However, the scale of the documentation has reached a new level with the increased use of computers, the internet, social media (i.e. smart phones, videos) and open source imagery to trace human rights violations.

This poses new challenges for authentication, verification and resources of investigators, and the fairness of proceedings. As the ICC Prosecutor noted in Strategic Plan 2016–2018: 'technology is evolving so rapidly that it will be impossible for the Office to keep current if it does not combine investing in its own expertise with developing strategic partnerships for the purposes of outsourcing, when needed, and for understanding and shaping how future technology can assist it to execute its mandate'.[417] New technologies offer fresh opportunities. For instance, in the context of the MH17 investigation, Bellingcat, an organization specialized in online investigation, used open source information, including links on Facebook and other social media, to identify the missile launcher that downed the aircraft and trace members of the organizations involved in the attack.[418] Aerial imagery from drones can establish essential information relating to crime sites. Video footage has played a key role in the investigation of crimes committed in Syria and Libya. There are numerous recorded instances in which alleged perpetrators have made media appearances or shot videos in which they expose their violations. For instance, a Swedish court relied inter alia on a public video to convict a former Syrian rebel for executing captives. The Court used YouTube and Facebook to specify the time and place of the crimes.[419] In August 2017, the ICC issued a warrant of arrest against Mahmoud Al-Werfalli, a Commander of the Al-Saiqa Brigade, for executing thirty-three persons, based on open source material. It formally cited four sources of evidence: '(i) recordings of witness

---

[415] See generally UC Berkeley School of Law, *Digital Fingerprints: Using Electronic Evidence to Advance Prosecutions at the International Criminal Court* (Berkeley: Human Rights Center, UC Berkeley School of Law, 2014); L. Freeman, 'Digital Evidence and War Crimes Prosecutions: The Impact of Digital Technologies on International Criminal Investigations and Trials' (2018) 41 *Fordham International Law Journal* 283, 316 et seq.

[416] For instance, the ICC admissibility assessment in relation to Afghanistan has been 'conducted primarily on the basis of public sources, including information submitted to and reported by United Nations bodies as well as the publicly available results of congressional and DOJ inquiries'. See *Situation in Afghanistan*, Public redacted version of 'Request for Authorisation of an Investigation Pursuant to Article 15', 20 November 2017, ICC-02/17-7-Conf-Exp, ICC-02/17-7-Red 20-11-2017, 20 November 2017, para. 27. See generally A. Whiting, 'Dynamic Investigative Practice at the ICC' (2013) 76 *Law & Contemporary Problems* 163–189.

[417] OTP, Strategic Plan 2016–2018, 6 July 2015, para. 60.

[418] See Bellingcat, 'MH17: The Open Source Investigation Three Years Later', at www.bellingcat.com/wp-content/uploads/2017/07/mh17-3rd-anniversary-report.pdf.

[419] C. Anderson, 'Syrian Rebel Gets Life Sentence for Mass Killing Caught on Video', *New York Times*, 16 February 2017.

interviews and summaries of witness interviews; (ii) video material and transcripts of video material; (iii) internal orders, and social media posts by the Media Centre of the Al-Saiqa Brigade; and (iv) reports of international organizations, non-governmental organizations, and research centres'.[420] However, the 'smoking gun' was seven videos depicting the incidents on social media. There is thus a trend to include material drawn from social media in evidence used for purposes of criminal investigation and prosecutions.

This trend raises a number of concerns. Digital evidence is easy to manipulate. For instance, video images may be modified or digital information can be changed. It is important to prove the reliability of footage. Crime scenes might be manipulated. Images alone do not necessarily prove that crimes occurred (e.g. that persons were actually killed). They provide circumstantial rather than direct evidence.

Second, there is a risk that prosecutors and criminal courts become overwhelmed by information. It is necessary to specify standards and practices for the security and authenticity of video evidence. NGOs have an important role in professionalizing human rights investigations, e.g. by filtering information, highlighting legal requirements or clarifying ethical duties.[421] For example, the International Bar Association has created a special app to facilitate the authentication and secure transfer of videos.[422] The sheer amount of material available also gives a new dimension to the duties of the Prosecution to disclose potentially exculpatory evidence.

Third, the legal value of open source material as evidence varies. It has different functions. It can provide helpful leads to seek other forms of evidence. It may corroborate evidence. It might be used to show that a person (e.g. a superior) is aware of the commission of violations.[423] Moreover, it may have relevance to establish 'context' in the early stages of proceedings. However, it is less critical in relation to the establishment of guilt and innocence. The use of open source material may raise serious concerns in relation to the rights of the Defence. The Defence must have a meaningful opportunity to challenge its reliability and probative value. One risk is that increased use of digital and technological evidence may affect the equality of arms to the detriment of the Defence and increase the length of trials, due to the need to involve witnesses and experts to authenticate and explain evidence. For example, in the *Ayyash et al.* case, the Defence faced problems challenging digital evidence in the same way as other evidence.

---

[420] *Prosecutor* v. *Al-Werfalli*, ICC-01/11–01/17, Warrant of Arrest, 15 August 2017, para. 3.

[421] The ICC Trial Chamber held in *Bemba* that 'NGOs Reports can be considered prima facie reliable, provided that they offer sufficient guarantees of impartiality'. *Prosecutor* v. *Bemba*, Decision on the admission into evidence of items deferred in the Chamber's 'Decision on the Prosecution's Application for Admission of Materials into Evidence Pursuant to Article 64 (9) of the Rome Statute', ICC-01/05–01/08, 27 June 2013, para. 21.

[422] The 'eyeWitness' app is a mobile camera app that includes metadata used to authenticate photos and videos. This allows investigators and prosecutors to verify information.

[423] In the *Bemba* case, a report by the International Federation for Human Rights was used to show that the defendant was aware that crimes were being committed. See *Bemba* Trial Judgment, para. 714 ('the FIDH Report, released on 13 February 2003 and concerning an investigative mission in Bangui between 25 November and 1 December 2002, included detailed accounts of alleged acts of murder, rape, and pillaging by MLC soldiers against civilians in, inter alia, Bangui, PK12, and PK22').

In several cases, ICC Judges have been reluctant to accept classical open source material as evidence for the confirmation of charges and requested further investigation. For instance, in the *Mbarushimana* case, pre-trial judges declined to confirm charges, due to an overuse of indirect evidence, such as NGO and UN reports.[424] The Pre-Trial Chamber was even more explicit in the *Gbabgo* case. It noted with 'serious concern' that the Prosecutor relied heavily on NGO reports and press articles with regard to key elements of the case, including the contextual elements of crimes.[425] It held that

> such pieces of evidence cannot in any way be presented as the fruits of a full and proper investigation by the Prosecutor in accordance with article 54(I)(a) of the Statute. Even though [they] may be a useful introduction to the historical context of a conflict situation, they do not usually constitute a valid substitute for the type of evidence that is required to meet the evidentiary threshold for the confirmation of charges.

In the *Lubanga* appeal, Judge Usacka expressed concern as to how the Chamber dealt with video evidence introduced at trial to establish guilt. She noted:

> the accused must always be given the benefit of any doubt as to the proof of guilt. In the present case, there is no video excerpt that truly 'speaks for itself', namely depicts an individual that is 'manifestly under fifteen'. Looking at the age estimates by witnesses in this case, I see a series of major problems in relation to reliance on indirect evidence only and a lack of reasoning on the part of the Trial Chamber as to how it reached its conclusion based on the evidence at hand without any explanation of these major issues.[426]

In the *Al Mahdi* case, open source material was used successfully. At trial, the Prosecution presented an interactive digital platform with videos, photos, satellite imagery and panoramas to show that Al Mahdi was involved in the destruction of the historic sites in Timbuktu.[427] This evidence played a role in the conviction. The case is exceptional though, since the defendant admitted his guilt.[428] The video was not the sole evidence. The destruction itself was shown by other means.

Digital and technological evidence will undoubtedly be used more regularly in the future. It is helpful in the investigation and early stages of proceedings. However, it is not a gateway for conviction. In a post-truth environment, courts and prosecutors become ever more important guardians of the veracity of facts and information. The use of open source information, such as social media videos, has not yet been

---

[424] See *Mbarushimana* Confirmation Decision, paras 113–239.
[425] *Prosecutor* v. *Gbagbo*, ICC-02/11-01/11-432, Decision Adjourning the Hearing on the Confirmation of Charges Pursuant to Article 61(7)(c)(i) of the Rome Statute, 3 June 2013, para. 35.
[426] *Lubanga* Appeal Judgment, ICC-01/04-01/06-3121-Anx2, Dissenting Opinion of Judge Anita Ušacka, para. 79.
[427] See *Prosecutor* v. *Al Mahdi*, ICC-01/12-01/15, Transcript trial Opening 22 August 2016, ICC-01/12-01/15-T-4-Red-ENG, 41 ('the Prosecution will use satellite images, photographs, videos and other material gleaned from the Internet which are included on the list of our evidence material to show the situation of the mausoleums before, during and after the destruction, including the participation of the accused. These elements are authentic and have been accepted by the Defence and which are solid proof corroborating the plea of guilt entered by the accused').
[428] *Al Mahdi* Judgment, para. 43.

'intensely challenged as evidence in an international courtroom'.[429] It remains risky to base a full trial on such forms of evidence. Authentication of data and digital evidence from open access sources may raise difficult fair trial and privacy issues. It should thus be used in connection with other types of evidence.[430]

4.4.2.4.3 Admissibility and Exclusion of Evidence

Regimes as to the admission of evidence differ.[431] Common law systems often have strict technical rules on the admissibility of evidence. They are meant to exclude irrelevant evidence, safeguard the rights of the Defence and protect a jury from exposure to unreliable or unfairly prejudicial evidence. Inquisitorial systems have a more liberal regime. They place more weight on the 'free evaluation of evidence'.[432] All evidence is generally admitted, and then evaluated by judges. This flexible approach is reflected in international criminal procedures.[433] Procedural instruments grant judges a wide degree of discretion to rule on the admissibility of evidence.[434] The idea is that evidence should be weighed at trial, rather than precluded per se. This approach takes into account the difficult context of international criminal investigations, including limited access to documentary evidence and witnesses. It is increasingly important in light of the multiplication of fact-finding and evidence-gathering bodies, and the absence of a single set of procedural rules governing investigations and prosecutions. It makes the acceptance of material as evidence dependent on the judgment of those who receive it.

The admissibility of evidence is generally determined in light of its relevance and probative value.[435] Evidence is relevant if it is sufficiently connected to a material issue at stake, e.g. allegations against the defendant or the case.[436] The probative value relates to the weight of the evidence to prove an issue at stake. The downside of judicial flexibility is the risk of different standards. For instance, at the ICC different trial chambers have adopted different approaches towards the admissibility of evidence,[437] including the admission of prior recorded testimony.[438] This may raise

---

[429] Freeman, 'Digital Evidence and War Crimes Prosecutions', 317.

[430] See IBA, *Evidence Matters in ICC Trials*, August 2016, 30–32.

[431] See generally M. Klamberg, *Evidence in International Criminal Trials* (Boston: Brill, 2013), 335 et seq.

[432] See *Prosecutor* v. *Lubanga*, ICC-01/04–01/06–1399, Decision on the admissibility of four documents, 13 June 2008, para. 24 ('the drafters of the Statute framework have clearly and deliberately avoided proscribing certain categories or types of evidence, a step which would have limited – at the outset – the ability of the Chamber to assess evidence "freely"'). See C. Buisman, M. Bouazdi and M. Costi, 'Principles of Civil Law', in K. Khan, C. Buisman and C. Gosnell, *Principles of Evidence in International Criminal Justice* (Oxford: Oxford University Press, 2010) 7, 28–30.

[433] Art. 19 of the Nuremberg Charter stated: 'The tribunal shall not be bound by technical rules of evidence'.

[434] See e.g. Art. 69 (4) of the ICC Statute.

[435] Ambos, *Treatise on International Criminal Law, Vol. III*, 448.

[436] On 'probative value', see C. Gosnell, 'Admissibility of Evidence', in Khan, Buisman and Gosnell, *Principles of Evidence in International Criminal Justice*, 375, 384–389.

[437] For instance, in the *Gbagbo* and *Blé Goudé* cases, the majority refused to rule on the admissibility of a given item of evidence at the time of its submission and deferred decisions on admissibility of evidence 'to the time of the judgment'. See *Prosecutor* v. *Gbagbo and Blé Goudé*, ICC-02/11–01/15–405, Decision on the submission and admission of evidence, 29 January 2015, para. 15.

[438] See *Prosecutor* v. *Ruto and Sang*, ICC-01/09–01/11–2024, Judgment on the appeals of Mr William Samoei Ruto and Mr Joshua Arap Sang against the decision of Trial Chamber V(A) of 19 August 2015 entitled 'Decision on Prosecution Request for Admission of Prior Recorded Testimony', 12 February 2016, paras. 95–96.

fairness concerns, since defendants receive different treatment depending on the judges they face.

Evidence may be excluded in case of a serious rights violation. One controversial issue is to what extent judges may take into account evidence obtained in violation of human rights or procedural standards.[439] This issue has raised many difficulties in national legal systems which apply different standards. Some domestic systems apply the 'fruit of the poisonous tree doctrine',[440] according to which evidence obtained through illegal means is excluded as evidence. International criminal courts and tribunals have adopted a more flexible test, based on the gravity of the crimes adjudicated and investigative challenges. They have weighed the interests of defendants against the broader interests of crime control. For instance, in the context of the ICC, evidence obtained in violation of international human rights standards is only inadmissible if the violation casts 'a substantial doubt' on its reliability (e.g. evidence obtained through coercion of a person), or if its admission would be 'antithetical to' and 'seriously damage the integrity of proceedings.[441] This dual test, requiring a violation and a detrimental effect is a 'balance of competing conceptions'.[442] Judges are encouraged to strike a balance 'between the seriousness of the violation and the fairness of the trial as a whole'.[443] The goal is to prevent proceedings being impugned by evidence that is unreliable or obtained in a way that calls into question the integrity of the proceedings themselves, such as evidence obtained by torture.[444]

In practice, judges have accepted illegally obtained evidence in a number of cases in which the violation was not committed by employees or agents of tribunals themselves. There is rich practice in relation to violations of the right to privacy.[445] For instance, in the *Brđanin* case, the ICTY accepted transcripts of intercepted telephone conversations that were recorded in violation of domestic constitutional provisions.[446] In *Lubanga*, the ICC failed to exclude evidence based on the grounds that it was collected through a search and seizure by domestic authorities that violated the Congolese Code of Procedure.[447]

---

[439] W. Jasiński, 'Admissibility of Illegally Obtained Evidence in Proceedings before International Criminal Courts', in B. Krzan (ed.), *Prosecuting International Crimes: A Multidisciplinary Approach* (Boston: Brill Nijhoff, 2016), 201–223.

[440] On the complexities, see R. M. Pitler, 'The Fruit of the Poisonous Tree Revisited and Shepardized' (1968) 56 *California Law Review* 579, 581 et seq.

[441] Art. 69 (7) ICC Statute. See generally P. Viebig, *Illicitly Obtained Evidence at the International Criminal Court* (The Hague: TMC Asser Press, 2016).

[442] See D. Piragoff and P. Clarke, 'Article 69', in Triffterer and Ambos, *Rome Statute of the International Criminal Court*, 1749.

[443] *Lubanga* Confirmation Decision, para. 89.

[444] See Piragoff and Clarke, 'Article 69', 1749; T. Thienel, 'The Admissibility of Evidence Obtained by Torture under International Law' (2006) 17 *EJIL* 349, 367.

[445] G. E. Edwards, 'International Human Rights Law Challenges to the New International Criminal Court: The Search and Seizure Right to Privacy' (2001) 26 *Yale Journal of International Law* 325.

[446] *Prosecutor* v. *Brđanin*, IT-99-36-T, Decision on the Defence Objection to the Use of Intercept Evidence, 3 October 2003, 29–31.

[447] *Lubanga* Confirmation Decision, para. 78 ('the unlawfulness of the search and seizure conducted ... was a breach of a procedural rule, but cannot be considered so serious as to amount to a violation of internationally recognised human rights)'.

By contrast, evidence obtained through coercion of a defendant is clearly inadmissible. In the *Čelebići* case, the ICTY confirmed that 'confessions made by accused persons in the absence of their volition and arising from threats, inducement or hope of favour by persons in authority' are inadmissible.[448] The tribunal also accepted that violations of the right to counsel during police interviews may render a statement inadmissible.[449]

The Convention against Torture contains an express exclusionary rule according to which statements made as a result of torture 'shall not be invoked as evidence in any proceedings, except against a person accused of torture'.[450] The scope of this provision was debated before the ECCC.[451] The co-prosecutors sought to introduce statements made by victims of torture at S-21 and other Khmer Rouge security centres as evidence against Khmer leaders at trial. The Prosecution intended to establish that the Communist Party of Kampuchea relied on the content of these confessions to carry out systematic crimes, i.e. arrest and execution of others. The Defence argued that the statements were inadmissible since they constituted evidence obtained through torture.[452] The Co-Investigating Judges accepted them. They argued that the statements were not deemed to be used against the person who was subject to torture. They claimed that barring the use of information would allow those who 'are accused of torture' to 'use the law designed to prevent torture to shield themselves from liability'.[453] The decision was affirmed by the Pre-Trial Judges.[454] It has been subject to critique since it disregarded the detrimental effect of the admission of evidence on the integrity of the proceedings.[455]

4.4.2.5 Investigative Choices

The process of investigation involves many delicate processes of inclusion and exclusion. In domestic jurisdictions, prosecutors may be duty-bound to investigate and prosecute. At the international level, investigation is mostly about making choices, and establishing priorities.

There is often an urgent pressure to act quickly. Resources are limited. One of the most controversial aspects of investigations is to decide where and whom to investigate, i.e. what situations, which regions, which incidents, what groups and entities.

---

[448] *Prosecutor* v. *Delalić et al.*, IT-96-21-T, Decision on Hasim Delić's Motions pursuant to Rule 73, 1 September 1997, para. 15.

[449] *Prosecutor* v. *Delalić et al.*, IT-96-21, Decision on Zdravko Mucic's Motion for the Exclusion of Evidence, 2 September 1997, paras. 50–55.

[450] See Art. 15 of the UN Convention against Torture.

[451] See D. McKeever, 'Evidence Obtained Through Torture Before the Khmer Rouge Tribunal: Unlawful Pragmatism?' (2010) 8 *JICJ* 615.

[452] M. P. Scharf, 'Tainted Provenance: When, If Ever, Should Torture Evidence Be Admissible?' 65 *Washington & Lee Law Review* (2008) 129.

[453] *Prosecutor* v. *Ieng Thirith*, 002/19-09-2007-ECCC-OCIJ, Order on use of statements which were or may have been obtained by torture, 28 July 2009, para. 24.

[454] *Prosecutor* v. *Ieng Thirith*, 002/19-09-2007-ECCC/OCIJ, Decision on the Admissibility of the Appeal against Co-Investigating Judges' Order on Use of Statements which were or may have been obtained by Torture, 18 December 2009.

[455] See Viebig, 'Illicitly Obtained Evidence', 178; Scharf, 'Tainted Provenance', 154.

Large parts of the decision-making process and the formulation of potential cases remain internal. Investigators take many implicit decisions in the course of their work. To the outside, certain choices may appear to be driven by opportunistic factors, rather than adherence to the law and the gravity of crimes. There is a risk that investigations may focus too easily on individuals, rather than crimes and context, or overemphasize the role of suffering and victimization, in order to justify investigative choices.[456]

4.4.2.5.1 Selecting Situations

Courts like the Nuremberg and Tokyo tribunals, the ad hoc tribunals, the Special Court for Sierra Leone or the Extraordinary Chambers in the Courts of Cambodia were provided with jurisdiction over a specific situation. States or the Security Council defined those situations and decided that the intervention of an international criminal court was appropriate. The ICC has to select the very situations in which it intervenes.[457]

The Statutes of international criminal courts and tribunals provide some general legal criteria. The ICC Statute uses concepts such as the 'most serious crimes of international concern',[458] gravity, the interests of victims or the interests of justice to guide the selection of situations and cases. These concepts frame the exercise of prosecutorial discretion. They are relatively vague. They have been specified through practice and OTP policies.

The ICC has been criticized for its approach towards the selection of situations.[459] The Statute requires the Prosecutor to consider whether crimes within the jurisdiction of the Court have been committed and whether the situation is of sufficient gravity to justify further action by the Court. This gravity determination requires a case-by-case assessment. The first eight situations that were investigated by the Court were all African. This has created a perception of bias. The Office of the Prosecutor has made it clear that 'geo-political implications of the location of a situation' or 'geographical balance between situations' are not relevant criteria for selection of situations.[460] It has tried to argue that the choices merely follow law and the evidence. However, the arguments on both sides have been misleading and lacked engagement with the underlying dilemmas.[461]

---

[456] X. Agirre, 'Methodology for Criminal Investigation of International Crimes', in Smeulers, *Collective Violence and International Criminal Justice*, 353, 377–358.

[457] See M. Hadi Zakerhossein, *Situation Selection Regime at the International Criminal Court* (Antwerp: Intersentia, 2017).

[458] See ICC Statute, Preamble and Art. 5.

[459] A. Smeulers, M. Weerdesteijn and B. Hola, 'The Selection of Situations by the ICC: An Empirically Based Evaluation of the OTP's Performance' (2015) 15 *International Criminal Law Review* 1–39; M. M. deGuzman, 'Choosing to Prosecute: Expressive Selection at the ICC' (2012) 33 *Michigan Journal of International Law* 265–320.

[460] Policy Paper on Preliminary Examinations, para. 29.

[461] Max Du Plessis has offered a fair account of the status quo: 'The perception of ICC bias against Africa and lack of consistency and fairness in the way the court is implementing international criminal justice may not correspond with the true reality, but it cannot be wished away by simply being ignored. There are real issues and concerns on both sides that need to be addressed in a serious, constructive and cooperative manner through honest dialogue'. M. du Plessis, T. Maluwa and A. O'Reilly, *Africa and the International Criminal Court*, Chatham House Brief, July 2013, 11.

It is wrong to assert that the ICC focused on African situations with some kind of 'malicious intent'. Formally, most situations were referred to the Court through state referrals (Uganda, DRC, Central African Republic, Mali) or Security Council referrals (Darfur, Libya). For governments in Uganda and the DRC, ICC action was a convenient instrument to counter military and political opponents. AU discourse mixed objections against ICC selection policy with broader discontents about the targeting of acting heads of state, the reluctance of the Security Council to listen to African concerns, and conditions under which African states were prompted to adhere to the Statute. The main critique was a political one, namely that the ICC is targeting politically weak states while ignoring more powerful ones. Anti-ICC rhetoric was driven by strong governmental self-interest. It negated the differentiated positions towards international criminal justice on the continent, including existing civil society support for the Court.[462]

The OTP downplayed its discretion and failed to seriously engage with the merits of critiques. The ICC has actively 'chased' some African referrals to attract cases.[463] The focus on Africa was partly a choice of convenience. For more than a decade, namely until the opening of the investigation in Georgia in 2016, situations outside Africa remained under preliminary examination while African situations passed on to investigation. Situations like Colombia or Afghanistan could have proceeded to investigation if a specific aspect of the situation had been selected for inquiry. The OTP sought to reduce this to a perception problem.[464] It argued that the focus on investigations in Africa was justified by gravity and the large numbers of victims in each situation. This argument is shaky. While all African situations were undoubtedly grave, other situations are not necessarily less grave.

One of the core problems in the debate on the ICC and Africa is that the Court was unable to respond to the broader structural critique voiced by African critics, namely that crimes committed on the continent are part of a larger global network in which violence, war, arms trade, mineral resource extraction and poverty are interconnected.[465] ICC discourse reduced the complexity of choice to law and avoided tackling the harder questions. This made it vulnerable to critique and triggered reflections on alternative forums of justice.

4.4.2.5.2 Selecting Cases

The selection of cases against specific individuals requires a different set of choices. It involves the identification of individual suspects, crime base and linkage elements.

---

[462] For a differentiated account, see L. J. M. Seymour, 'The ICC and Africa', in Clarke, Knottnerus and De Volder, *Africa and the ICC*, 107, 121 et seq.

[463] See P. Clark, 'Chasing Cases: The ICC and the Politics of State Referral in the Democratic Republic of Congo and Uganda', in Stahn and El Zeidy, *The International Criminal Court and Complementarity*, 1180.

[464] At the 14th session of the Assembly of States Parties, Fatou Bensouda stated that '[w]e have two problems with perceptions: first, that the ICC is targeting Africa and second, that the ICC is ignoring other criminals'. See www .africalegalaid.com/news/is-africa-a-participant.

[465] On the arms trade nexus, see S. Kendall and C. da Silva, 'Beyond the ICC', in Clarke, Knottnerus and De Volder, *Africa and the ICC*, 407.

This is a complex process. Within a given situation, there are often multiple incidents of crime. Investigators have to choose the incidents that they focus on, and then identify the crimes and potential perpetrators within a wide range of incidents.

The legal framework is limited. The Prosecution is mandated to ensure an effective investigation and prosecution of crimes. The framework of some tribunals (e.g. SCSL, ECCC, ICTY) encourages prosecutors to focus on a specific group or category of persons. This is not a firm jurisdictional requirement however. Case selection involves many strategic choices that are not regulated or within the discretion of the Prosecutor. The ICC Prosecution has formulated some guidelines that explain the legal framework and OTP policies.[466]

During the investigation, prosecutors are bound by a duty to investigate impartially and objectively.[467] As a principle, prosecutors must examine allegations against all groups or parties within a particular situation to assess whether persons bear criminal responsibility. The application of this principle has caused numerous problems. The SCSL has sought to create the appearance of parity between parties by bringing cases against all factions. The ICC, the ICTY and the ICTR have faced challenges of one-sided prosecution. These arguments are difficult to counter, since it is problematic to compare the criminality of different types of actors. Impartiality does not necessarily require 'equivalence of blame'. The ICC has therefore adopted a minimalist position to protect its discretion. It has argued that impartiality means that investigators must apply the same processes, methods, criteria and thresholds to all groups in order to assess their blameworthiness.[468] This is difficult to control, since compliance with this principle is not necessarily reflected in the outcome of investigations or subject to judicial scrutiny.

The question of whether a case is brought against an individual defendant depends on a range of factors, including the gravity of the crimes or the degree of responsibility of the alleged perpetrators and the potential charges.[469] It is also guided by pragmatic considerations, such as the quantity and quality of available evidence, the options to secure arrest and surrender, or the impact on ongoing or future crimes.[470]

A recurring challenge is the 'big fish vs. small fish' dilemma.[471] There has been a strong pressure to prosecute only the 'big fish' – this means people who are in senior positions, whether military or civilian, rather than mid-level or low-level offenders. For example, the completion strategy urged both ad hoc tribunals to concentrate on the prosecution and trial of the most senior leaders suspected of being most

---

[466] OTP, "Policy Paper on Case Selection and Prioritisation", 15 September 2016.
[467] Art. 54 ICC Statute.
[468] "Policy Paper on Case Selection and Prioritisation", para. 20.
[469] Ibid., paras. 34–46.
[470] Ibid., paras. 47–52.
[471] See H. Takemura, 'Big Fish and Small Fish Debate: An Examination of the Prosecutorial Discretion' (2007) 7 *International Criminal Law Review* 677; M. O'Brien, 'Prosecutorial Discretion as an Obstacle to Prosecution of United Nations Peacekeepers by the International Criminal Court: The Big Fish/Small Fish Debate and the Gravity Threshold' (2012) 10 *JICJ* 525.

responsible for crimes,[472] and to transfer cases involving intermediate- and lower-rank accused to competent national jurisdictions. The ICC OTP has adopted a strategy of focusing on the most responsible perpetrators. However, the persons who are most responsible for serious crimes are not always 'big fish'. For instance, it might make sense to prosecute lower-level perpetrators whose conduct has been particularly grave or notorious. Moreover, there may be a need to investigate and prosecute lower-level perpetrators to build the evidentiary foundations for cases against those most respon-sible. It is thus wrong to assume that gravity excludes mid- or lower-level offenders per se.

In the history of many international criminal courts and tribunals, relatively small cases broke the ice. At the ICTY, the first case was against Tadić, a mid-level leader of Bosnian Serb paramilitary forces.[473] At the ICTR, it was the case against a former mayor (Akayesu). At the ICC, it was *Lubanga* – a variation of *Tadić*.[474] They were followed by other important rulings against mid-level defendants (e.g. Furundzija[475]). It is thus rightly acknowledged that the prosecution requires a certain amount of discretion in the choice of perpetrators, in order to facilitate a 'strategy of gradually building [cases] upwards'.[476]

The 'big fish/small fish' dilemma has given rise to some curious case law.[477] Some defendants have argued that they could not be investigated and prosecuted before an international criminal court and tribunal because they were not important enough to satisfy the focus on 'senior' or 'most responsible' leaders. For instance, defendants before the SCSL argued that they were not within the jurisdiction of the Court, since the SCSL is mandated to 'prosecute persons who bear the greatest responsibility'.[478] One Trial Chamber claimed that this was an issue relating to the scope of personal jurisdiction.[479] A different Chamber found that this is a matter within the discretion of the Prosecutor.[480] The Appeals Chamber argued that the requirement must be applied with 'good faith' by the Prosecutor, but is subject to limited judicial review. It held

---

[472] The Security Council urged the ICTY and the ICTR to focus primarily on 'the most senior leaders suspected of being most responsible for crimes'. See SC Res. 1534 26 March 2004, para. 5.

[473] At the ICTY, the first indictment was against *Nikolić*. Richard Goldstone gave a pragmatic explanation: 'Just before the end of October 1994, we decided there was only one defendant against whom there was sufficient evidence available to justify an indictment. His name was Dragan Nikolic. We indicted him for a number of murders and the torture of innocent civilians. Now, Nikolic was not an appropriate first person for an indictment by the first international war crimes tribunal, but we had no option. In order for the work to continue, we had to get out an indictment quickly. That is the explanation for the Nikolic indictment.' See R. Goldstone, 'Prosecuting Rape as a War Crime' (2002) 34 *Case Western Reserve Journal of International Law* 277, 281.

[474] *Lubanga* was an easy pick since he was in detention by the DRC authorities.

[475] Anto Furundžija was the local commander of a unit of the Croatian Defence Council in the Vitez municipality of BiH, see *Furundžija* Trial Judgment, para. 39.

[476] See OTP, Strategic Plan 2012–2015, para. 22 ('The Office would therefore first investigate and prosecute a limited number of mid- and high-level perpetrators in order to ultimately have a reasonable chance to convict the most responsible. The Office will also consider prosecuting lower level perpetrators where their conduct has been particularly grave and has acquired extensive notoriety. Such a strategy will in the end be more cost-effective than having unsuccessful or no prosecutions against the highest placed perpetrators').

[477] C. C. Jalloh, 'Prosecuting Those Bearing "Greatest Responsibility": The Lessons of the Special Court for Sierra Leone' (2013) 96 *Marquette Law Review* 863.

[478] See Art. 1 (1) of the SCSL Statute.

[479] *Fonfana and Kondewa* Trial Judgment, para. 92.

[480] *Brima et al.* Trial Judgment, paras. 653–654.

that it would be 'inconceivable' if 'after a long and expensive trial the Trial Chamber could conclude that although the commission of serious crimes has been established beyond reasonable doubt against the Accused, the indictment ought to be struck out on the ground that it has not been proved that the Accused was not one of those who bore the greatest responsibility'.[481] The exact opposite argument was made before the ICTY by defendants in Rule 11 *bis* cases. The rule on transfer of cases from the ad hoc tribunals provides that only cases involving medium- and low-level perpetrators may be transferred to Bosnia or Serbia. Some defendants who had been detained at the ICTY wanted to be tried internationally, rather than before domestic forums. They argued before the tribunal that they were actually not 'small fish', but persons bearing great responsibility, in order to avoid transfer.

The ICC Pre-Trial Chamber gave a 'magical' interpretation to the gravity requirement under the admissibility test of the ICC Statute, when it declined to issue an arrest warrant against Bosco Ntaganda due to lack of gravity. The provision states that a case is inadmissible where it 'is not of sufficient gravity to justify further action by the Court'.[482] The Pre-Trial Chamber derived a full-fledged test from this text and a systematic interpretation of the Statute. It argued that the case lacked gravity since 'relevant person must fall within the 'category of most senior leaders of the situation under investigation' in light of his/her position in the State entity, organization or armed group, and [that] the role of the respective State entity, organization or armed group in the overall commission of crimes must be sufficiently important in the relevant situation'.[483] This ruling was rightly overturned by the Appeals Chamber. It overstretched the gravity requirement, restricted the potential scope of cases before the ICC, and made it impossible for the Prosecution to build cases through the investigation and prosecution of mid-level perpetrators.[484]

A further challenge is how to draw a balance between the main patterns of victimization in a situation and strategic considerations, such as the possible global impact of cases. Given the selectivity of their mandate, prosecutors may be tempted to focus the investigation on a specific theme or category of crime in order to facilitate the prosecution of such crimes ('thematic investigation and prosecution'). According to this logic, a case might be selected because of its thematic significance, or because the underlying paradigm is not sufficiently investigated or prosecuted in domestic courts. This type of prioritization derives the necessary gravity from the 'nature of the crime' and the expressivist function of charges.[485]

---

[481] *Brima et al.* Appeal Judgment, para. 283.
[482] Art. 17 (1) (d) ICC Statute.
[483] *Prosecutor* v. *Ntaganda*, Decision on the Prosecutor's Application for a warrant of arrest, 10 February 2006, para. 63.
[484] See ICC-01/04–159, Judgment on the Prosecutor's appeal against the decision of Pre-Trial Chamber I entitled 'Decision on the Prosecutor's Application for Warrants of Arrest', 13 July 2006, Art. 58, paras. 68 et seq.
[485] M. De Guzman, 'An Expressive Rationale for the Thematic Prosecution of Sex Crimes', in M. Bergsmo (ed.), *Thematic Prosecution of International Sex Crimes* (Beijing: Torkel Opsahl Academic Epublisher, 2012), 11.

This thematic approach has played in important role in practice. For instance, the ICTY focused on sexual violence as a theme in the *Furundžija* case.[486] The SCSL did signature cases crimes against children, in particular child soldiers and attacks on peacekeepers.[487] The ICC gave a new dimension to theme-based cases. It relied in two cases predominantly on thematic prioritization, without including other charges. *Lubanga* focused exclusively on child recruitment, *Al Mahdi* solely on protection of cultural property. This trend should remain an exception rather than the rule.[488] Thematic approaches are justifiable if theme-based charges are combined with other charges, or if these cases are complemented by other cases in the situation with a broader focus. However, they are likely to cause disappointment or increase the friction between global priorities and local expectations if they are the main focus of prosecutorial action. For instance, the narrow focus of the *Lubanga* case was heavily criticized in the light of the number of other charges that could have been brought.[489]

Among all international criminal courts and tribunals, the ICTY has had the most cases. Its overall record is mixed. It brought out major patterns of violence through its cases. It formally departed from the principle of victor's justice. Its selection policy remained contested, however. Discrepancies in the balance of cases were used to discredit the tribunal, or to accuse it of bias. Most cases concerned crimes committed in Bosnia and Herzegovina.[490] The majority of them focused on Serb-controlled Republika Srpska. This choice may be defended by the number and systematicity of crimes. Yet Russia and Serbia continued to argue that case selection reflected an implicit anti-Serb bias.[491] Roughly three-quarters of the indictees were Serb or Montenegrin. Crimes committed against Serbs received less attention. The lack of trials of high-level Croatian and Bosnian leaders remained a bone of contention.[492]

The Tribunal addressed crimes by Croatian forces during the conflict in several cases (*Gotovina et al.*,[493] *Prlić et al.*[494]). It found that former President Tuđman played an active role in a Croat Joint Criminal Enterprise against Serb populations during

[486] *Furundžija* Trial Judgment, paras. 165 et seq.

[487] See e.g. *Prosecutor* v. *Sesay, Kallon, and Gbao*, SCSL-04-15-T, Judgment, 2 March 2009, paras. 213 et seq.

[488] See K. Ambos, 'Thematic Investigations and Prosecution of International Sex Crimes: Some Critical Comments from a Theoretical and Comparative Perspective', in Bergsmo, *Thematic Prosecution of International Sex Crimes*, 291, 302.

[489] See Women's Initiatives for Gender Justice, Letter to Prosecutor Luis Moreno Ocampo, August 2006, at www .iccwomen.org/news/docs/Prosecutor_Letter_August_2006_Redacted.pdf ('grave concern at the narrow charges being brought by the Office of the Prosecutor in the case against Thomas Lubanga Dyilo'). See also J. McBride, *The War Crime of Child Soldier Recruitment* (The Hague: TMC Asser Press, 2013), 156–157; C. Ferstman, 'Limited Charges and Limited Judgments by the International Criminal Court: Who Bears the Greatest Responsibility?' (2012) 16 *International Journal of Human Rights* 796.

[490] D. Orentlicher, *That Someone Guilty Be Punished: The Impact of the ICTY in Bosnia* (New York: Open Society Institute, 2010).

[491] M. Ostojić, *Between Justice and Stability: The Politics of War Crimes Prosecutions in Post-Milošević Serbia* (Farnham: Ashgate, 2014).

[492] I. Vukušić, 'Judging Their Hero: Perceptions of the International Criminal Tribunal for the former Yugoslavia in Croatia', in J. Gow, R. Kerr and Z. Pajić (eds.), *Prosecting War Crimes: Lessons and legacies of the International Criminal Tribunal for the former Yugoslavia* (London: Routledge, 2014), 151–181.

[493] *Prosecutor* v. *Gotovina, Čermak and Markač*, IT-06-90-T, Judgment, 15 April 2011 (*Gotovina et al.* Trial Judgment). On Gotovina and 'Operation Storm', see V. Pavlaković, 'Croatia, the International Criminal Tribunal for the Former Yugoslavia, and General Gotovina as a Political Symbol' (2010) 62 *Europe-Asia Studies* 1707–1740.

[494] *Prosecutor* v. *Prlić et al.*, IT-04-74, Judgment, 29 May 2013.

Operation Storm, including plans to drive Serbs out of Krajina province.[495] In *Prlić et al.*, all defendants were convicted for a joint criminal enterprise aimed at creating a Croatian entity in Bosnia and Herzegovina through ethnic cleansing of the Muslim population.[496] Tuđman was not indicted since he passed away in 1999. Three generals of the Croatian Army, Ante Gotovina, Ivan Čermak and Mladen Markač, were acquitted. In particular, the acquittal of Gotovina was highly criticized.[497] Croatia has continued to dispute its role in the Bosnian conflict. It has rejected any ICTY judgments that challenged the Croatian narrative of self-defence against Serb aggression. This sense of denial was dramatically expressed by Slobodan Praljak's suicide in the ICTY courtroom ('Slobodan Praljak is not a war criminal') during the reading of the *Prlić et al.* Appeal Judgment,[498] and subsequent endorsements by Croatian officials.

The ICTY Prosecution sought to counter concerns about a Serb-focused charging strategy through indictments against members of the former KLA during the Kosovo conflict.[499] These cases remained controversial. In 2003, the Tribunal issued an indictment against three former KLA officials, Fatmir Limaj, Haradin Bala and Isak Musliu, for crimes against Serbian and Kosovo Albanian civilians in the KLA-run Llapushnik/Lapušnik prison camp. It was the first Kosovo case of the tribunal.[500] Only Haradin Bala was convicted.[501] In the *Haradinaj et al.* case, all defendants were acquitted following a trial, and a re-trial.[502] The Prosecution was unable to show that the defendants were part of a joint criminal enterprise to establish KLA control in western Kosovo using detention camps. The OTP claimed that trials were compromised by witness intimidation.[503] Opponents argued that the cases were unfounded and that Carla Del Ponte was abusing her power by pursuing them.[504]

---

[495] In *Gotovina*, the ICTY relied on the minutes of the Brioni meeting on 31 July 1995 to make that case. See *Gotovina et al.* Trial Judgment, paras. 1970 et seq.

[496] *Prosecutor v. Prlić et al*, IT-04-74-A, Judgment, 29 November 2017 (*Prlić et al.* Appeal Judgment).

[497] See *Prosecutor v. Gotovina and Markač*, IT-06-90-A, Judgment, 16 November 2012. Serb President Tomislav Nikolic stated: 'It is now quite clear the tribunal has made a political decision and not a legal ruling'. See B. Waterfield, 'Croatian Hero Ante Gotovina Acquitted of War Crimes', *The Telegraph*, 16 November 2012. Judge Agius and Judge Pocar dissented.

[498] For a discussion see A. Heinze, 'Slobodan Praljak's Suicide and International Criminal Justice', *E-International Relations*, 9 January 2018, at www.e-ir.info/2018/01/09/slobodan-praljaks-suicide-and-international-criminal-justice/ ('From ... the expressive view of punishment on an international level, Praljak did not escape punishment – at least, not completely. He received his formal judgement and the facts of his case were laid out in detail before the eyes of the world to establish, once and for all, the truth. However, he partly defeated the plan of the international community to use him for the purpose of showing the world that it is the world community that decides about the fate of war criminals, perpetrators of gross human rights violations and the like').

[499] See ICTY, 'View from The Hague: Tribunal Indictment Against the KLA', 28 January 2004, www.icty.org/x/file/Outreach/view_from_hague/balkan_040128_en.pdf.

[500] See P. Chifflet, 'The First Trial of Former Members of the Kosovo Liberation Army: Prosecutor v. Fatmir Limaj, Haradin Bala, and Isak Musliu' (2006) 19 *LJIL* 459.

[501] ICTY, 'The Tribunal's Appeals Chamber today upheld the Trial Chamber judgement in the case against former Kosovo Liberation Army (KLA) members Fatmir Limaj, Isak Musliu and Haradin Bala', 27 September 2007, at www.icty.org/sid/8841.

[502] *Prosecutor v. Haradinaj, Balaj, and Brahimaj*, IT-04-84bis-T, Judgment, 29 November 2012, paras. 682–685.

[503] In 2010, the Appeals Chamber ordered a re-trial since 'the Trial Chamber failed to take sufficient steps to counter the witness intimidation that permeated the trial'. See *Prosecutor v. Haradinaj, Balaj, and Brahimaj*, IT-04-84-A, Judgment, 19 July 2010, para. 49.

[504] Haradinaj's Defence counsel, Ben Emmerson requested De Ponye to apologize for 'her own, entirely personal, responsibility for the decision to issue this indictment without any reliable evidence to justify her decision'. See

Overall, it is misguided to blame the ICTY for ethnic bias in its charging strategy. In practice, however, case selection achieved only 'partial impartiality'.[505]

4.4.2.6 *Outsourcing Investigations*

Criminal investigators do not have a monopoly regarding investigations. Investigators are often limited to carrying out work in areas protected by the United Nations or other security actors. The output of investigations is mostly the result of a large network of organizations and individuals, which includes NGOs, lawyers and other entities willing to share information and evidence. A key dilemma is to what extent criminal investigations should rely on external providers to carry out investigative functions.[506]

The idea of involving private or other entities in criminal functions has gained increased importance in past years. At the domestic level, private actors have been entrusted with police functions or prison services.[507] At the international level, contingents of peace operations or private associations have been entrusted with investigative functions. For instance, in Syria the Commission for International Justice and Accountability (CIJA), a private NGO supported and advised by former investigators from international tribunals, has been charged with collecting evidence in relation to war crimes.[508] The MH17 investigation by Bellingcat shows that private entities may be more efficient than domestic criminal investigators in collecting and analysing open source material.[509] However, the outsourcing of criminal investigative work raises problems in relation to ethics, fairness, transparency and accountability. Third parties are often guided by other objectives, subject to specific donor dependencies and less accountable towards defendants.[510] They may lack the duty to look for exculpatory evidence. The reliance on external structures therefore requires caution and certain safeguards.

The ICC has struggled with reliance on third parties. A first problem is provider confidentiality. The Prosecution is entitled to receive information from external providers under the condition of non-disclosure. However, this option is meant to

---

O. Bowcott, 'Kosovan Former PM Cleared of War Crimes by Hague Tribunal', *The Guardian*, 29 November 2012, www.theguardian.com/world/2012/nov/29/kosovan-former-pm-cleared-war-crimes.

[505] Bruning, Scallon, Rudy and Whall, 'Partial Impartiality'.

[506] See E. Baylis, 'Outsourcing Investigations' (2009) 14 UCLA *Journal of International Law & Foreign Affairs* 121.

[507] R. Simmons, 'Private Criminal Justice' (2007) 42 *Wake Forest L Rev* 911; R. A. Fairfax, 'Outsourcing Criminal Prosecution? The Limits of Criminal Justice Privatization' (2010) 10 *University of Chicago Legal Forum* 266.

[508] William Wiley defines it as an 'an international non-governmental organization with a mandate from its donors to undertake international criminal investigations in the midst of the ongoing conflicts'. See Statement Mr. William Wiley (Executive Director, Commission for International Justice and Accountability) at the Subcommittee on International Human Rights, 22 November 2016, at https://openparliament.ca/committees/international-human-rights/42-1/33/william-wiley-1/only/. It assisted Western countries in the investigation and prosecution of Syrian regime officials. See M. Rankin, 'Investigating Crimes against Humanity in Syria and Iraq: The Commission for International Justice and Accountability' (2017) 9 *Global Responsibility To Protect* 395.

[509] J. D. Aronson, 'The Utility of User-Generated Content in Human Rights Investigations', in M. K. Land and J. D Aronson, *New Technologies for Human Rights Law and Practice* (Cambridge: Cambridge University Press, 2018), 129, 138 et seq.

[510] On CIJA's selectivity challenges, see Rankin, 'Investigating Crimes against Humanity in Syria and Iraq', 420.

serve as a lead for further investigation, i.e. geared 'solely for the purpose of generating new evidence'.[511] In the *Lubanga* investigation, the Prosecutor collected detailed documentary evidence from the United Nations and non-governmental organizations.[512] The amount of information collected from these sources nearly caused the case to collapse. More than 200 documents were provided under the condition of confidentiality. This meant more than 50 per cent of evidence was collected on the basis of confidentiality, i.e. with a proviso of non-disclosure without the consent of the provider. This included potentially exculpatory or mitigating evidence, e.g. information of *Lubanga*'s authority and efforts to demobilize child soldiers. The Trial Chamber stayed the proceedings since it was concerned about the fairness of the trial.[513] The Appeals Chamber argued that the Prosecutor had abused its power to receive confidential information during the investigation. This meant that the OTP had to reach agreement with the information providers to disclose all the material.

A second problem is the 'contracting out' of investigative functions. The ICC has relied heavily on intermediaries, i.e. external individuals or organizations, to assist it in identifying and interviewing witnesses. Intermediaries are go-betweens for the ICC and local actors.[514] Their status has not been regulated in the founding instruments of the Court. They are creatures of practice. They have been used for various purposes: identification of witnesses and victims, evidence collection, community outreach and victim assistance. Such contact points are essential for investigations and prosecutions, as well as victim participation, in particular in contexts where the ICC lacks access on the ground or confronts government criminality. The ICC Prosecutor even conceded that 'prosecutions themselves are impossible without the assistance of intermediaries'.[515] The way in which they have used has raised significant critique though.

In early investigations, the function of intermediaries went beyond establishing contact with potential witnesses. In the *Lubanga* case, the Trial Chamber reprimanded

---

[511] Art. 54 (3) (e) ICC Statute.

[512] On the UN perspective, see L. D. Johnson, 'Lubanga Case and Cooperation between the UN and the ICC: Disclosure Obligation v. Confidentiality Obligation' (2012) 10 *JICJ* 887.

[513] The Trial Chamber found that the Prosecution 'has incorrectly used Article 54(3)(e) [confidentiality agreement] when entering into agreements with information-providers, with the consequence that a significant body of exculpatory evidence which would otherwise have been disclosed to the accused is to be withheld from him, thereby improperly inhibiting the opportunities for the accused to prepare his defence'. See *Prosecutor* v. *Lubanga*, ICC-01/04–01/06, Urgent Decision on the Consequences of Non-Disclosure of Exculpatory Materials Covered by Article 54 (3) (e) Agreements and the Application to Stay the Prosecution of the Accused, Together with Certain Other Issues Raised at the Status Conference on 10 June 2008, 13 June 2008, para. 92.

[514] The ICC defines an intermediary as 'someone who comes between one person and another; who facilitates contact or provides a link between one of the organs or units of the Court or Counsel on the one hand, and victims, witnesses, beneficiaries of reparations and/or affected communities more broadly on the other'. See Guidelines Governing the Relations between the Court and Intermediaries for the Organs and Units of the Court and Counsel working with intermediaries, March 2014, 5 (Intermediaries Guidelines). See generally D. Clancy, '"They Told Us We Would Be Part of History": Reflections on the Civil Society Intermediary Experience in the Great Lakes Region', in De Vos, Kendall and Stahn, *Contested Justice*, 219–248; C. De Vos, '"Someone Who Comes between One Person and Another": Lubanga, Local Cooperation and the Right to a Fair Trial' (2011) 12 *Melbourne Journal of International Law* 217; E. Haslam and R. Edmunds, 'Managing A New "Partnership": Professionalization, Intermediaries and the International Criminal Court' (2013) 24 *Criminal Law Forum* 49.

[515] *Prosecutor* v. *Lubanga*, ICC-01/04–01/06–2310-Red, Prosecution's Submissions in Response to Trial Chamber's Oral Request of 10 February 2010, 25 February 2010, para. 12.

the Prosecution for its unchecked use of intermediaries and its 'negligence in failing to verify and scrutinise' the work of intermediaries which led to 'inaccurate or dishonest' testimony.[516] It found that 'the prosecution should not have delegated its investigative responsibilities to the intermediaries in the way set out above, notwithstanding the extensive security difficulties it faced'.[517] It suggested that some intermediaries exercised improper influence over witnesses, warranting contempt of court proceedings.[518] Such problems have also occurred in other contexts.[519]

Following the *Lubanga* ruling, the ICC developed more detailed guidelines for the use of intermediaries and a Code of Conduct[520]. They limit the investigative role of intermediaries more narrowly to 'assist[ing] a party or participant to conduct investigations by identifying evidentiary leads and/or witnesses and facilitating contact with potential witnesses'.[521] Investigators must thus maintain control over investigations and safeguard their integrity. However, many structural challenges remain.

According to the Guidelines, intermediaries are not meant to serve as 'a substitute for staff for the implementation of the mandate of the Court'.[522] However, the Guidelines recognize intermediaries as a new category of professional justice agents that complement ICC staff.[523] They are divided into three classes: contracted intermediaries, intermediaries 'approved by the ICC' (through an affidavit) and 'unapproved' intermediaries. This distinction may introduce difficult frictions on the ground between contracted intermediaries, who become quasi-institutional service providers with specific benefits and duties, and other information providers, who are deemed to offer their support on a more voluntary basis and free of charge. This formalization may reinforce the perception that international criminal investigations are part of a global justice industry that is driven by negotiation, market and demand. Potential witnesses are seen as business opportunities by intermediaries or witnesses themselves. For instance, in *Lubanga*, the Trial Chamber confirmed that some witnesses in Bunia viewed participation in ICC proceedings as 'an opportunity to secure free rehousing'.[524] This may make it harder to count on voluntary cooperation.

The contracting of intermediaries introduces a filter between 'locals' and 'internationals'. It may be more helpful to create mixed investigation teams, composed of domestic and international investigators, or to facilitate direct interaction between

---

[516] *Lubanga* Trial Judgment, para. 482.

[517] Ibid., para. 482.

[518] Ibid., para. 483 ('there is a risk that P-0143 persuaded, encouraged, or assisted witnesses to give false evidence; there are strong reasons to believe that P-0316 persuaded witnesses to lie as to their involvement as child soldiers within the UPC').

[519] In the Kenya situation, an intermediary of the Prosecution, Walter Barasa, was indicted for offering witnesses money to withdraw their testimony against Ruto and Sang. See *Prosecutor v. W. Osapiri Barasa*, ICC-01/09–01/13–1-Red2, Warrant of Arrest for Walter Osapiri Barasa, 2 August 2013, paras. 3–5.

[520] See ICC, Intermediaries Guidelines and Code of Conduct for Intermediaries, March 2014.

[521] Ibid., 6.

[522] Ibid., 3.

[523] In *Lubanga*, the Trial Chamber found that 'intermediaries were activists, most of whom were fully aware of developments within the sphere of international criminal justice and the objectives of the investigators'. See *Lubanga* Trial Judgment, para. 184.

[524] *Lubanga* Judgment, para. 147.

ICC staff and local communities.[525] The experience of using intermediaries for investigation and collection of witnesses and victims has shown that such go-betweens exercise significant factual power in local contexts. They may predetermine who ultimately becomes recognized as witness or victim. There is thus a risk that the use of intermediaries is perceived as a new form of 'legal hegemony' through which the ICC reasserts 'itself in multiple ways in the guise of protection and support'.[526]

4.4.2.7 Timing of Investigations

Timing and ending of investigations involves sensitive decisions, including a balancing of conflicting priorities.[527] Prosecutors have a duty to ensure effective investigations. This warrants swift investigatory measures. For instance, if an investigations runs late, important evidence may be lost, or the quality of the evidence may impaired. However, the dynamic nature of investigations, and their size and complexity, make it difficult to establish absolute time frames for their completion. There is not one investigative approach for all cases.

In many instances, prosecutors have continued to collect new evidence to refine the case during proceedings against the defendants. This poses problems from a fairness point of view since the defendant may face changing charges. For instance, at the ICTY prosecutors sometimes discovered during litigation that the case file had significant weaknesses, since investigators focused on establishing what happened, rather than on how crimes could be linked to the accused. Investigations continued through trial and led to requests for the amendment of charges. This created uncertainty and fairness concerns, since it affected the rights of defendants to prepare an effective defence.[528]

At the ICC, the timing of the investigation is subject to greater judicial scrutiny due to the role of the Pre-Trial Chamber. It has been controversial to what extent the Prosecution is entitled to continue building its investigation throughout the proceedings. There are two competing visions. Some voices suggest that the Prosecution should be allowed to continue its investigations beyond the confirmation of charges by the Pre-Trial Chamber, 'in order to insure that it fulfill its obligation to uncover the truth'.[529] Others argue that the OTP should be prevented from collecting evidence

---

[525] L. Ullrich, 'Beyond the "Global–Local Divide": Local Intermediaries, Victims and the Justice Contestations of the International Criminal Court' (2016) 14 *JICJ* 543, 555.

[526] Haslam and Edmunds, 'Managing a New Partnership', 85.

[527] A. Pues, 'Towards the "Golden Hour"? A Critical Exploration of the Length of Preliminary Examinations' (2017) 15 *JICJ* 435, 452.

[528] In *Kupreškić et al.*, the Appeals Chamber noted: 'the Prosecution is expected to know its case before it goes to trial. It is not acceptable for the Prosecution to omit the material aspects of its main allegations in the indictment with the aim of moulding the case against the accused in the course of the trial depending on how the evidence unfolds'. *Prosecutor v. Kupreškić et al.*, IT-95-16-A. Judgment, 23 October 2001, para. 92.

[529] A. Whiting, 'Dynamic Investigative Practice at the International Criminal Court' (2013) 76 *Law & Contemporary Problems* 163, 189.

which it could reasonably have been expected to have collected prior to confirmation.[530] The Prosecution should only proceed to charges when it is sufficiently ready in its preparation. The ICC Appeals Chamber adopted a middle ground. It held that the investigation 'should be largely completed by the time of the confirmation hearing'.[531] This limits the possibility of the Prosecution changing its case theory after pre-trial.

International prosecutors cannot investigate a situation forever.[532] Keeping investigations open-ended can have negative side effects on prevention, deterrence and the duty of domestic jurisdictions to investigate and prosecute. The right number of cases per situation will always be context-specific. At the ad hoc tribunals and the SCSL, the completion strategies specified criteria. The ICTY began to pass on evidence to domestic authorities that it gathered in investigations.[533] At the ICC, the Prosecution has failed to develop a comparable 'exit strategy', due to the differences between situations. Some voices have suggested that Pre-Trial Chambers 'should be authorized to interrupt investigations' that exceed 'a reasonable time-frame'.[534] At present, however, there are very limited means for judges to control prosecutorial inaction, including whether the OTP has lived up to its duty to investigate all sides to a conflict.[535] In many situations, the Prosecution was unable to able investigate the gravest incidents or the main types of victimization. The idea of incentivizing domestic jurisdictions to act has thus even greater weight. It depends largely on the will of political actors to support domestic justice efforts.

4.4.3   Pre-Trial

During the pre-trial stage, the focus shifts from investigation to prosecution. The pre-trial is a prelude to trial proceedings. The length of pre-trial may vary from several months to several years. Its format differs between international institutions. In most systems, the Prosecution remains the driving force. It must substantiate its case theory, but there is a greater degree of judicial control. The defendant is initially a suspect. Warrants of arrest require judicial approval. The Prosecution needs to disclose its evidence to the Defence. The Defence may challenge the evidence. The charges brought by the Prosecution are tested before a pre-trial judge or Chamber. Only once

---

[530] *Prosecutor v. Kenyatta*, ICC-01/09–02/11, Decision on Defence Application Pursuant to Article 64(4) and Related Requests, 26 April 2013, paras. 119–121.

[531] *Prosecutor v. Mbarushimana*, ICC-01/04–01/10, Judgment on the Appeal of the Prosecutor Against the Decision of Pre-Trial Chamber I of 16 December 2011 entitled 'Decision on the Confirmation of Charges', 30 May 2012, para. 44.

[532] R. J. Hamilton, 'Closing ICC Investigations: A Second Bite at the Cherry for Complementarity?', Research Working Paper Series, HRP 12–001, May 2012.

[533] On the 'Category Two' cases, see D. Tolbert and A. Kontic, 'The International Criminal Tribunal for the former Yugoslavia: Transitional Justice, the Transfer of Cases to National Courts, and Lessons for the ICC', in Stahn and Sluiter, *Emerging Practice of the International Criminal Court*, 135, 157.

[534] De Hemptinne, 'The Creation of Investigating Chambers at the International Criminal Court', 416.

[535] Art. 53 (3) (c) allows *proprio moto* review of prosecutorial inaction only in cases where the decision not to proceed is taken 'in the interests of justice' – a clause that has not been invoked by the Prosecutor.

charges are confirmed does the defendant become an accused. In some forums, states or victims (e.g. ICC, STL) may intervene in the course of pre-trial proceedings.

4.4.3.1 Competing Philosophies

The goals of pre-trial proceedings are contested. There are different philosophies. They are influenced by the balance between inquisitorial and accusatorial features.[536] According to one view, the main function of pre-trial is to test the charges of the Prosecution and to protect the fairness of proceedings. Pre-trial is thus essentially a filter to separate the cases that should go to trial from those that should not.[537] The judge is an arbiter. The trial is the main stage. This approach prevailed in the ad hoc tribunals and the SCSL. Pre-trial proceedings were initially relatively slim and straightforward. Disclosure obligations were limited to what needs to be proven at pre-trial. Judges used a prima facie test to assess whether prosecutorial charges can go to trial. Managerial approaches were only gradually developed to maintain efficient proceedings.

According to a second view, pre-trial proceedings may have a more elaborate function. Pre-trial serves not only to protect the Defence against unfounded charges or to specify the charges but also to streamline proceedings, prepare the trial and ensure trial readiness of the case.[538] This conception is based on the idea that time spent at pre-trial is time gained at trial. It grants judges more powers to ensure the efficient and effective management of proceedings. According to this vision, most of the evidence should be disclosed at pre-trial. Charges are tested more thoroughly. This approach was tested before the ICC. It was meant to give a thicker meaning to pre-trial. However, practice has varied considerably among Chambers. Judges have sought to mitigate differences through a (non-binding) 'pre-trial manual' which sets out certain common understandings.[539]

4.4.3.2 Politics of Warrants of Arrest or Summons to Appear

The first step of the Prosecution to concretize the case strategy and formalize the investigation of suspects is the application for a warrant of arrest or summons to appear. A warrant of arrest serves as a title to detain a defendant. A summons to appear is an invitation to appear voluntarily before the Court. It allows the defendant to appear before the Court, with or without restrictions of liberty. Both measures entail a high degree of social condemnation. Warrants may be directly geared at delegitimizing certain agents. A summons may have political costs. Public opinion does not await trial. For instance, in the Kenya situation, Kenyatta and Muthaura resigned from their offices as finance minister and cabinet secretary after the issuance

---

[536] See generally M. Fairlie, 'Revised Pre-Trial Procedure before the ICTY from a Continental/Common Law Perspective', in Sluiter and Vasiliev, *International Criminal Procedure*, 311.
[537] V. Nerlich, 'The Confirmation of Charges Procedure at the International Criminal Court' (2012) 10 *JICJ* 1339, 1347.
[538] See I. Stegmiller, 'Confirmation of Charges', in Stahn, *Law and Practice of the International Criminal Court*, 891, 892.
[539] ICC, Pre-Trial Manual, September 2015.

of the summons.[540] In the ICC context, domestic authorities are not entitled to review whether a warrant was lawfully issued by the Court.[541] Otherwise cooperation would remain without teeth.

The Prosecutor's request has to be based on evidence which satisfies judges that there are reasonable grounds to believe that the person committed the crime. The test is whether there is a certain probability that the person concerned committed the crime. The application can be made *ex parte* and based on a summary of available evidence.[542] The defendant is not given a voice at this stage.[543] The Prosecutor may request a confidential (i.e. a sealed) warrant[544] to maintain an element of surprise in relation to arrest, or to protect witnesses and victims. However, given the political significance of an arrest warrant and the high risks of leaks, such confidentiality is often fragile and difficult to preserve. As Christopher Gosnell has noted:

Arrest warrants are issued publicly precisely when it is apparent that the target is beyond the reach of any cooperative jurisdiction, or sheltered by states or entities that will not cooperate with the ICC. Rather than secrecy, the best chance of securing the target's arrest is publicity designed to galvanize international and domestic opinion so that pressure will induce the noncooperative state, or rebel group, to change its ways.[545]

A key element of case strategy is to decide on the right moment to apply for a warrant of arrest or a summons to appear. This is part of prosecutorial discretion. Often, years may pass between issuance of a warrant of arrest and transfer of a defendant to the Court. The existence of a warrant of arrest may, in theory, have a certain preventive effect. The Prosecution is even required to establish that arrest is necessary to avert the obstruction of the investigation or court proceedings, or to prevent the commission of further crimes.[546] However, a quick issuance of warrants may also have downsides. It can be a stumbling block for peace negotiations. For instance, the Juba peace talks with the LRA were heavily influenced by the ICC warrants.[547] Moreover, a premature targeting of the highest political leadership can easily entail deadlock for arrest strategies (i.e. a point of no return), and make an international court or tribunal look powerless, if the warrant is not executed. For example, the immediate targeting of heads of state in the Sudan and Kenya situations did not strengthen the credibility of the ICC system, but rather weakened it. The actual benefits of the warrants have been minimal, while the political costs have been high. One of the hard lessons learned from

---

[540] See Mégret, 'Practices of Stigmatization', 300.

[541] Art. 59 (4) ICC Statute. See generally M. El Zeidy, 'Critical Thoughts on Article 59(2) of the ICC Statute' (2006) 4 *JICJ* 448.

[542] The ICC evidentiary standard is 'reasonable grounds to believe'. See Art. 58 (1) (a) ICC Statute.

[543] This is sometimes used as an argument to criticize the fairness of international criminal procedures. See Damaška, 'What Is the Point of International Criminal Justice?', 348 n. 31.

[544] Sealed warrants were inter alia issued against Bosco Ntaganda and Jean-Pierre Bemba.

[545] C. Gosnell, 'The Request for an Arrest Warrant in Al Bashir' (2008) 6 *JICJ* 841, 845.

[546] See Art. 58 (1) (b) ICC Statute.

[547] See A. MacDonald, '"In the Interests of Justice?" The International Criminal Court, Peace Talks and the Failed Quest for War Crimes Accountability in Northern Uganda' (2017) 11 *Journal of Eastern African Studies* 628, 630 (arguing that 'both parties came to see the court as a perplexing intervention that needed to be contained').

these cases is that it may be necessary to build a broader pool of cases before bringing such charges, or to proceed after the individuals in question have lost power.

4.4.3.3 Dilemmas of Pre-Trial Detention

After arrest, defendants are held in pre-trial detention. This practice has raised critiques from a human rights perspective. The defendant has a right to a speedy trial. In several cases, defendants have been held for years in pre-trial detention before they were tried. During this period, individuals are in a legal grey area. As Fréderic Mégret has argued, even 'being implicitly branded a flight risk includes some stigmatizing dimension' due to its associative features:

Appearing in the seat of the accused, the seat previously occupied by others who have been convicted, and having one's picture taken and circulated the world over, framed by two square-jawed ICC security guards, already begins to shape the accused's body as that of a convict en puissance, rather than as an innocent in the wrong place.[548]

Some defendants spent over a decade in detention before trial judgment. Theoneste Bagsora and Anatole Nsengiyumva spent over five years in pre-trial detention.[549] The record was at the ICTR. The *Butare* case, a multi-accused case against six defendants, took twenty years from arrest to the appeal judgment. The defendants were arrested 1995 and 1998. The Prosecution used time to continue its investigations. The trial started in 2001 and took over eight years. Such practices clash with the right to be tried without undue delay.[550] The Appeals Chamber argued that the length of an accused's detention does not in itself constitute undue delay. However, it found that 'delays in the start of the trial due to the Prosecution's conduct and delays resulting from the Trial Chamber judges' simultaneous assignment to multiple cases' could not 'be reasonably explained or justified'.[551] Such delays may trigger a mitigation of sentence or compensation.[552] Tribunals have been reluctant to release persons based on violations of the right to be tried without delay.

4.4.3.4 Charging Strategy

One of the core functions of pre-trial is to clarify the charges. This is an essential element of fairness. The defendant must be provided with a detailed description of the

---

[548] Mégret, 'Practices of Stigmatization', 299.
[549] The ICTR noted: 'six years of pre-trial detention may be a factor in the consideration of exceptional circumstances warranting the release of an accused. However, the length of current or potential future detention of the Accused cannot be considered material in these circumstances because it does not mitigate in any way that the Accused . . . may be a flight risk or may pose a threat to witnesses or to the community if he were to be released'. See *Prosecutor v. Bagosora et al.*, ICTR-98-41-T, Decision on Defence Motion for Release, 12 July 2002, para. 27.
[550] Art. 14 (3) (c) ICCPR.
[551] See *Prosecutor v. Nyiramasuhuko et al.*, ICTR-98-42-A, Judgment, 14 December 2015, para. 378.
[552] In *Gatete*, the ICTR found that a seven-year pre-trial delay was not justified for a trial that lasted thirty days. See *Prosecutor v. Gatete*, ICTR-00-61-A, 9 October 2012, para. 29.

charges, including the alleged offence, the form of criminal liability and the factual basis of the charge.[553] Only what is properly charged may lead to conviction.

The choice of charges poses complex policy problems. Prosecutors face conflicting priorities. They must decide whether to charge a wide array of crimes to express criminality or broader patterns of victimization, or to focus on selected charges to secure conviction. This choice depends on the number of overall estimated cases related to the context. Judges must balance the accusatory function of the Prosecution against the necessity to maintain fair and efficient proceedings.

Since World War II, international criminal justice has been marked by a tendency to 'historicize' charges. The Nuremberg and Tokyo trials were driven by the ambition to express the cruelty of warfare through broad charges against the political and military leadership, as well as certain business agents. This is reflected in the counts. The indictment at Nuremberg contained four counts.[554] They covered the main historical incidents between 1923 and 1945 through broad charges, ranging from the establishment of totalitarian control by the Nazis to acts of aggression between 1936 and 1938 and after the invasion of Poland in 1939.[555] The five charges at Tokyo covered Japanese involvement in crime between 1928 and 1945.

Modern international criminal courts and tribunals have pursued more targeted charges. Practice has been marked by 'trial and error'. The ICTR started with broad indictments against multiple accused.[556] It first brought cases against government officials (Government I[557] and Government II cases[558]) and military leaders.[559] The initial idea was to show that genocide was the result of collective planning at the highest political and military levels. At one point, the Prosecutor even filed a joint indictment against twenty-nine persons. This approach caused multiple problems. Cases became too long and too complex. Trial proceedings started between four and five years after arrest and took between six and eight years. Prosecutorial strategy was therefore adjusted. Prosecutions changed from large thematic indictments directed against a group of defendants to more individual-focused cases.[560]

---

[553] See Regulation 52 of the Regulations of the Court.

[554] The four counts in the indictment were: Count 1: Conspiracy to commit crimes alleged in the next three counts; Count 2: Crimes against peace, including planning, preparing, starting, or waging aggressive war; Count 3: War crimes, including violations of laws or customs of war; and Count 4: Crimes against humanity, including murder, extermination, enslavement, persecution on political or racial grounds, involuntary deportment, and inhumane acts against civilian populations.

[555] See e.g. Count 1 ('The Common Plan or Conspiracy').

[556] See A. Obote-Odora, 'Drafting of Indictments for the International Criminal Tribunal for Rwanda' (2001) 12 *Criminal Law Forum* 335–358.

[557] The case was brought against André Rwamakuba and three co-defendants: Edouard Karemera, former Interior Minister, Mathieu Ngirumpatse, President of the National Republican Movement for Democracy and Development (MRND Party), and Joseph Nzirorera, General Secretary of the MRND.

[558] *Prosecutor* v. *Bizimungu et al.*, ICTR-99–50-T, Judgment and Sentence, 30 September 2011.

[559] *Prosecutor* v. *Bagosora et al.* (Military I), ICTR-98–41-T, Judgment and Sentence, 18 December 2008; *Prosecutor* v. *Ndindilyimana et al.* (Military II) ICTR-00–56-T, Judgment and Sentence, 17 May 2011.

[560] See J. Locke, 'Indictments', in Reydams, Wouters and Ryngaert, *International Prosecutors*, 604, 618.

The ICTY faced its 'Waterloo moment' in the *Milošević* case. The case turned into a tragic mega-trial.[561] The charges spanned a period of ten years. They covered three main areas of conflict: Kosovo, Croatia and Bosnia. The Prosecution sought to join the three indictments since it considered that the events form one 'transaction'. The joinder was meant to avoid duplication of testimony and inconsistency of evidence, but it expanded the case. It included sixty-six counts, twenty-three different crimes, based on two theories of liability: JCE and command responsibility. The challenges became evident during the trial. The Prosecution was unable to deal with its procedural burdens. It constantly changed its witness list and applied for extensions of time. The Defence was overburdened with the scope of the trial. The Prosecution disclosed 1.2 million pages of material to the Defence team.[562] The record of proceedings encompassed more than 46,000 pages. The problems were compounded by the fact that Milošević decided to represent himself in proceedings and suffered from declining health. The trial lasted more than four years. The case ended without judgment, when the defendant passed away in 2006 at the Detention Unit in The Hague. This prompted judges to amend the Rules of Procedure to streamline indictments. Judges were given the power to invite the Prosecution to 'reduce the number of counts charged in the indictment', to 'fix a number of crime sites or incidents' or to determine the number of witnesses.[563] In later proceedings (e.g. *Karadžić*), judges used this power to reduce the charges, crime sites and witnesses.[564] Such managerial control requires significant skill and knowledge. It presupposes that 'judges are sufficiently familiar with the case to be able to make these decisions wisely'.[565]

At the ICC, judges and the Prosecution have been eager to limit the scope of charges. The Prosecutor has adopted a more selective charging strategy. In the first cases, the OTP has been criticized for under-inclusive, rather than over-inclusive charging. Additional efforts were made to increase the specificity of charges. Charges must enable the Defence to 'identify the historical event(s) at issue and the criminal conduct alleged'.[566]

A delicate question is to what extent a defendant can be charged with many different crimes for the same act.[567] The ICTY Appeals Chamber argued that cumulative charges[568] are only possible if the conduct involves at least one distinct 'material element' (*Čelebići* test).[569] In *Bemba*, the Pre-Trial Chamber restricted the practice of

---

[561] G. Boas, *The Milošević Trial: Lessons for the Conduct of Complex International Criminal Proceedings* (Cambridge: Cambridge University Press, 2007).

[562] G. Higgins, 'The Impact of the Size, Scope, and Scale of the Milošević Trial and the Development of Rule 73 *bis* before the ICTY' (2009) 7 *Northwestern University Journal of International Human Rights* 239, 246.

[563] Rule 73 *bis*.

[564] ICTY, *Prosecutor* v. *Karadžić*, IT-95-5/18-PT, Order to the Prosecution under Rule 73 *bis* (d), 22 July 2009.

[565] Bonomy, 'The Reality of Conducting a War Crimes Trial', 354.

[566] ICC Chambers Practice Manual, 13.

[567] The ICTY Appeals Chamber argued that 'cumulative charging is to be allowed in light of the fact that, prior to the presentation of all of the evidence, it is not possible to determine to a certainty which of the charges brought against an accused will be proven'. See *Čelebići* Appeal Judgment, para. 400.

[568] C.-F. Stuckenberg, 'Cumulative Charges and Cumulative Convictions' in Stahn, *Law and Practice of the International Criminal Court*, 841.

[569] *Prosecutor* v. *Delalic et al.*, Appeals Chamber, Judgment, IT-96-21-A, 20 February 2001, paras. 412–413.

cumulative charges, i.e. the possibility to charge multiple crimes under the same set of facts.[570] The Chamber refused to confirm charges of torture and outrages against personal dignity, since the elements of these crimes were 'congruent with those of the crime of rape'[571] and thus captured by it as *lex specialis*. It was criticized by the OTP for failing to express the full extent of criminality and victimization.[572] At pre-trial, some flexibility may be allowed, since decisions on conviction and sentencing are made by the Trial Chamber.[573]

Alternative charges, i.e. the use of alternative crime labels or modes of liability, may be problematic from the perspective of fairness and specificity.[574] They provide an opportunity for the Prosecution to overload the Defence with imprecise charges and alternative characterizations of conduct. For instance, in *Ntaganda*, the defendant was charged with at least seven alternative modes of liability: (i) direct perpetration, (ii) direct or indirect co-perpetration, (iii) ordering, (iv) inducing, (v) common purpose liability, (vi) attempt and/or (vii) superior responsibility.[575] This turns charging into a 'fishing expedition'. The Prosecution can include every possible case hypothesis in the network of charges. The ICC Pre-Trial Chamber permitted alternative charges if 'the evidence is sufficient to sustain each alternative'.[576] This approach makes it difficult for the defendant to develop a succinct Defence strategy.[577] It stands in contrast to the aim of precise charging and the goal to promote trial readiness at pre-trial.[578] In the ICC context, there is no need to allow extensive alternative charging, since judges are vested with the power to modify the legal characterization of facts.[579] It allows the Trial Chamber to correct an incorrect legal qualification of conduct alleged in the charges at trial.[580]

---

[570] *Prosecutor v. Bemba*, ICC-01/05–01/08, Decision Pursuant to Article 61(7)(a) and (b) of the Rome Statute on the Charges of the Prosecutor Against Jean-Pierre Bemba Gombo, 15 June 2009, para. 202.

[571] *Prosecutor v. Bemba*, ICC-01/05–01/08–523, Decision on the Prosecutor's Application for Leave to Appeal the Decision Pursuant to Article 61 (7) (a) and (b) on the Charges of the Prosecution against Jean-Pierre Bemba Gombo, 18 September 2009, para. 54.

[572] *Prosecutor v. Bemba*, ICC-01/05–01/08, Prosecutor's Application for Leave to Appeal the Decision Pursuant to Article 61 (7) (a) and (b) on the Charges of the Prosecution against Jean-Pierre Bemba Gombo, 23 June 2009, paras. 27–28.

[573] *Ongwen* Confirmation Decision, para. 30.

[574] See Ambos, *Treatise on International Criminal Law, Vol. III*, 422.

[575] See *Prosecutor v. Ntaganda*, ICC-01/04–02/06–309, Decision Pursuant to Art. 61 (7) (a) and (b) of the Rome Statute on the Charges of the Prosecutor against Bosco Ntaganda, 9 June 2014, para. 99.

[576] Pre-Trial Manual, 18.

[577] Ambos rightly compares it to 'shadow-boxing'. See Ambos, *Treatise on International Criminal Law, Vol. III*, 423.

[578] In *Ruto and Sang*, Pre-Trial Chamber II noted that it 'is not persuaded that it is best practice to make simultaneous findings on modes of liability presented in the alternative. A person cannot be deemed concurrently as a principal and an accessory to the same crime'. See *Prosecutor v. Ruto and Sang*, ICC-01/09–01/11–373, Decision on the Confirmation of Charges Pursuant to Article 61 (7) (a) and (b) of the Rome Statute, 23 January 2012, para. 284.

[579] See Regulation 55. For an explanation, see C. Stahn, 'Modification of the Legal Characterization of Facts in the ICC System: A Portrayal of Regulation 55' (2005) 16 *Criminal Law Forum* 1; E. Fry, 'Legal Recharacterisation and the Materiality of Facts at the International Criminal Court: Which Changes Are Permissible?' (2016) 29 *LJIL* 577. For a critique, see K. J. Heller, '"A Stick to Hit the Accused with": The Legal Recharacterization of Facts under Regulation 55', in Stahn, *The Law and Practice of the International Criminal Court*, 990.

[580] See Ambos, *Treatise on International Criminal Law, Vol. III*, 423.

4.4.3.5 Disclosure Challenges

The disclosure process, i.e. the divulgation of evidence and information according to procedural rules, is a central element of pre-trial. In many inquisitorial systems, the very concept of 'disclosure' between Prosecution and Defence is unknown. The results of the investigations carried out by judges or prosecutorial authorities are contained in a case file (dossier) which contains exonerating and incriminating circumstances. It is open to the judge, and made accessible to both parties. Access to the dossier fulfils the role of disclosure.[581] In an adversarial setting, disclosure is a party-based process, with limited involvement of the judge. It is fundamental to a fair trial and the ideal of equality of arms. It ensures that the defendant is not ambushed by the Prosecution case at trial. The Defence does not have access to the investigation file as such. However, the Prosecution is required to disclose exculpatory and incriminating evidence.[582] Defence disclosure is more restricted, since the defendant has the right to remain silent and benefits from the prohibition of self-incrimination. Disclosure obligations are limited to defences or alibis.

In international criminal justice, disclosure has turned into a centrepiece of procedure, due to the large amount of evidence presented in proceedings and the need for protection of witnesses and victims.[583] Prosecution teams spend months preparing documents for disclosure and carrying out 'redactions', i.e. blacking out details or anonymizing names of witnesses, under the overall supervision of judges. There are often many different versions of the same document, namely (i) the original one, (ii) a publicly redacted document open to public view, (iii) a redacted document that is shared with the Defence, and (iv) in case of victim participation, a redacted version shared with victims. Defence teams routinely complain that disclosure is imprecise, due to redactions.[584]

The problems of party-based disclosure regimes are that they take a considerable amount of time and resources and can easily be abused by parties for their own purposes. The sanctions for violations of disclosure obligations are limited. For instance, failures to disclose exculpatory evidence can amount to an abuse of process, and lead to a stay of proceedings or disciplinary measures. However, this requires the knowledge of judges. Without sufficient information about the case, a judge is, drastically put, 'a blind and blundering intruder, acting in spasm as sudden flashes of seeming light may lead or mislead him at odd times'.[585] This is why judges have been vested with increased managerial functions in relation to the supervision of disclosure.

---

[581] See Klamberg, *Evidence in International Criminal Trials*, 270.

[582] For instance, at the ICC, the Prosecution is required to disclose to the Defence 'as soon as practicable' and on a continuous basis, all evidence related to the innocence of the person or mitigating circumstances. See Art. 67 (2) ICC Statute.

[583] See generally K. Gibson and C. Lussiaà-Berdou, 'Disclosure of Evidence', in Khan, Buisman and Gosnell, *Principles of Evidence in International Criminal Justice*, 306; A. Whiting, 'Disclosure Challenges at the ICC', in Stahn, *Law and Practice of the International Criminal Court*, 1007.

[584] See K. Khan and C. Buisman, 'Sitting on Evidence? Systemic Failings in the ICC Disclosure Regime: Time for Reform', in Stahn, *Law and Practice of the International Criminal Court*, 1029, 1049–1050.

[585] M. E. Frankel, 'The Search for Truth: An Umpireal View' (1975) 123 *University of Pennsylvania Law Review* 1031, 1042.

Early rulings at the ad hoc tribunals confirmed that exposure to the materials of the parties at pre-trial does not render a Chamber biased.[586] Both the ICTY and the ICTR started early to request parties to submit information (e.g. written witness statements and other documents) to judges.[587] Later, a pre-trial judge was vested with the power to facilitate communication between the parties and prepare the case for trial.[588]

At the ICC, judges are vested with a significant amount of control over disclosure. Disclosure is not merely a process between the parties, but is managed through the Registry, under the guidance of the Pre-Trial Chamber. Pre-Trial Judges have developed different models. The main dispute has been to what extent the case should be trial-ready and prepared through disclosure at pre-trial. Some Chambers have argued that pre-trial disclosure of incriminating evidence should be limited to material that the Prosecutor intends to rely on at pre-trial,[589] and that the 'bulk' of exculpatory evidence should be disclosed before trial.[590] This approach left some discretion to the Prosecution to determine the amount of evidence disclosed at pre-trial. Other Chambers invoked the 'truth-finding' mandate of judges to argue that Pre-Trial Judges should have 'access to evidence other than that on which the parties intend to rely at the confirmation hearing'.[591] They argued that all exculpatory evidence must be disclosed prior to confirmation and that all evidence disclosed should be communicated to the Chamber, in order to enable judges to decide whether a case should be sent to trial. This system introduced a 'quasi-dossier' approach.[592] It is based on the premise that pre-trial should be the main forum for disclosure of evidence.

Pre-Trial Judges have further insisted on the preparation of an additional analytical chart by the Prosecution (the 'in-depth analysis chart') in order to streamline disclosure and to provide the Defence with all 'necessary tools to understand the reasons why the Prosecutor relies on any particular piece of evidence'.[593] It must link the evidence to the 'elements of the crimes (context and individual acts) and the forms of participation'.[594] The advantage of this approach is that it encourages parties to focus their

---

[586] Schuon, *International Criminal Procedure*, 265.
[587] *Prosecutor* v. *Akayesu*, ICTR-96-4-T, Decision by the Tribunal on its request to the Prosecutor to submit the written witness statements, 28 January 1997, 2. For a discussion, see V. Tochilovsky, 'Rules of Procedure For the International Criminal Court: Problems to Address in Light of the Experience of the Ad Hoc Tribunals' (1999) 46 *Netherlands International Law Review* 343, 355–357.
[588] See Rules 73 *bis* and 73 *ter* of the ICTY Rules of Procedure and Evidence.
[589] *Prosecutor* v. *Lubanga*, ICC-01/04–01/06–102, Decision on the Final System of Disclosure and the Establishment of a Timetable, 15 May 2006, para. 41.
[590] Ibid., para. 124.
[591] *Prosecutor* v. *Bemba*, ICC-01/05–01/08–55, Decision on the Evidence Disclosure System and Setting a Timetable for Disclosure between the Parties, 31 July 2008, paras. 11, 16 and 44 (*Bemba* Disclosure Decision).
[592] See H. Friman, 'Trial Procedures', in Stahn, Law and Practice of the International Criminal Court, 909, 923.
[593] *Bemba* Disclosure Decision, paras 66–70; *Prosecutor* v. *Ruto, Kosgey and Sang*, ICC-01/09–01/11–44, Decision Setting the Regime for Evidence Disclosure and Other Related Matters, 6 April 2011, para. 21; *Prosecutor* v. *Muthaura, Kenyatta and Ali*, ICC-01/09–02/11–48, Decision Setting the Regime for Evidence Disclosure and Other Related Matters, 6 April 2011, para. 22.
[594] *Prosecutor* v. *Ongwen*, ICC-02/04–01/15, Decision Setting the Regime for Evidence Disclosure and Other Related Matters, 27 February 2015, para. 39. The Chamber required that '[e]ach piece of evidence must be analysed ... by relating each piece of information contained in that page or paragraph with one or more of the constituent elements of

analysis on 'truly relevant evidence' and helps to understand the 'underlying reasons' why a party seeks to use a particular piece of evidence.[595] The risk of the chart is that it relies on preliminary and incomplete information and may suggest a specific reading of evidence at pre-trial that might not necessarily correspond to its later use at trial.[596]

4.4.3.6 Judicial Review of Charges

The form of judicial review of charges at pre-trial varies across institutions. At Nuremberg and Tokyo, indictments were simply endorsed by a Committee of Chief Prosecutors. In modern international courts and tribunals charges are subject to judicial review. The timing and intensity of review differs.

The ad hoc tribunals, the SCSL and the STL have a relatively straightforward confirmation process. Charges are reviewed before the issuance of a warrant of arrest. The goal is not to make final determinations as to the reliability of evidence, but to inquire whether there is a sufficient basis to convict the person charged, if the evidence would be accepted.[597] Neither the defendant nor victims participate in this process. The test is to determine whether there is a prima facie case against the suspect. This may lead to the issuance of an arrest warrant. If counts are rejected, the Prosecutor may seek an amended indictment on the basis of new material or evidence. According to this model, the trial is the main playing field where the 'real confrontation' with the defendant takes place[598] and where challenges to the reliability and credibility of the evidence and the charges are examined. Pre-trial is mainly a prima facie check. The focus is on checking the work of the Prosecutor, rather than trying the defendant. The content of the trial is prepared through pre-trial brief of the parties, and status conferences.

The ICC has a more complex confirmation procedure.[599] It is a unique process without clear precedent. It is the result of many different factors: the desire to prevent futile charges and provide additional checks and balances on the independent prosecutor, compromises among inquisitorial and adversarial cultures, and the ambition to ensure fair and efficient proceedings. The Prosecutor is mandated to file a separate document containing the charges, after a warrant of arrest or a summons to appear. These charges are then subject to a more thorough judicial review, the confirmation of charges. This is an adversarial hearing in which victims are entitled to participate. It

---

one or more of the crimes with which the person is charged, including the contextual elements of those crimes, as well as the constituent elements of the mode of participation in the offence with which the person is charged'. Ibid., para. 37.

[595] Ibid., para. 40.

[596] *Prosecutor* v. *Ongwen*, ICC-02/04-01/15, Prosecution's appeal against the "Decision Setting the Regime for Evidence Disclosure and Other Related Material", 28 April 2015, paras. 21–38.

[597] See H. Friman, H. Brady, M. Costi, F. Guariglia and C. F. Stuckenberg, 'Charges', in Sluiter et al., *International Criminal Procedure*, 382, 398.

[598] See Marchesiello, 'Proceedings before the Pre-Trial Chambers', in Cassese, Gaeta and Jones, *Rome Statute of the International Criminal Court*, 1231, 1234.

[599] K. Ambos and D. Miller, 'Structure and Function of the Confirmation Procedure before the ICC from a Comparative Perspective' (2007) 7 *International Criminal Law Review* 335; Nerlich, 'The Confirmation of Charges Procedure', 1339.

generally takes place after the defendant has been apprehended or appeared before the Court.[600] Judges are mandated to conduct an independent assessment of the case, based on the evidence disclosed. The confirmation decision frames the content of the trial, since it sets out the charges in an authoritative way.

The confirmation procedure has two macro-purposes. The first one is a filtering function. The confirmation hearing serves as a safeguard before trial to 'detect deficiencies' that 'would otherwise flaw the entire proceedings'.[601] It contains a first probe into the evidence. It is geared at promoting prosecutorial fairness and efficiency, protecting the rights of the suspect and enhancing judicial economy. It is meant to secure that 'no case goes to trial unless there is sufficient evidence to establish substantial grounds to believe that the person committed the crime with which he or she has been charged'.[602] The Chamber can confirm or decline to confirm charges, or request the Prosecutor to present further evidence or amend the charges.

The second function is trial preparation. The confirmation process serves to organize the disclosure process and victim participation before trial proceedings, to specify the factual and legal base of charges, and to identify key issues for trial. This function is more contested, since it may encroach on the functions of the trial.

The experiences of the confirmation process are mixed. The confirmation hearing has had certain benefits. It protected certain defendants from lengthy trials or unfounded charges. The Pre-Trial Chamber declined to confirm charges against several defendants due to lack of sufficient evidence: Callixte Mbarushimana,[603] Bahar Idriss Abu Garda,[604] Henry Kiprono Kosgey[605] and Mohammed Hussein Ali.[606] It has thus served as a filter. Confirmation decisions have also clarified the factual allegations of charges. Judges have agreed that the decision must contain a narrative of the relevant events that forms the basis of the trial.[607] This is necessary to ensure that the Defence will 'not be presented with a wholly different evidentiary case at trial'.[608] However, the efficiency of the confirmation process has been questioned.

Critics claim that the confirmation process unnecessarily delays proceedings, and involves resources that the Court could use more meaningfully otherwise. On average,

---

[600] A confirmation of charges in the absence of the defendant is possible under specific conditions. See Art. 62 (2) (b) of the ICC Statute and Rule 125 of the Rules of Procedure and Evidence. For a discussion, see E. Trendafilova, 'Fairness and Expeditiousness in the International Criminal Court's Pre-Trial Proceedings', in Stahn and Sluiter, *Emerging Practice of the International Criminal Court*, 452–457.

[601] *Prosecutor v. Bemba*, ICC-01/05–01/08–532, Decision on the Prosecutor's Application for Leave to Appeal the 'Decision Pursuant to Article 61 (7) (a) and (b) of the Rome Statute on the Charges of the Prosecutor Against Jean-Pierre Bemba Gombo', 18 September 2009, para. 52.

[602] *Prosecutor v. Katanga and Ngudjolo Chui*, ICC-01/04–01/07, Decision on the admissibility for the confirmation hearing of the transcripts of interview of deceased Witness 12, 18 April 2008, 4.

[603] *Prosecutor v. Mbarushimana*, ICC-01/04–01/10–465-Red, Decision on the confirmation of charges, 16 December 2011.

[604] *Prosecutor v Abu Garda*, ICC-02/05–02/09–243-Red, Decision on the Confirmation of Charges, 8 February 2010.

[605] *Prosecutor v. Ruto, Kosgey and Sang*, ICC-01/09–01/11, Decision on the Confirmation of Charges Pursuant to Article 61 (7) (a) and (b) of the Rome Statute, 23 January 2012, paras. 293–298.

[606] *Prosecutor v. Muthaura, Kenyatta and Ali*, ICC-01/09–02/11, Decision on the Confirmation of Charges Pursuant to Article 61 (7) (a) and (b) of the Rome Statute, 23 January 2012, para. 430.

[607] Pre-Trial Manual, 17.

[608] *Prosecutor v. Gbagbo*, ICC-02/11–01/11–432, Decision Adjourning the Hearing on the Confirmation of Charges Pursuant to Article 61 (7) (c) (i) of the Rome Statute, 3 June 2013, para. 25.

the ICC has taken more than fourteen months to confirm charges.[609] The time for preparation of the confirmation hearings is similar to the time that might be required for trial preparation. The confirmation process adds to the overall length of trials. It has thus been proposed that its scale be reduced, and the amount of evidence relied on. Judges have officially claimed that confirmation hearings should not serve as a 'trial before the trial'. In practice, however, this has turned out to be lip service. At least in the first cases, they have de facto turned into 'mini-trials'. Decisions were long, i.e. over 150 pages,[610] and extensive in the development of the legal argument. It is difficult to measure to what extent confirmation processes have enhanced the 'trial readiness' of cases, or contributed to preparing the trial. On average, a Trial Chamber needed still more than a year for trial preparation, after the case had been transferred by the Pre-Trial Chamber.[611] Many substantive issues were re-litigated. There are thus criticisms that pre-trial has at times duplicated the functions of the trial, instead of preparing it.

During pre-trial, the Prosecutor remains the master of the case. This means that the Prosecution retains the power to withdraw charges and bring charges. Following pre-trial, the case is transferred to the Trial Chamber. The defendant is formally an 'accused'.

4.4.4   *Trying Perpetrators*

The trial is the main stage where the Prosecution and the Defence present their cases.[612] The core task is to decide on the guilt or innocence of the accused. It must be established 'beyond reasonable doubt'. The main purpose is to ensure that the defendant receives a fair and expeditious legal process.[613] At the end there are two choices: conviction or acquittal. However, there is more to it than meets the eye. The function of the trial goes beyond the interests of the Defence and the Prosecution. Trials typically serve additional didactic and pedagogic functions.[614] They educate, they explain and they illuminate. They seek to explain what happened, why it happened and who is responsible.[615] This is complex since the defendant is often only one piece in a large puzzle of crime. Judges must assess competing narratives and the credibility of evidence.[616] Trials also have a symbolic function that goes beyond

---

[609] War Crimes Research Office, *The Confirmation of Charges Process at the International Criminal Court: A Critical Assessment and Recommendations for Change* (Washington, DC: War Crimes Research Office, 2015), 1, 17–19.

[610] The length of decisions is 157 pages in *Lubanga*, 213 pages in *Katanga & Ngudjolo* and 196 pages in *Bemba*.

[611] War Crimes Research Office, *The Confirmation of Charges Process at the International Criminal Court*, 18.

[612] See generally S. Vasiliev, 'The Trial', in Reydams, Wouters & Ryngaert, *International Prosecutors*, 700.

[613] J. D. Ohlin, 'Goals of International Criminal Justice and International Criminal Procedure', in Sluiter et al., *International Criminal Procedure*, 55.

[614] Ibid., at 63; L. Douglas, *The Memory of Judgment; Making Law and History in the Trials of the Holocaust* (New Haven: Yale University Press, 2001; Wilson, *Writing History in International Criminal Trials*.

[615] E. Fry, 'The Nature of International Crimes and Evidentiary Challenges', in Van Sliedregt and Vasiliev, *Pluralism in International Criminal Law*, 251, 258 et seq.

[616] S. Zappalà, 'Comparative Models and the Enduring Relevance of the Accusatorial – Inquisitorial Dichotomy', in Sluiter et al., *International Criminal Procedure*, 44 et seq.

shame, sanction and stigma. They offer a space to re-humanize perpetrators and might bestow a certain sense of equality between victim and perpetrator. There is thus a certain virtue in the expressive features of proceedings that go beyond the judgment and the sentence. The trial is often an 'echo chamber' for broader discussions on responsibility or peace and justice more generally.[617]

4.4.4.1 *Nature of the Trial*

The culture of trials varies. In an adversarial setting, the trial is focused on the hearing of the evidence and the cases of both parties. In an inquisitorial system, it may be geared more towards the verification of evidence collected during a judicial investigation,[618] or the testing of cases through contradiction, including confrontation and dialogue, rather than contest.

Trials involve a high degree of communication and performance.[619] The trial is public in principle. The transparency of proceedings is necessary to relate narratives and testimony to affected constituencies. Exceptions are only allowed for specific purposes, such as public order, the safety and security of witnesses and victims, or the protection of confidential or sensitive information.[620] The principle of orality is the rule. It implies that live testimony, even by video or audio link, should be used where possible, since it can be better tested than out-of-court testimony by the parties and the Bench. The judgment must be based on evidence discussed at trial or submissions that are part of the trial record. The effects of trials outside the courtroom are difficult to control.

In many international criminal courts and tribunals, the adversarial structure dominates the nature of the trial.[621] Proceedings are generally set up as a contest between parties – like a sporting game. The Prosecution and the Defence present separate cases. There should be procedural equality between the parties. Both parties must have a fair and equal opportunity to present their case. The presumption of innocence imposes the burden on the prosecution to prove guilt. The Prosecutor must tell a story, put together a coherent narrative and prove every necessary element of the charges beyond a reasonable doubt. The Defence typically raises doubts, identifies weaknesses in the Prosecution case or offers counter-narratives.[622] The parties submit the evidence. Each party may call the witnesses it feels are necessary to present its evidence. It is the task of the judge to assess the strength of the evidence by the parties.

---

[617] Mégret, 'Practices of Stigmatization', 300.

[618] Friman, 'Trial Procedures', 918.

[619] T. Meijers and M. Glasius, 'Expression of Justice or Political Trial?: Discursive Battles in the Karadžić Case' (2013) 35 *Human Rights Quarterly* 720;

[620] See Art. 64 (7) ICC Statute.

[621] For a comparative survey, see G. Aquaviva, N. Combs, M. Heikkilä, S. Linton, Y. McDermott and S. Vasiliev, 'Trial Process', in Sluiter et al., *International Criminal Procedure*, 638–645; K. Ambos, 'International Criminal Procedure: "Adversarial", "Inquisitorial" or Mixed?' (2003) 3 *International Criminal Law Review* 1.

[622] On the narrative culture, see M. Glasius and T. Meijers, 'Constructions of Legitimacy: The Charles Taylor Trial' (2012) 6 *International Journal of Transitional Justice* 229, 231 ('the prosecution and the defence are simultaneously constructing narratives about the political legitimacy of the accused as an actor in a past or ongoing conflict, as well as the political legitimacy of the court itself as another such actor').

One of the weaknesses of this binary structure of trials is that it may prolong hearings or induce hostility between the parties. This is why judges have gradually introduced certain inquisitorial features. Trial management and preparation are under judicial control.[623] Judges have autonomous powers. For instance, at the ICC, judges may require that evidence becomes part of the record and even summon their own witnesses.[624] An admission of guilt obtained from the accused in exchange for commitments of the Prosecution in relation to charges or sentencing does not automatically bind the Trial Chamber.[625] Judges must assess whether a guilty plea is voluntary, informed and supported by the facts of the case. They may insist on an ordinary trial procedure where a more complete and public presentation of the facts is in the interests of victims or historical record.

4.4.4.2   Trial Stages

The trial can be divided into four stages: the opening stage, the presentation of evidence, the closing stage, and judgment and sentence.

The opening statements are often full of pathos and drama. As Sofia Stolk as noted: 'they are not part of the "actual" legal proceedings, but at the same time they transpire the big ideas behind the procedures and defend the relevance of the trial, the tribunal, and international criminal law like no other moment in the courtroom process ... They are both less than law and more than law'.[626] They combine case theory with advocacy.[627] For instance, in *Lubanga*, the ICC Prosecution mentioned sexual crimes against girls by the UPC that were not formally charged in order to illustrate the importance of the case.[628]

Most time at trial is spent with the presentation and testing of evidence. This can take several years. Evidence is typically presented in the following order: evidence for the Prosecution, evidence for the Defence, prosecution evidence in rebuttal, defence evidence in rebuttal. This is complemented by the possibility for victims to make submissions, potential evidence ordered by the Trial Chamber and any relevant information that may assist the Trial Chamber in determining the appropriate sentence.

In each case, an examination-in-chief, cross-examination and re-examination are allowed to both parties. The examination-in-chief is the initial questioning by the party calling the witness, subject to instructions by the Chamber. Parties are generally

---

[623] Ambos, *Treatise on International Criminal Law, Vol. III*, 353. In shortcomings, see M. Langer and J. W. Doherty, 'Managerial Judging Goes International, but Its Promise Remains Unfulfilled: An Empirical. Assessment of the ICTY Reforms' (2011) 36 *Yale Journal of International Law* 241.

[624] Art. 64 (6) (b) ICC Statute.

[625] Art. 65 ICC Statute.

[626] S. Stolk, *A Solemn Tale of Horror: The Opening Statement of the Prosecution in International Criminal Trials*, PhD Dissertation (2017), 14, at https://research.vu.nl/ws/portalfiles/portal/42578284.

[627] See S. Stolk, '"The Record on Which History Will Judge Us Tomorrow": Auto-History in the Opening Statements of International Criminal Trials', (2015) 28 *LJIL* 993, 1012 ('Opening statements position the tribunal as pivotal in the transition from chaos to peace and present their audience a saviour').

[628] *Lubanga* Trial Judgment, paras. 629 et seq.

not allowed to ask leading questions, i.e. questions which suggest an answer or assume facts not yet established.[629] Cross-examination involves questioning of a witness of the other party or a witness declared hostile. It is designed to cast doubt on matters raised during the examination-in-chief, the reliability of the witness, or to solicit information favourable to the cross-examining party.[630] Re-examination allows the calling party to have the last word with the witness in relation to matters or new facts arising out of cross-examination.[631] This method has posed several problems in practice. Often witnesses, defence counsel or even judges are 'unfamiliar with the adversarial method of examination and cross-examination'.[632] This may cause confusion and delays. The type of interrogation may easily intimidate witnesses. It may thus only be partly conducive to the determination of the truth.[633] It is even more difficult to conduct via video-link.

After the presentation of the Prosecution case, there is room for the Defence to request a 'mid-trial acquittal', the 'no case to answer motion'.[634] It derives from common law systems. Its purpose is to prevent accused persons having to defend themselves against charges for which there is insufficient Prosecution evidence.[635] The judge may render an acquittal without hearing the full Defence case. It is grounded in the presumption of innocence and the right to a fair and speedy trial. This motion was foreseen in the Rules of Procedure and Evidence of the ad hoc tribunals (motion for 'judgment of acquittal'),[636] but not expressly provided in the ICC Statute. The ICC Trial Chamber used it in a controversial way in the case against Ruto and Sang. The case collapsed following external interference with Prosecution witnesses. The Chamber recognized that it has authority to consider 'no case to answer' motions, despite the existence of the confirmation hearing procedure at pre-trial, since they 'contribute to a more efficient and expeditious trial' and are 'fully compatible with the rights of the accused under the Statute'.[637] In the decision on the Defence motion, the majority did not pronounce an acquittal, but found that the 'charges against the accused are vacated ... without prejudice to their prosecution afresh in future'.[638] It thereby left

---

[629] See C. Rohan, 'Rules Governing the Presentation of Testimonial Evidence', in Khan, Buisman and Gosnell, *Principles of Evidence in International Criminal Justice*, 499, 507 and 510–513 on exceptions to the prohibition of leading questions.

[630] Ibid., 513–519. In certain situations, leading questions may be allowed in cross-examination. See Aquaviva et al., 'Trial Process', 587.

[631] See Aquaviva et al., 'Trial Process', 593–598.

[632] See Kwon, 'The Challenge of an International Criminal Trial as Seen from the Bench', 364.

[633] See Ambos, *Treatise on International Criminal Law, Vol. III*, 467.

[634] V. Tochilovsky, *Jurisprudence of the International Criminal Courts and the European Court of Human Rights: Procedure and Evidence* (Leiden: Martinus Nijhoff Publishers, 2008), 535 et seq.

[635] *Prosecutor v. Milosevic*, IT-02–54-T, Trial Chamber Decision on Motion for Judgement of Acquittal, 16 June 2004, para. 11. See generally A. J. Burrow, 'The Standard of Proof in Pre-Trial Proceedings', in Khan, Buisman and Gosnell, *Principles of Evidence in International Criminal Justice*, 671, 686–687.

[636] See e.g. Rule 98 *bis* of the ICTY Rules of Procedure and Evidence ('At the close of the Prosecutor's case, the Trial Chamber shall, by oral decision and after hearing the oral submissions of the parties, enter a judgement of acquittal on any count if there is no evidence capable of supporting a conviction').

[637] *Prosecutor v. Ruto and Sang*, ICC-01/09–01/11–1334, Decision No. 5 on the Conduct of Trial Proceedings, 3 June 2014, para. 18. See Art. 64 (2) ICC Statute.

[638] *Prosecutor v. Ruto and Sang* ICC-01/09–01/11, *Decision on Defence Applications for Judgments of Acquittal*, ICC-01/09–01/11-2027-Red-Corr, 5 April 2016, 1 (*Ruto and Sang* Decision on Defence Applications).

the Prosecution the opportunity to re-prosecute the accused based on new evidence. Judge Chile Eboe-Osuji sought to declare a 'mistrial' due to 'a troubling incidence of witness interference and intolerable political meddling that was reasonably likely to intimidate witnesses',[639] and to leave victims the option of reparation. The reasoning conflicts with the prohibition of double jeopardy which prohibits that the defendant is prosecuted twice for the same conduct.

At the end of the trial, the Prosecution may present closing arguments, followed by the Defence and/or the legal representative of victims. The closing argument does not serve to present further evidence. It is meant to sum up elements of proof and suggest a verdict.

Following the presentation of evidence, the judges must assess the facts and legal issues. They are not meant to serve as Judge and Prosecutor. They are constrained by facts and circumstances that are part of the trial. In *Bemba*, the ICC Appeals Chamber acquitted the defendant partly because certain criminal acts were added after the Confirmation of Charges Decision, without a formal amendment of the charges. The majority disregarded eighteen acts of murder, rape and pillage, since they were described too broadly in the confirmation process and therefore did 'not form part of the "facts and circumstances described in the charges"'.[640] It found that the charges were not specific enough in relation to criminal acts of the accused since they implied that the defendant was responsible 'for all acts of murder, rape and pillaging committed by MLC soldiers in the CAR between on or about 26 October 2002 and 15 March 2003, i.e. covering a time frame of more than 4 months and a geographical area of more than 600,000 square kilometres'.[641] Judges have autonomy in the legal assessment of charges.[642] This is expressly specified in the ICC context. According to Regulation 55 of the Regulations of the Court, judges are allowed to enter a conviction for a different label of crime or mode of liability, if the underlying elements are enshrined in the charges. Fairness requires that judges can only do so if they have given prior notice to the parties during the proceedings.[643]

4.4.4.3 Deliberations

The closure of the trial is followed by the deliberation of the judges and the drafting. This is a difficult process. Parties have typically filed more evidence than needed, and judges have admitted evidence that later turns out to be peripheral to the case. The

---

[639] Ibid., para. 464.
[640] *Prosecutor* v. *Bemba*, Judgment on the appeal of Mr Jean-Pierre Bemba Gombo against Trial Chamber III's 'Judgment Pursuant to Article 74 of the Statute', ICC-01/05-01/08 A, 8 June 2018, para. 115.
[641] *Prosecutor* v. *Bemba*, Separate opinion Judge Christine Van den Wyngaert and Judge Howard Morrison, para. 23.
[642] The ICTY held the *iura novit curia* principle ('The Court knows the law') applies only to a limited extent in international criminal proceedings in light of the protection of the right of the accused. It argued that if the Trial Chamber finds in the course of trial that that 'the accused has committed a more serious crime than the one charged, it may call upon the Prosecutor to consider amending the indictment' or 'decide to convict the accused of the lesser offence charged'. It added that where 'only a different offence can be held to have been proved', judges should ask the Prosecutor to amend the indictment and would otherwise 'have no choice but to dismiss the charge'. See *Kupreškić* Trial Judgment, paras. 747–748.
[643] Regulation 55 of the Regulations of the Court.

transcripts of witness statements and documentary evidence often cover tens of thousands of pages. The task of judges is to apply the law to the facts and to evaluate the evidence.

Guilt or innocence is decided through deliberation of the judges. This process typically requires an element of private discovery or intuition that precedes the formal legal reasoning. This freedom is protected by the principle of the secrecy of the deliberations.[644] It is grounded in the independence and impartiality of the Bench. Judges must be free to discuss, develop or even change views. Otherwise, they might refrain from speaking freely during deliberations.

The responsibility of the accused must be determined based on the content of the trial, and the assessment of the totality of the evidence, rather than 'cherry-picking'. However, it is difficult to base this decision solely on the overall impression at the end of the case, often several years after hearing the evidence. The assessment of evidence, and the preparation of the judgment, requires ongoing filtering and analysis. Much of the groundwork for the deliberations is laid by internal memoranda and preparatory work undertaken during the trial. Judgments are thus mostly collective products that emerge in bits and pieces over years. The authority is created through a process of filtering arguments and weighing evidence.[645]

One of the main challenges is to reach agreement. This requires articulation, persuasion and sometimes negotiation and compromise. The ICC Statute contains an express obligation of judges 'to attempt to achieve unanimity' in their decision.[646] This principle reinforces the obligation to conduct common deliberations. No judge can be forced to vote with the others though. This is why separate or dissenting opinions are typically allowed. As in other highest courts, they are often the rule, rather than the exception.

Separate opinions and dissents may undoubtedly serve useful functions in the legal process. They are both an expression of the conscience and independence of judges and a means to constrain judicial power, i.e. make the majority answerable for their claims.[647] Some individual opinions or dissents have provided nuance to the argument of the majority, or contributed to the development of the law. This may improve the quality of a decision. Often the reasoning provides the ground for clarification or refinement of issues on appeal or in subsequent decisions. In some cases the minority of today becomes the majority of tomorrow.[648] More generally, a dissent may provide a space to bring out the limitations of the law in relation to human atrocity, problems

---

[644] Art. 74 (4) ICC Statute.

[645] M. D. Öberg, 'Processing Evidence and Drafting Judgments in International Criminal Trial Chambers' (2013) 24 *Criminal Law Forum* 113.

[646] 74(3) ICC Statute.

[647] See H. Mistry, 'The Paradox of Dissent: Judicial Dissent and the Projects of International Criminal Justice' (2015) 13 *JICJ* 449, 474.

[648] A key example is the dissenting opinion by the late Judge Cassese in the *Erdemović* case which became the prevailing view in the codification of defences in the ICC Statute. See Section 2.5.6.

that cannot be solved through judgment, or fundamentally different accounts of the historical and political context of trials that otherwise go unnoticed.[649]

There are also drawbacks, however. There are risks of abuse. The reasons for the issuance of separate opinions and dissents are not always clear. In certain cases, they are a means to avoid common deliberation of hard questions, or to express individual opinion on points of law that are only remotely connected to the case. This may compromise the quality of the judgment or invite future challenges.[650] Some types of 'whistle-blowing' may infringe on the secrecy of deliberations. Moreover, certain 'fundamental dissents' may undermine the authority of the judgment.[651] For instance, it may be difficult to explain how the required threshold of 'beyond reasonable doubt' is met if the reasoning of the majority does not engage with fundamental objections of the minority argument.[652] In *Bemba*, the divisions on appeal became evident: two majority judges voted to acquit the defendant on appeal, the two minority judges sought to uphold the conviction, while the fifth judge (the 'swing vote') originally wanted to order a re-trial. A re-trial was finally avoided due to the length of the trial, and to save a Trial Chamber from the dilemma of entering a conviction merely 'in order to "justify" the extended detention'.[653] The legitimacy of separate opinions and dissents at trial thus depends largely on how they are used.

Some problems have occurred at the MICT. It introduced a system of 'remote judging' in order to satisfy demands for cost efficiency.[654] Judges worked remotely, unless they were called to the seat of the Mechanism. This posed challenges in relation to the integrity of remote deliberations and the accessibility of judges. A 'lean' court management model may be efficient in terms of resources, but lack effectiveness in terms of fairness or quality of the justice process.

4.4.4.4 The Judgment

The special value of the judgment lies in the fact that it translates the different narratives of the trial into one authoritative account. It is of particular significance to the accused person who has the last word at trial. However, its reach extends beyond the accused. It is meant to provide a final narrative or sense of closure that extends beyond the individual submissions of parties.[655]

The judgment is a response to all participants in the case. The judgment must respond to all charges by the Prosecution. It is, further, of fundamental importance for victims. It is more likely to live up to this expectation if parties and participants have the impression that they are listened to, and that their claims are properly addressed in the legal

---

[649] See N. Jain, 'Radical Dissents in International Criminal Trials' (2017) 28 *EJIL* 1163.

[650] G. Sluiter, 'Unity and Division in Decision Making: The Law and Practice on Individual Opinions at the ICTY', in Swart, Zahar, and Sluiter, *The Legacy of the International Criminal Tribunal for the Former Yugoslavia*, 191 et seq.

[651] On the notion of 'fundamental dissent', see Mistry, 'The Paradox of Dissent', 450.

[652] See *Katanga* Trial Judgment, Minority Opinion of Judge Christine Van den Wyngaert.

[653] *Prosecutor* v. *Bemba*, Separate opinion Judge Christine Van den Wyngaert and Judge Howard Morrison, para. 73.

[654] Remarks of Judge Theodor Meron President, Mechanism for International Criminal Tribunals, Diplomatic Briefing, The Hague, 17 May 2017, at www.unmict.org/sites/default/files/statements-and-speeches/170517-remarks-of-judge-theodor-meron-president-en.pdf.

[655] Cryer, Friman, Robinson and Wilmshurst, *Introduction to International Criminal Law and Procedure*, 38–40.

reasoning. The act of judgment, and its findings on law and fact, may provide a form of satisfaction – even years after events. In specific cases, the determination of individual criminal responsibility of the defendant may serve as a basis for reparation to victims.

Moreover, the judgment has an important social and civic role. It provides legitimacy to the relevant institution, and the preceding legal process. The process of judgment produces an authoritative account of law and facts that earlier proceedings lack. Unfinished trials, such as the *Milošević* trial at the ICTY, leave a strong sense of dissatisfaction, despite all facts and legal battles fought in the courtroom. The judgment is thus clearly more than the sum of the parts of previous litigation.

There is a certain tension between purpose and form. The judgment must be understandable by the public. However, judgments in international criminal cases are often lengthy. For instance, the *Taylor* and *Mladić* judgment ran over 2,500 pages. The *Karadžić* judgment came close to 3,000 pages. This may be explained by the complexity of facts and the multiplicity of audiences. Judgments typically respond to claims and concerns by a broad range of actors: legal and political agents, local actors, or specific knowledge communities.

In a domestic setting, a judgment is perceived to be good if it is respected by the parties and not appealed. In international criminal justice, the reality is different. Almost every judgment is appealed by one of the parties. The benchmark is thus the quality of reasoning, rather than the rate of appeal.

The actual trial judgment must be delivered in public and in writing. This is necessary to explain the reasoning, to allow scrutiny by the public and to provide a record that can be appealed. Disagreements may remain. However, both the parties and the public are more likely to accept a decision if it is grounded in an objective and transparent application of law to the facts.

A significant part of its acceptance is related to procedural integrity. Judges must in particular indicate with sufficient clarity the grounds why and how they reached a decision. This includes the determination of facts, the legal assessment and the explanation of the assessment of evidence. The fact that there are separate or dissenting opinions is not bad per se. Such diversity may even strengthen the legitimacy of the judgment. The more the judgment ventures into creativity, the more it requires justification

Two types of decisions pose problems. In some cases, a decision is problematic since the reader does not know 'what' was decided. This is particularly troublesome if the result of a decision remains unclear. One example is the decision on the 'no case to answer motion' in the case against Ruto and Sang. Three judges expressed three different opinions. It remained unclear by the two majority opinions whether a mistrial was declared.[656]

---

[656] *Ruto and Sang* Decision on Defence Applications, para. 148 (lacking a reference to the notion of 'mistrial') and para. 484 (making reference to 'mistrial'). The entire judgment was composed of two separate reasonings, forming the majority opinion, and a separate dissent.

In other cases, it clear what was decided, but the reasoning is contradictory or does not explain fully 'how' it was decided. A drastic illustration is the acquittal of Vojislav Šešelj by the majority of the ICTY trial chamber. The 108-page judgment, delivered after several years of trial, deviates from many of the narratives established in other tribunal judgments. Šešelj made public appeals to forcibly remove Croats from Serbia by trucks and trains, rather than to kill them. The majority concluded that this did not constitute a criminal offence, such as incitement to genocide or instigating crimes against humanity (e.g. forcible transfer, persecution), but rather 'an expression of an alternative political programme'.[657] It interpreted calls to clean areas and to take revenge as statements 'meant to boost the morale of the troops', and qualified the provision of buses by Serb forces to deport civilians in municipalities under attack as 'acts of humanitarian assistance to non-combatants fleeing the zones'.[658] The dissenting judge, Judge Lattanzi, qualified the judgment as a 'big accident' that is reasoned so poorly that it lacks authoritative force.[659] She argued that the majority 'showed total disregard, if not contempt, for many aspects of the application and the interpretation of that law as set forth in the case-law of the ICTY and the ICTR'[660] and failed 'to provide sufficient reasons'.[661]

The Appeals Chamber reversed the acquittal. It entered a new conviction on appeal, sentencing Mr Šešelj to a largely symbolic penalty of ten years of imprisonment (which miraculously matched the ten years he had already spent in ICTY detention pending trial). It relied, in particular, on a speech given by the defendant on 6 May 1992 in Hrtkovci, Vojvodina (Serbia), which called for the expulsion of the Croatian population from Hrtkovci. It found that 'in light of Šešelj s influence over the crowd and the striking parallels between his inflammatory words and the acts subsequently perpetrated by, inter alia, members of the audience, no reasonable trier of fact could have found that, through his speech, he did not substantially contribute to the conduct of the perpetrators'.[662] Examples like this illustrate why both parties have a right to appeal both a conviction and an acquittal, due to errors of law, errors of fact and lack of reasoning.[663]

4.4.5　*Appeals*

The Nuremberg and Tokyo tribunals did not provide for a right to appeal. Today, however, anyone convicted of a crime is entitled to a review of the conviction and the

---

[657] *Prosecutor* v. *Šešelj*, IT-03-67-T, Judgment, 31 March 2016, para. 338 (*Šešelj* Trial Judgment).
[658] Ibid., para. 193.
[659] A. O. Rossini, Interview given by Judge Flavia Lattanzi, *Šešelj Verdict: The Dissenting Judge*, 8 April 2016, available at www.balcanicaucaso.org/eng/layout/set/print/content/view/print/169740.
[660] *Šešelj* Trial Judgment, Partially Dissenting Opinion of Judge Flavia Lattanzi, para. 143.
[661] Ibid., para. 10.
[662] *Prosecutor* v. *Šešelj*, MICT-16-99-A, Judgment, 11 April 2018, para. 154.
[663] The Nuremberg and Tokyo tribunals did not provide for a right to appeal. But today, anyone convicted of a crime is entitled to a review of the conviction and the sentence. The right to appeal is stipulated in ICCPR, Art. 14 (5): 'Everyone convicted of a crime shall have the right to his conviction and sentence being reviewed by a higher tribunal according to law'. General Assembly Resolution 2200A (XXI) of 16 December 1966.

sentence.[664] Appeals are typically not new trials, but corrective decisions. The Appeals Chamber reviews errors of law and errors of fact.[665] In egregious cases, it may remand a case back to the Trial Chamber.[666]

Parties to proceedings are also allowed to appeal certain decisions before judgment, i.e. through interlocutory appeals. For instance, in the ICC context, challenges to jurisdiction and admissibility are directly appealable, since they should be solved as early as possible by the Appeals Chamber.[667] Parties may seek leave to appeal in relation to issues that affect the fairness and expeditiousness of proceedings and might require immediate resolution by the Appeals Chamber.[668] One paradox is that such interlocutory appeals require leave by the same Chamber that has issued the decision that is subject to review.[669] Technically, considerations related to the merits of the appeal should be blended in such decisions on leave to appeal. In practice, it is often difficult for a Chamber to separate merits from criteria governing leave to appeal and to approach its own decision with a fresh mind, i.e. detached from considerations of merit.

4.4.6 Concluding Reflections

International criminal proceedings involve strong aspects of advocacy and drama. The courtroom is often compared to an arena. International trials may easily be blamed for 'demonizing' perpetrators.[670] The strength of the criminal process lies in the fact that it offers a forum where contradictions and contestations may legitimately coexist. It provides a space to allow different narratives, and test contradictions and contestations in order to counter such critiques.

The procedural law has been extended beyond domestic analogies, in order to reflect the nature and context of international crimes and the sheer size of cases. It is often more challenging to obtain evidence and bridge the distance to the crime site

---

[664] The right to appeal is stipulated in ICCPR, Art. 14 (5): 'Everyone convicted of a crime shall have the right to his conviction and sentence being reviewed by a higher tribunal according to law'.

[665] In practice, the Appeals Chamber mostly defers to the assessment of the evidence made by the Trial Chamber. The *Bemba* acquittal was severely criticized for deviating from this standard of review. See 'Statement of ICC Prosecutor, Fatou Bensouda, on the recent judgment of the ICC Appeals Chamber acquitting Mr Jean-Pierre Bemba Gombo', 13 June 2018.

[666] On appeals, see D. Re, 'Appeal', in Reydams, Wouters and Ryngaert, *International Prosecutors*, 797; Ambos, *Treatise on International Criminal Law, Vol. III*, 548 et seq. On ICC practice, see V. Nerlich, 'The Role of the Appeals Chamber', in Stahn, *Law and Practice of the International Criminal Court*, 963 et seq.

[667] Art. 82 (1) (a) ICC Statute.

[668] Art. 82 (1) (d) ICC Statute.

[669] The Appeals Chamber argued that 'Article 82 (1) (d) of the Statute does not confer a right to appeal interlocutory or intermediate decisions' and that a 'right to appeal arises only if the Pre-Trial or Trial Chamber is of the opinion that any such decision must receive the immediate attention of the Appeals Chamber'. See Situation in the DRC, ICC-01/04-168, Judgment on the Prosecutor's Application for Extraordinary Review of Pre-Trial Chamber I's 31 March 2006 Decision Denying Leave to Appeal, 13 July 2006, para. 20.

[670] Mamdani, 'Beyond Nuremberg', 81 ('The tendency to portray the perpetrator as the driving force behind the violence leads to freezing the two identities, perpetrator and victim, leading to the assumption that the perpetrator is always the perpetrator and the victim is always the victim. The result is to demonize the agency of the perpetrator – and diminish the agency of the victim').

and local actors. Courts need to strike a balance between many competing interests, such as trial expediency, fairness, truth-finding, protection of witnesses and victims, and budgetary constraints. This has led to certain procedural innovations. One of them is the more managerial role of judges. It has been instrumental to reconcile adversarial and inquisitorial features and to adjust procedures to the nature of criminality. A second one is the greater attention to the active role of victims in proceedings. It has been used as an instrument to relate these proceedings more closely to affected societies. Despite these efforts, international criminal proceedings struggle to challenge 'friend/enemy' clusters or the association of crime or victimhood with preconfigured collective identities, such as ethnic lines.

A key challenge is to express the scale and nature of atrocity in legal argument. Judgments are typically written in non-emotive language. They are mostly not great 'reads'. They may appear rather technical, since they are geared at an expert audience. They are constrained by the limits of rational argument and the limitations of language as a medium. As Judith Shklar has argued, certain 'causes of . . . war' may 'defy legal judgment'.[671] The search for some form of closure regarding atrocities creates a strong incentive to write morality into law. It is uncomfortable to accept that the law is silent or incomplete in light of moral outrage. Where existing legal notions do not fit, there is a temptation to use legal creativity to bridge gaps and silences.[672] This is why there is often only a thin line between legal interpretation and judicial development of law in key judgments, ranging from Nuremberg and Tokyo to modern atrocity trials.

Although legal procedures are governed by technical rules, they do not fully bar the expression of human elements. Judgments have often used expressivist language to validate victims' suffering and convey moral outrage, beyond the legalist determinations of guilt. A study of the ad hoc tribunals and the SCSL has shown that multiple judgments (e.g. *Krstić*, *Galić*, *Čelebići*, *Fonfana and Kondewa* or *Taylor*) have grappled with rational argument and legal form and used particular language and appeal to emotion in order to reveal the scale of human suffering, the brutality of acts and the damage caused.[673] As Rosa Aloisi and James Meernik note, this is often done in contradictory ways. Judges recognize that they are not supposed to express feeling or provide historical judgment, but then use expressive language to

speak to the whole of humanity and place the suffering of the victims into a historical context that recognizes their tragedy as a personal loss and as an exemplar of loss alongside other tragedies throughout history [or] . . . speak through the words of witnesses when their descriptions cannot resonate with same forceful and simple clarity of the victim's own words.[674]

---

[671] J. N. Shklar, *Legalism: Law, Morals, and Political Trials*, (Cambridge, MA: Harvard University Press, 1986) 188.
[672] See generally S. Darcy and J. Powderly (eds.), *Judicial Creativity at the International Criminal Tribunals* (Oxford: Oxford University Press, 2010).
[673] Alosi and Meeernik, *Judgment Day*, 134–150.
[674] Ibid., 149.

A second challenge is the establishment and verification of facts. The question of who is responsible cannot be answered without an account as to what happened. Trials require a 'theory of the case', i.e. an explanation of why the crimes occurred in the first instance, in order to establish individual criminal responsibility. However, the underlying facts are often more complex than revealed through evidence and testimony at trial. The judgment is constrained by this. It relies on constructed chains of causality or fiction. It is controversial to what extent it may serve as an authoritative account of facts. Often, a differentiated vision emerges only through a sequence of trials.

Third, international criminal proceedings face a constituency dilemma, since they relate to multiple audiences. The judgment is primarily concerned with fairness to the accused. International trials are often more than trials of individuals, however. The fact that there is a trial at all might be more important than the exhaustive prosecution of all crimes. Trials have a deeply didactic function. They express the nature of the crimes adjudicated and the communities affected by them. Through this, they seek to bestow confidence in the idea of public order and to shape a common conscience. Their persuasiveness is not only built on the correct application of facts and law, but also on the way in which the 'story' is conveyed to the respective audience. Trials are both a means to promote ideal norms of behaviour and an instrument to highlight alternative narratives to violence.

Trials struggle to confront ideology-fuelled criminality. Judicial proceedings need to provide space to challenge predetermined attitudes and biases or the heroization of agents in order to maintain their perception as a shared forum. This requires active, and sometimes better, judicial management of proceedings, deeper engagement with conflicting visions of history and causes of criminality, and space to highlight and challenge contradictions in ideology-tainted discourse.

Any truth produced by international criminal proceedings is a 'living truth'. It emerges through a diffuse set of truth-telling relations between actors during proceedings. It continues to be challenged, contested and expanded after trial. It excludes many elements, such as the role of bystanders or colonial histories. There is likely to be disagreement on the outcome, whatever is decided, since the allocation of blame to an individual is easily associated with wrongdoing by a specific state structure, community or political group. These tensions are impossible to resolve through legal reasoning alone. Judgments have to be translated into non-technical language. They need to be explained and related to domestic discourses in order to reach local communities.[675] The expressive potential of international criminal proceedings depends on the form of communication, i.e. its perception as a genuine process, and

---

[675] Former ICC Judge Elizabeth Odio Benito argued that there is a disconnect between 'court room justice' and the lived realities and justice needs of victims: 'Our notions of judicial justice are incomprehensible for those who are unable to survive without a permanent place to live in, without enough money to take care of their families' basic needs and without full recognition of the atrocities committed against them'. E. O. Benito, 'Foreword', in C. Ferstman, M. Goetz and A. Stephens, *Reparations for Victims of Genocide, War Crimes and Crimes Against Humanity* (Boston: Martinus Nijhoff Publishers, 2009), 1.

its degree of persuasiveness. As Paul Seils has aptly noted, the more procedures are seen by a society 'as a genuine means to establish and communicate responsibility for serious crimes, the more they will successfully meet their objectives. The more they are seen as a maneuver to subvert the exposure of crimes and those responsible for them, the more pointless and counterproductive they will become'.[676] The trial is at best one intermediate factor in such a process. It may take decades until it produces its full impact. A key element for the success is to create archives and sites of memory after the trial that tell a broader story.

[676] Seils, 'Squaring Colombia's Circle', 14.

5

Remedying Wrong

Remedying wrong is one of the greatest challenges of international criminal law. More than 130 perpetrators have been convicted by international criminal courts and tribunals over the past three decades. They are complemented by numerous domestic judgments. Determining appropriate sanctions and measures to repair harm entails multiple paradoxes, however. As Hannah Arendt put it in 1958: 'men are unable to forgive what they cannot punish and are unable to punish what turns out to be unforgivable'.[1] In public discourse, much emphasis has been placed on punishment and punitive measures. However, the function of international criminal law extends beyond punishment of individuals. International criminal courts and tribunals inflict punishment on a selected number of perpetrators. Crimes take place in times of chaos and social unrest. The collective nature of crimes complicates the allocation of individual culpability. The harm caused is often so great or diffuse that it exceeds the classical proportionality considerations of criminal punishment. Compared to local realities, the prospects of detention, international sentencing and enforcement of sentence in a liberal democracy are often not the worst form of 'punishment'. The ability of the judgment to remedy harm is limited. A court can judge, but only people can build or repair social relations.[2] Some harm may only heal with time, or remain beyond forgiveness. This creates difficulties for the justification of punishment, the definition of adequate penalties and the broader question of how the legal process as such can remedy harm.

Traditionally, incarceration is the main form of punishment for international crimes. This narrow focus is increasingly under critique. As Ian Ward noted: 'The imprisoning of individual soldiers and politicians does not rebuild schools, hospitals and roads. It does not rebuild trust within devastated societies either'.[3] With the rise of victims' rights, reparative measures have gained broader importance in international criminal proceedings, in addition to classical punishment. In domestic settings, there is

---

[1] H. Arendt, *The Human Condition* (Chicago: University of Chicago Press, 1958), 241.
[2] See J. Halpern and H. Weinstein, 'Rehumanizing the Other: Empathy and Reconciliation' (2004) 26 *Human Rights Quarterly* 561, 575.
[3] I. Ward, *Justice: Humanity and the New World Order* (Aldershot: Ashgate, 2003), 131.

greater creativity in relation to the forms of punishment. For instance, in transitional justice contexts, additional attention is given to alternatives to imprisonment for specific offenders or categories of crimes and measures to prevent re-occurrence of violations. They include suspended or reduced sentences, alternative penalties (e.g. financial penalties, house arrest, other restrictions of liberty), exclusion from political office and/or community service.[4]

International criminal law requires a holistic account of punishment. What type of punishment is adequate depends on the underlying goals. It is widely acknowledged that punishment needs to go beyond the infliction of suffering on the perpetrator in order to be meaningful.[5] A key question is to determine what type of punishment ensures adequate social condemnation of conduct, proper communication of wrongdoing, engagement of the offender with the wrong and non-repetition of offences.

5.1   Foundations of Punishment

International criminal law is still in search of adequate theories of punishment.[6] Punishment theories have a long tradition in domestic criminal law. But rationales from domestic settings cannot be directly transposed to international contexts.[7] In light of its global constituency and its inherent limitations (e.g. selectivity, limited enforcement, difficulty reflecting the gravity and collective nature of crime), international criminal law has generally been more concerned with rationales of norm affirmation, moral condemnation and prevention than perpetrator-centred justifications of punishment. There are at least four major theories: retribution, consequentialism, restorative justice and expressivism.

5.1.1   Rationales of Punishment

The most classical theory to justify punishment is the idea of retribution.[8] It is focused on the culpability of the accused. It implies that those who have committed crimes ought to be punished for the harm they caused. The notion is derived from the Latin term *retribuo* ('I pay back'). It relies on the premise that offenders are morally responsible for their actions and should receive the punishment that they 'deserve'

---

[4] See Seils, 'Squaring Colombia's Circle', 2.

[5] See M. Osiel, 'Why Prosecute? Critics of Punishment for Mass Atrocity (2000) 22 *Human Rights Quarterly* 118–147.

[6] See F. Hassan, 'The Theoretical Basis of Punishment in International Criminal Law' (1983) 15 *Case Western Reserve Journal of International Law* 39, 59 (1983); R. Henham, 'Developing Contextualised Rationales for Sentencing in International Criminal Trials' (2007) 5 *JICJ* 757; M. Bagaric and J. Morss, 'International Sentencing Law: In Search of a Justification and Coherent Framework' (2006) 6 *International Criminal Law Review* 191.

[7] See A. Werkmeister, *Straftheorien im Völkerstrafrecht* (Baden-Baden: Nomos, 2015).

[8] Immanuel Kant provided a secular grounding for retributivism in his *Metaphysics of Morals*. It combined aspect of deterrence and retribution. See S. Byrd, 'Kant's Theory of Punishment: Deterrence in Its Threat, Retribution in Its Execution' (1989) 8 *Law and Philosophy* 151–200. On modern retributive theory, see A. A. Haque, 'Retributivism: The Right and the Good' (2013) 32 *Law & Philosophy* 59; A. von Hirsch, 'Proportionality in the Philosophy of Punishment' (1992) 16 *Crime and Justice* 55, 59–63.

in light of the social harm caused and the comparative seriousness of offences in relation to other offenders.[9] It requires the imposition of a 'just and appropriate punishment'.[10] This justification faces several problems in international criminal law.[11] Unlike ordinary criminals, perpetrators of international crimes often act in compliance with domestic norms. It is difficult to reflect an 'equivalence' between the punishment, i.e. just deserts and the crime through sentencing.[12] As highlighted by tribunals, it is questionable whether any sentence of incarceration can 'duly express . . . the outrage of the international community at crimes'.[13]

Something more is required. Punishment requires that perpetrators face account-ability towards the public, and that victims have their rights vindicated. Modern retributivists have thus rightly argued that the virtue of punishment may lie more in the confrontation of the perpetrator with the wrong caused to the others, the reaffirm-ation of the value of the legal order and the expression of blame in relation to criminal conduct, than the infliction of 'just deserts'.[14] The fear is that without punishment the violation may become accepted in the norms of society or encourage self-help.[15]

Utilitarian theories acknowledge that punishment is an evil in itself that is justified by the positive effects that it produces. They place greater emphasis on the social benefits of punishment, such as deterrence or incapacitation. They claim that the impact of punishment on the minds of perpetrators may be more important than the length of the sentence. These theories are problematic.[16] A philosophical problem of utilitarian theories is that they use external factors to justify infliction of punishment on an individual. Many of the alleged benefits of punishment, such as incapacitation, general or individual deterrence or rehabilitation are difficult to establish.[17] They are largely grounded in faith. It cannot be shown that they work, but it has also not been established that they do not work.[18] Judges apply them because they may be useful, even if they cannot be proven scientifically. They are deeply linked to a 'moral view

---

[9] *Prosecutor v. Kordić & Čerkez*, IT-95–14/2, Judgment, 17 December 2004, para. 1075.

[10] *Prosecutor v. Nikolić*, IT-94–2-S, Sentencing Judgment, 18 December 2003, para. 140 (*Nikolić* Sentencing Judgment).

[11] For a critique of 'just deserts' in light of the selectivity of international criminal law, see Drumbl, 'Atrocity, Punishment and International Law', 151; Amann, 'Group Mentality, Expressivism, and Genocide', 117.

[12] A. K. Woods, 'Moral Judgments and International Crimes: The Disutility of Desert' (2011) 52 *Virginia Journal of International Law* 633.

[13] *Prosecutor v. Aleksovski*, IT-95–14/1, Judgment, 24 March 2000, para. 185; *Prosecutor v. Stakić*, IT-97–24, Judgment, 31 July 2003, para. 40.

[14] Greenawalt, 'International Criminal Law for Retributivists', 1016–1017. On the censuring aspects of punishment, see A. von Hirsch, *Censure and Sanctions* (Oxford: Clarendon Press, 1993), 11.

[15] See J. D. Ohlin, 'Towards a Unique Theory of International Criminal Sentencing', in Sluiter and Vasiliev, *International Criminal Procedure*, 373, 390–391 ('[I]f the victims feel as if the perpetrators will not get the punishment that they deserve – because they will not be caught, because there are no tribunals within which to try them, or because the sentences will be too low – then the victims may decide to engage in self-help measures and take matters into their own hands').

[16] See S. Dana, 'The Limits of Judicial Idealism: Should the International Criminal Court Engage with Consequentialist Aspirations?' (2014) 3 *Pennsylvania State Journal of Law and International Affairs* 30, 112 ('[M]ost utilitarian aspir-ations associated with international criminal prosecutions should be abandoned as sentencing rationales because they distort the individual perpetrator's culpability').

[17] See R. Henham, 'The Philosophical Foundations of International Sentencing' (2003) 1 *JICJ* 64, 77–80.

[18] On this dilemma, see Sloane, 'Expressive Capacity of International Punishment', 73.

that punishment for heinous crimes has genuine value in and of itself'.[19] However, these moral foundations are not articulated.

Restorative justice theories provide a stronger focus on the needs of victims, communities or group structures and their relevance in the legal process and sanction (e.g. restorative penalties).[20] The key idea is that 'crime should be understood not merely as an act against the state, but as an offense against a particular victim or victims and relevant communities'.[21] Punishment may have beneficial effects for victims.[22] As Pablo de Greiff has argued, one of the major assets of a criminal trial is that it provides a forum to discard any 'implicit claim of superiority made by the criminal's behaviour'.[23] Victims might be more willing to forgive, or at least temper their feelings of revenge, if they know that the perpetrator will be punished. In particular, the idea that the offender needs to confront victims of crimes in proceedings has gained broader importance in criminal justice. It is reflected in juvenile justice, victim impact statements at sentencing, and different modalities of victim participation in trials. There are positive examples. For instance, Auschwitz survivor Eva Moses Kor noted in the trial against camp guard Oskar Gröning that she could forgive because 'forgiveness does not absolve the perpetrator from taking responsibility for his actions' or diminish the 'need to know what happened there'.[24] However, the appropriate space of restorative justice in criminal processes remains contested. Sceptics caution that too many restorative features may distort the core function of criminal procedures and blur their distinction from transitional justice mechanisms.[25]

Expressivist theories see the merit of punishment in the message that the denunciation of the crime conveys to the perpetrator, victims and society at large.[26] They justify punishment by the moral authority and stigma associated with the condemnation,[27] its alert function, and its communicative function.[28] Expressivist theory goes

---

[19] See Woods, 'Moral Judgments and International Crimes', 640.

[20] See generally C. Menkel-Meadow 'Restorative Justice: What Is It and Does It Work?' (2007) 3 *Annual Review of Law and Social Science* 161; A. J. MacLeod, 'All for One: A Review of Victim-Centric Justifications for Criminal Punishment' (2008) 13 *Berkeley Journal of Criminal Law* 31; Henham, 'Philosophical Foundations of International Sentencing', 80–84.

[21] See DeGuzman, 'Choosing to Prosecute', 310.

[22] C. Garbett, 'The Truth and the Trial: Victim Participation, Restorative Justice, and the International Criminal Court' (2013) 16 *Contemporary Justice Review* 193–213.

[23] Report of the Special Rapporteur on the promotion of truth, justice, reparation and guarantees of non-recurrence, A/HRC/21/46, 9 August 2012, para. 30.

[24] B. Knight, 'Auschwitz Survivor Angers Co-Plaintiffs in SS Officer Trial by Saying Prosecutions Should Stop', *The Guardian*, 27 April 2015, www.theguardian.com/world/2015/apr/27/auschwitz-survivor-angers-plaintiffs-trial-forgiveness.

[25] DeGuzman, 'Choosing to Prosecute', 311; Aukerman, 'Extraordinary Evil, Ordinary Crime', 79–80.

[26] See Sloane, 'The Expressive Capacity of International Punishment', 36; W. Wringe, 'Why Punish War Crimes? Victor's Justice and Expressive Justifications of Punishment' (2006) 25 *Law and Philosophy* 159; E. Anderson and R. H. Pildes, 'Expressive Theories of Law: A General Restatement' (1999–2000) 148 *University of Pennsylvania Law Review* 1503.

[27] In *Erdemović*, the ICTY saw 'public reprobation and stigmatisation by the international community, which would thereby express its indignation over heinous crimes and denounce the perpetrators, as one of the essential functions of a prison sentence for a crime against humanity'. See *Prosecutor* v. *Erdemović*, IT-96–22-T, Sentencing Judgement, 29 Nov. 1996, para. 65.

[28] See also W. Schabas, 'Sentencing by International Tribunals: A Human Rights Approach' (1997) 7 *Duke Journal of Comparative and International Law* 461, 516 ('[T]he declaratory value of criminal law is probably its most important contribution to the struggle against impunity. Society declares that certain specific kinds of conduct are wrong ... and it adds it to the collective memory').

back to Durkheim, who argued that punishment serves the interest of social solidarity, i.e. to 'maintain social cohesion'.[29] Modern accounts have stressed the symbolic functions of punishment,[30] the role of punishment as ritual,[31] its means of social expression of norms, and its broader educational or didactic functions.[32] Some emphasize the importance of the trial process for the consideration of what constitutes adequate punishment.[33] Others submit that punishment is more about communication than expression. For instance, Antony Duff has argued that the purpose of a trial is not to inflict suffering on the offender, but to 'engage the defendant in a rational dialogue about the justice of the charge' and to make them accept the condemnation expressed through punishment.[34] Mark Osiel has defended the argument that trial proceedings and civil dissension in trials stimulate reflection on wrongdoing and future norms.[35] Still others argue that punishment has a confidence-building effect on victims. Traces of an expressive function of punishment were articulated in *Nikolić*:

One of the main purposes of a sentence imposed by an international tribunal is to influence the legal awareness of the accused, the surviving victims, their relatives, the witnesses and the general public in order to reassure them that the legal system is implemented and enforced. Additionally, the process of sentencing is intended to convey the message that globally accepted laws and rules have to be obeyed by everybody ... This fundamental rule fosters the internalisation of these laws and rules in the minds of legislators and the general public.[36]

Expressivist theories have a close link to prevention.[37] The problem is that they presuppose the existence of a discursive community and a willingness to engage, and may easily be perceived as a form of imposition.[38] Structurally, they highlight potential benefits of international punishment, but do not necessarily provide 'a factor for allocating sentence severity'.[39] They are aspirational in the sense that they declare 'certain conduct to be behavior to which people should aspire'.[40]

None of these theories alone is suited to address the complexities of mass atrocity crime.[41] As rightly argued in doctrine, international criminal law requires a 'holistic, integrated approach' to punishment that combines retributive factors with

---

[29] Durkheim, *Division of Labour in Society*, 108.
[30] J. Feinberg, 'The Expressive Function of Punishment' (1965) 49 *The Monist* 397, 400.
[31] Sloane, 'The Expressive Capacity of International Punishment', 89–90.
[32] Damaška, 'What is the Point', 347; Drumbl, *Atrocity, Punishment, and International Law*, 173–176.
[33] Seils, 'Squaring Colombia's Circle', 2.
[34] Duff, *Trial and Punishments*, 233.
[35] Osiel, *Mass Atrocity, Collective Memory and the Law*, 2, 50–51.
[36] *Nikolić* Sentencing Judgment, para. 139.
[37] See T. J. Farer, 'Restraining the Barbarians: Can International Criminal Law Help?' (2000) 22 *Human Rights Quarterly* 90, 91–92.
[38] Damaška, 'What is the Point', 349.
[39] Dana, 'The Limits of Judicial Idealism', 62. See also J. Nemitz, 'The Law of Sentencing in International Criminal Law: The Purposes of Sentencing and the Applicable Method for the Determination of the Sentence' (2001) 4 *Yearbook of International Humanitarian Law* 87, 100 '[I]t is rather difficult to determine what length of sentence will reassure the public that justice has been done'.
[40] See S. Mohamed, 'Deviance, Aspiration, and the Stories We Tell: Reconciling Mass Atrocity and the Criminal Law' (2015) 124 *Yale Law Journal* 1628, 1674.
[41] M. DeGuzman, 'Proportionate Sentencing at the ICC', in Stahn, *The Law and Practice of the International Criminal Court*, 932.

consideration of broader collective goals.[42] The justification of punishment relies on a combination of factors: retributive elements that express condemnation and sanction the social danger caused by the offender, and certain forward-looking features, such as crime prevention, repair of social harm or potential empowerment of victims.[43] As the ICTY stated in the *Furundžija* case

> it is the infallibility of punishment, rather than [...] the sanction, which is the tool for retribution, stigmatisation and deterrence ... penalties are made more onerous by its international stature, moral authority and impact upon world public opinion, and this punitive effect must be borne in mind when assessing the suitable length of sentence.[44]

Overall, the role of punishment is thus more complex in the context of international criminal justice than traditionally assumed. Often, the punishment lies not so much in the final sentence at trial, but rather the issuance of an indictment or the very prospect of a trial. The very process of facing justice for atrocity crimes in an international context entails certain forms of stigmatization that go beyond traditional domestic trials. The punishment of individuals may have less importance than the broader social significance of the trial.

5.1.2   Legal Principles

The perception of what constitutes a 'just' or an 'unjust' punishment differs greatly among societies. This makes it difficult to determine the purposes that punishment should serve.[45] The allocation of punishment is guided by two major principles: the principle of legality (*nulla poena sine lege*) and the principle of proportionality.

The principle of legality requires that punishment is prescribed by law.[46] The penalty must be contemplated,[47] but it is not necessary for the individual to know the precise punishment in advance with the same degree of specificity as in relation to crimes (*lex certa*).[48] The international sentencing system is thus less developed than domestic ones.[49] Domestic criminal codes sometimes define an appropriate penalty for an offence, including a minimum and a maximum term. For example, in Romano-Germanic systems, penal codes include sentencing ranges in order to ensure consistency in punishment. Sentencing guidelines play this role in common law systems.

---

[42] Ambos, *Treatise on International Criminal law, Vol. II*, 288.
[43] Report, UN SG, *The Rule of Law in Transitional Justice in Conflict and Post-Conflict Societies*, S/2004/616, 23 August 2004, para. 38.
[44] *Furundžija* Trial Judgment, para. 290.
[45] S. D'Ascoli, *Sentencing in International Criminal Law: The UN Ad Hoc Tribunals and Future Perspectives for the ICC* (Oxford: Hart, 2011).
[46] See Rome Statute, Art. 23.
[47] S. Dana, 'Beyond Retroactivity to Realizing Justice: A Theory on the Principle of Legality in International Criminal Law Sentencing' (2009) 99 *Journal of Criminal Law and Criminology* 857.
[48] K. Ambos, 'Nulla Poena Sine Lege in International Criminal Law', in R. Haveman and O. Olusanya (eds.), *Sentencing and Sanctioning in Supranational Criminal Law* (Antwerp: Intersentia, 2006), 17.
[49] See generally J. Meernik and K. King, 'The Sentencing Determinants of the International Criminal Tribunal for the Former Yugoslavia: An Empirical and Doctrinal Analysis' (2003) 16 *LJIL* 717.

International criminal justice lacks such a classification. Judges are given broad discretion to determine the length of the sentence, and the weight given to individual factors. The ICC Statute preserves legal pluralism in relation to penalties. It allows national jurisdictions flexibility to pass sentences in light of their own domestic traditions.[50] Some argue that international criminal courts and tribunals should follow domestic sentencing traditions.[51]

The second principle is the principle of proportionality. It has been traditionally linked to retributive theory. It requires that punishment must be proportionate to the gravity of the crime ('offence gravity')[52] and the culpability of the offender.[53] Both criteria pose particular problems in international criminal law. There is no formal hierarchy of crimes. It is difficult to determine the correlation between the seriousness of the crime and the penalty.[54] Is a ten-year sentence enough for war crimes? Is thirty years appropriate for genocide or crimes against humanity? For some crimes, no penalty may ever be appropriate enough to reflect the social harm caused. These might be so grave that they would require sentences prohibited by human rights law.[55] Moreover, the abstract categorization of a crime as genocide, crime against humanity or war crime might be less important than the actual impact of the offence, such as the specific harm caused or the actual suffering inflicted on victims. The gravity requirement is thus frequently related to individual factors, such as the position of the defendant and the role played in the situation.

There are difficulties in establishing an exact correlation between the sentence and the culpability of the offender. Proportionality implies that culpable defendants should receive higher sentences than less culpable defendants ('defendant relative proportionality').[56] It also mandates a certain degree of coherence. The penalty should be comparable to penalties in similar cases. This requires an approximation.

The principle of proportionality was initially conceived as a means for protecting the offender from excessive punishment (*Übermassverbot*).[57] A more controversial question is to what extent the principle of proportionality provides some minimum

---

[50] Art. 80 ICC Statute.

[51] A. K. A. Greenawalt, 'The Pluralism of International Criminal Law' (2011) 86 *Indiana Law Journal* 1063, 1099; N. Combs, 'Seeking Inconsistency: Advancing Pluralism in International Criminal Sentencing' (2016) 41 *Yale Journal of International Law* 1, 31 et seq.

[52] A. von Hirsch, 'Proportionality in the Philosophy of Punishment: From "Why Punish?" to "How Much?"' (1990) 1 *Criminal Law Forum* 259.

[53] See generally J. D. Ohlin, 'Proportional Sentences at the ICTY', in Swart, Zahar and Sluiter, *Legacy of the International Criminal Tribunal for the Former Yugoslavia*, 322.

[54] See A. M. Danner, 'Constructing a Hierarchy of Crimes in International Criminal Law Sentencing' (2001) 87 *Virginia Law Review* 415, 441.

[55] See on this problem M. deGuzman, 'Harsh Justice for International Crimes' (2014) 39 *Yale Journal of International Law* 2, 1–14. For a controversial argument on support of the death penalty on this ground, see J. D. Ohlin, 'Applying the Death Penalty to Crimes of Genocide' (2005) 99 *AJIL* 747, 768–769.

[56] B. Hola, 'Sentencing of International Crimes at the ICTY and ICTR: Consistency of Sentencing Case Law' (2012) 4 *Amsterdam Law Forum* 3, 9.

[57] R. S. Frase, 'Excessive Prison Sentences, Punishment Goals, and the Eighth Amendment: "Proportionality" Relative to What?' (2004) 89 *Minnesota Law Review* 571.

protection for the rights of victims, i.e. protection against insufficient punishment (*Untermassverbot*).[58] Human rights bodies have been critical towards illusory and disproportionate sentences. It is widely agreed that symbolic punishment is not enough. For instance, the Human Rights Committee has held that disciplinary measures or administrative penalties might not be sufficient to deal with crimes.[59] Fully suspended sentences may shield defendants from responsibility. Some scholars argue that there may be some room for compromise in relation to the form of the penalty (i.e. years of imprisonment) if the criminal process leading to the penalty involves exposure of wrongdoing, public accountability and acknowledgment.[60] However, there are many grey areas.

This dilemma has become relevant in the Colombian context in relation to the sentences pronounced by the Special Jurisdiction for Peace (five to eight years). The Colombian Constitutional Court has held that penalties imposed for the gravest international crimes must be compatible with an intent to bring the person concerned to justice and should not lead to impunity. It argued that the Special Jurisdictions for Peace should weigh the proportionality of the sentence with regard to the gravity of the crime, the degree of responsibility of the perpetrator, and the type and degree of restriction of the right to freedom.[61]

5.1.3   Types of Penalties

The types of penalties that international criminal courts and tribunals proscribe are rather orthodox.[62] Penalties are criminal in nature. The main form of punishment is imprisonment. There are two types: imprisonment for a specific number of years, and life imprisonment.[63] The Nuremberg and Tokyo tribunals pronounced death penalty sentences.[64] Neither UN tribunals nor the ICC foresee capital punishment.[65] Community-based measures, rehabilitation and more creative forms of punishment are relatively alien to international criminal law. Critics claim that this approach to

---

[58] See Ambos, *Treatise on International Criminal Law, Vol. II*, 287.

[59] Human Rights Committee, *Bautista de Arellana* v. *Colombia*, Communication 563/1993, Views of 27 October 1995, para. 8.2.

[60] Seils, 'Squaring Colombia's Circle', 14.

[61] Constitutional Court of Colombia, Press Release No. 55 of 14 November 2017, 14 November 2017, para. 23.

[62] See M. Drumbl, 'Punishment and Sentencing', in W. Schabas (ed.), *Cambridge Companion to International Criminal Law* (Cambridge: Cambridge University Press, 2016), 73. For an overview of penalties under domestic law, see ICRC, 'Analysis of the Punishments Applicable to International Crimes (War Crimes, Crimes Against Humanity and Genocide) in Domestic Law and Practice' (2009) 90 *International Review of the Red Cross* 461.

[63] D. van Zyl Smit 'Life Imprisonment as the Ultimate Penalty in International Law: A Human Rights Perspective' (1999) 9 *Criminal Law Forum* 5; E. Gumboh, 'The Penalty of Life Imprisonment under International Criminal Law' (2011) 11 *African Human Rights Law Journal* 75.

[64] The Nuremberg tribunal handed down twelve death sentences, the Tokyo tribunal seven.

[65] See W. Schabas, 'International Criminal Law and the Abolition of the Death Penalty' (1998) 55 *Washington & Lee Law Review* 797.

punishment masks some of the more imaginative ways in which offenders could be punished, including alternatives to imprisonment.[66]

The conditions are framed in rudimentary terms. There is no uniform framework to impose standardized sentences. The regime differs across courts and tribunals. Paradoxically, sentences for mass atrocity crimes may be lower than sentences for ordinary crimes at the domestic level.[67] Unlike in domestic systems, there is no specific minimum penalty. Imprisonment for a certain number of years is the ordinary penalty. At the ICC, there is a maximum penalty. Imprisonment is limited to thirty years.[68] This differs from the practice of the ad hoc or hybrid tribunals which have awarded higher sentences – sometimes over fifty years.[69] For instance, former Liberian President Charles Taylor was sentenced to fifty years by the Special Court for Sierra Leone.[70] The absence of guidance makes sentencing exceedingly challenging.

The option of life imprisonment caused controversy in the context of the negotiation of the ICC Statute.[71] Some states argued that life imprisonment is too indeterminate and might amount to cruel, inhumane or degrading punishment. Others felt that it is not severe enough. It was ultimately retained in the ICC Statute as a trade-off against the non-inclusion of the death penalty.[72] There are two caveats however. Life imprisonment must be justified by the 'extreme gravity of the crime and the individual circumstances of the convicted person'.[73] Moreover, life does not necessarily mean life. After twenty-five years there is a mandatory parole review.

Finally, courts may award fines. In this way, judges may ensure that perpetrators do not benefit from the wrongful acts committed.

5.1.4 Sentencing

Sentencing plays a key role in punishment. It matters greatly to victims of crimes. It serves to distinguish the culpability of perpetrators. It is often the only way to take into account the social context of the commission of the crimes in the determination of blameworthiness. The individualization of the sentence pays tribute to individual culpability.

---

[66] See M. Drumbl, 'Impunities', Washington & Lee Legal Studies Paper No. 2017–17, 2 November 2017, at SSRN: https://ssrn.com/abstract=3070346 or http://dx.doi.org/10.2139/ssrn.3070346 (arguing that impunity should be defined 'as freedom from harmful consequences, recrimination, reparations, shame, or pain', rather than lack of imprisonment). See also Seils, 'Squaring Colombia's Circle', 15 ('[P]unishment must be capable of being taken seriously as condemning the breach of the core values of society. It should be creative, embracing possibilities of restorative justice approaches, reparations funds, community service, and possibly some limited periods of political exclusion').

[67] Harmon and Gaynor, 'Ordinary Sentences for Extraordinary Crimes', 685.

[68] See Art. 77 (1) (a) ICC Statute.

[69] B. Holá, A. Smeulers and C. Bijleveld, 'International Sentencing Facts and Figures' (2011) 9 *JICJ* 411, 414.

[70] At the SCSL, Ivay Sesay was convicted to fifty-two years. Charles Taylor and Alex Brima received sentences of fifty years. A. Smeulers, B. Holá and T. van den Berg, 'Sixty-Five Years of International Criminal Justice: The Facts and Figures' (2013) 13 *International Criminal Law Review* 7, 23.

[71] On long-term sentences and human rights, see D. Scalia, 'Long-Term Sentences in International Criminal Law' (2011) 9 *JICJ* 669.

[72] See W. Schabas, *The International Criminal Court* (Oxford: Oxford University Press, 2010), 893.

[73] Art. 77 (1) (b) ICC Statute.

Judges enjoy a considerable amount of discretion in sentencing. At first sight, there are some striking discrepancies. For instance, the ICTR issued forty-seven convictions. Sentences at the ICTR tended to be higher than sentences at the ICTY.[74] According to estimates, the sentence was on average slightly more than twenty-two years.[75] At the ICTY, sentences were on average around fifteen years.[76] The first two convicted persons at the ICC, Thomas Lubanga and German Katanga, received terms of imprisonment below fifteen years. It is relatively easy to criticize the uncertainty of penalties and the incoherence of sentences.[77] However, the picture is more nuanced.

Some divergences may be explained by the historical and institutional context. The international sentencing system had to be built from scratch. International human rights law does not set specific penalties for crimes. Sentencing practices applied by other tribunals are instructive, but not formally binding. The ad hoc tribunals were required to take into account the general practice regarding prison sentences by domestic courts in Rwanda and the former Yugoslavia. It is thus no surprise that there is no uniform system.[78] The convergence lies in the methodology, rather than in the severity of sentences awarded.

There are some common features.[79] Judges typically apply different sentencing criteria: general factors that influence sentencing and case-specific factors.

Sentencing judgments start with an explanation of general sentencing rationales. These include retribution, deterrence (general and specific), prevention, incapacitation, expressivism and potential contributions to the restoration of peace.[80] The conceptual difficulty is that these goals cannot be immediately translated into the quantification of sentences. The individual weight given to these criteria in the actual sentencing differs across judgments, and in line with the purposes of the respective tribunal.

The second step is the assessment of case-specific criteria. They involve two main elements: the gravity of the offence and the individual characteristics of the perpetrator.

The gravity of the crime is crucial to distinguish sentences. Not all crimes are of equivalent gravity. Domestic judges typically assess gravity in abstract terms. They look at the range of applicable sentences stated in the law. International judges apply a different method, since the sentences are in theory equal for each of the core crimes. They put primary emphasis on the concrete situation of the defendant, namely the

---

[74] B. Holá, C. Bijleveld, and A. Smuelers, 'Consistency of International Sentencing: ICTY and ICTR Case Study' (2012) 9 *European Journal of Criminology* 539, 549.

[75] Smeulers, Hola and van den Berg, 'Sixty-Five Years of International Criminal Justice', 22.

[76] Ibid.

[77] J. R. W. D. Jones and S. Powles, *International Criminal Practice*, 3rd edn (Oxford: Oxford University Press, 2003), 778–780.

[78] S. Beresford, 'Unshackling the Paper Tiger – the Sentencing Practices of the Ad Hoc International Criminal Tribunals for the Former Yugoslavia and Rwanda' (2001) 1 *International Criminal Law Review* (2001) 33–90; D'Ascoli, *Sentencing in International Criminal Law*, 261.

[79] B. Holá, A. L. Smeulers and C. C. J. H. Bijleveld, 'Is ICTY Sentencing Predictable? An Empirical Analysis of ICTY Sentencing Practice' (2009) 22 *LJIL* 79.

[80] On the diverse sentencing goals, see D'Ascoli, *Sentencing in International Criminal Law*, 135–140.

particular circumstances of the crime at hand and the role and degree of participation of the convicted persons in the crime. The scope of victimization plays a key role. The ICC Rules of Procedure and Evidence mentions factors such as the extent of damage caused and the harm to victims and their families.[81] For instance, in *Lubanga*, the ICC took into account the vulnerability of children, their exposure to risk, and post-traumatic stress when assessing the gravity of the crime of using child soldiers.

The second element is the determination of the individual circumstances of the convicted persons.[82] They include factors such as the leadership level of the offender, the age,[83] education and condition of the convicted person, lack of previous criminal record,[84] and health.[85] For example, in *Lubanga* the Trial Chamber emphasized that the defendant understood the seriousness of the crime in light of his educated background.[86]

Additional considerations, such as expressions of remorse,[87] may serve as mitigating or aggravating factors for the sentence. They must be balanced. The final sentence must reflect each of the convictions, and the totality of the criminal conduct of the accused. In case of convictions for several different offences, judges cannot punish the defendant twice for the same acts, unless the material elements of the crime differ.

A particular difficulty is that judgments rarely relate the guilt for a specific charge to a corresponding length of sentence. This makes it difficult to compare sentences and identify correlating patterns.[88] Overall, coherence of sentences across tribunals remains an issue.[89] However, there are some comforting factors. Empirical analysis suggests certain correlations. Genocide convictions typically entail a high sentence.[90] For instance, Barbora Holá, Catrien Bijleveld and Alette Smeulers found that the sentence 'is increased by 16 years and 1 month' where a defendant 'is convicted of genocide', compared to those not convicted of genocide.[91] They also found that at the ICTY and the ICTR the 'lowest sentences' were given in relation to 'crimes that usually do not result in physical damage to victims', while 'the lengthiest sentences were meted out for violent offences'.[92] High-ranking perpetrators often face harsher sentences.[93] Studies suggest that sentences of 'top-level' military and political leaders

---

[81] Rule 145 of the Rules of Procedure and Evidence.
[82] Art. 78 (1) ICC Statute; Art. 24 (2) ICTY Statute; Art. 23 (2) ICTR Statute.
[83] See D'Ascoli, *Sentencing in International Criminal Law*, 167.
[84] Ibid., at 163.
[85] Ibid., at 170.
[86] *Prosecutor* v. *Lubanga*, Decision on Sentence pursuant to Art. 76 of the Statute, ICC-01/04–01/06–2901, 10 July 2012, para. 56.
[87] See D'Ascoli, *Sentencing in International Criminal Law*, 166.
[88] See Holá, Bijleveld and Smeulers, 'Consistency of International Sentencing', 539; U. Ewald, 'Predictably Irrational: International Sentencing and its Discourse against the Backdrop of Preliminary Empirical Findings on ICTY Sentencing Practices' (2010) 10 *International Criminal Law Review* 365.
[89] Some compare it to a 'lottery system'. See O. Olusanya, *Sentencing War Crimes and Crimes against Humanity under the International Criminal Tribunal for the Former Yugoslavia* (Groningen: Europa Law Publishing, 2005), 139.
[90] D'Ascoli, *Sentencing in International Criminal Law*, 259; R. D. D. Sloane, 'Sentencing for the "Crime of Crimes": The Evolving "Common Law" of Sentencing of the International Criminal Tribunal for Rwanda' (2007) 5(3) *JICJ* 713.
[91] Holá, Bijleveld and Smeulers, 'Consistency of International Sentencing', 546.
[92] Holá, Smeulers and Bijleveld, 'International Sentencing Facts and Figures', 424.
[93] D'Ascoli, *Sentencing in International Criminal Law*, 259.

are up to fourteen years longer than those of 'low-ranking' offenders.[94] Discrepancies between institutions may be partly explained by situational differences. The higher average sentence of the ICTR may be partly explained by the fact that it entered more convictions for genocide.[95] The high average sentence of the SCSL (38.6 years) results from the focus on leadership responsibility and the fact the 'SCSL could not hand down any life sentences and thus relied on long determinate sentences for those most culpable'.[96] A fully harmonized practice might neither be realistic nor desirable, given the differences across atrocity crime situations.[97] However, it would be helpful to provide further indicators for possible sentencing ranges of crimes.[98]

A popular complaint is that sentences are too lenient.[99] International courts and tribunals are said to apply ordinary sentences to extraordinary crimes.[100] This critique is superficial. The appropriateness of sanctions cannot be measured simply by the length of sentences. It rather depends on the approach towards punishment and sentencing goals.[101] The fact that international sentences may in some instances be lower than domestic sentences may appear unjust from a strictly retributive perspective. It becomes less important, however, if the essence of punishment is seen in the expression of moral condemnation, the stigma associated with public proceedings, the reaffirmation of globally accepted norms and the educative functions of trials.

What needs to be improved is the reasoning underlying sentencing. Existing decisions leave it unclear how general and case-specific sentencing factors are connected to specific years of imprisonment. It is thus important to develop a clearer taxonomy of sentencing ranges. Further guidance may be drawn from domestic systems.

5.1.5   The Role of Plea Bargaining

It is disputed to what extent defendants should be able to negotiate punishment in return for an acknowledgment of guilt. In many common law systems plea bargaining is a popular means to limit submissions by parties and avoid lengthy trials. For instance, in the US most criminal cases are solved through a guilty plea or a plea agreement by the parties. Inquisitorial systems are more hostile to this practice. They limit it to specific types of crimes (e.g. non-violent crimes), attach strict conditions to its validity and submit it to greater judicial scrutiny.

---

[94] Holá, Bijleveld and Smuelers, 'Consistency of International Sentencing', 546.
[95] Ibid., 549.
[96] Smeulers, Hola and van den Berg, 'Sixty-Five Years of International Criminal Justice', 22.
[97] In favour of greater consistency, see D. B. Pickard, 'Proposed Sentencing Guidelines for the International Criminal Court' (1997) 20 *Loyola of Los Angeles International and Comparative Law Review* 124.
[98] Ambos, *Treatise on International Criminal Law, Vol. II*, 303–304.
[99] Stover has argued that 'short – one might even say mind-bogglingly short – prison sentences have clearly embittered many witnesses towards the ICTY'. See E. Stover, *The Witnesses: War Crimes and the Promise of Justice in The Hague* (2007), 142. See also Ohlin, 'Towards a Unique Theory of International Criminal Sentencing', 381, 390.
[100] For discussion, see deGuzman, 'Harsh Justice for International Crimes', 2.
[101] Henham, 'Developing Contextualized Rationales', 775–776.

In international criminal law, the space of plea bargaining is contested. Originally, the Rules of the ad hoc tribunals did not contain provisions on plea bargains. The idea of 'negotiating' justice and punishment sits uneasily with the nature of international crimes, the multiple purposes of international criminal proceedings and the concerns of victims. It has only been accepted under strict conditions. As Judge Schomburg put it, any such promises, 'can not result in *de facto* granting partial amnesty/impunity by the Prosecutor, particularly not in an institution established to avoid impunity'.[102] Today, most international criminal courts and tribunals admit the possibility of plea bargaining, based on certain conditions.[103] Both the ICTY and the ICTR have accepted plea agreements leading to potential withdrawal of charges and sentencing discounts.[104] Judges are not bound by them however. This makes them acceptable to advocates and critics. The ICC does not follow the common law-oriented guilty plea model, but recognizes 'admissions of guilt'.[105]

Such procedures require a balancing of conflicting considerations. Plea agreements or admissions of guilt have undeniable benefits. They may provide prosecutors with insider knowledge, expedite proceedings, save testimony and resources.[106] They provide an incentive to defendants to publicly acknowledge their wrongdoing. This may be crucial to reconcile defendants with their deeds and society as a whole, or to challenge revisionist accounts of history. Such an approach also has costs, however. It may limit the potential scope and truth-finding process of the trial. For instance, the guilty plea in *Al Mahdi* may have encouraged judges not to address controversial issues relating to protection of cultural property, such as the scope of protection of cultural property (e.g. movable cultural property),[107] the nexus to armed conflict or the relevance of 'military necessity'. It also carries risks of abuse, since the motives of defendants and expressions of remorse are difficult to control. These factors may effectively reduce accountability and compromise the demonstration effect and educative functions of trials.

The ICC Statute seeks to accommodate these concerns through a *sui generis* construction. It allows admissions of guilt, but leaves room for additional presentation of evidence to support the facts of the case.[108]

In practice, the number of guilty pleas has differed across tribunals. Overall, the range of cases is limited. At the ad hoc tribunals they initially enjoyed some prominence.[109] Over time, the enthusiasm has waned. There is no clear rule as to what extent

---

[102] *Prosecutor v. Deronjić*, IT-02–61-S, Sentencing Judgment, 30 March 2004, Dissenting Opinion Judge Schomburg, para. 11.

[103] See N. Combs, *Guilty Pleas in International Criminal Law: Constructing a Restorative Justice Approach* (Stanford: Stanford University Press, 2006).

[104] The ICTY recorded twenty plea agreements.

[105] On the difference, see Ambos, *Treatise on International Criminal Law, Vol. III*, 434–445.

[106] See *Al Mahdi* Trial Judgment, para. 28.

[107] Y. Gottlieb, 'Criminalizing Destruction of Cultural Property: A Proposal for Defining New Crimes Under the Rome Statute of the ICC' (2005) 23 *Penn State International Law Review* 857, 866.

[108] Art. 65 ICC Statute. The Court used this for the first time in the *Al Mahdi* case.

[109] N. Jørgensen, 'The Genocide Acquittal in the Sikirica Case Before the International Criminal Tribunal for the Former Yugoslavia and the Coming of Age of the Guilty Plea' (2002) 15 *LJIL* 407.

a guilty plea benefits the defendant. It is generally accepted as a mitigating factor. The ICTY held that it 'should, in principle, give rise to a reduction in the sentence that the accused would otherwise have received'.[110] However, there is no guarantee. At both ad hoc tribunals some defendants received high sentences (e.g. life imprisonment, forty years) despite a guilty plea.[111] The 'sentencing discount' varies.[112] Chambers have departed from recommendations by the Prosecution.[113] There is scepticism as to whether they have a conciliatory effect. As Dragan Nikolić, commander of the Serb-run Sušica Detention Camp, argued in his guilty plea statement: 'mere words are not enough. Acts are needed'.[114]

5.1.6   Review of Sentence and Early Release

One factor which may affect the perception of sentencing is early release. In many domestic jurisdictions, defendants are allowed to apply for parole after serving two-thirds of their sentence. International criminal courts and tribunals rely on domestic states to enforce sentences. They retain supervisor power over enforcement and typically allow for a possibility to review sentences. The conditions under which early release may be justified in the context of international crimes are contested.

The ad hoc tribunals have initially applied different standards. At the ICTR, convicts were granted early release after having served three-quarters of their sentence.[115] The ICTY adopted a two-thirds rule, in light of the fact that many enforcement jurisdictions apply that standard.[116] This became the rule at the International Residual Mechanism for Criminal Tribunals (MICT) which dealt with the remaining cases. In 2012, MICT President Theodor Meron decided that 'all convicts supervised by the Mechanism should be considered eligible for early release upon the completion of two-thirds of their sentences, irrespective of the tribunal that convicted them'.[117] He argued that equal treatment was required by the *lex mitior* principle, i.e. the 'retro-active applicability of a more lenient criminal law to crimes committed and sentences imposed before the law's enactment'.[118] The decision noted that the completion of two-thirds of the sentence does not automatically entail early release.[119] In MICT

---

[110] *Prosecutor* v. *Todorović*, Case No. IT-95-9/1-S, Sentencing Judgment, 31 July 2001, para. 80.

[111] Jean Kambanda was convicted to life imprisonment despite a guilty plea. See *Prosecutor* v. *Kambanda*, ICTR 97-23-S, Judgment and Sentence, 4 September 1998, 28. Goran Jelisić was sentenced to forty years' imprisonment, although he pleaded guilty to thirty-one counts. See *Prosecutor* v. *Jelisić*, IT-95-10-A, Judgment, 5 July 2001, 41.

[112] Holá, Smeulers and Bijleveld, 'International Sentencing Facts and Figures', 434.

[113] See e.g. *Prosecutor* v. *Babić*, IT-03-72-A, Judgment on Sentence Appeal, 18 July 2005, paras. 29–33.

[114] Guilty Plea Statement Dragan Nikolić, 6 November 2003, at www.icty.org/en/content/dragan-nikoli%C4%87.

[115] *Prosecutor* v. *Muvunyi*, ICTR-OO-59A-T, Decision on Tharcie Muvuyni's Application for Early Release, 6 March 2012, para. 12 (*Muvunyi* Early Release Decision).

[116] *Prosecutor* v. *Dragan Zelenović*, IT-96-23/2-ES, Decision of President on Early Release of Dragan Zelenovic, 30 November 2012, para. 14; *Prosecutor* v. *Martinović*, IT-98-34-ES, Decision of the President on Early Release of Vinko Martinović, 16 December 2011, para.12.

[117] *Prosecutor* v. *Bisengimana*, MICT-12-07, Decision of President on Early Release of Paul Bisengimana, 11 December 2012, para. 20.

[118] Ibid.

[119] Ibid., para. 19.

practice, the two-thirds standard turned de facto into a presumption of release.[120] The Mechanism considered four criteria: the gravity of the crimes, the treatment of similarly situated prisoners, the defendant's demonstration of rehabilitation, as well as any substantial cooperation of the prisoner with the Prosecutor. The argument adopted was somewhat circular. In many cases, early release was justified based on signs of rehabilitation or comparison to other defendants. This justification overlooks the partly distinctive nature of international crimes.[121] The crimes of many perpetrators of international crimes are driven by context-related factors. Convicted persons often conform to detention requirements, have good prospects of reintegration and lack the means to re-commit offences once the underlying context has changed. Rehabilitation thus may not be a decisive criterion, or work differently than in relation to ordinary crimes.[122]

The application of the two-thirds standard of early release has been criticized. It amounts in fact to an 'unconditional reduction or commutation of the sentence', since international criminal courts and tribunals have limited 'means to supervise convicted persons on parole or to react if conditions for early release are being violated'.[123] It led to the release of defendants who did not show any remorse or other favourable factors that establish a change of circumstance post-conviction, such as new information, or cooperation with the Prosecutor after sentencing. Cynics claim that early release was partly driven by cost-related concerns.

The early release of ICTR genocide convicts by MICT raised concerns among survivors and the Rwandan government. A presumption of unconditional early release sits uneasily with the alleged gravity of international crimes and reinforces bias in relation to lenient sentencing. It may conflict with some of the underlying goals of international criminal law, including expressivist considerations in sentencing. As Prosecutor Serge Brammertz has argued, a more nuanced and substantiated assessment, including consideration of potential conditions, may be more feasible to avoid perception problems: 'There are many countries where early release is more of a conditional release where it is linked to a number of conditions to be imposed and a number of actors of the judicial process like victims or prosecutor are consulted before a decision is taken'.[124] At the ICC, the decision on early release is subject to additional constraints. Early release is possible after two-thirds of the sentence, or twenty-five years in the case of life imprisonment.[125] However, it requires a decision by three judges. The test is more demanding. 'Genuine dissociation' from the crime is an express criterion. Judges are mandated to take into account whether early release

---

[120] For a critique, see J. Choi, 'Early Release in International Criminal Law' (2014) 123 *Yale Law Journal* 1784.
[121] Ibid., 1817.
[122] J. M. Kelder, B. Holá and J. van Wijk, 'Rehabilitation and Early Release of Perpetrators of International Crimes: A Case Study of the ICTY and ICTR' (2014) 14 *International Criminal Law Review* 1177, 1197.
[123] *Muvunyi* Early Release Decision, para. 11.
[124] N. Bishumba, 'UN Prosecutor Faults Early Release of Genocide Convicts', *The New Times*, 16 February 2017, at www.newtimes.co.rw/section/read/208051/.
[125] Art. 110 (3) ICC Statute.

'would give rise to significant social instability', as well as 'any impact on the victims and their families'.[126] In *Lubanga*, judges denied early release, partly because the defendant had not 'acknowledge[d] his own culpability for conscripting and enlisting children under the age of fifteen years old and using them to participate actively in hostilities or express[ed] remorse or regret to the victims of the crimes for which he was convicted'.[127] It is necessary to distinguish pre-conviction and post-conviction criteria and to develop a fuller theory as to why sentences should be reduced in the absence of a change of circumstances.[128]

5.2   Repairing Harm

Trials contain multiple features that have reparative effects: the revelation of atrocities, acknowledgement of responsibility and clarification of facts. Some courts, like the ICC or the Extraordinary Chambers in the Courts of Cambodia, combine the criminal process with reparation to victims. Providing reparation is arguably 'the most victim-centered of the various approaches to fighting impunity'.[129]

The trend to combine a criminal trial with remedies for victims is relatively novel in international justice. It is grounded in the increasing recognition of the right to reparation under international law.[130]

5.2.1   Foundations

In human rights law, reparation is regarded as a key element of the right to an effective remedy for violations. States have a duty to provide reparation for victims of human rights violations. Several international treaties mandate states to include provisions on compensation[131] or reparation[132] for victims in their domestic law. Regional courts, such as the European and the Inter-American Court of Human Rights have developed a rich jurisprudence on state obligations.[133] The

---

[126] See Rule 223 (c) and (d) of the ICC Rules of Procedure and Evidence.
[127] *Prosecutor* v. *Lubanga*, ICC-01/04/01/06, Decision on the review concerning reduction of sentence of Mr Thomas Lubanga Dyilo, 22 September 2015, para. 46.
[128] Choi, 'Early Release in International Criminal Law', 1827.
[129] R. Carranza, 'The Right to Reparations in Situations of Poverty', ICTJ Briefing, September 2009, 4.
[130] L. Zegveld, 'Victims' Reparations Claims and International Criminal Courts: Incompatible Values?' (2010) 8 *JICJ* 79; C. Mc Carthy, *Reparations and Victim Support in the International Criminal Court* (Cambridge: Cambridge University Press, 2014); C. Mc Carthy, 'The Rome Statute's Regime of Victim Redress': Challenges and Prospects', in Stahn, *Law and Practice of the International Criminal Court*, 1203; A. Durbach and L. Chappell, 'Leaving Behind the Age of Impunity: Victims of Gender Violence and the Promise of Reparations' (2014) 6 *International Feminist Journal of Politics* 543.
[131] See e.g. Art. 14 (1) of the Convention against Torture ('enforceable right to fair and adequate Compensation'), Art. 6 (6) of the Palermo Protocol.
[132] See e.g. Art. 24 (4) and (5) of the International Convention for the Protection of All Persons from Enforced Disappearance.
[133] See J. M. Pasqualucci, 'Victim Reparations in the Inter-American Human Rights System: A Critical Assessment of Current Practice and Procedure' (1996) 18 *Michigan Journal of International Law* 1.

Inter-American Court was pioneering in awarding reparation to entire communities for human rights violations.[134]

Parties in armed conflicts must pay compensation for violations of international humanitarian law. This is specified in the 1907 Hague Convention regarding the Law and Customs of War[135] and Additional Protocol I to the Geneva Conventions.[136] The wording of these provisions leaves it unclear to what extent reparation can be directly claimed by victims, or what mechanisms should be used to pursue such claims. Some authorities claim that they provide an avenue for individual claims,[137] while others argue that they are geared towards states.[138] In practice, individual claims for violations have mostly been recognized through specific claims commissions. In its Advisory Opinion on the Construction of the Wall in the Occupied Palestinian Territory the ICJ recognized that states may have a duty to compensate individuals for violations of international law, including international humanitarian law.[139] However, the scope of such a duty remains contested. In *Germany* v. *Italy*, the Court noted that

against the background of a century of practice in which almost every peace treaty or post-war settlement has involved either a decision not to require the payment of reparations or the use of lump sum settlements and set-offs, it is difficult to see that international law contains a rule requiring the payment of full compensation to each and every individual victim as a rule accepted by the international community of States as a whole.[140]

The idea that duties of reparation arise not only in the relationship between individuals and states, but also in the relationship between individuals is enshrined in specific UN documents, such as the UN Basic Principles and Guidelines on the Right to a Remedy and Reparation for Victims. The Basic Principles state that natural or legal persons are liable to provide reparation for harm caused to victims of 'gross violations' of international human rights law and 'serious violations' of international humanitarian law. In a few cases victims have sued individual perpetrators, like *Karadžić*, through civil litigation in foreign courts.[141] Practice remains scarce, however.

---

[134] See IACtHR, *Case of the Plan de Sánchez Massacre* v. *Guatemala*, Judgment, 19 November 2004, paras. 86 et seq.

[135] Art. 3.

[136] Art. 91.

[137] F. Kalshoven, 'State Responsibility for Warlike Acts of the Armed Forces: From Article 3 of Hague Convention IV of 1907 to Article 91 of Additional Protocol I of 1977 and Beyond' (1991) 40 *ICLQ* 827, 830 (arguing that 'delegates sought not so much to lay down a rule relating to the inter- national responsibility of one State vis-a-vis another, as one relating to a State's liability to compensate the losses of individual persons incurred as a consequence of their direct (and harmful) contact with its armed forces').

[138] See C. Tomuschat, 'State Responsibility and the Individual Right to Compensation Before National Courts', in A. Clapham and P. Gaeta (eds.), *Oxford Handbook of International Law in Armed Conflict* (Oxford: Oxford University Press, 2014), 811, 821–828.

[139] ICJ, *Legal Consequences of the Construction of a Wall in Occupied Palestinian Territory*, 9 July 2004, para. 153 ('Israel also has an obligation to compensate, in accordance with the applicable rules of international law, all natural or legal persons having suffered any form of material damage as a result of the wall's construction').

[140] ICJ, Jurisdictional Immunities of the State (*Germany* v. *Italy: Greece Intervening*), 3 February 2012, para. 94.

[141] See United States District Court for the Southern District of New York, 93 Civ. 878, *Doe et al.* v. *Karadžić*, Judgment, 4 October 2000, https://ccrjustice.org/sites/default/files/assets/files/Chapter%2021.pdf. The District Court Judge ordered Karadžić to pay US$4.5 billion in damages. On the problems of collective action in relation to the Alien Torts Claims Statute, see M. G. Perl, 'Not Just Another Mass Tort: Using Class Actions to Redress International Human Rights Violations' (2000) 88 *Georgetown Law Journal* 773.

In transitional justice, there is a trend to argue that reparations should not only seek to remedy a status quo, i.e. to correct wrong, but to transform the experiences of individuals who have suffered from harm.[142] For instance, the 2007 Nairobi Declaration on Women's and Girls' Right to a Remedy and Reparation states that 'Reparation must go above and beyond the immediate reasons and consequences of the crimes and violations; they must aim to address the political and structural inequalities that negatively shape women's and girls' lives'.[143] This argument recognizes the reality that the restoration of the status *quo ante* is often no viable option in contexts where massive or systemic repression of marginalized groups has become the norm rather than the exception.[144]

Pursuing reparation directly through a criminal process is relatively novel at the international level. It may be explained by several considerations. Some of them are legal, others are policy-oriented. They encompass the increased attention to victims' rights in criminal procedure, including the idea of a 'right to reparation', the unique fact-finding powers of the criminal process, and the ambition to extend options for enforcement beyond domestic courts,[145] specific mass claims mechanisms[146] or regional human rights courts. Linking reparation to criminal proceedings mitigates in particular the critique that reparations are a convenient way to 'pay off' victims of crimes.

The adjudication of reparations by international criminal courts and tribunals compensates partly for the lack of reparation by state authority.[147] It is particularly important in relation to violations by non-state actors, which often remain without remedy. Its function is limited. In a criminal process, adjudication of victims' claims remains an annex function to the process of judgment. The award of reparations serves at least three important functions from a justice perspective.[148] Reparations introduce a new type of responsibility. The offender is not only held accountable for the crimes through a public process, but faces direct responsibility of the offender towards victims (principle of responsibility). The second important feature is the

---

[142] Committee on the Elimination of Discrimination against Women, 'General Recommendation No. 30 on Women in Conflict Prevention, Conflict and Post-Conflict Situations', UN Doc. CEDAW/C/GC/30, 1 November 2013, para. 79.

[143] Nairobi Declaration on Women's and Girls' Right to a Remedy and Reparation, March 2007, para. 3H. See generally V. Couillard, 'The Nairobi Declaration: Redefining Reparation for Women Victims of Sexual Violence' (2007) 1 *International Journal of Transitional Justice* 444; R. Rubin-Marín, 'The Gender of Reparations in Transitional Societies', in R. Rubin-Marín (ed.), *The Gender of Reparations: Unsettling Sexual Hierarchies While Redressing Human Rights Violations* (Cambridge: Cambridge University Press, 2009), 63, 66.

[144] See M. Urban, Walker 'Transformative Reparations? A Critical Look at a Current Trend in Thinking about Gender-Just Reparations' (2016) 10 *International Journal of Transitional Justice* 108, 116.

[145] On civil jurisdiction, see D. F. Donovan and A. Roberts, 'The Emerging Recognition of Universal Civil Jurisdiction' (2006) 100 *AJIL* 142.

[146] M. Henzelin, V. Heiskanen and G. Mettraux, 'Reparations to Victims Before the International Criminal Court: Lessons from International Mass Claims Processes' (2006) 17 *Criminal Law Forum* 317.

[147] In the *Habré* case, the government of Chad presented itself as a victim and requested to participate in proceedings before the Extraordinary Chambers as a civil party. It argued that Habré had taken funds from the treasury. The request was rejected, however, since Chad was not a party to proceedings. See Sperfeldt, 'The Trial against Hissène Habré', 1253.

[148] P. Dixon, 'Reparations, Assistance and the Experience of Justice: Lessons from Colombia and the Democratic Republic of the Congo' (2016) 10 *International Journal of Transitional Justice* 88, 95 et seq.

recognition of harm. Reparations recognize victims as holders of rights and the individual harm they have suffered (principle of recognition).[149] Third, reparations have a certain redistributive effect that is otherwise lacking in the criminal process. They provide not only symbolic, but also certain material benefits to victims of crime (principle of distribution).

5.2.2 Approaches towards Reparation

Domestic courts or specific civil mass claim mechanisms are typically the main forum for reparation claims. International criminal courts and tribunals have a complementary role. Many domestic jurisdictions allow civil plaintiffs to join a criminal case to seek reparation. In international law, this is still the exception. There are different approaches towards reparation.

In the context of the UN ad hoc tribunals, the SCSL or the Special Tribunal for Lebanon reparation was neglected.[150] It was essentially left to domestic courts. Victims were deemed to use a certified copy of the judgment to seek compensation through national courts or other competent bodies. The reasons for this approach differ. In the case of the ICTY and the ICTR it was feared that reparation would divert attention from the core mandate of the ad hoc tribunals[151] and prolong proceedings.[152] In the context of the SCSL and STL, the focus on domestic jurisdiction may be explained by the hybrid nature of the courts. This choice has been criticized for prioritizing retributive justice over reparative justice.[153] Obtaining a reparation award through domestic courts is often illusory in states affected by conflict.

The role of international criminal courts and tribunals to remedy harm to victims evolved gradually. There are at least two major models: a civil model and a criminal model.

In the 'civil model', adjudication of reparation is essentially an annex to criminal proceedings. For instance, before the ECCC, victims were allowed to act as civil parties in the criminal process, based on the domestic legal tradition.[154] The forms of

---

[149] N. Roht-Arriaza and K. Orlovsky, 'A Complementary Relationship: Reparations and Development', in P. de Greiff and R. Duthie (eds.), *Transitional Justice and Development: Making Connections* (New York: Social Science Research Council, 2009), 172, 179.

[150] F. Mégret, 'Justifying Compensation by the International Criminal Court's Victims Trust Fund: Lessons from Domestic Compensation Schemes' (2010) 36 *Brooklyn Journal of International Law* 124, 137 ('At best, victims who also happened to be witnesses (a very small minority) were eligible for some degree of protection and assistance before, during, and to a lesser extent, after their testimony').

[151] See V. Morris and M. Scharf, *An Insider's Guide to the International Criminal Tribunal for the Former Yugoslavia* (Irvington-on-Hudson, NY: Transnational Publishers, 1995), 283–289.

[152] Judges argued that 'it would result in a significant increase in the workload of the Chambers and would further increase the length and complexity of trials'. See letter dated 12 October 2000 from the President of the International Tribunal for the Former Yugoslavia addressed to the Secretary-General, UN.Doc. S/2000/1063, 3 November 2000.

[153] Findlay and Henham, *Transforming International Criminal Justice*, 283.

[154] For an account, see J. Herman, 'Realities of Victim Participation: The Civil Party System in Practice at the Extraordinary Chambers in the Courts of Cambodia' (2013) 16 *Contemporary Justice Review* 461.

reparation were limited. Chambers were allowed to award collective and moral reparations to civil parties, but no direct monetary payments.[155] In the *Habré* case, victims were allowed to participate as civil parties and receive individual reparation.[156]

The ICC framework expanded the ambit of reparative justice in the criminal process. It is the most comprehensive reparation regime in international criminal justice.[157] Reparation is an integral part of criminal proceedings and subject to specialized reparation proceedings involving victims and the defendant. It is in many ways a novel model[158] which combines retributive and restorative features. Accountability is grounded in the obligation to repair harm, but linked to the punitive dimensions of justice, such as conviction and the culpability for criminal acts. Reparations themselves are meant to be remedial, rather than punitive.[159] Drafters of the Statute excluded a provision 'empowering the Court to make a reparations order against a State in the event that the convicted person is unable fulfil the order him or herself'.[160]

The ICC regime is neither a pure replication of criminal responsibility nor a classical form of human rights accountability. It foresees two mechanisms: formal determinations of reparations against a convicted person by the Trial Chamber and measures of assistance to victims by the Trust Fund for Victims. The two categories differ fundamentally.[161]

Reparations against the convicted person are judicial in nature. They can be material, symbolic, individual or collective.[162] They are determined by an order of the Trial Chamber against the defendant. The modalities were clarified by a landmark decision of the Appeals Chamber in *Lubanga*. Lubanga was indigent. The Appeals Chamber made it clear that the establishment of accountability towards victims through reparation proceedings is an asset per se, even in cases where the defendant is indigent.[163] It specified that the liability for reparations needs to be established

---

[155] Rule 23 *quinquies* provides that if an accused is convicted, 'the Chambers may award only collective and moral reparations to Civil Parties'.

[156] Chambre Africaine Extraordinaire d'Assises d'Appel, Le Procureur Général c. Hissein Habré, Arrêt, 27 April 2017.

[157] L. Moffett, 'Elaborating Justice for Victims at the International Criminal Court: Beyond Rhetoric and The Hague' (2015) 13 *JICJ* 281–311.

[158] See C. Stahn, 'Reparative Justice after the Lubanga Appeal Judgment: New Prospects for Expressivism and Participatory Justice or "Juridified Victimhood" by Other Means?' (2015) 13 *JICJ* 801, 806.

[159] *Prosecutor* v. *Katanga*, ICC-01/04–01/07 A3 A4 A5, Judgment on the appeals against the order of Trial Chamber II of 24 March 2017 entitled 'Order for Reparations Pursuant to Article 75 of the Statute', 8 March 2018, para. 185 (*Katanga* Reparations Appeal).

[160] *Katanga* Reparations Appeal, para. 189. The Preparatory Committee Draft Statute contained a provision enabling the ICC to make an order or recommend 'that an appropriate form of reparations to, or in respect of, victims, including restitution, compensation and rehabilitation, be made by a State'. Proposal by France and the United Kingdom of Great Britain, A/AC.249/1998/WG.4/DP.19, 10 February 1998. See also *Prosecutor* v. *Lubanga*, ICC-01/04–01/06–3129, Judgment on the appeals against the 'Decision establishing the principles and procedures to be applied to reparations' of 7 August 2012, 3 March 2015, para. 105 (*Lubanga* Appeal Reparation).

[161] Moffett, *Justice for Victims before the International Criminal Court*, 147 ('[R]esponsibility for reparations distinguishes such measures from charity or humanitarian assistance by achieving some form of accountability').

[162] See Art. 75 ICC Statute, Rule 97 of the ICC Rules of Procedure and Evidence.

[163] *Lubanga* Appeal Reparation, para. 104 ('[I]ndigence at the time when the Trial Chamber issues an order for reparations is not an obstacle to imposing liability because the order may be implemented when the monitoring of the financial situation of the person sentenced reveals that he or she has the means to comply with the order').

separately in each case, in addition to conviction. It held that the Trial Chamber must clearly define the harm caused, establish causality, identify the modalities of reparations and specify the victims eligible.[164] These determinations cannot be delegated to non-judicial organs, such as the Trust Fund or the Registrar. This implies that reparation is a central feature of the ICC process. It is more detailed and judicialized than alternative mechanisms promoting dialogue between perpetrators and victims, such as victim/offender mediation.

Standards of proofs are more relaxed than at trial, due to the 'fundamentally different nature of reparation proceedings' and the potential 'difficulty victims may face in obtaining evidence'.[165] Causality does not have to be established 'beyond reasonable doubt'. It requires merely 'sufficient proof of the causal link' between the crime and harm suffered, which needs to be assessed 'in light of the specific circumstances of the case'.[166] Resources for reparations stem from different sources: fines or forfeiture of proceeds, property and assets derived directly or indirectly from the crimes of the perpetrator, potential earnings after conviction and enforcement of the sentence, and general resources of the ICC Trust Fund for Victims, which is supported by voluntary financial contributions.

Reparations from the convicted person are distinct from general assistance measures by the Trust Fund. Such measures are more 'need-based'.[167] They are, to some extent, a 'corrective to the limitations of retributive justice'.[168] They are meant to provide an immediate response to victims and their communities. They are not dependent on prosecutorial charges, accountability of a specific defendant or conviction but open to victims of 'crimes' falling in the jurisdiction of the Court. They are decided by the Board of Directors of the Trust Fund, in consultation with a relevant Pre-Trial Chamber,[169] and based on the needs of victims and available funds. The Trust Fund used this assistance mandate, for instance, to provide physical and psychological rehabilitation for victims in the situations in DRC and northern Uganda, including reconstructive surgery for mutilated women and children and individual and group-based trauma counselling.[170] Such assistance is financed

---

[164] It held that a judicial reparation order must contain at least five 'essential elements: (i) it must be directed against the convicted person; (ii) it must establish and inform the convicted person of his or her liability; (iii) it must specify, and provide reasons for, the type of reparations ordered, (iv) it must define the harm caused to victims as a result of the crimes for which the person was convicted, and 5) it must identify the victims who are eligible to benefit from reparations, or at least eligibility criteria. Ibid., para. 1.

[165] *Prosecutor v. Lubanga*, Order for Reparations, ICC-01/04–01/06–3129-AnxA, Appeals Chamber, 3 March 2015, para. 22.

[166] Ibid.

[167] Dixon, 'Reparations, Assistance and the Experience of Justice', 90 ('Assistance ... is a broader term that can refer to any number of measures provided in response not to injuries, but to needs, and can stem from development projects, humanitarian relief, aid initiatives, state subsidies and more').

[168] F. Mégret, 'Justifying Compensation by the International Criminal Court's Victims Trust Fund', 143.

[169] See Rule 98 (5) of the ICC Rules of Procedure and Evidence and Regulation 50 (a) of the Regulations of the Trust Fund.

[170] For a survey of projects carried in the DRC, Uganda and Ivory Coast, see Trust Fund for Victims, 'Assistance programmes', at www.trustfundforvictims.org/en/what-we-do/assistance-programmes.

through the resources of the Trust Fund. The main difference to reparations is that assistance is not provided in recognition of legal responsibility.

5.2.3   *Modalities and Forms of Reparation*

One of the main dilemmas of reparation in atrocity crime situations is that need and demand exceeds capacity. The UN Basic Principles promote 'adequate, effective and prompt reparation'.[171] Full and effective reparation should be provided 'as appropriate and proportional to the gravity of the violation and the circumstances of each case'.[172] There is thus a necessary degree of discretion.[173] Victims often associate reparations with individual material benefits. It is virtually impossible to provide full reparation, *restitution in integrum*. States in which crimes have occurred are often unable to support national reparation programmes. The resources available to international institutions are limited. In certain contexts, such as the case against Jean-Pierre Bemba, the former Vice-President of the DRC, the ICC has seized bank accounts, real estate and property for purposes of reparation. In the *Habré* proceedings, the Extraordinary African Chambers seized two bank accounts as well as a house in Senegal. In many cases, however, defendants are indigent. The budget of the ICC Trust Fund amounted to around €11 million in 2017 – for all ICC situations, including assistance measures and implementation of reparation awards.[174] This makes it necessary to apply a broad variety of modalities and forms of reparation.

In general, there are three main forms: restitution, that is restoration of the original situation of the victim before the violation (e.g. return to family, home and previous employment, return of property, education); compensation for economically assessable damage; and rehabilitation, such as provision of medical services and health care. These three forms of reparation are geared towards material benefit.[175] However, it is necessary to consider a fuller range of reparation measures available. This includes satisfaction, such as public statements, formal apologies, renaming of public spaces or memorials, and guarantees of non-repetition which are deemed to prevent a return to violence.[176] These measures may be as important as material benefits, or the only option given the resource constraints. For instance, in Case 001 the Trial Chamber in Cambodia found that the publication of statements of apology or expressions of

---

[171] Basic Principles and Guidelines on the Right to a Remedy and Reparation for Victims of Gross Violations of International Human Rights Law and Serious Violations of International Humanitarian Law, UN Doc. A/RES/60/147, I (2) (c).

[172] Ibid., Principle 18.

[173] The ICC Trust has argued that 'there is a margin of appreciation which authorizes departure from the principle of restitution in integrum towards providing "fair and adequate reparation"'. See ICC Trust Fund, ICC-01/04–01/06, Observations on Reparations in Response to the Scheduling Order of 14 March 2012, 25 April 2012, para. 79 (Trust Fund Observations Scheduling Order).

[174] See Report to the Assembly of States Parties on the projects and the activities of the Board of Directors of the Trust Fund for Victims for the period 1 July 2016 to 30 June 2017, ICC-ASP/16/14, 21 August 2017, 2.

[175] Curiously, satisfaction or non-repetition are not mentioned in the ICC context.

[176] See F. Mégret, 'The International Criminal Court Statute and the Failure to Mention Symbolic Reparation' (2009) 16 *International Review of Victimology* 127, 132 et seq.

remorse during the trial was 'the only tangible means by which [the accused] could acknowledge his responsibility and the collective suffering of victims'.[177] It included the names of all civil parties and their deceased relatives in the judgment and the publication of all statements of apology or acknowledgement of responsibility by the convicted person.[178]

There is a strong need to consider collective forms of reparation, i.e. reparations that benefit a larger collectivity of victims.[179] These include different types of measures: reparations which benefit a community as such ('community reparations')[180] and collective reparations which provide individual benefits to members of the group.[181] Such an approach has a compelling criminological explanation. International crimes are typically collective crimes carried out against specific groups or collectivities. In light of this, it makes sense to repair harm to individuals as members of targeted collectivities. This might include victims of gender-based violations, or populations of an affected area, such as villages or members of an indigenous community.[182] Approaching reparation through the lens of individual rights and entitlements is not always helpful.[183] Collective reparation is particularly relevant in cultural contexts where the role of the individuals is closely tied to the role of collectivities, such as families, communities and their environment.[184] Reparative practices might be most effective if they transform specific narratives, biases or communal relations. For instance, sexual and gender-based violence is often grounded in collective beliefs about male sexual entitlement and female subordination or biases in relation to masculinity and gender. Reparations may not be able to fully eliminate the structural causes of such violence, but they can challenge such stereotypes. For instance, 'collective measures that honour survivors of sexual violence may both diminish stigmatization within a community as well as encourage victims to speak openly about their experiences'.[185] The ICC framework recognizes this need. It specifies that collective reparation should be awarded when 'it is impossible or impracticable to make individual awards directly to each victim'.[186]

---

[177] *Duch* Trial Judgment, para. 668.

[178] C. Sperfeldt, 'Collective Reparations at the Extraordinary Chambers in the Courts of Cambodia' (2012) 12 *International Criminal Law Review* 457–489.

[179] F. Mégret, 'The Case for Collective Reparations before the International Criminal Court', in J.-A. Wemmers (ed.), *Reparations for Victims of Crimes against Humanity* (London: Routledge, 2014), 171.

[180] *Prosecutor* v. *Katanga*, ICC-01/04–01/07, Order for Reparations Pursuant to Article 75 of the Statute, 24 March 2017, para. 279.

[181] *Katanga* Reparation Order, para. 280.

[182] Ibid., para. 273.

[183] E. L. Camins, 'Needs or Rights? Exploring the Limitations of Individual Reparations for Violations of International Humanitarian Law' (2016) 10 *International Journal of Transitional Justice* 126.

[184] For a caveat, see Guidance Note of the Secretary-General, 'Reparations for Conflict-Related Sexual Violence', July 2014, 7 ('[C]ollective reparations may end-up benefitting more men than women, if they for example result into greater access to economic resources for the family or the community, where women traditionally do not control or have little access to such resources').

[185] Ibid., 7.

[186] Rule 98 of the ICC Rules of Procedure and Evidence.

The ICC adopted a broad approach in *Lubanga*. The Trial Chamber noted:

Reparations may include measures to address the shame felt by some former child soldiers, and to prevent any future victimisation, particularly when they endured sexual violence, torture and inhumane and degrading treatment following their recruitment ... [T]he Court's reparations strategy should, in part, be directed at preventing future conflicts and raising awareness that the effective reintegration of the children requires eradicating the victimisation, discrimination and stigmatisation of young people in these circumstances.[187]

It supported a community-based approach in light of the considerable number of people affected by the crimes and the limited number of individuals who have applied for reparations.[188] Jurisprudence has clarified that collective reparation is possible irrespective of whether the envisaged collectivity enjoys legal personality or specific group rights.[189] It includes education, memorials and health programmes for the benefit of victim populations. However, it should not be confused with basic services or general development programmes.[190]

A collective approach involves trade-offs in relation to 'meaningful reparation' for individuals. As Luke Moffett has observed:

victims become increasingly distant, shrinking objects in the rear view mirror as we move closer to tackling wider causes of violence, maximizing welfare or community benefits ... While in the Lubanga case transformative reparations may benefit female child soldiers who suffered sexual violence, by including them in rehabilitation or community, it negates the acknowledgement and more direct remedy of their individual harm.[191]

The need for collective reparation may contrast with requests for compensation. For instance, in the *Habré* case victims and survivors primarily sought compensation for their individual harm, even through symbolic payments.[192] As Souleymane Guengueng, the founder of the Association of Victims of Crimes of the *Habré* regime, noted: 'Money will never bring back my friends ... But money is important to heal the wounds, to take victims out of poverty, and to show that we have rights that must be recognised'.[193] Compensation is important from a restorative perspective. It may provide a means to show that the offender makes a contribution to repair harm caused to individuals. However, it raises difficult distributive challenges.[194] The restorative effect is limited. In the international context, direct offender–victim

---

[187] See *Prosecutor* v. *Lubanga*, ICC-01/04–01/06, 'Decision establishing the principles and procedures to be applied to reparations', 7 August 2012, para. 240.

[188] Ibid., para. 274.

[189] *Katanga* Reparation Order, para. 276.

[190] On the differences and the need for distinction, see Dixon, 'Reparations, Assistance and the Experience of Justice', 95 et seq.

[191] L. Moffett, 'Reparations for Victims at the International Criminal Court: A New Way Forward?' (2017) 2 *International Journal of Human Rights* 1204, 1213.

[192] See Sperfeld, 'The Trial against Hissène Habré: Networked Justice and Reparations at the Extraordinary African Chambers', 1252–1254.

[193] 'Hissène Habré Ordered to Pay Millions for Crimes against Humanity in Chad', *The Guardian*, 29 July 2016, www .theguardian.com/global-development/2016/jul/29/hissene-habre-compensation-90m-crimes-against-humanity-chad.

[194] C. L. Smith, 'Victim Compensation: Hard Questions and Suggested Remedies' (1986) *17 Rutgers Law Journal* 51.

reparation is the exception, rather than the rule, due to the context of the crimes. Funds are often provided through public channels, rather than the defendant. As cautioned in scholarship, 'Money changes the nature of dealing with victimization, connoting material and symbolic messages about the worth and deservingness of, and social solidarity with, the victim'.[195] A particular problem is to quantify individual harm. In the *Habré* case, 7,396 victims were recognized as civil parties. The Extraordinary African Chambers quantified the overall harm deriving from *Habré*'s criminal responsibility at approximately €124 million. Representatives of victims had argued that the Court should award compensation irrespective of the availability of funds at the time of the ruling. The Trial Chamber awarded each survivor of rape and sexual slavery approximately €30,489, each survivor of torture and arbitrary detention and each mistreated former prisoner of war €22,867, and family members of victims €15,244.[196] The Court recognized that the current assets of the defendant would not suffice to remedy the harm. It ordered that *Habré*'s financial situation be monitored, counted on recovery of future assets and invited the trust fund to work with victim associations for the realization of collective reparation. The quantification is thus largely symbolic. The award of collective reparation (e.g. education, memorials) faced severe challenges, since Chad failed to agree to assist in their implementation.[197]

The ICC has in general tried to acknowledge the individual victimization of victims in its reparation practice, and combined individual and collective reparations. It has adopted different approaches to the quantification of harm, depending on the nature and scope of crimes and the numbers of victims.

In the *Katanga* case, the ICC awarded individual reparations to victims for the first time. The Chamber first identified the number of victims eligible for reparation, namely 297 victims. It then determined the overall amount of reparations for the Bogoro attack (US$3.7 million). The Chamber determined the monetary value of the harm of all applicants for reparation based on an *ex aequo et bono* standard, in a document of over a thousand pages ('sum-total of the harm').[198] It then specified Katanga's individual liability in relation to the harm caused to eligible victims (US$1 million);[199] granted individual victims a symbolic compensation of US$250;[200] recognizing that this amount was not meant to indemnify damages in integrity, but rather was intended to enable victims to buy items for daily living or to start a small business.[201] It combined this symbolic compensation with collective reparation. This

---

[195] L. Moffett, 'Reparations for "Guilty Victims": Navigating Complex Identities of Victim-Perpetrators in Reparation Mechanisms' (2016) 10 *International Journal of Transitional Justice* 146, 166.

[196] See *Prosecutor* v. *Habré*, Judgment (Reparations), First Instance Chamber, 29 July 2016, para. 82, at http://forumchambresafricaines.org/docs/JugementCAEd'Assises_Penal&Civil_.pdf. See also N. I. Diab, 'Challenges in the Implementation of the Reparation Award against Hissein Habré' (2018) 16 *JICJ* 141–163.

[197] *Prosecutor* v. *Habré*, Appeal Judgment, 27 April 2017, paras. 868–869, at www.chambresafricaines.org/pdf/Arrêt_intégral.pdf.

[198] *Katanga* Reparation Order, paras. 32–33.

[199] Ibid., para. 264.

[200] It stressed that that 'the symbolic award is not intended as compensation for the harm in its entirety'. Katanga Reparation Order, para. 300.

[201] *Katanga* Reparation Order, para. 300.

methodology was, as the Appeals Chamber stated, 'time consuming, resource intensive and, in the end, disproportionate to what was achieved', since it required the Trial Chamber to 'analyse all individual applications in detail, only to then put a monetary value to the harm which did not reflect the reparations eventually awarded to the victims'.[202] It clarified that 'individual assessment of individual claims should only be done when there are very few applications',[203] since the 'primary consideration is the extent of the harm and the cost it takes to repair that harm'.[204]

In the *Al Mahdi* case, the Chamber had to quantify the harm caused by the attack on cultural property in Timbuktu. It conceded the attack affected the population in Mali, and the international community as a whole. However, it limited its assessment in the Reparation Order to consideration of 'harm suffered by or within the community of Timbuktu'.[205] It used expert opinions to quantify the damage caused to property, economic loss and moral harm; and held Al Mahdi 'liable for 2.7 million euros in expenses for individual and collective reparations'.[206] A major problem was the large number of unidentified victims. Timbuktu had around 70,000 inhabitants at the time of the attack, but only a small 'fraction of the victims in the case' had applied for reparation.[207] The Chamber recognized that it would be 'impracticable' to attempt 'to identify and assess' all claims by unidentified victims itself.[208] It created a novel 'administrative screening' procedure through the Trust Fund to award individual reparations, involving victims and the Defence.[209] This methodology was approved by the Appeals Chamber, subject to an option for excluded victims to seek review by the Trial Chamber.[210]

In the *Lubanga* case, the ICC awarded collective reparation. It determined the overall liability of Lubanga at €10 million.[211] It quantified the harm caused to 425 identified victims at US$3.4 million, with an average harm of US$8,000 per victim. It also awarded US$6.6 million to estimated non-identified victims.

A fundamental dilemma of ICC reparation policy is financial sustainability. Due to the indigence of defendants, the main burden falls on the strained budget of the Trust Fund. The allocations in the first three reparations orders alone consume a substantial part of the Trust Fund's resources for all situations. In order to enhance the financial

---

[202] *Katanga* Reparations, para. 69. The Appeals Chamber noted that 'rather than attempting to determine the "sum-total" of the monetary value of the harm caused, trial chambers' should determine 'the cost to repair', with 'the assistance of experts and other bodies, including the TFV'. See para. 72.

[203] *Katanga* Reparations Appeal, para. 147.

[204] Ibid., para. 184.

[205] *Al Mahdi*, ICC-01/12–01/15, Reparation Order, 17 August 2017, para. 56. It argued that it is ultimately 'the local population that is in the best position to preserve the heritage in question'. Ibid., para. 55.

[206] Ibid., para. 135.

[207] Ibid., para. 141.

[208] Ibid., para. 141.

[209] Ibid., para. 142.

[210] *Prosecutor* v. *Al Mahdi*, ICC-01/12–01/15 A, Judgment on the appeal of the victims against the 'Reparations Order', 8 March 2008, para. 72 ('It is within the discretion of a trial chamber to request, on a case-by-case basis, the assistance of, for example, the TFV to undertake the administrative screening of beneficiaries of individual reparations meeting the eligibility criteria set out by the trial chamber').

[211] *Prosecutor* v. *Lubanga*, ICC-01/04–01/06–3379-Red, TC II, Décision fixant le montant des réparations auxquelles Thomas Lubanga Dyilo est tenu, 15 December 2017, 123.

assets for reparation, it is necessary to carry out effective final investigations prior to arrest of defendants.

5.2.4   Tensions

Attempts to repair the harm caused by international crimes through reparation in criminal proceedings cause similar conceptual dilemmas to the presumed ability of criminal law to address evil.

Human rights law mandates individual consideration of complaints, effective remedies and a say for affected communities. However, these prerequisites cannot be transposed in a linear fashion to reparation proceedings between victims and defendants in a mass atrocity trial. Reparation under human rights law follows a rights-based approach, while criminal law places greater emphasis on the establishment of injury and a nexus to crimes.[212] The outcomes of criminal trials are deeply shaped by prosecutorial strategies and choices in relation to case selection and charges. Reparations cover only a fragment of the underlying criminality, due to the limited focus of trials. By linking reparation to individual criminal responsibility, the ICC adopted a 'perpetrator-centred' approach towards reparation. This may contrast with the need for a more inclusive approach towards reparation, and the need to award reparation without discrimination, which requires the Court to provide legitimate reasons for differential treatment. For instance, the *Lubanga* case was criticized for failing to include charges for sexual and gender-based violence. Victims of 'sexual violence' in the Ituri could thus only benefit from collective reparation awards as 'beneficiaries' rather than as 'victims'.[213] Further selectivity problems arose from the fact that the case involved predominantly perpetration and victimization within one group, i.e. the Hema population. Leaders of the Lendu community raised these concerns in a letter to the ICC Prosecutor in the *Lubanga* case. They noted:

[The focus] makes the Lendu community believe that there was no interethnic war in Ituri between the Lendu and Hema peoples. This implies that that the children enlisted were Hema subjects, the victims would be the Hema relatives and brothers and the reparations in damages or interests whether individual or collective, would be done in the Hema community. Therefore, these enlisted children were at the side of their Hema brothers and adult relatives to massacre, kill, rape, pillage, burn and destroy in Lendu areas. What does this say about Lendu victims?[214]

Reparations thus may not only raise difficulties in relation to victimization among different communities, but also in relation to complex victim–perpetrator relations

---

[212] See M. Brodney, 'Implementing International Criminal Court-Ordered Collective Reparations: Unpacking Present Debates' (2016) 1 *Journal of the Oxford Centre for Socio-Legal Studies*, III. B., at https://joxcsls.com/archive-4/teaser-volume-1-issue-2/.

[213] See P. Dixon, 'Reparations and the Politics of Recognition', in De Vos. Kendall and Stahn, *Contested Justice*, 326, 337.

[214] International Refugee Rights Initiative, 'Steps Towards Justice, Frustrated Hopes: Some Reflections on the Experiences of the International Criminal Court in Ituri', Discussion Paper No. 2, January 2012, 14, at https://reliefweb.int/report/democratic-republic-congo/steps-towards-justice-frustrated-hopes-reflecting-impact-icc-ituri.

inside such communities. For instance, collective community reparations can easily disregard that crimes may also entail patterns of victimization in the collectivity that is blamed for the crimes.[215]

Sometimes there is a risk that entire categories of victims are excluded. This may effectively 'erase' such victims 'from existence and social memory'.[216] For example, Case 002 before the ECCC included limited genocide charges. This caused considerable disappointment among minority groups.[217] Co-Investigating Judges initially barred a group of Khmer Krom survivors, i.e. ethnic Khmer with roots in Vietnam, from participating as civil parties because the provinces in which the victims suffered were not included in the Prosecutor's initial submissions. Civil parties complained that it would be

> an affront to the collective experience of this victim group, and an outright absurdity, if no Ethnic Vietnamese Civil Parties are admitted in these proceedings on the basis of persecution or Genocide of the Vietnamese . . . In the eyes of these victims, the decision of the Co-Investigating Judges to deny the participation at this Tribunal of members of the ethnic Vietnamese group is akin to a denial that these persons are victims of genocide.[218]

Following mass appeals, the Pre-Trial Chamber finally admitted them as civil parties. The incident showed 'how the reality of prosecutorial selectivity – a necessary feature of mass crimes investigations – could be at odds with the objective of safeguarding representativeness within and among the victim compositions participating in the judicial proceedings'.[219] In the Kenyan context, victims were largely left without reparations due to the collapse of cases of the Prosecution. In the *Ruto and Sang* case, Judge Eboe-Osuji claimed that the ICC should continue to deal with reparation even though the case was not further pursued. He argued there is 'no general principle of law that requires conviction as a prerequisite to reparation'.[220] However, this approach conflicts with the 'perpetrator'-based approach to reparations in the ICC context. The Trust Fund Assistance mandate is the only institutional option to repair harm independently of the status of the criminal case.

There is a risk that victim participation in criminal proceedings is driven by unrealistic expectations concerning reparation.[221] The ability of perpetrators to do harm is far greater than their ability to repair damage. There is a widespread perception among victims that participation in criminal proceedings leads to reparation.

---

[215] Regarding community reparation as 'double-edged sword', see Moffett, 'Reparations for "Guilty Victims"', 164.

[216] M. Mohan, 'Reconstituting the "Un-Person": The Khmer Krom and the Khmer Rouge Tribunal' (2008) 12 *Singapore Yearbook of International Law* 43, 49, making an analogy to George Orwell's 'un-person' who has been 'vaporized'.

[217] J. O'Toole and M. Titthara, 'Reassuring the Khmer Krom', *Phnom Penh Post*, 14 June 2010, at www.phnompenhpost .com/national/reassuring-khmer-krom.

[218] *Prosecutor v. Sary, Thirith, Chea and Samphan* (002/19–09–2007/ECCC-D404/2/4, Decision on Appeals against Orders of the Co-Investigating judges on the Admissibility of Civil Party Applications, 24 June 2011, para. 111

[219] L. Nguyen and C. Sperfeldt, 'Victim Participation and Minorities in Internationalised Criminal Trial: Ethnic Vietnamese Civil Parties at the Extraordinary Chambers in the Courts of Cambodia' (2014) 14 *Macquarie Law Journal* 97, 110.

[220] See *Ruto and Sang* Decision on Defence Applications, para. 201.

[221] On experiences, see Dixon, 'Reparations, Assistance and the Experience of Justice', 88–107.

This is problematic if the numbers of victims move up from several hundred to several thousand. The ICC has therefore already ruled that it is not required to rule on each and every individual request for reparation if only collective reparation can be awarded.[222]

The award of reparations raises problems of distributive justice. It involves complex processes of labelling[223] and recognition.[224] As Peter Dixon has noted, such processes involve struggles over 'interpreting, representing and rendering visible (and invisible) categories of people'.[225] They may privilege some harms and sideline the victimization of others. Like sentencing, reparations have a strongly expressive function. Sceptics note that 'individual victims may end up being more sensitive about how the reparations they receive stands in relation to reparation received by others, than about the amount in the absolute'.[226] In the ICC context, there are many different categories of 'victims': victims who are recognized as victims of international crimes in the abstract, but do not receive any material benefit; victims who benefit from assistance measures by the Trust Fund; victims who are entitled to reparation as a result of harm suffered at the hands of the convicted person; victims who are awarded collective reparation; victims who receive individual reparation; unidentified beneficiaries of collective reparation; and 'invisible' victims. The prioritizations established in the reparative process, and the social meaning attached to victim identity in this context, including misrepresentation or lack of recognition, may cause significant grievances.[227] For instance, victims whose harm is not reflected in a conviction may not be eligible for reparation, while other persons in the same town or community may receive material reparation because their harm is reflected in prosecutorial charges. In *Katanga*, the ICC rejected reparation for 'transgenerational harm' of victims, i.e. harm transferred from parents to children.[228] The *Al Mahdi* case has shown that reparation of cultural property may pose specific challenges. The ICC adopted an anthropocentric model of assessment, focused on the symbolic and emotional value of the Timbuktu sites and their use by citizens. Critics note that such an approach may easily entail a re-imagination of cultural meanings through law which is at odds with a longer historical trajectory.[229] Certain dimensions of cultural property can never be fully restored.

Reparations must reconcile the rights of victims with the rights of the convicted persons. The current regime contains an imbalance. The liability must be proportional

---

[222] *Lubanga* Appeal Reparation, para. 152 ('when only collective reparations are awarded pursuant to rule 98 (3) of the Rules of Procedure and Evidence, a Trial Chamber is not required to rule on the merits of the individual requests for reparations').

[223] See D. Miers, 'Victim Compensation as a Labelling Process' (1980) 5 *Victimology* 3.

[224] R. Elias, 'The Symbolic Politics of Victim Compensation' (1983) 8 *Victimology* 213.

[225] Dixon, 'Reparations and the Politics of Recognition', 326.

[226] F. Mégret, 'Reparations before the ICC: The Need for Pragmatism and Creativity', ICC Forum 2012, at http://iccforum.com/reparations#Megret.

[227] See Moffett, 'Reparations for "Guilty Victims"', 155; Dixon, 'Reparations and the Politics of Recognition', 339 et seq.

[228] *Prosecutor* v. *Katanga*, 'Décision relative à la question renvoyée par la Chambre d'appel dans son arrêt du 8 mars 2018 concernant le préjudice transgénérationnel allégué par certains demandeurs en réparation', ICC-01/04-01/07-3804-Red, 19 July 2018.

[229] M. Lostal, 'The Misplaced Emphasis on the Intangible Dimension of Cultural Heritage in the Al Mahdi Case at the ICC' (2017) *Inter Gentes* 45–58.

to the harm caused and the role of the perpetrator in the commission of the crime. However, there is no clear burden-sharing. The contribution of a single individual to collective harm is difficult to quantity. A single defendant, or a perpetrator who is convicted first, may easily bear the responsibility for the entire harm caused to a community through collective crimes. This dilemma raises fairness and equality concerns. It might be mitigated through a greater focus on assistance measures, such as those provided by the Trust Fund.

There is significant debate as to what extent reparations should aim to be 'transformative'. The UN Guidance note on 'Reparations for Conflict-Related Sexual Violence' states that 'Reparations should strive to be transformative, including in design, implementation and impact'.[230] This approach was endorsed by the ICC Trust Fund.[231] It relates reparations to guarantees of non-repetition. It is questionable to what extent such transformative rationales can be realized through reparation in criminal proceedings.[232] Measures that require structural and institutional reforms are highly dependent on state support and assistance. Existing courts with reparative mandates (ICC, ECCC, EAC) lack the power to order states to provide reparation. For example, the ICC may call upon states to provide assistance to give effect to a reparation order.[233] However, implementation relies on consent and incentives. Sceptics fear that combining reparation with 'an agenda of social-structural transformation' would make them 'even less politically viable than they already are',[234] or instrumentalize victims for broader purposes of social justice. The main challenge is to establish a system of 'reparative complementarity',[235] whereby reparation measures against defendants in criminal proceedings are complemented by broader national reparation programmes and longer-term state commitments to sustain collective reparation (e.g. education, memorialization, health) ordered by criminal courts. Complementarity has a crucial role in filling 'the gap between the limited number of victims who will be eligible for redress at the ICC and the larger population of individuals and groups who have suffered from international crimes in a situation'.[236] Finally, there are some concerns as to the effectiveness of judicial procedures and the governance of reparations. The judicialization of reparations, and in particular the individualization of harm in criminal proceedings, is burdensome. It tests the capacity limits of international criminal courts and tribunals, involves large operational costs and feeds into

---

[230] Guidance Note, 'Reparations for Conflict-Related Sexual Violence', 8.

[231] Trust Fund Observations Scheduling Order, para. 77.

[232] S. Williams and E. Palmer, 'Transformative Reparations for Women and Girls at the Extraordinary Chambers in the Courts of Cambodia' (2016) 10 *International Journal of Transitional Justice* 311, 321 ('[G]uarantees of nonrepetition or larger-scale projects aimed at restructuring the societal and economic status of women and girls are highly unlikely due to the need for government involvement in such measures and the absence of a clear link to the charges for which an accused is convicted').

[233] Art. 75 (4) gives the ICC the power to seek cooperation in order to give effect to a reparation order. Art. 93 (1) (l) covers a broad range of assistance measures. L. Moffett, 'Reparative Complementarity: Ensuring an Effective Remedy for Victims in the Reparation Regime of the International Criminal Court' (2013) 17 *International Journal of Human Rights* 368, 381.

[234] Walker, 'Transformative Reparations', 123.

[235] See Moffett, 'Reparative Complementarity', 383–384.

[236] Moffett, 'Reparations for Victims at the International Criminal Court', 1214.

the pockets of lawyers. At the ICC, many cases are dependent on the financial support of the Trust Fund. The delicate legal relationship between Chambers and the Trust Fund, and their different philosophies, have caused struggles over the implementation of reparations. They have disagreed on issues such as the use of the resources of the Trust Fund or the modalities of reparation (e.g. the feasibility of community-based reparations).

Reparation orders easily promise more than they can deliver. There are concerns that courts instrumentalize the experiences of victims to strengthen their own cause and legitimacy, remedy their own failings or push specific agendas (e.g. sexual and gender-based violence).[237] Ironically, the ICC may have had to pay more compensation to its own former ICC staff members as compensation for internal reorganization or lost labour law cases before the International Labour Organization[238] than actual judicial reparation to victims of crime. Some voices argue that reparative measures should be left entirely to targeted Trust Funds or other specialized institutions. For instance, judges at the ad hoc tribunals argued that a claims commission established by the UN Security Council would be better suited to address reparation than the criminal process.[239] Often, it might be better to help victims of crimes in the same way as victims of disaster, namely without linking the entitlement to reparation to the establishment of responsibility of individual perpetrators. Some authors have suggested the creation of a permanent victims claim commission.[240] Criminal courts thus should not try to emulate human rights mechanisms or to make up for the absence of adequate domestic reparations programmes, but rather try to find their own distinct place in the much broader picture of reparative and humanitarian support measures for victims and survivors.

---

[237] Walker, 'Transformative Reparations', 122 ('If the bar is set ... with respect to solutions to deep-running injustices, then what is targeted for repair are societies or their socioeconomic and political structures rather than particular victims, who become at best something less than the central priority and at worst serve instrumentally as emblems or symptoms of the real or important problem').

[238] On the estimated costs of internal reorganization of the Registry (ReVision), see ASP, 'Audit Report of the ReVision Project of the International Criminal Court's Registry', ICC-ASP/15/27, 9 November 2016, 14 et seq.

[239] Moffett, 'Reparations for Victims at the International Criminal Court', 1206.

[240] M. T. Kamminga, 'Towards a Permanent International Claims Commission for Victims of Violations of International Humanitarian Law' (2007) 25 *Windsor Yearbook of Access to Justice* 23.

6

Beyond the Status Quo: Rethinking International Criminal Law

International criminal law has taken a long journey over past decades. Its evolution is comparable to the myth of Daedalus and his son Icarus who used wax wings to flee from imprisonment by King Minos on the island of Crete. Daedalus warned Icarus not to fly too close to the sun. Icarus was too excited, he flew too high, his wings melted and he drowned in the sea. Daedalus survived the flight, but struggled with the loss of his son. The history of international criminal law has striking parallels.[1] It involves rise and fall and risks of failure.[2] Like the two historic protagonists, it relied on creativity and idealism to escape from the narrow confines of a state-centric system of international law. It has developed its own narratives, vocabulary and approach to legal sources. It has been emancipated from international humanitarian law, human rights law and domestic criminal law. Rather than developing the idea of state criminality or the responsibility of legal persons, it has placed the individual at the centre of its own normative universe. This journey is at a critical juncture.

6.1   Modesty

International criminal law has been strongly grounded in promise, moral ambition and faith.[3] Its appeal results from the belief in the egalitarian functions and social benefits of criminal law.[4] Ideas of an international 'ordre public' and common civility provided the virtual 'feathers' that helped it to rise above the realm of realpolitik.[5] International criminal law is driven by ideals of moral agency, the prevalence of law over politics, and the transformative power of justice. It continues to be influenced by the 'Durkheimian' idea that punishment constitutes an act of the affirmation of a

---

[1] See C. Stahn, 'Daedalus or Icarus? Footprints of International Criminal Justice Over a Quarter of a Century' (2017) 77 *Heidelberg Journal of International Law* 371–408.

[2] See P. Akhavan, 'The Rise, and Fall, and Rise, of International Criminal Justice' (2013) 11 *JICJ* 527.

[3] S. M. H. Nouwen, 'Justifying Justice', in J. Crawford and M. Koskenniemi (eds.), *The Cambridge Companion to International Law* (Cambridge University Press, 2012), 327.

[4] See generally J. D'Aspremont, *International Law as a Belief System* (Cambridge: Cambridge University Press, 2017).

[5] Douglas, *The Memory of Judgment*, 261, arguing that international criminal trials 'remind the world of the extraordinary power of the law to submit unprecedented atrocity to its institutional will'.

collective conscience'.[6] These beliefs have nourished the idealism of individuals, civil society networks, international organizations and alliances of states that have invested intellectual capital and resources in international criminal law as a global project. These hopes and ideals emerged at crucial historical moments. They became gradually more embedded in international law through practice (e.g. regulation, adjudication, judicial dialogue and cooperation), repetition and emulation. The underlying fabric has remained fragile, however – like the wings of Icarus.

International criminal law has gone through different types of alleged 'crisis' over time.[7] It continues to develop as a body of substantive law and continues to influence related fields. However, global institutions face opposition and threats of 'withdrawal'. They must develop new techniques to adapt to change and counter critiques. International criminal tribunals may become rarer in the future. The idea of international criminal jurisdiction continues to meet defiance from recalcitrant states. Hybrid and regional justice, and the role of domestic courts, are becoming more important in this context. Investigative or quasi-judicial bodies have gained a greater role in gathering evidence and identifying crimes. The legitimacy and credibility of international criminal law is continuously called into question.[8] The critical movement has revealed some of the darker sides of international criminal law as a justice project, including its disempowering effects, simplified narratives and risks of instrumentalization,[9] and its effect of naturalizing structural and systemic inequalities. Many of the proclaimed goals and expectations were overenthusiastic, or fuelled by slogans that require greater nuance (e.g. 'no peace without justice'). International criminal law remains in demand, but is in need of modesty and greater recognition of its own limitations.[10] Like Icarus, it should neither fly too close to the sun, nor too low to the sea.

6.2   Signposts for the Future

Mark Drumbl has identified some useful signposts for the future. He has argued that international criminal law would benefit from less faith and more science, more discomfort than convenience, greater nuance in the use of images and narratives, and a shift from legalism to justice.[11] These suggestions provide a good starting point to rethink some of the fundamental premises of international criminal law and its contemporary critiques.

---

[6] Tallgren, 'The Durkheimian Spell of International Criminal Law', 156 et seq.

[7] Robinson, 'Identity Crisis', 930.

[8] See S. Vasiliev, 'Between International Criminal Justice and Injustice: Theorising Legitimacy', in Hayashi and Bailliet, *The Legitimacy of International Criminal Tribunals*, 66.

[9] See e.g. T. Krever, 'International Criminal Law: An Ideology Critique' (2013) 26 *LJIL* 701–723.

[10] On the limitations, see B. Roth, 'Coming to Terms with Ruthlessness: Sovereign Equality, Global Pluralism, and the Limits of International Criminal Justice' (2010) 8 *Santa Clara Journal of International Law* 231–288.

[11] See M. Drumbl, 'The Future of International Criminal Law and Transitional Justice', in Schabas, McDermott and Hayes, *Ashgate Research Companion to International Criminal Law*, 541, 540–544.

6.2.1   *The Sovereignty Paradox*

The relationship between international criminal law and sovereignty requires critical reflection. This connection is often misrepresented or abused on different parts of the spectrum, i.e. from supporters and critics of international criminal law.[12]

Sovereignty is an indeterminate notion. International criminal law is vulnerable to sovereignty critiques since it involves repressive power. States invoke sovereignty as a political argument to counter interference in their own affairs. This argument is contradictory. There is powerful philosophical argument that the very existence of international criminal law is justified by the fact that states should not be arbiters over their own violations. Many international crimes are not committed by individuals on their own, but within and through collective structures or in an official capacity. They are grounded in abuses of state authority or a lack of sovereign authority.[13] International criminal law has gained acceptance because it has combined claims for a 'relative' understanding of state sovereignty,[14] i.e. one that makes state power answerable, with reaffirmations of state power, or even 'deference to sovereignty'. It is built on the premise that acts can at times be lawful and unlawful at the same time, namely 'valid within the domestic legal order, but in breach of international legal obligation'.[15] The main discontent is who gets to decide on a violation.

The recognition of international crimes strengthens the obligation-related side of sovereignty. It triggers duties to investigate, prosecute and prevent crimes. Yet it serves at the same time to protect or enable state sovereignty. A classical example is the prohibition of the crime of aggression.[16] The concept of universal jurisdiction extends the realm of state power. By promoting the responsible use of power, international criminal law is to some extent a guardian of sovereignty. It serves in some respects as a model for domestic jurisdiction (i.e. in terms of crime definition, due process standards).

One of the main problems is that the exercise of universal or international jurisdiction continues to be regarded as an illustration of asymmetric powers in the international legal order, or even as an instrument to promote sovereign inequality (unequal equality). International criminal law cannot be expected to solve inequalities entrenched by colonialism,[17] unequal distributions of power resulting from sovereign equality, or discontents about the outdated configuration of the collective security system. It is in need of better safeguards against abuse, however, if it seeks to maintain its vocation.

---

[12] Cryer, 'International Criminal Law vs State Sovereignty: Another Round?', 979.

[13] W.-C. Lee, 'International Crimes and Universal Jurisdiction', in L. May and Z. Hoskins (eds.), *International Criminal Law and Philosophy* (Cambridge: Cambridge University Press, 20100, 21.

[14] *Tadić* 1995, para. 58.

[15] B. R. Roth, *Sovereign Equality and Moral Disagreement: Premises of a Pluralist International Legal Order* (Oxford: Oxford University Press, 2011), 91.

[16] It criminalizes not only violations of rights of individuals or protected groups, but violations of sovereignty (e.g. territorial integrity, non-interference). See Section 1.3.4.

[17] A. Anghie, 'Finding the Peripheries: Sovereignty and Colonialism in Nineteenth Century International Law' (1999) 40 *Harvard International Law Journal* 1, 6–7.

Some voices have argued that '[i]nternational criminal law emerged partly because great powers saw it as an alternative to more forceful action in situations of massive human rights violations – but in which they could not see their individual interests in intervening directly'.[18] Others claim that the movement towards the repression of crime has broadened duties to intervene. The discourse that is used to build support for international criminal law bears synergies with the rhetoric underpinning the case for humanitarian interventions.[19] It draws on elements of crisis, sacrifice and saviour to mobilize empathy.[20] For example, the R2P doctrine uses crime notions as a trigger for intervention.[21] The nexus between international criminal law and intervention is a 'double-edged sword'.[22] It hardens suspicions against the abuse of international criminal law by those who view it as a tool of the powerful. The risks became apparent in the Libya crisis, where ICC justice was seen as part of a toolbox of intervention. International criminal law can easily be misused as a 'continuation of war by other means'.[23]

International criminal justice agents must be attentive to the risks of becoming complicit in the legitimation of structural injustices or the politics of intervention.[24] For instance, where international legal mechanisms need to stay at arm's length from strategies of military intervention. One-sided jurisdictional mandates are incompatible with the idea of equality before the law, and the impartiality of justice. Prosecutors and courts should use the interpretative authority and discretionary power that are inherent in their mandates to counter arising biases and inequalities, or distinctions between 'winners' and 'losers' of conflict. International criminal institutions need to pay greater attention to the potential disempowering effects that their authority may produce in relation to domestic or local actors.

There is a growing trend to ground international criminal law more thoroughly in domestic jurisdiction, in light of the limitations and critiques of international criminal courts and tribunals. Domestic or hybrid mechanisms are seen as important instruments to address accountability gaps. Various international institutions provide assistance to states to strengthen their own accountability infrastructure. Institutions such as the IIIM build an important bridge between international accountability

---

[18] K. Anderson, 'The Rise of International Criminal Law: Intended and Unintended Consequences' (2009) 20 *EJIL* 331, 334.

[19] See A. Orford, 'Muscular Humanitarianism: Reading the Narratives of the New Interventionism' (1999) 10 *EJIL* 679, 692–703; E. Bikundo, 'Saving Humanity from Hell: International Criminal Law and Permanent Crisis' (2013) 44 *Netherlands Yearbook of International Law* 89.

[20] Such elements are common in political arguments for the establishment of institutions, opening statements by prosecutors or storytelling at trial. They involve claims of exceptionalism, heroic narratives, binaries and narratives of progress (e.g. novelty vs. tradition, transition from chaos to peace). A good example is the opening remarks by David Crane in *Sessay, Kallon and Gbao*: 'Their alleged crimes against humanity cannot justly or practically be ignored, as they were the handmaidens to the beast – the beast of impunity that walked this burnt and pillaged land – its bloody claw marks in evidence on the backs of the hundreds of thousands of victims in this tragic conflict begun on 23 March of 1991'. See www.rscsl.org/Documents/Press/OTP/prosecutor-openingstatement070504a.pdf.

[21] See para. 138 of the World Summit Outcome Document.

[22] A. Tiemessen, 'The International Criminal Court and the Lawfare of Judicial Intervention' (2016) 30 *International Relations* 409.

[23] D. Kennedy, 'Lawfare and Warfare', in Crawford and Koskenniemi, *Cambridge Companion to International Law*, 158.

[24] On complicity as critique, see M. Farrell, 'Critique, Complicity and I', in Schöwbel, *Critical Approaches to International Criminal Law*, 96.

mechanisms and domestic jurisdictions, which has been lacking in other contexts. Ultimately, the future of international criminal law is thus neither fully international nor fully national. It rather lies in the cooperation and interaction between different accountability bodies. It requires a certain degree of openness, which transcends classical institutional silos.

6.2.2   Conceptualizing Crimes

Crime labels have emerged in a pragmatic fashion. As Frederic Mégret has argued, international criminal law has been driven by 'investment in a highly peculiar type of response to international crimes',[25] rather than by coherent criminalization. It has served as an umbrella for 'public' and 'private' types of criminality. There is no agreement on the underlying protected interests of specific categories of crime. Theory has followed practice, rather than vice versa. Existing crimes have extended, since they constitute an agreed *acquis*. This is an asset in terms of flexibility. Crime definitions are constantly adjusted to context in order to capture new criminological phenomena. However, this comes at a price. It makes it ever more difficult to maintain systemic coherence. Crime control prevails over due process.

Traditional theories of norm evolution (norm emergence, crystallization and internalization[26]) face challenges. There is a large degree of norm entrepreneurship.[27] Law is created by a small elite of judicial and policy actors. A particular crime conception is easily presented as being generally accepted, due to the high degree of moral ambition and advocacy, the strong communicative nature of international criminal courts and tribunals, and the stronger emphasis on *opinio juris* than state practice.[28] Benevolent critique is less developed, since there are fears that it might weaken the underlying project. Processes of norm internalization involve a high degree of imitation, since norms are presented as packages or agreed language. Domestic courts may lack the means, resources or time to critically examine findings of international criminal courts and tribunals.

Crime constructions are dominated by a strong focus on atrocity violence. This has created a perception that international criminal law deals with 'extraordinary' criminality.[29] This distinction is helpful to explain certain differences between international and domestic crimes, such as the relevance of contextual elements. The exceptionality argument is increasingly under challenge, however.

The distinction between macro-crime and transnational crime is fluid. For instance, in Africa and Latin America, corruption and money-laundering charges have been

---

[25] Mégret, 'Anxieties of International Criminal Justice', 218.
[26] M. Finnemore and K. Sikkink, 'International Norm Dynamics and Political Change', 52 *International Organization* 887–917.
[27] On judges as 'judicial entrepreneurs', see Roisini and Meernik, *Judgment Day*, 26 et seq.
[28] *Kupreškić et al.*, Trial Judgment, para. 527 ('This is however an area where *opinio iuris sive necessitatis* may play a much greater role than usus').
[29] Starr, 'Extraordinary Crimes at Ordinary Times', 1527; Aukerman, 'Extraordinary Evil, Extraordinary Crime', 39; Harmon and Gaynor, 'Ordinary Sentences for Extraordinary Crimes', 683.

used to accomplish some of the same rationales as core crimes, namely to combat abusive forms of government and target the highest political leaders and networks of criminality.[30] The nexus to peace and security is evolving. International crimes do not only protect negative peace, i.e. the absence of armed violence. They are inherently connected to the protection of certain public goods and the repression of certain social, cultural or economic drivers of crime (i.e. movements of people, hate crime, discrimination, illicit exploitation of goods or labour).[31]

The 'exceptionality' thesis is counterproductive from a sociological perspective. It tends to imply that international crimes are far from home. This may create an artificial distance from crimes and 'us vs. them' divides, which present one side as rational, orderly and stable, and the other as the opposite. Treating crimes as 'exceptional' may provide a moral comfort zone or an incentive to present such crimes as crimes of others.[32] It tends to marginalize the connection of crimes to broader 'non-exceptional' injustices that might implicate a wider range of actors. It might also inadvertently contribute to the normalization of 'ordinary' violations.

Institutional practices can produce meaning through silence. For example, Boaventura de Sousa Santos has argued in his 'sociology of absences'[33] that discourse may actively produce something as 'non-existent' and thus contribute to its marginalization or suppression. By failing to recognize injustices that are less tangible than atrocity crimes, international criminal law can actively contribute to their marginalization and validate dominating practices. Rather than conceptualizing international crimes as context-specific outbursts of criminality, it might be helpful to view them as part of a continuum of different spectrums of violence that is inherently connected to everyday life. They cannot be limited to physical violence against human beings, but involve attacks on other protected interests (e.g. the environment, cultural heritage).

Within such a broad vision, it is essential to recognize the modest role of criminal law. Criminal law remains a limited, formal and to some extent primitive response to violations. There is a need to reflect 'whether more criminalization is necessarily better than less'.[34] Over-criminalization may have negative side effects. As Paul Roberts and Nesam McMillan have argued, the 'best chance of success' for the project lies 'in a genuinely cooperative, multi-disciplinary enterprise'.[35] One of the most pressing challenges is to invest in more prevention rather than repression.[36]

---

[30] K. Olaniyan, *Corruption and Human Rights Law in Africa* (Oxford: Hart Publishing, 2016); Y. Krylova, 'Outsourcing the Fight against Corruption: Lessons from the International Commission against Impunity in Guatemala' (2018) 9 *Global Policy* 95.

[31] Schmid, *Taking Economic, Social and Cultural Rights Seriously in International Criminal Law*, 331.

[32] For a critique, see Roberts and McMillan, 'For Criminology in International Criminal Justice', 327–328.

[33] B. de Sousa Santos, 'Nuestra America: Reinventing a Subaltern Paradigm of Recognition and Redistribution' (2001) 18 *Theory, Culture & Society* 185, 191 et seq.

[34] K. Engle, 'Feminism and Its (Dis)contents: Criminalizing Wartime Rape in Bosnia and Herzegovina' (2005) 99 *AJIL* 778, 784.

[35] Roberts and McMillan, 'For Criminology in International Criminal Justice', 337.

[36] Reisman, 'Acting Before Victims Become Victims', 57.

6.2.3 International Criminal Law's Subjects

The subjects of international criminal law have remained rather limited.[37] Unlike domestic systems, international criminal law has predominantly focused on natural, rather than legal persons.

Crime provisions may trigger dual responsibility, namely state responsibility and individual responsibility. As the ICJ confirmed in the *Genocide* case, state responsibility itself is not criminalized.[38] It has been more comfortable to extend pathways for the criminal responsibility of individuals. The lack of recognition of the concept of crimes of state has meant that international criminal law and individual criminal responsibility have become the main vehicle to address state-orchestrated crimes. This has caused a certain normative overreach of the atrocity trial. State responsibility has been marginalized,[39] although the dividing line between individual crime and state crime is often more blurred than is assumed.[40]

The separation between individual and state responsibility serves important functions from a legal point of view. It provides different accountability regimes and remedies for violations. However, it is less convincing from a criminological perspective. One of the gaps in the existing system is the lack of possibility for victims to seek reparation from a state through criminal proceedings.[41] Existing mechanisms may at best make recommendations to states as to how reparations should be addressed.

International criminal law recognized relatively early the role of non-state actors in international crimes (e.g. piracy, terrorism). In contemporary practice, it has captured crimes committed by non-state actors and against other non-state actors under crime definitions (e.g. crimes against humanity, war crimes). Typically, responsibility remains attached to individuals rather than entities. For example, terrorist organizations or armed group have generally not been treated as legal subjects as such, due to the absence of formal legal personality and concerns of states against recognition of their status. Targeting such non-actors is convenient for governments and courts, but it can easily become a trap. It may detract from state-driven criminality and revive the traditional critique of international criminal law: namely that it is an instrument to fight political enemies or to legitimize governmental power.

The approach towards corporations is marked by contradiction. Corporations are considered as legal persons in domestic and international law. They may be as powerful as states, but they are only gradually recognized as subjects under

---

[37] See F. Mégret, 'The Subjects of International Criminal Law', in P. Kastner (ed.), *International Criminal Law in Context* (New York: Routledge, Taylor & Francis Group, 2017), 30 et seq.

[38] ICJ, *Application of the Convention on the Prevention and Punishment of the Crime of Genocide (Bosnia and Herzegovina v. Serbia)*, para. 173.

[39] For a critique, see P.-M. Dupuy, 'Crime Without Punishment' (2016) 14 *JICJ* 879.

[40] The close nexus between state action and individual agency is in particular visible in the context of the crime of aggression, where the state is involved by definition.

[41] See Section 5.2.2. Such claims are typically pursued in alternative forums, such as claims commissions, national proceedings or human rights courts.

international criminal law.[42] The exclusion of corporate criminal responsibility is artificial in cases where the criminality of conduct is predominantly rooted in corporate culture, rather than individual agency.[43] In these circumstances, the focus on corporate agents as individuals alone may not be effective and fail to reflect the criminality inherent in organizational conduct.[44] Theories of attribution make it possible to ascribe culpability and knowledge to corporations.[45] It is thus important to rethink the function of corporate criminal responsibility or to develop alternative forms of sanctions against corporations in the case of corporate involvement in international crime.[46]

6.2.4   Images of the Individual

International criminal law is focused on individuals as its main subject of reference. Its image of the individual is rather simplistic.[47] The legal process tends to downplay the complexity of human behaviour. The narrative shifts between extremes: the image of the evil agent (the villain) who defies global moral consciousness, and the concept of the rational and responsible actor who can be held responsible through law.

Throughout the legal process, the framing of the individual changes, depending on the underlying juridical construction. In jurisdictional claims and prosecutorial strategy, defendants are often presented as social outcasts. They are branded as enemies of humankind through their association with atrocity crime. These labels are used in order to justify the exercise of international or universal jurisdiction over crimes. This image has little to do with reality. As Alette Smeulers and Barbora Holá have shown, many perpetrators of international crimes 'are just ordinary people and . . . the reasons for their involvement in international crimes can be very banal rather than evil. Some perpetrators really seem to be nothing more and nothing less than a small cog in a big machine and they are part of something . . . of which the final outcome is beyond their control'.[48] This concept of the 'enemy' has been subject to intense debate in criminology (e.g. in relation to terrorists and sexual offenders).[49] It has been applied by some jurisdictions to justify exceptional measures against terrorists as part of the 'war on

---

[42] W. Huisman, 'Corporations and International Crimes', in Smeulers and Haveman, *Supranational Criminology: Towards a Criminology of International Crimes*, 181–213.

[43] Huisman and Van Sliedregt, 'Rogue Traders', 826.

[44] A. Clapham and S. Jerbi, 'Categories of Corporate Complicity in Human Rights Abuses' (2001) 24 *Hastings International and Comparative Law Review* 339.

[45] Ibid., 826.

[46] See e.g. UN Economic and Social Council, Resolution 1994/15, 'The role of criminal law in the protection of the environment', 25 July 1994, recommending 'criminal or non-criminal fines or other measures on corporations in jurisdictions in which corporate criminal liability is not currently recognized in the legal systems'.

[47] D. Joyce, 'Human Rights and Mediatization of International Justice' (2010) 23 *LJIL* 507–527.

[48] A. Smeulers and B. Holá, 'ICTY and the Culpability of Different Types of Perpetrators of International Crimes', in Smeulers, *Collective Violence and International Criminal Justice*, 175, 177.

[49] See G. Jakobs, 'On the Theory of Enemy Criminal Law', in M. Dubber (ed.), *Foundational Texts in Modern Criminal Law* (Oxford: Oxford University Press, 2014), 415; S. Krasmann, 'The Enemy on the Border' (2007) 9 *Punishment & Society* 301–318.

terror'.[50] This enemy-based reading of criminal law is counterproductive. It is based on social exclusion[51] and rationalizes a theory of legal exceptionalism or extra-legality. It suggests that certain individuals should not be treated as 'criminals' per se but rather as subjects that do not fit into usual categories of criminal law, since do not respect the authority of law or do not belong to a common civic community.[52] The notion of the 'enemy' is vague and runs counter to the liberal foundations of international criminal law, i.e. the dignity of the offender. International criminal law owes its authority to the equal application of norms and protections to all types of perpetrators. Its very vocation rests on the claim that it is able to constrain violence through law, rather than to exclude 'dangerous' subjects. 'Enemy'-based conceptions of international criminal law should be avoided.

The portrayal of defendants shifts in the framework of modes of liability and defences. The enemy of humankind and social outcast turns into a rational self-determined being. Perpetrators are treated as autonomous agents who choose to engage in conduct and accept opportunity costs. The reference point is a *homo economicus*,[53] who exercises moral choice, balances risks and calculates the consequences of action, rather than a *homo politicus*, whose action occurs in a specific situational context. Individual choices are in the foreground, while social relations are sidelined, or presented as part of network criminality. This framing pays limited attention to the political economy and material conditions under which individuals act, and their available 'social knowledge'. It involves a risk that individuals are held accountable for violations that transcend them (i.e. crimes committed as de facto or *de jure* agents of specific collectivities). The dialectic relationship, namely the reliance of collectives on the individual, and the dependence of the individuals on those collectives,[54] is often more nuanced than the law tends to admit.

At trial and sentencing, guilt is individualized. The conduct of the defendant is judged in its social context. The image of the defendant is deeply shaped by contrasting narratives at trial, and the power of images. Existing tensions in the production of perpetratorship and victimhood may be mitigated if procedures are construed as 'contradictorial' rather than 'adversarial', i.e. focused on 'elucidating the truth by way of contradiction, including confrontation' and '(controversial) dialogue' in 'a spirit of cooperation', rather than hostile contest.[55] At sentencing, it might be helpful to include more detailed information on the background of defendants and more

---

[50] See e.g. on the UK, S. Macdonald, 'Cyberterrorism and Enemy Criminal Law', in J. D Ohlin, K. Govern and C. Finkelstein (eds.), *Cyber War: Law and Ethics for Virtual Conflicts* (Oxford: Oxford University Press, 2015), 57.

[51] On 'juridical othering', see R. Jamieson and K. McEvoy, 'State Crime by Proxy and Juridical Othering' (2005) 45 *British Journal of Criminology* 504; G. P. Fletcher, *The Grammar of Criminal Law*, Vol. 1 (Oxford: Oxford University Press, 2007), 172.

[52] See generally M. D. Dubber, 'Citizenship and Penal Law' (2010) 13 *New Criminal Law Review* 190.

[53] C. Cramer, 'Homo Economicus Goes to War: Methodological Individualism, Rational Choice and the Political Economy of War' (2002) 30 *World Development* 1845–1864.

[54] A main trigger of individual responsibility is abuse of power structures, or failure to oppose them.

[55] A. Eser, 'Procedural Structure and Features of International Criminal Justice: Lessons from the ICTY', in Swart, Zahar and Sluiter, *Legacy of the Internatinal Criminal Tribunal for the Former Yugoslavia*, 108, 145.

explanation on the context in which they committed crimes. This would reduce binaries and allow a more nuanced account of offenders, social context and types of victimization.

6.2.5   Portraying 'the Other'

International criminal law faces similar paradoxes to other humanitarian projects in relation to the protection of subjects and engagement with constituencies. It invokes authority on behalf of others, or for their benefit (e.g. humanity, the international 'community' or victims). It seeks to promote equality, freedom and justice through disinterested agency and a commitment to alleviate human suffering. However, the portrayal of 'others' involves a large degree of social engineering and is often used as a means to legitimize international criminal law as a project.[56]

Carl Schmitt's warning that 'whoever says humanity wants to cheat'[57] has a grain of truth. The interest in the protected subject is coupled with self-interest. Constituency is a variable.[58] It shifts considerably. For example, international criminal courts and tribunals appeal to the interests of humanity when they seek to compensate for a lack of state consent. They stress international community interests when they wish to override specific national interests. They rely on local constituencies (e.g. affected communities, victims) in order to justify their global relevance. Use of notions such as 'humanity' or community interests leave little moral room for counterargument. They are guided by the aim to strengthen the appeal to morality.[59] However, they may at the same time have certain hegemonic features. They can be a means to silence dissent rather than to engage in reasoned dialogue.

The engagement with victims and 'the local' bears traces of experimentation. International criminal law draws legitimacy from its claim to remedy suffering. It may need 'victims' as much as they may need the law. The voices of victims provide immediacy and authenticity to the justice procedure. However, international criminal law is marked by a victim/saviour logic[60] that requires critical interrogation.

The type of victimhood that is presented in legal discourse is highly selective, shaped by the limited focus of proceedings, and conditioned by the interpretation of the underlying narrative of the conflict. There is a strong temptation to present victims

---

[56] See I. Tallgren, 'Come and See? The Power of Images and International Criminal Justice' (2017) 17 *International Criminal Law Review* 259, 277, arguing that trials bring 'to view suffering of individuals or groups identified, suffering presumably caused by suspects identified, too, all of them becoming characters in a narrative with chronological sequences that can be "evidenced", to create a beginning and an end'.

[57] See C. Schmitt, *The Concept of the Political* (Chicago: Chicago University Press, 2007), 54.

[58] Some argue that international criminal law essentially creates its own constituencies through the discourse of its agents. See F. Mégret, 'In Whose Name: The ICC and the Search for Constituency', in De Vos, Kendall and Stahn, *Contested Justice*, 44.

[59] On history as rhetorical strategy, see D. Joyce, 'The Historical Function of International Criminal Trials: Re-thinking International Criminal Law' (2004) 73 *Nordic Journal of International Law* (2004) 461, 464.

[60] See Mutua, 'Savages, Victims, and Saviors', 201–246.

as morally unambiguous subjects in order to appeal to sympathy.[61] The image of the innocent victim is often too simplistic. There is a risk that the images produced through justice procedures simply mirror those that are 'used by aid agencies and the media in the Western world to appeal to donors and stakeholders'.[62] This may exclude experiences of suffering that do not fit into this framework and precludes a more complex understanding of violence and victimization.

Some risks arise from the juridification of victimhood itself. Legal narratives may create stereotypes or artificial 'spectacles' of suffering.[63] For instance, it may be counterproductive to present criminal law as the 'main frame' to address sexual violence as a social phenomenon.[64] As critics have pointed out, the narrow lens of criminal law may detract from broader structural inequalities that have 'greater impact on women's lives and risks of being subjected to conflict-related sexual violence' than criminal prosecution.[65] The labels associated with legal determinations may have unintended consequences for persons affected. For example, humanitarian or development aid organizations often carry out programmes that provide support to specific target groups (e.g. child soldiers, victims of sexual and gender-based violence), while leaving others aside. The narrative produced in legal discourse may preclude victims from access to institutions or health and rehabilitation programmes.

These dilemmas are complemented by epistemic problems. Judicial agents make determinations about what is 'good' for victims. However, they may lack the underlying knowledge, or may make such claims without hearing or consulting them. Such practices are problematic from the perspective of the autonomy and self-determination of the affected subject. They may further produce overly homogenous treatments of victimhood, based on the assumption that the same approach will be beneficial for all of them. The discourse on victims needs demystification and better empirical grounding. Perspectives from anthropology, post-colonial or critical humanitarian studies offer an important means to understand the flaws and limitations in the process of 'judicial othering', highlight the complexity of victim identities and offer alternative accounts to certain stereotypes (e.g. constructions of ethnicity, gender biases or images of vulnerability or dependency).

Some of the existing shortcomings may be attenuated through greater involvement of expert input in proceedings (e.g. expert witnesses), less distance to affected societies (e.g. on-site presence, longer-term engagement in relation to situations), and better channels to 'listen' to and communicate with 'others' beyond outreach and gathering of material and testimony for investigations prosecutions.

---

[61] K. M. Clarke, 'The Rule of Law through Its Economies of Appearances: The Making of the African Warlord' (2011) 18 *Indiana Journal of Global Legal Studies* 7.

[62] C. Schwöbel-Patel, 'Spectacle in International Criminal Law: The Fundraising Image of Victimhood' (2016) 4 *London Review of International Law* 247, 272.

[63] Ibid.

[64] See Houge and Lohne, 'End Impunity', 780. See also K. Grewal, 'International Criminal Law as a Site for Enhancing Women's Rights? Challenges, Possibilities, Strategies' (2015) 23 *Feminist Legal Studies* 149–165; P. Kirby and L. J. Shepherd, 'The Futures Past of the Women, Peace and Security Agenda' (2016) 91 *International Affairs* 373–392.

[65] Houge and Lohne, 'End Impunity', 781.

6.2.6   Institutional Self-Reflexivity

Many institutional practices are geared at promoting international criminal law as a project. Existing practice would benefit from a greater degree of self-reflexivity.

International criminal courts and tribunals tend to stress the judicial dimensions of their work. However, they use language, produce decisions and trigger actions that other actors must relate to.[66] Even more than domestic courts, which can look back at a grown 'judicial' tradition, they have to conquer challenges of recognition and acceptance. Their power lies not so much in formal coercive features, but rather in their strong interpretative and symbolic authority, which may trigger certain political and legal actions.

International criminal law requires less universalistic rhetoric, and more cultural variation.[67] International criminal courts tend to argue that international criminal law is in need of greater universality in terms of jurisdiction, cooperation and crime definitions in order to reach its objectives.[68] The problem with this argument is that it fails to diagnose the underlying problems and relies on a one-sided vision of universality, namely the idea of universality embraced by the speaker. Lessons from international human rights suggest that '[e]ffective participation by states from different geographical and cultural contexts will not be sufficient to secure a genuine universal consensus, unless the state elites who act in the international sphere truly represent the cultures of those states'.[69] It is necessary to inquire more deeply into what type of universality is desirable, and how much space should be left for diversity.[70]

Human rights law has been marked for several decades by a rich debate about the relationship between 'universalism' and 'cultural relativism'.[71] Cultural relativist arguments have insisted that universal human rights must be flexible enough to allow differences in terms of emphasis and means of implementation of rights.[72] This tension has enriched the understanding of human rights. For instance, Onuma Yasuaki has pleaded for an intercivilizational approach to human rights which 'requires us to see the mechanism of human rights not merely within the West-centric modern civilization where it was born and raised, but from other

---

[66] See e.g. Tallgren, 'Sensibility and Sense of International Criminal Law', 594.

[67] For a critique of international law, see A. Roberts, *Is International Law International?* (Oxford: Oxford University Press, 2017).

[68] On universality, see A. P. Rubin, 'Is International Criminal Law Universal?' (2001) 10 *University of Chicago Legal Forum* 351; Stephen, 'International Criminal Law: Wielding the Sword of Universal Criminal Justice', 89.

[69] See S. Harris-Short, 'Listening to "the Other"? The Convention on the Rights of the Child' (2001) 2 *Melbourne Journal of International Law* 304, 313–314.

[70] K. E. Davis, 'Legal Universalism: Persistent Objections' (2010) 60 *University of Toronto Law Journal* 537, 541.

[71] C. Cerna, 'Universality of Human Rights and Cultural Diversity: Implementation of Human Rights in Different Socio-Cultural Contexts' (1994) 16 *Human Rights Quarterly* 740; A. Pollis, 'Cultural Relativism Revisited: Through a State Prism' (1996) 18 *Human Rights Quarterly* 316; R. Mullender, 'Human Rights: Universalism and Cultural Relativism' (2003) 6 *Critical Review of International Social and Political Philosophy* 70.

[72] For a discussion of the need of 'enculturation' of human rights, see A. Dundes Renteln, *International Human Rights: Universalism Versus Relativism* (Newbury Park, CA: Sage Publications, 1990), 74.

civilizational perspectives as well'.[73] In international criminal law, this debate is only now emerging. Pleas for greater context sensitivity have been voiced in transitional justice contexts.[74] They tend to see criminal justice and individual responsibility as part of a broader process of societal transformation. Existing discourse may benefit from a better understanding of the limits of universality[75] and the legitimate space of different traditions and approaches towards accountability. This is gradually becoming visible in different fields, such as complementarity, the hybridization of justice mechanisms and procedures, punishment and sentencing, or the rise of new regional mechanisms which postulate a better connection between global, national and local spheres of justice.[76] For instance, states should not simply replicate international crimes, doctrines or punitive practices, but rather 'internalize' them in equivalent form. Universality may require a certain degree of diversity and differentiation.

Some notions should be used with greater caution or be dropped from the vocabulary. For example, the term 'capacity-building' is misleading. It evokes a certain degree of paternalism.[77] It creates divides between global institutions and local constituencies. It entails an implicit challenge to the competence and legitimacy of local justice. The concept of the 'fight against impunity' deserves critical scrutiny.[78] It derives from human rights discourse, but has an ambiguous meaning in relation to criminal justice.[79] The notion involves a sense of 'heroism' that sits uneasily with the rational functionality of criminal trials. It associates international criminal law with an ideology that stands in contrast to the liberal foundations of the criminal trial. The purpose of international criminal law is not punishment and conviction per se, but to render fair and impartial justice or prevent crime. In a domestic context, criminal law cannot reasonably be expected to 'end impunity'. It is even less realistic to make such a pledge in relation to international crimes.

Institutional discourse requires a more nuanced engagement with the political dimensions of mass atrocity trials.[80] Recourse to formal legalism tends to reduce the

---

[73] See O. Yasuaki, 'Towards an Intercivilizational Approach to Human Rights', in J. Bauer and D. Bell, *The East Asian Challenge for Human Rights* (Cambridge: Cambridge University Press, 1999), 103, 119.

[74] K. McEvoy, 'Beyond Legalism: Towards a Thicker Understanding of Transitional Justice' (2007) 34 *Journal of Law and Society* 411–40; D. N. Sharp, 'Addressing Dilemmas of the Global and the Local in Transitional Justice' (2014) 29 *Emory International Law Review* 71.

[75] See also M. De Hoon, 'The Future of the International Criminal Court: On Critique, Legalism and Strengthening the ICC's Legitimacy' (2017) 17 *International Criminal Law Review* 591, 614 ('If international criminal justice is truly intent on developing as a universal system of justice throughout the world, it needs to be open to understanding what is universal and what is not').

[76] Drumbl, *Atrocity, Punishment and International Law*, 181–205.

[77] On the dichotomies and justifications of paternalism, see M. Barnett, 'International Paternalism and Humanitarian Governance' (2012) 1 *Global Constitutionalism* 485, 503 et seq.; M. Barnett, *Paternalism Beyond Borders* (Cambridge: Cambridge University Press, 2016).

[78] According to the Updated Set of Principles for the Protection and Promotion of Human Rights through Action to Combat Impunity (UN Doc. E/CN.4/2005/102/Add.1, 8 February 2005), impunity means 'the impossibility, de jure or de facto, of bringing the perpetrators of violations to account – whether in criminal, civil, administrative or disciplinary proceedings – since they are not subject to any inquiry that might lead to their being accused, arrested, tried and, if found guilty, sentenced to appropriate penalties, and to making reparations to their victims'.

[79] See J.-M. Silva Sanchez, 'Doctrines Regarding the Fight Against Impunity and the Victim's Right for the Perpetrator to be Punished' (2008) 28 *Pace Law Review* 865.

[80] K. A. Rodman, 'Justice as a Dialogue Between Law and Politics' (2014) 12 *JICJ* 437.

complexity of argument. By deciding what comes within the ambit of law, legal proceedings, trials or reparations, justice institutions inevitably produce new social realities, structural relations and forms of power. Rather than denying the elements of choice, discretion and power inherent in this exercise, they should better explain why and how certain choices are made, and by what constraints they are driven. As noted in scholarship: 'What is needed now is a more reflective understanding of the politics that international criminal law interacts, represents and reproduces; to engage with the critique seriously and consider what it can and cannot do; and on that basis manage and adjust expectations to a realistically achievable level'.[81] The benefits of international criminal law cannot be taken for granted. They must be assessed and readjusted, if necessary. Some of the methods require reconsideration. There is need for better epistemic grounding and broader openness to non-Western traditions in the process of knowledge production. More attention needs to be paid to the negative or unintended side effects. For instance, it is essential to trace what local effects international criminal law produces, and how it affects broader processes of social, political and institutional change at the local level. The exercise of authority over persons and the protection of subjects through criminal law create dependencies and relationships of care that do not stop with proceedings. There is a need for continuing protection of defence rights and protection witnesses and victims after situations and cases end.

6.2.7   *Justice*

Throughout past decades, international criminal law has mostly been considered as a legal project. The underlying justice dimensions have remained at the periphery. It is fundamental to examine what types of justice international criminal law can reasonably be expected to provide.

The turn to law and legal institutions has created an expectation that the underlying problems of atrocity can be solved through law. There is a temptation to present justice as an objective good that can be delivered or done. As Anette Bringedal Houge and Kjersti Lohne have argued: 'Politicians, lawyers and NGOs act as if international criminal law can fulfill the expectations its proponents claim it to have, as if it is a solution, as if it deters future crime, and as if it is a necessary precondition for peace, justice, and reconciliation'.[82] This is partly an illusion. International criminal law is better understood through tensions and complex dynamics that arise in the interaction of different justice agents.[83] Some of these tensions are positive, others create frictions. These contradictions are part of the 'DNA of international criminal law' and the structure of the legal process.

---

[81] See De Hoon, 'The Future of the International Criminal Court', 598.
[82] Houge and Lohne, 'End Impunity', 782.
[83] Simpson, *Law, War and Crime*, 1.

International criminal law is theorized and assessed through its contribution to justice goals. Several institutions have developed indicators to measure their contribution to such goals.[84] The problem is that the relevant indicators are often self-centred and focused on the 'economy and efficiency of prosecutions'.[85] They focus on factors such as 'input', i.e. the relevance of certain procedural and operational elements underlining judicial action (e.g. inclusiveness, transparency of proceedings), and 'output', i.e. fair and effective outcomes.[86] The relationship to affected constituencies and the subjective dimensions of justice are easily ignored.[87] What is considered as justice differs among and inside different constituencies. Justice may derive from the plurality of perspectives. It is important to take into account the experiential dimensions of trials and proceedings in order to gain a more nuanced picture of moments of justice and justice perceptions.[88]

In theory, international criminal law is associated with different types of justice (retributive, restorative, distributive or expressivist justice). The distinctions among these categories are not as clear as assumed.

International criminal law has a complex relationship to retribution. Individual punishment cannot provide adequate retribution for the social harm caused. International criminal law remains highly vulnerable to critique if retribution is merely associated with penalties and sentences for offenders.[89] However, retributive features extend far beyond the infliction of punishment. For instance, some of the most important 'punitive' features arise from the publicity and stigma of proceedings, and the very fact that a defendant is selected for prosecution at the international level. Retribution is closely connected to preventive rationales, such as social alarm, the

---

[84] The ICC identified four key goals as reference: expeditiousness, fairness and transparency of proceedings; effective leadership and management; adequate security of its work; and adequate access of victims to the Court. ICC, 'Report of the Court on the Development of Performance Indicators for the International Criminal Court', 12 November 2015, at www.icc-cpi.int/itemsDocuments/Court_report-development_of_performance_indicators-ENG.pdf; Second Court's Report on the Development of Performance Indicators for the International Criminal Court, 11 November 2016, at www.icc-cpi.int/itemsDocuments/ICC-Second-Court_report-on-indicators.pdf.

[85] Kotecha, 'The ICC's Office of the Prosecutor and the Limits of Performance Indicators', 543.

[86] For a broader account, see B. Oomen, 'Justice Mechanisms and the Question of Legitimacy: The Example of Rwanda's Multilayered Justice Mechanisms', in K. Ambos, J. Large and M. Wierda (eds.), *Building a Future on Peace and Justice: Studies on Transitional Justice, Peace and Development: The Nuremberg Declaration on Peace and Justice* (Berlin: Springer, 2009), 175.

[87] The Open Society Justice Initiative has suggested a wider taxonomy of indicators. It includes three main types: 'operational indicators' that are geared at assessing the Court's operations, broader 'systemic indicators' that view ICC operations in the broader context of the Rome Statute as a system of justice, and 'impact indicators' that take into account 'the degree to which people affected by the crimes … understand and engage with the process, as well as the court's legacy'. See Open Society Justice Initiative, Establishing Performance Indicators for the International Criminal Court 4 (November 2015), at www.opensocietyfoundations.org/sites/default/files/briefing-icc-perforamnce-indicators-20151208.pdf.

[88] A number of situation-specific surveys have been conducted over the past years. See Berkeley Human Rights Centre, *Forgotten Voices: A Population-Based Survey on Attitudes About Peace*, July 2005, at www.law.berkeley.edu/files/HRC/Publications_Forgotten-Voices_07-2005.pdf; *When the War Ends: A Population-Based Survey on Attitudes About Peace, Justice, and Social Reconstruction in Northern Uganda* (December 2007), at www.law.berkeley.edu/files/HRC/Publications_When-the-War-Ends_12-2007.pd ; *Living With Fear: A Population-Based Survey on Attitudes about Peace, Justice and Social Reconstruction in Eastern Congo* (August 2008), at www.peacebuildingdata.org/sites/m/pdf/DRCongo_2008_Living_With_Fear.pdf; *The Victims' Court? A Study of 622 Victim Participants at the International Criminal Court* (2015), at www.law.berkeley.edu/wp-content/uploads/2015/04/VP_report_2015_final_full2.pdf.

[89] See Section 5.1.

affirmation of violated norms and the impact of the legal process (i.e. not only punishment itself) on potential offenders and other individuals.

The distinction between retribution and restorative justice is becoming more porous. The role of punishment is partly to re-establish a certain degree of equality between the perpetrator and the victim.[90] Justice procedures may have certain restorative effects. They could help victims and survivors regain some of the humanity that they might have lost through crimes. The rise of the status of victims as subjects of international criminal law reinforces this trend. The victim and perpetrator may (re-) encounter each other as mutual holders of rights, or as members of a common polity. In certain contexts, retribution may be a necessary precursor to forgiveness or forgetting. One way to strengthen the restorative dimensions of trials is to recognize the names of victims in judgments.

The distributive dimensions of international criminal law have received limited attention.[91] Distributive elements are inherent in the power of international and domestic criminal institutions, their decision-making processes, and their role as global justice agents. International criminal law involves choices about the distribution of the benefits and burdens of prosecutions, the selection of crime sites, the identification of perpetrators that merit global attention, and the relationship between different layers of justice. It nurtures a broad field of professionals that are invested in the cause.[92] Critics have insisted that the 'frame' of international criminal law may displace alternative approaches to accountability or transform the way in which social phenomena are treated and addressed. Historical injustices with socio-economic dimensions, such as colonization or slavery, have been largely neglected. There is a risk that the strong focus on deviant individual behaviour may blur where responsibilities for violations lie, or detract attention from state responsibility or alternative mechanisms of justice. As Tor Krever notes, it is tempting to assume, [w]ith an end to individual impunity assured, we need not to worry about the responsibility of states, corporations, structures, political-economic interests and world-systemic forces'.[93] Some see international criminal law more as part of the 'problem' than as part of the solution, due to its structural reflection of global inequalities. It is important to pay greater attention to dilemmas of the political economy of international criminal law in justice discourse. The idea of protecting future generations deserves more consideration. It is only marginally reflected in existing statutory frameworks[94] and crime definitions (e.g. environmental crime, attacks against cultural property or

---

[90] G. Fletcher, 'The Place of Victims in the Theory of Retribution' (1999) 3 *Buffalo Criminal Law Review* 51, 61.

[91] Mégret, 'What Sort of Global Justice', 95; Schwöbel, 'Market and Marketing Culture of International Criminal Law', 264. Justice has been perceived as an abstract or immaterial concept.

[92] C. Kress, 'Towards a Truly Universal Invisible College of International Criminal Lawyers', FICHL Occasional Paper Series No. 4 (2014).

[93] T. Krever, 'Ending Impunity? Eliding Political Economy in International Criminal Law', in U. Mattei and J. D. Haskell (eds.), *Research Handbook on Political Economy and Law* (Cheltenham: Edward Elgar, 2015), 298, 313.

[94] The preamble of the ICC Statute contains a reference to 'the sake of present and future generations'.

buildings dedicated to education, art or science, deportation or forcible transfer of populations).[95]

International criminal law is a highly discursive project. In the future, as in the past, it will be difficult to demonstrate empirically how international criminal law contributes to justice. Many of its benefits can only be understood through an expressivist lens. It is an instrument of reasoning and persuasion. Its importance lies not only in the production of certain specific outcomes (i.e. cases, trials, reparation), but also in the transformation of certain normative discourses, the creation of common discursive spaces or the initiation of longer-term processes. Like domestic criminal law, it will continue to require a certain degree of faith. However, it must be more than a mere set of 'show trials of individuals' that provide moral comfort to the international community if it is to serve as meaningful project of justice.

6.2.8   A Relational Account

The existing normative foundation of international criminal law requires rethinking. Standard justifications raise difficult justificatory problems. Criminal lawyers and criminologists tend to justify international criminal law through the lens of punishment. Justifications such as retribution, general and special deterrence, incapacitation

---

[95] For a creative proposal in relation to crimes against future generation, see S. Jodoin, 'Crimes against Future Generations: Implementing Intergenerational Justice through International Criminal Law' (2010) 10 *Intergenerational Justice Review* 10, 13:

1. Crimes against future generations means any of the following acts within any sphere of human activity, such as military, economic, cultural, or scientific activities, when committed with knowledge of the substantial likelihood of their severe consequences on the long-term health, safety, or means of survival of any identifiable group or collectivity:
   (a) Forcing members of any identifiable group or collectivity to work or live in conditions that seriously endanger their health or safety, including forced labour, enforced prostitution and human trafficking;
   (b) Unlawfully appropriating or acquiring the public and private resources and property of members of any identifiable group or collectivity, including the large scale embezzlement, misappropriation or other diversion of such resources or property by a public official;
   (c) Deliberately depriving members of any identifiable group or collectivity of objects indispensable to their survival, including by impeding access to water and food sources, destroying water and food sources, or contaminating water and food sources by harmful organisms or pollution;
   (d) Forcefully evicting members of any identifiable group or collectivity in a widespread or systematic manner;
   (e) Imposing measures that seriously endanger the health of the members of any identifiable group or collectivity, including by impeding access to health services, facilities and treatments, withholding or misrepresenting information essential for the prevention or treatment of illness or disability, or subjecting them to medical or scientific experiments of any kind which are neither justified by their medical treatment, nor carried out in their interest;
   (f) Preventing members of any identifiable group or collectivity from enjoying their culture, professing and practicing their religion, using their language, preserving their cultural practices and traditions, and maintaining their basic social and cultural institutions;
   (g) Preventing members of any identifiable group or collectivity from accessing primary, secondary, technical, vocational and higher education;
   (h) Causing widespread, long-term and severe damage to the natural environment, including by destroying an entire species or ecosystem;
   (i) Unlawfully polluting air, water and soil by releasing substances or organisms that seriously endanger the health, safety or means of survival of members of any identifiable group or collectivity;
   (j) Other acts of a similar character intentionally and gravely imperilling the health, safety, or means of survival of members of any identifiable group or collectivity.
2. The expression 'any identifiable group or collectivity' means any civilian group or collectivity defined on the basis of geographic, political, racial, national, ethnic, cultural, religious or gender grounds or other grounds that are universally recognized as impermissible under international law).

or rehabilitation place the focus on the individual, neglect the institutional dimensions of international criminal justice, and may overestimate the benefits of punishment.[96] Public international lawyers rely heavily on the premise that penal power is an essential feature of sovereignty that needs to be legitimized through some form of consent (state consent, delegation of power) when it is exercised beyond the state. The problem with this argument is that it is strongly focused on formal legal authority, and the mediatization of the relationship between perpetrators and victims through state authority. It is necessary to develop a fuller justification.

In doctrine, there are at least three major types of justifications: consent-based justifications (e.g. state consent, social contract theories[97]), which focus on the source of authority and the answerability of justice agents; process- and outcome-based justifications, which link justification to agency of justice actors and its effects;[98] and expressivist accounts which legitimize international criminal law through norm expression and its discursive impacts.[99] What is missing is a communicative account of international criminal law that goes beyond mere engagement with the defendant as a subject.[100]

None of the three theories is sufficient as such. They must be seen in conjunction with each other. Different justifications may operate simultaneously for different stakeholders. For instance, defendants, victims, states, affected communities and global society all have different interests, expectations and relations to international criminal law. In light of its inherent tensions and contradictions, international criminal law will hardly ever enjoy full universal consent or societal acceptance. It is thus feasible to develop a more pluralist account, which draws on different agent–stakeholder relationships.

International criminal law needs to justify itself on a continuing basis in different relations and emerges in and through these relations.[101] It is shaped by the multiple roles and identities that agents take, balancing of competing interests (e.g. crime control vs. due process, collective vs. individual responsibility) and processes of rationalization, communication and internalization. Such a relational account helps us understand the apparent contradictions of international criminal law. It takes into account that the justification of legal norms and institutions is inherently linked to the social milieu and dynamics in which they evolve.

---

[96] See also Sloane, 'Expressive Capacity', 89 ('in ICL ... the standard justifications for and goals ostensibly served by criminal punishment – deterrence, retribution, rehabilitation, and incapacitation – seem less plausible, legitimate or efficacious').

[97] Bassiouni, *Introduction to International Criminal Law*, 926. Antony Duff has argued that the authority of criminal law stems from the fact that 'defendants are answerable to their fellow citizens (in whose names the courts act) for public wrongs that they commit, in virtue of their shared membership of the political community'. See Duff, 'Authority and Responsibility in International Criminal Law', in Besson and Tasioulas, *The Philosophy of International Law*, 589, 595.

[98] B. Wringe, 'Why Punish War Crimes?' (2006) 25 *Law and Philosophy* 159, 172.

[99] Meijers and Glasius, 'Trials as Messages of Justice', 437–438 ('The trial is a way to reaffirm legal order, establish truths, recognize the wrongs committed to the victims, and educate the public at large. It is not only a message about the crimes but also about the system of justice').

[100] On international criminal law as a communicative, rather than an expressivist project, see Duff, 'Authority and Responsibility in International Criminal Law', 593.

[101] On the 'relational' account, see A. Huque, 'Group Violence and Group Vengeance: Toward a Retributivist Theory of International Criminal Law' (2005) 9 *Buffalo Criminal Law Review* 273.

Index